BIM Handbook

BIM Handbook

A Guide to Building Information Modeling for Owners, Designers, Engineers, Contractors, and Facility Managers

Third Edition

Rafael Sacks
Charles Eastman
Ghang Lee
Paul Teicholz

WILEY

For general information about our other products and services, please contact our Customer Care Department within the United States at (800) 762-2974, outside the United States at (317) 572-3993 or fax (317) 572-4002.

Wiley also publishes its books in a variety of electronic formats. Some content that appears in print may not be available in electronic books. For more information about Wiley products, visit our web site at www.wiley.com.

Library of Congress Cataloging-in-Publication Data:

Names: Sacks, Rafael, author. | Eastman, Charles M., author. |
  Lee, Ghang, author. | Teicholz, Paul M., author.
Title: BIM handbook : a guide to building information modeling for owners,
  designers, engineers, contractors, and facility managers / by Rafael Sacks,
  Charles Eastman, Ghang Lee, Paul Teicholz.
Description: Third edition. | Hoboken, New Jersey : Wiley, 2018. | Includes
  bibliographical references and index. |
Identifiers: LCCN 2018001037 (print) | LCCN 2018001340 (ebook) | ISBN
  9781119287544 (pdf) | ISBN 9781119287551 (epub) | ISBN 9781119287568
  (oBook) | ISBN 9781119287537 (cloth)
Subjects: LCSH: Building information modeling—Handbooks, manuals, etc. |
  Building—Computer simulation—Handbooks, manuals, etc. | Building
  management—Data processing—Handbooks, manuals, etc. | Communication in
  the building trades—Handbooks, manuals, etc. | Architectural
  practice—Handbooks, manuals, etc. | Architects and builders—Handbooks,
  manuals, etc. | Construction industry—Information resources
  management—Handbooks, manuals, etc.
Classification: LCC TH437 (ebook) | LCC TH437 .E22 2018 (print) | DDC
  690.0285—dc23
LC record available at https://lccn.loc.gov/2018001037

Cover Design: Wiley
Cover Image: Courtesy Mortenson

Set in 10/12pt and LifeLTStd by SPi Global, Chennai, India

SKY10031172_110321

Contents

Foreword to the *Third Edition*

Designers and builders have struggled for centuries to describe three-dimensional buildings on two-dimensional paper, and their contractor partners have struggled to interpret the same drawings when constructing a building.

Occasionally very complex parts of significant buildings were described using a three-dimensional mockup, a smaller version of what was to be built. Brunelleschi created a detailed mockup for his magnificent dome at the Cathedral of Florence, and Bartholdi prepared mockups at different scales for his Statue of Liberty.

Architects then and today build study models to better understand their designs and presentation models to help clients understand how the finished building will look, but these models have little utility in helping the contractor to build.

As an architect, I was trained to describe buildings with drawings on paper. But buildings have three dimensions while paper has two dimensions, resulting in compromises. Drawings traditionally described *size and shape*, so other information about the building better described in words evolved as *specifications,* companions to drawings. The purpose of drawings and specifications was to provide adequate information for the contractor to build the building.

Early computers allowed architects to design electronically using Computer-Aided Design (CAD). However, this system was limited to two dimensions and not much of an improvement over drawing by hand. Improved computers at last allowed architects to design buildings in three dimensions using an electronic building model, called 3D CAD. These early efforts to electronically model buildings in three dimensions were helpful, but they were only a beginning.

Electronic building models began with architects, but soon engineers, contractors, and building owners began to dream of adding other useful information to the electronic Building Model, and the word *Information* was inserted in the center of *Building Model* to become *Building Information Model* (BIM).

It is appropriate that *Information* occupies the central place in BIM, for the rapidly-evolving use of *Information* is the main driver of a revolution in the building industry. The Building Model origins of BIM are still important but can now be viewed as a small part of the ocean of *Information* becoming available for use. Information-rich BIM has enabled dramatic change in the processes for designing and building, with big changes just beginning in how buildings are operated for their useful lifetime.

This Third Edition of the *BIM Handbook* distills the ocean of BIM information into a well-organized, clearly written and illustrated book describing the technology and processes supporting BIM and the business and organizational imperatives for implementation.

Architects, engineers, contractors, subcontractors, fabricators, and suppliers will gain an understanding of the advantages of effective BIM use. Building owners and operators will learn about business advantages generated by effective BIM use. Academic institutions will find the *BIM Handbook* an essential aid for teaching and research.

The first chapter provides an overview of the book, including building industry trends, the business imperative for BIM adoption, and challenges to implementation. Subsequent chapters survey BIM trends in detail for each building industry participant, and include a summary at the beginning and a list of questions at the end suitable for teaching.

Chapter 9, "The Future: Building with BIM" is an ambitious but well-informed look at what we can expect in the near and midterm future. It highlights the nature of the BIM revolution, explaining "the shift from paper drawing to computer drawing was not a paradigm change: BIM is." The authors predict that by 2025 we will see thoroughly digital design and construction processes; growth of a new culture of innovation in construction; diverse and extensive off-site prefabrication; strong progress in automated code-compliance checking; increased application of artificial intelligence; globalization of fabrication in addition to design; and continued strong support for sustainable construction.

The final chapter includes eleven detailed case studies in the design and construction industry that demonstrate BIM effectiveness for feasibility studies, conceptual design, detail design, estimating and coordination during construction, off-site prefabrication and production control, and BIM support for facility operation and maintenance.

Authoring a book chronicling the evolution of BIM with depth of detail, yet with clarity and purpose, is a major accomplishment. Yet three of the authors of this third edition of the *BIM Handbook*—Rafael Sacks, Chuck Eastman, and Paul Teicholz—have collaborated to accomplish this great feat three times (the first edition was published in 2008, followed by the second edition in 2011, both with Kathleen Liston). In this new edition, Professor Ghang Lee of Yonsei University in Seoul, South Korea, has joined the team. Each has been a keen observer and participant in the BIM revolution, and all have collaborated over many years.

Chuck Eastman is a world leading authority on building modeling and has been active in the field since the mid-1970s. He was trained as an architect at the Berkeley CED, where he focused on tool development for practitioners with early versions of Building Information Modeling. He initiated the PhD program at Carnegie Mellon University and founded ACADIA, the North American Academic Building Modeling Conference Group. He joined UCLA for eight years before coming to Georgia Tech, where he has been a professor and director of the Digital Building Laboratory. I have known Chuck for many years and worked with him to advise the Charles Pankow Foundation, which supports research and innovation in the building industry.

Paul Teicholz is professor emeritus of civil engineering at Stanford University. He saw the potential for computers to revolutionize the construction industry as a graduate student at Stanford when programming was still done using punch cards. In 1963, he became the first in the country to receive a PhD in construction engineering and has more than 40 years of experience applying information technology to the AEC industry. In 1988, Paul was invited back to Stanford to create the Center for Integrated Facility Engineering (CIFE), a collaboration between the Civil and Environmental Engineering and Computer Science Departments. He served as the center's director for the next decade, during which CIFE scholars developed computerized tools to significantly improve the AEC industry.

Rafael Sacks is a professor in the Faculty of Civil and Environmental Engineering at the Technion–Israel Institute of Technology, in Haifa, Israel, where he leads the Virtual Construction Lab. He earned a bachelor's degree in 1983 from the University of the Witwatersrand, South Africa, a master's degree in 1985 from MIT, and a PhD in 1998 from the Technion in Israel, all in civil engineering. In 2000, after a career in structural engineering, software development, and consulting, he returned to academia, joining the Technion as a member of faculty. Rafael's research interests extend from BIM to Lean Construction, and he is also the lead author of "Building Lean, Building BIM: Changing Construction the Tidhar Way."

Ghang Lee is a professor and the director of the Building Informatics Group (BIG) in the Department of Architecture & Architectural Engineering at Yonsei University in Seoul, Korea. He earned his bachelor's and master's degrees in 1993 and 1995 from Korea University, Seoul, Korea, and a PhD in 2004 from the Georgia Institute of Technology. Before his PhD studies he worked at a construction company and founded a dot-com company. In addition to publishing numerous BIM-related papers, books, and international standards, Ghang has developed various software and automation tools such as xPPM, a tower crane navigation system, a smart exit sign system, the global BIM dashboard, and the construction listener. He serves as a technical advisor to several government and private organizations in Korea and other countries.

It has been a pleasure to review the *BIM Handbook* prior to writing this Foreword. It will be of great value to everyone in the building industry who needs to understand the BIM revolution and its far-reaching effects on practitioners, owners, and society at large.

Patrick MacLeamy, FAIA
CEO and Chairman, HOK (retired)
Founder and Chairman, buildingSMART International

Preface

This book is about the process of design, construction, and facility management called *building information modeling* (BIM). It provides an in-depth understanding of BIM technologies, the business and organizational issues associated with its implementation, and the profound impacts that effective use of BIM can provide to all parties involved in a facility over its lifetime. The book explains how designing, constructing, and operating buildings with BIM differs from pursuing the same activities in the traditional way using drawings, whether paper or electronic.

BIM is changing the way buildings look, the way they function, and the ways in which they are built. Throughout the book, we have intentionally and consistently used the term "BIM" to describe an activity (meaning *building information modeling*), rather than an object (*building information model*). This reflects our belief that BIM is not a thing or a type of software but a socio-technical system that ultimately involves broad process changes in design, construction, and facility management. At a minimum, BIM systems function at the level of the organization (manifested as a construction project, company, or owner organization) shown in Figure 00–01.

Perhaps most important is that BIM creates significant opportunity for society at large to achieve more sustainable building construction processes and higher performance facilities with fewer resources and lower risk than can be achieved using traditional practices.

Why a BIM Handbook?

Our motivation in writing this book was to provide a thorough and consolidated reference to help students and practitioners in the construction industry learn about this exciting approach, in a format independent of the commercial interests that guide vendors' literature on the subject. There are many truths and myths in the generally accepted perceptions of the state of the art of BIM. We hope that *The BIM Handbook* will help reinforce the truths, dispel the myths, and guide our readers to successful implementations. Some well-meaning decision makers and practitioners in the construction industry at-large have had disappointing experiences after attempting to adopt BIM, because their efforts and expectations were based on misconceptions and inadequate planning. If this book can help readers avoid these frustrations and costs, we will have succeeded.

Collectively, the authors have a wealth of experience with BIM, both with the technologies it uses and the processes it supports. We believe that BIM

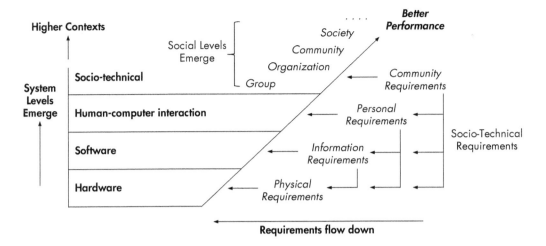

FIGURE 00–01   Socio-technical levels.

© Brian Whitworth, Alex P. Whitworth, and First Monday. This image appeared as Figure 1 in "The Social Environment Model: Small Heroes and the Evolution of Human Society" by Brian Whitworth and Alex P. Whitworth, published in *First Monday* (Volume 15, Number 11, November 2010), at http://firstmonday.org/article/view/3173/2647; http://dx.doi.org/10.5210/fm.v15i11.3173.

represents a paradigm change that will have far-reaching impacts and benefits, not only for those in the construction industry but for society at large, as better buildings are built that consume fewer materials and require less labor and capital resources and that operate more efficiently. We make no claim that the book is objective in terms of our judgment of the necessity for BIM. At the same time, of course, we have made every effort to ensure the accuracy and completeness of the facts and figures presented.

Who is *the BIM Handbook* for, and what is in it?

The BIM Handbook is addressed to building developers, owners, project managers, operators, facility managers, and inspectors; to architects, engineers of all disciplines, construction contractors, and fabricators; and to students of architecture, civil engineering, and building construction. It reviews building information modeling and its related technologies, its potential benefits, its costs, and needed infrastructure. It also discusses the present and future influences of BIM on regulatory agencies; legal practice associated with the building industry; and manufacturers of building products. It is directed at readers in these areas. A rich set of BIM case studies is presented in Chapter 10, and more, from the earlier editions of the book, are available on the *BIM Handbook*

This book is accompanied by a book companion site: www.wiley.com/go/bimhandbook3e.

companion website. The case studies describe various BIM processes, platforms, tools, and technologies. Current and future industry and societal impacts are also explored.

The book has four sections:

- Chapters 1, 2, and 3 provide an introduction to BIM and the technologies that support it. These chapters describe the current state of the construction industry, the potential benefits of BIM, the technologies underlying BIM including parametric modeling of buildings, and interoperability.
- Chapters 4, 5, 6, and 7 provide discipline-specific perspectives of BIM. They are aimed at owners and facility managers (Chapter 4), designers of all kinds (Chapter 5), general contractors (Chapter 6), and subcontractors and fabricators (Chapter 7).
- Chapter 8 discusses facilitators of BIM: BIM standards, guides and contracts, BIM education, and organizational change. Chapter 9 deals with potential impacts and future trends associated with the advent of BIM-enabled design, construction, and operation of buildings. Current trends are described and extrapolated through the year 2025, as are forecasts of potential long-term developments and the research needed to support them beyond 2025.
- Chapter 10 provides eleven detailed cases studies of BIM in the design and construction industry that demonstrate its use for feasibility studies, conceptual design, detail design, estimating, detailing, coordination, construction planning, logistics, operations, and many other common construction activities. The new case studies in Chapter 10 include buildings with signature architectural and structural designs (such as the Louis Vuitton building and the Hyundai Motorstudio), complex hospital projects (Saint Joseph Hospital in Denver, Dublin's New Children's Hospital, and the Stanford Neuroscience Center) as well as a wide range of fairly common buildings (a shopping mall, an office building, a student residence, an airport terminal, and a laboratory building). There is also a study of a complex infrastructure project: the Victoria Station upgrade for the London Underground.

What's new in this edition?

BIM is developing rapidly, and it is difficult to keep up with the advances in both technology and practice. There have been many changes since we completed the second edition, fully seven years ago. To name a few:

- Extensive adoption by government and other public owners, with a plethora of BIM mandates, guides, standards, execution plans, and more.
- The benefits of integrated practice are receiving wide review and being tested intensively in practice.
- BIM tools are increasingly used to support sustainable design, construction, and operation.

- BIM integration with lean design and construction methods, with many new software tools to support the new workflows and management practices.
- Models have become accessible in the field, with strong impact on the ways in which work is done.
- Off-site prefabrication and modular construction are benefitting from the quality of information BIM provides, and growing rapidly.
- BIM is being used for operations and maintenance, and owners can now clearly state their information requirements when buildings are delivered.
- Laser-scanning, photogrammetry, and drones are all common terms now in construction projects.
- AI, machine-learning, and semantic enrichment are at the forefront of the BIM research agenda.

This edition not only addresses these themes and updates the material related to the BIM applications; it also introduces sections on new technologies, and it includes eleven new case studies.

How to use *the BIM Handbook*

Many readers will find the *Handbook* a useful resource whenever they are confronted with new terms and ideas related to BIM in the course of their work or study. A thorough first reading, while not essential, is of course the best way to gain a deeper understanding of the significant changes that BIM is bringing to the AEC/FM industry.

The first section (Chapters 1–3) is recommended for all readers. It gives a background to the commercial context and the technologies for BIM. Chapter 1 lists many of the potential benefits that can be expected. It first describes the difficulties inherent in traditional practice within the U.S. construction industry and its associated poor productivity and higher costs. It then describes various approaches to procuring construction, such as traditional design-bid-build, design-build, and others, describing the pros and cons for each in terms of realizing benefits from the use of BIM. It describes newer integrated project delivery (IPD) approaches that are particularly useful when supported by BIM. Chapter 2 details the technological foundations of BIM, in particular parametric and object-oriented modeling. The history of these technologies and their current state of the art are described. The chapter then reviews the leading commercial application platforms for generating building information models. Chapter 3 deals with the intricacies of collaboration and interoperability, including how building information can be communicated and shared from profession to profession and from application to application. The relevant standards, such as IFC (Industry Foundation Classes) and IDM (Information Delivery Manual), BIM server technologies (a.k.a. common data environments), and other data interfacing technologies are covered in detail. Chapters 2 and 3 can also be used as a reference for the technical aspects of parametric modeling and interoperability.

Readers who desire specific information on how they can adopt and implement BIM in their companies can find the details they need in the relevant chapter for their professional group within Chapters 4–7. You may wish to read the chapter closest to your area of interest and then only the executive summaries of each of the other chapters. There is some overlap within these chapters, where issues are relevant to multiple professions (for example, subcontractors will find relevant information in Chapters 6 and 7). These chapters make frequent reference to the set of detailed case studies provided in Chapter 10.

Chapter 8 is an entirely new chapter. It discusses facilitators of BIM including BIM mandates, roadmaps, guides, education, certificates, and legal issues.

Those who wish to learn about the long-term technological, economic, organizational, societal, and professional implications of BIM and how they may impact your educational or professional life will find an extensive discussion of these issues in Chapter 9.

The case studies in Chapter 10 each tell a story about different professionals' experiences using BIM on their projects. No one case study represents a "complete" implementation or covers the entire building lifecycle. In most cases, the building was not complete when the study was written. But taken together, they paint a picture of the variety of uses and the benefits and problems that these pioneering firms have already experienced. They illustrate what could be achieved with existing BIM technology at the start of the twenty-first century. There are many lessons learned that can provide assistance to our readers and guide practices in future efforts.

Finally, students and professors are encouraged to make use of the study questions and exercises provided at the conclusion of each chapter.

Acknowledgments

Naturally, we are indebted first and foremost to our families, who have all borne the brunt of the extensive time we have invested in this book over the years. Our thanks and appreciation for the highly professional work of Margaret Cummins, our executive editor, Purvi Patel, our project editor, and their colleagues at John Wiley and Sons.

Our research for the book was greatly facilitated by numerous builders, designers, and owners, representatives of software companies and government agencies; we thank them all sincerely. We especially thank the contributors and correspondents who worked with us to prepare the all new case studies, and their efforts are acknowledged personally at the end of each relevant case study. The case studies were also made possible through the very generous contributions of the people who participated in the projects themselves, who corresponded with us extensively and shared their understanding and insights.

Finally, we are grateful to Patrick MacLeamy for his excellent foreword to this, the third edition. Likewise, we remain indebted to Jerry Laiserin and to Lachmi Khemlani for their enlightening forewords to the first and second editions respectively. Jerry helped initiate the original idea for *The BIM Handbook*, and Lachmi continues to make significant contributions to BIM through her publication of AECbytes.

CHAPTER 1

Introduction

1.0 EXECUTIVE SUMMARY

Building Information Modeling (BIM) has become established as an invaluable process enabler for modern architecture, engineering, and construction (AEC). With BIM technology, one or more accurate virtual models of a building are constructed digitally. They support all the phases of design, allowing better analysis and control than manual processes. When completed, these computer models contain precise geometry and data needed to support the construction, fabrication, and procurement activities through which the building is realized, operated, and maintained.

BIM also accommodates many of the functions needed to model the lifecycle of a building, providing the basis for new design and construction capabilities and changes in the roles and relationships among a project team. When adopted well, BIM facilitates a more integrated design and construction process that results in better-quality buildings at lower cost and reduced project duration. BIM can also support improved facility management (FM) and future modifications to the building. The goal of this book is to provide the necessary knowledge to allow a reader to understand both the technology and the business processes that underlie productive use of BIM.

This chapter begins with a description of existing construction practices, and it documents the inefficiencies inherent in these methods. It then explains the technology behind BIM and recommends ways to best take advantage of the new business processes it enables for the entire lifecycle of a building. It concludes with an appraisal of various problems one might encounter when converting to BIM technology.

1.1 INTRODUCTION

To better understand the significant changes that BIM introduces, this chapter begins with a description of paper-based design and construction methods and the predominant business models traditionally used by the construction industry. It then describes various problems associated with these practices, outlines what BIM is, and explains how it differs from 2D and 3D computer-aided design (CAD). We briefly describe the kinds of problems that BIM can solve and the new business models that it enables. The chapter concludes with a presentation of the most significant problems that may arise when using the technology, which, despite some 20 years of commercial application, is still evolving.

1.2 THE CURRENT AEC BUSINESS MODEL

Traditionally, the facility delivery process has been fragmented and dependent on communication using 2D drawings. Errors and omissions in paper documents often cause unanticipated field costs, delays, and eventual lawsuits between the various parties in a project team. These problems cause friction, financial expense, and delays. Efforts to address such problems have included alternative organizational structures such as the design-build method; the use of real-time technology, such as project websites for sharing plans and documents; and the implementation of 3D CAD tools. Though these methods have improved the timely exchange of information, they have done little to reduce the severity and frequency of conflicts caused by the use of paper documents or their electronic equivalents.

One of the most common problems associated with 2D-based communication during the design phase is the considerable time and expense required to generate critical assessment information about a proposed design, including cost estimates, energy-use analysis, structural details, and so forth. These analyses are normally done last, when it is already too late to make important changes to the design. Because these iterative improvements do not happen during the design phase, *value engineering* must then be undertaken to address inconsistencies, which often results in compromises to the original design.

Regardless of the contractual approach, certain statistics are common to nearly all large-scale projects ($10 M or more), including the number of people involved and the amount of information generated. The following data was compiled by Maged Abdelsayed of Tardif, Murray & Associates, a construction company located in Quebec, Canada (Hendrickson, 2003):

- Number of participants (companies): 420 (including all suppliers and sub-sub-contractors)
- Number of participants (individuals): 850
- Number of different types of documents generated: 50
- Number of pages of documents: 56,000
- Number of bankers' boxes to hold project documents: 25
- Number of 4-drawer filing cabinets: 6
- Number of 20-inch diameter, 20-year old, 50-feet-high, trees used to generate this volume of paper: 6
- Equivalent number of megabytes of electronic data to hold this volume of paper (scanned): 3,000 MB

It is not easy to manage an effort involving such a large number of people and documents, regardless of the contractual approach taken. Figure 1–1 illustrates the typical members of a project team and their various organizational boundaries.

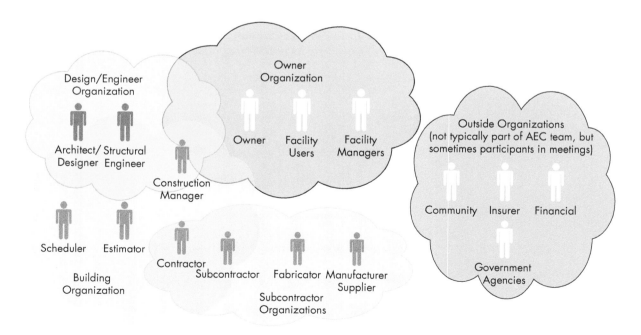

FIGURE 1–1 Conceptual diagram representing an AEC project team and the typical organizational boundaries.

There are three dominant contract methods in the United States: Design-Bid-Build (DBB), Design-Build (DB), and Construction Management at Risk (CM@R). There are also many variations of these (Sanvido and Konchar, 1999; Warne and Beard, 2005). A fourth method, quite different from the first three, called "Integrated Project Delivery (IPD)" is becoming increasingly popular with sophisticated building owners. These four approaches are now described in greater detail.

1.2.1   Design-Bid-Build

A significant percentage of buildings are built using the DBB approach. The two major benefits of this approach are more competitive bidding to achieve the lowest possible price for an owner and less political pressure to select a given contractor. (The latter is particularly important for public projects.) Figure 1–2 schematically illustrates the typical DBB procurement process as compared to the typical CM@R and DB processes (see Section 1.2.2)

In the DBB model, the client (owner) hires an architect, who then develops a list of building requirements (a program) and establishes the project's design objectives. The architect proceeds through a series of phases: schematic design, design development, and contract documents. The final documents must fulfill the program and satisfy local building and zoning codes. The architect either hires employees or contracts consultants to assist in designing structural, HVAC (heating, ventilation, and air-conditioning), piping, and plumbing components. These designs are recorded on drawings (plans, elevations, 3D visualizations), which must then be coordinated to reflect all of the changes as they are identified. The final set of drawings and specifications must contain sufficient detail to facilitate construction bids. Because of potential liability, an architect may choose to include fewer details in the drawings or insert

FIGURE 1–2 Schematic diagram of Design-Bid-Build, CM at Risk, and Design-Build processes.

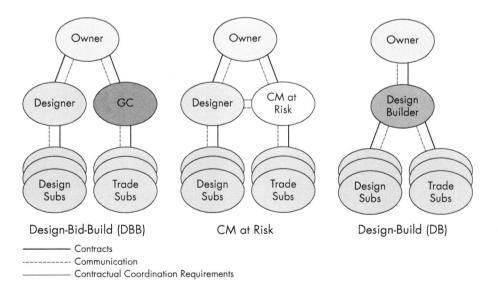

Design-Bid-Build (DBB)   CM at Risk   Design-Build (DB)

———————— Contracts
------------ Communication
———————— Contractual Coordination Requirements

language indicating that the drawings cannot be relied on for dimensional accuracy. These practices often lead to disputes with the contractor, as errors and omissions are detected and responsibility and extra costs reallocated.

Stage two involves obtaining bids from general contractors. The owner and architect may play a role in determining which contractors can bid. Each contractor must be sent a set of drawings and specifications that are then used to compile an *independent quantity survey*. Contractors use these quantities, together with the bids from subcontractors, to determine their *cost estimate*. Subcontractors selected by the contractors must follow the same process for the parts of the project that they are involved with. Because of the effort required, contractors (general and subcontractors) typically spend approximately 1 percent of their estimated costs in compiling bids.[1] If a contractor wins approximately one out of every 6 to 10 jobs that they bid on, the cost per successful bid averages from 6 to 10 percent of the entire project cost. This expense then gets added to the general and subcontractors' overhead costs.

The winning contractor is usually the one with the lowest responsible bid, including work to be done by the general contractor and selected subcontractors. Before work can begin, it is often necessary for the contractor to redraw some of the drawings to reflect the construction process and the phasing of work. These are called *general arrangement drawings*. The subcontractors and fabricators must also produce their own *shop drawings* to reflect accurate details of certain items, such as precast concrete units, steel connections, wall details, piping runs, and the like.

The need for accurate and complete drawings extends to the shop drawings, as these are the most detailed representations and are used for actual fabrication. If these drawings are inaccurate or incomplete, or if they are based on drawings that are out-of-date or contain errors, inconsistencies, or omissions, then expensive, time-consuming conflicts will arise in the field. The costs associated with these conflicts can be significant.

Inconsistency, inaccuracy, and uncertainty in design make it difficult to fabricate materials off-site. As a result, most fabrication and construction must take place on-site and only after exact conditions are established. On-site construction work is costlier, more time-consuming, and prone to produce errors that would not occur if the work were performed in a factory environment where productivity is higher, work is safer, and quality control is better.

Often during the construction phase, numerous changes are made to the design as a result of previously unknown errors and omissions, unanticipated site conditions, changes in material availabilities, questions about the design, new client requirements, and new technologies. These need to be resolved by the project team. For each change, a procedure is required to determine the cause, assign responsibility, evaluate time and cost implications, and address how the issue will be resolved. This procedure, whether initiated in writing or

---

[1] This is based on two of the authors' personal experience in working with the construction industry. This cost includes the expense of obtaining bid documents, performing quantity takeoff, coordinating with suppliers and subcontractors, and the cost estimating processes.

with the use of a web-based tool, involves a *Request for Information* (RFI), which must then be answered by the architect or other relevant party. Next, a *Change Order* (CO) is issued, and all impacted parties are notified about the change, which is communicated together with needed changes in the drawings. These changes and resolutions frequently lead to legal disputes, added costs, and delays. Website products for managing these transactions do help the project team stay on top of each change, but because they do not address the source of the problem, they are of marginal benefit.

Problems also arise whenever a contractor bids below the estimated cost in order to win the job. Faced with the "winner's curse," contractors often abuse the change process to recoup losses incurred from the original bid. This, of course, leads to more disputes between the owner and the project team.

In addition, the DBB process requires that the procurement of all materials be held until the owner approves the bid, which means that long lead time items may extend the project schedule. For this and other reasons (described next), the DBB approach often takes longer than the DB approach.

The final phase is commissioning the building, which takes place after construction is finished. This involves testing the building systems (heating, cooling, electrical, plumbing, fire sprinklers, and so forth) to make sure they work properly. Depending on contract requirements, final drawings are then produced to reflect all *as-built changes*, and these are delivered to the owner along with all manuals and warranties for installed equipment. At this point, the DBB process is completed.

Because all of the information provided to the owner is conveyed in 2D (on paper or equivalent electronic files), the owner must expend considerable effort to relay all relevant information to the facility management team charged with maintaining and operating the building. The process is time-consuming, prone to error, costly, and remains a significant barrier to effective building operation and maintenance. As a result of these problems, the DBB approach is probably not the most expeditious or cost-efficient approach to design and construction. Other approaches have been developed to address these problems.

1.2.2 Design-Build

The design-build (DB) process was developed to consolidate responsibility for design and construction into a single contracting entity and to simplify the administration of tasks for the owner (Beard et al., 2005). In this model, the owner contracts directly with the design-build team (normally a contractor with a design capability or working with an architect) to develop a well-defined building program and a schematic design that meets the owner's needs. The DB contractor then estimates the total cost and time needed to design and construct the building. After all modifications requested by the owner are implemented, the plan is approved and the final budget for the project is established. It is important to note that because the DB model allows for modifications to be made to the building's design earlier in the process, the amount of money and time needed to incorporate these changes is also reduced. The DB contractor establishes contractual relationships with specialty designers and subcontractors as needed. After this point, construction begins and any further changes to the design (within predefined limits) become the responsibility of the DB contractor. The same is true for errors and omissions. It is not necessary for detailed construction drawings to be complete for all parts of the building prior to the start of construction on the foundation and early building elements. As a result of these simplifications, the building is typically completed faster, with fewer legal complications, and at a somewhat reduced total cost. On the other hand, there is little flexibility for the owner to make changes after the initial design is approved and a contract amount is established.

The DB model has become common in the United States and is used widely abroad. An RS Means Market Intelligence report (Duggan and Patel, 2013) found that the share of DB among nonresidential construction projects in the United States grew from some 30 percent in 2005 to 38 percent in 2012. A particularly high share (above 80 percent) was reported for military construction.

The use of BIM within a DB project is clearly advisable. The Los Angeles Community College District (LACCD) has established and refined a clear set of guidelines for this use of BIM for its design-build projects (BuildLACCD, 2016). Figure 1–3, reproduced from the LACCD guide, shows the BIM-related workflow and deliverables for this standard, with clear demarcation of handover of the BIM facilitation role from the design to the construction phases.

1.2.3 Construction Management at Risk

Construction management at risk (CM@R) project delivery is a method in which an owner retains a designer to furnish design services and also retains a construction manager to provide construction management services for a project throughout the preconstruction and construction phases. These services may include preparation and coordination of bid packages, scheduling, cost control, value engineering, and construction administration. The construction manager is usually a licensed general contractor and guarantees the cost of the project (guaranteed maximum price, or GMP). The owner is responsible for the design before a GMP can be set. Unlike DBB, CM@R brings the constructor into the design process at a stage where they can have definitive input. The value of the delivery method stems from the early involvement of the contractor and the reduced liability of the owner for cost overruns.

1.2.4 Integrated Project Delivery

Integrated project delivery (IPD) is a relatively new procurement process that is gaining popularity as the use of BIM expands and the AEC facility management (AEC/FM) industry learns how to use this technology to support integrated teams. There are multiple approaches to IPD as the industry experiments with this approach. The American Institute of Architects (AIA), the Association of General Contractors (AGC), and other organizations have published sample contract forms for a family of IPD versions (AIA, 2017). In all cases, integrated projects are distinguished by effective collaboration among the owner, the prime (and possibly sub-) designers, and the prime (and possibly key sub-) contractor(s). This collaboration takes place from early design and continues through project handover. The key concept is that this project team works together using the best collaborative tools at their disposal to ensure that the project will meet owner requirements at significantly reduced time and cost.

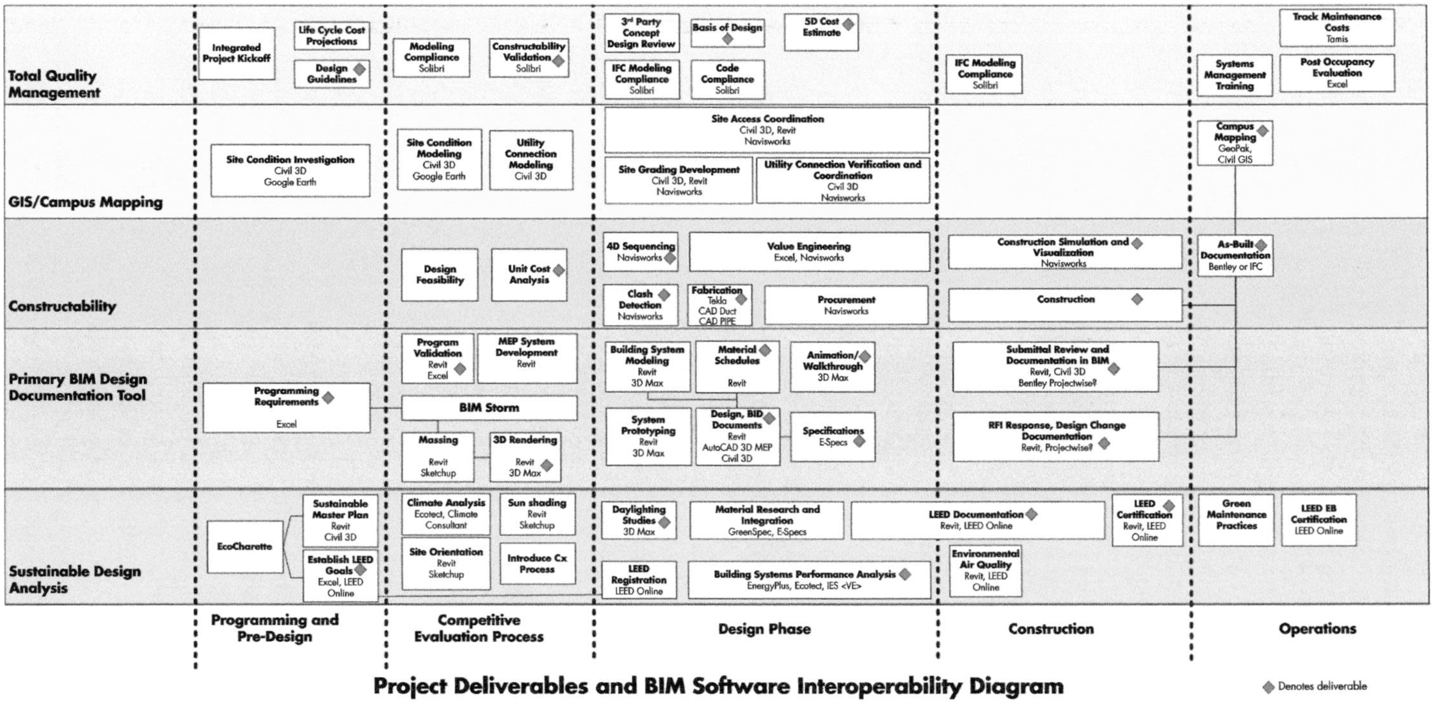

FIGURE 1-3 Los Angeles Community College District BIM process for Design Build projects (BuildLACCD, 2016).

Reproduced with permission of BuildLACCD.

8

Either the owner needs to be part of this team to help manage the process or a consultant must be hired to represent the owner's interests, or both may participate. The trade-offs that are always a part of the design process can best be evaluated using BIM—cost, energy, functionality, aesthetics, and constructability. Thus, BIM and IPD go together and represent a clear break with current linear processes that protect and restrict information flow with obscure product representations and adversarial relationships. Clearly the owner is the primary beneficiary of IPD, but it does require that they understand enough to participate and specify in the contracts what they want from the participants and how it will be achieved. The legal issues of IPD are very important and are discussed in Chapters 4 and 6. Several case studies of IPD projects are available in the *BIM Handbook* companion website. The St. Joseph Hospital project case study, in Chapter 10, is another example.

1.2.5 What Kind of Building Procurement Is Best When BIM Is Used?

There are many variations of the design-to-construction business process, including the organization of the project team, how the team members are paid, and who absorbs various risks. There are lump-sum contracts, cost-plus a fixed or percentage fee, various forms of negotiated contracts, and so forth. It is beyond the scope of this book to outline each of these and the benefits and problems associated with them (but see Sanvido and Konchar, 1999, and Warne and Beard, 2005).

With regard to the use of BIM, the general issues that either enhance or diminish the positive changes that this technology offers depends on how well and at what stage the project team works collaboratively on one or more digital models. The DBB approach presents the greatest challenge to the use of BIM, because the contractor does not participate in the design process and thus must build a new building model after design is completed. The DB approach may provide an excellent opportunity to exploit BIM technology, because a single entity is responsible for design and construction. The CM@R approach allows early involvement of the constructor in the design process, which increases the benefit of using BIM and other collaboration tools. Various forms of integrated project delivery are being used to maximize the benefits of BIM and "Lean" (less wasteful, uneven, and overburdened) processes. Other procurement approaches can also benefit from the use of BIM but may achieve only partial benefits, particularly if BIM technology is not used collaboratively during the design phase.

1.3 DOCUMENTED INEFFICIENCIES OF TRADITIONAL APPROACHES

This section documents how traditional practices contribute unnecessary waste and errors. Evidence of poor field productivity is illustrated in a graph developed by the Center for Integrated Facility Engineering (CIFE) at

Stanford University (Teicholz, 2001). The impact of poor information flow and redundancy is illustrated using the results of a study performed by the National Institute of Standards and Technology (NIST) (Gallaher et al., 2004).

1.3.1 CIFE Study of Construction Industry Labor Productivity

Extra costs associated with traditional design and construction practices have been documented through various research studies. Paul Teicholz first called attention to the significant difference in productivity between construction and nonfarm industries in a widely publicized discussion paper published in 2001. More recently compiled data, shown in Figure 1–4, shows that the trend of increasingly weaker construction productivity when compared with manufacturing has continued, but it also shows the gap between off-site and on-site construction activities. It is clear that fabrication off-site is more productive than construction on-site.

The data for the curves in Figure 1–4 were obtained from the U.S. Economic Census (U.S. Census Bureau, 2016a). The productivity index values were calculated by dividing constant value-added dollars by numbers of employees. The manufacturing sector includes all the NAICS 31-33 codes. The off-site construction values were calculated from a basket of fabrication sectors, including metal window and door manufacturing, fabricated structural metal bar joists and reinforcing, concrete product manufacturing, steel and precast concrete contractors, and elevator and moving stairway manufacturing. The on-site values used a basket of sectors that includes glass and glazing contractors, concrete contractors, and drywall and insulation contractors. During the 45-year-long period covered, the productivity of the manufacturing industries has more than doubled. Meanwhile, the productivity of construction work performed on-site is relatively unchanged. It is adversely affected from time to time by economic downturns, such as that following the 2008 economic crisis, which is expressed in the 2012 economic census. Off-site construction, most of which is considered part of the manufacturing industries for the purpose of the economic census, shows improvement in productivity, but is also subject to the influence of the economic climate in construction.

FIGURE 1–4 Indices of labor productivity for manufacturing, off-site construction trades, and on-site construction trades, 1967–2015.

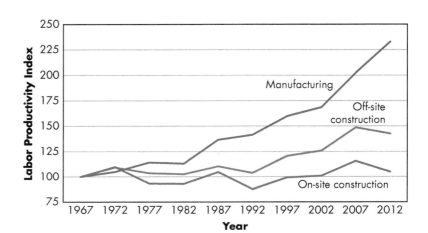

Of course, many material and technological improvements have been made to buildings in the last four decades. The results are perhaps better than they appear, because quality has increased substantially and off-site prefabrication is becoming a bigger factor.

Contractors have made greater use of off-site components that take advantage of factory conditions and specialized equipment. Clearly this has allowed for higher quality and lower cost production of components, as compared to on-site work (Eastman and Sacks, 2008).

While the reasons for the apparent decrease in construction productivity are not completely understood, the statistics are dramatic and point at significant structural impediments within the construction industry. It is clear that efficiencies achieved in the manufacturing industry through automation, the use of information systems, better supply chain management, and improved collaboration tools, have not yet been achieved in field construction. Possible reasons for this include:

- Sixty-five percent of construction firms consist of fewer than five people, making it difficult for them to invest in new technology; even the largest firms account for less than 0.5 percent of total construction volume and are not able to establish industry leadership (see Figure 6-1 in Chapter 6).
- The real inflation-adjusted wages and the benefit packages of construction workers have stagnated over this time period. Union participation has declined, and the use of immigrant workers has increased, discouraging the need for labor-saving innovations. While innovations have been introduced, such as nail guns, larger and more effective earth-moving equipment, and better cranes, the productivity improvements associated with them have not been sufficient to change overall field labor productivity.
- Additions, alterations, or reconstruction work represents about 29 percent and maintenance and repair represents about 16 percent of construction volume. It is more difficult to use capital-intensive methods for these kinds of work. It is labor intensive and likely to remain so. New work represents only about 55 percent of total construction volume (U.S. Census Bureau, 2016a).
- The adoption of new and improved business practices within both design and construction has been noticeably slow and limited primarily to larger firms. In addition, the introduction of new technologies has been fragmented. Often, it remains necessary to revert to paper or 2D CAD drawings so that all members of a project team are able to communicate with one another and to keep the pool of potential contractors and subcontractors bidding on a project sufficiently large. Almost all local authorities still require paper submittals for construction permit reviews. For these reasons, paper use maintains a strong grip on the industry.
- Whereas manufacturers often have long-term agreements and collaborate in agreed-upon ways with the same partners, construction projects

typically involve different partners working together for a period of time and then dispersing. As a result, there are few or no opportunities to realize improvements over time through applied learning. Rather, each partner acts to protect him- or herself from potential disputes that could lead to legal difficulties by relying on antiquated and time-consuming processes that make it difficult or impossible to implement resolutions quickly and efficiently. Of course, this translates to higher cost and time expenditures.

Another possible cause for the construction industry's stagnant productivity is that on-site construction has not benefited significantly from automation. Thus, field productivity relies on qualified training of field labor. Since 1974, compensation for hourly workers has steadily declined with the increase in use of nonunion immigrant workers with little prior training. The lower cost associated with these workers may have discouraged efforts to replace field labor with automated (or off-site) solutions, although automation in construction is less dependent on the cost of labor than on technological barriers to automation, such as the nature of field work environments and the relatively high setup costs for use of automated machinery.

1.3.2 NIST Study of Cost of Construction Industry Inefficiency

The National Institute of Standards and Technology (NIST) performed a study of the additional cost incurred by building owners as a result of inadequate interoperability (Gallaher et al., 2004). The study involved both the exchange and the management of information, in which individual systems were unable to access and use information imported from other systems. In the construction industry, incompatibility between systems often prevents members of the project team from sharing information rapidly and accurately; it is the cause of numerous problems, including added costs. The NIST study included commercial, industrial, and institutional buildings and focused on new and "set in place" construction taking place in 2002. The results showed that inefficient interoperability accounted for an increase in construction costs by $6.12 per square foot for new construction and an increase in $0.23 per square foot for operations and maintenance (O&M), resulting in a total added cost of $15.8 billion. Table 1–1 shows the breakdown of these costs and to which stakeholder they were applied.

In the NIST study, the cost of inadequate interoperability was calculated by comparing current business activities and costs with hypothetical scenarios in which there was seamless information flow and no redundant data entry. NIST determined that the following costs resulted from inadequate interoperability:

- Avoidance (redundant computer systems, inefficient business process management, redundant IT support staffing)
- Mitigation (manual reentry of data, request for information management)
- Delay (costs for idle employees and other resources)

Table 1–1   Additional Costs of Inadequate Interoperability in the Construction Industry, 2002 (in $M)

Stakeholder Group	Planning, Engineering, Design Phase	Construction Phase	O&M Phase	Total Added Cost
Architects and Engineers	$1,007.2	$147.0	$15.7	$1,169.8
General Contractors	$485.9	$1,265.3	$50.4	$1,801.6
Special Contractors and Suppliers	$442.4	$1,762.2		$2,204.6
Owners and Operators	$722.8	$898.0	$9,027.2	$10,648.0
Total	**$2,658.3**	**$4,072.4**	**$9,093.3**	**$15,824.0**
Applicable sf in 2002	1.1 billion	1.1 billion	39 billion	n/a
Added cost/sf	**$2.42/sf**	**$3.70/sf**	**$0.23**	**n/a**

Source: Table 6.1 NIST study (Gallaher et al., 2004).

Of these costs, roughly 68 percent ($10.6 billion) were incurred by building owners and operators. These estimates are speculative, due to the impossibility of providing accurate data. They are, however, significant and worthy of serious consideration and effort to reduce or avoid them as much as possible. Widespread adoption of BIM and the use of a comprehensive digital model throughout the lifecycle of a building would be a step in the right direction to eliminate such costs resulting from the inadequate interoperability of data.

1.4   BIM: NEW TOOLS AND NEW PROCESSES

This section provides an overview of BIM-related terminology, concepts, and functional capabilities; and it addresses how these tools can improve business processes.

1.4.1   BIM Platforms and Tools

All CAD systems generate digital files. They generate files that consist primarily of vectors, associated line types, and layer identifications. As these systems were further developed, additional information was added to allow for blocks of data and associated text. With the introduction of 3D modeling, advanced geometry definition and complex surfacing tools were added.

As CAD systems became more intelligent and more users wanted to share data associated with a given design, the focus shifted from drawings and 3D images to the data itself. A building model produced by a BIM tool can support multiple different views of the data contained within a drawing set, including 2D and 3D. A building model can be described by its content (what objects it describes) or its capabilities (what kinds of information requirements it can support). The latter approach is preferable, because it defines what you can do with the model rather than how the database is constructed (which will vary with each implementation). In Chapter 2, we describe BIM platforms in detail and define the way they use parametric modeling.

1.4.2   BIM Processes

For the purpose of this book, we define **BIM as a modeling technology and associated set of processes** to produce, communicate, and analyze building models. BIM is the acronym of "Building Information Modeling," reflecting and emphasizing the process aspects, and not of "Building Information Model." The objects of BIM processes are building models, or BIM models.

Building models are characterized by:

- Building components that are represented with digital representations (objects) that carry computable graphic and data attributes that identify them to software applications, as well as parametric rules that allow them to be manipulated in an intelligent fashion.
- Components that include data that describe how they behave, as needed for analyses and work processes, such as quantity takeoff, specification, and energy analysis.
- Consistent and nonredundant data such that changes to component data are represented in all views of the component and the assemblies of which it is a part.

The following is both the vision for and a definition of BIM technology provided by the National Building Information Modeling Standard (NBIMS) Committee of the National Institute of Building Sciences (NIBS) Facility Information Council (FIC). The NBIMS vision for BIM is "an improved planning, design, construction, operation, and maintenance process using a standardized machine-readable information model for each facility, new or old, which contains all appropriate information created or gathered about that facility in a format useable by all throughout its lifecycle" (NIBS, 2008). The NBIMS Initiative categorizes the Building Information Model (BIM) three ways:

1. as a product
2. as an IT-enabled, open standards–based deliverable, and a collaborative process
3. as a facility lifecycle management requirement

These categories support the creation of the industry information value chain, which is the ultimate evolution of BIM. This enterprise-level (industry-wide) scope of BIM is the area of focus for NBIMS, bringing together the various BIM implementation activities within stakeholder communities.

The methodologies used by NBIMS are rooted in the activities of building-SMART International (formerly the International Alliance for Interoperability) (buildingSMART, 2017). They include preparation of Information Delivery Manuals (IDM), Model View Definitions (MVD), and Industry Foundation Dictionaries (IFD), as will be explained in Chapter 3.

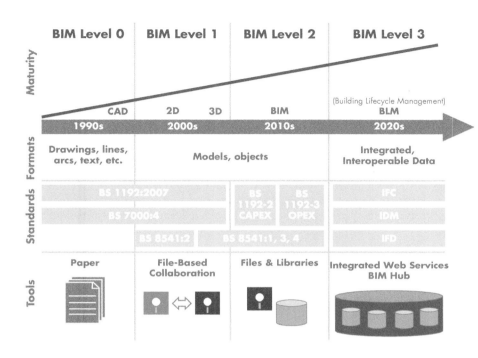

FIGURE 1–5 The BIM maturity model by Mark Bew and Mervyn Richards

Reproduced based on PAS 1192-2:2013 (BSI, 2013) and BS 1192-4:2014 (BSI, 2014a).

Another way to characterize BIM is to define a progression of levels of maturity of application of information technology in construction that expresses the degree of collaboration in the process as well as the levels of sophistication of use of the individual tools. In this view BIM is seen as a series of distinct stages in a journey that began with computer-aided drawing and is taking the industry into the digital age. Since the UK Government BIM Task Group adopted the concept of "BIM Levels," the following chart and the four levels it defines (Level 0 to Level 3) have become a widely adopted definition of the criteria for a project to be deemed BIM-compliant. In Figure 1–5, BS standards numbers refer to British Standards Institution and the description of each level is their definition (BS, 2017).

Level 0 BIM

This level is defined as unmanaged CAD. This is likely to be 2D, with information being shared by traditional paper drawings or in some instances, digitally via PDF, essentially separate sources of information covering basic asset information. The majority of the industry is already well ahead of this now.

Level 1 BIM

This is the level at which many companies are currently operating. This typically comprises a mixture of 3D CAD for concept work, and 2D for drafting of statutory approval documentation and

Production Information. CAD standards are managed to BS 1192:2007, and electronic sharing of data is carried out from a common data environment (CDE), often managed by the contractor. Models are not shared between project team members.

Level 2 BIM

This is distinguished by collaborative working—all parties use their own 3D models, but they are not working on a single, shared model. The collaboration comes in the form of how the information is exchanged between different parties—and is the crucial aspect of this level. Design information is shared through a common file format, which enables any organization to combine that data with their own in order to make a federated BIM model, and to carry out interrogative checks on it. Hence any CAD software that each party uses must be capable of exporting to a common file format such as IFC (Industry Foundation Class) or COBie (Construction Operations Building Information Exchange). This is the method of working that has been set as a minimum target by the UK government for all work on public-sector work, by 2016.

Level 3 BIM

This level represents full collaboration between all disciplines by means of using a single, shared project model that is held in a centralized repository (normally an object database in cloud storage). All parties can access and modify that same model, and the benefit is that it removes the final layer of risk for conflicting information. This is known as "Open BIM."

From "What is BIM and why do you need it?", TMD Studio, London and Prague, Jan Gasparek and Ondrej Chudy

Thus, BIM moves the industry forward from current task automation of project and paper-centric processes (level 0) (3D CAD, animation, linked databases, spreadsheets, and 2D CAD) toward an integrated and interoperable workflow where these tasks are collapsed into a coordinated and collaborative process that takes maximal advantage of computing capabilities, web communication, and data aggregation into information and knowledge capture (Level 3). All of this is used to simulate and manipulate digital models to manage the built environment within a repeatable and verifiable decision process that reduces risk and enhances the quality of actions and product industry-wide.

Virtual Design and Construction (VDC) is the practice of using building information modeling specifically as a first-run study of a construction process. First-run studies are standard practice in lean manufacturing and in lean construction—they support process improvement by focusing management attention very closely on the production process for the first of any series of products. With VDC, designers and builders test both the product and the construction process virtually and thoroughly before executing work in the field to construct the building. They examine integrated multidisciplinary performance models of design-construction projects, including the facilities, work processes, supply chains, and project teams in order to identify and remove constraints, thus improving project performance and the resulting facilities.

1.4.3   Definition of Parametric Objects

The concept of parametric objects is central to understanding BIM and its differentiation from traditional 2D objects. Parametric BIM objects are defined as follows:

- Consist of geometric definitions and **associated data and rules**.
- Geometry is integrated **nonredundantly**, and allows for no inconsistencies. When an object is shown in 3D, the shape cannot be represented internally redundantly, for example, as multiple 2D views. A plan and elevation of a given object must always be consistent. Dimensions cannot be "fudged."
- Parametric rules for objects **automatically modify associated geometries** when a new object is inserted into a building model or when changes are made to associated objects. For example, a door will fit automatically into a wall, a light switch will automatically locate next to the proper side of the door, a wall will automatically resize itself to butt to a ceiling or roof, and so forth.
- Objects can be defined at **different levels of aggregation**, so we can define a wall as well as its related components. Objects can be defined and managed at any number of relevant levels of a hierarchy. For example, if the weight of a wall subcomponent changes, the weight of the wall should also change.
- Objects' rules can identify when a particular change violates **object feasibility** regarding size, manufacturability, and so forth.
- Objects have the ability to **link to or receive, broadcast, or export sets of attributes**, for example, structural materials, acoustic data, energy data, and the like, to other applications and models.

Technologies that allow users to produce building models that consist of parametric objects are considered BIM authoring tools. In Chapter 2 we elaborate the discussion of parametric technologies and discuss common capabilities in BIM tools, including features to automatically extract consistent drawings and reports of geometric parameters. In Chapters 4 through 7 we discuss these capabilities and others and their potential benefits to various AEC practitioners and building owners.

1.4.4   Support for Project Team Collaboration

Open interfaces should allow for the import of relevant data (for creating and editing a design) and export of data in various formats (to support integration with other applications and workflows). There are four primary approaches for such integration: (1) to stay within one software vendor's products, (2) to use software from vendors who have themselves collaborated to provide direct file exchanges through the Application Programming Interface (API) of either or both of pairs of applications using the proprietary file format of one of the vendors, (3) to use software from various vendors that can exchange data using open industry-wide standards, primarily the Industry Foundation Classes (IFC) schema, or (4) model server-based data exchange through a database management system (DBMS).

The first approach may allow for tighter and easier integration among products in multiple directions. For example, changes to the architectural model will generate changes to the mechanical systems model, and vice versa. This requires, however, that all members of a design team use software provided from the same vendor.

The second and third approaches use either proprietary or open-source (publicly available and supported standards) to define building objects. These standards may provide a mechanism for interoperability among applications with different internal formats. This approach provides more flexibility at the expense of possibly reduced interoperability, especially if the various software programs in use for a given project do not support, or only partially support with some data loss, the same exchange standards. This allows objects from one BIM application to be exported from or imported into another. The fourth approach, using a DBMS on a local or a cloud server, is sometimes referred to as a model server, a BIM server, an IFC server, a data repository, or a product data repository. It has the advantage of allowing all users to work on the same information concurrently without any BIM software designed to work with the central model. See Chapter 3 for an extensive discussion of BIM collaboration technology.

1.5   BIM AS A LIFECYCLE PLATFORM

BIM supports a reevaluation of IT use in the creation and management of the facility's lifecycle. The stakeholders include real estate; ownership; finance; all areas of architecture, engineering, and construction (AEC); manufacturing and fabrication; facility maintenance, operations, and planning; regulatory compliance; asset management; sustainability; and disposal within the facility lifecycle. With society's growing environmental, sustainability, and security mandates, the need for open and reusable critical infrastructure data has grown beyond the needs of those currently supplying services and products to the industry. First-responders, government agencies, and other organizations also need this data.

BIM shares many similarities with *product lifecycle management (PLM)*, which originated in the automobile industry in the mid-1980s and became widespread in the late 1990s. PLM is the process of managing a product throughout its lifecycle, which aims to improve product quality and reduce waste as well as risks through integration of design and engineering processes and reuse of information. BIM and PLM are so similar in concept that many people refer to BIM as **project** *lifecycle management (PLM)* or *building lifecycle management (BLM)*, stressing the importance of BIM as a platform for the creation and management of information about buildings throughout their design, construction, and serviceable life.

Conceptually, BIM at Level 3 plays the role of lifecycle platform by providing a single information source, which enables project participants to query, view, and (re)use current information. With current commercial technology and practice however, information is still generated and managed by multiple systems and multiple parties through different phases of a project. Consequently, it is critical to have data interoperability and integration technologies that can minimize data loss during the data exchange, sharing, and integration processes. Data exchange through a standard data format such as IFC is one approach. An integrated single project data repository such as a cloud-based system is another. A federated or distributed database is the third approach. Data exchange through proprietary file formats or direct data links between different systems through an Application Programming Interface (API) is also a common approach in practice.

Although none of these methods is free from data loss, the role of BIM as a lifecycle platform is growing, resulting in new terms such as *BIM FM* (Chapter 4)*, green BIM* (Chapter 5), *field BIM* (Chapter 6), and *BIM to fabrication* (Chapter 7). BIM FM—the integration of BIM models with FM systems with the graphic and equipment data supported by both systems, which have traditionally been separate systems—is an area that has seen particularly strong progress. Chapter 4 contains a detailed discussion of BIM FM integration.

Another area of development is the use of internet-connected sensor devices (Internet of Things, IoT) linked to Building Automation Systems. Pärn et al. (2017) provide an excellent overview of lifecycle BIM opportunities and problem areas in their paper "The Building Information Modelling Trajectory in Facilities Management: A Review." They summarize as follows: "This early integration of both geometric and semantic data would prove invaluable to the FM team during building occupancy, particularly with respect to monitoring building performance. In turn, a more accurate measurement of building performance in-use provides a virtual circle and invaluable knowledge-based feedback opportunity for designers and contractors to improve the development of future projects commissioned."

1.6 WHAT IS NOT A BIM PLATFORM?

The term *BIM* encompasses both technology and process. Given the broad spread of both, the term is frequently used in a fairly superficial way, a popular buzzword used by software developers to describe the capabilities that their products offer and by professionals of many kinds to describe their services. This breeds confusion. To provide some clarity concerning BIM platforms, the following paragraphs describe modeling solutions that do not constitute

BIM platforms. (BIM environments, BIM platforms, and BIM tools are defined in Section 2.3.) These include applications that create the following kinds of models:

- **Models that contain 3D data only and no (or few) object attributes:** These are models that can only be used for graphic visualizations and have no intelligence at the object level. They are fine for visualization but provide little or no support for data integration and design analysis. Trimble's SketchUp application, for example, is excellent for rapid development of building schematic designs and for visualizing form, but has limited use for any other type of analysis because it has no knowledge of the function of the objects in the design. McNeel's Rhino 3D, when used for surface modeling, can feed into BIM workflows, but is not BIM modeling *per se*. These are BIM tools insofar as they support the BIM process, but they are not BIM platforms.

- **Models with no support of behavior:** These are models that define objects but cannot adjust their positioning or proportions because they do not implement parametric behavior. This makes changes extremely labor intensive and provides no protection against creating inconsistent or inaccurate views of the model.

- **Models that are composed of multiple 2D CAD reference files that must be combined to define the building:** It is impossible to ensure that the resulting 3D model will be feasible, consistent, or countable, and display intelligence with respect to the objects contained within it.

- **Models that allow changes to dimensions in one view that are not automatically reflected in other views:** This allows for errors in the model that are very difficult to detect (similar to overriding a formula with a manual entry in a spreadsheet).

1.7   WHAT ARE THE BENEFITS OF BIM? WHAT PROBLEMS DOES IT ADDRESS?

BIM technology can support and improve many business practices. Although not all of the advantages discussed below are achieved in all projects, we list them to show the entire scope of changes that can be expected as BIM processes and technology develop. BIM is at the heart of the ways in which the building design and construction process can respond to the increasing pressures for greater complexity, faster development, improved sustainability, reduced cost, and more effective and efficient operation and maintenance of buildings. Traditional practice is not able to respond to these pressures. The subsequent sections briefly describe how this improved performance can be achieved.

1.7.1 Preconstruction Benefits to Owner

Concept, Feasibility, and Design Benefits. Before owners engage an architect, it is necessary to determine whether a building of a given size, quality level, and desired program requirements can be built within a given cost and time budget. In other words, can a given building meet the financial requirements of an owner? If these questions can be answered with relative certainty, owners can then proceed with the expectation that their goals are achievable. Finding out that a particular design is significantly over budget after a considerable amount of time and effort has been expended is wasteful. An approximate (or "macro") building model built into and linked to a cost database can be of tremendous value and assistance to an owner. This is described in further detail in Chapter 4.

Increased Building Performance and Quality. Developing a *schematic model* prior to generating a *detailed building model* allows for a more careful evaluation of the proposed scheme to determine whether it meets the building's functional, sustainability, and other requirements. Early evaluation of design alternatives using analysis/simulation tools increases the overall quality of the building. These capabilities are reviewed in Chapter 5.

Improved Collaboration Using Integrated Project Delivery. When the owner uses Integrated Project Delivery (IPD) for project procurement, BIM can be used by the project team from the beginning of the design to improve their understanding of project requirements and to extract cost estimates as the design is developed. This allows design and cost to be better understood and also avoids the use of paper exchange and its associated delays. This is described further in Chapters 4 through 7 and is illustrated in the Sutter Medical Center Castro Valley case study in the online *BIM Handbook* case study archive.

1.7.2 Benefits for Design

Design involves the refinement and articulation of the project, in all aspects—economy, structure, energy, aesthetic, functional, and others—to meet the client's intentions. It impacts all later phases.

Earlier and More Accurate Visualizations of a Design. The 3D model generated by the BIM software is designed directly rather than being generated from multiple 2D views. It can be used to visualize the design at any stage of the process with the expectation that it will be dimensionally consistent in every view.

Automatic Low-Level Corrections When Changes Are Made to Design. If the objects used in the design are controlled by parametric rules that ensure proper alignment, then the 3D model will be free of geometry, alignment, and spatial coordination errors. This reduces the user's need to manage design changes (see Chapter 2 for further discussion of parametric rules).

Generation of Accurate and Consistent 2D Drawings at Any Stage of the Design. Accurate and consistent drawings can be extracted for any set of objects or specified view of the project. This significantly reduces the amount of time and the number of errors associated with generating construction drawings for all design disciplines. When changes to the design are required, fully consistent drawings can be generated as soon as the design modifications are entered.

Earlier Collaboration of Multiple Design Disciplines. BIM technology facilitates simultaneous work by multiple design disciplines. While collaboration with drawings is also possible, it is inherently more difficult and time consuming than working with one or more coordinated 3D models in which change control can be well managed. This shortens the design time and significantly reduces design errors and omissions. It also gives earlier insight into design problems and presents opportunities for a design to be continuously improved. This is much more cost-effective than waiting until a design is nearly complete and then applying value engineering only after the major design decisions have been made.

Easy Verification of Consistency to the Design Intent. BIM provides earlier 3D visualizations and quantifies the area of spaces and other material quantities, allowing for earlier and more accurate cost estimates. For technical buildings (labs, hospitals, and the like), the design intent is often defined quantitatively, and this allows a building model to be used to check for these requirements. For qualitative requirements (e.g. this space should be near another), the 3D model can also support automatic evaluations.

Extraction of Cost Estimates during the Design Stage. At any stage of the design, BIM technology can extract an accurate bill of quantities and spaces that can be used for cost estimation. In the early stages of a design, cost estimates are based either on formulas that are keyed to significant project quantities, for example, number of parking spaces, square feet of office areas of various types, or unit costs per square foot. As the design progresses, more detailed quantities are available and can be used for more accurate and detailed cost estimates. It is possible to keep all parties aware of the cost implications associated with a given design before it progresses to the level of detailing required of construction bids. At the final stage of design, an estimate based on the quantities for all the objects contained within the model allows for the preparation of a more accurate final cost estimate. As a result, it is possible to make better-informed design decisions regarding costs using BIM rather than a paper-based system. When using BIM for cost estimates, it is clearly desirable to have the general contractor and possibly key trade contractors who will be responsible for building the structure, as part of the project team.

Their knowledge is required for accurate cost estimates and constructability insights during the design process. The use of BIM for cost estimating is complex and is discussed in Chapters 4 through 7 and in a number of the case studies presented in Chapter 10.

Improvement of Energy Efficiency and Sustainability. Linking the building model to energy analysis tools allows evaluation of energy use during the early design phases. This is not practical using traditional 2D tools because of the time required to prepare the relevant input. If applied at all, energy analysis is performed at the end of the 2D design process as a check or a regulatory requirement, thus reducing the opportunities for modifications that could improve the building's energy performance. The capability to link the building model to various types of analysis tools provides many opportunities to improve building quality.

1.7.3 Construction and Fabrication Benefits

Use of Design Model as Basis for Fabricated Components. If the design model is transferred to a BIM fabrication tool and detailed to the level of fabrication objects (shop model), it will contain an accurate representation of the building objects for fabrication and construction. Because components are already defined in 3D, their automated fabrication using numerical control machinery is facilitated. Such automation is standard practice today in steel fabrication and some sheet metal work. It has been used successfully in precast components, fenestration, and glass fabrication. This allows vendors worldwide to elaborate on the model, to develop details needed for fabrication, and to maintain links that reflect the design intent. Where the intent to prefabricate or pre-assemble is introduced early enough in the design process, BIM effectively facilitates off-site fabrication and reduces cost and construction time. The accuracy of BIM also allows larger components of the design to be fabricated off-site than would normally be attempted using 2D drawings, due to the likely need for on-site changes (rework) and the inability to predict exact dimensions until other items are constructed in the field. It also allows smaller installation crews, faster installation time, and less on-site storage space.

Quick Reaction to Design Changes. The impact of a suggested design change can be entered into the building model, and changes to the other objects in the design will automatically update. Some updates will be made automatically based on the established parametric rules. Additional cross-system updates can be checked and updated visually or through clash detection. The consequences of a change can be accurately reflected in the model and all subsequent views of it. In addition, design changes can be resolved more quickly in a BIM system because modifications can be shared, visualized, estimated, and resolved without the use of time-consuming paper transactions. Updating in this manner is extremely error-prone in paper-based systems.

Discovery of Design Errors and Omissions before Construction. Because the virtual 3D building model is the source for all 2D and 3D drawings, design errors caused by inconsistent 2D drawings are eliminated. In addition, because models from all disciplines can be brought together and compared, multisystem interfaces are easily checked both systematically (for hard and clearance clashes) and visually (for other kinds of errors). Conflicts and constructability problems are identified before they are detected in the field. Coordination among participating designers and contractors is enhanced and errors of omission are significantly reduced. This speeds the construction process, reduces costs, minimizes the likelihood of legal disputes, and provides a smoother process for the entire project team.

Synchronization of Design and Construction Planning. Construction planning using 4D CAD requires linking a construction plan to the 3D objects in a design and supplementing the model with construction equipment objects (shoring, scaffolding, cranes, etc.), so that it is possible to simulate the construction process and show what the building and site would look like at any point in time. This graphic simulation provides considerable insight into how the building will be constructed day by day and reveals sources of potential problems and opportunities for possible improvements (site, crew and equipment, space conflicts, safety problems, and so forth).

Better Implementation of Lean Construction Techniques. Lean construction techniques require careful coordination between the general contractor and all subs to ensure that only work that can be performed (i.e., all preconditions are met) is assigned to crews. This minimizes wasted effort, improves workflow, and reduces the need for on-site material inventories. Because BIM provides an accurate model of the design and the material resources required for each segment of the work, it provides the basis for improved planning and scheduling of subcontractors and helps to ensure just-in-time arrival of people, equipment, and materials.

This reduces cost and allows for better collaboration at the job site. The model can also be used with tablet computers to facilitate material tracking, installation progress, and automated positioning in the field. These benefits are illustrated in the Mapletree and St. Joseph Hospital case studies presented in Chapter 10.

Synchronization of Procurement with Design and Construction. The complete building model provides accurate quantities for all (or most, depending upon the level of 3D modeling) of the materials and objects contained within a design. These quantities, specifications, and properties can be used to procure materials from product vendors and subcontractors (such as precast concrete subs).

1.7.4   Post Construction Benefits

Improved Commissioning and Handover of Facility Information. During the construction process the general contractor and MEP contractors collect information about installed materials and maintenance information for the systems in the building. This information can be linked to the objects in the building model and thus be available for handover to the owner for use in their facility management systems. It also can be used to check that all the systems are working as designed before the building is accepted by the owner. This can be achieved by a one-time download of data from BIM to FM systems using COBie standards or using integrated BIM-FM systems. This is illustrated by the Stanford University Medical Center case study in Chapter 10.

Better Management and Operation of Facilities. The building model provides a source of information (graphics and specifications) for all systems used in a building. Previous analyses used to determine mechanical equipment, control systems, and other purchases can be provided to the owner, as a means for verifying the design decisions once the building is in use. This information can be used to check that all systems work properly after the building is completed.

Integration with Facility Operation and Management Systems. A building model that has been updated with all changes made during construction provides an accurate source of information about the as-built spaces and systems and provides a useful starting point for managing and operating the building. A building information model supports monitoring of real-time control systems, as it provides a natural interface for sensors and for remote operation of facilities. Many of these capabilities are just starting to be implemented, but BIM provides an ideal platform for their deployment. This is discussed in Chapters 4 and 8 and illustrated in the Medina Airport and the Stanford University Medical Center case studies in Chapter 10.

1.8   BIM AND LEAN CONSTRUCTION

The key idea of lean construction is to optimize value to the customer through continuous process improvements that optimize flow and reduce waste. The basic principles are drawn from lean production, and much has been learned from the Toyota Production System (TPS). Naturally, significant adaptation is needed before the ideas and tools of TPS are applied to construction. Adaptation has been practical and theoretical, and the process has given rise to new ways of thinking about production in construction, such as the Transformation-Flow-Value (TFV) concept defined by Koskela (1992).

Many lean construction tools and techniques, such as the Last Planner System (Ballard, 2000), require commitment and education, but can generally be implemented with little or no software support. Nevertheless, there is a strong synergy between lean construction and BIM, in that the use of BIM fulfills some lean construction principles and greatly facilitates fulfillment of other lean principles. There are many causes of waste in construction that result from the way information is generated, managed, and communicated using drawings, such as inconsistencies between design documents, restricted flow of design information in large batches, and long cycle times for requests for information. BIM goes a long way to removing these wastes, but it also does something more—it improves workflow for many actors in the construction process, even if they make no direct use of BIM.

In a study of this relationship, Sacks et al. (2010) listed 24 lean principles (see Table 1–2) and 18 BIM functionalities and identified 56 explicit interactions between them, of which 52 were positive interactions.

The first area of significant synergy is that the **use of BIM reduces variation**. The ability to visualize form and to evaluate function, rapid generation of design alternatives, the maintenance of information and design model integrity (including reliance on a single information source and clash checking), and automated generation of reports, all result in more consistent and reliable information that greatly reduces the waste of rework and of waiting for information. This affects all members of a building's design team, but its economic impact on those involved directly in construction is greater.

The second area of synergy is that **BIM reduces cycle times**. In all production systems, an important goal is to reduce the overall time required for a product to progress from entry into the system to completion. This reduces the amount of work in process, accumulated inventory, and the ability of the system to absorb and respond to changes with minimal waste. This is relevant in design management, construction planning, and in production planning and control on site.

Thirdly, **BIM enables visualization, simulation, and analysis of both construction products and processes.** Visualization greatly enhances clients' understanding of the design of a building, and requirements capture is improved. BIM helps align the various project team members' mental models of the project, removing much of the waste that results from inconsistent designs across disciplines. Designers can simulate and analyze building performance to improve functional design. For contractors and their suppliers, visualizing the construction process supports better planning and production control.

Finally, and perhaps most obviously, where used effectively, **BIM improves information flows**.

Modular construction and increased prefabrication of building parts and assemblies, as described in the NTU North Hills project case study (Chapter 10), reveals how BIM's support for prefabrication leads to leaner practice in all of the areas listed previously. For more detailed discussion of these aspects, see Chapter 7.

Table 1–2   Lean Construction Principles (Sacks et al., 2010)

Principal Area	Principle
Flow process	**Reduce variability** Get quality right the first time (reduce product variability) Improve upstream flow variability (reduce production variability)
	Reduce cycle times Reduce production cycle durations Reduce inventory
	Reduce batch sizes (strive for single-piece flow) **Increase flexibility** Reduce changeover times Use multiskilled teams
	Select an appropriate production control approach Use pull systems Level the production
	Standardize **Institute continuous improvement** **Use visual management** Visualize production methods Visualize production process
	Design the production system for flow and value Simplify Use parallel processing Use only reliable technology Ensure the capability of the production system
Value generation process	**Ensure comprehensive requirements capture** **Focus on concept selection** **Ensure requirement flow down** **Verify and validate**
Problem-solving	**Go and see for yourself** **Decide by consensus, consider all options**
Developing partners	**Cultivate an extended network of partners**

Considering these synergies, it becomes clear why the American Institute of Architects document on Integrated Project Delivery, which is an essentially lean approach (Eckblad et al., 2007), states, "Although it is possible to achieve Integrated Project Delivery without Building Information Modeling, it is the opinion and recommendation of this study that it is essential to efficiently achieve the collaboration required for Integrated Project Delivery."

1.9 WHAT CHALLENGES CAN BE EXPECTED?

Improved processes in each phase of design and construction will reduce the number and severity of problems associated with traditional practices. Intelligent use of BIM, however, will also cause significant changes in the relationships of project participants and the contractual agreements between them. (Traditional contract terms are tailored to paper-based practices.) In addition, earlier collaboration between the architect, contractor, and other design disciplines will be needed, as knowledge provided by specialists is of more use during the design phase. The growing use of IPD project delivery for buildings and other types of structures reflects the strong benefits of integrated teams using BIM and lean construction techniques to manage the design and construction process.

1.9.1 Challenges with Collaboration and Teaming

While BIM offers new methods for collaboration, it introduces new challenges with respect to the development of effective teams. How to permit adequate sharing of model information by members of the project team is a significant issue. Where architects and engineers still provide traditional paper drawings, the contractor (or a third party) can still build the model so that it can be used for construction planning, estimating, and coordination. Where designers create their design using BIM and share the model, it may not have sufficient detail for use for construction or may have object definitions that are inadequate for extracting necessary construction quantities. This may require creating a new model for construction use. If the members of the project team use different modeling tools, then tools for moving the models from one environment to another or combining these models are needed. This can add complexity and introduce potential errors and time to the project.

These issues can be ameliorated by preparing a thorough BIM Execution Plan (BEP) that specifies the levels of detail that are required from each modeler at each stage, as well as the mechanisms for model sharing or exchange. Model exchange can be file-based or use a model server that communicates with all BIM applications. The practice of co-locating multidisciplinary design and construction teams in a "Big Room" office space—a collocated and collaborative work environment—is a very effective way to leverage the close coordination that BIM enables for improving project design quality and reducing project durations. The technical issues are reviewed in Chapter 3 and Big Room collaboration is discussed in Chapters 4, 5, and 6. A number of the case studies presented in Chapter 10 provide background for this issue.

The collaborative and open work environment that BIM creates can also raise security concerns. For example, if appropriate steps are not taken, a detailed BIM model of a security-sensitive facility such as an airport, a railway station, or other public and private buildings may fall into the hands of people with malicious intent. In response to this threat, the UK BIM Task Group developed the BS PAS 1192-5:2015, *Specification for Security-minded Building Information Modelling, Digital Built Environments and Smart*

Asset Management (BSI, 2015). ISO 27001:2013, *Information Technology—Security Techniques—Information Security Management Systems* (ISO, 2013) also provides guidance, although it is not specific to BIM. Many cloud-based BIM services seek ISO 27001 certification to demonstrate that their services are secure.

1.9.2 Legal Changes to Documentation Ownership and Production

Legal concerns, with respect to who owns the multiple design, fabrication, analysis, and construction datasets; who pays for them; and who is responsible for their accuracy, arose as BIM use grew. These issues have been addressed by practitioners through BIM use on projects. Professional societies, such as the AIA and the AGC, have developed guidelines for contractual language to cover issues raised by the use of BIM technology. These are discussed in Chapters 4 and 8.

1.9.3 Changes in Practice and Use of Information

The use of BIM encourages the integration of construction knowledge earlier in the design process. Integrated design-build firms capable of coordinating all phases of the design and incorporating construction knowledge from the outset will benefit the most. IPD contracting arrangements that require and facilitate good collaboration will provide greater advantages to owners when BIM is used. The most significant change that companies face when implementing BIM technology is intensively using a shared building model during design phases and a coordinated set of building models during construction and fabrication, as the basis of all work processes and for collaboration.

1.9.4 Implementation Issues

Replacing a 2D or 3D CAD environment with a building modeling system involves far more than acquiring software, training, and upgrading hardware. Effective use of BIM requires that changes be made to almost every aspect of a firm's business (not just doing the same things in a new way). It requires some understanding of BIM technology and related processes and a plan for implementation before the conversion can begin. A consultant can be very helpful to plan, monitor, and assist in this process. While the specific changes for each firm will depend on their sector(s) of AEC activity, the general steps that need to be considered are similar and include the following:

- Assign top-level management responsibility for developing a BIM adoption plan that covers all aspects of the firm's business and how the proposed changes will impact both internal departments and outside partners and clients.
- Create an internal team of key managers responsible for implementing the plan, with cost, time, and performance budgets to guide their performance.
- Allocate time and resources for education in BIM tools and practices, and ensure that people at all levels are prepared.

- Start using the BIM system on one or two smaller (perhaps already completed) projects in parallel with existing technology and produce traditional documents from the building model. This will help reveal where there are deficits in the building objects, in output capabilities, in links to analysis programs, and so forth. It will also allow the firm to develop modeling standards and determine the quality of models and level of detail needed for different uses.
- Use initial results to educate and guide continued adoption of BIM software and additional staff training. Keep senior management apprised of progress, problems, insights, and so forth.
- Extend the use of BIM to new projects and begin working with outside members of the project teams in new collaborative approaches that allow early integration and sharing of knowledge using the building model.
- Continue to integrate BIM capabilities into additional aspects of the firm's functions and reflect these new business processes in contractual documents with clients and business partners.
- Periodically replan the BIM implementation process to reflect the benefits and problems observed thus far, and set new goals for performance, time, and cost. Continue to extend BIM-facilitated changes to new locations and functions within the firm.

In Chapters 4 through 7, where specific applications of BIM over the lifecycle of a building are discussed, additional adoption guidelines specific to each party involved in the building process are reviewed. Chapter 8 discusses facilitators of BIM adoption and implementation, reviewing BIM standards and BIM guides, organizational change, and formal education in BIM.

1.10 FUTURE OF DESIGNING AND BUILDING WITH BIM

Chapter 9 describes the authors' views of how BIM technology will evolve and what impacts it is likely to have on the future of the AEC/FM industry and to society at large. There are comments on the near-term future (up to 2025) and the medium-term future (beyond 2025). We also discuss the kinds of research that will be relevant to support these trends.

It is rather straightforward to anticipate near-term impacts. For the most part, they are extrapolations of current trends. Projections over a longer period are those that to us seem likely, given our knowledge of the AEC/FM industry and BIM technology. Beyond that, it is difficult to make useful projections.

1.11 CASE STUDIES

Chapter 10 presents case studies that illustrate how BIM technology and its associated work processes are being used today. An additional 15 case studies are available in the online *BIM Handbook* case study archive. These cover the entire range of the building lifecycle, although most focus on the design and construction phases (with extensive illustration of off-site fabrication building models). For the reader who is anxious to "dive right in" and get a first-hand view of BIM, these case studies are a good place to start.

Chapter 1 Discussion Questions

1. What is BIM and how does it differ from 3D modeling?

2. What are some of the significant problems associated with the use of 2D CAD, and how do they waste resources and time during both the design and construction phases as compared to BIM-enabled processes?

3. Why was field labor productivity in the construction industry stagnant for much of the period from 1960 to 2010, despite the many advances in construction technology?

4. What changes in design and construction process are needed to enable productive use of BIM technology?

5. Why does the design-bid-build business process make it very difficult to achieve the full benefits that BIM can provide during design or construction?

6. How does integrated project delivery differ from the design-build and construction management at risk project procurement methods?

7. What kind of legal, collaboration, and/or communication problems can be anticipated as a result of using BIM with an integrated project team?

8. What techniques are available for integrating design analysis applications with the building model developed by the architect?

Core Technologies and Software

2.0 EXECUTIVE SUMMARY

This chapter provides an overview of the primary technology that distinguishes BIM design applications from earlier-generation CAD systems. Object-based parametric modeling was originally developed in the 1970s and 1980s for manufacturing. Unlike other CAD systems previous to this era, parametric modeling does not represent objects with fixed geometry and properties. Rather, it represents objects by parameters and rules that automatically determine the geometry and optionally nongeometric properties and features. The parameters and rules can be expressions that relate to other objects, thus allowing the objects to automatically update according to user control or changing contexts. Custom parametric objects allow for the modeling of complex geometries, which were previously not possible or simply impractical. In other industries, companies use parametric modeling to develop their own object representations and to reflect industry knowledge and best practices. In the AECO industry, BIM software companies have predefined a set of base building object classes for users, which may be added to, modified, or extended. An object class allows for the creation of any number of object instances, with forms that vary, depending on the current parameters and possibly according to their changed context.

How an object updates itself as its context changes is called its *design behavior*. The system-provided object classes predefine what is a wall, slab, or roof in terms of how they interact with other related objects. Companies should have the capability of developing user-defined parametric objects—both new ones and extensions to existing ones. Object attributes are needed to interface with analyses, cost estimations, and other applications, but these attributes must first be defined by the software firm or by the user.

Some BIM platforms let users associate 3D objects with simplified separately drawn 2D drawings, allowing users to determine the level of 3D detailing, then filling in missing model geometry with 2D projections. While still being able to produce complete drawings from the combination of the simplified 3D objects and 2D section details, objects drawn in 2D cannot be included in bills of material, in analyses, and other BIM-enabled applications. Most BIM projects and platforms, however, emphasize representing every object fully in 3D and produce 2D drawings from the 3D model. In such systems, the level of detail for cost estimation, scheduling, energy simulation, or other engineering analyses, as well as for drawings, is subject to the level of 3D modeling used. In any case, the required level of 3D modeling has to be carefully determined depending on the goals set for model use during different project phases. The level of modeling is referred to as *level of development (LOD)*. Many organizations and project-level BIM execution plans specify LOD as requirements for the subsystem projects at different phases.

Any BIM application addresses one or more of these types of services. At the BIM tool level, systems vary in important ways: the elaboration of their predefined base objects, in the ease with which users can define new object classes, in the methods of updating objects, in ease of use, in the types of shapes and surfaces that can be represented, in the capabilities for drawing generation, in their ability to manage large numbers of objects. At the platform level, they vary in the ability to manage large or very detailed projects, in their interfaces with other BIM tool software, in their interface consistency for using multiple tools, in their extensibility, in the external libraries that can be used and the data they carry to allow management, and in their ability to support collaboration. These issues are important criteria for building up BIM capabilities within and across organizations.

This chapter provides an overall review of the major BIM model generation technology and the tools and functional distinctions that can be used for assessing and selecting among them.

2.1 THE EVOLUTION TO OBJECT-BASED PARAMETRIC MODELING

A good craftsman knows his tools, whether the tools involve automation or not. This chapter begins by providing a strong conceptual framework for understanding the capabilities that make up BIM design applications.

The current generation of building modeling tools is the outgrowth of four decades of research and development on computer tools for interactive 3D design, culminating in object-based parametric modeling. One way of understanding the current capabilities of modern BIM design applications is by reviewing their incremental evolution historically. We start with a short history.

2.1.1 Early 3D Modeling

Since the 1960s, modeling of 3D geometry has been an important research area. Development of new 3D representations had many potential uses, including movies, architectural and engineering design, and games. The ability to represent compositions of polyhedral forms for viewing was first developed in the late 1960s and later led to the first computer-graphics film, *Tron* (in 1987). These initial polyhedral forms could be composed into an image with a limited set of parameterized and scalable shapes, but designing requires the ability to easily edit and modify complex shapes. In 1973, a major step toward this goal was realized. The ability to create and edit arbitrary 3D solid, volume-enclosing shapes was developed separately by three groups: Ian Braid at Cambridge University, Bruce Baumgart at Stanford, and Ari Requicha and Herb Voelcker at the University of Rochester (Eastman, 1999; Chapter 2). Known as *solid modeling*, these efforts produced the first generation of practical 3D modeling design tools.

Two forms of solid modeling were initially developed and competed for supremacy: the boundary representation (B-rep) approach and the Constructive Solid Geometry (CSG) approach. The B-rep approach represented shapes as closed, oriented sets of bounded surfaces. A shape was a set of these bounded surfaces that satisfied a defined set of volume-enclosing criteria, regarding connectedness, orientation, and surface continuity among others (Requicha, 1980). Computational functions were developed to allow creation of these shapes with variable dimensions, including parameterized boxes, cones, spheres, pyramids, and the like, as shown in Figure 2–1 (left). Also provided were swept shapes: extrusions and revolves defined as a profile and a sweep axis—straight or around an axis of rotation (Figure 2–1, right).

FIGURE 2–1 A set of functions that generate regular shapes, including sweeps.

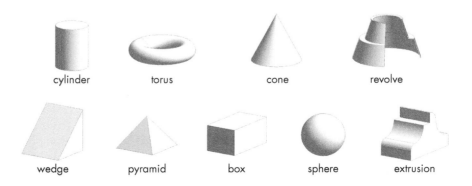

cylinder   torus   cone   revolve

wedge   pyramid   box   sphere   extrusion

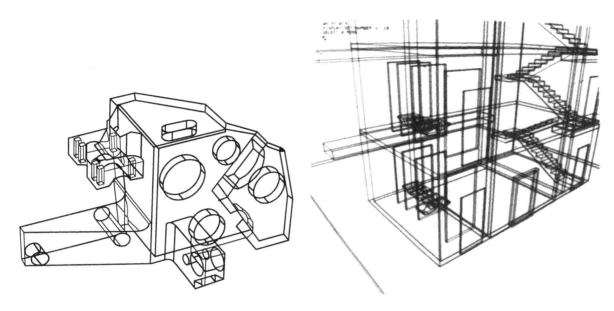

FIGURE 2–2 One of the first complex mechanical parts generated using B-reps and the Boolean operations (Braid, 1973) and an early solid modeler representation of a building service core (Eastman, 1975).

Each of these operations created a well-formed B-rep shape with explicit dimensions. Editing operations placed these shapes in relation to one another, possibly overlapping. Overlapped shapes could be combined using the operations of spatial union, intersection, and subtraction—called the Boolean operations—on pairs or multiple well-formed polyhedral shapes. These operations allowed the user to interactively generate quite complex shapes, such as the examples shown in Figure 2–2 from Braid's thesis or Eastman's early office building. The editing operations had to output shapes that were also well-formed B-reps, allowing operations to be concatenated. The shape creation and editing systems provided by combining primitive shapes and the Boolean operators allowed generation of a set of surfaces that together were guaranteed to enclose a user-defined volumetric shape. Shape editing on the computer began.

In the alternative approach, CSG represented a shape as a set of functions that define the primitive polyhedra like those defined in Figure 2–3 on the left, similar to those for B-rep. These functions are combined in algebraic expressions, also using the Boolean operations, shown in Figure 2–3 on the right. However, CSG relied on diverse methods for assessing the final shape defined as an algebraic expression. For example, it might be drawn on a display, but no set of bounded surfaces was generated. An example is shown in Figure 2–4. The textual commands define a set of primitives for representing a small house. The last line above the figure composes the shapes using the Boolean operations. The result is the simplest of building shapes: a single shape

FIGURE 2–3 A set of primitive shapes and operators for Constructive Solid Geometry. Each shape's parameters consist of those defining the shape and then placing it in 3D space.

THE CSG MODEL:

A set of primitives of the form:

PLANE (Pt$_1$, Pt$_2$, Pt$_3$)

SPHERE (radius, transform)

BLOCK (x, y, z, transform)

CYLINDER (radius, length, transform)

A set of operators:
UNION (S$_1$, S$_2$, S$_3$,.......)
INTERSECT (S$_1$, S$_2$)
DIFFERENCE (S$_1$, S$_2$)
CHAMFER (edge, depth)

FIGURE 2–4 The definitions of a set of primitive shapes and their composition into a simple building. The building is then edited.

BuildingMass := BLOCK(35.0,20.0,25.0,(0,0,0,0,0,0,));
Space := BLOCK(34.0,19.0,8.0,(0.5,0.5,0,1.0,0,0));
Door := BLOCK(4.0,3.0,7.0,(33.0,6.0,1.0,1.0,0,0));
Roofplane1 := PLANE((0.0,0.0,18.0).(35.0,0.0,18.0),(35.0,10.0,25.0));
Roofplane2 := PLANE((35.0,10.0,25.0),(35.0,20.0,18.0),(0.0,20.0,18.0));
Building := (((BuildingMass - Space) – Door) - Roofplane1) - Roofplane2;

EVALUATED MODEL:

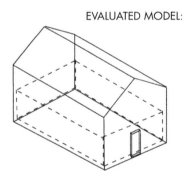

UNEVALUATED MODEL:
(primitives displayed):

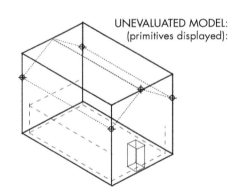

Space := BLOCK(34.0,19.0,14.0,(0.5,0.5,0,1.0,0,0));
Door := BLOCK(4.0,3.0,7.0,(33.0,6.0,1.0,1.0,0,0));

EVALUATED MODEL:

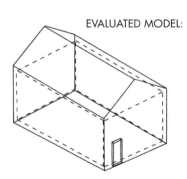

UNEVALUATED MODEL:
(primitives displayed):

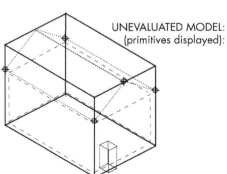

hollowed with a single floor space with a gable roof and door opening. The placed but not evaluated shapes are shown on the right. The main difference between CSG and B-rep is that CSG stores the parameters defining its shape components and an algebraic formula for composing them together, while B-rep stores the results of the sequence of operations and object arguments making up the component shape. The differences are significant. In CSG, elements can be edited and regenerated on demand. Notice that in Figure 2–4, all locations and shapes parameters can be edited via the shape parameters in the CSG expressions. This method of describing a shape—as text strings—was very compact, but took several seconds to compute the shape on desktop machines of that era. The B-rep, on the other hand, was excellent for direct interaction, for computing mass properties, rendering, and animation, and for checking spatial conflicts. Editing B-rep shapes was very difficult because their parametrization did not offer useful parameters for editing.

Initially, these two methods competed to determine which was the better approach. It soon was recognized that the methods should be combined, allowing for editing within the CSG tree (sometimes called the *unevaluated shape*). By using the B-rep for display and interaction to edit a shape, compositions of shapes could be made. The B-rep was called the *evaluated shape*. Today, all parametric modeling tools and all building models incorporate both representations, one CSG-like for editing, and the B-rep for visualizing, measuring, clash detection, and other nonediting uses. First-generation tools supported 3D faceted and cylindrical object modeling with associated attributes, which allowed objects to be composed into engineering assemblies, such as engines, process plants, or buildings (Eastman, 1975; Requicha, 1980). This merged approach to modeling was a critical precursor to modern parametric modeling.

The value of associating materials and other properties with the shapes was quickly recognized in these early systems. These could be used for preparation of structural analyses or for determining volumes, dead loads, and bills of material. Objects with material lead to situations where a shape made of one material was combined by the Boolean operation with a shape of another material. What is the appropriate interpretation? While subtractions have a clear intuitive meaning (walls in windows or holes in steel plate), intersections and unions of shapes with different material do not.

This conceptually was a problem because both objects were considered as having the same status—as individual objects. These conundrums led to the recognition that a major use of Boolean operations was to embed "features" into a primary shape, such as connections in precast pieces, reliefs, or bullnose in concrete (some added and others subtracted). An object that is a feature to be combined with the main object is placed relatively to the main object; the feature later can be named, referenced, and edited. The material of the main object applies to any changes in volume. Feature-based design became a major subfield of parametric modeling (Shah and Mantyla, 1995) and was another important incremental step in the development of modern parametric design tools. Window and door openings with fillers are intuitive examples of features within a wall.

Building modeling based on 3D solid modeling was first developed in the late 1970s and early 1980s. CAD systems, such as RUCAPS (which evolved into Sonata), TriCAD, Calma, GDS (Day, 2002), and university research systems at Carnegie-Mellon University and the University of Michigan developed these basic capabilities. (For one detailed history of the development of CADtechnology, see http://mbinfo.mbdesign.net/CAD-History.htm.) This work was carried out concurrently by teams in mechanical, aerospace, building, and electrical product design, sharing concepts and techniques of product modeling, and integrated analysis and simulation.

Solid modeling CAD systems were functionally powerful but often overwhelmed the available computing power. Some production issues in building, such as drawing and report generation, were not well developed, limiting their use in production. Also, designing 3D objects was conceptually foreign for most designers, who were more comfortable working in 2D. The systems were expensive, costing upward of $35,000 per seat in the 1980s (including hardware), the equivalent of an expensive sports car. The manufacturing and aerospace industries saw the huge potential benefits in terms of integrated analysis capabilities, reduction of errors, and the move toward factory automation. They worked with CAD companies to resolve shortcomings and led efforts to develop new capabilities. Most of the building industry did not recognize these benefits. Instead, they adopted architectural drawing editors, such as AutoCAD, Microstation, and MiniCAD that augmented the then-current methods of working and supported the digital generation of 2D design and construction documents.

Another step in the evolution from CAD to parametric modeling was the recognition that multiple shapes could share parameters. For example, the boundaries of a wall are defined by the floor planes, wall, and ceiling surfaces that bound it; how objects are connected partially determines their shape in any layout. If a single wall is moved, all other walls that abut it should update as well. That is, changes propagate according to their connectivity. In other cases, geometry is not defined by related objects' shapes, but rather globally. Grids, for example, have long been used to define structural frames. The grid intersection points provide parameters for placing and orienting shapes. Move one grid line and the shapes defined relatively to the associated grid points must also update. Global parameters and equations can be used locally too. The example for a portion of a façade shown in Figure 2–6 provides an example of this kind of parametric rule.

Initially, these capabilities for stairs or walls were built into object-generating functions, for example, where the parameters for a stairway were defined: a location; stair riser, tread, and width parameters given; and the stair assembly constructed virtually within the computer. These types of capabilities allowed the layout of stairs in AutoCAD Architecture and early 3D CAD tools, and in the development of assembly operations in AutoCAD 3D, for example. But this is not yet full parametric modeling.

Later in the development of 3D modeling, parameters defining shapes could be automatically reevaluated and the shape rebuilt, first on-demand under control by the users. Then the software was given flags to automatically mark what was modified, so only the changed parts were automatically rebuilt.

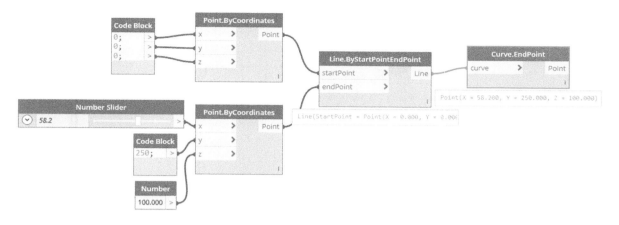

FIGURE 2–5   The parametric relation representation in some BIM applications.

Because one change could propagate to other objects, the development of assemblies with complex interactions led to the need to the development of a "resolver" capability that analyzed the changes and chose the most efficient order to update them. The ability to support such automatic updates was a further development in BIM and parametric modeling.

In general, the internal structure of an object instance defined within a parametric modeling system is a directed graph, where the nodes are object classes with parameters or operations that construct or modify an object instance; links in the graph indicate relations between nodes. Some systems offer the option of making the parametric graph visible for editing, as shown in Figure 2–5. Modern parametric object modeling systems internally mark where edits are made and only regenerate affected parts of the model's graph, minimizing the update sequence and maximizing speed.

The range of rules that can be embedded in a parametric graph determines the generality of the system. Parametric object families are defined using parameters and the relations between the parameters. Since the relations constrain the design behavior of a parametric model, parametric modeling is also referred to as *constraint modeling*. Three methods are commonly used to define parametric relations: geometric relations (e.g., distances and angles), descriptive relations (e.g., *coincident, parallel*, and *vertical*), and equational relations (e.g., parameter*2). Current tools allow additional "if-then" conditions. The definition of object classes is a complex undertaking, requiring embedding knowledge about how they should behave in different contexts. If-then conditions can replace one design feature with another, based on the test result or some condition. These are used in structural detailing, for example, to select the desired connection type, depending upon loads and the members being connected. Examples are provided in Chapter 5 and in Sacks et al. (2004). Also see Lee et al. (2006) for a brief history of parametric modeling and more details on parametric constraints.

Several BIM design applications support parametric relations to complex curves and surfaces, such as splines and nonuniform B-splines (NURBS). These tools allow complex curved shapes to be defined and controlled similarly to other types of geometry.

The definition of parametric objects also provides guidelines for their later dimensioning in drawings. If windows are placed in a wall according to the offset from the wall-end to the center of the window, the default dimensioning will be done this way in later drawings.

In summary, there is an important but varied set of parametric capabilities, some of which are not supported by all BIM design tools. These include:

- Generality of parametric relations, ideally supporting full algebraic and trigonometric capabilities
- Support for condition branching and writing rules that can associate different features to an object instance
- Providing links between objects and being able to make these attachments freely, such as a wall whose base is a slab, ramp, or stair
- Using global or external parameters to control the layout or selection of objects
- Ability to extend existing parametric object classes using subtyping, so that the existing object class can address new structures and design behavior not provided originally

Parametric object modeling provides a powerful way to create and edit geometry. Without it, model generation and design would be extremely cumbersome and error-prone, as was found with disappointment by the mechanical engineering community after the initial development of solid modeling. Designing a building that contains a hundred thousand or more objects would be impractical without a system that allows for effective low-level automatic design editing.

Figure 2–6, developed using Generative Components by Bentley, is an example custom parametric assembly. The example shows a curtain wall model whose main geometric attributes are defined and controlled parametrically. The model is defined by a structure of center lines dependent on control points. Different layers of components are propagated on and around the center lines, adapting to global changes on the overall shape and subdivisions of the curtain wall and the 3D orientation of the connections. The parametric models were designed to allow a range of variations that were defined by the person defining the parametric model. It allows the different alternatives shown to be generated in close to real time.

The current generation of BIM architectural design platforms, including Revit, AECOsim Building Designer, ArchiCAD, Digital Project, Allplan, and Vectorworks, as well as fabrication-level BIM design platforms, such as Tekla Structures and Structureworks, all grew out of the object-based parametric modeling capabilities developed and refined first for mechanical systems. Particular mention should be made of Parametric Technology Corporation (PTC). In the 1980s, PTC led efforts to define shape instances and other properties

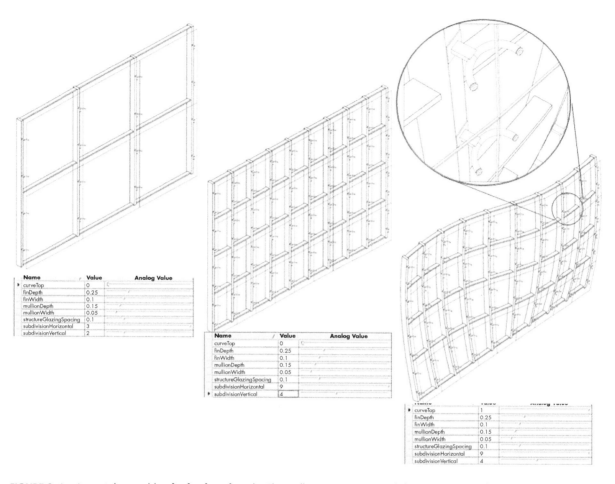

Name	Value	Analog Value
▶ curveTop	0	
finDepth	0.25	
finWidth	0.1	
mullionDepth	0.15	
mullionWidth	0.05	
structureGlazingSpacing	0.1	
subdivisionHorizontal	3	
subdivisionVertical	2	

Name	Value	Analog Value
curveTop	0	
finDepth	0.25	
finWidth	0.1	
mullionDepth	0.15	
mullionWidth	0.05	
structureGlazingSpacing	0.1	
subdivisionHorizontal	9	
▶ subdivisionVertical	4	

Name	Value	Analog Value
▶ curveTop	1	
finDepth	0.25	
finWidth	0.1	
mullionDepth	0.15	
mullionWidth	0.05	
structureGlazingSpacing	0.1	
subdivisionHorizontal	9	
subdivisionVertical	4	

FIGURE 2–6 A partial assembly of a freeform façade. The mullion partitioning and dimensions are defined in the parameter table, while the curvature is defined by a curved surface behind it. The surface drives automatic adjustment of the mullion profiles, glazing panelization, and bracket rotation. The faceted glazing panels are connected by brackets as shown in the blowup. This wall model and its variations were generated by Andres Cavieres using Generative Components.

defined and controlled according to a hierarchy of parameters at the assembly and at an individual object level. The shapes could be 2D or 3D.

In this sense, an object edits itself behaviorally, applying the rules used to define it. An example wall class, including its shape attributes and relations, is shown in Figure 2–7. Arrows represent relations with adjoining objects. Figure 2–7 defines a wall family or class, because it is capable of generating many instances of its class in different locations and with varied parameters. Wall families can vary greatly in terms of the geometry they can support, their internal compositional structure, and how the wall can be connected to other parts of the building. Some BIM design applications incorporate different wall classes, called *wall libraries*, to allow more of these distinctions to be addressed.

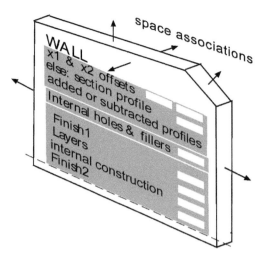

Using the parametric functionality of BIM modelers, users can embed domain knowledge into a model. Significant care must be taken to define even a generic wall. It is common for a parametric building element class to have more than 50 low-level rules for its definition and an extensible set of properties. These conditions show how architectural or building design is a collaboration between the BIM object class modeler, who defines the system of behaviors of BIM elements, and the architectural or building user, who generates designs within the products' rule set. It also explains why users may encounter problems with unusual wall layouts—because they are not covered by the built-in rules. For example, a clerestory wall and the windows set within it are shown in Figure 2–8. In this case, the wall must be placed on a nonhorizontal floor plane. Also, the walls that trim the clerestory wall ends are not on the same base-plane as the wall being trimmed. Some BIM modeling tools have trouble dealing with such combinations of conditions, leading to the need for workarounds.

In Figure 2–9, we present a sequence of editing operations for the semiautomatic design of a small theater. The designer explicitly defines the bounding

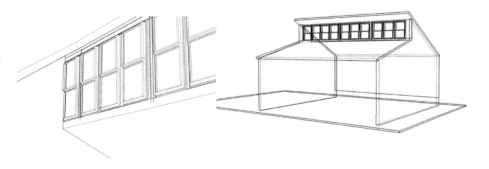

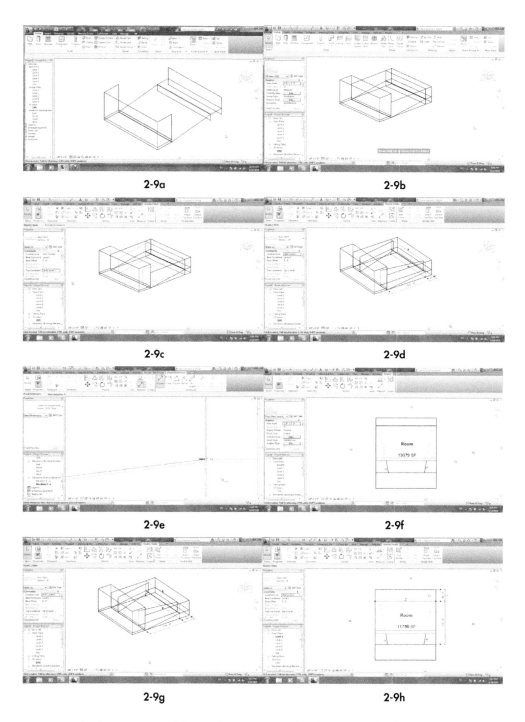

FIGURE 2–9   An example of parametric modeling: A theater is initiated with (a) a raised lobby at the rear, sloping house floor, and raised stage at the front; (b) the enclosing walls and roof are added; (c) angled side walls are added, but do not naturally attach to the sloped house floor; (d) these are aligned to the sloped floor; (e) rules are added to align the sloping wall with the lobby floor; (f) the areas of the house are used for quick estimates of seating; (g) the lobby depth is increased to provide more space, automatically changing the slope of the house floor and the bottom of the side walls; (h) the house space area is reviewed to consider seating implications.

relations of walls, including end-wall butting and floor connections, in order to facilitate later easy editing. When set up appropriately, changes such as the ones shown in Figures 2–9a to 9g become simple and it is possible to make quick edits and updates. Notice that these parametric modeling capabilities go far beyond those offered in previous CSG-based CAD systems. They support automatic updating of a layout and the preservation of relations set by the designer. These tools can be extremely productive.

2.1.2　Degrees of Parametric Modeling

There are many detailed differences between the domain-specific parametric modeling tools used in BIM and those used in other industries. Also, there are several different types of BIM design applications, with different object classes for dealing with different building systems. Buildings are composed of a very large number of relatively simple parts. Each building system has typical building rules and relations that are more predictable than for general manufactured objects. However, the amount of information in even a medium-sized building at construction-level detail can cause performance problems in even the most high-end personal workstations. Another difference is that there is a broad set of standard practices and codes in construction that can be readily adapted and embedded to define design behavior. Also, BIM design applications require drawing production capabilities that use architectural conventions, in contrast to mechanical systems, which often do not support drawing, or use simpler orthographic drawing conventions. These differences have resulted in only a few general-purpose parametric modeling tools being adapted and used for building information modeling.

Several different technologies are combined to provide a modern parametric modeling system.

1. At the simplest level is the definition of complex shapes or assemblies defined by a few parameters. This is often called *parametric solid modeling*. Editing consists of making changes to the parameters and regenerating the piece or layout automatically or when called by the user. The sequence of updates is specified in a tree structure, which is generally called a *feature tree*. Most architectural parametric modelers hide the feature tree to minimize the complexity of a system, but most mechanical or low-level parametric modelers allow the users to access and edit the feature tree.

2. An incremental improvement is the definition of *parametric assembly modeling* that allows the users to create an assembly of individual parametric objects by calling in instances of the individual parametric objects and specifying parametric relations between them. Parametric assembly modeling automatically updates when any shape's parameters are changed.

3. Another improvement allows the users to embed complex intelligence into a parametric model by adding topology-based parametric objects or script-based rules. For example, if a roof is composed of quadrilateral panels with different sizes, a topology-based parametric roof-panel

object can be created in a way to make the shape of each instance of the roof-panel object automatically adjust to the shape of a roof grid pattern. Most complex buildings today, including the Louis Vuitton Building and the Dongdaemun Design Plaza that are featured in Chapter 10, are designed and built using these technologies. See Glymph et al. (2004) for more technical details.

2.1.3 Predefined versus User-Defined Parametric Objects and Libraries

Using these parametric functions, object classes can be defined. A set of object classes is called a *BIM object library* or simply a *library* or a *family*. Each BIM application provides an expanding set of *predefined (or system) parametric object classes*, reflecting its target functionality, and most allow users to create their own *user-defined parametric object classes*.

Each BIM authoring application and the predefined objects that come with it are meant to capture the standard conventions in the area of building that the application targets. Most design and engineering domains have handbooks of standard practice. In architecture, this has for a long period been addressed by Ramsey and Sleeper's *Architectural Graphic Standards* (Ramsey and Sleeper, 2000). In other areas, standard practice is captured by handbooks such as the AISC handbook *Detailing for Steel Construction* (AISC, 2017), or the *PCI Design Handbook* (PCI, 2014). *Standard practice* reflects industry conventions, how to design building parts and systems, based on current practices, often addressing safety, structural performance, material properties, and usage. Design behavior, on the other hand, has not been codified, resulting in different design behaviors in each of the BIM design tools. The base objects in each different BIM design tool is a repackaging of standard practice, as interpreted by the software company's software developers, often with input from industry groups and experts.

In the real world, however, these predefined objects and their built-in behaviors will be limiting at the design and fabrication stages, for a variety of reasons, some enumerated below:

- *A different configuration of parts* is desired for construction, analysis, or aesthetic reasons. A few examples are a window with a Frank Lloyd Wright–inspired mitered glass corner; a custom window frame with modeled thermal breaks; custom connections, such as for glass or plastics; development of a set of custom connections for steel, precast, or wood structures; and connections for a space-frame.
- *The base parts do not address a specific design condition* encountered in a design or real-world context. Examples are a wall that sits on a stepped slab, a spiral ramp with varying slope, and rooms with a domed ceiling.
- *A building system whose structure and behavior is not available from the software or building system vendors*. Examples are curtain wall and building skin systems, complex space types that embed expertise in their layout, and also laboratories and medical spaces.

- *Some objects are not provided by the BIM design application.* Examples include renewable energy objects, such as photovoltaic systems, and cisterns for thermal storage.
- *Improved objects incorporating company best practices.* These may involve detailing that requires extension to base objects, specific attributes, and associated detailing.

If a needed parametric object capability does not exist in the BIM tool, the design and engineering team has these options:

1. Creating an object in another system and importing it into your BIM tool as a *reference object*, without local editing capabilities.
2. Laying out the object instance manually as a nonparametric solid model object, assigning attributes manually, and remembering to update the object details manually as needed.
3. Defining a new parametric object family that incorporates the appropriate external parameters and design rules to support automatic updating behaviors, but the updates are not related to other object classes providing needed parameters.
4. Defining an extension to an existing parametric object family that has modified shape, behavior, and parameters; the resulting object(s) fully integrate with the existing base and extended objects.
5. Defining a new object class that fully integrates and responds to its context.

The first two methods listed above reduce the capabilities of piece editing to the pure 3D-solid-object-level, without parametric representation. All BIM model generation tools support the definition of custom object families (methods 3 to 5). These allow users to define new object classes that can update according to the context defined within them. More challenging is the integration of new custom objects with existing predefined objects such as doors, walls, slabs, and roofs that are provided by the BIM tool. New objects need to fit into the BIM platform's already defined updating structures; otherwise, the interfaces of these objects with others must be edited manually. These extended objects, for example, might include how to frame a particular style of stairway, keeping the code-related parameters for riser and tread. These objects and rules, once created, can be used in any project in which a potential user wants to embed them. It is also important that the objects carry the attributes necessary for the various assessments that the object family's instances must support, such as cost estimation and structural or energy analyses. The updating structures in BIM applications are seldom documented by their developers, making this level of integration harder. Only a few BIM design tools support this level of custom objects. Software maintenance of such customizations is an important consideration before starting down any of these paths.

If a firm frequently works with some building type or system involving special object families, the added labor to define these parametrically is easily

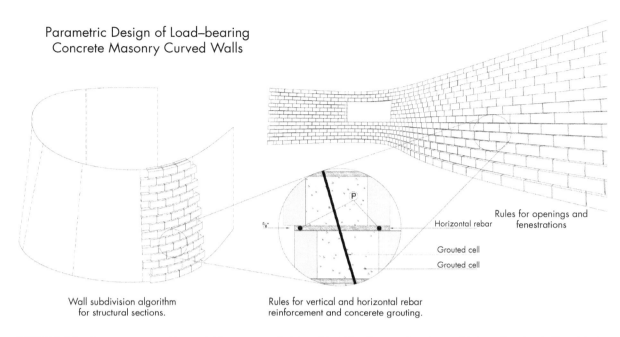

FIGURE 2–10 A custom parametric model for masonry (brick or block) freeform surface (curved in two directions). The object includes the management of trimming of pieces and the automatic assessment when reinforcing is required (from Cavieres, 2009).

justified. They provide automatic application of company best practices in the various contexts found in different projects and can be applied firm-wide. These may be at a high level for layouts or those needed for detailing and fabrication. Examples of such custom parametric objects are the custom masonry wall in Figure 2–10 (Cavieres et al., 2009) and the building core object, described in Chapter 5. The effect of these capabilities is to extend parametric modeling from a geometric design tool to a *knowledge embedding tool.* Any firm that considers itself BIM-capable should have the ability to define its own libraries of custom parametric object families to reflect the expertise and knowledge it has gained and can routinely apply.

Although BIM design tools are no longer new, they are continuously evolving and maturing. The largest effort has been directed toward addressing architectural design intent. The next level of effort has been to address some construction- and fabrication-level objects and behavior. BIM structural design tools are also available and are reviewed in Chapter 5. Other details are provided in Chapters 5, 6, and 7. As the range of renewable and sustainability procedures and control system issues grows, the need for BIM design tools for sustainability will also grow. The intellectual implications of defining object rules and behavior, vis-a-vis the degree of control maintained by BIM users, have not yet been explored thoroughly.

2.2   BEYOND PARAMETRIC SHAPES

In this section, we focus on issues that extend beyond parametric geometric modeling.

2.2.1   Property and Attribute Handling

Object-based parametric modeling addresses geometry and topology, but objects also need to carry a variety of properties if they are to be interpreted, analyzed, priced, and procured by other applications.

Properties come into play at different stages in the building lifecycle. For example, design properties address space and area names, properties for spaces such as occupancy, activities, and equipment performance needed for energy analysis. Zones (an aggregation of spaces) are defined with properties dealing with thermal controls and loads. Different system elements have their own properties for structural, thermal, mechanical, electrical, and plumbing behaviors. Later, properties also address materials and quality specifications for purchasing. At the fabrication stage, material specifications may be refined to include bolt and weld and other connection specifications. At the end of construction, properties provide information and links to pass operating and maintenance data onto operations.

BIM provides the environment to manage and integrate these properties over the project lifecycle. However, the tools to create and manage them are only starting to be developed and integrated into BIM environments.

Properties are seldom used singularly. A lighting application requires material color, a reflection coefficient, a specular reflection exponent, and possibly a texture and bump map. For accurate energy analysis, a wall requires a different set. Thus, properties are appropriately organized into sets and associated with a certain function. Libraries of property sets for different objects and materials are an integral part of a well-developed BIM environment. The property sets are not always available from the product vendor and often have to be approximated by a user, the user's firm, or from the American Society of Testing and Materials data (ASTM). Although various standards organizations are addressing these issues, the property sets needed for storing information for a wide range of simulation and analysis tools have not yet been adequately organized in a standard way for common use; currently, they are left to users to set up.

Even seemingly simple properties can be complex. Take space names, which are used in spatial program assessment, functional analysis, facility management and operations, and sometimes for early cost estimation and assigning energy loads. Space names are specific to building types. Some organizations have tried to develop space name standards to facilitate automation. The U.S. General Services Administration (GSA), for example, has three different space name classifications for courthouses: for building type spatial validation, another for lease calculations, and yet another set used in the U.S. Courts Design Guide. At both the department and individual space levels, Georgia Tech estimated there are about 445 different valid space names (Lee et al., 2010). They should therefore be defined explicitly in project BIM execution plans.

Current BIM platforms default to a minimal set of properties for most object types and provide the capability of extending the set. Users of an application must add properties to each relevant object to produce a certain type of simulation, cost estimate, or analysis and also must manage their appropriateness for various tasks. The management of property sets becomes problematic because different applications for the same function may require somewhat different properties and units, such as for energy and lighting.

There are at least three different ways to manage property instance values for a set of applications:

- By predefining them in the object libraries so they are added to the design model when an object instance is created
- By the user adding them as needed for an application from a stored library of property sets
- By the properties being assigned automatically from a database as they are exported to an analysis or simulation application, based on a unique identifier or key

The first alternative is good for production work involving a standard set of construction types but requires careful user definition for custom objects. Each object carries extensive property data for all relevant applications, only some of which may actually be used in a given project. Extra definitions may slow down an application's performance and enlarge a project model's size. The second alternative allows users to select a set of similar objects or property sets to export to an application. This results in a time-consuming export process. Iterated use of simulation tools may require the addition of properties each time the application is run. This would be required, for example, to examine alternative window and wall systems for energy efficiency. The third approach keeps the design application light but requires the development of a comprehensive material tagging system that can be used by all exporting translators to associate a property set for each object. The authors believe that this third approach is the desired long-term "solution" for property handling. The necessary global object classifications and name tagging required of this approach are still to be developed. Currently, multiple object tags must be developed, one for each application.

The development of object property sets and appropriate object classification libraries to support different types of applications is a broad issue under consideration by the Construction Specification Institute of North America and by other national specification organizations. Building Object Model (BOM) libraries, representing both objects and properties of specific commercial building products for managing object properties, are a potentially important part of a BIM environment. This type of facility is reviewed in Chapter 5, Section 5.4.

2.2.2 Drawing Generation

Even though a building model has the full geometric layout of a building and its systems—and the objects have properties and, potentially, specifications and can carry much more information than drawings—drawings will continue to be required as reports extracted from or as specialized views of the model, for some time into the future. Existing contractual processes and work culture, while changing, are still centered on drawings, whether paper or electronic. Drawings are referred to as the spatial representation in contracts of a building. If a BIM tool does not support effective drawing extraction and a user has to do significant manual editing to generate each set of drawings from cut sections, the benefits of BIM are significantly reduced.

With BIM, each building object instance—its shape, properties, and placement in the model—is represented only once. Based on an arrangement of building object instances, all drawings, reports, and datasets can be extracted; all drawings, reports, and analysis datasets are consistent if taken from the same version of the building model. This capability alone resolves a significant source of errors. With normal 2D architectural drawings, any change or edit must be manually transferred to multiple drawing views by the designer, resulting in potential human errors from not updating all drawings correctly. In precast concrete construction, this 2D practice has been shown to cause errors costing approximately one percent of construction cost (Sacks et al., 2003).

Current BIM design tool capabilities come close to automated drawing extraction.

The location of the drawn section is automatically recorded with a section-cut symbol on a plan or elevation as a cross-reference and the location can be moved if needed. An example is shown in Figure 2–11, with the figure on the left showing the extracted section and the one on the right showing the detailed section with drafted annotation. The section is then detailed manually with the needed wood blocks, extrusions, silicon beading, and weather stripping, and associated annotations provided in the fully detailed drawn section. In most systems, this detail is associated with the section cut it was based on. When 3D elements in the section change, they update automatically in the section but the hand-drawn details must be manually updated.

To produce drawings, each plan, section, and elevation is separately composed based on the above rules from a combination of cut 3D sections and aligned 2D drawn sections. They are then grouped into sheets with normal borders and title sheets. The sheet layouts are maintained across sessions and are part of the overall project data.

Drawing generation from a detailed 3D model has gone through a series of refinements to make it efficient and easy. Below is an ordered list of the levels of quality that can now be supported technically, though note that most systems have not realized the top level of capability for drawing generation. We start from the weakest level.

1. A weak level of drawing production provides for the generation of orthographic sections cut from a 3D model, and the user manually edits the line formats and adds dimensions, details, and annotations. These

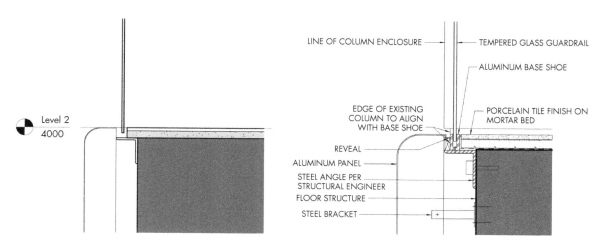

FIGURE 2–11 Sketch showing the initial section extracted from the building model (left) and the manually detailed drawing elaborated from the section (right).

Image courtesy of Yunhee Kim.

details are associative. That is, as long as the section exists in the model, the annotation setup is maintained across drawing versions. Such association capabilities are essential for effective regeneration of drawing versions for the design. In this case, the drawing is an elaborated report generated from the model. The drawing generation may be done either in an external drafting system or within the BIM tool.

2. An improvement upon this level is the definition and use of drawing templates associated with elements for a type of projection (plan, section, elevation) that automatically generates dimension formatting of the element, assigns line weights, and generates annotations from defined attributes. This greatly speeds up the initial drawing setup and improves productivity, though the initial setup of each object family is tedious. Template layout defaults of drawing views can be overwritten and custom annotations added. 2D drawing edits cannot be propagated to the model projections; these have to be made in the model view. In these first two cases, report management should be provided to inform the user that model changes have been made, but the drawings cannot automatically update to reflect these changes until they are regenerated.

3. Current top-level drawing functionality supports bidirectional editing between models and drawings. Changes to model annotations are the same as described above. However, model edits are supported in the drawing view and are propagated to the model. If displayed in windows alongside views of the 3D model, updates in any view can be referenced immediately in the other views. Bidirectional views and strong template generation capabilities further reduce the time and effort needed for drawing generation.

Door, window, and hardware schedules are defined in a similar way to the three alternatives described above. That is, they may be generated as reports and only locally edited. Schedules can also be treated as model views and in some systems can be updated directly, modifying the building model. A static report generator method is weakest, and a strong bidirectional approach is strongest. Such bidirectionality offers useful benefits, including the ability to trade hardware used on a set of doors with hardware recommended on the schedule, rather than from the model. Edits made to a model from a schedule require care, however, and model corruption is often encountered as a result of this type of editing.

In fabrication-level BIM modeling systems, this mixed system of automatic 3D sectional layout and 2D detailing is greatly reduced, and the design is assumed to be generated primarily from the 3D object model. In these cases, joists, studs, plates, plywood sills, and other pieces, shown in Figure 2–11, would be laid out in 3D.

An obvious current goal is to automate the drawing production process as much as possible, since most initial design productivity benefits (and costs) will depend on the extent of automatic generation. At some future point in time, most parties involved in the building delivery process will adapt their practices to BIM technology; they will no longer require drawings and will work directly from building models. We are slowly moving to a paperless world (see Chapter 9 for a discussion). Drawings will continue to be used for the foreseeable future, but increasingly as throw-away mark-up sheets by construction crews and other users. As these changes take place, the conventions regarding architectural drawings are likely to evolve, allowing them to be customized for the specific task in which they are used. Some examples are presented in Chapter 5. Despite advances in automated drawing generation, it is unlikely that automation will ever reach 100 percent because drawings can be generated in various ways depending on designs or drawing conventions.

Current BIM tools provide technologies to relieve some of these issues. BIM applications generally allow designers to choose the level of 3D modeling to use, with 2D drawing sections filling in the missing details. The BIM benefits of data exchange, bills of material, clash detection, detailed cost estimation, and other actions are lost on those elements defined only in 2D section drawings. While it can be argued that complete 3D object modeling is not warranted in every situation, advanced users of BIM are moving toward 100 percent modeling (see, for example, the Victoria Station upgrade, Medina Airport, St. Joseph Hospital, and Dublin New Children's Hospital case studies in Chapter 10) and are held back by those design consultants and fabricators who cannot provide 3D models for coordination.

2.2.3 Scalability

A problem that many BIM users encounter is scalability. Problems in scaling are encountered when a project model gets too large for practical review or editing. Operations become sluggish, so that even simple operations are laborious. Building models take a lot of computer memory space. Large buildings can contain millions of objects, each with a different shape. Scalability is affected by both the size of the building, say in floor area, by the level of detail in the model, and because of inefficient methods of modeling. Even a simple building can encounter scalability problems if every nail and screw is modeled individually.

Parametric modeling incorporates design rules that relate geometry or other parameters of one object with those of other objects. These come in a hierarchy of relations: *within object* parametric relations, *peer object* relations, adjusting one object's shape in response to the change of another object, and *hierarchical relations* between control grids and surfaces that determine the parameters of shape and placement of a set of associated objects. While within object and peer object relations update locally, hierarchical rule propagation may generate updates to the whole building. Local parametric rule propagation makes only reasonable demands on models, while some BIM system platforms limit the ability to manage propagation of large sets of hierarchical rules. Also, it is hard to partition a project into parts for separate development and still manage a large set of hierarchical rules.

The issue is memory size; all operations on object shapes must take place in memory. The simple solution to manage parametric updates is to carry the project in memory. This challenges scalability and places practical limits on the size of a project module that can be effectively edited. However, if rules can be propagated across files, where updating an object in one file can lead to automatic updates propagated to other files, the size limitation of a project disappears. Only a few BIM design applications developed especially for architecture have the means for managing parametric change propagation across multiple files. We call systems that must carry all updated objects in memory simultaneously *memory-based*. When the model gets too large to be held in memory, virtual memory-swapping occurs, which can result in significant degradation of BIM model performance. Other systems have methods of propagating relations and updates across files and can open, update, and then close multiple files during an edit operation. These are called *file-based* systems. File-based systems are generally a bit slower for small projects, but their speed decreases very slowly as project size grows.

User segmentation of projects into modules has been a time-tested way of sharing work and limiting the scale of automatic updates. Reference files are often used to also limit what can be edited. These work well if hierarchical relations in a project don't lead to global project changes. Some BIM tools impose these limitations.

Memory and processing issues will naturally decrease as computers get faster. Cloud computing is also expected to reduce performance issues on large BIM projects. Sixty-four-bit processors and operating systems also provide significant help. There will be the parallel desire, however, for more detailed building models and larger sets of parametric rules. Issues of scalability will be with us for some time.

2.2.4 Object Management and Links

Object Management. BIM models become quite large and complex. Multi-gigabyte models are becoming common. In such cases data coordination and management (what is referred to as "synchronization" in Chapter 3) becomes a large data management task and concern. The traditional approaches to updating versions of a project using files leads to two kinds of problems:

1. Files become huge and the project must be partitioned in some way to allow design to continue; the models are large, slow, and cumbersome.
2. Determining the changes within a file is still a manual management effort, replacing a red marker on drawings in drafting with notes in a 3D PDF or similar reviewing file. Traditionally, major project changes at the construction document stage were frowned upon because of their synchronization cost implications. BIM and model management are supposed to eliminate or greatly reduce this problem. While parametric updates resolve issues of local changes, the coordination of different discipline-specific models and their derived data for schedules, analyses, and reports is still an important project management issue.

The long-discussed but only recently realized capability of exchanging only the new, modified, or deleted object instances in a file, eliminating the "chaff" of the unmodified objects, is available in a production environment, notably Graphisoft BIM server (more fully reviewed in Chapter 3, Section 3.5.3). Transferring only the changed objects and importing them, called an *incremental update*, greatly reduces the size of the exchanges, and allows for immediate identification and targeting of the change issues. This capability requires object identification and version control at the object level, usually provided by timestamps. This capability will become increasingly important as BIM models grow. It will become a "must" feature on future releases of all systems for coordination across multiple BIM applications. It is a fundamental capability for cloud BIM systems.

External Parameter Management. A capability explored in a number of innovative projects has been to control the geometric layout of a design based on control parameters (often a 3D grid) generated and defined in a spreadsheet. An example application of using a spreadsheet to control and coordinate geometry is presented in both the building core model in Chapter 5 and the Aviva Stadium case study project (see the *BIM Handbook* companion website).

For certain types of projects, the ability to read from and write to spreadsheets provides an important level of interoperability among different design tools. Suppose the equivalent parametric models can be built in two different modeling softwares, say Rhino and Bentley, with the same parameters controlling the geometry. Design explorations can be made in Rhino, generally a friendly but information-limited design tool, then the parameters updated in Bentley Architecture, allowing the changes to be integrated in a BIM tool that might have cost or energy analysis capabilities. The spreadsheet provides an important level of geometric interoperability.

Another use of external spreadsheets of parameter lists is to exchange parametric objects by reference, rather than explicitly. The best-known example is steel structures. Steel handbooks, now in digital form, carry the different standard profiles for structural steel, such as W18X35 or L4X4. These profile names can be used to retrieve profile, weight, and mass properties from the steel handbooks. Similar profiles are available for precast concrete products, reinforcing bars, and some window manufacturer catalogs. If the sender and the receiver each have access to the same catalog, then they may send and retrieve the relevant information by reference (name); and the exchange is made by retrieving the appropriate catalog information and loading it into the appropriate parametric model for the part. This is a significant capability in many production areas.

Links to External Catalog Files. Another important capability is to provide links to external files. The primary use of this capability today is to link products with their associated manuals for maintenance and operation, for later association with facilities operation and maintenance (O&M). Some BIM tools offer this capability and enhance their value as a tool that can provide support during the O&M stage.

The functional capabilities outlined in this section are all important in assessing and selecting a BIM platform. They will be used later in this chapter when we review the major BIM design tools.

2.2.5 Some Commonly Asked Questions

There are many questions associated with BIM and parametric computer-aided design systems. This section attempts to answer the most common ones.

What are the Strengths and Limitations of Object-Based Parametric Modeling? One major benefit of parametric modeling is the intelligent design behavior of objects. Automatic low-level editing is built in, almost like one's own design assistant. This intelligence, however, comes at a cost. Each type of system object has its own behavior and associations. As a result, BIM design applications are inherently complex. Each type of building system is composed of objects that are created and edited differently, though with a similar user interface style. Effective use of a BIM design application usually requires months to gain proficiency in a single area of design.

Modeling software that some users prefer, especially for early concept design, such as SketchUp and Rhino, are not parametric modeling–based tools. Rather, they have a fixed way of geometrically editing objects, which varies only according to the surface types used. This functionality is applied to all object types, making them much simpler to use. Thus, an editing operation applied to walls will have the same behavior when it is applied to slabs. In these systems, attributes defining the object type and its functional intention, if applied at all, can be added when the user chooses, not when it is created.

All of these systems allow the grouping of surfaces, giving the group a name and maybe assigning attributes. Done carefully and with a matching interface, the object can be exported and used in other areas, say solar gain studies. This is similar to the kinds of workarounds people used to do to create 3D visual modes with 3D geometry modeling tools (such as AutoCAD) before BIM was commonplace. However, one would not take this kind of modeling into design development because such objects are not linked to other objects and must be spatially managed individually. An argument can be made that for concept design use, however, BIM technology with its object-specific behavior is not always warranted. This topic is explored further in Chapter 5.

Why Can't Different Parametric Modelers Exchange Their Models? It is often asked why firms cannot directly exchange a model from Revit with Bentley AECOsim, or open an ArchiCAD model with Digital Project. From the overview discussed previously, it should be apparent that the reason for this lack of interoperability is that the different BIM design applications rely on different definitions of their base objects and their behaviors. A Bentley wall behaves differently than a Vectorworks wall or a Tekla wall. This is the result of different capabilities involving rule types in the BIM tool and also the rules applied in the definition of specific object families. This problem applies only to parametric objects, not those with fixed geometry. If the shapes are accepted in their current form as fixed and their behavioral rules are dropped, an ArchiCAD object can be used in Digital Project; a Bentley object can be used in Revit. The issues of exchange are resolvable. IFC, an open standard for exchanging BIM data, also supports parametric definitions and is another solution. The problem is exchanging object behavior (which is not often needed). Behavior also could be exchanged if and when organizations agree on a standard for common building object definitions that includes not only geometry but also behavior. Until then, exchanges for some objects will be limited or will fail completely. Improvements will come about incrementally, as the demand to resolve these issues makes implementation worthwhile, and the multiple issues are sorted out. The same issue exists in manufacturing and it has not yet been resolved.

Are There Inherent Differences between Construction, Fabrication, and Architectural BIM Design Applications? Could the same BIM platform support both design and fabrication detailing? Because the base technology for all of these systems has much in common, there is no technological reason why building design and fabrication BIM design applications cannot offer products in each other's area. This is happening to some degree with Revit and other platforms which are developing some of the capabilities offered by fabrication-level BIM design applications.

On the other hand, there are cases where Tekla, a platform primarily intended for structural design and fabrication detailing, has been used to design and build houses. However, the expertise needed to support full production use in information-rich design areas will depend on major front-end embedding of requisite object behaviors, which are distinctly different for different building systems and their lifecycle needs. Expert knowledge of specific building system object behaviors is more readily embedded when it is codified, as it is, for example, in structural system design. The interfaces, reports, and other system issues may vary, but we are likely to see skirmishes in the middleground for a significant period of time, as each product attempts to broaden its market domains.

Are There Significant Differences Between Manufacturing-Oriented Parametric Modeling Tools and BIM Design Applications? Could a parametric modeling system for mechanical design be adapted for BIM? Some differences in system architecture are noted in Sections 2.1.3 and 2.3.1. Mechanical parametric modeling tools have already been adapted for the AEC market. Digital Project, based on CATIA, is an obvious example. Structureworks is a precast concrete detailing and fabrication product that uses Solidworks as a platform. These adaptations build in the objects and behavior needed for the target system domain. Building modelers are organized as top-down design systems, while manufacturing parametric tools were originally organized bottom-up. Because of manufacturing systems' structure, where different parts were originally different "projects," they have addressed the challenge of propagating changes across files, making them often more scalable. In other areas, such as plumbing, curtain wall fabrication, and ductwork design, we can expect to see both mechanical parametric modeling tools and architectural and fabrication-level BIM design applications vying for these markets. The range of functionality offered in each market is still being sorted out. The market is the battleground.

In this section, we have tried to articulate several different issues:

- The differences between previous CAD systems and BIM design applications
- The differences between BIM design applications used in architectural and engineering design and those used in fabrication
- The similarities and differences between BIM design applications and more general object-based parametric modeling systems used by other industries

2.3 BIM ENVIRONMENTS, PLATFORMS, AND TOOLS

This chapter has, so far, provided an overview of the basic capabilities of BIM design applications resulting from their development as object-based parametric design tools. We now turn to reviewing the main BIM design applications and their functional differences. We have considered parametric modeling applications up to this point in a homogeneous manner, primarily as tools for generating design information, and possibly for structuring it and managing it. In considering their use in more detail, we note that most BIM design applications aspire to be more than a design tool. Most BIM design applications also have interfaces to other applications, for rendering, energy analysis, cost estimation, and so forth. Some also provide multiuser capabilities that allow multiple users to coordinate their work.

In planning and developing BIM within an organization, it is useful to think of it in system architecture terms. BIM, in most organizations, will involve multiple applications for different uses. How are the different applications to be conceptualized and organized? Large firms will typically support and in some sense integrate tens of different applications for their employees' use.

We use the term *application* as the generic term to denote software. We make explicit use of some terms that long have been used informally to consider BIM applications in the following hierarchy:

- **BIM tool:** A BIM information sender, receiver, and processor used within a BIM process in association with BIM platforms. Note that many of these tools may not be generally regarded as BIM tools unless they are used within the context of a BIM process. Example BIM tools include applications such as specification generation tools, cost estimation tools, scheduling tools, and Excel-based engineering tools that do not include geometric definitions and are all text-based. AutoCAD for drawing production or other AutoCAD-based applications can be also regarded as BIM tools as far as they are used in the context of a BIM process. Some other examples include tools for model quality checking, rendering, navigation, visualization, facility management, early design generation, project management, and various types of engineering and simulation. Third-party applications are also included.

- **BIM platform:** A core BIM information generator with functions to maintain the integrity of a model based on the parametric and object-based modeling capability. It provides a primary data model that hosts the information from various BIM applications. Thus, strong interoperability capabilities are needed, and they typically incorporate interfaces to multiple other tools with varied levels of integration. Generally known object-based parametric BIM applications such as Revit, ArchiCAD, Tekla Structures, Vectorworks, Bentley AECOSim, and Digital Project fall into this category. Most BIM platforms internally incorporate tool functionality such as rendering, drawing production, and clash detection. Most platforms provide different sets of interfaces, libraries, and functions for different domains and trades. Examples include Revit Structure, ArchiCAD MEP, and different Workbenches in Digital Project.

- **BIM environment:** A set of BIM applications that are interfaced to support multiple information and process pipelines in a project, an organization, or a local construction sector. BIM environments encompass the various BIM tools, platforms, servers, libraries, and work flows within the project or the organization. See Figure 2–12.

When multiple platforms and thus multiple data models are used, additional levels of data management and coordination are required. These address

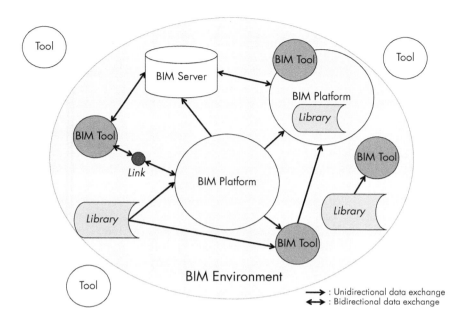

FIGURE 2–12 BIM environments, platforms, and tools.

tracking and coordinating communication between people as well as between multiple platforms. BIM environments also provide the opportunity to carry much wider forms of information than model data alone, such as video, images, audio records, emails, and many other forms of information used in managing a project. BIM platforms are not set to manage such diverse information. BIM servers, reviewed in Chapter 3, Section 3.5, are the new products targeted to support BIM environments. In addition, the BIM environment includes object and assembly libraries for reuse, interfaces to the applications the organization supports, and links to corporate management and accounting systems.

Adopting a BIM design application, as a tool and/or platform within a BIM environment, is a significant undertaking. Adoption is also discussed in later chapters, especially regarding their intended use for design and engineering in Chapter 5, for contractors and construction management in Chapter 6, and for fabricators in Chapter 7. The facility with which they integrate within a BIM environment is an essential aspect (see Chapter 3). Decisions about applications involve understanding new technologies and the new organizational skills needed, and then learning and managing those skills. These challenges will recede over time, as the learning curve and practices surrounding BIM use become more ingrained in practice. Because the functionality of BIM design applications is changing quickly, it is important to consider the reviews of the current versions in *AECBytes, Cadalyst, the BIM Hub*, or other AEC computer-aided design journals and special interest groups on collaboration sites such as LinkedIn. Within the common framework of providing object-based parametric modeling, BIM design applications embody many different kinds of capabilities. The sections below explain considerations for BIM design applications and BIM environments.

2.3.1   Considerations for BIM Design Applications

Next, we describe the design application capabilities in rough-rank based on our sense of their level of importance. We take parametric model generation and editing as fundamental. We assume that model definition and drawing production are the current primary uses for building modeling systems. Model generation and editing is considered multifaceted, in terms of user interface, custom objects, and complex surface modeling.

- **User Interfaces:** BIM design applications are quite complex and have much greater functionality than earlier CAD tools. Some BIM design applications have a relatively intuitive and easy-to-learn user interface, with a modular structure to their functionality, while others place more emphasis on functionality that is not always well-integrated into the overall system. Criteria to be considered here include consistency of menus across the system's functionalities following standard conventions; menu-hiding that eliminates irrelevant actions not meaningful to the current context of activities; modular organization of different kinds of functionality; and online help providing real-time prompts and command-line explanation of operations and inputs. While user interface issues may seem minor, a poor user interface results in longer learning times, more errors, and often to users' not taking full advantage of the functionality built into the application. A BIM application needs to be able to present a large range of information: geometry, properties, and relations between them to other applications. Typical uses include structural, energy, lighting, costs, and other analyses during design; clash detection and issue tracking for design coordination; purchasing and materials tracking; and task and equipment scheduling for construction. User interfaces of importance depend on the intended use of the BIM application, defined by particular patterns of workflow. We assess their appropriateness in the tools and workflows in the chapters that address their use in different contexts—Chapters 5, 6, and 7. User interface issues across a set of integrated applications are also important at the platform level; we review those issues in the next section.
- **Drawing Generation:** How easy is it to generate drawings and drawing sets and to maintain them through multiple updates and releases? Assessment should include quick visualization of the effects of model changes on drawings, strong associations so that model changes propagate directly to drawings and vice versa, and effective template generation that allows drawing types to carry out as much automatic formatting as possible. A more thorough review of functionality was provided in Section 2.2.2.
- **Ease of Developing Custom Parametric Objects:** This is a complex capability that can be defined at three different levels. The issue is explained further in Section 2.1.3.
- **Complex Curved Surface Modeling:** Support for creating and editing complex surface models based on quadrics, splines, and nonuniform

B-splines is important for those firms that currently do this type of work or plan to in the future. These geometric modeling capabilities in a BIM application are foundational; they cannot be easily added on later.

- **BIM Object Libraries:** Each BIM platform has various libraries of predefined objects that can be imported for use in that platform. These can be helpful by eliminating the need to define them yourself. In general, the more predefined objects, the more productive are users. There is a further level of discrimination regarding how good the objects are for different uses. During design, BIM objects may be generic and not a particular object: In construction, the product is likely to have a specific product ID. Currently, there is little effort to standardize the structure of object information beyond geometry. Here we are referring to specifications for selection, specifications for use in analyses, service manuals, material properties for use in rendering, and other similar uses. In considering different platforms, the availability of predefined building objects facilitates work on that platform. Organizations are recognizing the value of object libraries as a means to develop standards of detailing at the architectural or fabrication/detailing levels.

- **Extensibility:** Extensibility capabilities are assessed based on whether a BIM platform provides scripting support—an *interactive language* that adds functionality or automates low-level tasks, similar to AutoLISP in AutoCAD—an Excel format bidirectional interface, and a broad and well-documented application programming interface (API). Scripting languages and Excel interfaces are generally for end users, while an API is intended for software developers. These capabilities are needed depending on the extent to which a firm expects to customize capabilities, such as custom parametric objects, specialized functions, or interfaces to other applications.

- **Interoperability:** Model data is generated, in part, to share with other applications for early project feasibility studies, for collaboration with engineers and other consultants, and later for construction. Collaboration is supported by the degree to which the BIM application provides interfaces with other specific products and, more generally, its import and export support of open data exchange standards. Both these types of interfaces are reviewed in detail in Chapter 3. Open exchange standards are getting more elaborate and starting to support workflow-level exchanges. This requires varied export and import translations. An easily customizable import and export facility is highly beneficial. Both tool interfaces and the more general aspects of interoperability are considered.

- **Multiuser Environment:** More and more systems support collaboration among a design team and a cloud-based work environment. They allow multiple users to create and edit parts of the same project directly from a single project file and manage user access to these various information parts. These issues will become predominant as cloud services evolve.

- **Effective Support for Managing Properties:** Properties are an integral part of the data needed for most BIM support tools. Property sets need to be easily set up and associated with the object instances they describe. The properties vary by their use: fabrication, object performances, logistical issues, and so on. Thus property set assignment and management is part of system workflows.

- **Other Capabilities:** Support for design application capabilities beyond the basics include clash detection, quantity takeoffs, issue tracking, and incorporation of product and construction specifications. These are appropriate for different uses and workflows, and are considered in more detail in Chapters 5, 6, and 7.

In Section 2.5 below, we offer an overview of the current capabilities of the major BIM platforms. Some of those reviewed support only architectural design functions; others only various types of fabrication-level building systems; and others both. Each assessment is for the version of the software system noted; later versions may have better or worse capabilities. We review them according to the criteria developed earlier.

2.3.2   Considerations for a BIM Environment

At the beginning of the BIM age, it was thought that a single application could serve the needs at all three levels: as a tool, as a platform, and as an environment. That idealism has slowly waned, as the scale of a BIM project and the systems to support it have become understood. An important capability needed to globally support advanced BIM projects is to support work in a multiplatform and multirepresentation environment. A BIM environment needs the ability to generate and store object instances for different tools and platforms and to manage that data effectively, including change management at the object level. This issue is addressed more centrally in Chapter 3. This can be handled by a change flag and/or a timestamp that is updated whenever an object is modified. The goal is to exchange and manage objects and sets of objects rather than files.

2.4   BIM MODEL QUALITY AND MODEL CHECKING

As BIM use expands, model quality is quickly becoming an issue of overriding importance. BIM data application uses are increasingly automated because eliminating manual entry saves time and is potentially error-free. But in the enthusiasm for automation, some organizations can overlook that BIM also removes some intelligent human reviewers from the data flow. While inefficient and error prone, the manual user interface forces a round of visual checking that is eliminated by automation and integration. Furthermore, for BIM information to be useful for downstream applications—such as functional simulations, code-compliance checking, automated permitting, and the like—it must conform to the semantic content and syntax requirements defined for the receiving applications. Therefore, the move to automated rule checking is critical if the quality assumptions of BIM are to be realized.

Automated checking is clearly superior to manual checking. Rule sets can be prechecked by comparing the outcomes of automated checking with manual checks of the same model. Similar tests can also be run on different checking applications for comparison. Some errors may be missed because of errors in rule testing software; rule checking requires careful thinking through of the validation criteria.

The model aspects than can be checked range from physical and material correctness at one end of the spectrum to performance requirements defined in codes at the other end. Correctness concerns overlaps of solids in space and time that are not physically realizable, alignment of objects that are parts of different systems that may be meant to be connected (Belsky et al., 2016), construction practices regarding engineering requirements for the spaces needed for construction methods, and other rules regarding safety, user behavior, assembly, and construction and maintenance practices that may not explicitly be codified. Code requirements define the physical behavior of the building structurally, thermally, and so on. The list of issues to which rule checking can be applied is open-ended.

The definition and implementation of rule checking is expected to be a capability that all parties to the BIM process will need to employ as BIM matures: designers and owners to verify programmatic requirements, subsystem contractors and fabricators to check that the required system interface conditions are satisfied (such as connections), facility managers (maintenance operations supported), and others. In the expected future, then, rule checking should not be a capability that requires advanced programming expertise; it should be easily applied by a wide range of users.

Rule testing involves the application of two types of classification: (1) regarding the intent of the rule, the other (2) according to the process and implementation of the rule. In general, these classifications are orthogonal. The intent of the rule comes from the user and defines the purpose of the test. The implementation of the rule involves both the data representing the project and the process of checking. There are multiple methods of mapping intents to process, some ranging from crude approximations (such as overlapping bounding boxes to interpret spatial relations) to more accurate tests. They are open to the many ways that an intention can be resolved. For example, for quick egress in case of fire, the check can apply to circulation pathways, material enclosure of safe spaces, and to sprinklers and other technologies, each with different representational and rule checking algorithmic issues. Representations may be trivial, such as a maximum value, an allowed type of object, or a point in time; others may be complex, such as geometric relations only represented implicitly, such as the volume of space that must be empty to allow for maintenance access to a building part, such as an air-conditioning filter. Variations in representation are generally selected according to differences in their computational complexity. Some rule checks deal with temporary objects, including temporary structures (formwork, shoring, and required access paths for maintenance).

Thus a building model must be *qualified* in order to validate that it can meaningfully support a target array of tests. By qualified, we mean that the building model must satisfy certain rules in order for it to be further tested.

Qualifying checks are prerequisites that must pass before other checks can be applied. For example, in almost all buildings, rooms must have at least one door in their bounding walls for access. Another, even more basic set of tests are the syntax rules of the testing language, carried out by the language compiler/interpreter. All qualification tests need to have easy to understand documentation for use.

Model quality checking tools require that the information in a building model be complete, correct, and explicit. Unfortunately, users often leave much information implicit. For example, room boundaries are obvious to anyone viewing a model, and so are not necessarily defined explicitly. Space labels may be applied arbitrarily, not conforming to a set standard, which can also confound model checking systems. From the perspective of a vendor providing a rule checking software, the easiest manner to obtain the information needed for testing is to get the user to enter the needed information in the building model. In fact, all current rule checking systems require preprocessing, or normalizing, to supplement the model with semantic information before it can be checked.

The extension of BIM models to address implicit rules not explicitly represented are exemplified in circulation analysis tests. These are usually implemented by the automatic generation of a scaled metric circulation graph pre-calculating the circulation distances between circulation spaces and the distance to adjacent doors. The graph is an extension to the qualifying model view for checking circulation distances. Other rule checks apply to objects not represented in normal building designs or models. Access to equipment that has maintenance requirements, scaffolding, and other temporary structures require walk space and spaces to allow access and necessary work. Many analyses of building behavior rely on automatic derivation of behavior from geometry and material properties (Belsky et al, 2016; Lee et al, 2016; Solihin and Eastman, 2015). These are considered separately in Chapter 3 (Section 3.6.2).

Another important part of rule checking is to traverse the logic tree identifying the context of the test. Does the rule apply to every entity? If not, which does it apply to? This is essentially a decision tree to precheck that the conditions are necessary for applying the test. Effective rule checking allows the application rule to easily depict and reference the specific parts of the model being checked and the nature of all failing conditions.

Although there is still a clear need for much research and development in this area, a number of model checking systems are available. They are reviewed in Section 2.6.3 below.

2.5   BIM PLATFORMS

BIM platforms may be used in diverse ways in building construction: by the architect for design modeling and drawing production; by an engineer for structural or energy data management; by a contractor for developing a construction coordination model, for fabrication detailing, or for facility management. For example, they include varying types of tool functionality. Some are marketed to multiple types of user. The different marketing strategies lead to packages with different collections of functionality. In this review, we do not address these different uses but consider the major BIM platforms generically, from the perspective of the platform's primary product with references to other products running on the same platform. Their uses and limitations will be considered more explicitly in the chapters associated with the different types of BIM users. We consider each platform from the three levels outlined in Section 2.3: as a tool, as a platform, and as an environment.

As is broadly understood, the acquisition of a software package is very different from most other purchases we make. Whereas the purchase of a physical tool is based on a very specific product and set of features, a software package involves both its current capabilities and the development path of enhancements that are released regularly, at least annually, by the vendor or third parties. A purchaser is buying into both the current product and its future evolution, as projected by the company. One is also purchasing a support system that at least one person in a firm will be dealing with. The support system is an augmentation of the user-provided documentation and online support built into the BIM tool. Apart from the vendor's support network, an organization receiving services for a platform level software system is also part of a broader user community. Most provide blog communication for peer-to-peer help and open portals for the exchange of object families. These may be free or available at a small cost. The availability of product libraries for a BIM platform is another critical consideration. However, many systems have a very large set of product libraries. For example, at the time of writing, BIMobject.com carried information for about 19,250,000 different products from 967 companies. The products were defined in a variety of 49 file types: RVG, DWG, DWF, DGN, GSM, SKP, IES, TXT, and more. Object libraries should be considered in the acquisition of a BIM platform.

Note: The reviews that follow are ordered alphabetically according to the application names, and do not represent any order of preference or chronological sequence. We are grateful to Meir Katz, Sibenik Goran, and the many other graduate students who assisted with reviews of the various BIM platforms.

2.5.1 Allplan

The first version of Allplan appeared in 1984, and it has been a brand of the Nemetschek Group ever since. It is a family of products with software modules for architecture, engineering, and facility management. It is a parametric-based design software with a lot of automation. Model integrity remains high when changing between different views. Allplan is light and copes well with large scale projects, but users often divide them into smaller projects to more easily manage large amounts of information.

The modeling approach differs significantly from other BIM platforms, using 2D drawings, 3D models, and combining 2D and 3D elements in a unique project structure that facilitates creation of combined 2D and 3D information. Allplan relies heavily on the use of layers, which represent horizontal planes.

The layering allows for quick and easy designation of levels, floor height, and spacing as well as easy presentation of desired elements by turning the visibility of layers on and off. When creating layouts, one can choose exactly which layers will appear for export or printing. However, users familiar with other BIM software find that this structure requires time to get used to.

Starting with the 2016 version, Allplan incorporates the Parasolid 3D modeling kernel. Parasolid allows complex modeling with Bezier surfaces and NURBS. Users can create complex free-form geometry thanks to the use of the Parasolid modeling kernel.

Parametric objects are called "Smart Parts" in Allplan. The software has a large built-in library of standard Smart Parts, and users can build custom Smart Parts as well. The Smart Parts are parametric and lend themselves to customization, but sophisticated use requires programing skills: Allplan also has a python-based API, which allows for deeper customization, including access to Parasolid 3D modeling functions.

The software has a clear visual interface that allows one to work in 2D, 3D, or mixed views. Placement of structural elements, such as reinforcing bars, is quite intuitive. However, it can be complex to operate at times, as it relies on the user mastering all its shortcuts to be proficient.

Allplan is commonly used in combination with other software. It provides many import and export possibilities, for both 2D and 3D files.

Allplan strengths: Allplan is a thoroughly parametric rule-based modeling software that can cope with complex geometry. Reports, quantity takeoffs, and schedules are easily exported in a readable format with little customization. The working interface allows one to easily visualize elements in a variety of ways. The BIM+ cloud-based tool allows sharing of both native and IFC models and elements. Allplan supports European planning practices, such as creating detailed plans of the structure of the building (e.g., formwork and reinforcement plans), effectively and efficiently. 2D and 3D elements and plans can be used together easily. Its support for detailed structural design is particularly strong, including quantity and cost calculation.

Allplan weaknesses: The interface is complex. Although it provides many options and possibilities, and most of the attributes can be defined, significant manual setup is needed to generate elements correctly. The mix of 2D drawing and 3D modeling allows users to continue using 2D drawing exclusively when switching to BIM. Allplan model elements are less associative than other software. For example, should a hosting element be deleted or moved, the changes are not propagated to elements within it (e.g., rebar arrays in a reinforced concrete wall). Allplan relies on third party apps to model MEP systems.

2.5.2 ArchiCAD

ArchiCAD is the oldest continuously marketed BIM application for architectural design. Graphisoft began marketing ArchiCAD in the early 1980s. Headquartered in Budapest, Hungary, Graphisoft was acquired in 2007 by Nemetschek, a German CAD company. ArchiCAD supports the Mac platform in addition to Windows.

ArchiCAD's user interface is well-crafted, with smart cursors, drag-over operator hints, and context-sensitive operator menus. Its model generation and ease of use are loved by its loyal user base. Drawing generation in ArchiCAD is automatically managed by the system; every edit of the model is automatically placed in document layouts; details, sections, and 3D images can be easily inserted into layouts. All sections, elevations, plans, and 3D documents are bidirectionally editable. As a parametric modeling tool, ArchiCAD incorporates a very broad range of predefined parametric objects. It includes modeling capabilities for site planning and for interiors, and provides strong space planning capabilities. In addition, there are a large number of external websites that define both static and parametric objects for ArchiCAD (the majority are from Europe).

It supports the generation of custom parametric objects through its Geometric Description Language (GDL) scripting language, which relies on CSG-type constructs and a Visual Basic-like syntax. It contains extensive object libraries for users, organized by systems: precast concrete, masonry, metals, wood, thermal and moisture protection, plumbing, HVAC, electrical, and so forth. Its user-defined parametric modeling has some limitations; its sketch tool and parametric rule generation do not support algebraic expressions or conditionals. Existing object classes can be extended and customized using GDL. It also has an Open Database Connectivity (OBDC) interface. Global grids or controls are possible but complex. It can depict and reference shapes made with complex curved surfaces using the Shell tool, the Morph tool, or other external add-ons. When ArchiCAD was acquired by Nemetschek, it strengthened its design focus, releasing its early move into construction management with Vico.

ArchiCAD has links to multiple tools in different domains including structural, mechanical, energy, and environmental engineering tools, visualization tools, and facility management tools. Some are direct links through GDL and others are through IFC. The latest list of compatible software and file formats supported by ArchiCAD is available at the "Import/Export File Formats in Archi-CAD" page under the Graphisoft official website (http://helpcenter.graphisoft .com/technotes/setup/software-technologies/file-formats-in-archicad/). Other tools include BIMx (formerly, Virtual Building Explorer), a navigation tool.

ArchiCAD has further strengthened its interactions with IFC and provides good bidirectional exchange. Its IFC exchange functions include object classification, filtering by object types, and object-level version management. ArchiCAD has the Graphisoft BIM Server backend repository, which comes with the ArchiCAD platform. See Chapter 3 for more detail on Graphisoft BIM Server.

ArchiCAD's strengths: ArchiCAD has an intuitive interface and is relatively simple to use. It has large object libraries and a rich suite of supporting applications in design, building systems, and facility management. It supports all phases of design work except fabrication detailing.

ArchiCAD's weaknesses: It has some minor limitations in its custom parametric modeling capabilities.

2.5.3 Bentley Systems

Bentley Systems offers a wide range of related products for architecture, engineering, infrastructure, and construction. The Bentley AECOsim is an evolutionary descendant of Triforma, an earlier product. Bentley is a major player in the civil engineering, infrastructure, and plant marketplace.

As a building modeling and drawing production tool, Bentley has a standard set of predefined parametric objects. The predefined parametric objects have relations between each other. Global- or assembly-level parametric modeling is supported by GenerativeComponents. Bentley has good freeform B-spline surface and solid modeling capabilities. Its rendering engine is fast and provides high-quality renderings and animations. For drawing production, 2D detailing and annotation on a 3D model section are well supported. For drawing editing, the predefined objects are bidirectional, but the other objects must be edited in the model to be updated. Its drawing capabilities are strong, showing printed line weights and text. It is easy to add properties to object classes. Bentley AECOsim, with its various modules, is a large system with lots of functionality but is less easy to access and become proficient in. Bentley AECOsim supports import of external objects and clash detection.

Bentley AECOsim platform applications are file-based systems, meaning that all actions are immediately written to a file and result in lower loads on memory. The system scales well.

In addition to its base design modeling tools, Bentley has a large array of additional systems (approximately 40 applications), many of which were acquired in support of its civil engineering products. The full list of Bentley software is available at Bentley's official website at www.bentley.com/en/products.

Some of these products were acquired by purchasing small third-party companies and have only limited compatibility with others within the Bentley environment. Thus a user may have to convert model formats from one Bentley application to another. Similarly, user cognition sometimes must change because user interface conventions also vary.

Primavera and other scheduling systems can be imported and grouped with Bentley objects for 4D simulation. Bentley AECOsim interfaces include: DWG, DXF, PDF, U3D, 3DS, Rhino 3DM, IGES, CGM, STEP AP203/AP214, STL, OBJ, VRML, Google Earth KML, SketchUp, COLLADA, and ESRI SHP. Its public standard support includes IFC, CIS/2, STEP, and SDNF. Bentley products are extensible. It supports user-defined macros: Microsoft VBA, VB.NET, C++, C#, and Bentley MDL. Bentley offers a well-developed and popular multiproject server called ProjectWise (see Chapter 3). It supports replication of files to a prearranged set of local sites, managing the consistency of all files. It is file-based, not object-based. It supports links to manage relationships between DGN, DWG, PDF, and Microsoft Office documents. Bentley supports Object IDs and timestamps and their management on round trips.

Bentley System's strengths: Bentley offers a very broad range of building modeling tools, dealing with almost all aspects of the AEC industry. It supports modeling with complex curved surfaces, including Bezier and B-splines. It includes multiple levels of support for developing custom parametric objects, including the Parametric Cell Studio and GenerativeComponents.

Its parametric modeling plug-in, GenerativeComponents, enables definition of complex parametric geometry assemblies and has been used in many prize-winning building projects. Bentley provides scalable support for large projects with many objects. It provides multiplatform and server capabilities.

Bentley System's weaknesses: Bentley's large product offerings are partially integrated, at the data consistency and user interface levels. It thus takes more time to learn and navigate. Its heterogeneous functional modules include different object behaviors, further adding to learning challenges. The weaknesses in the integration of its various applications reduce the value and breadth of support that these systems provide individually.

2.5.4 DESTINI Profiler

DESTINI Profiler (Design ESTImating INtegration Initiative) is a product of Beck Technology, Ltd. It is based on a parametric modeling platform acquired from Parametric Technologies Corporation (PTC) in the late 1990s, after PTC decided not to enter the AEC market. DESTINI Profiler is an application and platform that has evolved from the software acquired from PTC. DESTINI Profiler functionality is unique; it addresses conceptual design from a cost of construction, and, to a degree, an operating cost basis. It supports quick definition of the conceptual design of given building types, based on the room types, and building structural and site parameters. The high-level components of a project are site, consisting of soils, parking, and detention ponds; and Massing, referring to cladding, features, mechanical, slabs, and rooms. These are building model objects that carry links to the cost definitions. A concept-level model can be laid out in an easy 3D sketch manner, using intuitive editing operations. A building can be composed as a set of spaces, floor by floor, or alternatively as a shell that is then decomposed into floors that are assigned spaces or some mixture of the two. The site plan can be an imported terrain model or Google Earth segment. Each of these can be defined in little or great detail, using defaults, or overriding them if desired.

Defaults are set up for different building types, using the RS Means Masterformat 16 divisions, or further down to line-item detailed categories, or alternatively to Timberline's more detailed ones. Each object, such as wall or slab, is associated with an assembly cost class. Objects can be changed from one construction type to another without necessarily changing the geometry. This means that a cost estimator has almost complete control of the project costing, defining types of slabs and details of cladding and construction. It has increasingly detailed site development definition and costing. Cost parameters are carried as fixed units for the building type or location, while others are under explicit user control (such as the type of films on glazing or number of fume hoods in a laboratory), while the building geometry defines the spatial properties. The design model can be simple or complex from a cost standpoint, where the design intent is defined by the associated cost categories. Thus the strength of the system is the articulation of intent in the cost-estimating side, organized hierarchically as components, collections, assemblies, and line items. These multiple levels allow contractors or other users to map to their own cost databases, if that is desired.

The resulting cost estimates are detailed, based on quantity of materials in place that start out being estimates, but that can be tracked downstream as the project is detailed, then constructed, to compare with the actual quantities and costs for quality assurance. In addition, it provides a full economic cash-flow development proforma for the project, optionally including occupancy and operation. The cost estimating database accessed by DESTINI Profiler is centralized and maintained by the Dallas office.

DESTINI Profiler supports a range of graphical inputs that can be used as 2D underlays over which the user can model, including DWG, DXF, PDF, JPG, and other image files. It can import SketchUp geometry as features, and with the aid of a customized Revit plugin, one can import slabs, cladding, and massing objects as native geometry. It supports output to eQuest for energy analysis, used to estimate operating costs and output to XLS spreadsheets and various image formats.

Beck Technology also provides DESTINI Estimator and DESTINI Optioneer software. The latter application is unique in its capabilities to help users optimize early phase design decisions, such as identifying the best location and configuration for a building. The system generates and then evaluates very large numbers of possible project permutations by enumerating across a range of design parameters, allowing users to follow trends and identify design scenarios they may not have considered otherwise. The Hillwood-Beck Multiuse Building case study (discussed in Chapter 9 of the *BIM Handbook*, second edition, and available on the *BIM Handbook* companion website) presents an example of DESTINI Profiler's use.

DESTINI Profiler strengths: DESTINI Profiler functionality allows it to be easily adapted to almost any building type, based on costing of assemblies and line items. Its strength is in the value analysis of alternative concept designs based on a wide range of construction specifications and their associated cost estimates. Some case studies show that a well-developed DESTINI Profiler project is reliable to within 5 percent of construction costs, and it has supported project models that have come within 1 percent of project costs. Its ability to generate detailed economic assessments on a conceptual-level project, together with the model enumeration capability of DESTINI Optioneer, is powerful and unique.

DESTINI Profiler weaknesses: DESTINI Profiler is not a general-purpose BIM tool. Its major purpose is financial evaluation of a construction project, with financial exploration of alternative finishes and system choices, usually without modeling them geometrically. Once a model is complete, its interface to support full development is limited currently to exporting the model to Revit.

2.5.5 Digital Project

Developed by Gehry Technologies, Digital Project (DP) is an architectural and building customization of Dassault's CATIA V5, a powerful parametric modeling platform for large systems in aerospace and automotive industries. Gehry Technologies was acquired by Trimble in 2014. DP requires a powerful workstation to run well, but it is able to handle even the largest projects.

DP is a complex tool that is learned in incremental steps. Its smart cursor presents selection options. Online documentation is readily available. Menus are customizable. As a parametric modeler, DP supports both global parameters to define object classes and assemblies and local rules and relations to be maintained between objects. Its rules for defining objects are complete and general. It is excellent in developing complex parametric assemblies, such as for dealing with fabrication issues. Subtypes of an object class can be generated and their structure or rules elaborated. Curved surface modeling is excellent, as befits a tool whose major users include automobile designers. Until the third release, DP did not include built-in base objects for buildings. Users could reuse objects developed by others, but these were not supported by DP itself. DP is complex and has a steep learning curve. It has good interfaces for importing and exporting object data to spreadsheets and XML. It continues to expand its IFC capabilities. Like most applications, annotations in DP are associative with a drawing view and are not bidirectional with the model; drawings are treated as annotated reports. DP supports clash detection. DP's Knowledge Expert provides rule-based checking that can augment the rules used in defining shapes, but can apply between objects in different parametric trees.

Digital Project is file-based, but very scalable. The DDP and Louis Vuitton case studies in Chapter 10 provide examples of DP's ability to model geometrically and functionally very complex buildings. The logical structure of CATIA involves tool modules called *workbenches*. DP comes with several workbenches in addition to the Architectural and Structures Workbench. Imagine & Shape is a fully integrated freeform sketch design tool, based on CATIA; Knowledgeware supports rule-based checking of design; the Project Engineering Optimizer allows for easy optimization of parametric designs based on any well-defined objective function; and Project Manager tracks parts of a model and manages their release. These are sophisticated tools with major potential benefits, but which require significant technical knowledge for effective use. It also includes capabilities for mechanical, electrical, and plumbing (MEP) layout in its MEP Systems Routing. Other products organized as CATIA Workbenches can also be easily integrated. Of note is Delmia, a Monte Carlo simulation system allowing assembly and fabrication modeling and assessment. Its user interface is consistent across workbenches. In addition to the integrated workbenches, DP has interfaces with Ecotect for energy studies, 3DVia Composer for documentation production, and 3DXML for lightweight viewing. It has links to Microsoft Project and Primavera Project Planner for scheduling, and ENOVIA for project lifecycle management. DP supports definition of new object and family classes. It supports Visual BASIC scripting and has a strong API that uses .NET for developing add-ons. It has the Uniformat and Masterformat classifications embedded, which facilitates integration of specifications and cost estimating. It supports the following exchange formats: CIS/2. IFC Version 2x3, SDNF, STEP AP203 and AP214, DWG, DXF, VRML, TP, STL, CGR, 3DMAP, SAT, 3DXML, IGES, STL, and HCG.

DP was designed as a platform, with a suite of tools tailored to integrate manufactured product design and engineering. It supports concurrent users with the open source SVN version control manager. It has additional related features that provide integration at the environment level. ENOVIA is the major Dassault PLM (Product Lifecycle Management) product (see Chapter 3). DP carries multiple timestamps and object IDs at the object level for supporting object-level version management.

Digital Project's strengths: It offers very powerful and complete parametric modeling capabilities. It is able to directly model large, complex assemblies for controlling surfaces, features, and assemblies. It can support fabrication. Digital Project relies on 3D parametric modeling for most kinds of detailing. It is a complete solution at the platform level. It has a powerful set of integrated Workbench tools.

Digital Project's weaknesses: DP requires a steep learning curve, has a complex user interface, and has a high initial cost. Its predefined object libraries for buildings are limited, as are external third-party object libraries. Drawing capabilities for architectural use are not as fully developed as other AECO platforms. DP is still based on CATIA V5, which is not the latest version. It does not (yet) benefit from the latest functionality of CATIA.

2.5.6   Revit

Revit is a well-known and popular BIM platform, introduced by Autodesk in 2002 after Autodesk acquired the Revit software from a start-up company.

Revit provides an easy-to-use interface with drag-over hints for each operation and smart cursor. Its menus are well organized according to workflow, and its operator menus gray out unavailable actions within the current system context. Its drawing generation support is very good; its drawing production is strongly associative, so that drawing releases are easily managed. It offers bidirectional editing from drawings to and from the model, and also bidirectional editing from schedules for doors, door hardware, and the like. Revit supports the development of new custom parametric objects and customization of predefined objects. Its rule set for defining objects has improved with each release and includes trigonometric functions. It can constrain distances and angles and the number objects in an array. It also supports hierarchical relations of parameters. Thus, an object can be defined by using a group of sub-objects with parametric relations. It is more difficult to set up global parameters that can constrain assemblies of objects' layout and sizes. The release of the current API provides good support for external application development.

Revit is a strong platform, especially because of its range of supporting applications. Revit has the largest set of associated applications. Some have direct links through Revit's Open API, and others are linked through IFC or other exchange formats.

Revit interfaces with AutoCAD Civil 3D for site analysis, with Autodesk Inventor for manufacturing components, and with LANDCADD for site planning. It interfaces with US Cost, Cost OS by Nomitech, Innovaya, and Sage Timberline and also with Tocoman iLink for quantity takeoff for cost estimation. Innovaya also provides 4D simulation links with Primavera and MS Project schedules. Revit also supports links to Autodesk Navisworks. Vico Office supports both scheduling and quantity takeoffs. Revit has links with specifications to e-SPECS and BSD SpecLink through the BSD Linkman mapping tool.

Revit is able to import models from SketchUp, AutoDesSys form•Z, McNeel Rhinoceros, Google Earth conceptual design tools, and other systems that export DXF files. Previously, these were visible but could not be referenced. They could be referenced from Revit Version 2011 ("referenced" here means that users can select points on the objects, allowing dimensionally accurate referencing, rather than visual dimensional alignment).

Revit supports various file formats including DWG, DXF, DGN, SAT, IFC (for building components), gbXML, and ODBC (Open DataBase Connectivity). The latest information about the file formats supported by Revit can be found online at Autodesk Knowledge Network.

Revit carries object IDs. However, version and change information is carried at the file level, not at the object level. This limits synchronization of objects with different views in different files.

The strengths and weaknesses of Revit are as follows:

Revit's strengths: As a design tool, Revit 2018 is strong; it is intuitive; its drawing production tools are excellent. However, many designers wishing to go beyond the built-in objects' limitations use other tools to design in a more freeform manner, and then import the results into Revit for production modeling. Revit is easy to learn and its capabilities are organized in a well-designed and user-friendly interface. It has a very broad set of object libraries, developed both by themselves and by third parties. Because of its dominant market position, it is the preferred platform for direct link interfaces with other BIM tools. Its bidirectional drawing support allows for information updates and management from drawing and model views, including schedules. It supports concurrent operation on the same project. Revit includes an excellent object library (bimobject.com).

Revit's weaknesses: Revit is an in-memory system that slows down significantly for projects larger than about 100 to 300 MB in case of Revit 2018 when the memory size is 4 GB. It has a few limitations on parametric rules. It also has limited support for complex curved surfaces. Lacking object-level timestamps, Revit does not yet provide needed support for full object management in a BIM environment. See Chapter 3 for more information.

2.5.7 Tekla Structures

Tekla Structures is offered by Tekla Corp., a Finnish company founded in 1966 with offices worldwide. In 2012, Trimble purchased Tekla. Tekla has multiple divisions: Building and Construction, Infrastructure, and Energy. Its initial construction product was Xsteel, which was introduced in the mid-1990s and grew to be a widely used steel detailing application throughout the world. It is largely file-based and scales well. It supports multiple users working on the same project model on a server. It does not currently support B-spline or NURBS surfaces.

In the early 2000s, Tekla added timber and precast concrete design and fabrication-level detailing for structural and architectural precast. In 2004 the expanded software product was renamed Tekla Structures to reflect its expanded support, including for steel, precast concrete, timber, reinforced concrete, and for structural engineering. Recently, it has added Construction

Management capabilities and a structural design application. It is a platform supporting a growing range of products. In addition to full detail editing licenses it also offers Engineering, Project Manager, and Viewing licenses. All of these tools provide the functionality needed for fabrication and automated fabrication. It has good functionality to customize existing or create new parametric objects. Nevertheless, it is a complex system with rich functionality that takes time to learn and keep abreast of.

Tekla offers interface support for a wide range of other applications, and it has an open application programming interface. It also supports a very broad range of exchange formats. The latest list of supported file formats can be found at Tekla's "Compatible Formats" webpage. Tekla supports concurrent user access to the same project, allowing reservations at the object or higher aggregation of objects level. It carries object IDs and timestamps, supporting object-level management.

Tekla Structures' strengths: It features versatile ability to model structures that incorporate a wide range of structural materials and detailing, and the ability to support very large models and concurrent operations on the same project and with multiple simultaneous users. It supports user-defined parametric custom component libraries, including customization of its provided objects.

Tekla Structures' weaknesses: While a powerful tool, its full functionality is quite complex to learn and fully utilize. The power of its parametric components is impressive and, while a strength, requires dedicated operators who must develop high levels of skill. It is able to import objects with complex multicurved surfaces from outside applications, and these can be referenced but not edited.

2.5.8 Vectorworks

Vectorworks began as MiniCAD, an Apple Computer Mac CAD system developed by Diehl Graphsoft in 1985. It was adapted to Windows in 1996. Diehl Graphsoft was acquired by Nemetschek in 2000. It has always stressed strong customer support and a strong worldwide user base, targeting smaller firms. In 2009, it adopted the Parasolid geometry engine for its core geometric modeling platform; Vectorworks previously had parametric capabilities similar to AutoCAD Architecture. Now its parametric modeling is similar to others, but with the ease of use, fine-grained user-friendliness, and rich presentation capabilities for which it has been noted.

Vectorworks 2018 provides a very wide variety of tools, organized into separate products serving different industries. These include:

- *Architect*—for architectural, interiors, and BIM applications.
- *Landmark*— for landscaping, site design, and urban design applications with plant library, irrigation, digital terrain, and GIS capabilities.
- *Spotlight*—for lighting and production design of theatrical venues and staged events. Spotlight has two companion products: *Vision* (for simulation and light control interface) and *Braceworks* (for static analysis of temporary structures).
- *Fundamentals*—for general purpose 2D/3D modeling and integrated rendering.

These different products provide a wide range of functionality, all with a consistent user interface and style and with drag-over operator hints, smart cursor, pre-selection highlighting, content-sensitive operator display, and customizable menus and tool-bars. Vectorworks' drawing capabilities associate drawn section annotations with model projections. Vectorworks has a reasonable set of object libraries to import and use. Its NURBS surface modeling is very good. It supports customizing its predefined object classes and also supports new object definition, using any of its four APIs:

- SDK, a C++ based API
- Python / VectorScript: scripting languages using Python and Pascal syntaxes respectively
- Marionette: a graphical algorithmic programming tool

It has incorporated a Design Constraint Manager from Siemens PLM that facilitates the management of dynamic dimension-shape interaction. Attributes are carried in a project database and associated with objects for use when needed. Vectorworks is a 64-bit system supporting both Mac and PC. Its exchange formats include DXF/DWG, Rhino 3DM, IGS, SAT, STL, Parasolid X_T, 3DS, OBJ, COLLADA, FBX, KML, and more. The latest list of supported file formats is available at the Vectorworks Import/Export File Format webpage.

Vectorworks has strengthened its interactions with IFC and provides good bidirectional exchange, supporting both IFC 2x3 and IFC4. Its IFC functions include object classification, assignment of property sets, COBie support, and owner/history data. Its IFC exchange capabilities have been tested with ArchiCAD, Bentley Microstation, AutoCAD Architecture, Revit, Solibri Model Checker, and Navisworks. Vectorworks supports cloud services and free model viewers. Vectorworks also has a full implementation of BCF (BIM Collaboration Format).

2.5.9 AutoCAD-Based Applications

Whether AutoCAD-based applications can be classified as BIM platforms is questionable. Although AutoCAD can model objects using "blocks," it does not maintain parametric relationships and integrity between objects as a true BIM platform would. Nevertheless, we include a short review here because of its widespread use. Autodesk's AutoCAD software became the mainstay of 2D and 3D building design before Autodesk's acquisition of Revit. Although there were fully-fledged 3D parametric building modeling applications available earlier, Autodesk Architecture—Autodesk's building application on the AutoCAD platform—remained the most popular architectural modeling software because it was based on the AutoCAD geometry platform, which itself was in widespread use for 2D drawing. To some extent AutoCAD Architecture can be considered to have provided users a comfortable transition from 2D drafting to BIM.

AutoCAD has solid and surface modeling extensions, and supports the definition of "blocks" of 3D geometry. AutoCAD provides some of the functionality offered by parametric tools, including the ability to make custom objects with adaptive behaviors.

Third-party application developers can build on this base to add predefined sets of objects and limited sets of rules for those objects, thereby implementing parametric behavior within the defined object or assembly (like a stair or roof). However, it is much more difficult to achieve the full functionality of design intent behavior that is a hallmark of a BIM authoring application. Auto-CAD remains a useful legacy BIM platform only in so far as it is still the core technology of many BIM tools that have been built upon it.

Drawing Space in AutoCAD is linked to Model Space from the 3D model, and in current interpretation, provides one-way links from the model to the annotated drawings. The model views are simple orthographic projections, with limited view management. Interfaces include DGN, DWG, DWF™, DXF™, and IFC.

Autodesk encouraged third parties to use AutoCAD as a platform and to develop new sets of objects in different AEC domains by providing powerful application programming interfaces, including AutoLISP, Visual Basic, VB Script, and ARX (C++) interfaces. This led to growth of a worldwide developer community with a plethora of independent companies, offering packages for structural design and analysis, piping and plant design, control systems, electrical system design, structural steel, fire sprinkler systems, ductwork, wood framing, and many other applications.

AutoCAD-based applications' strengths: Ease of adoption for AutoCAD users because of user interface consistency; easy use because they build upon AutoCAD's well-known 2D drafting functionality and interface. There is an extensive API with numerous programming languages for developing new applications, well supported with appropriate Software Development Kits (SDK).

AutoCAD-based applications' weaknesses: Their fundamental limitations are that they are not parametric modelers that allow nonprogrammers to define new objects (without API-level programming), object rules, and constraints; they have limited interfaces to other applications; their use of external references (XREFs) (with inherent integration limitations) for managing projects; they are an in-memory system with scaling problems if XREFs are not relied upon; and they need to propagate changes manually across drawings sets.

2.6   DESIGN REVIEW APPLICATIONS

Design review is recognized as the most common way of using BIM (Kreider et al., 2010). Contrary to the general perception, even very experienced practitioners cannot easily detect errors from drawings (Lee et al., 2003; Lee et al., 2016). BIM, however, can help a project team virtually inspect a building or even automate a design review process. This section reviews methods and applications that help users review designs effectively and efficiently. It reviews model viewing and navigation applications (*model viewers*), model integration and review applications (*model integration tools*), and model checking applications (*model checkers*) that are partially automated.

Note: In this section too, as for the BIM Platforms, the applications are listed alphabetically. The order does not represent any preference or chronological sequence.

2.6.1 Model Viewers

A large number of model viewers are available for visualizing and navigating BIM models. Model viewers have been used as the primary method for reviewing designs by single users or by teams. Some remain pure model viewers with simple annotation functions, while others have evolved into applications with more advanced functions, such as clash-checking. Another trend is to develop model viewers using game engines for fast and high-quality rendering and for easy navigation of large and complex BIM models. Most model viewers also run on a mobile environment, which allows designers and field engineers to quickly review or present a design.

Adobe Acrobat 3D is a 3D PDF (Portable Document Format) viewer. The 3D PDF format is a lightweight 3D format developed by Adobe not for creating building model information, but rather for "publishing" information to support various workflows. Adobe Acrobat 3D supports a dynamic and viewable 3D object or animation to be embedded in a document. It supports model comparison.

Allplan BIM+ enables merging of submodels from different disciplines and different BIM platforms. It includes clash-checking capability and management of design tasks.

Autodesk BIM 360 Glue is a cloud-based BIM coordination application with its own lightweight geometry viewer that can automatically translate and view objects from multiple BIM platforms and supports most major 3D file formats (b4.autodesk.com/file_compatibility.html). This greatly facilitates collaboration. It supports management of IFC and native files as well as both its own and Navisworks' clash detection; its particular strength is providing open communication links and change record tracking.

Autodesk Design Review is a free downloadable viewer supporting review, checking, and other forms of collaboration. It supports 2D drawings and 3D models converted to DWF (Design Web Format), developed by Autodesk. Models can be spatially reviewed by fixed position or walking or flying through them; views may be fixed orthogonally to various surfaces or by cutting sections through the project. Distances and angles between object surfaces may be selected and measured. Queries using object names are also supported, with the object names returned, which when selected are highlighted in the view. Two-dimensional documents may be rotated, and markups may be applied to any point on surface for recording review comments. Reports with markups are easily generated. A digital signature is provided, allowing the user to check if changes have been made to the file since the signature was applied.

Autodesk Navisworks Freedom is a free model viewer, acquired by Autodesk in 2007. The original Navisworks Jetstream application became popular as a BIM tool because it supported a wide range of 3D file formats and a model file aggregation function.

BIMx (previously Building Model Explorer) is a model viewer developed by Graphisoft. It supports cross-references between 2D and 3D views and, like many other model viewers, allows users to measure the distance between points located in a model. It also displays 3D stereo images for use in Google Cardboard and similar stereo viewing tools.

Fuzor is a proprietary game-engine-based BIM rendering and navigation tool. Unlike the other BIM viewers, it provides easy and fast rendering and light visualization functions based on preset rendering options. It also has a function to maintain the link between a BIM authoring tool and Fuzor. That is, any change in a BIM model will be reflected in a Fuzor model. Fuzor provides a direct link with Revit and ArchiCAD, and can read in various files such as Rhinoceros 3D, SketchUp, Navisworks, FBS, and 3DS while maintaining previous Fuzor model settings. Another strength is that Fuzor supports virtual reality (VR) with audio effects.

Kubity facilitates publication and distribution of 3D models to any device, desktop or mobile, in standard or immersive virtual reality, using Sketchup's geometry file format. It makes sharing 3D models simple and intuitive, providing easy access to people who are not construction industry professionals. However, BIM files, such as Revit, must be exported to Sketchup's file format, which means that all of the nongraphic information is lost.

Oracle AutoVue is a lightweight 2D drawing and 3D model viewer for review, walkthroughs, accurate spatial measurements, and 3D identification of clashes. It supports 3D PDF.

ProjectWise Navigator provides an overlay display capability for dealing with heterogeneous project files. It handles DGN, i-Model, PDF, DWG, and DGN overlays, user indices to key files for access and viewing, incorporates internal applications for multiproduct clash detection and allows grouping for managing product data, purchases, review, and so forth. It supports 4D simulation, rendering, and markups for review, but only limited editing. The ProjectWise products do not yet provide object-level management of data, although Bentley has had earlier products with this capability.

Solibri Model Viewer is a free model viewer developed by Solibri using IFC as the native data format. It works on both Windows and Mac OS. Solibri series is another case which evolved as a BIM tool with advanced functions. These include real-time section cuts and making selected objects transparent for better viewing, and the ability to measure lengths and angles between points in imported models. Solibri products also include IFC model compression. A Solibri series with rule-based model checking functions is called Solibri Model Checker. Solibri Model Checker is reviewed in detail in the following section.

Tekla BIMSight is a free lightweight model viewer developed by Tekla (Trimble) mainly for model aggregation, clash detection, and issue reporting. It supports IFC (.ifc), IFC XML (.ifcxml), IFC ZIP (.ifczip), DWG (.dwg), DGN (.dgn) and XML (Tekla Web viewer file), IGES (*.igs,*.iges), STEP (*.stp, *.step), and SketchUp (*.skp) file types.

VIMTREK is a cloud-based converter of Revit project models to the Unity game engine. It manages all geometries, textures, and lighting supported by Revit. It has an associated furniture and occupant library. While it is a general viewing engine, it excels at providing tours for clients or users as a replacement of a physical model. Beside furniture, hardware, and window decoration, it includes backdrop skies and horizons. VIMtrek supports VR hardware, including Oculus Rift and Gear VR. The furniture library is actually much more than the materials needed for visual appearance, but includes product specs, carbon counts, and other sustainability data. This is the SMARTbim Product library, described more fully in Chapter 5.4.

xBIM Xplorer is an open-source IFC model viewer application. It is one of many applications that use the "xBIM Toolkit," a library of open-source code resources for working with IFC files (see www.openbim.org). Using the xBIM content provided on GitHub, software developers can quickly build applications. xBIM itself is just one of a variety of open source IFC resources that are freely available.

2.6.2 Model Integration Tools

Model integration tools provide users the ability not only to merge multiple models to form a federated model and to check for clashes, as some of the more sophisticated viewers do; they also provide construction management functions that can operate on the integrated models. Common functions are construction planning and definition of work zones; scheduling and 4D simulation; quantity take-off and estimation; and production monitoring and control.

DP Manager (Digital Project Inc., a Trimble company): DP manager offers tools for project collaboration, measuring and quantity takeoff, 4D modeling, and schedule integration. It does not have a cost estimation function. Its main advantage is its ability to work with models of very large and geometrically complex buildings, by virtue of the fact that it works directly with Digital Project BIM models on the CATIA 3D platform. A second advantage is that changes to the model do not require export and realignment of the model with the schedule, again because it runs within the BIM platform.

Navisworks Manage (Autodesk): Navisworks is a multipurpose construction management tool, incorporating tools for model review, clash detection, 4D simulation and animation, 5D quantity takeoff, and rendering. Navisworks became popular originally due to its ability to import BIM models and 3D geometry in a wide variety of formats, and this is still a major advantage. Navisworks can also import and view point cloud data from laser scans or photogrammetry.

iTWO (RIB): iTWO's platform uses a proprietary SQL database to store model objects, estimating data and scheduling resources in a single integrated database and solution environment. One or many models can be imported from various BIM platforms and coordinated using iTWO's BIM manager. iTWO enables estimation, tendering, subcontractor management, cost controlling, and invoicing processes. The BIM model can be enhanced with historical cost and price data or other internal data, accelerating the performance and quality of estimating. Its open interfaces support XML data exchange, including ifcXML, thus enabling integration with both BIM and ERP systems. It also provides facilities for managing the bidding and subcontract award process. Within iTWO, one or many detailed schedules can be developed in parallel, allowing for the direct alignment of cost, quantities, and activity schedules among subcontractors. Schedules can be created and maintained directly in iTWO or derived from commercial scheduling applications such as Microsoft Project, Oracle Primavera P6, and more. Given that the schedule is aligned to the cost, quantity, and model, multiple full 5D simulations can be analyzed within iTWO allowing for detailed virtualized planning and optioning. As the model matures, the mappings are maintained and new versions are integrated into the project with clear visualization of changes as well as cost and schedule implications. Finally, it supports monitoring of installed quantities and progress as the project moves into execution, providing cost controlling and forecasting capabilities.

Vico Office (Trimble): Vico is arguably the most comprehensive and sophisticated integrated BIM tool for construction management. It is comprehensive in that it covers model review, quantity takeoff and estimating, scheduling, and project controls. It is sophisticated because it incorporates advanced functions such as zone definitions to define work packages, integrated quantity take-off, estimating, and 4D scheduling using recipes that define the work content for construction products represented by model objects, Monte-Carlo simulation for risk analysis of costs and schedules, location-based scheduling, line-of-balance charts and schedule analysis, and comparison of planned vs. actual schedules with 4D views. Perhaps not surprisingly, it is also more difficult to learn and to operate than the other tools.

2.6.3 Model Checkers

Rule checking systems need to have the following functionality, and all of the systems reviewed below apply these steps:

1. Identify rulesets that are to be applied.
2. Identify the aspects of the model needed to provide the data for the rules to be tested, usually defined as a model view.
3. Use methods to select the parts of the building model the check is applied to.
4. Apply the rule or rulesets to the building instance model.
5. Identify all instances in the selected part of the model where failures occurred.

As discussed in Section 2.4, a common requirement of all of the tools is that the information in the building model being checked must be complete, correct, and explicit. They all therefore require preprocessing by the user to make sure that the information is provided as needed by the clauses of the rule sets.

BIM Assure. Invicara was incorporated in Singapore in the early 2010s, as a BIM application development company, and benefits from the many years of automation and code checking experience of Singapore's Building Construction Authority (BCA). Invicara introduced their first product, BIM Assure, in mid-2016. Assure is a cloud-based rule checking application that takes over much of the tedious but important rule checks, especially addressing rule checking during design. It is bidirectionally linked with Revit for authoring models and for correcting errors in models. Assure supports workflows by quality assurance of data, reducing model errors and rework. Like most rule checkers, Assure addresses the following processes:

- Preparing the BIM model for checking
- Identifying the types of checks to apply
- Identifying the part of the project to be checked (if not the whole project)
- Reporting the errors and set-up to fix the errors in the authoring tool

BIM Assure organizes rules through classifications. To do this it maps the Revit objects with the object classes in the rulesets, a process called "normalization." Normalization initially frees users from entering object information according to a predefined set of object classes, but it must be done at some point later in the normalization process. The Assure model has bidirectional access to the nongeometric properties of the Revit model. Assure has particular strength in medical facilities.

Solibri Model Checker. In the late 1990s, the founders of Solibri Model Checker (SMC) realized that the quality of BIM models was critical, and introduced a product in 1999 as an initial response to the problem. SMC applies tests to all or parts of a building model instance.

To support the range of BIM platforms on the market, SMC developed the checks to be applied to an IFC project model. Regardless of the platform, the same set of rules can be applied. If the different platforms model the identical project, the test results will be the same and the same test results reported. By default, SMC relies on the IFC Coordination View as a default model subset, but it also has other predefined views for focusing on various design review issues, based on the roles of the reviewer: architectural, structural, mechanical, and so on. Advanced users have the ability to modify model views and to develop new checking rules.

SMC assumes that users will compile libraries of checks for different project types, space types, materials, special functions, and so forth. Rulesets are selected and managed in the Solibri Solution Center (SSC) in the cloud. Each rule or set includes documentation regarding its definition and use, the entities and attributes it requires from the model to carry out the tests, and example instance models. The SSC is set up to support teams of users and sharing rule sets. SMC supports multiple construction classification schemes: Omniclass, Uniclass, Masterformat, Uniformat, DSTV, and others.

General checks provided include spatial conflicts, needed properties, duplicated objects (including across different BIM platforms), space program check (optionally applying ANSI-BOMA algorithms for area calculations, as shown in Figure 5-15), completeness of zone closures, and others. SMC includes Building Coordination Format (BCF) for tracking rule failures, which are tracked at project level. Error reports can be highlighted visually, formatted by function, user role, floor level, and more. SMC also supports data mining: rule failures may be grouped by task, implementer, context, and other classifications, and exported for analysis.

Autodesk Revit Model Review is an add-on for Revit that enables checking of model content, suitability of model data for energy or other analyses, connectivity of MEP systems, modeling or geometry inconsistencies, object visibility, and annotation graphics. Users can compile rules for checks in the interface and collect and save sets of rule assessments in check files (with BCF extension). Model content rules can check whether specific objects are present and if object parameters have specific required values, for example, so that Revit Model Review could be used to compile a Model View compliance ruleset. In some cases, the add-on can facilitate correction of an error once it is identified, by bringing the user to the model object or set of objects that violate a particular condition. Revit Model Review supports both automated and interactive rule checking.

SmartReview APR is a new rule checking product that addresses building model compliance with the building construction codes. It applies rules from the International Building Code (IBC) directly to Revit building models. The IBC defines the base building code requirements used by the United States and many international public bodies. The IBC is elaborated by local code checking bodies to address local conditions. At present, the software checks code sections of particular importance in building layout and construction from Chapters 5, 6, 7, 8, and 10 of the IBC, including building area, building height, number of stories, fire ratings of assemblies, flame spread classifications, occupant loads, exit access paths, common path of travel, location of exit discharge, and others. The software checks the Revit model directly, collecting data and sending it to a cloud-based analysis service. By storing the rules on a cloud server, processing can be off-loaded, rules can be easily maintained, and new rules shared rapidly with the user base. APR has a bidirectional interface with the Revit model and uses the Revit UI, facilitating learning by new users. The bidirectional interface allows updates of nongeometric properties either within Revit or within the SmartReview APR user interface, easing model updates. The results are linked back to the Revit model, allowing the user to pinpoint which elements are out of compliance. Building code information is "ready-at-hand" to the design model, aiding the user in acquiring a tacit understanding of the building code in the context of design decisions. The code checking engine requires a fairly simple model of the building. SmartReview APR provides built-in Revit families for walls for exterior and interior, doors for exterior and interior, windows, floors, roofs, rooms, property lines, levels, and areas. In addition, Wall types have a built-in parameter for fire ratings, using values of 0, 1, 2, 3, and 4. SmartReview APR searches for the above entity types and relies on them for carrying out checks. Missing data is flagged; nonrequired additional object data is skipped.

2.7   CONCLUSION

Object-based parametric modeling is a major change for the building industry that is facilitating the move from a drawing-based and handcraft technology to one based on digitally readable models that can generate consistent 3D models and drawings, schedules, and data interfaces to applications that address issues of design performance, construction, and facility operating information. Parametric modeling facilitates the design of large and complex models in 3D. The cost of these benefits is that BIM imposes a style of modeling and planning that is foreign to most users. Like CADD, it has been most directly used as a documentation tool separate from designing. A growing number of firms, however, use it directly for design and for generating exciting results. Some of these uses are taken up in Chapter 5. The case studies in Chapter 10 provide further examples.

The ability to extract geometric and property information from a building model for use in design, analysis, construction planning, and fabrication, or in operations, has large impacts on all aspects of the AEC industry; many of these are discussed in the succeeding chapters. The full potential of this enabling capability will not be fully known for at least another decade, because its implications and new uses are being discovered incrementally. What is currently known is that object-based parametric modeling resolves many of the fundamental representational issues in architecture and construction geometric modeling and allows quick payoffs for those transitioning to it, even with only partial implementation. These early payoffs include a reduction in drawing errors due to the built-in consistency of a central building model, improved engineering productivity, and the elimination of design errors based on spatial interferences. Because the models are 3D and much closer to everyday reality, they facilitate communication among the actors in a project: owners, architects and their consultants, contractors, fabricators, and facility managers and operators.

While object-based parametric modeling has had a catalytic influence on the emergence and acceptance of BIM, it is not synonymous with BIM design tools or the generation of building models. There are many other design, analysis, checking, display, and reporting tools that can play an important role in BIM procedures. Many information components and information types are needed to fully design and construct a building. Fundamentals of these other types of data, dealing with relations and attributes, have not been as fully developed as the geometry component nor have they been standardized. Many types of software can facilitate the development and maturing of building information modeling. The BIM design tools and platforms considered here, and the BIM environments in the next chapter, are only the newest in several generations of tools, but are already proving to be revolutionary in their impact.

Chapter 2 Discussion Questions

1. Summarize the major functionalities that distinguish the capabilities of a BIM design tool from 3D CAD modeling tools.

2. Most BIM design tools support both 3D object models as well as 2D drawn sections. What considerations should be made

when determining the changeover level of detail, such as when to stop modeling in 3D and complete the drawings in 2D?

3. Why is it unlikely that a single integrated system will incorporate a unified parametric model of all of a building's systems? On the other hand, what would be the advantages if it could be achieved?

4. In what ways are some popular design tools not BIM platforms? SketchUp? 3D Max Viz? FormZ? Rhino?

5. How do parametric rules associated with the objects in BIM improve the design and construction process?

6. What are the limitations that can be anticipated with the generic object libraries that come with BIM systems?

7. What are the essential differences between a manufacturing parametric modeling tool, such as Autodesk Inventor, and a BIM design tool, such as Revit?

8. Do you think there may be additional manufacturing-oriented parametric modeling tools used as a platform to develop BIM applications? What are the marketing costs and benefits? What are the technical issues?

9. You are part of a small team of friends who have decided to start an integrated design-build firm comprised of both a small commercial contractor and two architects. Lay out a plan for selecting one or more BIM-model creation tools. Define the general criteria for the overall system environment.

10. What are the different aspects of a BIM model that must be checked? How can automation of model-checking improve design and construction workflows?

Collaboration and Interoperability

3.0 EXECUTIVE SUMMARY

AECO is a collaborative activity. Multiple participants deploy multiple applications with overlapping data requirements to support various tasks of design, construction, operation, and maintenance. Consequently, the next threshold for better design and construction management is to improve *collaborative workflows*—collaborative work processes supported by smoothly sharing and exchanging information among project participants. *Interoperability* is the ability to exchange data between applications, which smooths workflows and sometimes facilitates their automation. There are various ways to share and exchange data, and it is critical for BIM managers and users as well as software developers to clearly understand the benefits and limitations of each method for effective work process management.

Interoperability has traditionally relied on file-based exchange formats limited to geometry, such as DXF (Drawing eXchange Format) and IGES (Initial Graphic Exchange Specification). Direct links based on the Application Programming Interfaces (APIs) are the oldest and still-important route to interoperability. Starting in the late 1980s, *data models* or *schemas* were developed to support *product* and *object model* exchanges within different industries, led by the ISO-STEP (ISO 10303) international standards effort.

Two main building product data models are the *Industry Foundation Classes* (IFC)—an international standard model, ISO 16739 for building planning, design, construction, and management, and *CIMsteel Integration Standard Version 2,* (CIS/2)—for structural steel engineering and fabrication. In addition to IFC and CIS/2, many XML-based data models such as Green Building XML (gbXML) and OpenGIS have been developed and are in use.

Different product data models represent different kinds of geometry, relations, processes and material, performance, fabrication, and other properties needed for different domains. They, however, include overlapping definitions or different definitions of the same objects. To resolve these issues, efforts to harmonize different product data models are being undertaken by the National BIM Standard (NBIMS) and buildingSMART International (bSI). Their approach is to specify information requirements for specific information use cases in a structured manner called an *Information Delivery Manual (IDM)* and to use predefined subsets of product data models called *Model View Definitions (MVDs)* for specific information use cases. Construction Operations Building Information Exchange (COBie) is an example of a subset data model, which focuses on operation and maintenance of facilities and assets.

While file and XML-based exchanges facilitate data exchange between pairs of applications, there is a growing need to coordinate data in multiple applications through a *BIM server* (a *common data environment*, a *building model repository,* or *a BIM repository*)—a database management system for BIM data. A critical aspect of BIM servers is that they allow collaborative management of projects at the building object level, rather than at a file level. A fundamental purpose of a BIM server is to help manage the synchronization of multiple models representing a project. BIM servers are slowly being integrated into traditional file-based Project Management Information Systems (*PMISs*) and will become a common technology for managing BIM projects.

3.1   INTRODUCTION

In the 1970s, the United States Air Force (USAF) initiated the Integrated Computer Aided Manufacturing (ICAM) project to develop aerospace manufacturing technologies that could integrate and automate design, engineering, and production processes and reduce costs. The project team, however, soon faced data exchange problems because parts were designed by different CAD systems. The Initial Graphics Exchange Specification (IGES) file format was developed to solve this problem. Similar *interoperability* issues exist in BIM processes, and were recognized as the main barrier to data sharing even in the early days of BIM (Young et al., 2007). *Interoperability* is the ability to exchange data between applications, which smooths workflows and sometimes facilitates their automation.

The design and construction of a building is a team activity. Increasingly, each activity and each type of specialty is supported and augmented by its own computer applications. Besides the capability to support geometry and material layout, there are structural and energy analyses that rely on their own building representation. A schedule of the construction process is a nongeometrical representation of the project, closely aligned to the design; the fabrication models used for each subsystem (steel, concrete, piping, electrical) are other representations with specialized detailing, in addition to others. *Interoperability* is the ability to pass data between applications and for multiple applications to jointly contribute to the work at hand. Interoperability, at the minimum, eliminates the need to manually copy data already generated in another application. Manual copying of partial project data greatly discourages iteration during design, as required for finding best solutions to complex issues, such as structural or energy design. It also leads to errors, where manual copying inevitably leads to some level of inconsistency. It also is a great restriction to the automating of business practices.

People have exchanged geometry data between applications using CAD file formats such as DXF, IGES, and SAT for many years. How is BIM model exchange different? While geometry has been the main concern for drafting and CAD systems, BIM represents not only multiple kinds of geometry, but also relations, attributes, and properties for different behaviors, as described in Chapter 2. The model, while integrated, must carry much more information than CAD files do. This is a large change and the supporting information technology methods and standards for achieving this are only incrementally being put in place.

Then why should architects, contractors, engineers, and fabricators be interested in these interoperability issues and standards and technologies associated with them? Aren't these technological issues for computer scientists and software companies to resolve? Why is this chapter important to read and understand?

First of all, to find an effective solution to any problem, it is critical to understand the problems in detail as well as potential solutions. For example, knowing the differences between 2G, 3G, and LTE telecommunication technologies sounds very technical, but is critical for a person to find the most appropriate mobile phone. Interoperability technologies are not very different. BIM as a process and a collaboration platform is about exchanging and reusing information. Effective collaboration among project participants has been recognized as one of the critical factors for successful BIM projects (Won et al., 2013b). Many studies identified poor interoperability as a key obstacle to collaborative BIM environments. Interoperability problems are inevitable once a team starts exchanging data among team members. Different data exchange methods are required to solve different types of interoperability issues. Without clearly understanding the advantages and limitations of each interoperability method, it is difficult to select the right method for different interoperability problems.

Secondly, standards have played and will continue to play important roles in AEC business practice—material performance standards, graphic standards, standards for defining products, drawing set standards, classification standards, layering standards. Architects, engineers, contractors, and fabricators, however, are the knowledge experts who know what the information content of an exchange and standards should be. In AEC, no one organization has the economic clout or knowledge to define effective interoperability for the whole industry. User-defined exchange standards seem an imperative. Consider the meaning of R-values, lumens, thermal breaks, and wythes.[1] Different construction domains define needed terms and these are part of that field. In some ways building model exchanges deal with the varied building information with which a field works. To play a role as an information provider to the standard community and potentially a standard developer, it is critical for architects, engineers, contractors, and fabricators to understand why the standards are important, how they work, and to know their current status.

Thirdly, software applications as well as data models and interoperability solutions are developed based on use-case scenarios. The use-case scenarios are defined by architects, engineers, fabricators, and owners, not by computer scientists or programmers.

Different types of exchange methods are the focus of the first part of this chapter. The second part focuses on the issues and methods for synchronizing and managing the multiple representations of a building project and the management of these heterogeneous representations.

3.2   DIFFERENT KINDS OF DATA EXCHANGE METHODS

Even in the earliest days of 2D CAD in the late 1970s and early 1980s, the need to exchange data between different applications was apparent. The most widely used AEC CAD system at that time was Intergraph. A set of businesses arose to write software to translate Intergraph project files to other systems, especially for process plant design—for example, exchanging data between the piping design software and the applications for piping bills of material or pipe flow analysis.

Later, in the post-Sputnik era, NASA found that they were expending significant amounts of money paying for translators among all their CAD developers. The NASA representative, Robert Fulton, brought all the CAD software companies together and demanded that they agree on a public domain exchange format. Two NASA-funded companies, Boeing and General Electric, offered to adapt some initial efforts they had undertaken separately. The resulting exchange standard was reviewed, extended, and christened IGES (Initial Graphics Exchange Specification). Using IGES, each software company need only develop two translators (it was thought), for exporting from and importing to their application, instead of developing a translator for every pair-wise exchange. IGES was an early success that is still widely used throughout many design and engineering communities.

---

[1] A wythe is a continuous vertical section of masonry one unit in thickness, typically called out on wall sections.

McGraw-Hill and Dodge surveys on BIM identify interoperability as a critical issue for advanced BIM users (Jones and Laquidara-Carr, 2015; Young et al., 2007).The interoperability (especially data loss) problems are attributed mainly to the following four technical reasons (Lee, 2011).

1. *Limited coverage of a data model*: The data of interest are not within the scope of a data model or an exchange file format. For example, IGES is developed to support only certain types of complex doubly curved surfaces, and thus cannot support some forms of geometric data. Similarly, IFC cannot support exchange of data that are not included in the scope of IFC.

2. *Translator problems*: A translator does not support the data of interest, although the data are specified in a data model.

3. *Software bugs or implementation issues*: The data are successfully exchanged and read into a software application, but the software application has a problem loading or visualizing the data due to a software bug or other implementation issues.

4. *Software domain problems*: The data of interest is outside of the scope of a software application. For example, a general cost estimation software application includes the length, volume, and area data extracted from a 3D model, but does not internally store 3D model data.

In addition to the previous technical factors, procedural factors are also common causes of interoperability problems, especially when multiple people collaborate on a project using multiple BIM models throughout different phases of a project.

5. *Version control and concurrent engineering issues*: If an architect updates a design while a structural engineer analyzes the structural stability of a building based on the previous version of design, the structural analysis results will become redundant when a new design is created.

6. *Level of development (LOD) issues*: It would be ideal to incrementally develop a single BIM model that can support all different types of BIM uses throughout the lifecycle of a project. It is, however, practically impossible to include all the details required by different uses of BIM models throughout different phases of a project in a single model. A recent BIM capability has been to provide a guideline for the proper levels of detail or development of BIM models for different BIM uses. BIM models on different LODs are not only different in terms of level of details, but also on the contents of information. Harmonization of LOD with performance and economic assessments are being explored to realize further workflow integration. Consequently, BIM model data on different LODs require additional data adjustments. More discussions and a historical review of LODs (also known as LOx) are available in Section 8.3.2.

Not all, but many of these technical and procedural problems can be overcome by deploying different data exchange strategies or proper work processes as far as project participants agree to share information with team members. In practice, however, it is not rare to meet project participants who are unwilling to share information with team members. This human factor is one of the most difficult hurdles to overcome.

7. *Unwillingness to share information*: Some team members are unwilling to share information with team members due to intellectual property, security, or contractual issues, but sometimes, without a rational reason. BIM experts around the world identified willingness of project participants to share information as one of the critical success factors for BIM projects (Won et al., 2013b). Contrarily, this means that this willingness problem is not easy to resolve. Since the willingness problem is not a technical problem, this and other interoperability problems due to human factors can be resolved only through negotiation or contractual mandate.

How do we achieve interoperability—the easy, reliable exchange of project data? First of all, a *data model* or *schema* must be defined. A *data model* or *schema* conceptually defines elements required for a target domain and the relationships between the elements. In general, data models between applications are defined on three levels, characterized in Figure 3–1 (ANSI/X3/SPARC, 1975). The three-level definition is often referred to as the *ANSI/SPARC architecture (for databases)*.

The first tier is the user's view on information exchange requirements. This tier is called the *external level*. Each user may need a different set of information to process his or her work. A data model specified from a specific user perspective is called a *subset*, a *view*, a *model view*, a *view definition*, a *model view definition (MVD)*, or *a conformance class*. The first and the last steps of data modeling are to specify and generate these views. The first step is called the *requirements collection and modeling* phase—a phase to collect and specify users' information requirement. An international standard that

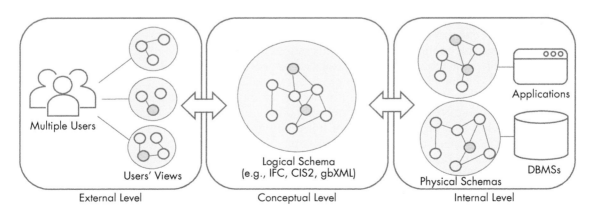

FIGURE 3–1 Three-level definitions of information exchange requirements.

defines this process and the documentation format for BIM is the ISO 29481 Information Delivery Manual (IDM) (ISO TC 59/SC 13, 2010). The last step is to develop an export module in a software application or a view specification in a database management system based on a view definition.

The second tier is the *conceptual level*, which is independent of an implementation method or an application system. The data model specified on this level is referred to as a *logical schema*. A logical schema can be viewed as a data model that is generated by consolidating multiple users' views. Examples of a logical schema include Industry Foundation Classes (IFC) (bSI, 2017) and CIMsteel Integration Standard, version 2 (CIS/2) (Crowley, 2003a). IFC is discussed in detail in Section 3.3.

The third tier is the *internal level*. A logical schema that is generated on the second level can be implemented in various ways such as a translator between two different systems or a database management system. Each software application has its own data structure. To implement a logical schema into a software application, a mapping process between a logical schema and an internal data structure of an application is required. The internal data structure or a data model on the internal level is referred to as a *physical schema*.

Given the schema dimensions, different data exchange methods can be deployed depending on the causes of interoperability problems. Exchanges can be classified in one of the three main ways listed below:

- **Direct links** between two applications through an Application Programming Interface (API) of one system can be deployed when a data model is not mature enough to support data exchange between two applications. Some may write a temporary file in the exchange between two independent applications; others may rely on real-time exchanges calling one application from the other. Some applications provide proprietary interfaces, such as ArchiCAD's GDL, Revit's Open API, or Bentley's MDL. Direct links are implemented as programming level interfaces, typically relying on C++, C#, or Visual Basic languages. The interfaces make some portion of the application's building model accessible for creation, export, modification, checking, or deletion, and the other programming interface provides capabilities for import and adaptation for the receiving application's data. Many such interfaces exist, often within a company's own product family and sometimes through a business arrangement between two or more companies.

  Software companies often prefer to provide direct link or proprietary exchanges to specific software; they can support them better. The interfaces can be tightly coupled with, for example, an analysis tool directly embedded in a design application. These interfaces allow capabilities not easily supported through current public exchanges. The functionality of exchanges that are supported is determined by the two companies (or divisions within the same company) that identify certain use cases, defining where it lies in the design-build lifecycle and the assumed purpose(s). Sometimes the use cases that motivated the exchange capabilities are documented, but often they are not and thus are difficult to evaluate. Public definitions of BIM standards for use cases are driving the recognition that all building model exchanges need to have a use case specification, if they are to be relied upon. Because direct exchanges have been developed, debugged, and maintained by the two companies involved, they are typically robust for the versions of the software for which they were designed, and the use-case functionality and LOD intended. Many exchanges fail because the translators were developed with different use cases in mind. The interfaces are maintained as long as the business relationships hold.

- **File-based data exchange** is a method to exchange data through a model file either using a proprietary exchange format or a publicly open standard format. A *proprietary exchange format* is a data schema developed by a commercial organization for interfacing with that company's application. The specification for the schema may be published or confidential.

Some well-known proprietary exchange formats in the AEC area are DXF and RVT, both defined by Autodesk, PLN by Graphisoft, and DGN by Bentley. Other proprietary exchange formats include SAT (defined by Spatial Technology, the implementer of the ACIS geometric modeling software kernel), and 3DS for 3D-Studio. Each of these has their own purpose, dealing with different kinds of geometry. *Data exchange in a standard exchange format* involves using an open and publicly managed schema. IFC and CIS/2 are examples of standard data formats for AEC. These will be described in more detail shortly.

- **Model-server based data exchange** is a method to exchange data through a database management system (DBMS). A DBMS for BIM models is sometimes referred to as *a model server, a BIM server, an IFC server, a data repository, a product data repository*, or *a common data environment (CDE)*. A BIM server is structured often based on standard data models such as IFC or CIS/2 to provide a common data environment. Examples of model servers include the IFC model server (IMSvr) developed by VTT, Finland (Adachi, 2002), the CIS2SQL server by Georgia Tech, US (You et al., 2004), the Eurostep Model Server (EMS) developed by Eurostep (Jørgensen et al., 2008), Express Data Manager Server (EDMServer), developed by Jotne EPM Technology, Finland (Jotne EPM Technology, 2013), the Open Source BIMserver by TNO, the Netherlands (BIMserver.org, 2012), and the OR-IFC server by Yonsei, Korea (Lee et al., 2014).

The model-server based data exchange approach has an advantage over the file-based data exchange approach in that it can relieve aspects of the version control and concurrent engineering issues. Moreover, the model-server based data exchange approach has the potential to reduce many interoperability problems by adding artificial intelligent functions to a model server and by enabling an automated analysis of the status and quality of data and filling in missing and conflicting information based on the analysis results.

A summary of the most common exchange formats in the AEC area is provided in Table 3–1. Table 3–1 groups file exchange formats with regard to their main usage. These include 2D raster image formats for pixel-based images, 2D vector formats for line drawings, 3D surface and solid shape formats for 3D forms. Three-dimensional object-based formats are especially important for BIM uses and have been grouped according to their field of application. These include the ISO-STEP-based formats that include 3D-shape information

Table 3–1   Common Exchange Formats in AEC Applications

Image (Raster) Formats

JPG, GIF, TIF, BMP, PNG, RAW, RLE	Raster formats vary in terms of compactness, number of possible colors per pixel, transparency, compression with or without data loss.

2D Vector Formats

DXF, DWG, AI, CGM, EMF, IGS, WMF, DGN, PDF, ODF, SVG, SWF	Vector formats vary regarding compactness, line formatting, color, layering, and types of curves supported; some are file-based and others use XML.

3D Surface and Shape Formats

3DS, WRL, STL, IGS, SAT, DXF, DWG, OBJ, DGN, U3D PDF(3D), PTS, DWF	3D surface and shape formats vary according to the types of surfaces and edges represented, whether they represent surfaces and/or solids, material properties of the shape (color, image bitmap, and texture map), or viewpoint information. Some have both ASCII and binary encodings. Some include lighting, camera, and other viewing controls; some are file formats and others XML.

3D Object Exchange Formats

STP, EXP, CIS/2, IFC	Product data model formats represent geometry according to the 2D or 3D types represented; they also carry object type data and relevant properties and relations between objects. They are the richest in information content.
AecXML, Obix, AEX, bcXML, AGCxml	XML schemas developed for the exchange of building data; they vary according to the information exchanged and the workflows supported.
V3D, X, U, GOF, FACT, COLLADA	A wide variety of game file formats vary according to the types of surfaces, whether they carry hierarchical structure, types of material properties, texture and bump map parameters, animation, and skinning.
SHP, SHX, DBF, TIGER, JSON, GML	Geographical information system formats vary in terms of 2D or 3D, data links supported, file formats and XML.

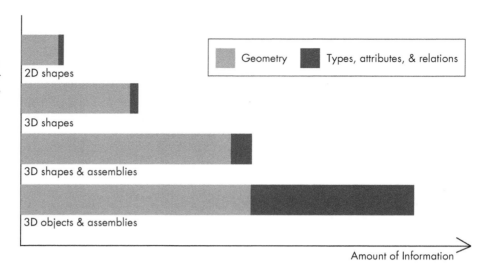

along with connectivity relations and attributes, of which the IFC building data model is of highest importance. Also listed are various gaming formats, which support fixed geometry, lighting, textures along with actors, and dynamic, moving geometry, and GIS public exchange formats for 3D terrain, land uses, and infrastructure.

As the computer-aided design field has progressed from 2D to 3D and more complex shapes and assemblies, the number of data types represented has grown tremendously. An ordinal charting of this phenomenon is shown in Figure 3–2. While 3D geometry of assemblies is complex, the additions of properties, object types, and relations has led to a large increase in the types of information represented. It is not surprising, then, that the purpose of data exchange has taken on increasing attention and importance, becoming the most important issue for advanced BIM users. As the richness of data about a building grows, the issues of data exchange shift from accurate translation to filtering just the information needed, and the quality of the information (e.g., is the data an estimated or nominal shape or property or those of a specific product?).

A natural desire is to "mix and match" software tools to provide functionality beyond what can be offered by any single software platform. This is especially true when diverse organizations collaborate on a project as a team. Gaining interoperability of different systems used by the team is much easier than forcing all team firms onto a single platform. The public sector also wishes to avoid a proprietary solution that gives any one software platform a monopoly. IFC and CIS/2 (for steel) are public and internationally recognized standards. Thus they are likely to become the international standard for data exchange and integration within the building construction industries.

3.3 BACKGROUND OF PRODUCT DATA MODELS

With BIM, the number and range of AEC applications is expanding quickly for design, fabrication, construction, and building operations. The need for interoperability can only grow, not shrink. Until the mid-1980s, almost all data exchange in all design and engineering fields was based on various fixed schema file formats. DXF and IGES are well-known examples. These provided effective exchange formats for 2D and 3D geometry. However, object models of piping, mechanical, electrical, and other systems were being developed at this time. If data exchange was to deal with models of complex objects with their geometry, attributes, and relations, any fixed file exchange format quickly became very large and so complex as to be uninterpretable. These issues arose in both Europe and the United States at about the same time. After some back and forth, the International Standards Organization (ISO) in Geneva, Switzerland, initiated a Technical Committee, TC184, to start a subcommittee to develop a standard called STEP (STandard for the Exchange of Product model data), numbered ISO-10303, to address these issues. They developed a new approach and a set of technologies to deal with advanced data exchange issues.

Surrounding the STEP standard is a collection of software companies providing toolkits for implementing and testing software based on EXPRESS. Text file and XML reading and writing is broadly supported, along with model viewers, navigators, and other implementation tools. A few BIM applications use IFC as their native data model; that is, they use IFC as their internal data structure to read, write, and save data within the system. The following subsections review these modeling languages, data models, and BIM servers in more detail.

3.3.1 Modeling Languages

Schemas are defined using graphical data modeling languages such as EXPRESS-G, Entity Relationship Diagrams (ERD), or UML Class Diagrams, or textual data modeling languages such as EXPRESS or XSD (XML Schema Definition).

One of the main products of ISO-STEP was the EXPRESS language, developed by Douglas Schenck and later contributed to by Peter Wilson (Schenk and Wilson, 1994). The EXPRESS language has become the central mechanism to support the modeling of products across a broad range of industries: mechanical and electrical systems, process plants, shipbuilding, furniture, finite element models, and others, as well as buildings and bridges. It also includes a large number of libraries of features, geometry, classifications, measurements, and others to provide common foundations for product data models. Both metric and imperial measurements are supported and intermixed. As a machine-readable language, it is excellent for computational use, but difficult for human users; thus a graphical display version of the language, called EXPRESS-G, was developed and is commonly used. All ISO-STEP information is in the public domain.

XML (eXtensible Markup Language) is a subset of ISO 8879:1986 Standard Generalized Markup Language (SGML) and a sibling of HTML, the base language of the web. XML can be used as both a schema language and an instance data representation language. A schema defined in XML is called XSD or XML schema. Some XML schemas are published and public, while others are proprietary. XML schemas for AEC include BACnet (Building Automation and Control networks; BACnet, n.d.), a standard protocol for building mechanical controls; AEX (Automating Equipment Information Exchange; FIATECH, n.d.) for identifying mechanical equipment; AECxml, an XML version of the IFC schema (bSI, 2017); and cityGML (City Geography Markup Language; CityGML, n.d.), an exchange for representing buildings within a GIS (Geographical Information System) format for urban planning, emergency services, and infrastructure planning.

An XML instance file can be generated according to an XML schema. An instance file or an instance data representation is a set of data defined based on a schema. For example, the "Building Archive" schema may include entities such as building type, building name, and completion year. Instance data of this schema will be healthcare facility (building type), John Hopkins Hospital (building name), and 1989 (completion year). An XML instance file has an extension of .xml and an XML schema file has an extension of .xsd.

With the advent of the World Wide Web, several different alternative schema languages were developed. These took advantage of streaming of information packets that could be processed as they were received, in contrast to file transfers that require the complete transfer of data before they can be processed. While file-based data transport is still common, XML provides streaming data packaging that is attractive for many uses. With cell phones and other devices, other transport media, such as GSM (Groupe Spécial Mobile), GPRS (General Packet Radio Service), and WAP (Wireless Application Protocol) can be expected to be applied to building data.

3.3.2   ISO-STEP in Building Construction

AEC organizations initially participated in ISO-STEP meetings and initiated some early STEP exchange models. Also, non-STEP organizations can use the STEP technologies to develop industry-based product data models, and there are two major efforts of this type. Up to now, the following product models related to buildings have been developed, all based on the ISO-STEP technology and defined in the EXPRESS language (Table 3–2):

- **ISO 10303 AP 225**—Building Elements Using Explicit Shape Representation is the only completed building-oriented product data model developed and approved by ISO STEP. It deals with the exchange of building geometry. AP 225 has been used in Europe, mostly in Germany, as an alternative to DXF. Only a few CAD applications support it.
- **IFC**—Industry Foundation Classes is an industry-developed product data model for the design and full lifecycle representation of buildings, supported by buildingSMART. It has broad support from most software companies; it is weakened by various inconsistent implementations.

Table 3-2 Standards Developed by the ISO/TC 59/SC 13 Technical Committee (Organization of Information About Construction Works)

Standard Number	Title	Stage	Catalog
ISO 12006-2:2015	Building construction, Organization of information about construction works; Part 2: Framework for classification	Published	Construction industry
ISO 12006-3:2007	Building construction, Organization of information about construction works; Part 3: Framework for object-oriented information	Published	Construction industry
ISO 16354:2013	Guidelines for knowledge libraries and object libraries	Published	Construction industry
ISO 16757-1:2015	Data structures for electronic product catalogues for building services; Part 1: Concepts, architecture and model	Published	Construction industry
ISO 16757-2:2016	Data structures for electronic product catalogues for building services; Part 2: Geometry	Published	Construction industry
ISO 22263:2008	Organization of information about construction works; Framework for management of project information	Published	Construction industry
ISO 29481-1:2016	Building information models, Information delivery manual; Part 1: Methodology and format	Published	Construction industry
ISO 29481-2:2012	Building information models, Information delivery manual; Part 2: Interaction framework	Published	Construction industry
ISO/DIS 19650-1.2	Organization of information about construction works, Information management using building information modeling; Part 1: Concepts and principles	Under development	IT applications in building and construction industry
ISO/DIS 19650-2.2	Organization of information about construction works, Information management using building information modeling, Part 2: Delivery phase of assets	Under development	IT applications in building and construction industry
ISO/NP 16739-1	Industry Foundation Classes (IFC) for data sharing in the construction and facility management industries; Part 1: Data schema using EXPRESS schema definitions	New project	Industrial process measurement and control
ISO/NP 21597	Information container for data drop (ICDD)	New project	Not assigned
ISO/TS 12911:2012	Framework for building information modelling (BIM) guidance	Published	Construction industry

IFC is an ISO standard (ISO 16739) and developed based on the ISO-STEP technologies, but is not part of ISO STEP. International efforts to develop IFC extensions for infrastructures such as roads, highways, bridges, and railways are underway. Main participants include France, Japan, Korea, China, the Netherlands, Germany, and others. The efforts are called the IFC for Infrastructure (IFC Infra) projects, and include IFC Alignment, IFC Bridge, and IFC Road.

- **CIS/2**—CIM (Computer-Integrated Manufacturing) Steel Integration Standard, Version 2, is an industry-developed standard for structural steel design, analysis, and fabrication, supported by the American

Institute of Steel Construction and the Construction Steel Institute in the United Kingdom. CIS/2 is widely used and deployed in the North American structural steel engineering and fabrication industry.

- **ISO 10303 AP 241**—Generic Model for Life Cycle Support of AEC Facilities addresses industrial facilities, and overlaps with IFC functionality; proposed in 2006 by buildingSMART Korea (bSK). The purpose of AP 241 is to develop a product data model for factories and their components in a fully ISO-STEP-compatible format. This project faded out as the focus of the buildingSMART International community shifted toward the IFC Infra projects.

- **ISO 15926**—A STEP standard for *industrial automation systems and integration:* Integration of lifecycle data for process plants including oil and gas production facilities. It addresses the whole lifecycle, from planning and design to maintenance and operation. Because a process plant is continuously maintained, objects are naturally 4D. ISO 15926 evolved from an earlier European Community EPISTLE project and was strongly supported by Det Norske Veritas, known as DNV (www.dnv .com). It brought together various ISO STEP part models, for 2D plant schematics, for plant physical layout, and for plant process modeling. ISO 15926 was adopted by a consortium of firms under FIATECH, and was refined and adopted for North American use. The schema supports the concept of Facades, which is similar to model views. ISO 15926 relies on EXPRESS and other ISO-STEP formats.

  ISO 15926 has seven parts:

  - *Part 1*—Introduction, information concerning engineering, construction, and operation of production facilities is created, used, and modified by many different organizations throughout a facility's lifetime. The purpose of ISO 15926 is to facilitate integration of data to support the lifecycle activities and processes of production facilities.
  - *Part 2*—Data Model, a generic 4D model that can support all disciplines, supply chain company types, and lifecycle stages, regarding information about functional requirements, physical solutions, types of objects, and individual objects as well as activities.
  - *Part 3*—Geometry and Topology, defining, in OWL, the geometric and topology libraries of ISO-STEP.
  - *Parts 4, 5, 6*—Reference Data, the terms used within facilities for the process industry.
  - *Part 7*—Implementation methods for the integration of distributed systems, defining an implementation architecture that is based on the W3C Recommendations for the Semantic Web.

  An important part of ISO 15926 is its large set of libraries, covering fluids, electrical, and mechanical components.

- **ISO 29481**—*Building information models: information delivery manual (IDM).* A data model or a schema is often developed inclusively to support as much as possible. Data exchange in practice, however, uses only a small subset of a data model. The ISO 29481 specifies a methodology and a format for defining information exchange requirements for specific information exchange scenarios. Another purpose of an IDM is to allow users to define their information requirements independently of any specific data model, such as IFC or CIS/2.

ISO 29481 has two parts and is expected to grow:

Part 1 Methodology and format—An IDM is mainly composed of three parts: a process map (PM), exchange requirements (ER), and a model view definition (MVD). A PM graphically illustrates a target data exchange scenario in terms of a process model. As a notation for a PM, BPMN (Business Process Modeling Notation) is recommended, but not mandated. An ER is a set of specific information items required for a PM and descriptions about the information items in a natural language. An MVD is a translation of an ER to a specific data model. An MVD can be regarded as part of IDM, but is often treated separately. An MVD is also called a subset model, and an MVD generally means a subset model of IFC.

Part 2 Interaction framework—Instead of using a PM, a data exchange scenario can be expressed as interaction between actors. ISO 29481 Part 2 defines how to represent a data exchange scenario as interaction between actors.

- **ISO 12006-3**—Building construction, Organization of information about construction works, Part 3: Framework for object-oriented information. A data dictionary is a collection of terms and definitions used to develop a data model. ISO 12006-3 stemmed from the buildingSMART Data Dictionary (bSDD) project. It specifies a framework for defining a data dictionary for AEC.

- **ISO/DIS 19650**—*Organization of information about construction works: Information management using building information modeling*. ISO/DIS 19650 specifies concepts and principles for generating, managing, and handing over information during the lifecycle of built assets. Part 1 describes general concepts and principles, and Part 2 specifies the specific requirements for information management during the delivery of built assets. Part 2 owes a lot of its contents to COBie.

There are multiple building product data models with overlapping functionality, all using the EXPRESS language. They vary in the AEC information they represent and their intended use, but with overlaps. IFC can represent building geometry, as can AP 225 and ISO 15926. There is overlap between CIS/2 and IFC in the design of structural steel. ISO 15926 overlaps IFC in the piping and mechanical equipment areas. These largely separate efforts will need to be harmonized. Harmonization efforts are being discussed between ISO 15926 and IFC, especially in the mechanical equipment area and structural steel design areas.

3.3.3 buildingSMART and IFC

The IFC, the most commonly used data model in AEC, has a long history. In late 1994, Autodesk initiated an industry consortium to advise the company on the development of a set of C++ classes that could support integrated application development. Twelve U.S. companies joined the consortium. Initially called the Industry Alliance for Interoperability, the Alliance opened membership to all interested parties in September 1995 and changed its name in 1997 to the International Alliance for Interoperability (IAI). The new Alliance was reconstituted as a nonprofit industry-led international organization with the goal of publishing the Industry Foundation Classes (IFC) as a neutral AEC product data model responding to the building lifecycle. It would be based on ISO-STEP technologies, but independent of its bureaucracy. In 2005, it was felt that the IAI name was too long, confusing (for example, with AIA), and complex for people to understand. At a meeting in Norway of the IAI Executive Committee, IAI was renamed buildingSMART, reflecting its ultimate goal. The umbrella international organization is called buildingSMART International, and subgroups are called buildingSMART chapters. A good historical overview of buildingSMART and IFC is available on the buildingSMART website.

As of 2017, buildingSMART had 17 chapters in 22 countries. The buildingSMART members meet twice every year to develop or update international standards and to share and document best practices for BIM. One of the ongoing international efforts is to extend IFC to cover road, bridge, tunnel, and railroad projects. The BIM Collaboration Format (BCF), a data format for exchanging design review and coordination data, is another outcome of such international efforts. Building Room, Infra Room, Product Room, Regulatory Room (for government representatives), Construction Room, and Airport Room are examples of international efforts to share and document best practices for BIM.

3.3.4 What Is the IFC?

The Industry Foundation Classes (IFC) is a schema developed to define an extensible set of consistent data representations of building information for exchange between AEC software applications. It relies on the ISO-STEP EXPRESS language and concepts for its definition, with a few minor restrictions on the EXPRESS language. While most of the other ISO-STEP efforts focused on detailed software exchanges within specific engineering domains, it was thought that in the building industry this would lead to piecemeal results and a set of incompatible standards. Instead, IFC was designed as an extensible "framework model." That is, its developers intended it to provide broad, general definitions of objects and data from which more detailed and task-specific models supporting particular exchanges could be defined. In this regard, the IFC has been designed to address all building information, over the whole building lifecycle, from feasibility and planning, through design (including analysis and simulation) and construction, to occupancy and operation (Khemlani, 2004). Because of its central role in AEC interoperability, we describe it here in some detail.

The latest version of IFC before this book went to press, IFC 4 Addendum 2, was published in 2016. This release of IFC has 776 entities (data objects), 413 property sets, and 130 defined data types. While these numbers indicate the complexity of IFC, they also reflect the semantic richness of building information, addressing multiple different systems, reflecting the needs of different applications, ranging from energy analysis and cost estimation to material tracking and scheduling. All of the major BIM design tool and platform software companies have developed interfaces for this version. IFC 4 Addendum 2 is available for review at the buildingSMART website.

The conceptual organization of IFC can be considered in several ways. Figure 3–3 illustrates an example of specific domain uses of a single IFC project model. A system architecture perspective is diagrammed in Figure 3–4. At the bottom are 21 sets of base EXPRESS definitions, defining the base reusable constructs, such as Geometry, Topology, Materials, Measurements,

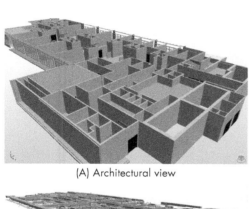

(A) Architectural view

(B) Mechanical system view

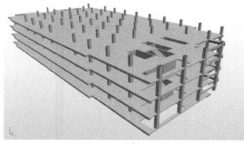

(C) Structural frame view

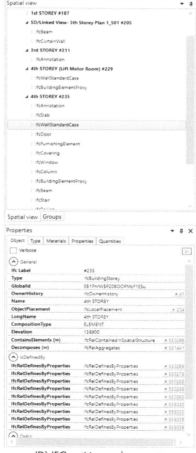

(D) IFC entities and property values of a view

FIGURE 3–3 IFCs consist of a library of object and property definitions that can be used to represent a building project and support use of that building information for a particular purpose. The figure shows three examples of specific domain uses from a single IFC project: (A) an architectural view, (B) a mechanical system view, and (C) a structural view. Also shown are (D) a sample IFC object or entity and sample properties and attributes.

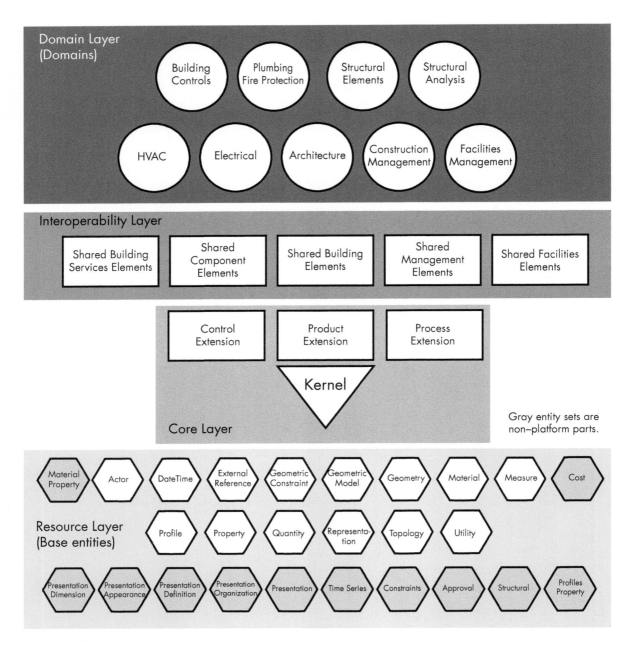

FIGURE 3–4   The system architecture of IFC subschemas. Each Resource and Core subschema has a structure of entities for defining models, specified at the Interoperability and Domain Layers.

Adapted from www.buildingsmart-tech.org/ifc/IFC4/Add2/html/introduction.htm.

Actors, Roles, Presentations, and Properties. These are generic for all types of products and are largely consistent with ISO-STEP shared library resources, with minor extensions.

The base entities are then composed to define commonly used objects in AEC, termed Shared Objects in IFC. These include building elements, such as generic walls, floors, structural elements, building service elements, process elements, management elements, and generic features. Because IFC is defined as an extensible data model and is object-oriented, the base entities can be elaborated and specialized by subtyping[2] to make any number of subentities.

Conceptually, IFC is structured as objects (e.g., *IfcObjectDefinition*) and their relations (entities whose names start with *IfcRel*). At the top level of the IFC data model are the domain-specific extensions of these object and relation entities. These deal with different specific entities needed for a particular use. Thus there are Structural Elements and Structural Analysis Extensions, Architectural, Electrical, HVAC, and Building Control Element Extensions.

All IFC models provide a common general building spatial structure for the layout and accessing of building elements. IFC organizes all object information into the hierarchy of *Project → Site → Building → BuildingStorey → Space*. Each higher-level spatial structure is an aggregation of lower-level ones, plus any elements that span the lower-level classes. For example, stairs usually span all building stories and thus are part of the Building Aggregation. Walls typically bound two or more spaces on one or multiple stories. They are typically part of the BuildingStorey, if structured within a single story, and part of the Building Aggregation if they span multiple stories. Because of the IFC hierarchical object subtyping structure, the objects used in exchanges are nested within a deep sub-entity definition tree. All physical objects, process objects, actors, and other basic constructs are abstractly represented similarly. For example, a simple wall entity has a trace down the tree shown in Figure 3–5.

Each level of the tree in Figure 3–5 introduces different attributes and relations to the wall entity. *IfcRoot*, the highest-level abstract entity in IFC, assigns a Globally Unique ID (GUID) and other information for managing the object, such as who created it and when. *IfcObjectDefinition* places the wall into the aggregate building story assembly. This level also identifies the components of the wall, including windows, doors, and any other openings. The *IfcObject* level provides links to properties of the wall, based on its type (defined lower down in the hierarchy tree). *IfcProduct* defines the location of the wall and its shape. *IfcElement* carries the relationship of this element with others, such as wall bounding relationships, and also the spaces that the wall separates. It also carries any openings within the wall and optionally their filling by doors or windows. If the wall is structural, a structural element representing the wall can be associated with it.

Walls are typed as one of the following: *Standard*: extruded vertically with a fixed width along its control line; *Polygonal*: extruded vertically but with

---

[2] Subtyping provides for defining a new class of building object that "inherits" the properties of its "parent" class and adds new properties that make it distinct from its parent and any possible "sibling" classes. IFC superclasses, subclasses, and inheritance behavior conform to accepted principles of object-oriented modeling. For more detail, see Booch, 1993.

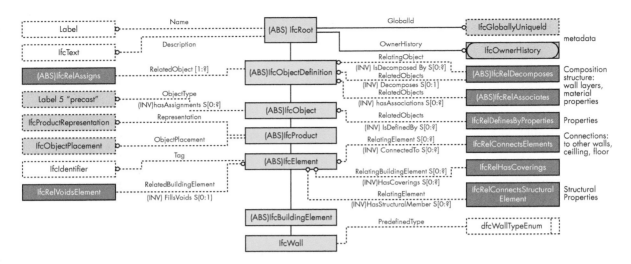

FIGURE 3-5   The IFC structure for defining a wall.

varying cross section; *Shear*: walls not extruded vertically; *ElementWall*: walls composed of elements such as studs and sheathing; *PlumbingWall*: wall with embedded routing space; *Userdefined*: all other types; *Undefined*. Many of these attributes and relations are optional, allowing implementers to exclude some of the information from their export routines. It is possible that not all BIM design tools can create or represent all of the different wall types.

Properties are carried in optional P-sets. The *PSetWallCommon* provides fields to define: Identifier, AcousticRating, FireRating, Combustibility, SurfaceSpreadOfFlame, ThermalTransmittance, IsExterior, ExtendToStructure (to slab above), LoadBearing, Compartmentation (firewall). Other more detailed P-sets are also supported if needed. Openings, notches and reveals, and protruding elements, such as pilasters, are supported, along with walls clipped by irregular ceilings.

From this wall example, one gets a sense for how all building elements in IFC are defined. There are many types of assemblies, P-sets, and features that can support structural, mechanical, and other system elements. Analysis models, load data, and product performance parameters can also be represented in some areas. Objects' geometry can also be represented parametrically using the IFC schema, but this use is not yet common.

There are significant efforts to apply the IFC in various parts of the world including the U.S., the UK, Norway, Finland, Denmark, Germany, Korea, Japan, China, Singapore, and other countries. The U.S., Norway, Korea, and Singapore have initiated efforts to develop automatic building code-checking capabilities and e-submission systems based on IFC. Also, the number of successful BIM and IFC projects increases every year. Award-winning IFC-based BIM projects can be found at the buildingSMART BIM Awards web page.

3.3.5 IDM and MVD

As the AEC field has matured, the focus of the issue of interoperability has moved from data exchange between two BIM applications to supporting the use cases defined by workflows. The major benefits of interoperability are not only to automate an exchange (although replicating the data in another application is certainly redundant activity), but the larger benefits that refine workflows, eliminate steps, and improve processes. The new phrase is to better "manage lean workflows."

Task and workflow information requirements have become recognized as critical for successful data exchanges. IFC, developed to respond to the different needs of designers, contractors, building product suppliers, fabricators, government officials, and others, is too large and complex to get a data set of interest by clicking simple user interface buttons for "IFC export" and "IFC import." What is needed are task-related exchanges based on subsets of the IFC schema, for example, an "architect's structural export for preliminary structural analysis" or a "curtain wall fabricator detail export to construction manager for fabrication-level coordination." Such exchanges are called *model views* and they are defined by *model view definitions (MVDs)*, drawing from the notion of a database view. This level of specificity involves identifying the exchanges to be supported and then specifying the IFC model view of the information that the exchange needs.

The specification of information requirements is called an *information delivery manual (IDM)*, which is composed of a definition of a target work process (a *process map, PM*) and a specification of information required by the target process (*exchange requirements, ER*) (ISO TC 59/SC 13, 2010). MVDs are another level of specification, above the IFC schema. The National Institute of Building Science (NIBS) lays out a process to be followed in developing MVDs (NIBS, 2012). This is characterized in Figure 3–6.

Specification of IDM/MVD is both the beginning and end of data modeling. Information that is not included in IFC can be specified by IDM/MVD and added to IFC. IDM/MVD can also be used to specify a subset of IFC for a specific data exchange scenario, which can be used by software developers as a guide to develop an IFC export/import function to support the data exchange scenario. Today, the focus is more on the latter than the former, but the role of IDM/MVD is expanding. For example, IDM/MVD can be used to define the handover specifications for different phases of project delivery (for example, from design to construction, and for construction to operation), such as defined by Construction Operations Building information exchange (COBie); see Section 3.4.3. Another example is Employers Information Requirements (EIRs) requested by the UK Government. EIR is BIM information that must be submitted as part of deliverables. These are part of the definition of project scope and defined within contracts to specify milestone handovers. They will then need to be defined for direct exchange between applications as well as public data schema exchanges. The point is that IDM/MVDs respond to very important needs in building procurement, far beyond IFC interoperability.

FIGURE 3–6 The four major steps for defining and implementing an NBIMS of Program, Design, Construct, and Deploy (NIBS, 2012).

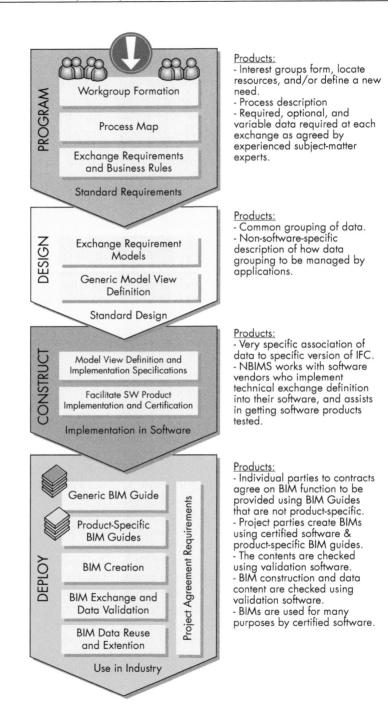

PROGRAM

Workgroup Formation

Process Map

Exchange Requirements and Business Rules

Standard Requirements

Products:
- Interest groups form, locate resources, and/or define a new need.
- Process description
- Required, optional, and variable data required at each exchange as agreed by experienced subject-matter experts.

DESIGN

Exchange Requirement Models

Generic Model View Definition

Standard Design

Products:
- Common grouping of data.
- Non-software-specific description of how data grouping to be managed by applications.

CONSTRUCT

Model View Definition and Implementation Specifications

Facilitate SW Product Implementation and Certification

Implementation in Software

Products:
- Very specific association of data to specific version of IFC.
- NBIMS works with software vendors who implement technical exchange definition into their software, and assists in getting software products tested.

DEPLOY

Generic BIM Guide

Product-Specific BIM Guides

BIM Creation

BIM Exchange and Data Validation

BIM Data Reuse and Extention

Project Agreement Requirements

Use in Industry

Products:
- Individual parties to contracts agree on BIM function to be provided using BIM Guides that are not product-specific.
- Project parties create BIMs using certified software & product-specific BIM guides.
- The contents are checked using validation software.
- BIM construction and data content are checked using validation software.
- BIMs are used for many purposes by certified software.

3.4 OTHER EFFORTS SUPPORTING STANDARDIZATION

IFC is only one piece of a huge puzzle regarding conventions and standards in the construction industry. While IFC addresses the data structures dealing with geometry, relations, and attributes, how will the attributes be named and used? How will the Chinese and other people who don't use the Roman alphabet work with those who do? Interoperability is a wider issue than is addressed by IFC or any current XML schema. While industries have grown up dealing with the classification and testing of construction materials, the same now needs to be done regarding other types of construction information. Here we provide a quick reference and overview of other BIM-related standards efforts.

3.4.1 buildingSMART Data Dictionary

The European community early saw an issue in the naming of properties and object classes. "Door" is *porte* in French, *Tür* in German, and 門 in Chinese. Each of its properties also has different names. Objects specified in IFC may have names and attributes in different languages and their meanings need to be properly interpreted. Fortunately, IFC deals well with measures in different units (SI and Imperial). Moreover, one may encounter different standards, such as CIS/2 and IFC, that have overlapping objects and properties that are treated differently, even though they are in the same spoken language. The building-SMART Data Dictionary (bSDD; also known as International Framework for Dictionary, IFD) team was formed to address these issues and can be found at the bSDD website. It is developing mappings of terms between different languages, for eventual wide use in building models and interfaces. Another important effort being undertaken by bSDD is the development of standards for building product specifications, particularly specification data, so these can be used in different applications, such as energy analysis, carbon footprint, and cost estimation.

The bSDD is being undertaken by the Construction Specifications Institute (CSI) in the United States, Construction Specifications Canada, building-SMART in Norway, and the STABU Foundation in the Netherlands.

3.4.2 OmniClass

A related activity is the review and replacement of existing building-related classification systems for their use in BIM. Both Masterformat and Uniformat are building element and assembly classification schemes used for specifications and cost estimation in the United States, and are overseen by the Construction Specification Institute. Both Masterformat and Uniformat are outline document structures that are excellent for aggregating information from project drawings, but do not always map well to the individual objects within a building model (although they can be mapped). Their limitations are described in Section 5.4.2 As a result, Europeans and Americans have embarked on a new set of outline structured classification tables, called OmniClass. OmniClass has been developed by the International Organization for Standardization (ISO) and the International Construction Information Society (ICIS) subcommittees and workgroups from the early 1990s to the present. In the UK, Uniclass (managed by NBC) is used instead of OmniClass. Currently OmniClass consists of 15 tables.

Table 11	Construction Entities by Function	Table 32	Services
Table 12	Construction Entities by Form	Table 33	Disciplines
Table 13	Spaces by Function	Table 34	Organizational Roles
Table 14	Space by Form	Table 35	Tools
Table 21	Elements	Table 36	Information
Table 22	Work Results	Table 41	Materials
Table 23	Products	Table 49	Properties
Table 31	Project Phases		

These tables of classification terms are being defined and structured by volunteer industry members. They are evolving quickly for adoption and use in BIM tools and methods. See Section 5.4.2 for more discussions on OmniClass and BIM.

3.4.3 COBie

Construction Operations Building information exchange (COBie) addresses the handover of information between the construction team and the owner. It deals with operations and maintenance (O&M), as well as more general facility management information. Traditionally, O&M information is provided in an ad hoc structure at the end of construction. COBie outlines a standard method for collecting the needed information throughout the design and construction process, as part of the deliverable package to the owner during commissioning and handover. It collects data from designers, as they define the design, and then by contractors as the building is constructed. It categorizes and structures the information in a practical and easy-to-implement manner.

Specific COBie objectives are as follows (East, 2012):

- Provide a simple format for real-time information exchange for existing design and construction contract deliverables.
- Clearly identify requirements and responsibilities for business processes.
- Provide a framework to store information for later exchange/retrieval.
- Add no cost to operations and maintenance.
- Permit direct import to owner's maintenance management system.

COBie specifies deliverables throughout all stages of design and construction, with specific deliverables in each of the phases below:

- architectural programming phase
- architectural design phase
- coordinated design phase
- construction documents phase

- construction mobilization phase
- construction 60 percent complete phase
- beneficial occupancy phase
- fiscal completion
- corrective maintenance

COBie was updated at the beginning of 2010 and is now called COBie2. It has formats for human as well as machine readability. The human readable format for COBie2 information is a conventional spreadsheet, provided in Microsoft Excel Spreadsheet format, on the WBDG COBie website. COBie2 has also been implemented for exchange of facility management data using the buildingSMART Industry Foundation Classes (IFC) open standard (or its ifcXML equivalent). Translators between IFC-Express and ifcXML to and from the COBie2 spreadsheet are available, free of charge, without technical support at the NIBS COBie web page.

COBie addresses the normal submittals required for handover at the end of a construction project, but puts them in a structured form, amenable to computer-based management. It includes the sections outlined in Table 3–3.

COBie2 has been developed to support the initial data entry into Computerized Maintenance and Management Systems (CMMS). Maximo, TOKMO,

Table 3–3   COBie2 Data Sections

Object Type	Definitions
Meta Data	Exchange file
Project	Attributes, Units, Decomposition
Site	Attributes, Address, Classification, Base Quantities, Properties
Building	Attributes, Address, Classification, Base Quantities, Properties
Story	Attributes, Base Quantities, Classification, Properties
Spatial Container	Attributes, Classification, Quantities, Properties, Space Boundaries,
Space Boundary	Doors, Windows, Bounding Space
Covering	Attributes, Type, Covering Material, Classification, Base Quantities
Window	Attributes, Type, Classification, Material, Base Quantities, Properties
Door	Attributes, Type, Classification, Material, Base Quantities, Properties
Furnishing	Attributes, Type, Material, Classification, Properties
MEP Elements	Attributes, Type, Material, Classification, Properties
Proxy Furniture, Fixture, Equipment	Attributes, Type, Material, Classification, Properties
Zone	Attributes, Classification, Properties, Spatial Assignment
System	Attributes, Classification, Properties, Component Assignment, System Service Buildings

NOTE: Attribute, Type, Classification attribute types vary by object type.

Onuma, and Archibus support COBie2, as do several European FM and design applications. It has been adopted as a required deliverable by VA hospitals, the U.S. Army Corps of Engineers, and NASA, as well as several university systems. It is also adopted by Norwegian, Finnish, and UK governments with some variations. ISO/DIS 19650 Part 2 is under development as an internationally standardized version of COBie.

3.4.4   XML-Based Schemas

Extensible Markup Language (XML) provides alternative schema languages and transport mechanisms, especially suited for web use. In the same way that some exchange formats are strictly file-oriented, some of the new exchange formats are only XML-based. XML provides user-defined tags to specify an intended meaning for data transmitted. XML has become very popular for exchange of information between web applications, for example, to support e-commerce transactions or collect data.

XML Schemas in AEC Areas

OpenGIS and the OpenGIS implementation standards have been developed by the OGC (Open Geospatial Consortium). OpenGIS defines an open set of common, language-independent abstractions for describing, managing, rendering, and manipulating geometric and geographic objects within an application programming environment (see list of OGC standards at the OGC website).

   gbXML (Green Building XML) is a schema developed to transfer information needed for preliminary energy analysis of building envelopes, zones, and mechanical equipment simulation (gbXML n.d.). Multiple platforms provide an interface.

   ifcXML is a subset of the IFC schema mapped to XML, supported by buildingSMART. It also relies on XML Schema, XSD, derived from the IFC EXPRESS release schema for its mapping. The language binding, for instance, the method of how to translate the IFC EXPRESS model into the ifcXML XSD model, follows the international standard ISO 10303-28ed2 "XML representation of EXPRESS schemas and data." The ISO/CD 10303-28ed2 version of 05-042004 is used for the language binding.

   aecXML is administered by FIATECH, a major construction industry consortium supporting AEC research, and by buildingSMART. It initially developed an integration framework that attempted to harmonize ifcXML and aecXML, as an umbrella schema, that could support multiple subschemas. It relied on XML business technology developed by the United Nations Centre for Trade Facilitation and Electronic Business. The integration schema is called Common Object Schema (COS) that consists of level XML structures of names, addresses, amounts, and other base information units. aecXML was initiated to represent resources such as contract and project documents [Request for Proposal (RFP), Request for Quotation (RFQ), Request for Information (RFI), specifications, addenda, change orders, contracts, purchase orders], attributes, materials and parts, products, equipment; meta data such as organizations, professionals, participants; or activities such as proposals, projects, design, estimating, scheduling, and construction. It carries descriptions and specifications of buildings and their components, but does not model them geometrically or analytically. Bentley was an early implementer of aecXML.

agcXML The Associated General Contractors (AGC) developed agcXML in 2007, a schema that supports construction business processes, based on the COS master schema of the aecXML effort. Its schemas include the exchange of information commonly included in the following document types:

- Request for Information
- Request for Pricing/Proposals
- Owner/Contractor Agreements
- Schedule of Values
- Change Order
- Application for Payment
- Supplemental Instructions
- Change Directive
- Bid, Payment, Performance, and Warranty Bonds
- Submittals

agcXML has been implemented by a few companies, including VICO and Newforma.

BIM Collaboration Format (BCF) is an XML format that supports exchange of design review data during a BIM collaboration process. During design reviews, various action items are identified. These are then acted upon by the various members of the project team. But how should these action items be transmitted? The answer comes from clash detection tools that identify a clash in 3D coordinates, associates an offset camera position to display the condition, then appends the action item to be taken, as identified by the parties involved. Originally this capability was limited to clash detection applications, such as Navisworks. However, transmitted in XML, the action item can be imported into any BIM platform and displayed for the user to act on. The use can be much wider than clash detection; it can be used for any type of review, whether automated (such as generated by Solibri Model Checker) or carried out manually through an in-person meeting or an online meeting. The benefit of BCF is that it directly loads and runs in the BIM design platform that generated the component of interest. BCF was initially proposed and defined by Tekla and Solibri in 2010, and has received commitments for support from Autodesk, DDS, Eurostep, Gehry Technologies, Kymdata, MAP, Progman, and QuickPen International. Now it is a part of buildingSMART standards. The second version, bcfXML v2, was released in 2014.

CityGML is a common information model for the representation of 3D urban objects. It defines classes and relations for relevant topographic objects in cities and regional models with respect to their geometrical, topological, semantic, and appearance properties. Included are generalization hierarchies between thematic classes, aggregations, relations between objects, and spatial properties. This thematic information goes beyond graphic exchange formats and supports virtual 3D city models for sophisticated analysis tasks in different application domains like simulation, urban data mining, facility management, and thematic inquiries. The underlying model differentiates five levels of detail (LOD). CityGML files can (but don't have to) contain multiple representations for each object in different LOD simultaneously. For more information, see the CityGML website.

There are multiple methods for defining custom tags, including Document Type Definitions (DTDs) that are developed for defining the valid structures and elements of an XML document. There are multiple ways to define XML schemas, including XML Schema, RDF (Resource Description Framework), and OWL (Web Ontology Language). Research is proceeding to develop even more powerful tools around XML and ever more powerful schemas, based on precise semantic definitions called *ontologies*. Practical results for these more advanced approaches have thus far been limited.

Using current readily available schema definition languages, some effective XML schemas and processing methods have been developed in AEC areas. Seven of them are described in the box on the previous page.

Each of these different XML schemas defines its own entities, attributes and relations, and rules. They work well to support work among a group of collaborating firms that implement a schema and develop applications around it. However, each of the XML schemas is different and incompatible. ifcXML provides a global mapping to the IFC building data model for cross-referencing. Efforts are underway to harmonize the OpenGIS schema with IFC. Translators do exist for mapping IFC models to CityGML. A data file specified in XML with tags is generally some two to six times larger than that specified in an plain text format. However, it can be processed significantly faster than a plain text file and thus works more effectively than file exchanges in most cases. The longer-term issue is to harmonize the other XML schemas with equivalence mappings between them and with data model representations. The analogy is when the railroads in the United States all rapidly built tracks over the country, each with their own gage; they worked fine within their own community, but could not link up.

Two important XML formats for publishing building model data are DWF and 3D PDF. These provide lightweight mappings of building models for limited uses.

3.5 THE EVOLUTION FROM FILE-BASED EXCHANGE TO BIM SERVERS

This chapter reviews the technology already developed or being developed to support the reuse of information created in one application in other applications. But a basic point made in the introduction is that buildings require multiple models for their full design, engineering, and construction. We now return to that point to examine its implications.

Production use of IFC or XML file exchanges and other XML-based e-business exchanges began with application-to-application exchanges. Typically, one person in each department or consulting team is responsible for managing versions within a project; when the architect or engineer releases an update to the design, it is passed to the consultant organizations for their reconciliation and model synchronization. As projects grow and project file structures get more complex, this style of coordination becomes increasingly complex. Project management at each firm, which is the historical way of doing it, is not effective when exchanges need to be processed rapidly. The management task can explode if the management of files is replaced with the management of objects.

The technology associated with the resolution of these types of data management issues is a *BIM server* (*building model repository, IFC server, or BIM repository*). A BIM server is a server or database system that brings together and facilitates management and coordination of all project-related data. It is an adaptation and expansion of existing project data management (PDM) systems and web-based project management systems. PDM systems have traditionally managed a project as a set of files and carried CAD and analysis package project files. BIM servers are distinguished by providing object-based management capabilities, allowing query, transfer, updating, and management of model data partitioned and grouped in a wide range of ways to support a potentially heterogeneous set of applications. The evolutionary change in the AEC field from managing files to managing information objects has only begun to take place.

BIM server technologies are a new technology that has different requirements than the equivalent systems developed for manufacturing. Their functional requirements are only now being sorted out. We provide an overview of their desired functionality, as now understood. We then survey the major current products at the end of this section.

3.5.1 Project Transactions and Synchronization

An important concept in databases is the definition of *transaction*. Transaction is a unit sequence of reading, writing, and creating data. Transactions are easy for single-user applications and for nonconcurrent updates. For single-user applications or nonconcurrent updates, traditional file-level data management and version control are sufficient because the entire file or model can be saved and managed as a new version. The *file-level transaction or data management* is a method to save the entire model file as one piece of information. An example of a file-level data management system is a project management system that stores the entire model as a file (e.g., *.rvt, *.dgn, *.pln, and *.ifc) in a database with additional submission information (the submission date, the user, and comments).

Most collaborative project management systems today are file-level management systems with web or cloud support. Many of them shifted from a web-based system to a cloud-based software as a service (SaaS) system and support both web and cloud environments. The functions are similar although the level of functions may vary by system.

Commonly supported functions include document (model files and project-related references) management; contract tracking; version control; search capabilities; design issue management; user management; notifications of work orders, design issues, and RFIs; generation and management of transmittals, meeting minutes, work orders, change orders, and other reports; workflow management; and project management dashboards. Dashboards are

Table 3-4   File-Based Collaborative Project Management Systems

Main Function \ Application	Aconex	Procore	Vault	ConstructWare	Projectwise	FINALCAD	BIM 360 Field
Cloud and mobile support	O	O			O	O	O
Document management	O	O	O	O	O	O	
Project management	O	O		O	O	O	
Project summary (dashboard)	O	O		O	O	O	O
Workflow management	O	O	O				
RFIs, mails, and form management	O	O			O		
Model viewer/BIM integration	O					O	
Punch list management	O	O			O	O	O
Version control	O		O		O		
Cost estimation		O		O			
Accounting		O		O			
Handover to O&M	O						O
Quality and safety management	O	O				O	

a graphical display of a statistical summary of a project, which can help project participants identify the status of a project or work to be done at a glance.

Some tools support cost management with budget and expenditure tracking and forecasting, data exchange with accounting systems to enable tracking of individual projects, and advanced schedule management. Table 3-4 lists several popularly used commercial file-level collaborative project management tools.

The approach that competes with file-level transaction is *object-level transaction or data management*. The object-level transaction or data management is a method to parse and save a model on an object level (e.g., column, beam, and slab). Compared to object-level transaction and data management, file-level data management has several drawbacks (Lee et al., 2014):

1. The system cannot tell which parts of a design have been modified by whom.
2. The users cannot query data directly from a model in a database. For example, a user cannot get information about the number of columns on a floor from a model stored in a database.
3. A subset of a model cannot be extracted from the model file.
4. The users cannot directly interact with a model in a database and conduct activities such as adding notes to a column with a problem.
5. Different access privileges cannot be assigned to different users by data type.
6. When multiple users work on the same design, synchronization problems occur. File-level data management does not have a function to resolve synchronization issues.

Synchronization is also referred to as *concurrent engineering,* and is a method of resolving conflicts that occur during simultaneous updates of product designs. *Project synchronization* means that all the various heterogeneous project models are maintained so as to be consistent with one another. The process of keeping a record of changes and maintaining models to be synchronized is referred to as *change management.* A method of managing a history of object or model changes is referred as *version control.*

A good example of common synchronization problems can be found from online reservation systems for airline or movie tickets. A general reservation step is to initiate a booking process, select a seat, and pay for the ticket. This process may take a while because you may need to think about the seat you would like to reserve and also need some time to find your credit card number. In the meantime, if one of millions of the system users logs onto the system and pays for the seat before you pay for the seat, you may lose the seat that you selected. To prevent such problems, online reservation systems usually have a locking system that "locks" your seat for a limited time (say, 15 minutes).

Such transaction problems are classified as the *long transaction* problem (Gray and Reuter, 1992). The long transactions are more serious problems in BIM than the above online reservation system example because the size of BIM models are very large and, thus, a transaction takes longer. In general, guaranteeing the integrity of design, engineering, and construction transactions with a building model server using concurrent, long transactions is a fundamental requirement for a building or product model server. Transaction capabilities are fundamental, and apply to single, parallel, or "cloud" configurations of servers.

A transaction is both the unit of change and also a unit of consistency management (or synchronization). A system's transaction management system determines how concurrent work is undertaken and managed, for example, by managing partitions of the building model at different levels of granularity, which might be a model (file) level, a floor level, an assembly level, or an object level. The information granules may be locked, allowing only single users to write, or allowing sharing by multiple users to write data but with automatic notification of updates and other concurrency management policies. These will become more important as we move to object-level management of data, potentially allowing high levels of concurrency. Today, most transactions are directly initiated by human users and only on a model (file) level. But many engineering database transactions will become *active,* in that they may fire automatically, for example, to identify a change in read-only objects being used by others, or to update a report when the data the report was based on has been updated.

An important goal capability of a BIM server is project synchronization. While the generation of multiple 2D drawing views and schedules from a single parametric model platform resolves synchronization among a set of drawings derived from the same model, it does not resolve the case involving multiple functionally different models running on tools that use data derived from the concurrently synchronized model. Even less easily synchronized are multiple platforms' models, say, used in different fabrication processes on the same project. Here, synchronization addresses all the coordination issues among the different systems, including spatial clashes, intersystem connections, and load transfers between systems (energy loads, structural loads, electrical or fluid flow loads).

Synchronization across heterogeneous models is still largely carried out manually but is one of the major benefits of an effective BIM server. Manual methods of data consistency management have been relied on but are onerous, as they help only a little when it is known that the information in one file depends on the contents of another file. Human management based on objects (carried in one's head) does a better job. But if synchronization is to be realized at the object level with millions of objects, manual maintenance is not practical, and automatic methods will have to be implemented and relied upon. It should be noted that the updating associated with synchronization cannot yet be fully automated, as many revisions to achieve consistency involve design decisions; some aspects of synchronization require person-to-person collaboration. So automatic synchronization can only now be achieved in degrees.

Automatic synchronization can be carried out by comparing the geometry and property values of each object in a model, but it takes too many resources and too much time to perform the comparison task. A practical solution that allows effective object-level coordination across heterogeneous project models is globally unique identifiers (GUIDs). A GUID is an identifier that is unique across software applications and hardware systems. It is also known as a UUID (universally unique ID) and usually composed of timestamps and system identifiers. Currently it is a 128-bit (16-byte, hexadecimal) integer and not human-readable. Each object in a BIM model receives a GUID.

Since GUIDs are system-independent, GUIDs identify an object regardless of what application is using it and allow reliable tracking and management of changes. Timestamps are another metadata type that allows tracking of the most recent update time. *Metadata* was coined as a term to addresses "the data about the data," allowing data to be managed.

The status of objects can be determined using GUIDs based on the logic described in Table 3–5 (Lee et al., 2011). If the GUID of an object (e.g., beam or column) in a new model is the same as that in an existing model, and the timestamps for the last update are the same, then the status of the object is determined to be "preserved." If the GUID exists in both models, but the timestamps for the last update are different, then the object is determined to be "revised." If an object with the GUID exists only in the new model, the object

Table 3–5   Determination of the Status of an Object by GUID (Adapted from Lee et al., 2011)

GUID in a New Model	GUID in an Existing Model	Timestamp for the Last Update	Status
Exists.	Exists.	Maintained	Preserved
Exists.	Exists.	Changed	Revised
Exists.	Does not exist.	N/A	New
Does not exist.	Exists.	N/A	Deleted

is determined to be "new" regardless of the timestamp. If an object with the GUID exists only in the existing model, the object is determined to be "deleted," regardless of the timestamp.

This logic can be applied to determining whether an object has been changed during a design and engineering process within a system by comparing an input model and an output model of the system instead of comparing new and existing models.

To allow the status check of an object based on GUIDs and timestamps, any application that can create, modify, or delete the design or engineering data must support:

- Creation of new GUIDs and timestamps, whenever a new object is created (or stored) or exported
- Reading the GUIDs and timestamps with imported objects and carrying this data for later export
- Exporting the timestamp and GUID data with other exported data and objects that have been created, modified, or deleted

The GUID capability of an application can be easily checked through a *roundtrip test*—a method to test the interoperability of an application by exporting and importing a model into the application without any revision, and analyzing any changes in the model. Based on the GUID analysis results, a model can be updated (synchronized) in two ways:

- **Full updates:** The entire model can be updated and saved as a new model.
- **Partial updates:** Only the explicitly modified objects and associated entities can be updated.
- **Logical updates:** These updates are the result of applying the reverse derivation of the previous design inferences that are logically invalidated by the current design operation. This concept is called *logical patching* (Eastman et al., 1997).

Partial updates can be subcategorized into automatic and assigned updates:

- **Automatic partial updates:** Many derived object views are simple and can be updated automatically. This class of synchronization transaction automatically updates those objects whose view is inconsistent with the exchange capabilities within the BIM server. These would apply to geometric changes of B-rep shapes, the generation of Building Object Models (BOMs) and other schedules, and attribute changes. The updated objects would also have their timestamps updated, possibly leading to additional automated or manual updates.
- **Manual partial updates:** Where automatic updates are not deterministic, a manual update transaction is required, such as for some types of clash detection. Here, each user receives a list of objects he or she is responsible for that need to be reviewed because of clash checks and

possibly updated. After the corrections have been made and agreed upon by the responsible parties, the transaction is considered complete. This is the lowest level of synchronization enforcement.

Initially, synchronization will be mostly manual, but as time progresses, methods will be developed to automatically derive updated views of modified objects. Synchronization can be extended, for example, to include automatic clash detection, where the clash is between a clearly dominant object and a subsidiary one. This is likely to be an early example of an automated synchronization transaction.

Synchronization guarantees that all data has been checked to be consistent up to the most recent timestamp. Synchronization is not addressed in the middle of some design activity, such as when one temporarily saves current files at dinner time. It applies only when changes are considered adequate for external sharing and review, i.e. when the 'submit' actions are made. Objects that are not current, not synchronized, should not have their data exported to other systems. This may result in propagating erroneous data; only fully synchronized objects should be the basis for exchanges. Status flags are often carried at the object level in order to distinguish temporary updates from complete transactions, and also objects lacking synchronization. Based on such status information, a background transaction identifies what objects have been created, modified, or deleted, and identifies what other files have those objects within them. Alternative mechanisms can be applied to flag the affected objects in the different application datasets. After identifying the potential inconsistencies, the type of synchronization transaction determines which are manual and which are automated.

3.5.2   Functionality of BIM Servers

The base functional requirements for a BIM server are fairly straightforward. Some are common to most database management systems. Others are basic needs articulated within the AEC industries. All BIM servers need to support access control and information ownership. They need to support the range of information required of its domain of application. The base requirements for a BIM server can be summarized as follows:

- *Manage users* associated with a project, so their involvement, access, and actions can be tracked and coordinated with workflows. *User access control* provides access and read/write/create capability for different levels of model granularity. Granularity of model access is important, since it identifies how much model data must be impounded for a user to revise it.
- *Import and parse BIM models* in a proprietary data format such as *.rvt or *.dgn or in an open standard format such as *.ifc into object-level data instances. The imported files can be saved in their original file format as well and managed in association with the project data.

- *Query and export object-level data instances* in a BIM server as an independent BIM model file in a proprietary data format such as *.rvt or *.dgn or in an open standard format such as *.ifc.
- *Manage object instances* and read, write, and delete them based on update transaction protocols.
- *Control versions of stored data. Version control*—a capability to keep and manage a record of transactions and changes of data is a critical requirement for concurrent management of data especially in a multi-user environment.

A BIM server may additionally support the following functions:

- *Visualize BIM data in the server.*
- *Support visual query of BIM data* for enabling the users to visually query, review, and select the information they need directly from a visualized 3D model stored in a BIM server.
- *Support web- or cloud-based functions* with a high level of security for protecting data from hacking and virus attacks.
- *Support product libraries* for incorporating product entities into BIM models during design or fabrication detailing.
- *Support storing product specifications* and other product maintenance and service information, for linking to as-built models for owner handover.
- *Store e-business data* for costs, suppliers, orders shipment lists, and invoices for linking into applications.
- *Manage unstructured forms of communication and multimedia data*: email, phone records, and notes from meetings, schedules, photographs, faxes, and videos.

These provide basic and additional content capabilities of a BIM server. However, more capabilities are required to manage complex object models and all their ancillary data.

The functional requirements of a BIM server can be also discussed by market. We believe that the BIM server market consists of multiple markets, at least three, based on their different functionality:

1. *A design-engineering-construction market*. This is the kernel market and is described in more detail below. It is project-oriented, needs to support a wide range of applications, and be able to support change management and synchronization.
2. *A made-to-order market*, primarily applied to engineered-to-order products, such as process plant units, steel fabrication, curtain walls, escalators, and other prefabricated and modular units for a given project.

However, this system must track multiple projects and facilitate production coordination across them. This market is similar to the small business Product Lifecycle Management (PLM) systems market.

3. *A facilities operation and management market*, addressing the monitoring of facility operations, possibly capturing sensor data from one or more facilities, with real-time monitoring and lifetime commissioning.

Each of these markets will grow to maturity in the next decade, responding to their different uses and functionality, responsible for managing different types of data.

Here, we address the needs of the first of the three uses listed above: a project-centric design, engineering, and construction server. It is probably the most challenging, with many diverse applications. In practice, each design participant and application is not involved with the complete representation of the building's design and construction. Each participant is interested in only a subset of the building information model, defined as particular views of the building model. Similarly, coordination does not apply universally; only a few users need to know reinforcing layouts inside concrete or weld specifications. Drawings were naturally partitioned and model servers will follow that tradition with model views as their specifications where synchronization must take place.

The general system architecture and exchange flows of an idealized BIM server are shown in Figure 3–7. BIM server services are complicated by the challenges of storing the required data in the appropriate format to archive and re-create the native project files required by the various BIM authoring and user tools. Neutral formats are inadequate to re-create the native data formats used by applications, except in a few limited cases. These can only be re-created from the native application datasets themselves, due to the basic heterogeneity of the built-in behavior in the parametric modeling design tools. Thus any neutral format exchange information, such as IFC model data, must be augmented by or associated with the native project files produced by the BIM authoring tools. The requirements and exchanges shown in Figure 3–7 reflect the mixed formats that have to be managed.

Future areas where BIM servers are expected to provide important automated synchronization services include dataset preparation and prechecking for multiple types of analyses, such as energy analyses of building shell, of interior energy distribution and mechanical equipment simulation; bills of material and procurement tracking; construction management; building commissioning; and facility management and operations. Also, these server capabilities will also be able to check project models to determine whether they fulfill information requirements to meet various milestones, such as construction tendering or owner pass-off upon completion.

While potential candidate BIM servers can be assessed in terms of the previous capabilities, other considerations, regarding application integration, training, and support required, are all part of the ROI calculation.

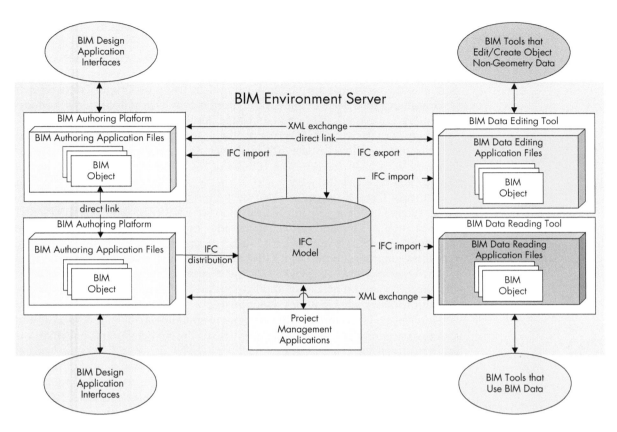

FIGURE 3-7   Example internal structure of exchanges supported by a BIM server. In order to support synchronization, all BIM tools must be accessible and checked by the server. Active transactions communicate between applications to define project/user action items. In some cases, active transactions may initiate updates. The synchronization management system is controlled by the BIM administrator.

3.5.3   BIM Server Review

The history of BIM servers is short because data models required for developing a BIM server such as IFC and CIS/2 became available only in 1997 and 1999, respectively. The IFC model server (IMSvr)—one of the earliest BIM servers—was developed by VTT in Finland and SECOM in Japan in 2002 (Adachi, 2002). In parallel, a BIM server based on CIS/2 was developed by Georgia Tech in the United States (You et al., 2004). These BIM servers were developed using a relational database (RDB) management system as a platform, and suffered from long transactions due to the time required to convert the object-based structure of IFC and CIS/2 into a RDB structure, and vice versa. To overcome the long transaction problem of RDB-based BIM servers, several BIM servers were developed using the object-oriented database (OODB), the NoSQL database, and the object-relational database (ORDB). Examples of such servers include the Express Data Manager (EDM) (Jotne EPM Technology, 2013), Open BIMserver (BIMserver.org, 2012), and the OR-IFC server (Lee et al., 2014). These are IFC-based BIM servers, but many other BIM servers were also developed or are under development using proprietary data models as a database. Examples include 3D Experience by Dassault Systems, i-Model by Bentley, Graphisoft BIMcloud and BIM Server, and Tekla BIMSight.

Many of the existing BIM server products are young, and their system architectures and functionality are still evolving. As a result, their functionality is changing with each release. The following list provides a quick overview of most products in this industry.

Express Data Manager (EDM) by Jotne IT supports any EXPRESS language schema with a full implementation of EXPRESS and any EXPRESS schema, such as IFC and CIS/2. It includes multi-language support (spoken language) with IFD. It supports EXPRESS-X, an ISO model mapping language that allows mapping between EXPRESS schemas. This could be used to map between model views or ISO-15926, for example. EXPRESS-X also supports rule checking and interfaces to applications on the server. It uses MVDs as one of multiple query/access modes. It supports both TCP and HTTP, for direct and web interfaces. It has limited version control and allows object level access and updates; updates always overwrite the stored version. Selection for checkout is limited (Jørgensen et al., 2008).

EuroSTEP Share-A-Space Model Server is a model server initially developed for aerospace, being adapted to AEC. It uses Oracle (soon also Windows SQL Server) as its host database. It is an object model server that relies on IFC as internal representation but also supports native models at the file level; it applies ISO10303-239 STEP and the OGC Product Life Cycle Support (PLCS) schema for change management, versioning, consolidation, requirements, status, and so forth. It uses MS Biztalk for XML-based communication and incorporates a web client portal. It supports strong business process capabilities, for part and product entities, testing, and requirements, status, and people-tracking. It includes email services and has interesting workflow capabilities; it includes a Mapper function that translates one object view to another, implemented in XML and C#; its imports can have associated rules that apply to change updates that can be automatic, partial, or manual. It incorporates Solibri Model Checker, for applications and requirements checking; it also uses VRML for visualization. This PLM-type system is being adapted to AEC applications.

Open BIMserver (an open source BIM server)—from TNO Netherlands and TU Eindhoven—supports import/export of IFC, which is the basis of the BIMserver data structure. It includes incremental updates and change management. It provides an easy-to-use (web) user interface with the IFC Browser. It provides IFC versioning, and can go back in time and see who made what changes and when. It supports Filter & Query, such as "get only the windows from a model," or "get one specific wall," using direct Objectlinks. It has a web service client for exploration of the BIMserver. It has SOAP (Simple Object

Access Protocol) and REST (which supports URL-based object access) for the web service interface. Mostly written in Java, it currently runs on Berkeley Database. RSS feeds are provided for real-time change alerts. It includes some support for bSDD. It is developing a clash detection embedded application. It supports CityGML export of IFC Models to CityGML, including the BIM/IFC-Extension. Several client applications are based on BIM Server: clash detection, rendering, gbXML energy interface, KML, and SketchUp export to Google Earth, XML export, and COBie export for construction operations handover. Open BIMserver is a shareware system with a user development team and source code access.

Bentley i–Model is an extensible XML format with its own schema for publishing DGN and other Bentley data. A plug-in for generating i-Model data from Revit is also available. i-Model data can be derived from STEP models including CIS/2, IFC, and ISO 15926, as well as DWG and DGN file formats. This provides a platform for markup and review, and for integrating applications within Bentley.

Graphisoft BIM Server and BIMcloud. Graphisoft provides both web-based and cloud-based project management systems with simple project access control, version and change management for ArchiCAD and IFC-based projects. The web-based tool is called Graphisoft BIM Server and the cloud-based tool is called Graphisoft BIMcloud. The two systems share similar basic model management functions. The difference is that BIMcloud provides more multi-user environment and management functions than BIM Server. Graphisoft BIM Server is one of the first major BIM design platforms with a backend database whose unit of management is objects rather than files. This allows selecting objects to work on, while the BIM server manages those accesses and access locks. In most cases, object reading and use of reference objects for context greatly reduces the scope of each transaction. Updates then are limited to those objects actually modified, reducing file transfer size and the time it takes to make the updates. All users can graphically see what other users have reserved. Updates are trimmed of unchanged objects and called Delta updates. Synchronization is an important issue—when are the changes to one object propagated to others that may not be reserved? ArchiCAD provides three options: real-time and automatic when objects are selected and worked on without checking them out; semiautomatic synchronization for the objects checked out and modified, only for those objects requested; or on-demand. It supports the use of 2D DXF files for coordination.

Dassault 3D Experience. Other industries have recognized the need for product model servers. Their implementation in the largest industries—electronics, manufacturing, and aerospace—has led to a major industry involving Product Lifecycle Management (PLM). These systems are generally adapted through custom software engineered for a single company and typically involve system integration of a set of tools including product model management, inventory management, material and resource tracking and scheduling, among others. They rely on supporting model data in one of a few proprietary native formats, possibly augmented by ISO-STEP-based exchanges. An example is Dassault 3D Experience. Dassault 3D Experience provides a cloud-based platform for multiple PLM solutions including Dassault CATIA and Enovia SmartTeam. Lack of a ready-to-use product that can support medium or small-scale organizations has been a limitation, but the limitation has been slowly overcome by lowering the cost barrier.

BIM 360 Design is a cloud-based collaborative design environment provided by Autodesk, which allows multiple users to review and comment on a design. Autodesk also offers other BIM 360 products, which cover different phases of a project. For example, BIM 360 Field is a cloud-based platform for construction field management, and BIM 360 Glue is a cloud-based collaboration tool that can compile and visualize models from different trades for review. At the time of writing the BIM 360 series was not fully integrated and some of the BIM 360 products were not object-level management systems, but the direction of the next step was obviously heading toward integration of these tools.

Konstru is a web-based collaborative design environment developed specifically to support iterative design and structural engineering processes. Users can create, edit, and analyze BIM models using general BIM design and engineering tools, and upload the latest model to the Konstru server using the Konstru add-on embedded in each tool. Konstru manages a history of changes, which allows the users to roll back to a specific version. Konstru supports Tekla Structures, Revit, Rhino, Grasshopper, Bentley Ram, SAP2000, ETABS, and Excel.

In addition to the above tools, many other object-level collaborative project management systems exist. Examples include project requirement management systems such as dRofus or Onuma System. These tools are introduced in Chapter 5, BIM for Architects and Engineers. Recently, file-level collaborative management tools have been extending their data management capability to an object level by providing modules that allow the users to review and manipulate data on an object level. Another good review on BIM collaboration tools and functions can be found in Shafiq et al. (2013).

3.6　INTERFACING TECHNOLOGIES

When BIM was first introduced, the notion of a BIM model as a "single source of information" was often cited as one of its major benefits. It quickly became apparent that BIM models should be configured in different ways and required different sets of information for different purposes and for different project phases. Terms for distinguishing BIM models for different purposes were coined. Examples of such terms include design BIM, construction BIM, FM BIM, record BIM, 4D BIM (BIM for schedule planning and management), and 5D BIM (BIM for cost estimation) models.

Another lesson learned was that a BIM model cannot be repurposed through a simple model "exchange" process, but rather requires a model "conversion" process. The difference is that each intended use of the model—analysis, simulation, and so on—requires new information. During a model

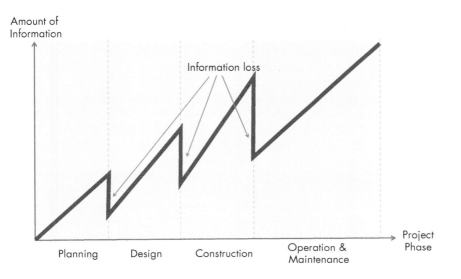

Amount of
Information

Information loss

Planning   Design   Construction   Operation &
Maintenance

Project
Phase

FIGURE 3–8 Loss of information between project phases.

Adapted from Teicholz, 2013.

conversion process, information loss is unavoidable in many cases (Figure 3–8). Interfacing technologies are software tools or functions that fill in such gaps between BIM models for different purposes and phases. This section briefly reviews two approaches for interfacing technologies: the semi-automated approach and the semantic approach.

3.6.1 Semi-Automated Approaches

Ideally, missing or newly required information could be added automatically when someone wants to reuse a BIM model for a purpose different to that for which it was created. Although such fully automated interfacing technologies are still at an early development stage, quite a few semi-automated ways to fill in missing or newly required information are commercially available. For example, many engineering analysis tools support semi-automated or step-by-step conversion of a design model to an analysis model (such as an energy analysis model or a structural analysis model). Automated structural detailing tools such as Tekla Structures, SDS/2, and RAM Steel are another example.

Some tools such as CATIA (Digital Project), GenerativeComponents, and Grasshopper use topology-based library objects to automatically generate and update building elements. The topology-based libraries are referred to as Knowledge Templates, Power Copies, and User Features in CATIA.

The functional requirements for design tools between the early phases and the later phases of a project are significant, and there are different work processes for the early and the late phases of a project. Early phase design tools require rapid and easy-to-use geometry study tools, whereas late phase design tools require accurate and object-based modeling tools. Examples of early phase design tools include SketchUp and Rhino. Examples of later phase design tools include Revit, ArchiCAD, AllPlan, Vectorworks, and Digital Project, as well as a large number of detailing tools that are used in the construction phases of a project. Model synchronization and transition between early phase design tools and late phase design tools have been a critical problem (see the DDP case study in Section 10.4, for example). Several approaches to convert early models into detailed models have been developed. For example, SketchUp models and Revit models can be synchronized through Flux.io and Dynamo. Another approach is to use Grevit. SketchUp and Rhino-Grasshopper models can be simultaneously imported into Revit through Grevit. Another possible method is to use a cloud-service for data exchange such as Konstru, introduced in Sections 3.5.3 and 5.3.3.

Another example is a 2D to BIM conversion tool. In many projects, it is still common to receive designs as a set of 2D drawings. Glodon and BuilderHub can generate a structural frame BIM model from 2D drawings with reinforcement details through a step-by-step process. They automatically check and report any discrepancies between drawings during the conversion process. The automatically generated model can be exported to other BIM tools such as Revit or Tekla Structures, can be linked to structural analysis tools for structure optimization, and can be used to produce a quantity takeoff. BuilderHub reported that the model conversion process could be reduced from three months to one day and that the error rate in the amount of reinforcement was also reduced from 10% to 1% in their case studies.

In general, BIM library objects developed for one platform cannot be used in other platforms. BIMscript and LENA, developed by bimobject.com, can convert BIM objects created in one platform for use in other platforms. BIMscript and LENA also support IFC, 3DS, and DWG formats.

These types of automated and semi-automated model conversion technologies are rapidly developing because they reduce the time and effort needed to fill in the information gaps between BIM models for different purposes and project phases.

3.6.2 Semantic Approaches

When you look at or walk through a BIM model on a computer screen, what do you see? This depends very much on your professional training and your experience, but whatever your expertise, you can usually infer from the model more information about the building than is explicitly recorded in the model. For example, an architect who sees a long, narrow space that connects to many rooms through doors understands that this is a corridor, even if it is not labeled or if the space and space boundary objects have not been defined. A structural engineer who sees longitudinal reinforcement adjacent to the top face of a beam above a column knows that the beam-column connection condition is fixed. Models contain cues—geometry, topology, and so on—that people interpret to build their perception of the model.

Semantic enrichment for BIM models is the idea that artificial intelligence techniques can be applied to models to supplement information, interpreting their contents in much the way a human expert might and writing the inferred, implicit information into the model explicitly. The lack of explicit information in models is one of the reasons why models cannot be used directly for automated building code review and other applications that require thoroughly defined information.

Supplementing models with the information needed by a specific use case can help in situations where there is no tailored export routine, where neutral exchange files (such as IFC files) are inadequate, or where the source file contains only 3D geometry. The central idea of the founders of the Industry Alliance for Interoperability (IAI, later renamed buildingSMART) was to establish the IFC standard as a *lingua franca* for all BIM exchanges. Unfortunately, due to significant differences across the different domains within the AEC industry in the ways that people understand buildings, how they simulate building behavior, and therefore in the way they conceptually model the data that represents the buildings, the IFC standard has had to be made very generic. As a result, there are many ways that one can represent a building in IFC, and they are not uniform (which is why MVDs are needed, as explained in section 3.3.5).

To quickly and easily understand this limitation, open a BIM model in your favorite software, export the model as an IFC file, close the model, open a blank model, and finally, import the IFC file. Does the model resemble the original model you exported? It probably looks like the same geometry, but try to use the imported objects with the standard functions of your system—insert a window, connect a beam, whatever—and you will likely find that the model you now have is decidedly less functional than the one you started with. This exercise is called a BIM "round trip," and for all but the simplest of models, it cannot be done with the interoperability technology available at the time of writing.

Semantic enrichment for BIM models potentially overcomes these problems because it allows a receiving BIM tool to infer any information it needs as long as it is carried implicitly. The kinds of information that can be inferred and added to a BIM model are:

1. Object classification (type)
2. Object Identity
3. Properties and property values
4. Parametric geometry
5. Aggregation relationships (part of)
6. Functional relationships (connected to)
7. Association relationships
8. Parametric constraints

In mechanical engineering, semantic enrichment has been applied to carry design intent, modeled in the form of parametric constraints between objects (for example, the relationship between the diameter of an axle and the diameters of the bearings in which it is mounted), when data is transferred from one tool to another. This kind of information is typically not carried in standard product data models; it requires semantic enrichment on the part of the receiving CAD tool. Innovative PLM technologies can infer such relationships from the geometry and spatial topology. Tools such as Siemens Synchronous Technology (Siemens, 2014), for example, can use data from multiple CAD systems. Given a model in B-rep the tool can process it into a feature-based CSG representation and in doing so infer parametric dimensions and constraints that can be used to position and size its objects and control their shapes.

In building design and construction, semantic and topological reasoning techniques have been applied to query models and extract subsets of information from BIM models (e.g., Won et al., 2013a, and Borrmann and Rank, 2009). Semantic enrichment using rule-inferencing has been successfully demonstrated for domains such as precast concrete cost estimation and for reconstructing BIM models of bridges from CAD files generated from point cloud data. Machine learning with artificial neural networks has been applied successfully to classify apartment space uses for permitting (Bloch and Sacks, 2018). It is, however, still the subject of research and development, and is discussed further in Chapter 9.

Chapter 3 Discussion Questions

1. What are the major differences between DXF as an exchange format and an object-based schema like IFC?
2. Choose a design or engineering application that has no effective interface with a BIM design tool you use. Identify the types of information the BIM design tool needs to send to this application.
3. Extend this to think what might be returned to the BIM design tool as a result of running this application.
4. Take a simple design of some simple object, such as a Lego sculpture. Using IFC, define the IFC entities needed to represent the design. Check the description using an EXPRESS parser.
5. For one or more of the following coordination activities, identify the information that needs to be exchanged in both directions:
    a. Building design that is informed by energy analysis of the building shell
    b. Building design that is informed by a structural analysis
    c. Steel fabrication level model that coordinates with a shop scheduling and materials tracking application
    d. Cast-in-place concrete design that is informed by a modular formwork system
6. What are the distinguishing functional capabilities provided by a BIM server as compared to a file-based system?

7. Explain why file exchange between design systems using IFC can result in errors. How would these errors be detected?

8. You are manager of a project BIM server that has both a structural analysis model and an energy analysis model. You make a change in placement to the physical (architectural intent) model. How should the synchronization process work so as to make the BIM environment model consistent?

9. Define a data exchange scenario between all software applications that will be used in your project. This will become a section of your BIM execution plan.

BIM for Owners and Facility Managers

4.0 EXECUTIVE SUMMARY

Owners can realize significant benefits on projects by using BIM processes and tools to streamline the delivery of higher-quality and better-performing buildings. BIM facilitates collaboration between project participants, reducing errors and field changes and leading to a more efficient and reliable delivery process that reduces project time and cost. There are many potential areas for BIM contributions. Owners can use a building information model and associated processes to:

- **Improve building performance and sustainability** through BIM-based energy and lighting design and analysis to improve overall building performance.
- **Reduce the financial risk** associated with the project using the architect's and/or contractor's BIM models to obtain earlier and more reliable cost estimates and improved collaboration of the project team.
- **Shorten project schedule** from approval to completion by using building models to coordinate and prefabricate portions of the design with reduced field labor time.

- **Support lean construction practices** that focus on value generation for owners, such as target-value design and integrated project delivery.
- **Assure program compliance** through ongoing analysis of the building model against owner and local code requirements.
- **Optimize facility management and maintenance** by exporting or integrating relevant as-built building models and equipment information to the systems that will be used over the lifecycle of the facility.
- **Support lifecycle value of the BIM model** by maintaining the accuracy of the as-built model as changes and additions are made to the building over its life.

These benefits are available to all types of owners on almost all types of projects; however, most owners have yet to realize all the benefits associated with a lifecycle approach to BIM or employ all the tools and processes discussed in this book. Significant changes in the delivery process, selection of service providers, and approach to BIM use on projects are necessary to fully realize BIM's benefits. Owners are rewriting contract language, specifications, and BIM execution plans (BEPs) to incorporate the use of BIM-based collaborative processes and technologies into their projects as much as possible. Most owners who have initiated and/or participated in BIM efforts are reaping advantages in the marketplace through faster and more reliable delivery of higher-value facilities and reduced operational costs. In concert with these changes, some owners are actively leading efforts to implement BIM tools on their projects by facilitating and supporting BIM education for their facility development and FM employees.

4.1 INTRODUCTION: WHY OWNERS SHOULD CARE ABOUT BIM

Lean processes and digital modeling have revolutionized the manufacturing and aerospace industries. Early adopters of these production processes and tools, such as Toyota and Boeing, have achieved manufacturing efficiencies and commercial success (Laurenzo, 2005). Late adopters were required to catch up in order to compete, and although they may not have encountered the technical hurdles experienced by early adopters, they still faced significant changes to their work processes.

The AEC industry is facing a similar revolution, requiring both process changes and a paradigm shift from 2D-based documentation and staged delivery processes to digital modeling and documentation to support collaborative workflows. The foundation of BIM is one of more coordinated and information-rich building models with capabilities for virtual prototyping, analysis, and virtual construction of a project. These tools broadly enhance 3D CAD and surface modeling capabilities with an improved ability to link design information with business processes, such as estimating, sales forecasts,

FIGURE 4–1 Comparison of information quality between drawing and BIM-based processes over life of building.

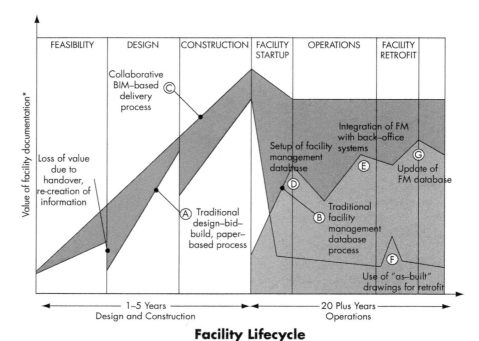

and operations. These tools support a collaborative rather than a fragmented approach to project procurement. This collaboration builds trust and common goals that serve the owner rather than creating competitive relationships where each team member strives to maximize their individual goals. In contrast, with drawing-based processes, analyses must be done independently of the building design information, often requiring duplicate, tedious, and error-prone data entry. The result is loss of value in information assets across phases, many more opportunities for errors and omissions, and increased effort to produce accurate project information, as the conceptual diagram in Figure 4–1 shows. Consequently, such analyses can be out of sync with design information and lead to errors. With BIM-based processes, the owner can potentially realize a greater return on his or her investment as the result of improved integrated design and construction process, which increases the value of project information in each phase and allows greater efficiency for the project team. Simultaneously, owners can reap dividends in project quality, cost, and future operation of the facility.

Traditionally, owners have not been agents of change within the building industry. They have long been resigned to typical construction project problems, such as cost overruns, schedule delays, and quality issues (Jackson, 2002). Many owners view construction as a relatively small capital expenditure compared to the lifecycle costs or other operational costs that accrue over time.

The firms that provide services to owners (AEC professionals) often point to the shortsightedness of owners and the frequent owner-requested changes that ultimately impact design quality, construction cost, and schedule. These changes often result from inadequate analysis and simulation during the design and engineering phase and the stovepipe processes that are often used by professional services. These are associated with the use of drawings that are difficult to keep aligned as changes are made.

Because of the considerable potential impact that BIM can have on these problems, the owner is in the position to benefit most from its use. Thus, it is critical that owners of all types understand how BIM applications can enable competitive advantages and allow their organizations to better respond to market demands and yield a better return on their capital investments. In those instances, in which service providers lead the BIM implementation—seeking their own competitive advantage—educated owners can better leverage the expertise and know-how of their design and construction team.

Table 4–1 summarizes the BIM applications reviewed in this chapter from the owner's perspective and the respective benefits associated with those applications. Many of the applications referenced in this chapter are elaborated on in greater detail in Chapters 5, 6, and 7, and in the case studies presented in Chapter 10.

4.2 OWNER'S ROLE IN A BIM PROJECT

In the following sections, we provide an overview of drivers that motivate all types of owners to adopt BIM technologies, and we describe the different types of BIM applications available today. These drivers are:

- design assessment early and often
- complexity of facilities
- time to market
- cost reliability and management
- product quality, in terms of leakages, malfunctions, unwarranted maintenance
- sustainability
- asset management
- changes to the facility over its lifetime.

4.2.1 Design Assessment
Owners must be able to manage and evaluate the scope of the design against their own requirements at every phase of a project. During conceptual design, this often involves spatial analysis. Later on, this involves evaluating whether the design will meet its functional needs. In the past, this was restricted to the use of 2D media and limited to a manual process, and owners relied on designers to walk through the project with drawings, images, or rendered animations. Requirements often change, however, and even with clear requirements, it can be difficult for an owner to ensure that all requirements have been met.

Table 4–1 Summary of BIM Application Areas and Potential Benefits to All Owners, Owner-Operators, and Owner-Developers

Service Providers (Relevant Chapters)	Specific BIM Application Areas for Owners	Market Driver	Benefits to All Owners	Relevant Case Studies in Chapter 10 and *BIM Handbook* Companion Website
Designers and Engineers (Chapter 5)	Space planning and program compliance	Cost management; marketplace complexity	Ensure project requirements are met	Victoria Station Upgrade NTU North Hills
	Energy (environmental) analysis	Sustainability	Improve sustainability and energy	Marriott Hotel Renovation* Helsinki Music Hall*
	Design configuration/ scenario planning	Cost management; complexity of building and infrastructure	Design quality communication	Dublin New Children's Hospital
	Building system analysis/simulation	Sustainability	Building performance and quality	Fondation Louis Vuitton
	Design communication and review	Marketplace complexity and language barriers	Communication	All case studies
Designers, Engineers, and Contractors (Chapters 5 and 6)	Quantity takeoff and cost estimation	Cost management	More reliable and earlier estimates during the design process	St. Joseph Hospital Project
	Design coordination (clash detection)	Cost management and infrastructure complexity	Reduce field errors and reduce construction costs	Hyundai Motorstudio Goyang
Contractors and Fabricators (Chapters 6 and 7)	Schedule simulation and 4D	Time to market, labor shortages, and language barriers	Communicate schedule visually	Dublin New Children's Hospital
	Project controls	Project controls	Track project activities	NTU North Hills
	Prefabrication	Prefabrication	Reduce on-site labor and improve design quality	Hyundai Motorstudio Goyang NTU North Hills St. Joseph Hospital
Owners (Chapter 4)	Pro forma analysis	Cost management	Improve cost reliability	Hillwood Commercial Project, Dallas*
	Operation simulation	Sustainability; Cost management	Building performance and maintainability	Victoria Station upgrade
	Commissioning and asset management	Asset management	Facility and asset management	Stanford Univ. Med. Bldg.
	Bldg. upgrades	Faster evaluation	Faster time to mkt	Stanford Univ. Med Bldg.

*These case studies can be found in the *BIM Handbook* companion website.

Additionally, an ever increasing proportion of projects involve either the retrofit of existing facilities or building in an urban setting. These projects often impact the surrounding community or users of the current facility. Seeking input from all project stakeholders is difficult when they cannot adequately interpret and understand the project drawings and schedule. The following paragraphs show how owners can work with their design teams to obtain these results:

- **Integrate development of programmatic requirements**: During the programmatic and feasibility phase, owners, working with their consultants, develop programs and requirements for projects. They often perform this process with little feedback with respect to feasibility and costs of various programmatic features or project requirements. One potential tool to facilitate this process is BIMStorm (http://bimstorm .com/Data/) an environment and process developed by Onuma Systems, which allows owners and multiple participants and stakeholders to conceptualize a project, solicit input from multiple sources, and assess in real time various design options from cost, time, and sustainability perspectives. Figure 4–2, for example, shows one of these sessions. The team develops a conceptual building model to develop in real time a realistic program.

- **Improve program compliance through BIM spatial analyses**: Owners such as the United States Coast Guard are able to do rapid spatial analyses with BIM authoring tools. (See Coast Guard Facility Planning case study in the *BIM Handbook* companion website.) The case study includes figures demonstrating how a building model can communicate in real time, both spatially and in data form, to check compliance with requirements. Different colors are automatically assigned to rooms based on their dimensions and function. In some cases, the color-coding can alert designers or owners of rooms that exceed or don't meet existing requirements. This visual feedback is invaluable

FIGURE 4–2 Snapshot of team collaboration using Onuma Systems (OS) during BIMStorm event.

Image courtesy of Onuma Systems and the Computer Integrated Construction Research Program at Penn State.

FIGURE 4–3 Snapshot showing the owner (GSA) and judges in a Virtual Reality Cave environment while interactively reviewing the design.

Image courtesy of Walt Disney Imagineering.

during conceptual and schematic design. Thus, the owner can better ensure that the requirements of their organization are met and that operational efficiencies of the program are realized.

- **Receive more valuable input from project stakeholders through visual simulation:** Owners often need adequate feedback from project stakeholders, who either have little time or struggle with understanding the information provided about a project. Figure 4–3 is a snapshot of judges reviewing their planned courtroom. Figure 4–8 shows a 4D snapshot of all floors of a hospital to communicate the sequence of construction for each department and get feedback on how it will impact hospital operations. In both projects, the building information model and rapid comparison of scenarios greatly enhanced the review process. The traditional use of real-time and highly rendered walkthrough technologies are one-time events, whereas the BIM and 4D tools make what-if design explorations far easier and more viable economically.
- **Rapidly reconfigure and explore design scenarios:** Real-time configuration is possible either in the model generation tool or a specialized configuration tool. Figure 4–4 shows an example from the Aditazz automated space planning capability that uses customer room requirements for a hospital combined with patient traffic patterns to create an optimized room layout and simulated traffic results for a given layout. Another approach specifically targeted to help owners rapidly assess the feasibility of alternative building designs is provided by the DESTINI Profiler system developed by Beck Technology, Ltd. (http://www.beck-technology.com/products/destini-profiler/). This system starts with a

1. Define functional and spatial requirements

2. Layout rooms with content

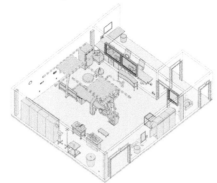

3. Place rooms in building

4. Identify and measure traffic patterns between rooms

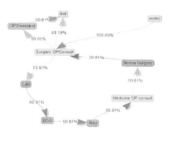

5. Measure space (room) utilization functional performance metrics

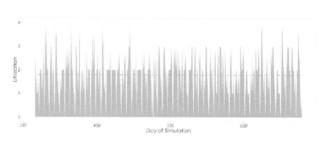

FIGURE 4–4 Example of automated space planning from conceptual requirements to simulation of circulation.

Image courtesy of Aditazz, Inc.

rough graphic model that allows rapid evaluation of alternatives that incorporate cost data and functional requirements from an owner. It is discussed in detail in further examples in this chapter.

- **Evaluate use of prefabricated and modular construction during the design phase:** In order to make effective use of prefabricated modules as an alternative to built-in-place construction, these options are best evaluated during the early design phase. This allows the project team to consider the design, time, and cost opportunities afforded by use of off-site manufactured components that can be incorporated into the design BIM model. It is difficult to do this after detail design has started. This is illustrated by the NTU Student Residence Hall case study in Chapter 10.

- **Simulate facility operations:** Owners may need additional types of simulations to assess the design quality beyond walkthroughs or visual simulations. These may include crowd behavior or emergency evacuation scenarios. Figure 4–5 shows an example crowd simulation for a

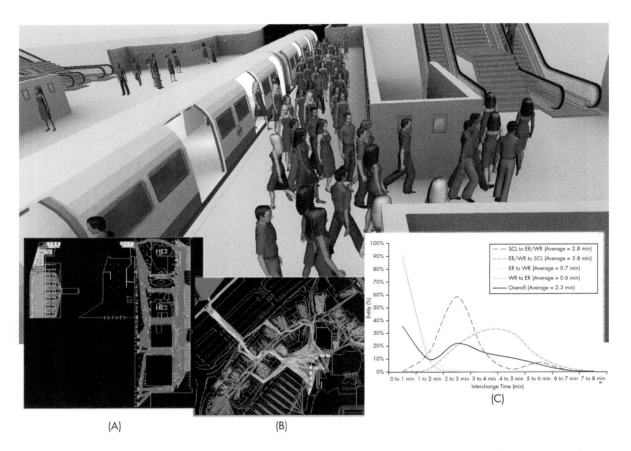

FIGURE 4–5   Examples of Legion Studio's visual and analytical outputs based on 2D and 3D building information data. The main 3D rendering shows a simulation of a metro station during a weekday morning peak. (A) A map of an airport uses color to show average speed, with red indicating slow movement and blue indicating free-flowing movement; (B) a map of a stadium with access routes and adjacent retail facilities showing mean density, with red and yellow indicating the locations of highest density; and (C) a graph comparing passenger interchange times between several origin-destination pairs.

Image courtesy of Legion Limited.

typical day at a metro station with related analysis. The simulations used the building information model as a starting point for generating these scenarios. Such simulations are labor intensive and involve the use of specialized tools and services. For facilities where such performance requirements are critical, however, the initial investment in a building information model can pay off due to the more accurate 3D input that these specialized tools require. These capabilities are illustrated in the Victoria Station Upgrade case study in Chapter 10.

4.2.2 Complexity of Building Infrastructure and Building Environment

Modern buildings and facilities are complex in terms of the physical infrastructure and the organizational, financial, and legal structures used to deliver them. Complicated building codes, statutory issues, and liability issues are now common in all building markets and are often a bottleneck or a significant hurdle for project teams. Often, owners must coordinate the design and approval efforts simultaneously. Meanwhile, facility infrastructures have grown increasingly complex. Traditional MEP systems are being integrated with data/telecom, building sensors or meters, and in some cases sophisticated manufacturing or electrical equipment. BIM tools and processes can support owners' efforts to coordinate the increasingly complex building infrastructure and regulatory process by the following methods:

- **Coordinating infrastructure through fully integrated 3D models of MEP, architectural, and structural systems:** A building information model enables virtual coordination of a building's infrastructure across all disciplines. The owner of a facility can include its own representatives from its maintenance and operations staff to provide input and review of the model. Rework due to design flaws can potentially be avoided. The Fondation Louis Vuitton, Hyundai Automobile Complex, and Victoria Station Upgrade project case studies (and others) in Chapter 10 demonstrate how an owner can work with a construction team to coordinate complex concrete, steel, and MEP systems using digital 3D models.

- **Producing higher-quality and maintainable infrastructure through interactive review of coordinated models:** Many owners need to go beyond typical MEP coordination to ensure that the MEP, data/telecom, and equipment are accessible and maintainable. This is particularly crucial for companies that depend heavily on these systems, such as biotech and technology companies, which demand reliable 24/7 service. Interactive review of an integrated BIM-FM system allows owners to virtually access and simulate maintenance procedures. This is discussed in detail in the Howard Hughes Medical Center case study in Chapter 10.

- **Preventing litigation through collaborative creation and sign-off of building information models:** Today, many projects invoke litigation to resolve payment issues due to changes. These issues include designers citing owner-initiated changes; owners arguing that designers did not meet contractual requirements; and contractors arguing about scope of work and lack of information or inaccurate project documentation. Processes that center on a building model can mitigate such situations simply due to the level of accuracy and resolution necessary for creating a model; the collaborative effort of creating the model often leads to better accountability among project participants.

4.2.3 Sustainability

The green building trend is leading many owners to consider the energy efficiency of their facilities and the overall environmental impact of their projects. Sustainable building is good business practice and can lead to greater marketability of a facility. Building models provide several advantages over traditional 2D models due to the richness of object information needed to perform energy or other environmental analyses. Specific BIM analysis tools are discussed in detail in Chapters 2 and 5. From the owner's perspective, BIM processes can help achieving the following goals:

- **Reduce energy consumption through energy analysis**: In the U.S., the lighting, heating, and cooling of buildings accounts for roughly 40% of total energy use. It is a very significant part of an owner's cost of operation. For this reason, investment in energy-saving building systems, such as enhanced insulation or improved control systems, are often cost effective. The challenge when making such assessments is to compute the actual reduction in energy consumption achievable by any specific design. There are many tools for owners to evaluate the payoff and return on energy-saving investments, including lifecycle analysis, and these are discussed in Chapter 5. While these analysis tools do not absolutely require the use of a building information model for input, a model greatly facilitates their use. The NTU North Hills case study in Chapter 10 and the Helsinki Music Hall case study in the *BIM Handbook* companion website illustrate the kinds of energy conservation analyses that can be integrated using BIM tools.

- **Improve operational productivity with model creation and simulation tools**: Sustainable design can greatly impact overall workplace productivity. Ninety-two percent of operating costs are spent on the people who work in the facility (Romm, 1994). Studies suggest that daylighting in retail and offices improves productivity and reduces absenteeism (Roodman and Lenssen, 1995). BIM technologies provide owners with tools needed for assessing the appropriate trade-offs when considering the use of daylighting and the mitigation of glare and solar heat gain, as compared with project cost and overall project requirements. The designers of the Helsinki Music Hall compared different scenarios to maximize the potential benefits of different glazing systems. Once the facility is complete, owners can use the building model and design data to monitor energy consumption and compare real-time use.

4.2.4 Public Construction Agencies: BIM Adoption Guidelines

There are many government agencies that have issued regulations and guidelines for the design and construction work for which they are responsible. They cover the processes, procedures, and deliverables that are expected from their vendors at each phase of design, construction, and turnover. For a more complete discussion of some of these guidelines (particularly for the GSA), see Chapter 3 of *BIM for Facility Managers* (Teicholz, et al., 2013). Sacks et al. (2016) provides a textural analysis of a number of owners' BIM Guideline documents. The following topics are those most covered in a large sample of guidelines from public agencies:

1. **Interoperability** (open architecture, data management): Requirements that stipulate how service providers are to provide their building model data, and specifically in what formats, so that information can be exchanged between providers in any given project team and between the project and downstream information clients, such as facilities maintenance and operations.

2. **Role of the BIM Manager** (project coordination manager, project model manager, BIM model manager, DB team BIM facilitator): What are the responsibilities and functions of the person or persons nominated to manage the building models in a project?

3. **Modes of Collaboration** (coordination, clash detection): Some guides dictate how project partners are to collaborate, in some cases defining technical information sharing arrangements, and in others going so far as to define the contract forms that are to be used (such as IPD).

4. **Prequalification of Designers** (BIM proficiency): What is the minimum set of skills and experience in BIM required for designers and other partners to participate in a construction project, and what are the methods for establishing conformance to that set?

5. **BIM Functions through Project Phases** (design phases): What are the major phases of the project? What are the deliverables in each phase?

6. **Level of Development/Level of Detail** (level of maturity, modeling requirement, level of model definition): Most guides specify the degree to which a model should be developed or detailed by each design discipline at each phase of the project.

7. **Operation and Maintenance Requirements** (Construction Operations Building information exchange [COBie]: What are the contents and formats of building information required for handover to the operations and maintenance functions?

8. **BIM Execution Plan** (project BIM work plan, BIM management plan. BIM data acquisition guidelines, asset information model [AIM] maintenance): Many guides call for each project team to establish a formal and specific plan for integration of BIM in a project's information flows, rather than stipulating these conditions in the document itself.

9. **Simulations** (analysis, simulation, energy modelling): Much of the value of BIM lies in the ability to run software simulations of the behavior of the designed building to check compliance to specifications. Some of the documents seek to ensure the use of these tools by mandating specific simulations and analyses.

10. **Schedule of Payments** (changes to design fees): When designing with BIM, designs are generally developed in greater detail earlier in the project than they would be using traditional design tools. Some documents, particularly those prepared by construction client organizations, stipulate changes to the payment schedules for designers to recognize this, moving some percentage of the designers' fees to be paid earlier in project lifecycles.

Section 8.4 contains a discussion of BIM guidelines (public and private) from various parts of the world.

4.3 COST AND TIME MANAGEMENT

4.3.1 Cost Management

Owners are often faced with cost overruns or unexpected costs that force them to either "value engineer," go over budget, or cancel the project. To mitigate the risk of overruns and unreliable estimates, owners and service providers add contingencies to estimates or a "budget set aside to cope with uncertainties during construction" (Touran, 2003). Figure 4–6 shows a typical range of contingencies that owners and their service providers apply to estimates, which vary from 50 to 5% depending on the project phase. Unreliable estimates expose owners to significant risk and artificially increase all project costs.

The reliability of cost estimates is impacted by a number of factors, including market conditions that change over time, the time between estimate and

FIGURE 4–6 Chart showing the upper and lower limits that an owner typically adds to the contingency and reliability of an estimate over different phases of a project and the potential targeted reliability improvements associated with BIM-based estimating.

Data adapted from Munroe (2007), and from Oberlender and Trost (2001).

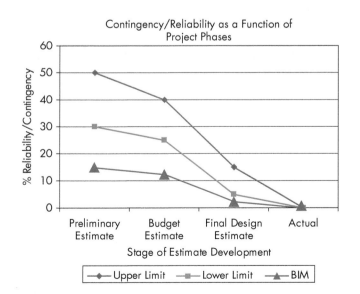

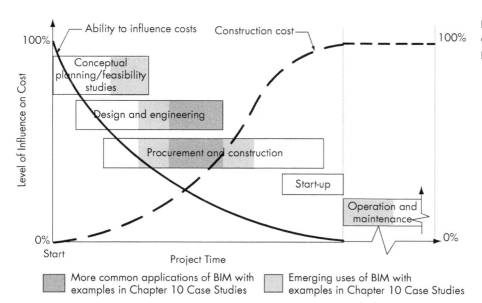

FIGURE 4–7 Influence on overall project cost over the project lifecycle.

execution, design changes, and quality issues (Jackson, 2002). The accurate and computable nature of building information models provides a more reliable source for owners to perform quantity takeoff and estimating and provides faster cost feedback on design changes. This is important because the ability to influence cost is highest early in the process at the conceptual and feasibility phase, as shown in Figure 4–7. Estimators cite insufficient time, poor documentation, and communication breakdowns between project participants, specifically between owner and estimator, as the primary causes of poor estimates (Akintoye and Fitzgerald, 2000).

Owners can manage cost with BIM applications to provide:

- **more reliable estimates early in the process with conceptual BIM estimating:** Estimates that use conceptual building information models consisting of components with historical cost information, productivity information, and other estimating information can provide owners with quick feedback on various design scenarios. Accurate estimates can be very valuable early in the project, particularly for assessing a project's predicted cash flow and procuring finance. The Hillwood Commercial project case study, discussed in the *BIM Handbook* companion website, illustrates this benefit.

- **faster, better-detailed, and more accurate estimates with BIM quantity takeoff tools:** Both owners and estimators struggle with the ability to respond to design and requirement changes and understand the impact of those changes on the overall project budget and estimate.

By linking the design model with the estimating processes, the project team can speed up the quantity takeoff and overall estimating process and get faster feedback on proposed design changes (see Chapters 5 and 6). The Hillwood Commercial project case, discussed in the *BIM Handbook* companion website, cites evidence that an experienced estimator using conceptual estimating software linked to BIM model early in design can result in significant time reduction and produce the estimate with small variance between the manual and BIM-based processes. It also provides a visual model that illustrates the basis of the quantities included in the estimate. In the One Island East Office Tower case study, discussed in the *BIM Handbook* companion website, the owner was able to set a lower contingency in their budget as a result of the more reliable and accurate design using BIM and the resulting BIM-based estimate. In the St. Joseph Hospital and the new Dublin Children's Hospital case studies (Chapter 10), the teams performed model-based cost estimates frequently to ensure that the design was kept within the budget. Owners, however, must realize that BIM-based takeoff and estimating is only a first step in the whole estimating process; it does not thoroughly address the issue of omissions. Additionally, the more accurate derivation of components that BIM provides does not deal with specific site conditions or the complexity of the facility, which depend on the expertise of an estimator to quantify. BIM-based cost estimation helps experienced cost estimators to be more productive and accurate, but it does not replace them.

4.3.2 Time to Market: Schedule Management

Time to market impacts all industries, and facility construction is often a bottleneck. Manufacturing organizations have well-defined time-to-market requirements, and must explore methods and technologies that enable them to deliver facilities faster, better, and cheaper. BIM provides owners and their project teams with tools to partially automate design, simulate operations, and employ off-site fabrication. These innovations—initially targeted toward manufacturing or process facilities—are now available to the general commercial facility industry and its service providers. The innovations discussed next provide owners with a variety of BIM applications to respond to market timing needs:

- **Reduce time to market using parametric models and target value design:** Long building cycles increase market risk. Projects that are financed in good economic times may reach the market in a downturn, greatly impacting the project's ROI (return on investment). BIM processes, such as BIM-based design and prefabrication, can greatly reduce the project duration, from project approval to facility completion. The component parametric nature of the BIM model makes design changes easier and the resulting updates of documentation automatic. When parametric design is combined with cost models based on the components in a BIM model, then it is possible to iterate on a design to quickly evaluate forecast cost. Target value design in particular is facilitated by the use of BIM for quantity take-off and cost-estimation, as illustrated both in this chapter's Working Backward from a Budget section and in the Temecula Valley Hospital project (Do et al., 2015).

- **Reduce schedule duration with 3D coordination and prefabrication:** All owners pay a cost for construction delays or lengthy projects, either in interest payments on loans, delayed rental income, or other income from sales of goods or products. In the NTU Student Residence Hall Project (see the case study in Chapter 10), the Nanyang Technological University (NTU, as represented by the NTU Office of Development & Facilities Management) had to provide a student resident facility in a very short time of 26 months. They decided to use Prefinished Prefabricated Volumetric Construction (PPVC) for development of a new 1,660-unit student hostel and apartment accommodation. The application of BIM to support early coordination, constructability analysis including manufacturing and shipping, and field installation led to improved design, manufacturing, and field productivity, resulting in a confident forecast of on-time delivery. It should also be noted that there have been some significant failures using modular solutions when planning and coordination did not occur early in the design process.

- **Reduce schedule-related risk with BIM-based planning:** Schedules are often impacted by activities involving high risk, dependencies, multiple organizations, or complex sequences of activities. These often occur in projects such as renovations of existing facilities, where construction must be coordinated with ongoing operations. For example, a construction manager representing the owner used 4D models (see Figure 4–8 and Chapter 6) to communicate a schedule to hospital staff and mitigate the impact of activities on their operations (Roe, 2002). Use of 4D during the planning phase of a project can improve understanding of alternative design decisions on cost, profit, and construction options.

- **Quickly respond to unforeseen field conditions with 4D-coordinated BIM models:** Owners and their service providers often encounter unforeseen conditions that even the best digital models cannot predict. Teams using digital models are often in a better position to respond to unforeseen conditions and get back on schedule. For example, a retail project was slated to open before Thanksgiving for the holiday shopping season. Three months into the project, unforeseen conditions forced the project to stop for three months. The contractor used a 4D model (see Chapter 6) to help plan for the recovery and open the facility on time (Roe, 2002).

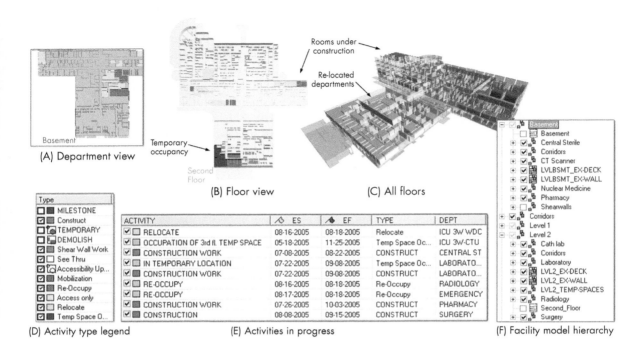

FIGURE 4–8   Views of a 4D model for a nine-floor hospital facility showing concurrent retrofit activities across departments and floors: (A) 4D view of a department; (B) 4D view of a floor; (C) 4D view of all floors; (D) activity type legend showing the types of activities the construction management team and owner communicated in the 4D model; (E) the activities in progress; and (F) the 4D hierarchy showing the organization by floor and department.

Image courtesy of URS.

Working Backward from a Budget

If there's one thing an estimator rarely hears, it's the phrase "Money is no object." On the contrary, it's rare to encounter a project in which the budget doesn't weigh heavily on design decisions. But when construction firms help owners get the absolute most out of every dollar of their investment, not only can they win the work—they can earn a client for life.

Rather than letting design drive the budget—which often results in the need to "value engineer" later in the process—target value design is an approach in which the budget drives design decisions, occurring very early in preconstruction. The concept allows the entire preconstruction team to begin with a validated, estimated cost in mind and then work backward from that amount to maximize the owner's budget.

Because Beck Technology's DESTINI Profiler combines 3D modeling with costs tied to each design element, the software provides a tool for estimators to evaluate the cost impact of various design and material options, helping owners make realistic choices that deliver the most "bang for the buck."

Informed Design Decisions, in Real Time

At Yates Construction, DESTINI Profiler plays a key role in target value design for construction management. Estimators frequently use the software in the early stages of concept development, showing owners what's possible within their established budget.

"We can get the architect, construction managers, and the owner in the same room for a roundtable session, shoot a bunch of ideas out, and make changes to the design really quickly," says Yates Estimator Stanley Wielgosz. "If owners say, 'What if we do this? Push this part of the building in? Add these many rooms? How will it look and what is the cost?,' we can show the impact during the meeting using DESTINI Profiler."

On a recently awarded school project, for example, Yates brought schematic drawings into DESTINI Profiler to create a 3D model and then applied costs to the elements from the firm's cost database.

"We presented the model in front of the district superintendent and CPA," Wielgosz says. "They were very impressed with how it looked and that the building was able to have costs loaded already. If they needed to make changes, we could give them pricing quickly based on the design at this early stage. We sold them with the immediacy and transparency."

Target Value Design Profile

"Working backwards ensures that we stay on budget as well as allowing us to offer smart, cost-conscious design options for clients."

In a presentation to the school board, the Yates team made changes to the DESTINI Profiler model on the fly, trying out various options to demonstrate how the district might stretch its construction dollars. For example, estimators were able to visually demonstrate how the district could save $5 per square foot by choosing a different ceiling material for classrooms. They were able to work backwards and ensure that they kept the school district in budget by suggesting cost-conscious design options.

Cross-Functional Collaboration

The Beck Group's Director of Preconstruction, Jeff Ratcliff, notes that the preconstruction and architecture/design teams must launch from the same spot at the same time, keep communication flowing, and work together to reach the same destination. Although the preconstruction team is more cost-driven and the architecture team is more aesthetics-driven, agreeing on elements from the very start is critical to keeping the project on course. One key is for everyone involved to focus on delivering value to the owner, Ratcliff says. DESTINI Profiler helps achieve this by enabling the preconstruction and design teams to explore options together and to communicate those choices to owners so that they can make informed decisions.

Because DESTINI Profiler contains historical cost data, including design packages for various types of rooms, the preconstruction team can quickly create a model based on various assumptions and supply a model-based room schedule to the design team. Cost data are broken down into bid tabs, with

(continued)

smaller budget targets for various elements, such as roofing, exterior, interiors, or site work. Each element is assigned a cluster team that makes decisions about how to meet budget targets.

"We let the architects focus on the creativity, and we can price that creativity, easily," Ratcliff says. "Using bid tabs lets us focus on targets while bidding out the work." The cross-functional team continuously tracks progress against the original budget, updating data along the way to understand the cost impact of each modification.

4.3.3 Facility and Information Asset Management

Every industry is now faced with understanding how to leverage information as an asset, and facility owners are no exception. Today, information is generated during each project phase and often reentered or produced during handoffs between phases and organizations, as shown in Figure 4–1. At the end of most projects, the value of this information drops precipitously, because it is typically not updated to reflect as-built conditions or in a form that is readily accessible or manageable. Figure 4–1 shows that a project involving collaborative creation and updating of a building model potentially will see fewer periods of duplicate information entry and opportunities for information loss. Owners who view the total lifecycle ownership of their projects can use a building model strategically and effectively.

- **Commission a building more efficiently**: According to the Building Commissioning Association (see www.bcxa.org/), "Building commissioning provides documented confirmation that building systems function according to criteria set forth in the project documents to satisfy the owner's operational needs." Unfortunately, the commissioning process from 2D records is both time consuming and error prone. Collecting all the needed equipment data and ensuring that it is the most current version (reflecting all change orders) can take many months. During this time, the data in the FM systems cannot be used to manage the building. This is a serious and costly issue. In addition, the 2D data is stored in rolls of drawings and related paper files. These are difficult to access and often do not reflect current conditions in the facility (particularly after some time has passed). This is true even when the 2D data is stored as pdf files in computer storage. Fortunately, there are much more efficient approaches that involve the use of BIM data that is entered during the design and construction process and then either transferred to FM systems (using COBie or other formats), or directly integrated with the FM system at project completion. The Stanford Hospital case study in Chapter 10 illustrates how they studied their own 2D processes and concluded that an integrated BIM-FM system would provide many advantages to the hospital. These included reduced FM maintenance cost, higher availability, and better service to their clients. Another example of the benefits of an integrated BIM-FM system is described in the Howard Hughes case study, also in Chapter 10.

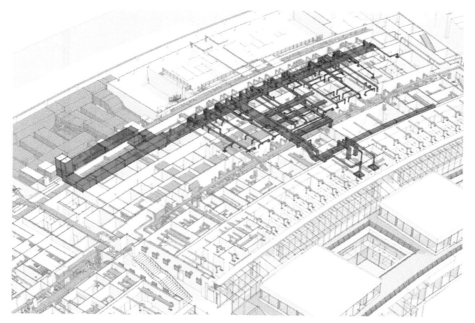

FIGURE 4-9 Example of using a building model to manage facility assets such as MEP systems. If power were lost to such a system, this graphical view would quickly allow FM staff to show all areas impacted by this failure.

Image courtesy of Howard Hughes Medical Center

- **Rapidly evaluate the impact of maintenance work on the facility**: Another example is the use of visual and intelligent models to help facility managers assess the impact of system failures on a facility. The maintenance team at the Howard Hughes Medical Center used an integrated BIM-FM system to visually assess which areas would be affected when power was lost to a given air handling unit as shown in Figure 4–9. It also showed what facilities (laboratories and other spaces) would be impacted and how to best repair the problem. This is described in detail in the case study in Chapter 10. Chan et al. (2016) describe a novel system for streamlining fault localization developed in Hong Kong. The system integrates BIM, system topology, RFID technology, and real-time data acquisition interfaces including building automation system (BAS) wireless sensors, closed circuit television (CCTV), and a real-time location system. It provides significant time savings (two hours or more) on fault localization in a typical air-conditioning fault system. This would represent an average of at least 160 hours of time savings per year in responding to the 80 faults on the 8,000 buildings in the Hong Kong Special Administrative Region. The system is in its early stages and has not yet been fully implemented, but does indicate that system integration involving these disparate systems can be helpful in complex facilities that require high levels of availability.

4.3.4 BIM Tool Guide for Owners

In the previous sections, we reference several BIM technologies that owners and their service providers are employing. In this section, we provide an overview of BIM tools or features of those tools intended to fulfill owners' needs and other owner-specific BIM applications. Chapter 3 discussed model servers and Chapters 5 through 7 discuss the specific BIM design and construction technologies, such as model generation tools, energy analysis, 4D, and design coordination. Here, the discussion addresses specific tools targeted to owners. Table 4–2 contains some information about a number of BIM tools for owners, some of which are described in the following sections.

4.3.5 BIM Cost Estimating Tools

Owners use estimates to baseline their project cost and perform financial forecasting or pro forma analyses. Often, these estimates are created early in design before the team develops a fully detailed building model. Estimates are created using square foot or unit cost methods, by an owner representative or estimating consultant. The DESTINI Profiler discussed earlier uses a conceptual building model to generate cost and pro forma estimates. The unit cost data on which the estimates are based can use data from prior projects or from Beck Technology. The model can be quickly modified to evaluate a range of alternative designs.

Microsoft Excel, however, is the software most commonly used for estimating. Exporting data from a BIM model rather than using takeoff from drawings is an easy way to continue use of existing estimating processes. There are many software products that provide this functionality. In 2007, U.S. Cost provided their customers with functionality to extract quantity takeoff information from a building model created in Autodesk Revit. Another product targeted to owners is Exactal's CostX product (see https://www .exactal.com/en/costx/products/costx/), which imports building models and allows users to perform automatic and manual takeoffs. Chapter 6 provides a more detailed overview of BIM-based estimating tools.

4.3.6 Facility and Asset Management Tools

Most existing facility management tools either rely on polygonal 2D information to represent spaces or numerical data entered in a spreadsheet. From most facility managers' perspectives, managing spaces and their related equipment and facility assets does not require 3D information; but 3D, component-based models can add value to facility management functions.

Building models provide significant benefits in the initial phase of entering facility information and interacting with that information. With BIM, owners can utilize "space" components that define space boundaries in 3D, thus greatly reducing the time needed to create the facility's database, since the traditional method involves manual space creation once the project is complete. This was a very important contribution for the Medina Airport project described in Chapter 10, because the spaces in an airport are both complex and difficult to describe. The use of the BIM model to define these spaces and then link them to an asset management system was an important advantage

Table 4–2   Table of BIM Tools That Are Useful to Owners

Main Use	Tool	Company	Main Functions
Asset Management	Maximo	IBM www.ibm.com/bs-en/marketplace/ maximo	Asset management Work management Procurement and materials management Service management Contract management
	EcoDomus FM	EcoDomus, Inc. http://ecodomus.com/	Filtering information by locations and disciplines Online 3D navigation Product documentation review Laser scanning interface BIM and Building Automation Systems (BAS) Surface finish queries
	ARCHIBUS	ARCHIBUS www.archibus.com/	Space management Move management Project management Maintenance Real estate and leasing management Asset management
	FM:Systems	FM:Systems Group, LLC https://fmsystems.com/	Space management Move management Project management Maintenance Strategic space portfolio planning Energy or water usage monitoring Real estate and leasing management Asset management Mobile tools
	AssetWORKS Solutions	AssetWORKS www.assetworks.com/iwms/ operations-and-maintenance-software	Space management Move management Project management Maintenance Energy management Capital planning Operations and maintenance Real estate management
	FAMIS	Accruent www.accruent.com/products/famis	Estate acquisitions Lease Project management Operations and maintenance Facilities management Asset management Inventory control Space management

(Continued)

Table 4–2 (continued)

Main Use	Tool	Company	Main Functions
	WebTMA	TMA Systems www.tmasystems.com/products/ webtmasolutions/	Request management Materials management Project management Time management Contract management Executive dashboard Capital planning Custodial management General inspections Room inspections Utility service management IT service management Knowledge base Facility scheduler Key management Event scheduler Fleet management GIS Solution BIM interface
	Corrigo	Corrigo Inc. www.corrigo.com/	Cloud-based FM solutions
	Building Operations	Autodesk www.autodesk.com/products/ building-ops/overview	Mobile-first facilities asset and maintenance management software for contractors and owners
Early Cost Estimation	DESTINI Profiler	Beck Technologies www.beck-technology.com/ products/destini-profiler/	Conceptual cost estimating 3D modeling Design evaluation
Early Time Management using 4D	Synchro	Synchro Software https://www.synchroltd.com/	4D planning by linking schedule to conceptual BIM model allow enhanced planning understanding of project. This can be extended to detail BIM model for construction planning.
	Assemble linked to P6 schedule	Assemble Systems + Oracle, Inc. https://assemblesystems.com/	4D planning as described above, but with more emphasis on construction phase
BIM Execution Plan	LOD Planner	LOD Planner https://www.lodplanner.com/	Develop BEP plan that specifies the appropriate level of development of the BIM model at each stage of design and construction, standards to be used, etc.
IoT based FM	BIM Watson IoT for FM	IBM https://www.ibm.com/internet-of-things/business-solutions/facilities-management	Analysis of building sensors (IoT)

Table 4–2 (*continued*)

Main Use	Tool	Company	Main Functions
Smart City based on Informed Decisions	Virtual Singapore Platform	National Research Foundation of Singapore www.nrf.gov.sg/programmes/virtual-singapore	Virtual experimentation and test-bedding Planning, decision-making, and research and development using a 3D city model with semantic information
	The City of Seoul, Big Data Platform	The city of Seoul seoulsolution.kr/en/content/7594	Analysis of traffic, optimal project sites, and others using big data Support for the making of tourism marketing policies, senior welfare policies, and other policies Analysis and improvement of the city administration process

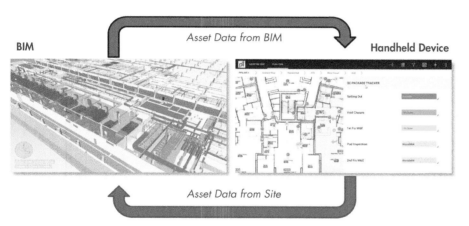

BIM   *Asset Data from BIM*   **Handheld Device**

Asset Data from Site

FIGURE 4–10 illustrates how the space data in the BIM model for the Medina airport can be displayed on hand-held computers.

Image courtesy of TAV Construction.

to the owner. Figure 4–10 illustrates how the space data in the BIM model for the airport could be displayed on hand-held computers.

According to an ENR article from May, 2015, "On average, building owners in the U.S. with at least a moderate ability to leverage BIM for facilities management report that architects and contractors are using BIM on a higher percentage of their current projects—on average, about 55%—than building owners with less ability to leverage BIM for FM, with an average of 37% of projects involving BIM" (Jones and Laquidara-Carr, 2015). Thus, owner BIM capabilities are becoming increasingly important for the management of their facilities.

Leveraging a building information model for facility management may require moving to specific BIM facility tools, or to third-party BIM add-on tools, such as that demonstrated in the Medina airport case study. This project illustrates how the owner's maintenance team worked with the construction team to integrate a building model (Revit) with its IFS Computerized Maintenance Management System (www.ifsworld.com/us/solutions/) tool using EcoDomus-FM middleware (ecodomus.com/products/).

One of the challenges with the handover from BIM to the CMMS is the standards and file formats common in BIM tools are not always readily accepted by CMMS tools. One standard effort, COBie (see Chapter 3), supports the downloading of maintenance information.

The use of BIM to support facility management is in its early days and the tools have only recently become available to support this area. Owners should work with their facility management organizations to identify whether current facility management tools can support BIM data or whether a transition plan to migrate to BIM-capable facility management tools is required.

4.3.7 Operation Simulation Tools

Operation simulation tools are another emerging category of software tools for owners that use data from a building information model. These include crowd behavior tools, such as Legion Studio, ViCrowd eRena, and Crowd Behavior; hospital procedure simulation; and emergency evacuation or response simulations, such as IES Simulex or EXODUS. Many of them are provided by firms that also offer the services to perform the simulations and add necessary information. In all cases, the tools require additional input of information to perform the simulations; and in some cases, they only extract the geometric properties from the building information model. An interesting example of crowd simulation is discussed in the Victoria Station Upgrade case study in Chapter 10 where they analyzed how the station would accommodate various numbers of people during the construction phase of the project.

4.4 AN OWNER AND FACILITY MANAGER'S BUILDING MODEL

4.4.1 Information Content of BIM-FM Model

Owners need not only be conversant in the kinds of BIM tools available; they must also understand the scope and level of detail they desire for a building model that can be used to FM requirements. Figure 4–11 illustrates the function of models developed at each stage in the building lifecycle.

It is important to understand that the models created for design and construction and turnover are normally not suitable for FM for the following reasons:

- The architectural model lacks adequate detail and information about building systems and equipment data, many facility elements are not modeled due to either complexity of the modeling process, or they are considered nonessential to design drawings and visualization.

FIGURE 4–11 BIM for Operations and Maintenance and how it relates to the other models used over the lifecycle.

Image courtesy of EcoDomus.

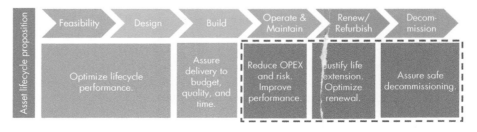

- The construction model normally contains too much information about construction details that have no relevance to FM, lacks proper definitions for space management, and lacks systems connectivity information and equipment data needed for FM.
- The BIM as-built model, if requested by the owner, is created by the general contractor, subcontractors, and suppliers. Traditionally this information has been provided as a set of working drawings that were annotated to reflect change orders and field changes with accompanying equipment cut sheets and shop drawings. This model represents the authoritative source and a reference for the building as constructed.

To provide guidance on how best to integrate BIM with FM needs, the BIM FM Consortium was formed in 2015 as an industry-academic group hoping to benefit from the experience of leading industry firms working with FM:Systems, Inc. and Georgia Tech (Kathy Roper) providing general oversight and guidance. Their suggestions for the BIM FM Model are as follows:

- The BIM FM Model is derived from the BIM As-Built Model with the following modifications.
- Extraneous information is removed, including construction details and working drawing sheets. This information can be obtained from the as-built model if needed, but otherwise encumbers the BIM FM Model.
- Where linked models have been used to distinctly represent building core, building shell, and tenant improvements, these are merged into a single model.
- If practical, linked models representing architectural, mechanical, electrical, fire protection, and specialized equipment are merged. For large buildings this may not be practical with current technology, so there may be the need to maintain multiple models that are linked.
- Occupancy room numbers are derived from construction room numbers with numbers matching building signage.
- For office space, workstations and offices are defined separately from rooms and are numbered with an occupancy numbering system. This is key to matching office occupants to desks, cubicles, and offices and is also essential for management of work orders.
- Building equipment items are numbered with unique asset IDs.
- The BIM FM model is linked to the facility management system that tracks ongoing work orders, maintenance operations, occupancy information, equipment and material replacement costs, and other data related to building operations.

4.4.2 Alternative Approaches to Creating a BIM-FM Model

Much has been written about the "handover" of information between design, construction, and operations phases. There are four basic approaches to transferring information from construction to facility management or for direct integration of this information:

1. Manual entry of data from drawings, manufacturers documents, and so on into CMMS files. This is tedious, error prone, and significantly delays the use of CMMS systems after turnover of the building. It cannot be seriously considered for modern buildings of moderate and larger size.
2. Transfer of data from a BIM model to a CMMS system using some standard format such as COBie.
3. Direct integration of the BIM and the facility management system.
4. Use of a middleware system that integrates with both the BIM authoring system and the CMMS.

The one-way transfer to a CMMS system has been used for a number of years since the development and maturity of COBie standards. COBie was developed by the U.S. Army Corp of Engineers (USACE) and is currently being further developed and maintained by the buildingSMART alliance and provides a framework for the information attributes required for major building systems. A number of BIM and facility management software developers have developed interfaces for importing and exporting COBie data. When the COBie data is exported to a stand-alone CMMS system, however, users should be aware that the data will need to be validated after import since the source system is not integrated with a target system. The COBie standard is also a useful reference for attributes to track various types of building equipment. Users should use judgment in determining the subset of attributes that can be kept accurate. A "lean" approach to BIM data, tracking the information that is deemed essential for ongoing maintenance, will be more successful than tracking every possible attribute of all equipment items. For an extended discussion of COBie, see East (2007) and Teicholz (2013).

There are significant advantages derived from direct integration between the BIM model and the facility management system. These include:

- **Better validation of data.** With the BIM and facility management systems linked, data is validated upon entry and there is no need for a "data scrubbing" activity on handover.
- **Better access to BIM data.** Facility management systems that provide floor plan and model viewing functionality open access to the BIM model up to anyone with a web browser. This greatly reduces the need for FM staff to research data from drawings and other documents.
- **Better ongoing updates to the building.** By maintaining a working BIM model throughout building occupancy, the owner has an accurate record of the building as a base for future remodeling and expansion.

The advantages of the middleware approach are that it provides additional flexibility to support various views of the CMMS data such as visualization of HVAC systems, which systems impact what spaces, and so forth. Another potential advantage is that APIs can be written to interface with various BIM

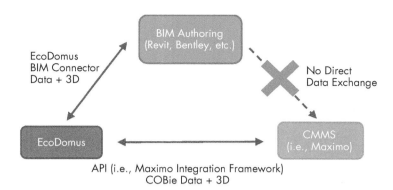

FIGURE 4–12 Integration between BIM and CMMS system as implemented using EcoDomus middleware system.

Image courtesy of EcoDomus.

and CMMS software vendors rather than supporting only one direct linkage. This allows greater flexibility to meet the needs of an owner who may already be using existing BIM and/or CMMS systems. This type of integration is illustrated in Figure 4–12.

The big X in the link between BIM authoring tools and CMMS reflects the various reasons why this linkage is difficult to establish and maintain. They include:

- The data in BIM authoring apps is almost never good enough for the direct push into CMMS; it needs extensive preparation and "cleaning." As an example, the naming standards used for equipment are not implemented in the BIM models and need to be entered or revised before they can be used by the CMMS.
- Nonmaintainable assets do not go into CMMS, and therefore are not accessible to FM personnel via easy-to-use interfaces.
- CMMS do not support model phases or versions and often require complex change management workflows.

When BIM and FM systems are integrated, the data about the facility may be located in either system, but not both. It is critical to determine the source for each set of data. The BIM-FM Consortium guidelines are shown in Table 4–3 (Schley et al., 2016).

4.4.3 Classification of Model Data and Standards

Regardless of how the data in BIM is linked to the data in an FM system, standards are needed for the naming of the data in the integrated system. There are existing naming standards called OmniClass that are useful for this approach (Tables 21 and 23); see examples in Figures 4–13 and 4–14. Many owners have established naming standards for their legacy FM systems (not integrated with BIM), but there are significant benefits in using the OmniClass standards to make it easier to work with external consultants, vendors, and suppliers who have adopted industry naming standards. It is strongly recommended that each organization implement and enforce the adoption of well-defined standards,

Table 4–3   Guidelines for Sources of Facility Information in an Integrated BIM FM System

BIM FM Model Is Authoritative Source	Facility Management System Is Authoritative Source
Building structure and base building architecture, including structure, walls, doors, stairs, elevators, and building core areas.	Real estate information, including property records and lease information.
Interior architecture, including walls, doors, floors, and ceilings.	N/A
Rooms with "as-occupied" room numbers consistent with building signage. Room numbers should be unique by building.	N/A
Workspace areas that include closed-wall offices but also include open-plan workstations. Areas should include space ID numbers that are consistent with occupancy management systems for occupant workspace assignment. Workspace numbers should be unique by building.	Occupants with unique occupant IDs and referencing workspace numbers. Move management information including from, to, move date, move project, and move details. Department or cost center codes.
Building equipment by general type and dimensions with unique asset ID numbers for reference by other systems. The BIM model should also carry the model, manufacturer, and serial number for major equipment. BIM is typically authoritative on the existence of an item of equipment. In other words, it is placed in BIM first and if removed from the building, deleted from the BIM model.	Equipment warranty information, information on date placed in service, replacement costs, asset values, depreciation schedules, and service contracts. Equipment preventative maintenance schedules and inspection results. Work requests and work orders. Service level agreements by activity.
Furniture panels, desks, and work surfaces but not fittings, components, shelves, or drawers.	N/A
Electrical outlets and switches with circuit information.	N/A
Lighting fixtures with circuit information.	N/A
Plumbing fixtures and piping.	N/A
Fire sprinklers and fire protection systems.	N/A
Special equipment such as food service equipment and lab equipment.	N/A
N/A	System user information, including system privileges.
N/A	Project management schedules and costs.
N/A	Sustainability information, including certifications and resource initiatives.
N/A	Strategic plans.
N/A	Lifecycle management information, including service life by system, replacement costs, annual upkeep costs, and capital budget forecasts.

Table 21   Elements

OmniClass Number	Level 1 Title	Level 2 Title	Level 3 Title	Level 4 Title	Table 22 Reference
21-04 40 30 70				Fire Extinguisher Accessories	22-10 44 43
21-04 50		Electrical			22-26 00 00
21-04 50 10			Facility Power Generation		
21-04 50 10 10				Packaged Generator Assemblies	22-26 32 00
21-04 50 10 20				Battery Equipment	22-26 33 00
21-04 50 10 30				Photovoltaic Collectors	22-26 31 00
21-04 50 10 40				Fuel Cells	22-48 18 00
21-04 50 10 60				Power Filtering and Conditioning	22-26 35 00
21-04 50 10 70				Transfer Switches	22-26 36 00
21-04 50 10 90				Facility Power Generation Supplementary Components	
21-04 50 20			Electrical Service and Distribution		
21-04 50 20 10				Electrical Service	22-26 21 00
21-04 50 20 30				Power Distribution	22-26 20 00
21-04 50 20 70				Facility Grounding	22-26 05 26
21-04 50 20 90				Electrical Service and Distribution Supplementary Components	
21-04 50 30			General Purpose Electrical Power		
21-04 50 30 10				Branch Wiring System	
21-04 50 30 50				Wiring Devices	22-26 27 26
21-04 50 30 90				General Purpose Electrical Power Supplementary Components	
21-04 50 40			Lighting		22-26 50 00
21-04 50 40 10				Lighting Control	22-26 09 23
21-04 50 40 20				Branch Wiring for Lighting	
21-04 50 40 50				Lighting Fixtures	22-26 50 00
21-04 50 40 90				Lighting Supplementary Components	

FIGURE 4–13   A portion of OmniClass Table 21.

Courtesy of OmniClass Development Committee.

Table 23   Products

OmniClass Number	Level 1 Title	Level 2 Title	Level 3 Title	Level 4 Title	Level 5 Title	Level 6 Title	Level 7 Title	Synonym
23-25 69 13			Laboratory And Scientific Equipment					
23-25 69 13 11				Microscopes				
23-25 69 13 11 11					Acoustic Microscopes			
23-25 69 13 11 13					Binocular Microscopes			
23-25 69 13 11 13 11						Phase Contrast Binocular Microscopes		
23-25 69 13 11 13 13						Binocular Light Compound Microscopes		
23-25 69 13 11 15					Bore Scope Inspection Equipment			
23-25 69 13 11 17					Combination Electron And Light Microscopes			
23-25 69 13 11 19					Dark Field Microscopes			
23-25 69 13 11 21					Digital Image Varityping Microscopes			

FIGURE 4–14   A portion of OmniClass Table 23.

Image courtesy of OmniClass Development Committee. Additional information on OmniClass tables is available at http://www.omniclass.org/.

which can include naming conventions, formats, and classifications. The BIM FM Consortium Guidelines contain specific information about OmniClass standards as follows:

- The OmniClass Construction Classification System is recognized by the construction industry as the authoritative source for classification of information related to building construction. OmniClass tables 21 and 23 are beneficial to the building owner and using both may need to be required as they each serve a different purpose.
- OmniClass Table 21–Elements is recommended as a general framework for BIM information. Elements are systems or major assemblies and as such lend themselves to the migration of information from conceptual design through construction and operations. Table 21 is based on the Uniformat system that was developed in the 1980s for conceptual cost estimating.

Table 23–Products is also relevant as a classification for final building equipment items and manufactured products. Manufacturers are beginning to provide downloadable BIM content, which is typically referenced by Table 23. These tables are also used in the Construction Operations Building Information Exchange (COBie) standard.

4.5   LEADING THE BIM IMPLEMENTATION ON A PROJECT

Owners control the selection of design service providers, the type of procurement and delivery processes, and the overall specifications and requirements of a facility. Unfortunately, many owners accept the traditional status quo and may not perceive their ability to change or control how a building is delivered. They may even be unaware of the benefits that can be derived from a BIM process.

Owners cite challenges with changing standard design or construction contracts produced by governing associations such as the American Institute of Architects (AIA) or the Association of General Contractors (AGC). The federal government, for example, faces many barriers to changing contracts since these are governed by agencies and legislatures. These challenges are real and the AIA, AGC, and federal agencies such as the GSA and Army Corps of Engineers are working toward instituting the contracting methods necessary to support more collaborative and integrated methods of procurement (see Chapters 5 and 6 for a discussion of these efforts). Yet the case studies and the various projects cited in this book demonstrate a variety of ways in which owners can work within current contractual arrangements and overcome the barriers presented in Section 4.6. Owner leadership and involvement is a prerequisite for optimal use of BIM on a project.

The Integrated Project Delivery (IPD) approach to procuring construction projects (introduced in Chapter 1, Section 1.2.4) aims to achieve close collaboration among all members of a project team. BIM has proved to be a key enabling technology for IPD teams. The owner's role in initiating and sustaining IPD projects is central and critical, and starts with the first project contract, sometimes called the "Integrated Form of Agreement for Lean Project Delivery" (IFOA; Mauck et al., 2009). There are also standard IPD contracts published by the AIA and ConsensusDocs (ConsensusDocs 300 series). An excellent discussion of how IPD can support owners' needs with an analysis of contractual issues can be found in a paper by a team of lawyers who have considerable experience with this form of project procurement (Thomsen et al., 2007). The legal issues associated with BIM in general and the use of an IPD contract in particular are discussed in detail in Chapter 4 of *BIM for Facility Managers* written by Kimberly Agular and Howard Ashcraft (Teicholz et al., 2013). These authors address the following owner-related issues:

1. What is the model's contractual status (including the role of the BIM execution plan)?
2. Who owns the modeling information (during and after turnover)?
3. Who owns the intellectual property generated during design?
4. Will the use of BIM increase the risks of project participants (including the owner), and how can these be mitigated?

The IPD contract usually defines the BIM software tools the various team members will use, as well as the information-sharing server solutions the project will support for the benefit of the team as a whole. Under IPD contracts, the owner plays an active role through the life of the project, taking part in decision making at all levels. BIM tools are essential for owners to understand the intent and the considerations of the designers and builders who make up the IPD team. IPD is discussed further in Chapters 1, 5, and 6 (Sections 1.2.4, 5.2.1, and 6.3).

Owners can deliver maximum value to their organization by reviewing and developing BIM guidelines, building internal leadership and knowledge, selecting service providers with BIM project experience and know-how, and educating the network of service providers and changing contractual requirements. Fortunately, increasing BIM adoption and the use of integrated project teams and contracts that require close collaboration are making this more common and easier to achieve.

4.5.1   Develop Guidelines for Use of BIM on Projects

Many organizations, particularly owners that build and manage multiple facilities, have developed guidelines for BIM. These guidelines contain the following key components:

- Identification of goals for BIM use and its alignment with organizational goals
- Scope and use of BIM across the phases of project (for example, a checklist of BIM applications, such as use of BIM for energy analysis or clash detection)
- Scope of standards or formats related to BIM and the exchange of BIM
- Roles of participants in the BIM process and a clear specification of what participant will be responsible for what data at each significant point in the project. This detailed specification is called a BIM Execution Plan (BEP), and it ensures that each member of the team knows what is expected from them for successful turnover of BIM data so that it can be used for FM and other functions.
- Owners should review these guidelines as a starting point and over time develop guidelines that fit their project goals. Figure 4–15 provides some guidelines for BEP development. This plan can be developed by the owner or in conjunction with a consultant with expertise

FIGURE 4–15 Guidelines for developing a BIM Execution Plan for a project.

Image courtesy of EcoDomus, Inc.

BIM Execution Plan

Be Clear
Guidelines should be unambiguous: all data and geometry requirements clearly defined, provide examples.

Focus on Lifecycle
Think about BIM implementation for all phases of facility lifecycle: not only design and construction, but O&M and FM as well.

Use Open Standards
Apply open standards where it makes sense. Don't blindly go with it just because it's free: calculate total ROI.

in this process. The Stanford Hospital case study in Chapter 10 contains a summary example of the BEP they use. One software tool that can assist an owner in developing a clear BEP is LOD Planner (https://www.lodplanner.com/product), which provides a means to specify the level of detail needed in the BIM model at each stage of design and construction, who will provide this information, and what standards will be used for identifying the objects in the design. This can then be refined with the project team to assure a lean use of BIM on the project.

An article by Robert Cassidy (Cassidy, 2017) discusses the BEP that was developed for the complete renovation of the Corcoran Gallery of Art in Washington, D.C., which is now managed by George Washington University (GWU). A portion of this article is shown in the sidebar and provides a good insight into the goals and methods used on this project.

Putting it All in Writing

All these efforts were conducted to comply with GWU's Facilities Information Management Procedures Manual, an 86-page document that governs all construction on the 43-acre Foggy Bottom campus. GWU's Planning, Development & Construction Department completed the FIM manual in 2014.

A key component is the "BIM Project Execution Plan," which defines the roles and responsibilities of the project team and proffers detailed guidelines on BIM goals, project deliverables, electronic communications, collaboration procedures (such as BIM coordination meetings), and content requirements of the BIM model.

The BIM execution plan also defines the required level of development (LOD) for project deliverables, from exterior walls, windows, and roofs, to interior partitions, conveying systems, MEP/LS systems, equipment and furnishings, and site work. For example, interior doors must attain 100 LOD at schematic design, 200 at design development, 300 at construction documents, and 500 LOD at turnover.

Andrew Graham, AIA, NCARB, Associate Architect in the D.C. office of Leo A Daly, has been impressed with GWU's BIM process. "They're clearly stating up front everything they expect to have for future operations and maintenance," he says. "Their O&M staff have a system in place to get the data they need. It's very organized."

Graham says GWU's thinking about BIM was eye opening. "We architects tend to think of BIM as 'the model,' but on the facility management side, it's more about the database," he says. In fact, only one GWU facilities staffer had a Revit license.

"Too many architects look at the BIM model. They should be looking at how to run the building and the equipment," says Doug Williams, director of digital practice at Leo A Daly. He notes that GWU's BIM execution plan concentrates on collecting data on the building's equipment—up to 16 data points for each

(continued)

piece of equipment: model number, lifespan, warranty information, installer, and so on. Much of the data from the surveys went into the Revit model, but some is being collected separately to meet the FIM requirements.

At turnover, sometime late this year, Leo A Daly and Whiting-Turner will be responsible for making sure the as-built information and additional materials like O&M manuals for the equipment are incorporated into the final Revit model. (Whiting-Turner is collecting some of the FIM-required data in Excel, which is fine with the university, as long as they get the data.) Then GWU will put all the data into an AssetWorks format (www.assetworks.com) for future reference.

Williams, who joined Leo A Daly last July from Perkins+Will, says there aren't a lot of institutional owners who have as sophisticated a BIM execution plan as GWU's. He credits Penn State University as an early proponent. The University of Texas Southwestern Medical Center, with whom he worked while at P+W, was "very intense" about tracking medical equipment. "It had to be bar coded for CMMS purposes," says Williams. (CMMS refers to "computerized maintenance management systems.") Williams says UTSW also wanted extensive modeling of the MEP system to identify components like valve cutoffs and service zones.

Another higher education institution, Brigham Young University, asks for a detailed inventory of the square footage of all materials for lifecycle budgeting. "They know the carpeting has a seven-year replacement cycle, so they can run schedules and reports for O+M budgeting," he says, "to include not only the cost of purchasing and installing new carpet every seven years or so, but also the cost of cleaning materials and maintenance staff time."

Williams says facilities staffs should be involved in the BIM modeling at the front end of major projects. "They have to run the building for the next 30 to 50 years," he says. "They have to ask: What's important to me as a client?" Graham seconds his colleague on that point. "You can't get the facilities people involved halfway through the project," he says. "You have to get them involved at the beginning."

4.5.2 Build Internal Leadership and Knowledge

The owner-led BIM efforts presented in Chapter 10 (Stanford Hospital, Howard Hughes, Victoria Station Upgrade) share two key processes: (1) the owner first developed internal knowledge about BIM technologies; and (2) the owner dedicated key personnel to lead the effort. For example, in the Stanford Hospital project, the owner examined internal work processes intensively and identified the tools that could be used to support FM operations more efficiently. They hired consultants to help them implement these systems on a selected subset of typical and critical tasks. They then compared how these tasks would be supported using the new integrated systems that allowed immediate access to data as opposed to referencing paper documents. These comparisons led to the strong conclusion to adopt integrated BIM FM systems and train all owner management and staff in the use and support of these new processes. This required considerable time and effort, but created very significant cost and client support benefits.

The Howard Hughes case study illustrates an owner that was already working with an integrated BIM FM system, but desired greater insight into systems that served multiple locations, particularly in the case of shutdowns and failures. They studied alternative approaches to incorporating this knowledge into their system and carefully examined how their response time could be reduced to better serve their clients. The case study describes their approach and results.

These case studies demonstrate owners that developed knowledge through an exploration of their own internal business models and work processes related to delivering and operating facilities. They understood the inefficiencies inherent in their current work processes and how they impacted the bottom line. In so doing, key members of the staff were equipped with the knowledge and skills to lead the BIM FM effort.

4.5.3 Service Provider Selection

Unlike the case in global manufacturing industries, such as that of automobiles or semiconductors, no single owner organization dominates the building market. Even the largest owner organizations, which are typically government agencies, represent only a small fraction of the overall domestic and global facility markets. Consequently, efforts to standardize processes, technologies, and industry standards are far more challenging within the AEC industry than in industries with clear market leaders. With no market leaders, owners often look at what their competition is doing or to industry organizations as guides for best practice or latest technology trends. In addition, many owners build or initiate only one project and lack expertise to take a leadership position. What all owners share, though, is the control over how they select service providers and the format of project deliverables.

The McGraw Hill SmartMarket Report from 2014 contains much useful information on how an owner can benefit from BIM and how best to achieve these benefits. This sidebar contains suggestions from this document by Kristine Fallon of KFA BIM Consultants (http://i2sl.org/elibrary/documents/Business_Value_of_BIM_for_Owners_SMR_(2014).pdf).

BIM Consultants Can Provide Three Main Values to Owners:

1. **BIM Strategy:** Consultants provide internal and designer/contractor requirements, with goals and metrics, and a plan to achieve them. Owners should seek consultants who know all BIM perspectives—designer, contractor, CM, and owner—and understand project delivery, contracts, licensing, liability, business processes, and culture. They should ask for a BIM implementation plan with milestones and budgetary pricing.

2. **Implementation Guidance:** For example, getting COBie output from BIM software may be an opaque process. A BIM consultant can provide training, videos, documentation, templates, object libraries, and the like for owners' internal use and with project teams. Owners should seek consultants with the prerequisite software skills, discuss the intended

(continued)

results, agree on deliverables, and have end-user review of deliverables to ensure quality.

3. **Doing BIM:** Consultants can outsource modeling, checking of BIMs and COBie data from project teams, transfer of COBie data to owner systems, or maintenance of BIMs. Owners should seek consultants who understand industry work flows and who automate processes rather than billing a lot of hours.

Develop Guidelines for Selection of Service Providers. Owners can use a number of methods to ensure that the service providers working on their project are conversant in BIM and its related processes:

- **Modifying job skill requirements to include BIM-related skills and expertise:** For internal hires, owners can require prospective employees to have specific skills, such as 3D and knowledge of BIM or component-based design. Many organizations are now hiring employees with BIM-specific job titles such as *BIM Specialist, BIM Champion, BIM Administrator, 4D Specialist,* and *Manager, Virtual Design and Construction.* Owners may hire employees with these titles or find service providers that bear similar ones.

- **Including BIM-specific prequalification criteria:** Many requests for proposals (RFPs) by owners include a set of prequalification criteria for prospective bidders. For public works projects, these are typically standard forms that all potential bidders must fill out. Commercial owners can formulate their own prequalification criteria. An excellent example is the qualification requirements formulated by hospital owner Sutter Health that are described in the Medical Building case study in the *BIM Handbook* companion website. These include explicit requirements for experience and the ability to use 3D modeling technologies.

- **Interviewing prospective service providers:** Owners should take the time to meet designers face to face in the prequalification process, since any potential service provider can fill out a qualification form and note experience with specific tools without having project experience. One owner even prefers meeting at the designer's office to see the work environment and the types of tools and processes available in the workplace. The interview might include the following types of questions:
  - What BIM technologies does your organization use and how did you use them on previous projects?
  - What organizations collaborated with you in the creation, modification, and updating of the building model? (If the question is asked to an architect, then find out if the structural engineer, contractor, or prefabricator contributed to the model and how the different organizations worked together.)
  - What were the lessons learned and metrics measured on these projects with respect to the use of the model and BIM tools? And how were these incorporated into your organization? (This helps to identify evidence of learning and change within an organization.)

- How many people are familiar with BIM tools in your organization and how do you educate and train your staff?
- Does your organization have specific job titles and functions related to BIM (such as those listed previously)? (This indicates a clear commitment and recognition of the use of BIM in their organization.)
- In the absence of an owner-specified BEP, how will you turn over the BIM model(s) used on this project and how can I transfer the information needed for my facility management system? What prior experience does your organization have with owner specified BIM FM requirements?

Examples of Job Skill Requirements

- Minimum three to four years' experience in the design and/or construction of commercial buildings structures
- B.S. Degree (or equivalent) in construction management, engineering, or architecture
- Demonstrated knowledge of building information modeling
- Demonstrated proficiency in one of the major BIM applications and familiarity with review tools
- Working knowledge and proficiency with any of the following: Revit, ArchiCAD, Navisworks, SketchUp (or other specific BIM applications that your organization uses)
- Solid understanding of the design, documentation, and construction processes and the ability to communicate with field personnel

4.5.4 Provide for Use of a "Big Room" for Design and Construction

The owner is in a unique position to require the use of a "big room" for the most significant members of the project team to closely collaborate their efforts during the early design phase of a project. This allows the owner, architect, engineers, and FM staff to all gain a better understanding of project requirements and evaluate alternative design options. It also allows consideration of off-site prefabrication and modularization options at an early design stage when these options are most easily considered. The use of a "big room" on an IPD project is thoroughly discussed in the case study Sutter Medical Center Castro Valley on the *BIM Handbook* companion website. The use of a "big room" during construction is further discussed in Section 6.6.2. Chapter 7 discusses various prefab options and how they are best implemented (see Section 7.2).

4.6 BARRIERS TO IMPLEMENTING BIM: RISKS AND COMMON MYTHS

There are risks associated with any changes to work processes. Real and perceived barriers and changes related to implementing BIM applications on projects are no exception. These barriers fall into two categories: process barriers to the business, including legal and organizational issues that prevent BIM implementation, and technology barriers related to readiness and implementation. These are summarized below.

The Market Is Not Ready—It's Still in the Innovator Phase. Some owners believe that if they change the contracts to require new types of deliverables, specifically requiring BIM uses, they will not receive competitive bids, limiting their potential pool of bidders and ultimately increasing the price. Fortunately, with BIM now being adopted at some level of depth by a large majority of architects, engineers, and contractors in the United States and other advanced countries, this is not generally a problem. In fact, professionals, particularly those dealing with larger projects, would probably not be considered by many owners if they did not use BIM.

In February, 2014, Engineering News-Record (ENR) magazine discussed a *SmartMarket Report* (Jones and Bernstein, 2012) that reported "building information modeling (BIM) is accelerating the pace of positive change for contractors of all types, sizes and locations." The findings, sampled in 2012 for nine major global markets in Western Europe, Asia, and North America, show the following results:

ROI

- Two-thirds of the construction companies that responded perceived a positive ROI on their BIM program and have clear ideas about how to further improve it (Figure 4–16).
- Firms in Japan, Germany, and France were the leaders. Over 95% of the respondents perceived a positive ROI.
- Perceived ROI increases directly with a contractor's level of BIM engagement, represented by its BIM experience, skill level, and commitment to doing a high percentage of its work in BIM.

FIGURE 4–16 Proportion of contractors perceiving a positive ROI for BIM (by country) (Jones and Bernstein, 2012).

Image courtesy of McGraw Hill.

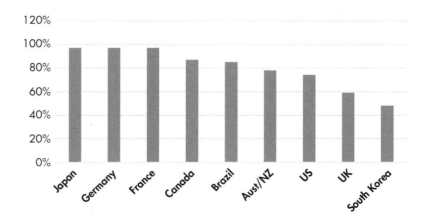

BIM Benefits

- Fewer errors and omissions, less rework, and lower construction cost are among the top project-related BIM benefits cited by contractors.
- Better cost control/predictability and reduced cycle time for workflows and approvals are also acknowledged as important process benefits of BIM.
- Leveraging BIM capabilities to win new work, maintain repeat business, and offer new services brings key internal benefits.

BIM Investments

- Contractors are increasingly assuming the central role on BIM projects; therefore, the top planned investment categories focus on IT infrastructure for hosting and sharing models and collaborative process between companies.
- While construction companies in the less advanced BIM markets are still focused on basic software and hardware investments, the more mature BIM users are planning heavy investments in mobile technology to get the value of BIM to the field.

Expansion of BIM Usage. From 2013 to 2015, contractors expected that the percentage of their work that involves BIM would increase by 50% on average. Growth markets such as Brazil are forecasting to triple the current number of companies using BIM at high levels. See Figure 4–17.

The Project Is Already Financed and Design Is Complete—It's Not Worth It to Implement BIM. As a project nears construction, it's true that owners and the project team will miss valuable opportunities available through the use of BIM applications, such as conceptual estimating and program compliance.

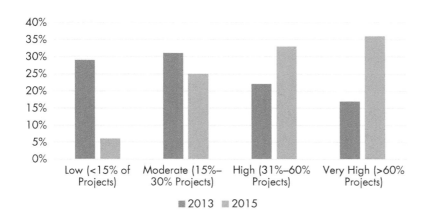

FIGURE 4–17 Contractors' current and future expected BIM implementation levels, averages for all regions.

Image courtesy of McGraw Hill.

There is still ample time and opportunity, however, to implement BIM in the latter stages of design and through the early phases of construction. For example, the BIM implementation in the Medina Airport case study (see Chapter 10) began after construction documents were started. The contractor suggested the use of BIM to improve the accuracy and clarity of collaboration. The benefits were immediate and extended after handover since the as-built BIM became the starting point for an integrated BIM FM system.

Training Costs and the Learning Curve Are Too High. Implementing new technologies such as BIM is costly in terms of training and changing work processes and workflows. The dollar investment in software and hardware is typically exceeded by the training costs and initial productivity losses. An Engineering News Record article (Grose, 2016), "BIM Adoption in the MEP World," illustrates this "skills gap" problem: "For MEP design firms attempting to transition to 3D BIM from 2D programs such as AutoCAD, the biggest obstacle is staffing. The older generations of engineers have been using 2D software for twenty years or more, and they are understandably resistant to learning new programs. But, surprisingly, the younger generation of MEP engineers are not yet learning to use BIM software in school." Fortunately, as we discuss in Chapter 8, education for architects, engineers, and construction engineers has attempted to make a significant transition to the use of digital collaborative technology.

Everyone Must Be on Board to Make the BIM Effort Worthwhile. It is often difficult to ensure that all project participants have the know-how and willingness to participate in the creation or use of the building information model. Many of the case studies in Chapter 10 demonstrate the benefits of BIM implementation without full participation from the start of a project that then present challenges with re-creating information from organizations not participating in the modeling effort. The owner can prevent this problem by requiring all or at least major project participants to demonstrate BIM competence as a precondition for participation in a project.

Too Many Legal Barriers Exist and They Are Too Costly to Overcome. Contractual and legal changes are required on several fronts to facilitate the use of BIM and more collaborative project teams. Even the digital exchange of project information is sometimes difficult, and teams are often forced to exchange only paper drawings in very specific formats and rely on old-fashioned contracts. Public institutions face even greater challenges, since they are often governed by laws that take considerable time to change. Nonetheless, government agencies and private companies have overcome these barriers and have prepared contract language that not only changes the nature of how information is exchanged within the project team but the liability and risks associated with a more collaborative effort. Governmental requirements for BIM use on all but the most minor projects are now quite common (see government requirements in Section 4.2.4 and government BIM mandates in Section 8.2).

The primary challenge is the assignment of responsibility and risk. BIM implementation centralizes information that is "broadly accessible," depends on constant updating, and subjects designers to increased potential liability (Ashcraft, 2006). The legal profession recognizes these barriers and the necessary risk-allocation changes that need to take place. This is a real barrier, one that will continue to persist and that will only fade once professional organizations revise standard contracts and/or owners revise their own contract terms.

Issues of Model Ownership and Management Will Be Too Demanding on Owner Resources. BIM potentially requires insight across multiple organizations and aspects of the project. Typically, a construction manager (CM) provides the oversight by managing communication and reviewing project documentation. The CM also oversees that the process is aligned with specific deliverables and milestones. With BIM, issue discovery and problem identification occur early and more frequently, enabling teams to resolve issues early, but this often requires owner input, which should be seen as a benefit and not a drawback. The current slack in the delivery process caused by multiple turnovers is significantly reduced, demanding more direct owner involvement. The process is more fluid and interactive. Managing this process and the related management of the model are critical to the project. Using a BIM Execution Plan, owners need to establish clear roles and responsibilities and methods to communicate with the project team and ensure that an owner representative is available as needed.

4.7 ISSUES FOR OWNERS TO CONSIDER WHEN ADOPTING BIM

Adopting BIM alone will not necessarily lead to project success. BIM is a set of technologies and evolving work processes that must be supported by the team, the management, and a cooperative and knowledgeable owner. BIM will not replace excellent management, a good project team, or a respectful work culture. Here are some key factors an owner should consider when adopting BIM.

Perform a Pilot Project with a Short Time Frame, a Small Qualified Team, and a Clear Goal. The initial effort should use either internal resources or trusted service providers that your organization has worked with. The more knowledge an owner builds with respect to the implementation and application of BIM, the more likely future efforts will succeed, as the owner develops core competencies to identify and select qualified service providers and forge cooperative teams.

Do a Prototype Dry Run. When doing a pilot project, it's always best to do a dry run and make sure the tools and processes are in place to succeed. This may be as simple as giving the designer a small design task that showcases the desired BIM applications. For example, the owner can ask the design team to design a conference room for twenty people, with specific targets for budget and energy consumption. The deliverable should include a building information model (or models to reflect two or three options) and the related energy and cost analyses. This is an example of a design task that is achievable in one or two days. The architect can build the model and work with an MEP engineer and estimator to produce a set of prototype results. This requires that the project participants work out the kinks in the process, so to speak, and also allows the owner to provide guidance regarding the types of information and formats of presentation that provide clear, valuable, and rapid feedback.

Focus on Clear Business Goals. While this chapter cites many different benefits, few projects have achieved all of them. In many cases, the owner started with a specific problem or goal and succeeded. The GSA's pilot project efforts (Daken, 2006), for example, each involved one type of BIM application for nine different projects. The application areas included energy analysis, space planning, laser scanning to collect accurate as-built data, and 4D simulation. The success in meeting focused and manageable goals led to expanded use of multiple BIM applications on projects such as the evolving use of BIM reported in the Medina Airport case study (Chapter 10).

Select a Project Team that Has Demonstrated Prior BIM Experience. With the growing adoption of BIM, it is now possible to find vendors with demonstrated capabilities to successfully use BIM in a collaborative team. It is also desirable to use a procurement approach that ensures that collaboration will be maximized over the entire design and construction period. Make sure that FM staffs are involved from the beginning of the process and that turnover requirements are incorporated into the BIM Execution Plan.

Establish Metrics to Assess Progress. Metrics are critical to assessing the implementation of new processes and technologies. Many of the case studies in Chapter 10 include project metrics, such as reduced change orders or rework, variance from baseline schedule or baseline cost, and reduction in typical square footage cost. (See also Section 8.3 for more discussions on BIM metrics and measures.) There are several excellent sources for metrics or goals relevant to specific owner organizations or projects, including:

- **Construction Users Roundtable** (CURT). This owner-led group holds workshops and conferences and issues several publications on their website (http://www.curt.org/) for identifying key project and performance metrics.

- **CIFE Working Paper on Virtual Design and Construction** (Kunz and Fischer, 2007; Kunz, 2012). These papers document specific types of metrics and goals along with case study examples.

Participate in the BIM Effort. An owner's participation is a key factor of project success, because the owner is in the best position to lead a project team to collaborate in ways that exploit BIM to its fullest benefit. All of the case studies in which owners took leadership roles demonstrate the value of the owner's participation in proactively leading the BIM implementation. They also highlight the benefits of ongoing involvement in that process. BIM applications, such as those for BIM design review, enable owners to better participate and more easily provide the necessary feedback. The participation and leadership of owners is critical to the success of the collaborative project teams that exploit BIM.

Chapter 4 Discussion Questions

1. List three types of project procurement methods and explain how these methods do or do not support the use of BIM technologies and processes. Also discuss ways to maximize the benefits of using BIM under different procurement methods.

2. Imagine you are an owner embarking on a new project and have attended several workshops discussing the benefits and limitations of BIM. What issues would you consider when deciding whether you should support and promote the use of BIM on your project? As an owner, why are they important to consider to make a project successful?

3. If the owner did decide to adopt lifecycle BIM, what types of evaluation and submittals would be needed to ensure the project team's success in using BIM at each stage of the building lifecycle? What risks need to be anticipated and how can they be mitigated?

4. Imagine you are an owner developing a contract to procure a project using a collaborative approach through the use of BIM. What are some of the key provisions that the contract should include to promote team collaboration, the use of BIM, and project success?

5. List the topics that need to be covered in a BIM Execution Plan (BEP) that is developed at the start of a project.

6. What methods can be used to transfer a building's FM data (equipment, piping, valves, electrical, etc.) to an owner so that it can be used for the management of the building? What standards are available for this data? How can the owner ensure that they will get what they need using the appropriate data and naming standards? What are the typical deficiencies of the as-built model used for construction when used for FM functions?

7. Given that FM knowledge is needed during the early design stage of a project, how can an owner ensure that this knowledge is available when it is needed?

BIM for Architects and Engineers

5.0 EXECUTIVE SUMMARY

Building Information Modeling (BIM) can be considered an epochal transition in design practice. Unlike Computer-Aided Design and Drafting (CADD), which primarily automates aspects of traditional drawing production, BIM is a paradigm change. By partially automating the detailing of construction-level building models, BIM redistributes the allocation of effort, placing more emphasis on conceptual design, where the most impactful decisions are made.

Other benefits include easier methods for guaranteeing consistency across all drawings and reports, automating spatial interference and other types of model checking, providing a strong base for interfacing analysis/simulation/cost applications, and enhancing visualization/communication at all scales and phases of the project.

There is no "standard" design process, and parallel actors result in complex nonsequential and integrated processes. Rather than trying to constructively describe the full range of practices in design, we offer a sampling of divergent subprocesses that anticipates parallelism and integration. We examine the impact of BIM on design from four viewpoints:

1. *Conceptual design* addresses the conceptual and spatial organization of the project. BIM potentially makes easier generation of complex building shells and potentially supports more thorough exploration and assessment of concept design, but the workflows to support strong assessment of concept designs are only partially in place.

2. *The integration of engineering services.* BIM supports new information workflows and integrates them more closely with existing simulation and analysis tools used by consultants over the design and construction lifecycle. BIM supports consultant integration in assessing the costs and benefits regarding sustainability, lifecycle costs, maintenance, and similar trade-offs, including those used by subcontractors. Subcontractors are encouraged to undertake detail engineering using their chosen detailing and fabrication BIM tools, to support multiple detailing, fabrication, delivery, and erection functions, in a manner that can be coordinated with the other component and system contractors. BIM addresses engineering integration by facilitating the workbench integration of these tools, and also supports workflows that can streamline processes both within a single system, and also across the multiple systems that rely on shared equipment, time, and schedules.

3. *Construction-level modeling* applies best practices and sometimes advances to detailing, specifications, fabrication and erection, and cost estimation resulting from visible management control of construction processes. This is the base strength of BIM. This phase also addresses what potentially can be achieved through a collaborative design-construction process, such as with design-build and Integrated Project Delivery (IPD).

4. *Building type specialization* addresses the special requirements of a particular building type. Hospitals, airports, sports stadia, shopping centers, and churches all have requirements, implicit functions, and traditions that are unique for that type and require special consideration. Unique requirements often result in specialized workflows suited to specific building types.

Overarching these issues, contractual provisions under which design services are offered are changing. New arrangements, such as design-build and IPD, affect communication and collaboration, altering the processes of design. Different design projects can be categorized according to the level of information development required for realizing them, ranging from predictable franchise-type buildings to experimental architecture. The information development concept facilitates distinguishing the varied processes and tools required for designing and constructing all varieties of buildings.

This chapter also addresses issues of adoption of BIM into practice, such as the evolutionary steps to replace 2D drawings with 3D digital models; automated drawing and document preparation; managing the level of detail within building models; the development and management of libraries of components and assemblies; and new means for integrating specifications and cost estimation. The chapter concludes with a review of the practical concerns that design firms face when attempting to implement BIM, including: the selection and evaluation of BIM authoring tools; training; office preparation; initiating a BIM project; and planning ahead for the new roles and services that a BIM-based design firm will evolve toward.

5.1   INTRODUCTION

In 1452, Renaissance architect Leon Battista Alberti in his *De re aedificatoria* (On the Art of Building) distinguished architectural "design" from "construction" by proposing that the essence of design lay in the thought processes associated with conveying lines on paper (Alberti, 1988). His goal was to differentiate the intellectual task of design from the craft of construction. Prior to Alberti, in the first century BCE, Vitruvius, in his *Ten Books of Architecture*, discussed the value inherent in using plans, elevations, and perspectives to convey design intent. Throughout architectural history, drawing has been the dominant mode of representation and fundamental to architecture's self-identification. Even now, contemporary writers critique how different architects use drawings and sketches to enhance their thinking and creative work (Robbins, 1994; Scheer, 2014). The extent of this time-honored tradition is further apparent in the way that computers were first adopted in architecture, as CADD—computer-aided design and drafting.

Because of this history, building information modeling (BIM) is revolutionary in the way it transforms architectural representation, replacing drawings with 3D virtual building models, potentially reintegrating Alberti's dichotomy. It changes the way that a representation is thought of and manipulated, fundamentally changing the line-by-line layout of old and the thought processes that went with it. Learning the tools of BIM is just the first-level step, leading to new ways in which design concepts are formed, refined, and evaluated. These changes suggest major rethinking regarding the degree to which designs are generated conceptually in a designer's head and recorded externally, or whether they emerge from an internal dialog between the designer and their external representations, or emerge through a shared set of design documents that provide a scaffold for different specialists' thought processes—or some combination of all three. The point is that the current intellectual tasks are being transformed because of the new representation.

A change in representation is, in the end, only an instrumentality for achieving the ends, in this case, the development and realization of an architectural project and addressing the multiple intents that it realizes. Does BIM facilitate designing for sustainability? Does it facilitate more efficient construction methods? Does it support higher-quality design? These are the value questions that this chapter attempts to address. Design, though not adequately taught this way, is a team effort, involving the owner/client; the architect; specialist designers and engineers; and with growing recognition, others involved in the project's detailing, fabrication, and erection. A project's realization involves prodigious levels of coordination and collaboration.

This chapter also reviews the changing contract structure facilitating team solutions in AEC projects. Coordination and collaboration involve multiple levels of communication. At one level, it involves communication between people regarding values, intent, context, and procedures. At another level, it also involves different tool representations and the need for data exchange between tools for costs and various dimensions of facility performance. Different members of a project team use different digital tools to support their particular work. The 3D models that are the basis of BIM provide major improvements in the human communication of spatial layouts. 3D layouts not in the orthogonal plane could only be approximated on 2D planar projections. Recent practice came to rely on on-site correction of complex layouts because the paper-based representations were fundamentally inadequate. Those issues are eliminated with virtual 3D modeling of the project's systems' layouts. Anyone can visually see how their work spatially relates to the work of others. At the data exchange level, building models, because of the machine readability and explicit coding, support automatic translation of building model data, improving the availability of design information for other uses throughout the design and later construction processes. While the current realization of this goal is inadequate, as described in Chapter 3, the goal will see its realization using BIM model views.

Outline of Traditional Architectural Services

Feasibility Study
Nonspatial quantitative and textual project specification that deals primarily with cash flows, function, or income generation; associates areas and required equipment; includes initial cost estimation; may overlap and iterate with predesign; may overlap and iterate with production or economic planning.

Predesign
Fixes space and functionality requirements, phasing and possible expansion requirements; site and context issues; building code and zoning constraints; may also include updated cost estimation based on added information.

Schematic Design (SD)
Preliminary project design with building plans, showing how the predesign program is realized; massing model of building shape and early rendering of concept; identifies candidate materials and finishes; and identifies all building subsystems by system type.

Design Development (DD)
Detailed floor plans including all major construction systems (walls, façades, floor, and all systems: structural, foundation, lighting, mechanical, electrical, communication and safety, acoustic, etc.) with general details; materials and their finishes; site drainage, site systems and landscaping.

Construction Detailing (CD)
Detailed plans for demolition, site preparation, grading, specification of systems and materials; member and component sizing and connection specifications for various systems; test and acceptance criteria for major systems; all chaises, block-outs, and connections required for intersystem integration.

Construction Review
Coordination of details, reviews of layouts, material selection, and review; changes as required when built conditions are not as expected or due to errors.

These new communication capabilities provide new opportunities for improving design services. BIM supports semiautomatic interfaces with analysis and simulation programs that provide feedback during the design development process. Coordination with fabricators through building models is expanding the level of coordination with construction. These changes are, in turn, affecting the way designers think and the processes they undertake. These changes have only just begun. But even at this early stage, BIM is redistributing the time and effort designers spend in different aspects of design.

This chapter addresses how BIM influences the entire range of design activities, from the initial stages of project development, dealing with feasibility and schematic design, to design development and construction detailing. In a narrow sense, it addresses building design services however this role is realized: carried out by autonomous architectural or engineering firms; as either part of a large integrated architecture/engineering (AE) firm or through a development corporation with internal design services. Within these varied organizational structures, a wide variety of contractual and organizational arrangements may be found. This chapter also introduces some of the new roles that will arise with this technology and considers the new needs and practices that BIM supports.

5.2 SCOPE OF DESIGN SERVICES

Design is the activity where a major part of the information about a project is defined. A summary of the often found services provided within the traditional phases of design is shown in Figure 5–1. Antitrust laws prohibit the AIA

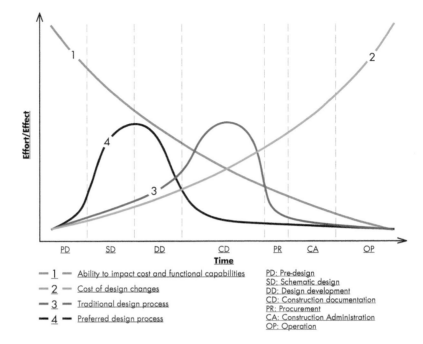

— 1 — Ability to impact cost and functional capabilities
— 2 — Cost of design changes
— 3 — Traditional design process
— 4 — Preferred design process

PD: Pre-design
SD: Schematic design
DD: Design development
CD: Construction documentation
PR: Procurement
CA: Construction Administration
OP: Operation

from publishing standard fee structures, but the earlier traditional contract for architectural services suggests a payment schedule (and thus the distribution of effort) to be 15 percent for schematic design, 30 percent for design development, and 55 percent for construction documents and project supervision (AIA, 1994). This distribution reflects the effort traditionally required for the production of construction drawings.

Due to its ability to automate standard forms of detailing, BIM significantly reduces the amount of time required for producing construction documents. Figure 5–1 illustrates the general relationship between design effort and time, indicating how effort is traditionally distributed (line 3) and how it can be redistributed as a result of BIM (line 4). This revision aligns effort more closely with the value of decisions made during the design and build process (line 1) and the differences in the cost of making changes over the project lifetime (line 2). The chart emphasizes the impact of early design decisions on the overall functionality, costs, and benefits of a building project. The fee structure in some projects is already changing to reflect the value of decisions made during schematic design and the decreased effort required for producing construction documents. The change in distribution of effort also makes assumptions about delivery method and contracting. Below we explore some of these implications.

5.2.1   Collaborative Forms of Project Delivery

Traditional forms of contract rely on two major partitions of the procurement process, called design-bid-build. Such projects typically involve the design of the project, followed by hiring of the contractor through an open bidding process, often to obtain the lowest cost bid. For a fuller review, see Chapters 1, 4, and 6.

From a design perspective, the design-bid-build procurement process is based on the following now-discredited assumptions:

1. Buildings are constructed using standard construction practices, well understood by both architects and contractors. Construction methods can be fully anticipated by the architects and engineers, who can optimize designs for cost and construction duration.

2. Construction relies primarily on management practices that are not affected by design details.

3. Design changes during construction have well-defined, discrete, and measurable impacts on the construction process.

4. Design-bid-build and the lowest responsible bid provide the best value for the project.

The inherent need to merge the expertise of architectural and engineering design with the expertise of construction in the final production documentation has led to distortion of the services offered. Current practice has been to specify the architect's drawings being limited to "design intent," with all aspects of construction detailing and coordination being resolved in an additional set of drawings, called construction coordination documents (for managing building system coordination) and shop drawings for fabrication and often the erection of the actual built elements. In practice, "design intent" drawings exist to isolate the intellectual contribution of architects and engineers from that of fabricators and constructors, and to indemnify designers from liability for design coordination and other problems.

This partition and redundant process is an inefficient use of time and dollars. It has evolved in parallel with a high level of litigation on construction projects. The potential for litigation leads architects to withhold information useful to the contractor and reduce communication and collaboration because the information is not covered in the architect's liability coverage. It also results in contractors relying on design and documentation errors as a basis for profit on a project through the additional charges associated with change orders. The resulting processes are dysfunctional, in the sense that they are not in the owner's interest and negatively contribute to the success of a project.

Design-build contracts establish a commercial relationship between the owner/client and a single legal entity for execution of the project, which covers both design and construction. A downside of this approach is that architecture firms, because of their low levels of capitalization, are almost always junior partners in such undertakings, which are usually led by contractors with generally greater capitalization. A related phenomenon is the coalescing of design services into large corporate entities, such as AECOM, WSP, Stantec, Gensler, HOK, and others. One of the reasons for this evolution is to address the capitalization limitation and become able to lead on large integrated projects.

Integrated Project Delivery (IPD) is a new option, quite different than both design-bid-build and design-build. In IPD projects the owner, designers, and leading contractors and suppliers enter into a single collaborative contract. The key goal of IPD is to form a cohesive team by carefully defining common and interdependent commercial interests and the technical and social means of communication and collaboration. Another important aspect of IPD is its designation of how risks, time, and costs are allocated (see the Sutter Medical Center case study in the *BIM Handbook* companion website). In IPD contracts, architects and engineers are full partners, accepting potential costs and benefits within the project (Fischer et al., 2017). This is an important change because it potentially provides a financial mechanism for designers to benefit from any contribution of design performance to construction performance. If the project is completed early, or below the target cost, the designer benefits with the other members of the collaborative team. These construction performance aspects open the door to measurement of other forms of design performance, such as energy use, organizational performance within the facility, and sustainability. An example of built performance might be the maximum air leakage of single-zone residences. Performance-based project metrics are expected to become more common and central to design services in the future. IPD projects typically use a Big Room, a working and meeting space for all team members, typically on the construction site. Big Rooms have been used by some contractors to repeatedly facilitate coordinated problem solving. They are also sometimes adopted to facilitate the work of design teams also in non-IPD projects. For a review of their use for design, see Sacks et al. (2017, Chapter 14).

Collaborative single-unit contracting for projects offers a new basis for contracting for services. These changes to design practices, project contracting, methods of delivery, and of new roles transform design in fundamental ways. The design services provided are not likely to disappear, but rather become more articulated and sharpened.

5.2.2   The Concept of Information Development

Building projects begin at different levels of information development, including definition of the building's function, style, and method of construction. At the low end of the information development spectrum are franchise buildings, including warehouses and roadside service stations, often called "big boxes," and similar buildings with well-defined functional properties and fixed building character. Sometimes the building is even predesigned and only needs adaptation to a particular site. With these, minimal information development is required, and the client knows ahead of time what is going to be delivered. Knowledge of the expected outcome is prescribed, including design detailing, construction methods, and environmental performance analyses.

At the other end of the spectrum—involving the highest level of information development—are owners interested in developing facilities for new social functions or attempting to rethink existing functions, such as combining an airport with a seaport, an undersea hotel, or a theater for experimental multimedia performances or an iconic visual edifice. Other instances of high information development involve agreements between the owner and designer to explore the application of nonstandard materials, structural systems, or environmental controls. One of the case studies in Chapter 10—the Fondation Louis Vuitton—is one of several excellent examples of a project with a high level of information development. The project, designed by Frank Gehry, applied new and untried systems that were generated from first principle analyses. For some time, progressive architecture firms and students have expressed an interest in fabricating buildings using nonstandard materials and forms, following the inspiration of Frank Gehry, Sir Norman Foster, Zaha Hadid, and others. These projects involve higher levels of information development in the short term, until such cladding or construction practices become accepted as part of the arsenal of standard practices. The development of initial master designs for projects that will be replicated, such as branch buildings of a chain, is also often initiated with a high-information content prototype.

In practice, most buildings are functionally and stylistically a composition of well-understood social functions with some variations in detail practices and procedures, styles, and image. On the construction side, most architecture conforms to well-understood construction practices, with only occasional innovations regarding materials, fabrication, and on-site or off-site assembly. That is, they are largely conventional projects with a few areas of new information development, often reflecting site conditions. Owners are just beginning to understand the issues of level of information development in contracting for design services. In projects with well-defined data for function and construction, the initial phase may be abbreviated or omitted, with design development (DD) and construction detailing (CD) being the main tasks. In other instances, feasibility, predesign, and schematic design (SD) may be of critical importance, where the major costs and functional benefits are determined. Different levels of information development justify different levels of remuneration.

The scope of design services, considered from the level of information development, can be simple or elaborate, depending on the needs and intention of the client. Traditionally, the level of information development is conveyed in the scope of contracts that define architectural services, as shown in the highlighted box "Range of Often Used Technical Services" and the range of special services, some of which are listed above. While some of the services listed in this box are carried out by the primary design firm, they are often undertaken by external consultants. In a study of collaborative architectural services (Eastman et al., 1998) with the firm of John Portman and Associates in Atlanta, a large building project in Shanghai was found to include more than twenty-eight different types of consultants.

From this overview, we can appreciate that building design is a broad and collaborative undertaking, involving a wide range of issues that require technical detailing and focused expertise. It is in this broad context that BIM must operate, supporting collaboration at both the human/social scale and at the computation/model level. We can also see from the diversity of contributors that the main challenge in adopting BIM technology is getting all parties of a design project to engage in the new methods of documentation and communication of their work at the design, engineering, fabrication, erection, and other scales of endeavor. In the end, everyone will have to adapt to the practices associated with this new way of doing business; it is becoming the new standard of practice. This point is emphasized—implicitly and explicitly—in the case studies in Chapter 10.

Range of Often Used Design Technical Services

Financial and cash flow analyses

Analysis of primary functions including services in hospitals, rest homes, airports, restaurants, convention centers, parking garages, theater complexes, and so forth

Site planning, including parking, drainage, roadways

Design and analysis/simulation of all building systems, including:

- Structure
- Mechanical and air handling systems
- Emergency alarm/control systems/sensors
- Lighting
- Acoustics
- Curtain wall systems
- Energy conservation, water conservation, and air quality
- Vertical and horizontal circulation
- Security
- Cost estimation
- Accessibility assessment
- Landscaping, fountains, and planting
- External building cleaning and maintenance
- External lighting and signage

5.2.3 Civil and Infrastructure Design

The fundamental paradigm of BIM—object-oriented digital modeling of buildings, enabling simulation and analysis for design, construction, and operations—applies equally to infrastructure projects, such as roads, highways, railways, subway systems, airports, harbors, bridges, dams, pipelines, and power plants. As such, infrastructure projects can expect to realize the same benefits from application of BIM processes that building projects derive.

From the perspective of BIM software platforms, infrastructure projects are different to buildings in that objects with extruded geometry with varying cross-sections and nonlinear extrusion paths are far more common, and far larger, than they are in buildings. Road, rail, bridge, and tunnel alignments are almost all of this type. (Figure 5–2 shows the curved alignment of the Crusell bridge in Helsinki, for example.) The spatial representation utilizes different

FIGURE 5–2   The structural BIM model of the Crusell Bridge, Helsinki, Finland. Note the curvature of the bridge's longitudinal alignment.

Image courtesy of WSP, Helsinki.

operations that reflect the ways traditional representations have evolved for the different object types. For these reasons, most vendors offer BIM software that is specifically tailored to infrastructure design, such as **Autodesk Infraworks**, **Autodesk Civil 3D**, **Bentley OpenRoads,** and **Bentley OpenRail**. These applications have specialized operations for generating and editing the longitudinal alignments. They provide specialized libraries of appropriate parameric objects for use in design, they facilitate integration of the designed objects with the existing terrain using digital terrain modeling (DTM), and they have analysis operations such as cut/fill optimization for earthworks. Naturally, they provide standard output templates for civil drawings, but they also provide digital data to drive earthworking equipment through LandXML and other interfaces.

An important caveat with regard to some of the civil specific tools is that some of them (such as **Autodesk CivilCAD 3D**) still use CAD software as their core geometry engines. As we explained in Section 2.5.9, this imposes limitations on their ability to reflect object behavior and design intent, one of the key features of BIM platforms.

Far from removing the potential to express the objects with parametric geometry, longitudinal objects of the kind common in infrastructure projects lend themselves to the use of parametric alignment curves and parametric cross-sections. Infrastructure specific BIM tools offer these parametrizations as built in features. Parametric modeling tools with visual programming like Dynamo, Grasshopper, and others (described in Section 5.3.3) provide excellent opportunities for parametric manipulation of geometry based on alignment curves.

Terrain is modeled as (usually orthogonal) grids with surface elevation values at each node in an approach called Digital Terrain Modeling (DTM). These naturally irregular surfaces do not lend themselves to parametric modeling, but the artificial surfaces generated by engineering design, such as the surfaces of roads, landscaping, or a building's footprint, do; and so the volumes generated by Boolean subtraction of a designed surface from a natural terrain can in general be represented as volumes with parametric controls. This enables application of optimization algorithms that can seek optimal solutions (expressed as sets of parameter values) for cut and fill, line-of-sight, and other goal functions.

A significant engineering consideration for BIM models of projects that extend over distances measured in kilometers instead of meters (or miles instead of yards) is that the dimensional accuracy obtained using Cartesian coordinate systems is insufficient as the earth's curvature begins to be significant. The dimensioning error becomes significant if flat surveys are used, and likewise, the idealized orthogonal coordinate systems that most BIM platforms use are inadequate. Instead, for such projects, curved coordinate systems must be used. Transport for London projects, such as the Victoria Station Upgrade (case study 10.6 in Chapter 10), use the London Survey Grid coordinate system. Bentley infrastructure software, such as **OpenRoads** and **OpenRail,** provide suitable tools for managing these coordinate systems and the transformations between them and the orthogonal representations used for buildings.

BIM models used for civil and infrastructure projects must interface not only with models of distinct structures that are part of or interact with them, such as subway stations along a tunnel or bridges along a road, but also with geographic information systems (GIS) that capture urban scale systems. IFC is appropriate for interoperability with building structures designed using different BIM platforms, and the current schema (IFC4 Add 2 at the time of writing) requires workarounds to represent alignments and infrastructure specific objects. BuildingSMART is continuing development of extensions, such as IFC Bridge and IFC Alignment (IFC Road) and even has a specific "Airport" room to explore what is needed for that domain. At the other end of the scale, cityGML offers tools for exchanging data with GIS platforms. Full integration between BIM and GIS models is still a topic of research and development (Liu et al., 2017), with researchers proposing exchanges, live data links, and simultaneous querying of models using cityGML and IFC (Daum et al., 2017).

5.3 BIM USE IN DESIGN PROCESSES

The two technological foundations of building information modeling reviewed in Chapters 2 and 3—object-oriented parametric design tools and interoperability, together with the growing array of BIM tools for specific functions, offer many process improvements and information enhancements within traditional design practices. These benefits span all phases of design. Some new uses and benefits of BIM have yet to be conceived, but several tracks of development have evolved far enough to demonstrate significant payoffs. Here, we consider the role and process of design from four of those viewpoints that apply in varying degrees to different projects, depending on their level of information development. In lieu of the project generic milestones found in traditional design contracts, we now consider four important example subprocesses that are embedded subdesign tasks that make up the overall design. Because of the potentially unique combination of foci, different combinations of issues create new contexts with unique objectives in current design development sequences. We consider concept design, prefabrication, integration of analyses, and consideration of special building types. We also address a number of practical issues: model-based drawing and document preparation; development and management of BIM object libraries; and integration of specifications and cost estimation. The practical issues of design practice, such as selecting BIM platforms and tools, training, and staffing issues, are covered in Chapters 2 and 8 respectively.

5.3.1 Concept Design

The first viewpoint addresses **conceptual design** (sometimes called schematic design in AIA contracts), as it is commonly conceived. The importance and refocus on concept design is well articulated in the MacLeamy curves presented in Figure 5–1, where the Schematic Design contract phase takes the burden of concept design, thus reducing the potential for design errors and changes during the later phases of a project. Concept design determines the basic framework of the design to be developed in later stages, in terms of its massing, structure, general spatial layout, approach to environmental conditioning, and response to site and other local conditions. It is the most creative part of the design activity. It brings to bear all aspects of the project, in terms of its function, costs, construction methods and materials, environmental impacts, building practices, and cultural and aesthetic considerations, among others. It anticipates and considers the full range of expertise of the design team.

Conceptual design typically involves development and refinement of the building program—the specification of the project in terms of spatial areas, functions, types of material and construction, and the basic assessment of its functional and economic viability. It may also assess the project's potential historical, visual, and cultural relevance. Concept design determines the basic framework of the design to be developed in later stages, in terms of its massing, structure, general spatial layout, approach to environmental conditioning, and response to site and other local conditions. Architects are often the lead in the development of the building program; sometimes the program is provided by client or consultants. The client provides an initial program with desired elaborations. The expressed statement is frequently inconsistent, identifying conflicting objectives. These may require immediate zoning or planning actions, or recognition that certain risks and resolutions will be required in the future, negotiations regarding needs and wants. After building program elaboration, the core of conceptual design is generated in the project's basic building layout in floor plans, its massing and general appearance, determining the building's placement and orientation on the site, its structure and its internal environmental quality, and how the project will realize the basic building program, taking into account its social neighborhood and site context.

These initial decisions of program and concept are of tremendous importance to the overall project, as shown in Figure 5–1. It is considered the most creative part of the design activity. The program largely determines the cost, utilization, complexity of construction, time to deliver, and other critical aspects. Building programs are now becoming properly recognized as fundamental and present a direct challenge to the traditional processes used in concept design. In the past, concept design heavily relied on the experience and expertise of the lead designer or design team, working from her or his knowledge and intuition, with feedback from the other members of the design team.

Because of the requirement of quick generation and assessment of sketch-level alternatives, assessment has been made intuitively from recall. Quickness of exploration and low cognitive demands of the tool user interface have kept the pencil (or other paper marker) as the dominant concept design tool. Freehand sketches have been a common documentation for recording and internal communication. In the same vein, some architects argue that BIM does not support conceptual design, because of its complexity and cognitive load. We partially accept this critique. Most current BIM design applications require too much of a learning curve, have many state-dependent operations, and require attention to object-dependent behaviors. The cognitive attention demanded of their operations and user interface almost prohibit "creative exploration."

Lightweight tools such as SketchUp, Rhinoceros, and FormZ Pro, however, have been accepted as concept design tools. These tools focus on quick 3D sketching and form generation. They facilitate communication of spatial and visual considerations by the design team. They do not have building object types and have no object type-specific behavior, so geometry operations apply consistently to all shapes, reducing complexity to the user. Some limit their surfaces to NURBS (non-uniform rational B-splines), a freeform surface type that can represent a very broad range of surfaces, including simple planar and spherical surfaces. These tools support reasonable object complexity and quick feedback, allowing intuitive visual assessment. With repeated use they can be learned so as to become "invisible" in the designer's thinking process. As stand-alone tools, they only partially respond to the challenge to concept design, of empowering the quality of decision making. These limitations are changing, however. They have evolved significantly since the second edition of this book and the tools have growing features and capabilities.

Other software tools support concept design focusing on a particular approach to development, such as spatial programming or energy usage or financial feasibility. The companies providing BIM platforms are also aware of the perceived limitations of their tools. Some have added concept design capabilities that compete with the sketch-level tools in this market area. This section reviews each of these types of products to examine their perceived role in concept design.

3D Concept Design Sketching Tools. Here we offer quick overviews of SketchUp, Rhinoceros, and FormZ Pro, paying special attention to the workflows to support BIM functionality.

SketchUp. Trimble SketchUp is a favorite sketch and exploration tool for many architects. It began as a surface modeler with a very intuitive user interface. Its professional version has increasingly powerful functional capabilities. We focus this review on the Pro version.

The base capability of SketchUp is its ease for defining a 3D line and stretching it into a surface that aligns with other points in space, supporting easy-to-use direct manipulation. Lines can be used to define a polygon on a surface that can be extruded into or out of the surface, to punch holes or define new shapes. Dimensioning feedback allows a user to be precise or vague. SketchUp allows 3D shapes and buildings to be defined quite simply with minimal or no training (see Figure 5–3). There are large libraries of predefined shapes, in Trimble's 3D Warehouse and the FormFonts library. SketchUp supports Ruby Script and a SketchUp System Development Kit (SDK) for creating plug-ins. There are hundreds of plug-ins that greatly extend SketchUp functionality, most of which work with both basic SketchUp and Pro. 3D photo-textured building models can be easily uploaded to Google Earth.

SketchUp Pro provides both 2D drawing generation from a model and interfaces to other applications through various file interfaces. The free Layout 3 plug-in supports the generation of dimensioned drawings from a 3D SketchUp model, while Style Builder provides filters that stylize a model rendering in terms of drawing style. It supports Generic Components that allows associating attributes with entities. Collections of faces can be defined as "objects." With version 2017, well-formed groups of surfaces can be turned into solids—and can have associated properties. The uses of these solid objects and their export into other tools will surely expand in succeeding releases.

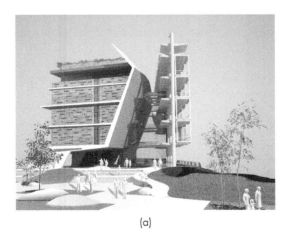
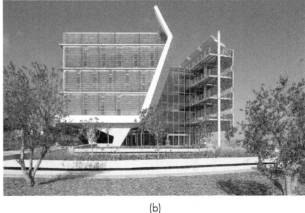

(a)   (b)

FIGURE 5–3   (a) A Sketchup model of the Porter Environmental Sciences research building at Tel Aviv University. The image was part of the winning bid for the design competition for this Leed Platinum building. (b) A photograph of the Porter Building after completion of construction.

Images courtesy of Axelrod Grobman Architects, Chen Architects, Geotectura and Shai Epstein.

An important SketchUp plug-in is IES VE, which provides a number of performance interfaces. IES uses an efficient simplified building model to interface to both SketchUp and sustainability performance assessment applications. It supports the simple construction of a building as single-line or double-line walls (actually thermal zones) on slabs that are used for the energy analysis and carbon assessment. These are assigned properties to designate their thermal behavior, and with location and orientation, IES uses APACHE-Sim to run quick "indicative" energy performance for both heating and cooling. Other IES tools address solar gain, sun shading, water, and carbon use. Another similar application is OpenStudio that provides a similar interface to EnergyPlus mapped through the IDF input representation. The new OpenStudio Version 1.0.5 supports smart matching of zonal interfaces, assignment of internal space loads, and other enhancements. A third option is Greenspace Research's Demeter plug-in. It responds to the gEnergyEPC requirements in the United Kingdom. It generates a common gbXML input interface, similar to ones developed for Revit, ArchiCAD, and Microstation. It appears that all three plug-ins reported here require a custom-developed version of the SketchUp model to support energy interfacing and manual assignment of properties for undertaking the simulations.

SketchUp Pro can read as background DXF, DWG, and IGES geometry input. It can also import IFC geometry—for some object types. SketchUp Pro also supports export of 3DS, AutoCAD DWG, AutoCAD DXF, FBX, OBJ, XSI, and VRML (for the functionality of these file formats, see Chapter 3). Some of these can be read into BIM platforms and the geometry recreated from the imported background images.

The workflows around SketchUp are not yet very extensive or user-friendly, limited to the geometry input for energy analysis. Each step requires data entry and manual manipulation. But these incremental steps show they are filling in a path for smooth flows for conceptual design assessment and then later into building models.

Rhinoceros. Rhinoceros (Rhino in short) is a popular NURBS geometric surface modeling tool by employee-owned McNeel (www.en.na.mcneel.com/default.htm). Rhino is a very attractive system for architects, industrial designers, animators, jewelry makers, and others interested in 3D freeform modeling. Rhino supports many surface modeling capabilities for generating, editing, viewing, combining, and analyzing simple or complex surface forms (see Figure 5–4). Rhino supports operations for creating and editing of curves and joining surfaces. These are used for designing many types of complex forms, including building skins, cast concrete forms, and various interior forms and fixtures. Rhino supports generating solid primitives and converting sets of surfaces into solids. Solids can be edited with Boolean operations and by extracting surfaces. Surfaces can be converted to meshes, and shapes may be analyzed and dimensioned. Rhino supports reasonable projection of forms to a plane and adding drafting annotation. With care, users can define large and complex building forms.

Rhino is a very open system, allowing easy user customization with both Rhinoscript, a version of Visual Basic scripting language, and Grasshopper,

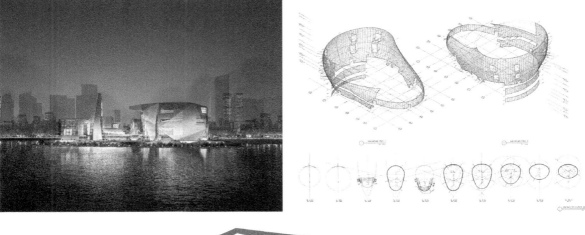

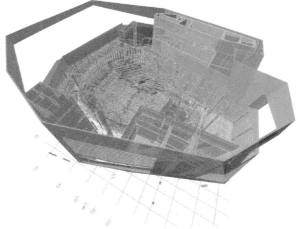

FIGURE 5–4   Incheon Arts Centers Concert Hall. Design can be freeform or structured in Rhino.

Images courtesy of dmp, Seoul, Korea

a Rhino-specific scripting language that requires little or no computing background. An easy beginning in scripting is to capture operations in a history file of operations, then automatically repeat them. In addition to making your own scripts, there is a large library of several hundred plug-ins, many supporting architectural use. This includes Paracloud Modeler and Paracloud Gem that enable generative workflows for managing arrays of objects parametrically (www.paracloud.com). Savannah3D provides libraries of architectural interior objects for populating models. Rhino supports a wide range of rendering engines as plug-ins, including V-ray, Lightworks, Maxwell, and others. Geometry Gym (http://ssi.wikidot.com/examples) provides interfaces to structural modeling applications. Available analysis model formats include OasysGSA, Robot, SAP2000, Sofistik, SpaceGASS, and Strand7. Neutral detailing format

SDNF is available with development on CIS/2 and IFC (for the functionality of these file formats, see Chapter 3). Rhino to Revit and the reverse mappings are available.

VisualARQ is a particularly interesting tool. It supports conversion of Rhino objects into BIM objects of the following classes: Wall, Slab and Roof, Column, Door and Window, and Space. Spaces can be reported in a table for space program validation. VisualARQ also provides default parametric object classes for the different types described here. Currently in development and beta release is an IFC Export Module. It supports converting the six object classes in VisualARQ into IFC models for importing into production BIM tools or to analysis applications that accept IFC input.

With the plug-ins, Rhino appears to provide capabilities for exploratory architectural design, followed by the incremental conversion of Rhino's surfaces into solids and then into VisualARQ's building elements and Geometry Gym's structural elements. These can then be exported into IFC for production work. This provides a potentially very attractive workflow.

IFC interfaces are supported with the following concept-level design applications: for cost estimation, Timberline, U.S. Costs, Innovaya; for spatial program validation, Solibri Model Checker and Trelligence. While there are internet listings for these interfaces, it is unclear whether they are supported in current releases.

FormZ Pro. FormZ Pro is a NURBS and faceted sketch modeling tool from AutoDesSys, the company that developed formZ and Bonzai. FormZ Pro is a solids modeling sketch tool that has very easy-to-use direct manipulation editing operations, like SketchUp. Indeed, much of the information about FormZ Pro discusses its style of operation as being like SketchUp. Being a solid modeling tool, however, many operations are easier; for instance, making thick walls with all the closing faces is managed automatically. Because it is NURBS-based, it supports many operations that are similar to Rhino, although the operations are different. For architects, it defines a few parametric assemblies: stairs, windows and doors, and roofs. It incorporates Renderzone for quick rendering and has access to Lightworks, Maxwell, and others through external file formats. These formats include DWG, DXF, FACT, and OBJ, SAT and STL, and 3DS and COLLADA. A scripting language is available.

Sketching Concepts with BIM Applications. The perceived limitations of BIM applications have been recognized by their developers. Several of them have developed concept-level design exploration tools using generic type objects, called "mass" or "proxy" objects. These can be parametrically customized to define families of shapes. They are meant to fill the void regarding BIM's weakness to support freeform shapes, particularly as the basis for generating building skins, which then can be refined in downstream design or for the generation of grills and other types of complex geometries. These freeform tools also support partitioning of these shapes into floor levels and into panels for "skinning." For example, Revit added capabilities to its massing tools to enable a greater range of freeform edit operations and ways to put a grid on its surface and to assign parameterized objects or shapes to the grid (see Figure 5–7). ArchiCAD

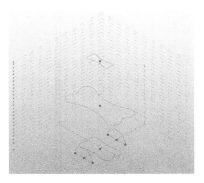 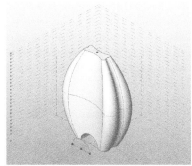 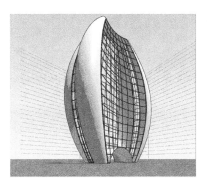

FIGURE 5–5 Revit mass objects can have freeform shapes that become more detailed with added object types.

Model images made available by David Light, Revit specialist, HOK London.

FIGURE 5–6 (A) Vectorworks supports a wide variety of massing shapes and surfaces. (B) A design can be freeform or planar in Bonzai.

(A)

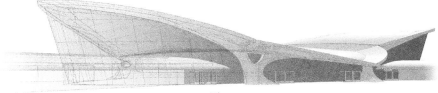
(B)

and Vectorworks both provide a similar capability using Cinema 3D. A Vectorworks example is shown in Figure 5–6a and a Bonzai example is shown in Figure 5–6b. Bentley Architecture's Generative Components is another but more powerful example. The Aviva Stadium case study (available in the *BIM Handbook* companion website) is an outstanding example.

These sketching tools also have potential interfaces to energy analysis; for example, Revit's sketch design can be interfaced with Green Building Studio. Similarly, ArchiCAD supports interfaces to EcoDesigner, an energy analysis and carbon use application for conceptual design. Bentley also supports gbXML for online energy assessment. The capabilities of these environmental sketch models are indicated in Table 5–1.

Sketching with Function-Specific Applications. Other early design tools emphasize specific functional workflows. Trelligence provides space planning layouts with feedback on space programming against target spatial relations. Trelligence supports export and two-way links with both Revit and ArchiCAD,

Table 5–1   Environmental Analyses Supported by Sketch Models

IES—own building model plus direct link with Autodesk Revit

ApacheCalc	Heat loss and gain
ApacheLoads	Heating and cooling loads
ApacheSim	Dynamic thermal simulation
ApacheHVAC	HVAC plant simulation
SunCast	Sun shading
MacroFlo	Simulates natural ventilation and mixed-mode systems
MicroFlo	Interior computational fluid dynamics application
Deft	Value engineering
CostPlan	Capital cost estimates
LifeCycle	Estimates lifetime operating costs
IndusPro	Ductwork layout and sizing
PiscesPro	Pipework systems
Simulex	Building evacuation
Lisi	Elevator simulation

gbXML—XML link from Autodesk Revit, Bentley Architecture, and ArchiCAD

DOE-2	Energy simulation
Energy	Energy simulation
Trane2000	Equipment simulation
	Building product information

and import into SketchUp. Vectorworks has its own space planning tool, as does Revit. Visio also supports space planning, in its Space Planner application. IES has its own stand-alone simple building models that allow quick schematic layout that interfaces to energy, solar gain analysis, and lighting, as described before. It supports multizone analysis using EnergyPlus. gbXML provides another information flow for energy assessment that is simple, with single-zone thermal behavior. Another important area for conceptual design is cost assessment, which is offered by DESTINI Profiler (see Section 2.5.4) and RIB iTWO (see Section 2.6.2).

Unfortunately, none of these programs provides the broad spectrum of functionality needed for general concept design, and workflows are currently challenging, requiring rigid modeling conventions to be followed or alternatively restructuring of the model. A smooth workflow using these tools is coming, but not quite a reality. In practice, most users rely on one of the aforementioned software tools. Of these, only a few are able to interface easily and efficiently with existing BIM authoring tools. Environmental analysis tools also require significant amounts of non-project-specific information, including details that may affect incident sunlight and any objects or effects that may restrict sunlight or views of existing structures, such as geographic location, climatic conditions, structures, or topography. This information is not typically carried within BIM design tools but by secondary analysis tools. These distributed datasets often introduce management-level problems, such as determining which analysis run gave which results and based on which version of the design. In this respect, BIM server repositories can play an important role (see Chapter 3).

Existing Conditions: Reality Capture. Another aspect of understanding the building context is in capturing the current as-built conditions. This is a critical issue for retrofit work and remodeling. Laser scanning and photogrammetry technologies can be used to rapidly compile point cloud data (PCD), offering valuable information on as-built conditions. Once the point cloud files collected in the field have been registered to one another and to the project coordinate system, they are extremely useful "as-is" if all that is needed is to situate new construction in relation to existing objects. Software tools such as **Autodesk RECAP**, **Trimble RealWorks**, **Leica Cloudworx,** and **Bentley Descartes** all support preparation of point clouds for use with BIM models, and some of the BIM platforms allow users to load point clouds directly as reference models that can be snapped to.

However, if one needs to work with existing building or infrastructure objects, PCD is no magic bullet; significant effort is required on the part of BIM operators to prepare native BIM models of existing conditions. Essentially, modelers rebuild the objects from scratch based on their observations and measurements of the conditions in the PCD. Where objects in the real world have occluded a building's parts, they recreate the objects using alternative data sources and/or their professional intuition.

A great deal of research effort is being invested toward automation of the "Scan to BIM" process, and in some very specific and well-defined domains,

FIGURE 5–7   (A) Point cloud data of a concrete highway bridge near Cambridge, UK. (B) A reconstructed BIM model of the same bridge.

Images courtesy of Dr. Ioannis Brilakis, Laing O'Rourke Centre for Construction Engineering and Technology, University of Cambridge.

(A)

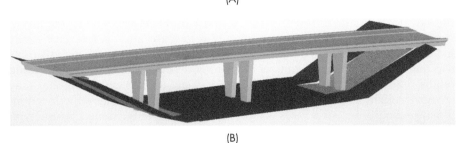

(B)

good results have been achieved. For example, the EU Infravation research project "SeeBridge" has made progress in reconstructing BIM models of concrete highway bridges (see Figure 5–7; Sacks et al., 2017). Generic automated "scan to BIM" processes will likely require application of artificial intelligence techniques. We discuss their future development in Chapter 9.

Concept Design Summary. Concept design tools must balance the need to support the intuitive and creative thinking process with the ability to provide fast assessment and feedback based on a variety of simulation and analysis tools, allowing more informed design. Unfortunately, each of the commercially available tools only does part of the overall task, requiring translation between them and later with the major BIM tools discussed in Chapter 2. However, we are beginning a new era of assessment. When the opportunity exists to gain technical assessment of design concepts at the sketch level for energy, costs, and some aspects of function, the interaction between design generation and assessment will become more articulated and convenient. With almost real-time feedback, the shift between cognitive resources, currently based on recall and intuition, will expand to include computational assessments and interpretation. This change will affect both the direction and quality of concept development and the cognitive processes that support it. The new generation of architectural designers are gaining familiarity with working with such "almost real-time" feedback.

5.3.2 Prefabrication

Construction fabrication refers to operations on a project that are carried out *in situ* on the construction site. Prefabrication refers to construction operations carried out in a shop or factory, preassembled into modules. Minimal variation between modules facilitates prefabrication, although prefabrication is sometimes driven by constrained site conditions where the modules are highly varying. 3D modeling has encouraged the development and application of prefabrication. The overhead costs of prefabrication are the transportation and logistics of aggregated units and the additional coordination required. The benefits of prefabrication are the safety and worker benefits of working in a controlled environment and the reduction of operations required on-site, with attendant improved quality control allowed by rationalized operations, reduction of worker congestion, and improved productivity.

Prefabrication and modular construction are discussed in detail in Sections 6.11, 7.2.3, and 7.2.5, but we emphasize here, for architects and for engineers, that prefabrication is most effective when it is considered early and applied throughout the design process. Prefabrication naturally addresses the different systems being integrated, as the interaction between prefabricated modules is a central concern.

5.3.3 Analysis, Simulation, and Optimization

As design proceeds past the conceptual stage, systems require detailed specification. Mechanical systems need sizing, structural systems must be engineered, and mechanical systems must be connected and sized. These tasks are usually undertaken in collaboration with engineering specialists, internal or external to the design organization. Effective collaboration among these activities provides an area for market differentiation.

In this section, we review the general issues associated with applying analysis and simulation methods to design. First, we focus on the use of such applications as part of the normal performance assessment process during the detailing of building systems in the later stages of design. In contrast to the earlier applications, the applications in this phase are specific, complex, and usually operated by technical domain specialists. They are mostly tools, not platforms, as defined in Chapter 2, supporting model transfer to analysis model and parameters. We consider areas of application and existing software tools, some of the issues concerning their use and exchange of building model data between them, and general concerns relating to collaboration. We conclude by examining the special use of analysis and simulation models that explore innovative applications of new technologies, materials, controls, or other systems to buildings. It is important to note that experimental architecture generally requires specialized tools and configurations.

Analysis and Simulation. As design development proceeds, details concerning the building's various systems must be determined in order to validate earlier estimates and to specify the systems for bidding, fabrication, and installation. This detailing involves a wide range of technical information.

All buildings must satisfy structural, environmental conditioning, fresh-water distribution and wastewater removal, fire retardance, electrical or other power distribution, communications, and other basic functions. While each of these capabilities and the systems required to support them may have been identified earlier, their specification for conformance to codes, certifications, and client objectives require more detailed definition. In addition, the spaces in a building are also systems of circulation and access, systems of organizational functions supported by the spatial configuration. Tools for analyses of these systems are also coming into use.

In simple projects, the need for specialized knowledge with respect to these systems may be addressed by the lead members of a design team, but in more complex facilities, they are usually handled by specialists who are located either within the firm or hired as consultants on a per-project basis.

Over the past four decades, a great many computerized analysis capabilities and software tools were developed, starting well before the emergence of BIM. One large set of these is based on building physics, including structural statics and dynamics, fluid flow, thermodynamics, and acoustics. Many of these tools required 3D modeling of buildings. For example, structural analysis software such as GT-STRUDL has enabled structural engineers to model and analyze three-dimensional frames since 1975. Although early users had to define 3D geometry for input by listing coordinates, nodes, and members in lines of text, graphic and parametric preprocessor capabilities were added to the core structural analysis tools as soon as the necessary computer hardware became available. Thus, structural engineers have been familiar with 3D parametric modeling for a long time, including parametric constraints and definition of members by reference to parametric cross-section profiles. In this respect, 3D parametric modeling aspects of BIM are seemingly less novel for them and one might expect adoption of BIM tools to be natural and rapid.

However, this is not the case, and rates of adoption among structural engineering practices are slower than for other construction professions (Young et al., 2007; Young et al., 2009; Bernstein et al., 2012). The explanation appears to lie in the philosophical and commercial separation that divides engineering designers and analysts, with their strict focus on building physics, from construction engineers and builders, who deal directly with the real world. The philosophical gap is reflected in the dichotomy between idealized analytical models and actual physical geometry (e.g., difference between idealizations of theoretically "pinned" or "fixed" connections versus the messy reality of connections whose behavior falls between the modeled ideals). Traditionally, structural designers model structures in ways suitable for analysis, and those models cannot be translated directly into building models that are useful for construction, because they are conceptually different. The conceptual gap exists to such an extent that in many countries, such as the United States, common practice is that the detailing of structures for fabrication is left to the builders. Professional organizations tend to reinforce this practice with narrow definitions of their members' scope of professional services.

Yet apart from the benefits BIM provides to the overall design process through multidisciplinary collaboration, BIM can provide direct and localized economic benefit for engineers by eliminating rework and improving design productivity. Almost all existing analysis software tools require extensive pre-processing of the model geometry, defining material properties, and applying loads. But with appropriate BIM interfaces, a model representing the actual geometry can be used to derive both the analytical model and the drawing set, thus eliminating or highly simplifying preparation of the analysis input data sets.

An effective interface between a BIM platform and an analysis tool involves at least three aspects:

1. Assignment of specific attributes and relations in the BIM platform consistent with those required for the analysis.

2. Functions for compiling an analytical data model that contains appropriate abstractions of building geometry for it to validly and accurately represent the building for the specified analysis software. The analytical model that is abstracted from the physical BIM model will be different for each type of analysis.

3. A mutually supported exchange format for data transfers. Such transfers must maintain associations between the abstracted analysis model and the physical BIM model and include ID information to support incremental updating on both sides of the exchange.

Where BIM tools incorporate these three capabilities, the geometry can be derived directly from the common model; material properties can be assigned automatically for each analysis; and the loading conditions for an analysis can be stored, edited, and applied. These aspects are at the core of BIM's fundamental promise to do away with the need for multiple data entry for different analysis applications, allowing the model to be analyzed directly and within very short cycle times. The major BIM software vendors have achieved this by incorporating engineering analysis software (structural, energy, etc.) within their software suites, providing these capabilities by programming the functionality within their platforms. Some BIM platforms maintain dual representations internally. **Autodesk REVIT**, for example, supplements the physical representation of the basic objects commonly used by structural engineers—such as columns, beams, walls, slabs, and the like—with automatically generated idealized "stick-and-node" representations. **Tekla Structures** allows users to specify the location of connection nodes on its objects, including definitions of the degrees of freedom, and also has objects to model structural loads and load cases. These capabilities provide engineers with direct interfaces for running structural analysis applications because they facilitate data exchange with structural analysis packages. Figure 5–8 shows a model of a shear wall in a BIM tool and the results of an in-plane lateral load analysis of that wall in such a configuration.

When working across platforms, however, problems still remain and exchanges must be made through files, either using dedicated bidirectional plug-ins (such as the **CSiXRevit** plug-ins for Revit that enable exchange with SAP2000 and ETABS), or using OpenBIM exchanges, such as IFC or

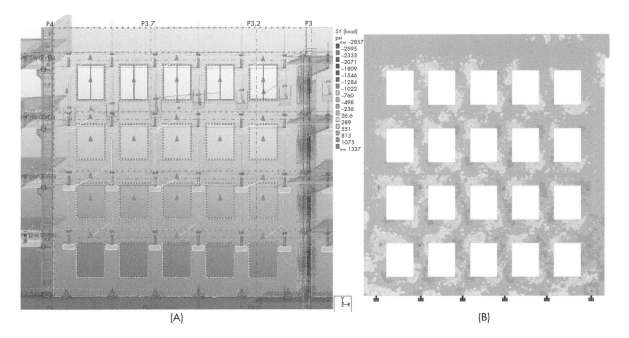

FIGURE 5–8   (A) A stack of lite-wall precast pieces in a Tekla Structures model with loads defined. (B) The same section in the STAAD PRO finite element analysis package.

CIS/2 (for structural steel), which are discussed in detail in Chapter 3. Cloud services, such as ***flux.io*** or ***konstru.com***, provide an alternative route. Konstru maintains a central model of a structure, allowing users to upload or download files from the central model for a range of both BIM modeling platforms and structural engineering analysis applications. Conversions between each tool's native model and Konstru's central model are performed by plug-in translator modules provided by Konstru for each tool. Thus Konstru takes care of the translations and change propagation across tools. It also maintains versions of design, allowing backward and forward traversal of the solution space as it develops through the normal iterations of a design.

Energy analysis has its own special requirements: one dataset set for representing the external shell for solar radiation; a second set for representing the internal zones and heat generation usages; and a third set for representing the HVAC mechanical plant. Additional data preparation by the user, usually an energy specialist, is required. By default, only the first of these sets are represented in a typical BIM design tool.

Lighting simulation, acoustic analysis, and air flow simulations based on computational fluid dynamics (CFD) each have their own particular data needs. While issues related to generating input datasets for structural analysis are well understood and most designers are experienced with lighting simulations (through the use of rendering packages), the input needs for conducting other kinds of analyses are less understood and require significant setup and expertise.

Providing the interfaces for preparing such specialized datasets is an essential contribution of the special-purpose environmental analysis building models reviewed in Section 5.3.1 and Table 5–1. It is likely that a suite of preparation tools for performing detailed analyses will emerge embedded within future versions of BIM environments and platforms. These embedded interfaces will facilitate checking and data preparation for each individual application, as will be done for preliminary design. A properly implemented analysis filter will: (1) check that the minimum data is available geometrically from the BIM model; (2) abstract the requisite geometry from the model; (3) assign the necessary material or object attributes; and (4) request changes to the parameters needed for the analysis from the user.

The above review focuses on quantitative analysis dealing with the physical behavior of buildings. Less complex but still complicated criteria must also be assessed such as fire safety, access for the disabled, and building code requirements. The availability of neutral format (IFC) building models has facilitated multiple products for rule-based model checking. The principles for checking BIM models are outlined in Chapter 2 (Section 2.4), and some of the more common tools are reviewed in Section 2.5.3.

Buildings are built to house various functions, such as healthcare, business, transportation, or education. While the physical performance of a building's shell is obviously important to fulfilling its intended function, computer simulation tools can also be applied to predict the degree to which the constructed spaces will support the efficient functioning of the operations carried out within the building. These are obvious in manufacturing facilities, where the layout of operations is well understood to have an effect on efficient production, with a large literature (Francis, 1992). The same logic has been applied to hospitals, based on the recognition that doctors and nurses spend a significant time each day walking (Yeh, 2006). More recently, issues of developing space layouts that can support varied emergency procedures in trauma units and intensive care facilities have also been studied.

The processing time in airport security is something all travelers face and is strongly affected by airport planning. Software for simulating people flows through facilities can be addressed with such products as **Legion Studio**, **Simwalk**, and **Pedestrian Simulations** from Quadstone Parametrics. As the workforce becomes more oriented toward creative production, the open, friendly work environments found in Silicon Valley have become commonplace everywhere. The increasing percentage of gross domestic product (GDP) devoted to healthcare indicates that improvements that can be generated through improved design—associated with new procedures—are an area worthy of intense analysis and study. Integration of building designs with models of organizational processes, human circulation behavior, and other related phenomena will become an important aspect of design analysis. These issues are generally driven by owner recognition of need, and are discussed in Section 4.5.

Cost Estimation. While analysis and simulation programs attempt to predict various types of building behavior, cost estimation involves a different kind of analysis and prediction. Like the previous analyses, it needs to be applicable at different levels of design development, taking advantage of the information available and making normative assumptions regarding what is missing. Because cost estimation addresses issues relevant to the owner, contractor, and fabricator, it is also discussed from these varying perspectives in Chapters 4, 6, and 7, respectively.

Until recently, the product or material units for a project were measured and estimated through manual counting and area calculations. Like all human activities, these involved errors and took time. However, building information models now have distinct objects that can be counted easily, and along with volumes and areas of materials, can be computed automatically, almost instantaneously. The specified data extracted from a BIM design tool can thus provide an accurate count of the building products and material units needed for cost estimation. The DESTINI Profiler system, reviewed in Chapter 2, provides a strong example of the mapping from material units in a BIM application to a cost-estimating system. Target costing with short cycle times, as applied in IPD projects such as the Sutter Medical Center in Castro Valley (see *BIM Handbook* companion website), is an even more powerful use of BIM-enabled cost estimation. It becomes an effective guide for designers throughout the project.

While most BIM platforms enable immediate extraction of item counts and area and volume calculations for many of their components and/or materials, more sophisticated quantity takeoff from a model requires specialized software, such as **Autodesk's QTO** (quantity takeoff) or **Vico Takeoff Manager**. These tools allow the estimator to associate objects in a building model directly with assemblies, recipes, or items in the estimating package or with an external cost database such as R.S. Means. A full review of cost-estimating systems is provided in Section 6.9. As with most model simulation and analysis software, there are two ways to exchange information with these tools:

- Through dedicated plug-ins to various BIM platforms. **Innovaya Visual Estimating, RIB iTWO** and **Vico Takeoff Manager**, for example, provide plug-ins.
- Using OpenBIM file exchange with IFC. **Nomitech CostOS, Exactal CostX** and **Vico Takeoff Manager** are examples.

The importance of cost estimation for designers is that it allows them to carry out target value design (P2SL, 2017) while they are designing, considering alternatives as they design that meet the client's needs in an optimal fashion. Eliminating the traditional cost or value engineering practice that eliminates cost items at the end of a project is an important benefit of BIM, in tandem with lean construction practice. Incremental target value design while the project is being developed allows practical assessment throughout design.

Design Optimization. As BIM technologies advance, data-driven design and optimization became another option. Data-driven design is a method

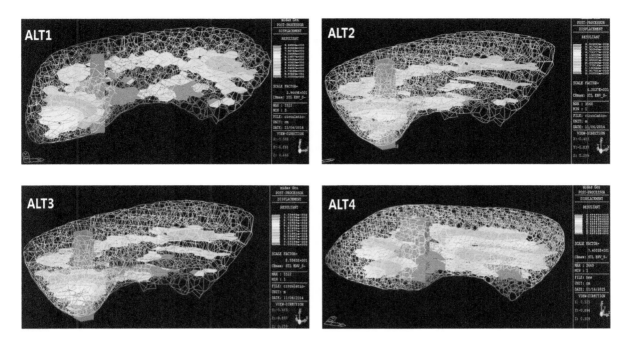

FIGURE 5–9   Optimization of a structural design of a building.

Image courtesy of ChangSoft I & I.

to produce and optimize a design based on the integration of design and big data. Parametric modeling provides building model definitions that can represent a family or space of designs, such as the set of structural alternatives shown in Figure 5–9. Plug-ins can be written that combinatorily explore that space of designs and to retain those parameter settings that best achieve some set of goals, which can be expressed in a utility function. Thus the second optimization component is a setup goal definition module that retains the best parametric configuration according to the goal. Some high-end parametric modeling tools in manufacturing include modules that facilitate such optimization. Currently the use of optimization is mostly a research topic exploring various AEC applications (Gerber, 2014).

Example applications include façade designs generation based on natural ventilation, solar gain or reduction methods, energy consumption, wind, and/or daylighting; structure optimization considering construction costs and methods as well as structural soundness; façade design rationalization based on construction costs and fabrication technologies; urban planning based on potential energy consumption; optimal form finding; and more. Various mulitobjective optimization methods, including pareto optimization and machine learning approaches, support goal definition and search, where goals need not be commensurate, providing search and feedback allowing optimization with conflicting goals (Gero, 2012).

Parametric modeling tools, some with visual coding, are key enablers of data-driven design. **GenerativeComponents**, a pioneering application, is still used. **Grasshopper** for Rhinoceros and **Dynamo** for Revit are newer and more commonly used visual-coding parametric tools. Many design firms build upon these proprietary tools to develop design generation or design optimization solutions in-house. An example is Aditazz—a Silicon Valley–based healthcare facility design and construction firm, which deploys a manufacturing-based design, simulation, and modular construction method. In the University Medical College Cancer Hospital project in Southeast China, Aditazz used clinical pedestrian flows and best practices of a cancer hospital to find the optimal and minimum number of clinical rooms without affecting patient care, which resulted in reductions in capital expenditure and operating expenses (see the Aditazz website for more information on the project).

5.3.4   Construction-Level Building Models

Designers can approach the development of a construction-level model in at least three different ways:

1. As traditionally conceived, the designers' building model is a detailed design expressing the intent of the designer and the client. In this view, the contractors are expected to develop their own independent construction model and documents from scratch and based on their knowledge and experience of construction methods.
2. Alternatively, the building model is regarded as a partially detailed model to be further detailed for use in all aspects of construction, planning, and fabrication. In this view, the design model is the starting point for elaboration by the construction team.
3. The design team can collaborate with contractors and fabricators from the beginning, being informed about fabrication issues as they model. They provide a model later that incorporates fabrication knowledge along with design intent.

The main reason why the first approach has traditionally been adopted by architects and engineers is to eliminate liability for construction issues by taking the approach that they are not providing construction information but only design intent. This is apparent in the text disclaimers that commonly appear on drawings, which transfer responsibility for dimensional accuracy and correctness to the contractors. Of course, technically this means that the contractor or fabricators should develop their models from scratch, reflecting the intent of the designer, and requiring repeated rounds of submittals, design reviews, and corrections.

The authors consider such practices—based strictly on design intent—to be inherently inefficient and irresponsible to clients. We encourage designers to take the second or third view, providing their model information to fabricators and detailers and allowing them to elaborate the design information as needed to both maintain the design intent and refine the design for fabrication. The benefits that derive from sharing models between designers and builders, and developing them in close collaboration, are a major driver for new procurement methods like Integrated Project Delivery (IPD; see Chapters 1 and 6 and Section 5.2 of this chapter for more details). At the same time, BIM is an essential facilitator for IPD.

The structural engineer's model of the USC School of Cinematic Arts provides an excellent example of this approach. As can be seen in Figure 5–10, the structural engineer has provided all of the structure geometry with cast-in-place concrete rebar and steel connection details. The different fabricators can all refine their details using the same model; coordination between the different systems is ensured. The Crusell Bridge (see case study in the *BIM Handbook* companion website) clearly illustrates how a design model was carried through directly into detailing, fabrication, and installation on-site.

Almost all existing platforms for generating building models support a mixture of full 3D component representation, 2D representative sections, plus symbolic 2D or 3D schematic representations, such as centerline layouts. Pipe layouts may be defined in terms of their physical layout or as a centerline logical diagram with pipe diameters annotated alongside them. Similarly, electrical conduit can be placed in 3D or defined logically with dotted lines. As reviewed in Chapter 2, the building models resulting from this mixed strategy are only

FIGURE 5–10   A view of a design engineer's Tekla Structures model of the USC School of Cinematic Arts. The model contains details for three subcontractors—structural steel, rebar fabricator, and cast-in-place concrete—and enables the engineer to ensure design coordination among these systems.

Image provided courtesy of Gregory P. Luth & Associates, Inc.

partially machine-readable. The level of detail within the model determines how machine-readable it is and the functionality that it can achieve. Automated clash checking can only be applied to 3D solids. Decisions regarding the level of detail required of the model and its 3D geometry of elements must be made as construction-level modeling proceeds.

Today, recommended construction details supplied by product vendors cannot yet be defined in a generic form allowing insertion into a *parametric* 3D model. This is because of the variety of underlying rule systems built into the different parametric modelers (as described in Section 2.2). Construction details are still most easily supplied in their conventional form, as drawn sections. The potential benefits for supplying parametric 3D details, to strengthen vendor control of how their products are installed and detailed, has large implications regarding liability and warrantees. This issue is developed in Chapter 8. On the designers' side, however, the current reliance on 2D sections is both a rationale not to undertake 3D modeling at the detail level and a quality control handicap to be overcome.

Building Systems Layout. Different construction types and building systems involve different kinds of expertise for detailing and layout (see Table 5–2). Curtain walls, especially for custom-designed systems, involve specialized layout and engineering. Precast concrete, structural steel, and ductwork are other areas that involve specialized design, engineering, and fabrication expertise. Mechanical, electrical, and plumbing (MEP) systems require sizing and layout, usually within confined spaces. In these cases, specialists involved in the design require specific design objects and parametric modeling rules to lay out their systems, size them, and specify them.

Specialization, however, requires a careful approach for integration in order to realize efficient construction. The designers and the fabricators/ constructors for each system are typically separate and distinct organizations. While 3D layout during the design phase carries many benefits, if it is undertaken too early it may result in wasteful iteration. Prior to selecting a fabricator, the architects and MEP engineers should only generate "suggested layouts," ideally consulting a fabricator in a "design assist" role. After the fabricator is selected, the production objects may be detailed and laid out, and this layout may differ from the original due to production preferences or other advantages that are unique to the fabricator. Designers and builders are beginning to deal with the issue of level of development (LOD) for BIM modeling. An early example is the "Model Progression Specifications" that explicitly define the LOD required from designers and fabricators for each object type through each project phase (Bedrick, 2008). Various types of LODs are reviewed in more detail in Section 8.4.2.

BIM tools will be most effective when used in parallel—and as seamlessly as possible—by all system designers and fabricator subcontractors. BIM tools provide strong advantages for design-build and IPD contractual arrangements for building systems. The use of construction detail–level models—where design

Table 5–2 Building System Layout Applications

Building System	Application
Mechanical and HVAC	Carrier E20-II HVAC System Design
	Vectorworks Architect
	AutoCad MEP
	Autodesk Revit MEP
	CAD-DUCT
	CAD-MEP
	CAD-MECH
Electrical	Bentley Building
	Vectorworks Architect
	Autodesk Revit
	MEP CADPIPE Electrical
Piping	Bentley Building
	Vectorworks Architect
	ProCAD 3D
	Smart Quickpen Pipedesigner 3D
	Autodesk Revit MEP
	AutoCad MEP
	CADPIPE
Elevators/Escalators	Elevate 6.0
Site Planning	Autodesk Civil 3D
	Bentley PowerCivil
	Eagle Point's Landscape & Irrigation Design
Structural	Tekla Structures
	Autodesk Revit Structures
	Bentley Structural

models are used directly for fabrication detailing—will become more prevalent due to cost and time savings.

Numerous applications are available to facilitate operations within or in concert with the primary BIM design platforms used by an A/E firm or consultant. A representative sample is shown in Table 5–2, which contains a list of mechanical and HVAC, electrical, piping, elevators, and trip analyses and site planning applications. These support areas are undergoing rapid development by specialized building system software developers. The software under development is also being integrated with major BIM design platforms. As a result, BIM vendors will be able to offer increasingly complete building system design packages.

Readers interested in more detailed discussion of the role of BIM in fabrication for construction are referred to Chapter 7, which focuses on these aspects.

Drawing and Document Production. Drawing generation is an important BIM production capability, and is likely to remain so for some time. At some point, drawings will stop being the design information of record and instead the model will become the primary legal and contractual source of building information. The American Institute of Steel Construction, in its code of standard practice, has adopted contractual text saying that if the structural steel of a project is represented by both a model and drawings, the design of record is the model. Even when such changes become widespread, design firms of record will still need to produce various drawings; to fulfill contract requirements; to satisfy building code requirements for contractor/fabricator estimation; and to serve as the documents between designer and contractors. Drawings are used during construction to guide layout and field work. General drawing production requirements from BIM tools are presented in Chapter 2, Section 2.2.2

In the world of BIM, construction and other types of drawings are reports filtered and extracted from the BIM model. The generation and use of drawings involve two aspects:

- The proper layout for different drawing formats: line weights, hatching, annotations, dimensioning, spacing between drawings, and so on. These techniques were developed in the 1980s. One hundred percent automatic generation is theoretically possible but challenging. Reconstruction of chained dimensions require rechaining; conversion of distances to the needed scale, and optionally architectural dimensioning are challenges. Hatching edits require redefinition of the hatched region, Dimensions may overwrite each other, requiring respacing. Most of these anomalies can be corrected by simple manual edits. All automatic drawing generation requires some level of manual cleanup. Automatic drawing generation is provided by all BIM tools, with something like 90 to 98 percent accuracy.
- Drawings are edited and changed. What must be reformatted and regenerated when an edit is made? Do I edit the model or the drawing? This is approached by associativity between the drawing marks and the elements of the building model. In a report, the authoritative data is the model and updates are most frequently made by logically marking all the drawing marks associated by an edited model object. These are redrawn automatically, with the cleanups entered manually, for reapplication of the editing. Some BIM environments support bidirectional updates, also supporting updates to a drawing to be propagated to the model.

With the development of BIM and its report-generating capabilities, once the legal restrictions on the format of drawings is eliminated, options arise that can further improve the productivity of design and construction. Already, fabricators that have adopted BIM tools are developing new drawing and report-generation layouts that better serve specific purposes. These apply not only to rebar bending and bills of material, but also layout drawings that take advantage of the 3D modeling of BIM tools. An aspect of BIM research is the development of specialized drawings for different fabricators and installers. An excellent example is provided in Figure 5–11. New representations facilitating

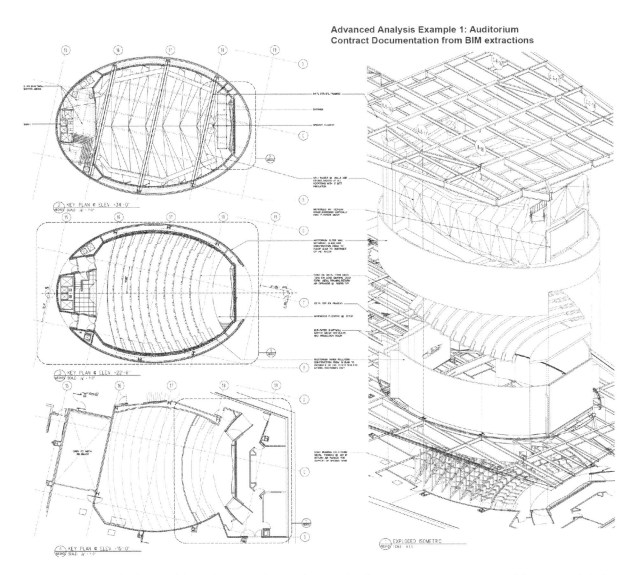

FIGURE 5–11 Detailed layout of the auditorium at the Merck Research Laboratories in Boston. Associated drawings included panel fabrication layout. The design was especially complicated because of the skewed structural grid.

Image provided courtesy of KlingStubbins.

easy interpretation of research results during design is another area where research is enhancing BIM capabilities.

The midterm goal is to completely automate the production of drawings from a model by applying predefined templates for drawing layouts. However, a close look at special conditions makes it evident that various special cases arise in most projects that are themselves so rare that planning for them and preparing template rules is not worth the effort. Thus review for completeness and layout of all drawing reports prior to release is likely to remain a needed manual task for the foreseeable future.

Specifications. A fully detailed 3D model or building model does not yet provide sufficiently definitive information for constructing a building. The model (or historically, the corresponding drawing set) omits technical specifications of materials, finishes, quality grades, construction procedures, and other information required for managing the realization of a desired building outcome. This additional information is packaged as the project specifications. Specifications are organized according to types of materials within a project and/or classes of work. Standard specification classifications are UniFormat (of which there are two slightly different versions) or MasterFormat. For each material, type of product, or type of work, the specification defines the quality of the products or materials and identifies any special work processes that need to be followed.

Various IT applications are available for selecting and editing the specifications relevant to a given project, and in some cases, to cross-link them with relevant components in the model. One of the earliest specification systems to cross-reference with a BIM design model was **e-Specs**, which cross-links with objects in Revit. e-Specs maintains consistency between the reference object and the specification. If the reference object is changed, the user is notified that the relevant specification must be updated. Specifications can also be associated with library objects, so that a spec is automatically applied when the library object is incorporated into the design. Another application is **linkman·e**, which coordinates between Autodesk Revit models and specification documents compiled using the companion **Speclink·e** tool.

UniFormat defines a document structure that was conceived as a companion to a construction drawing set. One limitation of UniFormat is that the specification structure covers broad areas with multiple possible applications within a given building project. Logically, this limits links to one-way functions, because a single specification clause applies to multiple but somewhat diverse objects in the design. One cannot directly access the objects that a spec paragraph applies to. This limitation restricts the management of specification quality. The Construction Specification Institute (the owner of UniFormat) is decomposing the structure of UniFormat to support a bidirectional relationship between building objects and specifications. The classifications, called Omni-Class, provide a more easily managed structure for specification information of model objects (OmniClass, 2017).

5.3.5 Design-Construction Integration

The third viewpoint is the conventional BIM viewpoint of its use in **developing construction-level information**. Building modeling software includes placement and composition rules that can expedite the generation of standard or predefined construction documentation. This provides the option of both speeding up the process and enhancing quality. Construction modeling is a basic strength of current BIM authoring tools. Today, the primary product of this phase is construction documents. But this is changing. In the future, the building model itself will serve as the legal basis for construction documentation. This viewpoint involves design and construction integration. At the more obvious level, this view applies to well-integrated design-build processes in conventional construction, facilitating fast, efficient construction of the building after design, or possibly in parallel with design. This phase also addresses generating input for fabrication-level modeling. In its more ambitious aspect, this view involves working out nonstandard fabrication procedures, working from carefully developed detailed design models that support what mechanical designers call "design for fabrication."

The historical separation of design from construction did not exist in medieval times and only appeared during the Renaissance. Throughout long periods of history, the separation was minimized through the development of close working relationships between construction craftspeople, who in their later years would work "white collar jobs" as draftspeople in the offices of architects (Johnston, 2006). But in recent years, that link has weakened. Draftspeople are now chiefly junior architects and the communication channel between field craftspersons and the design office has atrophied. In its place, an adversarial relationship has arisen, largely due to the risks associated with liabilities when serious problems arise.

To make matters worse, the complexity of modern buildings has made the task of maintaining consistency between increasingly large sets of drawings extremely challenging, even with the use of computerized drafting and document control systems. The probability of errors, either in intent or from inconsistency, rises sharply as more detailed information is provided. Quality control procedures are rarely capable of catching all errors, but ultimately, all errors are revealed during construction or facility operation.

A building project requires design not only of the built *product* but also design of the *process* of construction. This recognition lies at the heart of design-construction integration. It implies a design process that is conscious of the technical and organizational implications inherent in how a building and its systems are put together as well as the aesthetic and functional qualities of the finished product. In practical terms, a building project relies on close collaboration between experts situated across the spectrum of building construction knowledge, as well as particularly close collaboration between the design team and the contractors and fabricators. The intended result is a designed product and process that is coherent and integrates all the relevant knowledge.

Different forms of procurement and contracting are reviewed in Chapters 1 and 4. While the contractor perspective is given in Chapter 6, here we consider teaming from the designer's perspective. Below, we list a few of the benefits of integration:

- Early identification of long lead-time items and shortening of the procurement schedule. (See the Sutter Medical Center case study in the *BIM Handbook* companion website.)
- Value engineering as design proceeds, with continuous cost estimates and schedules, so that trade-offs are integrated fully into the design rather than after-the-fact in the form of "amputations."
- Early exploration and setting of design constraints related to construction issues. Insights can be gained from contractors and fabricators so that the design facilitates constructability and reflects best practices, rather than making changes later with added cost or accepting inferior detailing. By designing initially with fabrication best practices in mind, the overall construction cycle is reduced.
- Facilitating identification of the interaction between erection sequences and design details and reducing erection issues early on.
- Reducing the differences between the construction models developed by designers and the manufacturing models needed by fabricators, thus eliminating unnecessary steps and shortening the overall design/production process.
- Significantly shortened cycle times for fabrication detailing, reducing the effort required for design intent review and for addressing consistency errors.
- Greatly reducing coordination errors between systems during construction.

Part of the design-construction collaboration involves (and requires) deciding when the construction staff is to be brought on. Their involvement can begin at the project's outset, allowing construction considerations to influence the project from the beginning. Later involvement is justified when the project follows well-tried construction practices or when programmatic issues are important and do not require contractor or fabricator expertise. Increasingly, the general trend is to involve contractors and fabricators earlier in the process, which often results in the gaining of efficiencies that would not be captured in a traditional design-bid-build plan.

5.3.6 Design Review

Throughout design, collaborative work is undertaken between the design team, engineering, and specialist consultants. This consultative work involves providing the appropriate project information, its use and context to the specialists to review, gaining feedback/advice/changes. The collaboration often involves team problem-solving, where each participant only understands part of the overall problem.

Traditionally, these collaborations have relied on drawings, faxes, telephone calls, and physical meetings. The move to electronic drawings and models offers new options for electronic transfer, email exchanges, and online conferencing with online model and drawing reviews. Regular reviews with all of the parties involved in a design or construction project can be undertaken using 3D BIM models along with online conferencing tools. Conference participants may be distributed worldwide and are limited only by work/sleep patterns and time-zone differences. Newer tools such as Bluebeam's Studio feature in its **PDF Revu** software allow online but asynchronous review and markup of design documents, which can be of particular use where teams are distributed across time zones. With voice and desktop image-sharing tools—in addition to the ability to share building models—many issues of coordination and collaboration can be resolved.

Co-location of all of the professional designers and the detailers for a whole project in the same office space is a new mode of collaboration that is becoming common for large and complex projects. This is a common feature of projects where IPD is used. The project team's office space usually includes a "Big Room," where different groups of people can meet to collaborate in planned or ad hoc sessions, reviewing and discussing aspects of the design in process on large screens. Most major BIM systems include support for model and drawing review and online markups. These lightweight view-only applications rely on formats similar to external reference files used in drafting systems, but are quickly becoming more powerful. A sharable building model in a neutral format, such as VRML, IFC, DWF, or Adobe3D, is easy to generate, compact for easy transmission, allows markups and revisions, and enables collaboration via web conferences. Some of these model viewers include controls for managing which objects are visible and for examining object properties. Other tools, such as Navisworks and Solibri, allow multiple models, generated in a variety of authoring tools, to be overlaid and displayed together, and include features such as clash-checking and version comparison. Some of these applications are reviewed in Chapter 2. Collaboration takes place minimally at two levels: among the parties involved, using web meeting and desktop displays like those just described. The other level involves project information sharing. The human interaction level requires the following review capabilities for addressing each issue identified:

1. Identification of the relevant design issue by convention currently resolved as a camera looking at the point in space from where the issue is visible
2. Notes or data associated with the issue identifying the problem
3. Easy reporting of the issue back to the design application and users responsible for the part of the building with the issue
4. Ability to track the issues until they are resolved

Tools such as Navisworks and Solibri Model Checker have provided one level of this functionality. BIM Collaboration Format (BCF) is an open source collaboration tool that provides these services, implemented by most of the BIM authoring platforms. BCF is described in Chapter 3. These collaboration services will take new forms when BIM servers become the environments that are worked within.

The two-way capabilities at the model level have been realized in the interfaces with some structural analyses. Both the IFC and CIS/2 building data models support the definition of a globally unique ID (GUID). See Section 3.5.1 for more discussion on GUID. BIM platforms such as ArchiCAD allow users to filter and select load-bearing building objects for their two-way exchanges using IFC, and support filtered display of updated objects back in the building model once objects have been returned from the structural analysis, as can be seen in Figure 5–12.

Effective collaboration using two-way workflows can generally be achieved between BIM design applications and structural analyses. Effort is still required to create effective two-way exchanges in most other analysis areas. For a fuller discussion of model exchange, interoperability, and model synchronization, refer to Chapter 3.

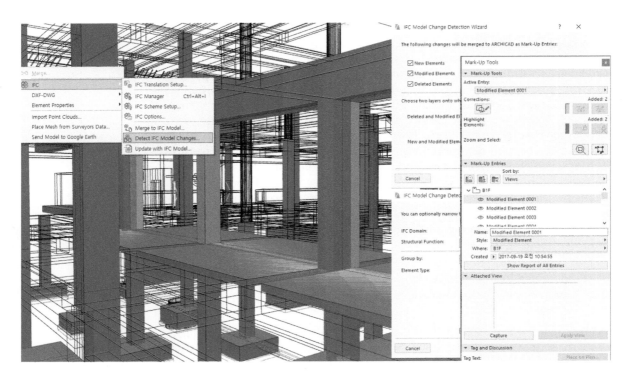

FIGURE 5–12 Display of ArchiCAD objects modified, added, or deleted in a structural analysis cycle using the IFC Model Change Detection Wizard. The exchanges were made using IFC files filtered for structural load-bearing content.

Image courtesy of ARCHITOP KL.

Use of virtual reality (VR), augmented reality (AR), and mixed reality (MR), 3D printing, and digital prototyping (digital mockup) for design review is also becoming common during the design and construction phases (see the Dublin New Children's Hospital and the Hyundai Motorstudio Goyang case studies in Chapter 10 for examples). The VR, AR, and MR technologies are implemented with VR rendering software and a variety of hardware, including head-mounted displays (HMD), computer-aided virtual environments (CAVE), and large curved immersive screens (Whyte and Nikolic, 2018). Examples of VR rendering software for commonly used BIM tools include Enscape, V-Ray, and Autodesk 360 Rendering.

The rationale for quicker iterations between designers and consultants is part of the lean design philosophy. Long iterations result in both sides multitasking, often on multiple projects. Multitasking results in lost time remembering issues and context of the designs on each return to a project, and makes human errors more likely. Shorter iteration cycles allow continuous work on projects. The result is less wasted time and better progress on each design task.

5.4 BUILDING OBJECT MODELS AND LIBRARIES

BIM involves the definition of a building as a composed set of objects. BIM design tools each provide different predefined libraries of fixed geometry and parametric objects. These are typically generic objects based on standard on-site construction practices that are appropriate for early-stage design. As a design is developed, object definitions become more specific as architects and engineers elaborate them with expected or targeted performances, such as for energy, lighting, sound, cost, and so forth. Designers also add visual features to support rendering. Technical and performance requirements can be outlined so that object definitions specify what the final constructed or purchased product should achieve. This product specification then becomes a guide for selecting or constructing the final object.

Previously, different models or datasets were hand-built for these different purposes and not integrated. It is very desirable to define an object once and use it for multiple purposes. These may be of different kinds:

1. Object models of products, either generic and partially specified, or specific products
2. Building assemblies that have been found to be valuable for reuse in the company's work

The challenge is to develop an easy-to-use and consistent means for defining object models appropriate for the current stage of design and supporting the various uses identified for the stage. Later, the selected product supersedes the specification. Thus, multiple levels of object definition and specification are needed. Throughout this process, objects undergo a sequence of refinements of performance and material properties used to support analyses, simulation, cost estimation, and other uses. Some issues of managing object properties are reviewed in Section 2.3.2. Over time, we expect these sequences to be better defined as phases, expected to be different from SD, DD, and CD, to become more structured and part of regular practice. At the end of construction, the building model will consist of hundreds or thousands of building objects—many of these can be transferred to a facility management organization to support downstream operations and management (see Chapter 4).

5.4.1   Embedding Expertise into Building Components[1]

Part of the development of a design office's intellectual capital is the knowledge it brings to bear on its projects. Sometimes this expertise is held by just a few people. Development of parametric assemblies that embed this expertise is an important means to transfer the expertise from the individual to the organization, and to allow it to be used more widely without constant demands on the individual expert.

Many complex programmatic, building system, and code compliance requirements are addressed in the design of a high-rise building core. Spatial efficiency is required in the core organization to achieve operational and financial efficiencies. Core design currently requires significant involvement by senior architects and engineers with substantial expertise in this specific aspect of architectural practice.

Core design issues are resolved by applying basic layout typologies that can be repeated from project to project. A sampling of these is shown in Figure 5–13. These basic typologies can be parametrically modified only slightly, based on informal yet complex design rules, to optimally address the specific occupancy loading and dimensional characteristics of the particular tower's floor plates. A detailed example of a plan layout is shown in Figure 5–14.

Gehry Technologies (GT) and SOM conducted joint research into the feasibility of developing parametric tools for the automated design and layout of building tower cores. This exercise was implemented in Digital Project and reviewed in detail in Chapter 5 of the second edition of the *BIM Handbook*. Newer visual programming tools for parametrizing building models support rapid development of powerful parametric design tools. **Grasshopper** was used in The Fondation Louis Vuitton case study (Section 10-3) and **Generative Components** in the Aviva Stadium case study (see *BIM Handbook* companion website), both of which are good examples of this use.

---

[1] This section presents work conceived of and directed by Skidmore, Owings & Merrill LLP, New York and with support from Gehry Technologies and adapted from work developed by Dennis Shelden. The work and technology presented have patent(s) pending.

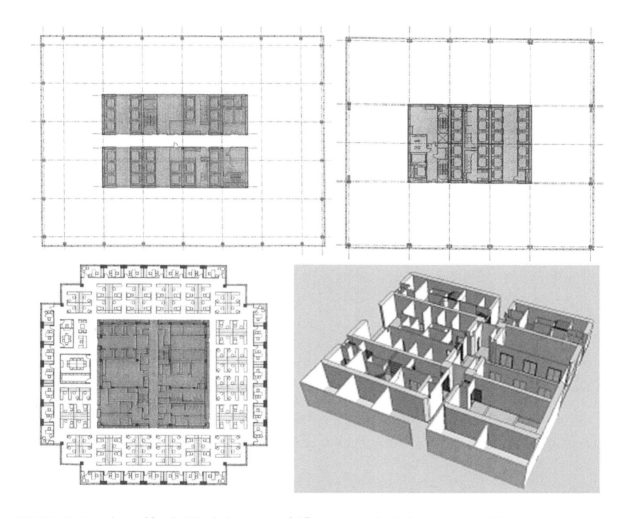

FIGURE 5–13 Sample set of four building high-rise cores of different types with a high-rise using one of them.

Image courtesy of Dennis Shelden.

5.4.2 Object Libraries[2]

There are over 10,000 building product manufacturers in North America. Each manufacturer produces a few to tens of thousands of products resulting in over twenty million products and product applications for fulfilling a broad range of architectural and facility uses.

Building Object Models (BOMs) are 2D and 3D geometric representations of physical products such as doors, windows, equipment, furniture, fixtures,

---

[2] This section was adapted from information provided by James Andrew Arnold, courtesy of SmartBIM LLC.

FIGURE 5–14   Detail layout of a sample building core, with partial development.

Image courtesy of Dennis Shelden.

and high-level assemblies of walls, roofs, ceilings, and floors at the various levels of detail needed during design and construction, including specific products.
For design firms involved in particular building types, parametric models of
space types may also be represented in libraries—for example, hospital operating suites or radiation treatment rooms—to enable their reuse across projects.
These spatial and construction assemblies can also be considered as BOMs.
Over time, the knowledge encoded in these model libraries become a strategic
asset. They represent best practices, as design and engineering firms incrementally improve and annotate them with information based on project use
and experiences. Building owners will develop object libraries that represent
corporate standards for contractor-installed products and assemblies in their
facilities. They will distribute these libraries to consulting A/E firms for project
development, and use them to check/validate BIM designs received from A/E
firms. These workflows involving object libraries will decrease the risk for
errors and omissions, particularly as firms realize success in developing and
using high-quality object models from previous projects.

It is anticipated that BOM libraries will reference useful information for a range of contexts and applications throughout the project delivery and facility maintenance lifecycle.

Developing and managing BOMs introduces new challenges for AEC firms, because of the large number of objects, assemblies, and object families that firms must organize and distribute, possibly across multiple office locations.

Object Definitions. Here we outline the primary information content needs for advanced object model specifications:

- 2D or 3D geometry (2D for carpeting, and filmlike finishes)
- Material representation, with name and model graphical finish (texture map)
- Parametric geometry, if not fixed
- Connection locations and requirements with other systems: electrical, plumbing, telecommunications, structural, airflow
- Performance specifications, operating life, maintenance cycle, light transmittance, and other specs used in selection (varies by type of equipment)
- Luminous Intensity Distribution Curve (for light fixtures)
- Links to product distribution channels

These properties allow an object to be embedded into applications developing an advanced BIM model, then later for specific product selection.

Organization and Access. A review of current BIM design platforms shows that they have each defined and implemented a heterogeneous set of object types, using their own object families, some with predefined attribute fields. Library objects are accessed within, and integrated into, projects using the standard nomenclature defined within that BIM platform for proper interpretation. Full integration includes object classification, naming conventions, attribute structure, and possibly the designation of topological interfaces with other objects reflected in the rules used to parametrically define them. This enables the imported object to support interoperability and interfacing with such tools as cost estimation, system analysis, and eventually building code and building program assessment applications, among others. This likely involves translation of objects to a common structure or defining a dynamic mapping capability that allows them to maintain their "native" terms but also allows them to be interpretable with synonym and hyponym relations.

The complexity and investment required to develop BOM content emphasizes the need to plan and rely on library management tools for object management and distribution that allow users to organize, manage, find, visualize, and easily use BOM content.

Classification hierarchies, such as CSI MasterFormat and UniFormat, are useful indices for organizing and grouping BOMs into project models. For example, assigning CSI MasterFormat codes to BOMs placed in projects can organize them for project specifications. Similarly, assigning UniFormat and Work Breakdown Structures (WBS) to BOMs can organize them for quantity takeoff, cost estimating, and construction planning. However, classification hierarchies are often inadequate for describing the configuration or application of a product or assembly for a specific project. (See Section 3.4.2 for more information about OmniClass.)

The OmniClass classifications developed by CSI are expected to provide more detailed object-specific classification and property definition structures (OmniClass, 2017). CSI, in partnership with Construction Specifications Canada, buildingSMART Norway, and STABU Foundation (Dutch) is implementing OmniClass terminology in the buildingSMART Data Dictionary (bSDD) project, to establish a computer-interpretable representation of OmniClass product and property definitions that can serve as an object reference and validation tool for BIM objects in a project. Given these new indexing and classification tools for standardizing terminology for object names and properties, it will be possible to organize objects at an international scale for access and project use. A well-designed library management system should support navigating multiple classifications to find object models; functionality to manage BOM libraries, including the ability to create catalogs of objects in a library (library views) for specific projects or building types; and functionality for resolving discrepancies between object names and property sets across catalogs of objects.

5.4.3 BOM Portals

BOM portals serve as web access points for building objects; both public and private portals have emerged in the marketplace. Public portals provide content and promote community through forums and indexes to resources, blogs, and the like. The content tools primarily support hierarchical navigation, search, download, and in some cases upload of BOM files. A comparison of the major portals is presented in this section. Private portals permit object sharing between firms and their peers that subscribe to joint sharing agreements under control of server access and management. Firms or groups of firms that understand the value in BOM content and the value/cost relation in different application areas may share BOMs or jointly support their development. Private portals enable firms to share common content and protect content that encodes specific, proprietary design knowledge. Public portals provide a range of services for different market uses.

BIMobject is a prominent portal that aggregates content in multiple formats from partners, such as Reed Construction Data, and McGraw-Hill, ArCAT, CADdetails.com, and from end users. BIMobject has received the data and replaced AutoDesk Seek (which was a public library), and adapted it to a private cloud portal. It provides fully parametric objects with topological connectivity for Revit. BIMobject provides libraries to help building product companies develop compliant construction objects in different BIM formats. BIMobject Apps are currently available for SketchUp, Revit, ArchiCAD, Vectorworks, and AutoCAD and are free to download and use. All apps integrate the BIMobject Cloud directly into the user's BIM program of choice so you can browse, filter, and download BIM objects to your project without switching between windows. We assume that the offerings of BIMobject will evolve quickly as it matures.

The Form Fonts EdgeServer product is an example of server technology that supports controlled sharing between peers. It supports SketchUp objects. ArchiBase.net is an ArchiCAD website with several thousand ArchiCAD objects and other ArchiCAD related products. Most appear to be for visualization, without product specs or quality control. CadCells is a Microstation and Bentley Architecture cell and AutoCAD block library site. The objects contain only geometry without materials or properties.

3D Warehouse is a public repository for SketchUp content that represents building products and buildings. It permits anyone to create a segmented area of the warehouse and create a schema and classification hierarchy for library search. It offers free storage and other back-end services and the ability for a developer to link from a Web page to a model in 3D Warehouse, thereby putting up a *storefront* that uses 3D Warehouse as a back end. It also provides integration with Google Earth, so Google Earth serves as a location-based search tool for building models uploaded to 3D Warehouse. These capabilities are intended to create new business opportunities. For example, McGraw-Hill Sweets experimented earlier with 3D Warehouse by creating a McGraw-Hill Sweets' Group and placing Sweets-certified manufacturer BOM models in SketchUp format in the Warehouse. The potential is strong for combining Google-distributed service, search, semantic modeling, and storage technology with a business entity that has AEC-specific knowledge; however, a focused effort has not yet materialized.

Other websites that provide graphical BOMs (and more) include Revit-City, ArchiBase Planet, cad-blocks.net, CadCells.com, and SmartBIM Library. These mostly focus on U.S. products.

A good website for learning and using BOM libraries and portals is BIMobject.com. Various apps for BOM object users are provided for downloading and embedding in applications and other applications for manufacturers or other product providers. In addition, BIMobject provides management support for product uploading into projects and support for purchase of products through manufacturers/distributors. BIMobject Apps are currently available for SketchUp, Revit, ArchiCAD, Vectorworks, and AutoCAD and are free to download and use. All apps integrate the BIMobject Cloud directly into user's BIM program of choice so you can browse, filter, and download BIM objects to your project without switching between windows.

5.4.4 Desktop/LAN Libraries

Private libraries are desktop software packages designed to distribute and manage building object content and closely integrate it with the user's file system. They automate the loading of BOMs into a stand-alone catalog in the library management system from a BIM tool, such as Revit, or from the user's file system, or a corporate network. They provide a schema for classifying objects and defining property sets upon entry that can be used later for searches, for inspection and for retrieval. They assist searching—for example, 3D visualization of objects outside the CAD system, inspection of categories, types, and property sets. The companies providing such tools also plan public portals for sharing BOMs across firms (file upload and download, community tools, and so forth) and distributing manufacturer-specific BOMs for building products.

One example of these products is the SmartBIM Library (SBL), shown in Figure 5–15. The products for various Revit Families are in a catalog, which a user can create from the file system or a Revit project. SBL displays multiple object catalogs; supports filtering across catalogs by object name, properties, user-defined tags, CSI MasterFormat, UniFormat, and OmniClass codes; and permits users to copy and move objects between user-defined catalogs. It also includes best practice guidelines for BOM modeling on the Revit platform. Similar products include CAD Enhancement Inc.'s FAR Manager and BIM Manager.

As presented, BOM portals have different functions: to represent normative product descriptions for design and client discussions during concept design, products with an intermediate level of development for cost checking of value trade-offs typically during design development, detailed product comparisons for performance level trade-offs during the construction document

FIGURE 5–15 A screenshot of the SmartBIM Library.

Image courtesy SmartBIM LLC.

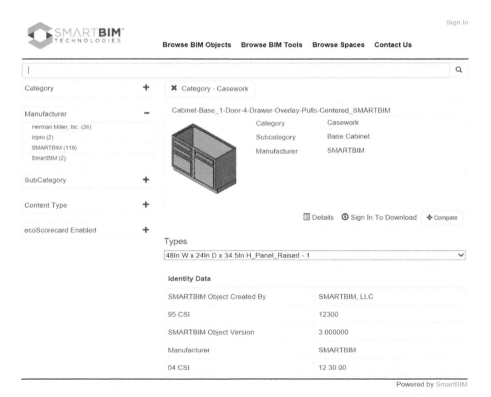

phase, to management of company assemblies and details as corporate knowledge, and others. These different uses have different needs, which we have tried to distinguish. We expect continuing development of BOM libraries and portals in the near-term, as cloud services continue to expand the potential services.

5.5 CONSIDERATIONS IN ADOPTION FOR DESIGN PRACTICE

Moving the base representation of building design from a set of drawings, even if produced digitally, to a building model has many potential direct benefits, not only for designers, but also for all those involved in the construction, operation, and maintenance of buildings and infrastructure. However, the move requires significant investment of time and money for design firms. We offer advice for those making the transition.

5.5.1 Justification and Platform Selection

While BIM offers the potential to realize new benefits, these benefits are not free. The development of a 3D model, especially one that includes information that supports analyses and facilitates fabrication, involves more decisions and incorporates more effort than producing the current set of construction documents. Considering the inevitable additional costs of purchasing new systems, retraining staff, and developing new procedures, it is easy to rationalize that the benefits do not seem worthwhile. Most firms that have taken these steps, however, have found that the significant initial costs associated with the transition result in productivity benefits at the construction document level. Even the initial transition to producing consistent drawings from a model makes the transition worthwhile.

In the existing business structure of the construction industry, designers are usually paid a fee calculated as a percentage of construction cost. Success in a project is largely intangible, involving smoother execution and fewer problems, improved realization of design intent—and realizing a profit. With the growing awareness of the capabilities offered by BIM technology and practices, building clients and contractors are exploring new business opportunities (see Chapters 4 and 6), and designers can offer new services that can be added to the fee structure. These services can be grouped into two broad areas:

1. Concept design development, applying performance-based design using analysis applications and simulation tools to address:
   - Sustainability and energy efficiency
   - Cost and value assessment during design
   - Programmatic assessment using simulation of operations, such as in healthcare or pedestrian-centric facilities
2. Integrating design with construction:
   - Improved collaboration with the project team: structural, MEP, and other consultants; subcontractors, fabricators, and other suppliers.

BIM use among a project team improves design review feedback, reduces errors, lowers contingency issues, and leads to faster construction

- Facilitating off-site fabrication of assemblies, reducing field work, and increasing safety
- Automation in procurement, fabrication, and assembly and early procurement of long lead-time items

What is the value of better functional design? Comparing initial costs with operating costs is notoriously difficult, with varying discount rates, varied maintenance schedules, and poorly tracked costs. However, studies by Veterans Administration (VA) hospitals have found that less than eighteen months of functional operations of a VA hospital are equal to its construction costs (see Figure 5–16), meaning that savings in hospital operations, even with higher first cost, can be hugely beneficial. The VA has also found that the lifetime fully amortized costs of energy are equal to one-eighth of construction costs and this percentage is likely to increase. Fully discounted plant operating costs (including energy and building security) are roughly equal to construction costs. These examples provide an indication of the reduction in operating costs and increases in performance that building owners/operators will be seeking.

Evaluation of functional design can use the triple bottom line (TBL) approach, which considers the financial, social, and environmental impact of a building project. Web services such as **Autocase for Buildings** enable designers to prepare their own TBL analyses, including LEED assessments. This means that designers using BIM can refine their design iteratively, optimizing for the triple bottom line.

The benefits of integrating BIM design with construction and manufacturing are already well articulated in Section 5.3.4, and in Chapters 6 and 7.

BIM Design Productivity Benefits. One way to indirectly assess the production benefits of a technology such as BIM is according to the reduction of errors. These are easily tracked by the number of Requests for Information (RFIs) and Change Orders (COs) on a project. These will often include a component based on the client's change of mind or changes in external conditions. However, changes based on internal consistency and correctness can be distinguished and their numbers on different projects collected. These indicate an

FIGURE 5–16 The various components of the lifetime capital and operating costs of a veterans' hospital.

Image courtesy of Veteran's Administration (Smoot, 2007).

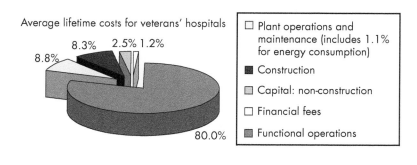

Average lifetime costs for veterans' hospitals

8.3%   2.5% 1.2%

8.8%

80.0%

- ☐ Plant operations and maintenance (includes 1.1% for energy consumption)
- ■ Construction
- ☐ Capital: non-construction
- ☐ Financial fees
- ■ Functional operations

important benefit of BIM and have been reported in several of the case studies in Chapter 10.

Design firms are often not familiar with methods of assessing productivity. An initial step in making such an assessment is to establish a baseline for comparison. Few firms keep track of the unit costs associated with design development and construction drawing detailing, for example, based on building floor area, façade area, or project type. These can provide a baseline metric to evaluate the costs or benefits of a transition to new design technologies (such a method is described by Thomas et al., 1999).

The second step is to estimate the productivity gain of the new technology, in this case BIM. Apart from the productivity enhancement figures provided by various BIM vendors, there is little data available within design firms that have already adopted BIM, or even in the research literature. Research into the productivity gain for producing structural engineering drawings with rebar detailing has yielded gains between 21 and 59 percent, depending on the size, complexity, and repetitiveness of the structures (Sacks and Barak, 2007). A few figures are also provided in the different case studies in Chapter 10. Of course, benefits for a particular design firm are necessarily speculative until real projects are undertaken. An assessment should distinguish time saved weighted according to the average wage of those doing the work and its percentage of the firm's annual labor cost. This will provide a weighted productivity gain. The resulting percentage can be multiplied by the annual direct labor costs for design activities to compute the annual benefit.

The third step is to estimate the increase in business that can be obtained through marketing the firm's BIM capabilities. These will vary by market but may be significant in some regions of the country.

The last step is to calculate the investment costs of adoption. The largest cost will be the labor cost of training time, which should include both direct costs for time spent and also the "learning curve cost" of initially reduced productivity as people learn to use the new tools. Hardware and software costs can be estimated in consultation with a BIM vendor. Finally, the total annual benefit divided by the total cost should provide a quick measure of the annual return on investment and the time needed to recoup the cost.

Platform Selection. Section 2.3.1 outlines criteria for evaluation of BIM platforms and provides brief reviews of the major platforms. Yet modeling tools are not only for internal use—the needs of companies that are frequent design partners should be considered, as should those of specific projects. Indeed, selection need not be restricted to a single platform. Some firms prefer to support multiple BIM platforms and tools, recognizing that some have nonoverlapping benefits.

5.5.2 Phased Utilization

In addition to the new external services discussed earlier, other services can be gradually introduced into a firm's BIM practice. Among these are:

- Integration with cost estimation to allow continuous tracking throughout project development

- Integration with specifications for better information management
- Design level integration with performance analyses for energy, air flows, and lighting to address issues only considered intuitively up to now
- Development of proprietary company libraries of detailing, room configurations, and other design information to embed specialized staff knowledge as corporate knowledge

Each type of integration involves its own planning and development of workflows and methods. Taking a step-by-step approach will allow for incremental training and adoption of advanced services without undue risks, which will lead to radically new capabilities within the overall design firm.

Chapter 5 Discussion Questions

1. Thinking about the level of information needed for cost estimation, scheduling, and purchasing, outline your recommendation regarding the level of detail that should be defined in a design model at the beginning of design development. How would it be different from concept design? Consider and recommend what the role of designers should be in supporting these activities.

2. Consider case studies 10-1, 10-2, 10-3, 10-5, and 10-11, all of which present the work of architects and engineers. Then, identify a building designed with extensive use of BIM, and prepare a brief case study of your own. Review and report how the design was carried out, how information was shared among designers and between design and analysis applications, and what information was carried over for fabrication and construction. The stories of many buildings built with BIM can be found on the websites of the major BIM application vendors and of many design firms.

3. Consider any specific type of building system, such as hung ceiling systems or an off-the-shelf curtain wall system. For that system, identify how it could be supported by automation tools for its custom adaptation to a particular project. What kinds of library objects could facilitate its design? How could the design be supported by parametric objects? What levels of detail are appropriate for each phase of design?

4. Obtain the recommended set of details for installing a manufactured door, window, or skylight. Examine and identify, using paper and pencil, the variations that might apply the detail. List these variations as a specification for what an automated parametric detailer needs to do and design a graphic user interface dialog for configuring the product.

5. Propose a new service for a design firm, based on the capabilities of BIM. Outline how the service would be of value to the owner. Also outline a fee structure and the logic behind that structure.

6. Conceptual design is often undertaken in such nontraditional BIM tools as SketchUp or Maya. Lay out an alternative design development process utilizing one of these tools, in comparison to one of the BIM platforms (from the list in Section 2.5). What are the considerations for selecting one type or the other for schematic design? Assess the costs and benefits of both development paths.

CHAPTER 6

BIM for Contractors

6.0 EXECUTIVE SUMMARY

Utilizing BIM technology has major advantages for construction that save time and money. An accurate building model benefits all members of the project team. It allows for a smoother and better-planned construction process and reduces the potential for errors and conflicts. Compiling a general contractor's building model is an opportunity to perform a virtual "first-run study" of the construction process itself, something that was not possible before the advent of BIM. This chapter explains how a general contractor can obtain these benefits and what changes to construction processes are desirable.

While there is great value in modeling for a contractor even where designers do not model, the earlier the contractor is involved in a project and the closer the collaboration with designers, the greater the potential to leverage BIM to optimize the construction process. Contractors who push for early involvement in construction projects and prefer owners who require early participation will find themselves at an advantage. In the absence of owner- or designer-driven BIM efforts, it is vital that contractors establish leadership in the BIM process if they are to gain the advantages for their own organization and better position themselves to benefit from industrywide BIM adoption.

Contractors and owners should also include subcontractors and fabricators in their BIM efforts. The traditional design-bid-build approach limits contractors' ability to contribute their knowledge to a project during the design phase, when they can add significant value. Integrated Project Delivery (IPD), where a joint contract requires that the owner, architect, designers, general contractor, and key trade contractors work together from the start of a project, makes the best use of BIM as a collaborative tool. Where an IPD contract is not possible, a formal collaboration agreement that focuses on the BIM Execution Plan, like the one adopted by the St. Joseph Hospital project team (see case study 10.5), can be used.

Whether or not the potential value of a contractor's knowledge has been realized once the design phase is complete, significant benefits to the contractor and the project team can still be realized by using a building model to support a variety of construction work processes. These benefits are best achieved by developing a model in-house with the collaboration of subcontractors and fabricators. The level of detail of the information in a building model depends on what functions it will be used for. For example, for accurate cost estimating, the model must be sufficiently detailed to provide the material quantities needed for cost evaluation. For 4D CAD schedule analysis, a less detailed model is adequate, but it must contain temporary works (scaffolding, excavation) and show how the construction will be phased (how deck pours will be made, the sequence of wall erection, the reach of tower cranes, and so forth). One of the most important benefits is the close coordination that a contractor can achieve when all of the major subcontractors use the building model for detailing their portions of the work. In the best case, partners will use the model to coordinate general routings and spaces for building systems in advance of detailing. When coordination *a priori* is weak, accurate clash detection using BIM is still effective for correction of clashes before they become problems in the field. The same reviews allow construction problems to be identified and solved in the most expeditious manner. Another major benefit is that BIM strongly supports offsite prefabrication which reduces field cost and time and improves accuracy. The St. Joseph Hospital and the North Hills Residential Hall NTU case studies (Sections 10.5 and 10.9) provide very good examples of these benefits, and more detail can be found in Chapter 7.

In the field, BIM can be used to deliver design information directly to crews using a variety of mobile devices. This has the advantage of direct access to the most up-to-date information, and it can also provide an effective direct channel for feedback of information about the work back to the model. These tools can also provide process information, which is one of the key ways in which contractors can implement and benefit from the synergies between BIM and lean construction.

BIM can make commissioning and handover procedures efficient and, if project data is managed correctly, it can provide the information needed to support facility operations and maintenance. Contractors should be aware of the great value that the information asset represents to owners and view it as an integral part of the products and services they provide. Chapter 4 describes the use of BIM for FM in detail, including specifications for information handover.

Any contractor contemplating the use of BIM technology should be aware that there is a significant learning curve. The transition from drawings to a building information model is not easy because almost every process and business relationship is subject to some change in order to exploit the opportunities offered by BIM. Clearly, it is important to plan these changes carefully and to obtain the assistance of consultants who can help guide the effort.

The spread of BIM into construction companies and onto construction sites is slowly but surely supporting the growth of construction tech innovators. Many start-up companies are working to apply remote-sensing, communications, monitoring, data-mining, machine vision, augmented reality, and a host of other advanced technologies to construction. BIM provides the information without which these technologies are useless. As such, BIM is a long-awaited, fundamental agent for change in construction.

6.1 INTRODUCTION

This chapter begins with a discussion of the various types of contractors and how BIM can provide benefits for their specific needs. It then goes into depth on important application areas that apply to most contractors. These include:

- BIM support for process change, including Lean Construction
- Constructability analysis and clash detection
- Quantity takeoff and cost estimating
- Construction analysis and planning
- Integration with cost, schedule, quality, and safety control
- Off-site fabrication
- BIM in the field
- Improved handover of the completed building to the owner

It follows with a discussion of the contractual and organizational changes that are needed to fully exploit the benefits that BIM offers, and concludes with some thoughts on how BIM can be implemented in a construction company.

As the practice and use of BIM increases, new business and engineering processes evolve. The case studies in Chapter 10 highlight a variety of ways in which contractors are adapting their work processes to leverage BIM: the Mapletree Business Park, the St. Joseph Hospital, and the Victoria Station upgrade project all illustrate novel ways in which contractors leveraged BIM to good effect, implementing many of the practices described in the following sections of this chapter.

BIM also enables radically new business models, in which contractors offer comprehensive construction procurement services with new values for customers. We will discuss some of these in Chapter 9.

6.2 TYPES OF CONSTRUCTION FIRMS

There is a tremendous range of construction companies, from large companies that operate in many countries and offer a wide range of services to small companies that work on one project at a time and provide a highly specialized service. There are far more of the latter (small-scale companies) than the former, and they perform a surprisingly large percentage of the total construction volume. Data for 2012 is shown in Figure 6–1.

A large percentage of firms were composed of just 1 to 19 people (90.9%), but a majority of construction employees worked in firms larger than 19 people (60.9%). A very small percentage of firms (0.07%) had over 500 workers, and they employed 9.1% of the workforce. The average firm size was 9.5 employees.

The range of contractors is also very large in terms of the services they offer. The bulk of the industry consists of contractors who start with a successful bid or a negotiated maximum price or fee, self-perform some of the work, and hire subcontractors for specialized services. Some contractors limit their service to managing the construction process, hiring subcontractors for all construction work. Design-build firms take responsibility for both the design and construction processes but subcontract most of the construction work. Almost all contractors end their responsibilities when construction is complete, but some offer services in the handover and management phases of the finished building (build-operate-maintain).

Fabricators of components produced off-site function as a hybrid between manufacturers and contractors. Some fabricators, such as precast concrete manufacturers, produce a range of standard products as well as custom items designed for a given project. Steel fabricators fall into the same category.

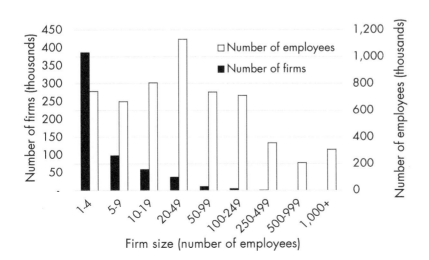

FIGURE 6–1 Distribution of 598,066 construction firms and total employees by size of firm for 2012.

U.S. Census Bureau, NAICS 23—Construction (U.S. Census Bureau, 2016b).

A third group includes specialty fabricators that manufacture structural or decorative items from steel, glass, wood, or other materials.

Finally, there are many types of subcontractors that specialize in one area or type of work, such as electrical, plumbing, or mechanical detailing. The general contractor selects these subcontractors based on competitive bids or they are preselected based on previous business relationships that have demonstrated effective collaboration. The specialized construction knowledge of these subcontractors can be very valuable during design, and many of them perform design review (also called design assist) as well as construction services. The percentage of work done by subcontractors varies widely depending on the type of work and contract relationship. The majority of all construction firms are specialty trades (mainly small subcontractors).

The Integrated Project Delivery (IPD) and Design Build (DB) contracts provide the best opportunities for exploiting the advantages of BIM because the team can be integrated early in the design process. Expertise is available for building the model and sharing it with all team members. (The DB and IPD processes are described in detail in sections 1.2.2 and 1.2.4, respectively.) This important advantage, however, cannot be achieved unless the traditional barriers between disciplines are removed and/or if the designers work with 2D or 3D CAD tools that produce drawings or other documents that are merely handed off to the construction group when the design is complete. In this case, or in the standard design-bid-build process, much of the value that BIM brings to a project is lost if the building model is only created after the design is complete. While this can still provide value, it overlooks one of the major benefits of BIM for a construction organization—the ability to overcome the lack of true integration between design and construction. This lack of integration is the Achilles' heel of many projects.

6.3   INFORMATION CONTRACTORS WANT FROM BIM

Given the diversity of contractor types described in the previous section, it is not surprising that there is a wide range of processes and tools currently in use across the industry. Larger firms typically use IT systems for almost all of their key work processes, including estimating, construction planning and scheduling, cost control, accounting, procurement, supplier and vendor management, marketing, and so forth. For traditional contractors who have not adopted BIM, paper plans and specifications are the typical starting point for tasks related to the design, such as estimating, coordination, and scheduling, even if the architect used 2D or 3D CAD systems for the design. These require contractors to manually perform quantity takeoffs to produce an accurate estimate and schedule, which is a time-consuming, tedious, error-prone, and expensive process. For this reason, cost estimates, coordinated drawings, and detailed schedules are often not performed until late in the design process. Perhaps even more important, the contractor is not involved during the design process and is not able to offer suggestions that would reduce costs without sacrificing quality and sustainability.

Fortunately, this methodology is beginning to change, as contractors recognize the value of BIM for project team collaboration and construction management. By using BIM tools, architects are potentially able to provide models earlier in the procurement process that contractors can use for estimating, coordination, construction planning, fabrication, procurement, and other functions. At a minimum, the contractor can use this model to quickly add detailed information. To permit these capabilities, ideally a building model would provide contractors with the following types of information:

- **Detailed building information** contained in an accurate 3D model that provides graphic views of a building's components comparable to that shown in typical construction drawings and with the ability to extract quantity and component property information.

- **Specification information associated with each building component** with links to textual specifications for every component that the contractor must purchase or construct. This information is needed for procurement, installation, and commissioning.

- **Connectivity between components,** including engineering details of connections, piping joints, electrical systems, and so on. Increasingly, general contractors are contractually required to provide owners with an "as-built" model that can be used for the owner's facility operation and maintenance systems. The COBie standard defines the information required. The relationships that bind building systems into functional systems are needed in addition to the information on individual components. Meeting this requirement is not trivial, requiring either sophisticated model quality control or later reconstruction of system connectivity. In the Medina Airport project (Section 10.9), for example, all of the building systems had to be modeled again by the owner for facility management.

- **Analysis data related to performance levels and project requirements** such as structural loads, connection reactions, maximum expected moments and shear, heating and cooling loads for tonnage of HVAC systems, targeted luminance levels, and the like. This data is for MEP detailing, fabrication and procurement.

- **Design and construction status** of each component to track and validate the progress of components relative to design, approval, procurement, installation, and testing (if relevant).

- **Major temporary components** to represent temporary structures, equipment, formwork, and other components that may be critical to the sequencing and planning of the project.

Very few projects achieve comprehensive models that provide all of this information in a single unified model. Most BIM platforms support the first and second items in the list, but even when project teams use BIM extensively from the start, each participant might use different tools. While merging the model objects with their geometry and basic information for coordination and review is straightforward, merging all of the information is often very difficult. Hence, the need for interoperability using the methods described in Chapter 3, many of which are used in the case studies in Chapter 10.

An accurate, computable, and relatively complete federated building model that includes the above information is needed to support critical contractor work processes for estimating, construction planning, fabricating components off-site, coordinating trades and building systems, and production control. It is important to note that each new work process often requires that the contractor add information to the model, since the architect or engineer would not traditionally include means and methods information such as equipment or production rates (needed for estimating, scheduling, and procurement).

Additionally, if the scope of work for the contractor includes turnover or operations of the facility, links between BIM components and owner control systems, such as maintenance or facility management, will facilitate the commissioning and handover process to the owner at the end of the project. The building model needs to represent information related to all these processes.

6.4 BIM-ENABLED PROCESS CHANGE

BIM's primary contribution for general contractors, subcontractors, and fabricators is that it enables **virtual** construction. From the perspective of those directly responsible for producing buildings, whether on-site or in off-site fabrication facilities, this is not just an improvement but a new way of working. For the first time, construction managers and supervisors can practice putting the pieces together before they actually commit to the labor and materials. They can explore product and process alternatives, make changes to parts, and adapt the construction procedures in advance. And they can perform all of these activities in close collaboration with one another across different trades continuously and as construction progresses, allowing them to cope with unforeseen situations as they emerge. They can also deal in this same way with changes introduced by owners and designers.

Despite the fact that virtual construction is not yet simple nor commonplace, best practices by leading construction teams throughout the world are resulting in the process changes described in Section 6.4.1. Some construction companies have developed a strong track record of projects in which they achieved a high degree of coordination among all of a project's fabrication and erection partners. Construction project teams continually refine their methods. They succeed not because they are expert at operating any one or other software, but as a result of the integrated way they exploit BIM technology to build virtually and in a collaborative fashion.

6.4.1 Leaner Construction

In the manufacturing world, lean production methods evolved to meet individual clients' demands for highly customized products, without the waste inherent in traditional methods of mass production (Womack and Jones, 2003).

In general, the principles developed apply to any production system, but given the differences between production of consumer products and building construction, adaptation of the manufacturing implementations was needed.

Lean construction is concerned with process improvement, so that buildings and facilities may be built to meet clients' needs while consuming minimal resources. This requires thinking about how work *flows,* with an emphasis on identifying and removing obstacles and relieving bottlenecks. Lean construction places special focus on workflow stability. A common cause of long construction durations are the long buffer times introduced by subcontractors to shield their own productivity where quantities of work made available are unstable and unpredictable. This occurs because subcontractors are reluctant to risk wasting their crews' time (or reducing their productivity) in the event that other subcontractors fail to meet their commitments to complete preceding work on time, or in case materials are not delivered when needed, or design information and decisions are delayed, and so forth.

One of the primary ways to expose waste and improve flow is to adopt *pull flow control,* in which work is only performed when the demand for it is made apparent downstream in the process, with the ultimate pull signal provided at the end of the process by the client. Workflow can be measured in terms of the overall cycle time for each product or building section, the ratio of activities that are completed as planned, or the inventory of work in progress (known as "WIP"). Waste is not only material waste but process waste: time spent waiting for inputs, rework, and the like.[1]

BIM facilitates leaner construction processes that directly impact the way subcontractors and fabricators work in at least four ways[2]:

1. **Greater degrees of prefabrication and preassembly** driven by the availability of error-free design information resulting from virtual construction (the ways in which BIM supports these benefits are described in Section 7.3.6) translates to reduced duration of on-site construction and a **shortened product cycle time** from the client's perspective. Increased prefabrication also leads to enhanced safety as more work, much of which was previously done at height, is moved from the site to factory conditions.

2. **Shared models:** Sharing models is not only useful for identifying physical or other design conflicts; shared models that are linked to planned installation timing data using 4D CAD techniques enable exploration of construction sequences and interdependencies between trades. Careful planning of production activities at the weekly level and proactive

---

[1] Readers interested in a brief introduction to the concepts of lean thinking are referred to the work of Womack and Jones (2003); references and links to the extensive literature on the subject of lean construction specifically can be found at the website of the International Group for Lean Construction (www.iglc.net).

[2] For a detailed discussion of the interaction between BIM and Lean Construction, see Sacks et al., 2010.

removal of constraints are standard lean construction practices, commonly implemented using the Last Planner System (Ballard, 2000), in which the people tasked with performing the work filter activities to avoid assigning those that may not be able to be carried out correctly and completely. Thus, a priori identification of spatial, logical, or organizational conflicts through step-by-step virtual construction using BIM *improves workflow stability*.

3. **Enhanced teamwork:** the ability to coordinate erection activities at a fine level of detail among different trades means that traditional interface problems—involving the handover of work and spaces from team to team—are also reduced. When construction is performed by better integrated teams, rather than by unrelated groups, *fewer and shorter time buffers* are needed.

4. **Time reduction:** When the gross time required for actual fabrication and delivery is reduced—due to the ability to produce shop drawings faster—fabricators are able to reduce their lead times. If lead times can be reduced far enough, then fabricators can reconfigure their supply to sites more easily to take advantage of the improved pull flow. This extends beyond just-in-time delivery to just-in-time production, a practice that substantially *reduces inventories* and their associated waste: costs of storage, multiple-handling, damaged or lost parts, shipping coordination, and so forth. Also, because BIM systems can generate reliable and accurate shop drawings at the last responsible moment— even when late changes are made—fabricators of all kinds can be more responsive to clients' needs, because pieces are not produced too early in the process.

6.4.2 Less Paper in Construction

When CAD was adopted initially, electronic transfers became a partial alternative to communicating paper drawings. The more fundamental change that BIM introduces is that drawings are relegated from the status of information archive to that of communication medium, whether paper or electronic. In cases where BIM serves as the sole reliable archive for building information, paper printouts of drawings, specifications, quantity takeoffs, and other reports serve only to provide more easily legible access to the information.

For fabricators exploiting automated production equipment, as described in Section 7.3.5, the need for paper drawings largely disappears. For example, parts of timber trusses that are cut and drilled using CNC machines are efficiently assembled and joined on beds, where the geometry is projected from above using laser technology. Productivity for the assembly of complex rebar cages for precast concrete fabrication improves when the crew consults a color-coded 3D model, which they can manipulate at will on a large screen, instead of interpreting traditional orthogonal views on paper drawings. The delivery of geometric and other information to structural steel erectors on-site, using tablet computers that graphically display 3D models of steel structures is a similar example.

The need for paper reports is greatly reduced as information from BIM fabrication models begins to drive logistics, accounting, and other management information systems and is aided by automated data collection technologies. It is, perhaps, only the slow pace of legal and commercial change that prevents this section from being titled "Paperless Construction."

6.4.3 Increased Distribution of Work

The use of electronic building models means that communication over long distances is no longer a barrier to the distribution of work. In this sense, BIM facilitates increased outsourcing and even globalization of two aspects of construction work that were previously the domain of local subcontractors and fabricators.

First, it is possible for design, analysis, and engineering to be carried out more easily by geographically and organizationally dispersed groups. In the structural steel industry, it is becoming commonplace for individuals, armed with powerful 3D parametric detailing software, to become freelancers providing services to fabricators that have greatly reduced their in-house engineering departments.

Second, better design coordination and communication means that fabrication itself can be outsourced more reliably, including shipping parts over long distances. In the case study describing the building at 100 11th Avenue in New York City (available on the *BIM Handbook* companion website), accurate BIM information enabled the production of façade components in China for installation in New York City.

6.5 DEVELOPING A CONSTRUCTION BUILDING INFORMATION MODEL

Interestingly, many medium- to large-size general contractors have been at the forefront of BIM adoption. This stems in part from the fact that the business case for BIM for contractors is very compelling, and in part from the fact that these organizations are large enough to support structured adoption of sophisticated information systems. They have access to capital, they are familiar with evaluating and implementing investments in equipment and processes, and they can support formal learning. Error-free product information makes construction less wasteful in every respect, and the savings can improve a contractor's productivity and profit margin, making BIM a worthwhile investment.

Given the variation in adoption among designers in terms of the quality of models they provide, and the different information needs of contractors, contractors apply many different approaches to leverage BIM. Where design teams have not created models, contractors often take ownership of the modeling process by preparing and implementing a BIM Execution Plan for designers and suppliers alike. Even where architects and engineers are adept in applying BIM, contractors still need to model additional components and add construction-specific information to make building models useful.

FIGURE 6–2 BIM process flow for a project where the contractor builds the construction model from 2D drawings and then uses it for system coordination and clash detection, construction planning and scheduling, quantity takeoff and estimating.

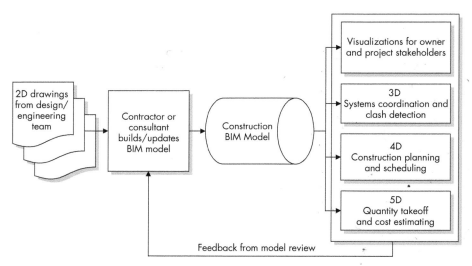

Consequently, many leading-edge contractors create their own building models from scratch to support coordination, clash detection, estimating, 4D CAD, procurement, and so forth.[3]

Figure 6–2 shows a workflow in which a contractor creates a building information model from 2D paper drawings. The need to continually update the construction BIM model whenever changes are made to the design is a significant drawback, requiring careful management.

Note that in cases where a contractor uses a 3D modeling software such as Sketchup to compile a visual representation of the project, the models do not contain parametric components nor relations between them. In these cases, use of the model is limited to clash detection, constructability review, visualization, and visual planning, such as 4D, because the 3D model does not define discrete quantifiable components to support quantity takeoff, purchasing, and production control.

Where some designers provide models, their models can be integrated with the contractor's model, as depicted in Figure 6–3. Typically, the contractor or the consultant manages the integration of these various models, which are developed independently by different members of the project team but then merged into a collaborative model. The shared model can be used by the project team for coordination, planning, quantity takeoff, and other functions. While this approach does not take advantage of all the tools that a full-featured building information model supports, it reduces costs and time compared to traditional practices. The shared 3D model becomes the basis for all construction activity and allows for much greater accuracy than 2D drawings. However, this approach does open the team to the risk that the

---

[3] The stories of companies like Lease Crutcher Lewis in Seattle and Tidhar in Tel Aviv, told in the book *Building Lean, Building BIM,* are good examples of this (Sacks et al., 2017).

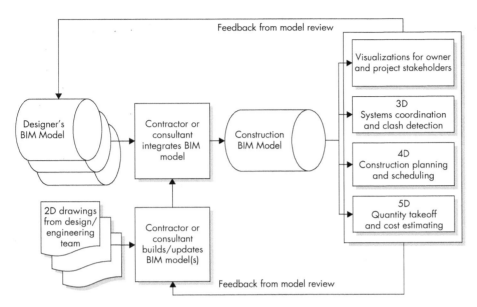

FIGURE 6–3 Process flow for a project, where the architect and other designers and subcontractors use 3D modeling tools or have a consultant develop 3D models from 2D drawings and contribute to a shared 3D construction model.

shared model will not contain the most recent changes that have been made outside the model (either in 2D or 3D in a separate model). This needs to be very carefully monitored to avoid errors, omissions, and (even more) rework.

Note that the shared model can be compiled in two ways:

- As a *single platform model*, by opening and managing the discipline-specific models in a single BIM platform;
- As a *federated model*, by importing all of the discipline-specific models, which are managed by different modeling tools, into a BIM integration tool (**Navisworks Manage**, **Solibri SMC**, **RIB iTWO**, **VICO Office** or similar tools).

The benefit of the single platform model is that the discipline models can be edited and coordinated within the platform, whereas with the federated model, any edits must be done in each model's original platform and then the model must be imported again. The single platform model approach is rarely used in large projects. The use of one or the other option will usually be determined in the project's BIM Execution Plan. Note that Figures 6–3 and 6–4 do not distinguish between these two options. In the figures, the "Construction BIM Model" symbol represents either the single platform model or the federated model.

6.5.1 Production Detailing

As a project proceeds, the fabricators of the various building systems and components add production detail level information about the part of the

FIGURE 6–4 Fabricators contribute production detail level information about the components and systems they provide. Where they prepare models, their information can be integrated directly into the construction BIM model. Where they provide 2D shop drawings, the details must be modeled before they can be integrated.

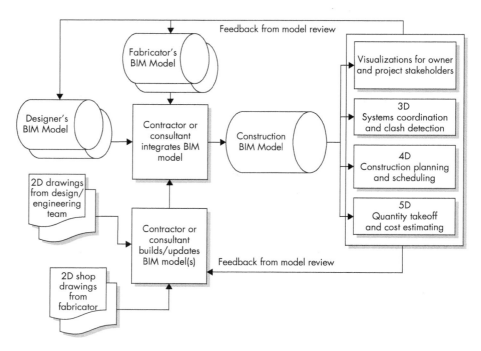

building they are responsible for. Ideally, where the contractual relationships allow, fabricators can model their components directly within the construction model. More commonly, however, fabricators will prepare their own trade-specific models and these will be integrated into the construction model.

Integrating BIM component information from subcontractors and various trades may be difficult to manage if different BIM platforms are used. In such cases effective integration of the information requires careful planning, which is usually achieved through specification of a common BIM Execution Plan for all project partners. This is easier to achieve with a design-build approach or a contract that integrates the main project participants from the beginning of the project (such as IPD) than with a Design-Bid-Build approach. Once again, early integration and collaboration are the keys to effective use of BIM technology. The AGC *Contractor's Guide to BIM* emphasizes this point (AGC, 2010).

As before, the use of 2D shop drawings should of course be discouraged as far as possible, because the opportunities for human error in system coordination using this method are far more numerous than with the use of models.

6.5.2 Big Room Co-location On-site

Bringing client representatives, designers, contractors, subcontractors, and fabricators to work together in a "Big Room" in an office space at the construction site is an excellent way to achieve the close cohesion and information integration needed for complex construction projects. The use of a Big Room during preconstruction and during construction itself is popular despite the expense involved because of the high quality of information that can be prepared in very short periods of time. Design and fabrication alternatives can be discussed and evaluated and issues resolved on the spot, without waiting for the cycles of coordination meetings that are common in other projects. Design and construction can be coordinated thoroughly, as teams work with shared models. The contractor usually maintains an integrated (federated) model with all of the discipline models, which is updated continuously.

Fischer et al. (2017), describe in their book "Integrating Project Delivery" how modern high-performance buildings have integrated building systems, which require integrated construction processes to build them. Integrated processes need integrated organizations, and integrated organizations require integrated information. The Big Room is an expression of an integrated organization, whether constituted by IPD contracts or by simpler agreements among the parties, and its primary purpose is to generate well-integrated project information using BIM.

6.6 USING A CONTRACTOR BUILDING INFORMATION MODEL

Contractors and/or project managers use BIM for fabrication level design coordination and quality control for planning, scheduling, and production system design; for quantity takeoff, cost estimation, budgeting, and procurement; for production control (production flow, schedule and budget control); and for delivery of as-built information to clients when buildings are handed over. The terms 3D, 4D, and 5D BIM are commonly used to refer to 3D design visualization and coordination, visual scheduling, and cost estimating, respectively, in the context of BIM.

There is a wide array of software tools available to contractors for all of these functions. Most are single-purpose tools that can take information from the construction model and process it to prepare the necessary outputs, but others are more comprehensive in the functions they cover. Figure 6–5 depicts a situation in which a contractor extracts information for use in stand-alone tools. This includes direct export of quantity takeoff information to data files, such as Excel, and export of IFC files for use in model coordination or 4D visualization. Figure 6–6 depicts the use of integrated tools, where the model is exported as a generic IFC file or as a tool-specific model file and then opened in the integrative construction tool (such as **DDP Manager, Navisworks Manage, RIB iTWO,** and **VICO Office**).

The following subsections outline the use of a contractor's BIM model for each of the three main functions: design coordination (3D), scheduling (4D), and cost estimating and control (5D). The integrative BIM for construction tools are reviewed in a box following Section 6.8, and information delivery to the client is discussed in Section 6.13.

FIGURE 6–5 Information flow from the construction model to various stand-alone tools for the different contractor BIM applications.

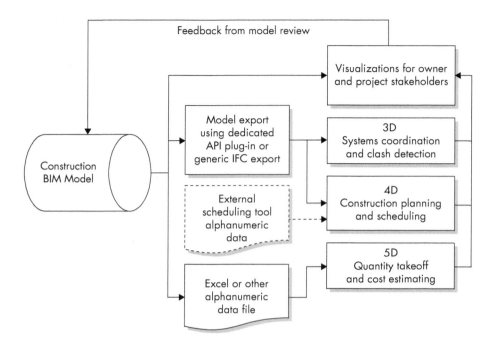

FIGURE 6–6 Information flow from the construction model to integrated contractor BIM tools that provide most of the functionality that is needed.

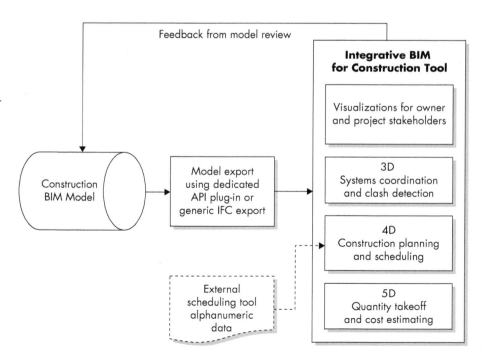

6.7   3D: VISUALIZATION AND COORDINATION

Trade and system coordination is a central responsibility for any contractor. BIM can be used proactively, to coordinate the work of trades as they detail and build the different systems, or reactively, to identify conflicts in space and time through the planned construction process.

For contractors, automated clash detection—in which spatial conflicts between building objects belonging to different systems are identified by superimposing the different disciplines' BIM models and applying solid modeling algorithms—is the "low-hanging fruit" among the benefits of BIM. It is effective and efficient, solving one of the Achilles's heels of traditional construction. Before BIM, people worked hard to identify physical conflicts by overlaying 2D drawings, either on a light table or on a computer screen. Given the limitations of the tools, the cognitive limitations of human beings, and the likelihood of human error, many clashes were only found during construction itself, causing significant rework costs and schedule delays. Automatic detection of conflicts is an excellent method for identifying design errors, where objects either occupy the same space (a hard clash) or are too close (a soft clash) for adequate access, insulation, safety, maintenance, and so forth. In some publications, the term "clearance clash" is used instead of "soft clash." The terms are synonymous.

However, clash detection is reactive. As BIM use has become more widespread among contractors, people have realized that spatial coordination prior to laying out building systems can avoid the majority of the design rework that ensues when clash detection is performed. Using a shared BIM model in multidisciplinary design meetings, designers and builders insert virtual volumetric "placeholder" objects for each building system. As long as detailers restrict their HVAC ducts, pipes, electrical cable trays, and other equipment to their designated spaces—and this can be checked by computing whether they are contained in those volumes—the number of clashes that need to be resolved later can be kept to a minimum.

For effective clash detection, the contractor must ensure that the building is modeled with an appropriate level of detail. While LOD 200 may be sufficient for the larger parts of a building, piping, ducts, structural steel (primary and secondary members) and attachments, and other components should be modeled to LOD 300 (see Chapter 8 for details on LODs). For parts with volumes that are not modeled at LOD 300, such as thermal insulation around piping, LOD 400 may be needed. The information to be included or excluded in an LOD 400 model should be determined beforehand in the BIM Execution Plan to avoid unnecessary modeling effort. For example, small, thin, or flexible objects such as electric cables are usually unnecessary in a model for clash detection because even if clashes occur, they can be easily fixed in the field. However, pipe or duct hangers, although they are also very slender, must be modeled to detect clashes between them and the other components.

Suppliers of building systems and components, whether internal or subcontracted, should participate in model development from the earliest stages

FIGURE 6–7 Snapshot of contractors and subcontractor using a building information model to support MEP coordination.

Courtesy of Swinerton, Inc.

of construction detailing. Ideally, design coordination and subsequent clash re-solution would take place in a common project site office, where each problem can be shown on a large display and each discipline can contribute their expertise to the solution. Figure 6–7 shows a snapshot of two employees from the contractor and subcontractor using a building information model to support MEP coordination. This was done in a trailer at the job site.

There are two predominant types of clash-detection technologies available in the marketplace: (1) clash detection within BIM design tools and (2) separate BIM integration tools that perform clash detection. All major BIM design tools include some clash-detection features that allow the designer to check for clashes during the design phase. But the contractor often needs to integrate these models and may or may not be able to do so successfully within the BIM authoring tool due to poor interoperability or the number and complexity of objects.

BIM integration tools are the second class of clash-detection technologies. These tools allow users to import 3D models from a wide variety of modeling applications and visualize the integrated model. Examples are ***Autodesk's Navisworks Manage***, ***Solibri Model Checker***, and ***RIB iTWO***, reviewed in Chapter 2. The clash-detection analyses that these tools provide tend to be more sophisticated, and they are capable of identifying more types of soft and hard clashes. Currently, identified clashes cannot be fixed immediately because the integrated model is not directly associated with the original model. In other words, the information flow is one way and not bidirectional. This is not a critical problem because it generally takes some time to update a model. Thus the current coordination process requires subcontractors to revise their own models after coordination meetings and to send the revised models to a BIM coordinator (usually on the general contractor's staff) for another round of review. Of course it would be preferable if minor adjustments or changes could be made during coordination meetings, but this is not current practice where people use different BIM platforms.

To ameliorate this problem, a publicly available standard has been defined to help modelers locate the clash issues, identified by the dedicated clash-checking software within the original BIM authoring software. The BIM Collaboration Format (BCF) defines an XML file format that can be saved from the clash-checking software. When BCF files are opened in the authoring software, the list of issues is available. The user's view of the model can be set to focus on and display each issue, together with additional information about the issue.

"What is the value of construction coordination using BIM?" is a question often asked but rarely answered with clear-cut numbers, especially in terms of reduction of the change order costs. Lease Crutcher Lewis, a general contractor from the U.S. Northwest, carefully recorded the costs of change orders for a science and technology building they completed recently for the University of Washington. The university maintains performance records for all of its projects, which enabled comparison of Lewis's project, built with thorough BIM integration led by Lewis as the main contractor with three very similar earlier projects. For the first three, the average cost for structural changes alone, including direct materials, labor, and overtime, was $20.77/m^2 ($1.93 per square foot). The costs for the structural changes in the Lewis building were $3.77/m^2 ($0.35 per square foot). The new building had 6,960 m^2 (75,000 square feet), which implies a predicted cost of $118,500. The actual cost of the BIM integration effort attributed to the structure was $46,000. Thus even for this relatively small, albeit complex, project, the saving was estimated at $72,500, or 158%.

Given that this represents the cost of structural changes alone, one may safely assume that the real value of the BIM coordination, which covered all of the construction trades, was significantly greater than this figure. Furthermore, because the costs for BIM integration include both fixed costs and costs that are in proportion to the building's size, the return on investment for a larger building would be even greater.

Data for the Lease Crutcher Lewis project courtesy of Ms. Lana Gochenauer, Lease Crutcher Lewis, Seattle, Washington.

6.8   4D: CONSTRUCTION ANALYSIS AND PLANNING

Construction planning and scheduling involves sequencing activities in space and time, considering procurement, resources, spatial constraints, and other concerns in the process. Traditionally, bar charts were used to plan projects but were unable to show how or why certain activities were linked in a given sequence; nor could they calculate the longest (critical) path to complete a project. Following invention of the Critical Path Method (CPM) in the 1950s, it became the industry standard approach to construction scheduling.

More recently, researchers and practitioners have recognized that CPM is unsuitable for the more detailed aspects of production management in construction, and its use is now focused on the master schedule. For fine-grained scheduling and control, the *Last Planner System* (LPS) of production control is used instead (Ballard, 2000). The LPS, a Lean Construction tool, implements "pull driven" scheduling. Its guiding principle is that work packages should be proactively prepared and screened to ensure that all constraints—materials, space, crews, equipment, preceding tasks, information, and external conditions—have been satisfied before a work package is assigned to a crew for execution. In practice, this often implies that work teams assume assignments only when all conditions are fulfilled, essentially delaying tasks until the "last responsible moment." This approach to detail level scheduling (the next one to three weeks) is in fact production control, and is discussed in Section 6.9.

Location-based scheduling (also known as *linear scheduling* and as the *line of balance* method) has also become popular for building construction projects, often bridging the gap between master scheduling using standard CPM software and production planning and control using LPS. Location-based scheduling tools use the CPM algorithms, but introduce space (location) dependency constraints explicitly, adding to the technological and the resource constraints that are used in standard CPM tools (Kenley and Seppänen, 2010). Location-based scheduling is particularly useful in visualizing cyclic tasks, such as a sequence of repetitive interior works for high-rise buildings or large apartment complexes.

Project schedulers typically use CPM software such as **Microsoft Project**, **Primavera SureTrak**, or **Primavera P6** to create, update, and communicate the master schedule using a wide variety of reports and displays. These systems show how activities are linked and allow for the calculation of critical path(s) and float values that improve scheduling during a project. Location-based scheduling software packages, such as **Vico Office Schedule Planner**, are better suited to building construction, because they help to schedule crews doing repetitive work in multiple locations. Sophisticated planning methods for resource-based analysis, including resource-leveling and scheduling with consideration of uncertainty, such as Monte Carlo simulation, are also available in some of the packages.

6.8.1   4D Models to Support Construction Planning

When CPM tools are used independently of the design model, the resulting plans tend to capture the spatial components related to the activities inadequately. Scheduling is therefore a manually intensive task, and it often remains out of sync with the design. Project stakeholders struggle to understand the schedule and its impact on site logistics. Figure 6–8 shows a traditional Gantt chart that illustrates how difficult it is to evaluate the construction implications of this type of schedule display. Only people thoroughly familiar with the project and how it will be constructed can determine whether this schedule is feasible.

FIGURE 6–8 Sample Gantt chart of a construction schedule for a project involving three buildings and multiple floors and areas. Assessing the feasibility or quality of a schedule based on a Gantt chart is often difficult for many project participants and requires manually associating each activity with areas or components in the project since there are no visual associations with the referenced areas to a drawing or diagram.

With the early availability of tools to compile 3D geometric models in mainframe CAD systems in the 1980s, an approach known as 4D CAD was developed to overcome this problem. 4D models and tools were initially developed by large organizations involved in constructing complex infrastructure, power, and process projects in which schedule delays or errors impacted cost. As the AEC industry adopted 3D tools more broadly in the late 1980s, construction organizations built "manual" 4D displays by combining snapshots of models of each critical phase or period of time in the project. Custom and commercial 4D CAD tools evolved in the mid- to late-1990s, facilitating the process by linking 3D geometry, entities, or groups of entities to construction activities in schedules (see Figures 6–9 and 6–10).

4D tools have subsequently been implemented for BIM models, and given the simplicity of the idea and the facility of its implementation, many commercial software tools are available. In a 4D model, the construction schedule is linked to the BIM objects, represented in 3D, allowing visualization of the sequential construction of the building. While some 4D tools simply allow this manual linking of objects and tasks, more sophisticated tools incorporate BIM components and construction method information to optimize activity sequencing and detailing. These tools incorporate spatial, resource utilization, and productivity information. They also support *4D* or *time-based clash detection*. Whereas standard clash detection identifies clashes between static objects such as beams, columns, pipes, and ducts, 4D clash detection can detect clashes between permanent and temporary objects, whether static or moving (such as tower cranes and trucks). Advanced 4D clash detection tools can help users check access for vehicles, determining, for example, whether a parking garage ramp is wide enough for a large bus to maneuver, or whether a mobile crane can move around a narrow structural frame on a tight urban site.

FIGURE 6–9 4D view of construction of the NTU North Hills student residence buildings (see case study 10.7 in Chapter 10), showing construction of concrete building cores and assembly of prefabricated modular units. The tower cranes were included in the model to review crane reach, clearances, and conflicts.

Courtesy Singapore Piling & Civil Engineering Pte Ltd., BBR

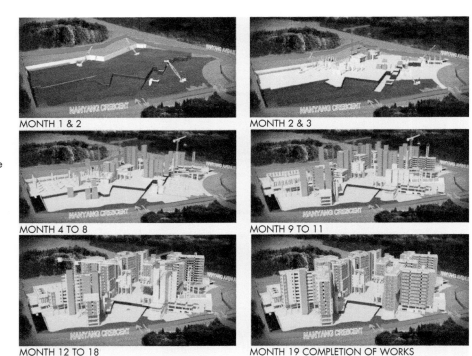

MONTH 1 & 2

MONTH 2 & 3

MONTH 4 TO 8

MONTH 9 TO 11

MONTH 12 TO 18

MONTH 19 COMPLETION OF WORKS

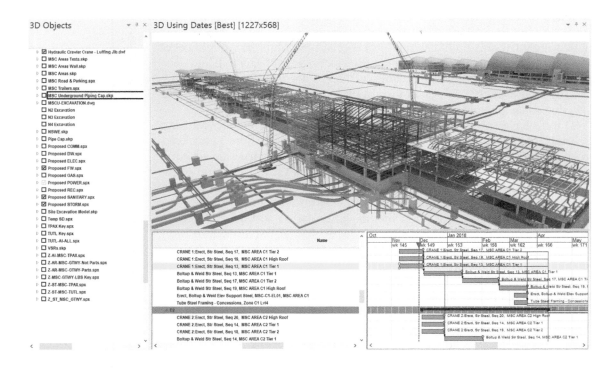

FIGURE 6–10 4D schedule of an airport terminal building prepared using Synchro PRO 4D scheduling and project management software.

Image courtesy of Synchro Software.

BIM allows schedulers to create, review, and edit 4D models more frequently, which has led to the implementation of better and more reliable schedules. The following sections discuss the benefits of 4D models and the various options schedulers have when producing them.

6.8.2 Benefits of 4D Models

4D CAD tools allow a contractor to simulate and evaluate planned construction sequences and share them with others in the project team. Objects in the building model should be grouped according to the phases of construction and linked to appropriate activities in a project schedule. For example, if a concrete deck will be placed in three pours, then the deck must be detailed into three sections so that this sequence can be planned and illustrated. This applies to all objects needed for these three pours: concrete, steel, embeds, and the like. In addition, the excavation areas and temporary structures such as scaffolding and lay-down areas should be included in the model (see Figure 6–11 and the Starfield Hanam 4D scaffolding animation on the *BIM Handbook* companion website). This is a key reason why contractor knowledge is beneficial when defining a building model. If the model is built by the architect or the contractor while the building is still being designed, the contractor can provide rapid feedback regarding constructability, sequencing, and estimated construction cost. Early integration of this information is of great benefit to the architect and owner.

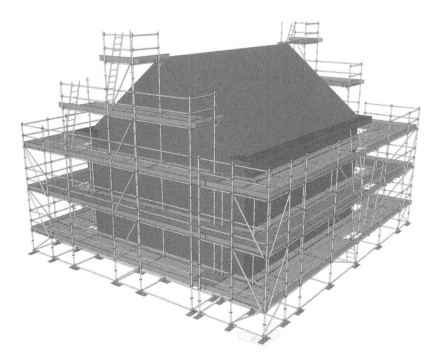

FIGURE 6–11 A 4D model snapshot showing scaffolding in Tekla Structures. Adding temporary equipment is often critical for determining the feasibility of the schedule; the details allow subcontractors and planners to visually assess safety and constructability issues.

Model courtesy of Skippon BV; image by Trimble Inc.

4D simulations function primarily as communication tools for revealing potential bottlenecks and as a method for improving collaboration. Contractors can review 4D simulations to ensure that the plan is feasible and as efficient as possible. The benefits of 4D models are:

- **Communication:** Planners can visually communicate the planned construction process to all project stakeholders. The 4D model captures both the temporal and spatial aspects of a schedule and communicates this schedule more effectively than a traditional Gantt chart.
- **Multiple stakeholder input:** 4D models are often used in community forums to present to laypersons how a project might impact traffic, access to a hospital, or other critical community concerns.
- **Site logistics:** Planners can manage laydown areas, access to and within the site, location of large equipment, trailers, and so forth.
- **Trade coordination:** Planners can coordinate the expected time and space flow of trades on the site as well as the coordination of work in small spaces.
- **Compare schedules and track construction progress:** Project managers can compare different schedules easily, and they can quickly identify whether the project is on track or behind schedule.

These considerations make the use of 4D a relatively expensive process to set up and manage during a project. Prior experience and knowledge of the level of detail needed to produce an accurate linked schedule are necessary to achieve the full benefits associated with this tool. When used properly, however, the associated cost and time benefits have been found to far exceed the initial implementation cost. For good examples, see the One Island East project case study in the *BIM Handbook* companion website and the NTU North Hills Residences project case study in Section 10.7. On the former project, detailed 4D analysis of the construction steps required for each floor allowed the contractor to ensure that a construction cycle of four days per floor could be safely maintained.

6.8.3 BIM Tools with 4D Capability

One way to generate 4D snapshots is through features that automate filtering of objects in a view based on an object property or parameter. For example, in **Revit** each object can be assigned to a "phase" that is entered as text, such as "June 07" or "existing." Users can then apply filters to show all objects in a specified phase or previous phases. This type of 4D functionality is relevant for basic phasing but does not integrate the model with schedule data. Additionally, functions to interactively play back a 4D model that are common in specialized 4D tools are not provided. **Tekla Structures**, on the other hand, features a built-in scheduling interface, providing multiple links between physical objects and task objects in the model. A given physical object can link to one or more tasks and a given task can link to one or more physical objects. Models can be used for 4D evaluations of construction sequences, with appearance and disappearance of temporary facilities. Model objects can also be color-coded based on time-dependent attributes. The use of these capabilities is explained in the Crusell Bridge case study in the *BIM Handbook* companion website.

Most BIM platforms don't have built-in phasing or scheduling capabilities, and stand-alone 4D BIM tools are needed. These tools facilitate the production and editing of 4D models and provide the scheduler with numerous features for customizing and automating production of the 4D model. Typically, they require that a 3D model be imported from a CAD or BIM application. In most cases, the extracted data is limited to geometry and a minimal set of entity or component properties, such as "name," "color," and a group or hierarchy level. The scheduler imports relevant data into the 4D tool, then "links" these components to construction activities, and associates them with types or visual behaviors. Figure 6–12 shows the types of datasets that are used by 4D software to generate the 4D model.

Here are some things to consider when evaluating specialized 4D tools:

- **BIM import capabilities:** What geometry or BIM formats can users import and what types of object data can the tool import (for example, geometry, names, unique identifiers, and the like)? In some cases, the tools only import geometry, geometry names, and hierarchy. This may be sufficient for basic 4D modeling, but other data may be needed so users can view object properties or filter or query based on this data.

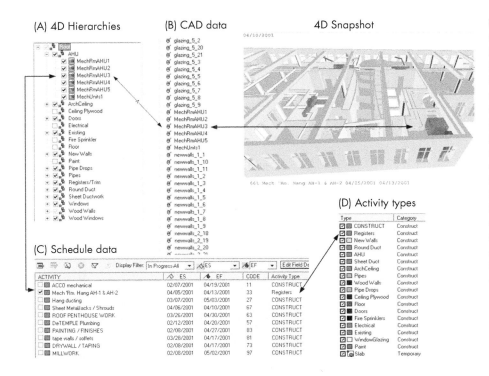

FIGURE 6–12 Diagram showing the key data interfaces of a 4D model. (A) Four-dimensional hierarchy or grouping of components related to activities in the schedule. (B) Organization of geometry data provided by design and engineering organizations. (C) Schedule data that can be illustrated hierarchically but is typically a set of activities with properties, such as start and finish dates. (D) Activity types that define the visual behavior of the 4D model.

- **Schedule import capabilities:** What schedule formats does the tool import and are the formats native files or text files? Some scheduling applications like Primavera work with a database. If so, the tool will need to support connections to the database and extraction of the schedule data.
- **Merge/update for 3D/BIM building models:** Can users merge multiple files into a single model and update portions or all of the model? If a project involves models created in multiple BIM tools, the 4D modeling process will require import and merging of these models. The 4D tool must provide this capability.
- **Reorganization:** Can you reorganize the data after it has been imported? (See the discussion in the following section.) Tools that support easy reorganization of model components will greatly expedite the modeling process.
- **Temporary components:** Can users add (and later remove) temporary components such as scaffolds, excavation areas, storage areas, cranes, and so forth to the 4D model? In many cases, users have to create these components and import them with the model geometry. Ideally, the 4D tool would have a library to allow users to quickly add these components.
- **Animation:** Can you simulate detailed crane operations, or other installation sequences? Some 4D tools allow users to animate objects over a specified time period to allow visualization of equipment movement.
- **Analysis:** Does the tool support specific analyses, such as time-space conflict analysis, to identify activities happening in the same space?
- **Output:** Can users easily output multiple snapshots for specified periods of time or create movies with predefined views and time periods? The custom output features will facilitate sharing the model with the project team.
- **Automatic linking:** Can users automatically link building components to schedule items based on fields or rules? This is useful for projects with standard naming conventions.

The need to revise links between the model objects and the schedule activities whenever there is a major change to the model makes maintaining the 4D schedule time-consuming. This has tended to reduce the use of 4D schedules for detail planning, restricting their use to specific planning problems and external presentations to owners, public agencies, and so on. Thus, functions that automate the linking process are especially important where changes to the model are frequent. The zoning functions provided in the **VICO Office** suite are the most sophisticated example of this functionality. Construction planners define volumes to represent zones. Construction activities are defined according to work type and the objects on which they operate. The software can then compose the scheduling tasks by automatically grouping all of the BIM model objects in each zone belonging to an activity type. The expected duration of each task is computed from the quantities of work defined by summing the appropriate quantities (surface areas, volumes, lengths) of the model objects according to the work type definition and dividing by the standard work rate of the activity and the size of the crew assigned to it. Any changes to the model objects, the zone geometry, the crew sizes, or the work rates can be automatically reflected in the resulting schedule, without the user needing to update any links.

Box 6–1 provides a brief overview of tools for 4D modeling, covering both BIM platforms with built-in or add-in 4D features and dedicated stand-alone 4D BIM tools.

Box 6–1   Selected BIM Platforms with 4D Capability and Dedicated 4D BIM Tools

Revit (Autodesk): Each Revit object includes parameters for "phasing" that allow users to assign a "phase" to an object and then use Revit's view filter to show different phases and create 4D snapshots. It is not possible to play back a model, however.

Tekla Structures (Trimble): A full-fledged Gantt chart scheduling interface allows definition of tasks and association of model objects to one or more tasks. The model can be played between dates and objects can be color-coded according to time-dependent attributes.

DP Manager (Digital Project Inc., a Trimble company): An add-on product to the core ***Digital Project*** BIM platform, DP Manager allows users to link 3D components to activities defined in the Delmia simulation tool or in Primavera or MS Project to generate 4D simulation analysis. Changes to Primavera or MS Project schedule are propagated to a linked DP model.

ProjectWise Navigator and ConstructSim Planner (Bentley): This is a stand-alone application that can import multiple 2D and 3D design files. Users can review 2D drawings and 3D models concurrently, check interferences (clashes), and view and analyze schedule simulations.

Visual 4D Simulation (Innovaya): Links any 3D design data with either MS Project or Primavera scheduling tasks and shows projects in 4D. Generates simulation of construction process. It color-codes potential schedule problems, such as objects assigned to two concurrent activities or objects not assigned to any activity.

Navisworks Manage (Autodesk): The Timeliner module includes all the features of Naviswork's visualization environment and supports a large number of BIM formats and has good visualization capabilities. The Timeliner module supports automatic and manual linking to imported schedule data from a variety of schedule applications.

Synchro PRO (Synchro Software): This is a well-developed, sophisticated stand-alone 4D BIM tool. To take advantage of its risk and resource analysis features, users will require deeper knowledge of scheduling and project management than required for basic 4D animation. It accepts building model objects and schedule activities from a variety of sources. These objects are then linked using a visual interface and managed on either a single computer or a server. Synchro features a two-way update capability that keeps the data in a Synchro model in sync with data in a linked schedule.

Vico Office Schedule Planner and 4D Manager (Trimble): Virtual Construction 5D construction planning system consisting of Constructor, Estimating, Control, and 5D Presenter.

(continued)

The building model is developed in Constructor or imported from another BIM-authoring system and objects are assigned recipes that define the tasks and resources needed to build or fabricate them. Quantities and costs are calculated in Estimator, schedule activities are defined and planned using line-of-balance (LOB or location-based) techniques in Schedule Planner, and then the 4D construction simulation is visualized in Presenter. As an alternative to scheduling within Vico Office, schedule dates can be imported from Primavera or MS Project. Changes in the scheduling system are automatically reflected in the 4D visualization.

6.8.4   BIM-Supported Planning and Scheduling Issues and Guidelines

While the mechanics of the planning and scheduling process may vary depending on the planner's tools, there are several issues that any planner or 4D modeling team should consider when preparing and developing a 4D model.

Level of Detail. The level of detail is affected by the size of the model, the time allotted for building it, and what critical items need to be communicated. Whereas an architect may represent a floor slab as a single solid object, a contractor may need to show the concrete slab and the ceramic tiling as different layers, because they are built in different stages. This dichotomy is true for other purposes too, such as material quantity takeoff and estimating too, as the level of detail needed for construction budgeting is greater than that for architectural design. The opposite also occurs: a highly detailed decorative façade may be relevant for an architectural rendering, but a single wall may be sufficient to represent the timing of its construction.

Reorganization. 4D tools often allow the scheduler to reorganize or create custom groupings of components or geometric entities. This is an important feature because the way that architects or engineers organize a model is often insufficient for relating components to activities. For example, the designer may group systems of components for ease of duplicating when creating the model, such as a column and a footing. The planner, however, will organize these components into zones of slabs or footings. Figure 6–13 shows a design hierarchy and a 4D hierarchy for two different organizations of a model. This ability to reorganize is critical for developing and supporting a flexible and accurate 4D model.

Decomposition and Aggregation. Objects shown as a single entity, such as a slab, may need to be broken into portions to show how they will be constructed. Another issue that planners face is how to break up specific components, such as walls or roofs, that a designer or engineer would model as a single component but the planner would divide or break up into zones. Most specialized tools do not provide this capability, and the planner must perform these "break-ups" within the BIM tool prior to import into the 4D tool.

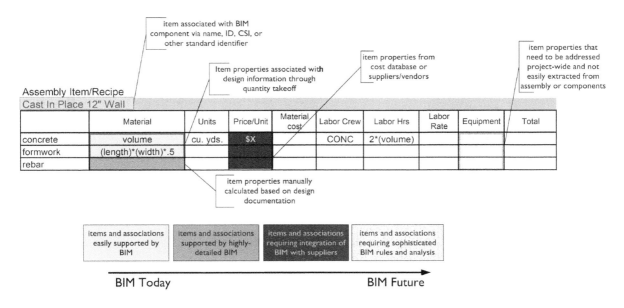

FIGURE 6-13 Example of how BIM component definitions relate to estimating assembly items and recipes.

Schedule Properties. Early start and completion dates are often used for 4D simulation. It may be desirable, however, to explore other dates, such as a late start or finish or a leveled start or finish, to view the impact of alternative schedules on the visual simulation of the construction process. Additionally, other schedule properties are valuable in the 4D modeling process that are often project-specific.

For example, in one hospital renovation study a team associated specific activities with the number of hospital beds that were either taken out of service or made operational, so that the team could visualize, at any time, the number of hospital beds available and ensure that a minimum number could remain in use. It is also possible to code each activity with a property titled "Area" or "Responsibility" so that the model can show who is responsible for certain activities and quickly identify trades working near one another to improve coordination.

6.9 5D: QUANTITY TAKEOFF AND COST ESTIMATING

Many types of estimates can be developed during the design process. These range from approximate values early in the design to more precise values after the design is complete. Clearly, it is undesirable to wait until the end of the design phase to develop a cost estimate. As the design progresses, interim estimates help to identify problems early so that alternatives can be considered.

This process allows the designer and owner to make more informed decisions, resulting in higher-quality construction that meets cost constraints. BIM greatly facilitates the development of interim estimates. The advantage of BIM use is that more detailed information can be generated earlier in a project, as indicated by the MacLeamy curve shown in Figure 5-1, and this translates into better cost estimates earlier. Furthermore, the earlier the contractor becomes engaged in the project, the more accurate and reliable the estimates can be; this is one of the advantages of the IPD procurement method, which emphasizes the use of BIM models as a basis for collaboration.

During the early design phase, the only quantities available for estimating are those associated with areas and volumes, such as types of space, perimeter lengths, and so forth. These quantities might be adequate for what is called a *parametric cost estimate,* which is calculated based on major building parameters. The parameters used depend on the building type, for example, number of parking spaces and floors for a parking garage, number and area of each type of commercial space, number of floors, quality level of materials for a commercial building, location of building, number of elevators, external walls area, roof area, and the like. Unfortunately, these quantities are not generally available in early schematic design because they do not define object types, such as those created by a BIM design system. Therefore, it is important to move the early design model into BIM to allow for quantity extractions and approximate cost estimates. **DESTINI Profiler** (Beck Technology) is a good example of a BIM platform that supports parametric estimating of this kind. (See additional description of this system in Chapter 2, Section 2.5.4.)

As the design matures, one can rapidly extract more detailed spatial and material quantities directly from the building model. All BIM tools provide capabilities for extracting counts of components, area and volume of spaces, material quantities, and to report these in various schedules. These quantities are more than adequate for producing approximate cost estimates. For more accurate cost estimates prepared by contractors, problems may arise when the components (typically assemblies of parts) are not properly defined and are not suitable for extracting the quantities needed for cost estimating. For example, BIM software might provide the volume or length of concrete footings, but not the quantity of reinforcing steel embedded in the concrete; or the area of interior partition walls but not the quantity of studs in the walls. These are problems that can be addressed, but the approach depends on the specific BIM tool and associated estimating system.

Note that while building models provide adequate measurements for quantity takeoffs, they are not a replacement for estimating. Estimators perform a critical role in the building process far beyond that of extracting counts and measurements. The process of estimating involves assessing conditions in the project that impact cost, such as unusual wall conditions, unique assemblies, and difficult access conditions. Automatic identification of these conditions by any BIM tool is not yet feasible. Estimators should consider using BIM technology to facilitate the laborious task of quantity takeoff and to quickly visualize, identify, and assess conditions, and provide more time for constructability reviews and to optimize prices from subcontractors and suppliers. A detailed building model is a risk-mitigation tool for estimators that can significantly reduce bid costs, because it reduces the uncertainty associated with material quantities.

6.9.1 Extracting Quantities from BIM Models for Estimating

Estimators use a variety of options to leverage BIM for quantity takeoff and to support the estimating process. No BIM tool provides the full capabilities of a spreadsheet or estimating package, so estimators must identify a method that works best for their specific estimating process. Four primary options are:

1. **Export building object quantities to estimating software using the BIM platform's own reporting capabilities**. This route is illustrated in Figure 6–5 by the lowest arrow in the figure. The quantity takeoff schedules produced using the platform's generic quantity functions are exported into text files or spreadsheet formats such as the computable document format (CDF). The information is alphanumeric only, with no graphics or geometry. Any changes in the model invariably require renewed generation of the quantity schedule within the platform, export to the estimating software, and recalculation of the estimate. Most BIM platforms include features for quantifying BIM component properties and exporting the resulting data to files in different file formats. There are hundreds of commercial estimating packages that can import data in this form, and many are specific to the type of work estimated. However, surveys have shown that MS Excel is the most commonly used estimating tool (Sawyer and Grogan, 2002). Thus for many estimators, the capability to extract and associate quantity takeoff data using custom Excel spreadsheets is often sufficient.

2. **Export building objects and/or quantities to estimating software using a proprietary add-in tool** that must be installed within the BIM platform. Many of the larger estimating software packages offer plug-ins to export quantity information from various BIM tools using their own formats. This route is also illustrated in Figure 6–5, in this case by the arrow feeding into the 5D Quantity takeoff and estimating activity. The add-ins may help users organize the information within the BIM platform in preparation for export, or they may export first and then offer a user interface that shows the model and enables users to perform more sophisticated quantity take-off measurements. This route allows estimators to use a takeoff tool specifically designed for their needs without having to learn all of the features contained within a given BIM tool. Examples of such tools include ***Innovaya Visual Estimating***, ***Vico Takeoff Manager,*** and ***Assemble***. These tools typically include specific features that link directly to items and assemblies, annotate the model for "conditions," and create visual takeoff diagrams. Changes to the building model require that any new objects be linked to proper estimating tasks so that accurate cost estimates can be obtained from the building model, depending on the accuracy and level of detail already modeled.

To help manage this process, some tools provide a 3D view of the objects imported from the BIM model, highlighting in color those objects that have been changed since the last time the building was estimated, and they can also highlight any objects that have not been included in the cost estimate.

3. **Export building objects using IFC or other model exchange formats,** as illustrated in Figure 6–5. This route has the advantage of using models from any BIM platform that has an IFC export function. Here too, no knowledge of the BIM platform is required, although by the same token, if the BIM model has not been modeled correctly, the input data may be flawed and lead to incorrect estimates. Examples of such tools include **Nomitech CostOS** and **Exactal CostX**. **Vico Takeoff Manager** can also use IFC files.

4. **Export BIM model objects, including their geometry, to a multi-functional integrative construction management software tool**, as illustrated in Figure 6–6 and detailed in Box 6–2. **RIB iTWO** and **Vico Office** are examples of such software. They have their own tools for viewing and manipulating the model once imported into their systems. The exchange can be done using IFC open BIM file exchange export, but in practice dedicated add-in routines that run in the BIM platform and extract proprietary format files provide more comprehensive data.

6.9.2   Guidelines and BIM Implementation Issues to Support Quantity Takeoff and Estimating

Estimators and contractors should understand how BIM can support specific estimating tasks by reducing errors and improving accuracy and reliability within the estimate. More importantly, they can benefit from the ability to respond rapidly to changes during critical phases of the project, a challenge many estimators face on a daily basis. There is a good discussion of model-based estimating in the Sutter Medical Center case study in the *BIM Handbook* companion website. It describes the process used for extracting quantities from various models and then making cost estimates from these quantities. There were many difficulties that had to be overcome, and expert assistance was needed to make it possible. Here are some guidelines to consider:

- **BIM is only a starting point** for estimating. No tool can deliver a full estimate automatically from a building model. Figure 6–13 illustrates that a building model can provide only a small part of the information needed for a cost estimate (material quantities and assembly names). The remaining data comes either from rules (called *recipes* in Vico Estimator) or manual entries provided by a cost estimator.
- **Start simple.** If you are estimating with traditional and manual processes, first move to on-screen takeoff to adjust to digital takeoff methods. As estimators gain confidence and comfort with digital takeoff, consider moving to a BIM-based takeoff.

Box 6–2   Integrative BIM Tools for Construction Management

DP Manager (Digital Project Inc., a Trimble company): DP Manager offers tools for project collaboration, measuring and quantity takeoff, 4D modeling, and schedule integration. It does not have a cost estimation function.

Navisworks Manage (Autodesk): Navisworks is a multipurpose construction management tool, incorporating tools for model review, clash detection, 4D simulation and animation, 5D quantity takeoff, and rendering. Navisworks can also import and view point cloud data from laser scans or photogrammetry.

iTWO (RIB): iTWO enables estimation, tendering, scheduling, subcontractor management, cost controlling, and invoicing processes. It also provides facilities for managing the bidding and subcontract award process. Within iTWO, one or many detailed schedules can be developed in parallel, allowing for the direct alignment of cost, quantities, and activity schedules among subcontractors. Given the schedule is aligned to the cost, quantity, and model, multiple full 5D simulations can be analyzed within iTWO allowing for detailed virtualized planning and optioning. Finally, it supports monitoring of installed quantities and progress as the project moves into execution, providing cost controlling and forecasting capabilities.

Vico Office (Trimble): Vico provides model review, quantity takeoff and estimating, scheduling, and project controls. It is sophisticated because it incorporates advanced functions such as zone definitions to define work packages, integrated quantity take-off, estimating, and 4D scheduling using recipes that define the work content for construction products represented by model objects, Monte-Carlo simulation for risk analysis of costs and schedules, location-based scheduling, line-of-balance charts and schedule analysis, and comparison of planned versus actual schedules with 4D views.

NOTE: The tools featured here are reviewed in more detail in Chapter 2, Section 2.6.2, "Model Integration Tools."

- ***Start by counting.*** The easiest place to start is to use BIM to support quantity takeoff and estimating for the tasks that involve counting, such as doors, windows, and plumbing fixtures. Many BIM tools provide scheduling functionality and simple functions to query and count specific types of components, blocks, or other entities. These can also be verified and validated.

- ***Start in one tool, and then move to an integrative process.*** It's easiest to start by doing takeoff in the BIM software or a specialized takeoff application. This limits potential errors or issues with respect to translating data and moving model data from one application to another. Once the estimator is confident that the data provided by a single software package is accurate and valid, then the model's data can be transferred to a secondary takeoff tool for validation.

- ***Set explicit Level of Development (LOD) expectations.*** The level of detail in the BIM takeoff reflects the level of development in the overall building model. If rebar isn't included in the building model, these values won't be auto-calculated. The estimator needs to understand the scope of the model information and what is represented.

- *Start with a single trade or component type* and work out the kinks.
- *Automation begins with standardization.* To fully leverage BIM, designers and estimators will need to coordinate methods to standardize building components and the attributes associated with those components for quantity takeoff. In addition, to generate accurate quantities of subcomponents and assemblies, such as the studs inside a wall, it is necessary to develop standards for these assemblies. It may be necessary to modify the object definitions in the BIM system you are using to correctly capture the quantities needed for cost estimating. For example, a wall object might not provide linear feet of taping needed for installing sheetrock wallboard.

It is important to note that BIM provides only a subset of the information estimators need to compute cost, and BIM components provide takeoff information but often lack the detailed capability of automatically computing labor, job (nonpermanent) material, and equipment costs.

6.10   PRODUCTION PLANNING AND CONTROL

The spread of lean construction has raised awareness of the need to proactively plan and control the flows of work, information, materials, crews, and equipment through construction projects. The "central command and control" model, in which plans are set by managers and crews are expected to execute them as planned, has been shown to be inadequate in the quick, uncertain environment of most construction projects. The Last Planner System (LPS; Ballard, 2000) is a popular process for production planning and control that engages people at all levels in planning and monitoring production.

BIM can support construction teams to remove process constraints in numerous ways. Detailed 4D simulations of construction operations can help people identify spatial and other constraints that might otherwise have been overlooked. The **smartCON Planner** add-in application for **Graphisoft's ArchiCAD** BIM platform, originally developed by the Kajima Construction Company, for example, provides 1:1 detail for site layout and organization planning, enabling testing the efficacy of construction equipment of all kinds within a BIM construction model.

More comprehensive support for LPS can be provided by tools that visualize the construction process and the status each of a work package's constraints using the BIM model. The **KanBIM** experimental prototype (Gurevich and Sacks, 2013, Sacks et al., 2013) was the forerunner of such systems, and DPR Construction's **ourPLAN** was an early commercial software for this purpose. Subsequently, a number of cloud-based "software-as-a-service" (SaaS) tools became available for LPS scheduling. Some of these, such as **VisiLean** (based on KanBIM) use the BIM model directly, enabling users to associate activities and constraints with model objects. Others, like **vPlanner**, **touchplan.io**, **BIM 360 Plan** (a retooled edition of ourPLAN), and **LeanSight**, provide visual planning tools but no links to the model.

The Crusell Bridge case study (on the *BIM handbook* companion website) explains how a model, maintained by the contractor at the site and synchronized with the designers' and the steel fabricator's models, was used to provide detailed product views for rebar installers and others that boosted productivity, as well as being used with 4D animations to support exploration of the process plans before and during Last Planner System meetings. Where BIM systems are integrated with supply chain partner databases, they provide a powerful mechanism for communicating signals to pull production and delivery of materials and product design information. This was exemplified in the Meadowlands Stadium project (available on the *BIM Handbook* companion website), where thousands of precast concrete risers were tracked through fabrication, delivery, and erection with status results displayed on a color-coded building model (Sawyer 2008). Some 3,200 precast concrete components were tracked through fabrication, shipment, erection, and quality control by RFID tags read by field staff using rugged tablet PCs. The tag ID values corresponded with the virtual objects in the building model, allowing managers to track, report, and visualize the status of all precast pieces. The major benefit is that day-to-day operational decisions that have far-reaching cost implications can be made on the basis of clear, accurate, and up-to-date information.

6.11 OFF-SITE FABRICATION AND MODULAR CONSTRUCTION

Off-site fabrication requires considerable planning, coordination and accurate design information. As BIM makes provision of information at the level of detail needed for it faster, cheaper, and much more accurate and reliable, off-site fabrication is becoming increasingly common by reducing construction durations, labor costs, and the risks associated with fabrication on-site. An increasing variety of building component types are produced and/or assembled off-site in factories and delivered to the site for installation. Here, we briefly discuss the benefits from the perspective of the contractor. The benefits from the perspective of the fabricator are explained in detail in Chapter 7.

Coordination of subcontractors' activities and designs constitutes a large part of a contractor's added value to a project. BIM enables contractors to automate modeling and detailing of building components, including 3D geometry, material specifications, finishing requirements, delivery sequence, scheduling, and supply chain control. Contractors able to exchange accurate BIM information with fabricators can save time by verifying and validating the model. The use of BIM for virtual prototyping—a direct application of "virtual design and construction (VDC)"—reduces errors and allows fabricators to participate earlier in the preplanning and construction process.

These advantages translate into moving work off-site, with associated safety, quality, and productivity benefits. The St. Joseph Hospital project case study (Section 10.5) describes in detail how the general contractor led the team to design and install fully prefabricated bathroom pods, exterior wall panels, multi-trade MEP racks, and patient headwalls. The overall return on investment in prefab for that project was 13%. Furthermore, an estimated 150,500 hours of labor on-site were avoided, replaced by 29,500 hours of work in factory settings. Perhaps most significant of all, the prefab process had zero safety incidents, compared with a predicted seven incidents that would potentially have occurred on-site according to the average accident rates for this kind of construction.

Similarly, the general contractor for the Hyundai Motor Studio project—the subject of the case study in Section 10.2—used prefabrication of multitrade MEP racks for the fifth to the eighth floors of the office tower (Figure 6–14).

FIGURE 6–14 One-cycle of the multitrade prefabrication method applied on floors 5–8 of the Hyundai Motor Studio project (see also Section 10.2 for more information on this project).

This helped reduce the schedule by one month. Although labor hours for the prefabrication and installation of the fifth-floor systems were slightly more than what would have been required using sequential work on-site, by the time the team reached the eighth floor, productivity had improved and the labor hours were some 95.6% of the expected hours for work on-site. Projects with larger scope for learning, such as Skanska Finland's headquarters building in Manskun Rasti, Helsinki, have shown larger productivity gains. Skanska's building had some 96 MEP rack modules and on-site labor was reduced from 60 hours to 5 hours per module (Sacks et al., 2017, Ch. 5).

Modular construction is the most comprehensive implementation of off-site fabrication. In modular construction, volumetric units are assembled together to form large parts of buildings. Each module is prefabricated with most of the structural components, building systems, and finishes prepared before delivery to site. The NTU Student Residence project case study (Section 10.7) is a thorough example of this method and explains the role of BIM in providing the high degree of integration among the trades and the general contractor that is required for modular construction. A detailed discussion of BIM and modular construction can be found in Chapter 7, Section 7.3.3, "Engineered-to-Order Component Fabricators."

6.12   BIM IN THE FIELD

The use of BIM in the field grew dramatically in the ten years since the first edition of the *BIM Handbook* was published in 2008 (Eastman et al., 2008). Advances in mobile computing devices, platforms, and communications have made handheld devices ubiquitous throughout developed counties. Tablet computers and smartphones are more convenient for construction workers than rugged laptops and information kiosks, and this has facilitated widespread development of field BIM applications by the traditional BIM vendors and by a plethora of start-up companies. Field BIM apps have three main uses: to deliver design information to workers in the field, to coordinate the construction process between all project partners, including trade crews, and to collect information about site conditions.

6.12.1   Delivering Design Information to the Field

- **Viewing and querying models in the field:** A wide range of software applications is available on mobile platforms to aid construction workers access model views, drawings, and other documents on-site (Figure 6–15). The important functions for such apps are ease of navigation within the model, filtering of objects, the ability to cut section views, links to product and supply chain information from databases, access to design metadata (versioning, approval status, and so on), and the ability to measure model objects and distances. To automate navigation, some apps provide features such as the use of

FIGURE 6–15   Viewing HVAC ducts in the BIM model on an iPad on site using the BIM 360 Glue app, during construction of the Mapletree Business Park II, Singapore. See Case Study 10-8 for more information on this project.

Image courtesy of Shimizu Corporation.

QR code labels in the field that, when read, change the model view to the local scene. Some apps require users to download models to their mobile device before going out to the field, while others provide direct access to the models in the cloud. Among the many available apps are ***BIMAnywhere, BlueBeam Revu, Autodesk BIM 360 Field, Graphisoft BIMx, Tekla BIMsight Mobile, Dalux Field, Assemble,*** and ***Bentley Navigator Pano Review.***

- **Augmented Reality applications:** This technology overlays information from a model onto a scene in a mobile device's camera viewport. In construction, this means that a user can view content from a BIM model, both graphic and alphanumeric, overlaid directly on their view of the building in the correct context in space and in time. Some use cases, among many, include construction workers reviewing where ducts and piping are to be installed in a building *in situ*; quality inspection to compare actual to design; accessing maintenance data about an object within a building by looking at it; viewing hidden objects, such as the reinforcement in a concrete beam or electric conduits behind a drywall; receiving step-by-step construction method directions; and viewing animated sequences of construction in preparation for their execution.

    Some augmented reality applications require markers to be placed in the scene so that the app can orient the display of virtual information with the real world, but more sophisticated tools can interpret the scene and identify their own location, sometimes with the aid of accelerometers, gyroscopes, and GPS. These technological aspects determine the accuracy of the matching, which should be appropriate for the purpose. Mobile devices (smartphones, tablets) with cameras produce overlaid images (as in Figure 6–16a), but more sophisticated headsets, such as the Microsoft HoloLens and DAQRI Smart Helmet/Smart Glasses enable workers to remain "hands free," projecting

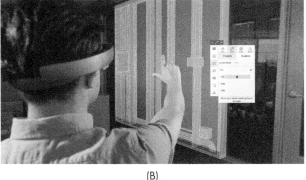

(A)   (B)

FIGURE 6–16   (A) Viewing HVAC ducts concealed behind a false ceiling using the as-built model viewed on an iPAD, at the Mapletree III Business Park project in Singapore (see case study 10-8). (B) Using Trimble BIM software with a Microsoft Hololens AR visor to superimpose a model of a drywall on the actual background scene.

(A) Image courtesy of Shimizu Corporation. (B) Image courtesy of Trimble Inc.

the virtual information directly onto the scene using a transparent visor (Figure 6–16b). A similar technique has also been applied to provide "heads up" displays on the cabins of earthmoving equipment.

- **Model-supported layout:** The typical process of VDC is to first compile a building model that serves as a prototype, then to metaphorically "get rid of the bugs" from the virtual building, and finally to "build the model" in concrete, steel, and wood. An effective and highly efficient way to ensure that the actual building is built according to the model information is to lay out the building work directly from the model. Laying out concrete formwork and penetrations by using a robotic total station to identify spot points is a good example of this. Apps like ***Trimble VICO Office Layout Manager*** and ***Autodesk BIM 360 Layout*** are just two of many that allow users to identify points in the model whose location they would like to establish in the field, to save the data to a robotic total station, and then to use the total station to identify those points precisely on site, as shown in Figures 6–17 and 6–18.

- **Machine-guidance technologies:** Earthwork contractors can use computer-controlled earthmoving equipment that can guide and verify grading and excavation activities based on dimensions extracted from a 3D/BIM model. These rely on various technologies, including laser scanning and differential GPS.

- **GPS technologies:** Rapid advances in global positioning systems (GPS) and the availability of mobile GPS devices offer contractors the ability to link the building model to GPS to verify locations. In some situations, GPS is essential. For example, the height of tall buildings cannot be measured using typical survey tools (such as a total station or a laser scanner). In such cases, Real-Time Kinematic (RTK) GPS can be used to check the height of a building against the building's design.

FIGURE 6–17 Tablet interface showing the BIM model being used for point layout with Autodesk BIM 360 Layout.

Images courtesy of Autodesk, Inc.

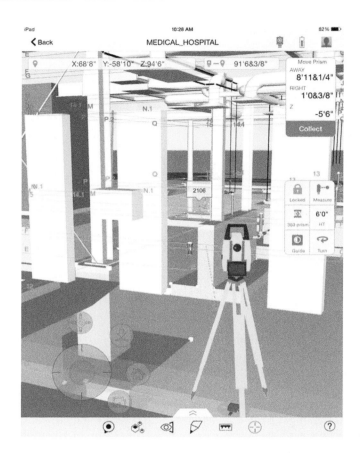

On the Letterman Digital Arts Center (LDAC) in San Francisco, the project team drew on their "virtual construction" experience to identify and correct errors in advance. The following excerpt describes how the team's familiarity with the BIM enabled them to catch what could have been an expensive field error (Boryslawski, 2006):

"During one of the daily rounds of onsite photography, we recognized a critical error shown in the positioning of concrete formwork, which was quickly confirmed by referencing the BIM. This error occurred when the formwork layout person measured from a column that was off the standard grid to the edge of the concrete slab. Pouring more concrete in this complex post-tension slab construction would have had serious consequences not only for the contractor but also for the entire project, as there were three more floors to be built above this floor. The problem was solved just as the concrete was being poured, saving what would have most definitely been a major expense."

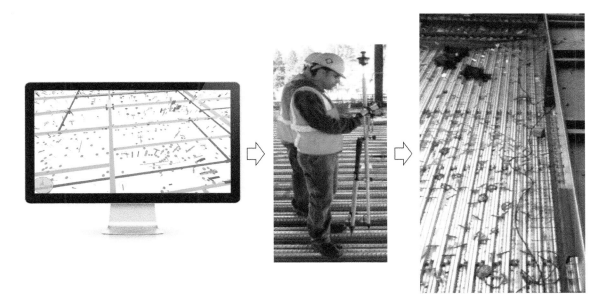

FIGURE 6–18   From model to field: layout of hangers for MEP installation in a flex deck slab shutter system prior to pouring concrete.

Image courtesy of DPR Construction.

6.12.2 Coordinating Production

Maintaining smooth work flow requires people to adapt their plans to conditions on-site as construction progresses, and their ability to adapt wisely is dependent on the quality of information they have about the conditions on-site and in the supply chain. BIM tools help both to collect and to deliver project status information to crews in the field. These are all cloud applications, which means that the information is immediately available to all.

The ability to take photos of site conditions and associate them with building objects in the model is the most basic functionality for collecting status information. Many applications also allow users to enter richer information about physical conditions (such as RFIs and quality control check list data), and a few also enable reporting of process status. Apps like Fira's **SiteDrive** and **VisiLean** include mobile reporting interfaces for crews to report work status (illustrated in Figure 6–19). Apps that can read barcodes, Quick Response (QR) codes, and Radio Frequency Identification (RFID) tags enable workers to report the status of building components as they move through production, delivery, and installation, further enriching the status information. An example of large-scale use of this capability can be found in the Maryland General Hospital case study in the *BIM Handbook* companion website.

In the future, computer vision and artificial intelligence tools will likely be added to provide remote-sensing of production status; as discussed in

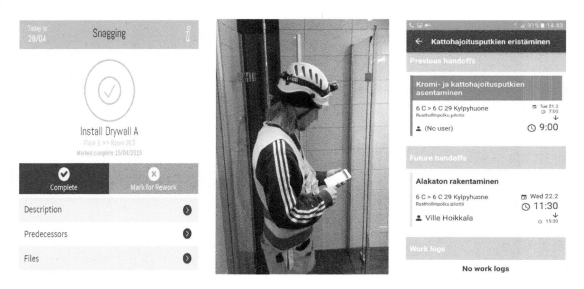

FIGURE 6–19   Reporting work status using the mobile app interfaces of VisiLean and Sitedrive.

Left image courtesy of Visilean Oy, center and right images courtesy of Fira Oy.

Chapter 9, this is currently the subject of academic research and is being developed by construction tech start-up companies.

Delivering project process information consists primarily of providing crews and suppliers with the status of their upcoming tasks and their constraints. In lean construction terms, the goal is to filter tasks for maturity so that the "last planners"—the crews themselves—can evaluate whether they can commit to them within the next planning period (usually the next week). This requires bringing together information from multiple sources, and BIM models are a convenient vehicle for storing and displaying such information on digital "ANDON" boards. Prototypes of such tools have been demonstrated in research (e.g., "KanBIM" system in Sacks et al., 2013) and are likely to become available in commercial applications as the monitoring and reporting hardware and software develops.

6.12.3   Surveying Site Conditions

Contractors must field-verify the installation of building components to ensure that dimensional and performance specifications are met. The building model can be used to verify that actual construction circumstances match those shown in the model. Capturing field conditions for engineering purposes requires a level of accuracy that previously could only be achieved by qualified surveyors using theodolites and other survey equipment. Laser scanning and photogrammetry technologies, using scanners on tripods or cameras borne by drones, provide a more cost-effective alternative for many construction site

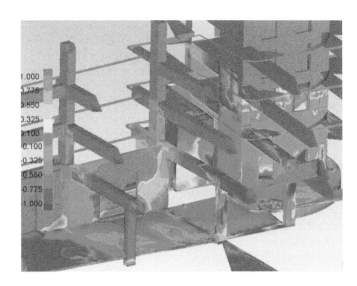

FIGURE 6–20   Laser scanning point cloud data can be mapped onto BIM objects to show deviations of the as-built geometry from the designed geometry. The colors represent the degree of deviation from the planned (gray) surfaces, according to the scale at the left of the figure.

Image courtesy of Elsevier (Akinci et al., 2006).

survey applications, and their outputs—point cloud data files—can be merged with BIM models for rapid and easy interpretation of their data.

- Laser scanning technologies: Contractors can use laser technologies, such as laser measurement devices that report data directly to a BIM tool, to verify that concrete pours are situated in exactly the correct location or that columns are properly located, as shown in Figure 6–20. Laser scanning can also be used effectively for rehabilitation work and capturing as-built construction details. Laser scanning services are widely available; buildings are scanned and operators then interactively generate the building model objects that represent the scanned components. For infrastructure applications, laser scanners may be carried on a vehicle or indeed be airborne. The end result can then be imported into a BIM system. Good examples of laser scanning use are presented in the Crusell Bridge and the Portland Marriott Hotel case studies on the *BIM Handbook* companion website.

- Photogrammetry: Computer algorithms can identify the same anchor points in a series of images, whether video frames or multiple photographs of the same scene, and use them to compute the pose and position of the camera for each image, and thus the position of the reference points in 3D space. The result is a point cloud representing the geometry of the scene, which is in principle similar to the data produced using laser scanning. The differences are that whereas scanners record only the location and color of each point, cameras maintain the photographic images and can wrap them onto a mesh generated from the points. Point clouds from photogrammetry are usually less dense and accurate than those from laser scanning. The accuracy of photogrammetry can be improved by increasing the number and/or the resolution of the images.

Laser scanning and photogrammetry are sophisticated technologies. Laser scanning requires fairly expensive equipment, and photogrammetry requires advanced software that in many cases has patented algorithms. Photogrammetry has an advantage over laser scanning in that a 3D model can be created even using several mobile phone pictures, whereas laser scanning takes more time. It is not surprising therefore that many general contractors find it convenient to subcontract data processing to dedicated service providers, be they local surveyors or cloud systems to which video or point cloud data can be uploaded for processing. Start-up companies like Pix4D, Pointivo, and Datumate offer cloud photogrammetry processing services, with data collection by drones or by cameras mounted on high vantage points around a construction site (such as atop tower cranes). **Bentley ContextCapture** is another powerful photogrammetry tool, producing surface models with overlaid images that can be viewed with **Bentley Acute3D**. **Indoor Reality** provides a portable data collection pack that incorporates range finders, cameras, laser scanners, and other sensors to compile a 3D mesh of an indoor scene with high resolution raster images mapped onto it, enabling engineers to view, measure, and annotate the models.

However, for recording as-built conditions and comparing with design intent, there is a significant caveat. As we discussed in Section 5.3.1, point cloud data cannot be converted into BIM data automatically. There are numerous research efforts in this direction, but it remains a problem to be solved and is discussed in Chapter 9. From a contractor's point of view, this means that the data collected using these methods will require work on the part of engineers to extract useful information such as quantities, volumes, or object identities.

6.13 COST AND SCHEDULE CONTROL AND OTHER MANAGEMENT FUNCTIONS

During the construction process, organizations use a variety of tools and processes to manage and report on the project's status. These range from schedule and cost control systems to systems for accounting, procurement, payroll, safety, and the like. Many of these systems report or rely on design and building component information, yet they are not typically linked or associated with design drawings or BIM models. This leads to redundant efforts of manually entering design information and identifying problems associated with the synchronization of various systems and processes. BIM software can provide vital support for these tasks, because it has detailed quantity and other component information that can be linked to other applications. Furthermore, contractors and project stakeholders can gain new insights by leveraging a graphic model to visually analyze project progress and highlight potential or existing problems. Following are some examples of how organizations are using BIM to support these tasks.

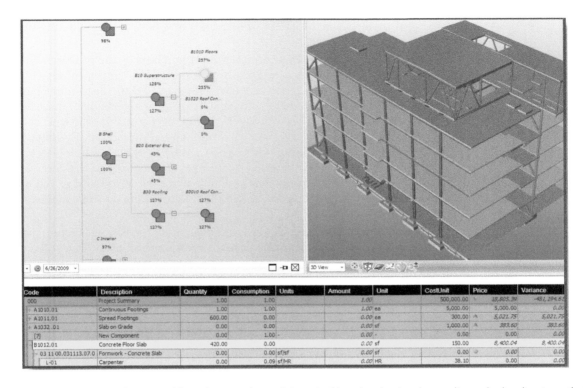

Code	Description	Quantity	Consumption	Units	Amount	Unit	CostUnit	Price	Variance
000	Project Summary	1.00	1.00		1.00		500,000.00	18,805.39	-481,294.61
A1010.01	Continuous Footings	1.00	1.00		1.00	ea	5,000.00	5,000.00	0.00
A1011.01	Spread Footings	600.00	0.00		0.00	ea	300.00	5,021.75	5,021.75
A1032.01	Slab on Grade	0.00	0.00		0.00	sf	1,000.00	393.60	393.60
[?]	New Component	0.00	1.00	-	0.00	-	0.00	0.00	0.00
B1012.01	Concrete Floor Slab	420.00	0.00		0.00	sf	150.00	8,400.04	8,400.04
03 11 00.031113.07.0	Formwork - Concrete Slab	0.00	0.00	sf/sf	0.00	sf	0.00	0.00	0.00
L-01	Carpenter	0.00	0.09	sf/HR	0.00	HR	38.10	0.00	0.00

FIGURE 6–21 Vico Cost Planner. Building objects in the model can be filtered and colored according to budget line items that reflect their cost, budget, or other financial properties.

- **Track variances between budget and actual cost:** Using the **Vico Cost Planner**, a user can import actual costs into the Vico model, and then visually see where there are significant variances between cost and budget using the model. This allows quick understanding of project performance and where the key problems are, as illustrated in Figure 6–21.

- **Viewing project status:** Each model object can have a field named "status," and depending on the project, values may be "in design," "approved for construction review," "in fabrication," and so forth. These fields can then be associated with colors so that the team can quickly determine the status of the facility and identify bottlenecks or areas that are behind schedule. Animations of models with as-built schedule records can be compared with 4D plans to get a sense of the pace of work, or for forensic analysis of schedules. The same can be done with sequences of 3D mesh models obtained over time from point cloud data.

- **Procurement, purchasing:** Since BIM objects define what needs to be purchased, it is possible to locate products and make purchases directly using the BIM tool. Product manufacturers provide models of their products on Internet servers. A good example of a BIM procurement application is **bimobject's BIMsupply** service, with which users can create bills of materials and tenders, solicit bids, and place orders directly from a model.

- **Supply chain tracking:** Another important issue is the procurement status of services and materials. Often, schedules consist of large numbers of construction activities, which makes it difficult to relate parallel design and procurement activities. By tracking the status of these activities, planners can perform queries to easily identify gaps in the procurement process as they relate to design and construction. By linking the schedule to a building information model, it is also possible to visualize where procurement delays are likely to impact the building. Cloud services such as **ManufactOn** enable contractors to manage the whole specification, procurement, detailing, fabrication, delivery, and installation process.

- **Safety management:** Safety is a critical issue for all construction organizations. Any tool that supports safety training and education, and reveals unsafe conditions is valuable to the construction team. A visual model allows teams to assess conditions and identify unsafe areas that might otherwise go unrealized until the team is in the field. For example, on a theme park project, a team modeled envelopes for testing rides to ensure that no activities were taking place during the testing period within the test envelope. Using 4D simulation, they identified a conflict and resolved it ahead of time. For construction of a large steel frame that envelops two buildings of the Yas Island project in Abu Dhabi, cylinders were used to model the spaces occupied by the activities of welding crews; clash detection between cylinders was then used to identify possible exposures of workers to dangers posed by other teams from time to time.

New York City's Department of Buildings is responsible for regulating construction, including site safety, across the city's numerous construction sites. In 2013, the department pioneered the use of BIM models for safety reviews, allowing construction companies to file Site Safety Plans as BIM models. *"The program enables the Department to virtually tour sites and see step-by-step how a building will be built and visualize its complexities and challenges. Under the program, Site Safety Plans are digitally submitted, amended and reviewed, improving the compliance review process and accelerating the approval process like never before."* (NYC, 2013).

6.14 COMMISSIONING AND TURNOVER

At the end of construction there are two important issues that must be addressed. The first is *commissioning,* which consists of testing that all the systems installed in the building (or other type of facility) are working properly. This includes HVAC, electrical, plumbing, and so forth. The second important process is the *turnover* of the data that was generated during the design and construction phases so that it can be used for facility management (FM). What data is given to the owner and its format are of vital importance and will determine its utility to the owner. There are at least three approaches to turning over the information the owner will need for FM:

1. Give the owner the paper drawings (or equivalent pdf files), system diagrams, project change orders, logs, and other information about the equipment and systems used. This traditional approach has proven to be costly and very ineffective in supporting owners' FM needs. This approach is not recommended.

2. Assuming that BIM has been used and the appropriate equipment and systems data has been entered into the model, this data can be extracted according to the COBie (East, 2007). The key to successful use of COBie is the inclusion of the appropriate data and naming standards by the contractor and subs at the proper points in time so that this information will be available at turnover. This process needs to be covered by the BIM execution plan (BEP) between the owner or the owner's representative and the members of the project team (see Section 4.5.1 in Chapter 4).

3. To obtain lifecycle support of the BIM model for both FM functions and for use of the model for building modifications, one can integrate these systems in BIM for FM services such as ***Ecodomus***. This has many benefits for building management, but to achieve these the model must include all appropriate equipment and systems connectivity information. Connectivity can be effectively modeled in BIM systems like ***I&E Systems' DAD software***, which builds a "Systems Information Model" (SIM; Love et al., 2016) during design that is naturally carried over to operations and maintenance. It also requires early integration of FM staff into the project team, so that their needs will be reflected in the building design and use of the model when linked to the FM systems.

These issues are discussed in Section 4.4.2 and in three case studies in Chapter 10 (Medina Airport, Stanford Hospital, and Howard Hughes Research Facility) and in the Maryland General Hospital case study in the *BIM Handbook* companion website. Another useful reference is *BIM for Facility Managers* (Teicholz, et al., 2013).

Chapter 6 Discussion Questions

1. Why does the use of BIM favor the design-build contract over design-bid-build contracts? For public projects, why are design-bid-build contracts often preferred (see also Chapter 1, Section 1.2.5)?

2. What are the key innovations in procurement in IPD contracts? How do they change the commercial interests of construction contractors in construction projects? What uses

of BIM are enabled by an IPD contract, as opposed to design-bid-build or even design-build contracts?

3. What kinds of information do contractors expect to obtain from a BIM model? What part of this information can designers (architects and/or engineers) provide, and what can they not provide?

4. What are the key synergies between BIM and Lean Construction? How can the use of BIM improve production flow for a general contractor?

5. Sometimes BIM models are available to a contractor, but sometimes only 2D drawings are provided. Depending on the types of available information, the contractor must deploy a different approach to implement BIM in a construction project. What approaches are available to the contractor? What are the limitations and benefits of each approach?

6. What level of detail is needed in a building model for useful clash detection? What are the reasons for detecting soft as opposed to hard clashes? What role do subcontractors play in the clash detection process?

7. What are the key benefits of co-locating construction detailing teams in a Big Room? How does BIM support their collaboration?

8. What are the main advantages and limitations of using BIM to prepare a cost estimate? How can an estimator link the building model to an estimating system? What changes are likely to the model to provide support for accurate quantity takeoff?

9. What are the basic requirements for performing a 4D analysis of a construction schedule? What are the contractor's options for obtaining the information needed to carry out this analysis? What major benefits can be obtained from this analysis?

10. What are the requirements for using a building model for offsite fabrication?

11. Consider the St. Joseph Hospital Mortenson case study (Section 10.5). In what specific ways did use of BIM make the project processes leaner? In what ways did the contractor fail to exploit the model to apply lean construction?

12. What modes of communication can BIM fulfill for workers on-site? How can the extensive and detailed information collected on-site serve contractors best?

13. How can a contractor ensure that the model information can be used for FM after turnover?

BIM for Subcontractors and Fabricators

Buildings are becoming increasingly complex. They are one-of-a-kind products requiring multidisciplinary design and fabrication skills. Specialization of the construction trades and economies of prefabrication contribute to increasingly larger proportions of buildings' components and systems being preassembled or fabricated off-site. Unlike mass production of off-the-shelf parts, however, complex buildings require customized design and fabrication of "engineered to order" (ETO) components, including: structural steel; precast concrete structures and architectural façades; curtain walls of various types; mechanical, electrical and plumbing (MEP) systems; timber roof trusses; and reinforced concrete tilt-up panels.

By their nature, ETO components demand sophisticated engineering and careful collaboration between designers to ensure that pieces fit within the building properly without interfering with other building systems and interface correctly with other systems. Design and coordination with 2D CAD systems is error-prone, labor-intensive, and reliant on long cycle times. BIM addresses these problems in that it allows for the "virtual construction" of components and coordination among all building systems prior to producing each piece. The benefits of BIM for subcontractors and fabricators include: enhanced marketing and rendering through visual images and automated estimating; reduced cycle times for detailed design and production; elimination of almost all design coordination errors and concomitant reduction of requests for information (RFIs) and their associated costs and delays; lower engineering and detailing costs; data to drive automated manufacturing technologies; and improved preassembly and prefabrication.

Accurate, reliable, and ubiquitous information is critical to the flow of products in any supply chain. For this reason, BIM systems can enable leaner construction methods if harnessed across an organization's many departments or through the entire supply chain. The extent and depth of these process changes goes hand in hand with the extent to which the building information models developed by participating organizations are integrated.

To be useful for fabrication detailing, BIM platforms need to support at least parametric and customizable parts and relationships, provide interfaces to management information systems, and be able to import building model information from building designers' BIM platforms. Ideally, they should also provide good information for model visualizations and export data in forms suitable for automation of fabrication tasks using computer-controlled machinery. Within this chapter, the major classes of fabricators and their specific needs are discussed. For each fabricator type, appropriate BIM software platforms and tools are listed and the leading ones are surveyed.

Finally, the chapter provides guidance for companies planning adoption of BIM. To successfully introduce BIM into a fabrication plant with its own in-house engineering staff, or into an engineering detailing service provider, adoption must begin with setting clear, achievable goals with measurable milestones. Human resource considerations are the leading concern not only because the costs of training and setup of software to suit local practices far exceed the costs of hardware and software, but also because the success of any BIM adoption will depend on the skill and goodwill of the people tasked with using the technology.

7.1   INTRODUCTION

The professional gap between designers and builders that became pronounced during the European Renaissance has continued to widen over the centuries, while building systems have grown increasingly complex and technologically advanced. Over time, builders became more and more specialized and began to produce building parts off-site, first in craft shops and later in industrial facilities for subsequent assembly on-site. As a result, designers had less and less control over the entire design; expert knowledge for any given system lay within the realm of specialized fabricators. Technical drawings and specifications on paper became the essential medium for communication. Designers communicate their intent to builders, and builders detail their proposed solutions. The builder's drawings, commonly called "shop drawings," serve two purposes: to develop and detail the designs for production and, no less importantly, to communicate their construction intent back to the designers for coordination and approval.

In fact, the two-way cycle of communication is not simply a review but an integral part of designing a building. Furthermore, where multiple systems are fabricated—and this is the case for all but the simplest buildings—their design must be integrated consistently to properly coordinate the location and function of various building system parts. In traditional practice, paper drawings and specifications prepared by fabricators for designers fulfill additional vital purposes. They are a key part of commercial contracts for the procurement of fabricators' products. They are used directly for installation and construction, and they are also the primary means for storing information generated through the design and construction process. For subcontractors and fabricators, BIM supports the whole collaborative process of design development, detailing, and integration. In many recorded cases, BIM has been leveraged to enable greater degrees of prefabrication than was possible without it, by shortening lead times and deepening design integration. As noted in Chapter 2, object-based parametric design platforms had already been developed and used to support many construction activities, such as structural steel fabrication, before the earliest comprehensive BIM platforms became available.

Beyond local impacts on productivity and quality, BIM enables fundamental process changes, because it provides the power to manage the intense amount of information required for "mass customization," which is a key precept of lean production (Womack and Jones, 2003). As the use of BIM and lean construction methods (Howell, 1999) becomes widespread, subcontractors and fabricators increasingly find that market forces compel them to provide customized prefabricated building components at price levels previously appropriate for mass-produced repetitive components. In manufacturing, this is called "mass customization." The facades of the Dongdaemun Design Plaza project in Seoul, South Korea (Section 10.4), and of the 100 11th Avenue, project in New York City (see the *BIM Handbook* companion website) provide good examples—every piece had different geometry. The lack of skilled labor in developed economies is another driver of increased prefabrication and modular construction.

After defining the context for our discussion (Section 7.2), this chapter describes the potential benefits of BIM for improving various facets of the fabrication process from the perspective of the subcontractor or fabricator responsible for making and installing building parts (Section 7.3). BIM system requirements for effective use by fabricators are listed and explained for modeling and detailing in general (Section 7.4). Detailed information is provided for a number of specific trades (Section 7.5) and for the case of comprehensive modular construction, and the significant software packages for fabricators are listed. Pertinent issues concerning the adoption and use of BIM are discussed (Section 7.6).

7.2   TYPES OF SUBCONTRACTORS AND FABRICATORS

Subcontractor trades and fabricators perform a very wide range of specialized tasks in construction. Most are identified by the type of work they do or the type of components they fabricate.

The type of work done on-site ranges from craft work, in which raw materials are transformed into finished products on one end of the scale, to erection and installation of prefabricated components on the other end. Building partitions from masonry blocks or from gypsum drywall boards are examples of trades where the work done on-site is the major part of the value they add. By contrast, installation on-site of machinery or prefinished modular volumetric units is a small part of the value of such components.

The types of components fabricated for use in construction can be classified by the degree of engineering design required in their manufacture. Looking beyond bulk raw materials, building components can be classified as belonging to one of three types:

- **Made-to-stock components (MTS)** are mass produced and available for immediate delivery. Examples include standard plumbing fixtures, dry-wall panels and studs, pipe sections, and the like.
- **Made-to-order components (MTO)** are predesigned but only fabricated once an order is placed. Prestressed hollow-core planks,[1] windows, and doors selected from catalogs are all MTO components.
- **Engineered-to-order components (ETO)** require engineering design before they can be fabricated. Examples are the members of structural steel frames, structural precast concrete pieces, façade panels of various types, custom kitchens and other cabinet-ware, and any other component customized to fit a specific location and fulfill certain building functions. Modular construction with off-site prefabrication is a special case, in which thoroughly integrated engineering design is required.

Made-to-stock and made-to-order components are designed for general use and not customized for specific applications.[2] Most BIM platforms enable suppliers to provide electronic catalogs of their products, allowing designers to embed representative objects and direct links to them in building information models. The suppliers of these components are rarely involved in their installation or assembly on-site, nor are they participants in the design and construction process. For this reason, this chapter focuses primarily on the needs of designers, coordinators, fabricators, and installers of building components of the third type: engineered-to-order (ETO) components.

---

[1] Hollow-core planks are pre-engineered but can be custom-cut to arbitrary lengths.

[2] They are distinguished in that MTO components are only produced as needed, usually for commercial or technological reasons, such as high inventory costs or short shelf life.

7.2.1 Subcontractor Trades

Most of the trades that perform work on-site can benefit from the BIM functionality that is useful also for the general contractor, for spatial coordination, scheduling, budgeting, production planning, and so on. However, they can also benefit in a number of ways from BIM support for production planning and control, all of which have the highly desirable effect of reducing waste and making processes leaner, but this requires that models be detailed to fabrication levels (LOD 400). The following list details specific ways in which the trades can leverage the information contained in models, and more detail can be found in Sacks et al. (2017). Where the subcontractor has its own BIM capabilities, these can be exploited directly, but where trade crews do not have the resources to manipulate the model themselves, they should demand the necessary modeling from the general contractor.

- **Estimating and bidding:** Quantities taken off from a BIM model are, in general, far more accurate and reliable than quantities measured from drawings. This removes a degree of uncertainty from the bidding process, reducing the potential for risky cost estimates and for conflicts concerning scope and quantity of work.

- **Optimizing production level details:** The small details of the work can sometimes have a big impact on productivity. For example, the layout of floor or wall tiles, or of masonry blocks, can be optimized to reduce the quantity of cut tiles or blocks that are needed. This is quite easily done in BIM (as shown in Figure 7–1, for example), and it can reduce the amount of non-value-adding work that is needed for cutting or otherwise shaping raw materials on-site, thus improving productivity.

- **Logistics:** Detail the work to be done to obtain precise quantities of materials, and ensure that the right amounts are delivered to the right place at the right time (see Figure 7–2). This will save much time in material handling, whether due to shortfalls that have to be brought in or for removing excess materials. Shortfalls also lead to waiting for the trade crews until the quantities are brought in, lowering productivity.

- **Spatial coordination:** Fabrication level detailing and coordination between systems will also allow resolution in advance of many of the physical conflicts that might otherwise arise on-site. For example, if a wall is detailed with all of its layers—masonry, insulation, interior finish, and so on—the intersections where walls meet can be properly planned and workers do not need to improvise.

- **Layout:** As described in Section 6.12.1, there are numerous ways in which models can be used to provide design information directly to the field. These are labor-saving techniques that not only save the time of reading drawings and measuring distances, but they also ensure that the right information (i.e., up to date) is used, greatly reducing the probability of rework.

- **Measuring and updating the as-built state:** Measuring the work done, whether for submitting accounts or for recording as-built documentation, is both more efficient and more accurate using models. It is also essential for spatial coordination of fabricated parts to match existing conditions on site.

FIGURE 7–1 A masonry partition wall detailed for fabrication (LOD 400). This level of detail allows optimization of the block layout to reduce the need for cutting blocks to a minimum, and it also enables accurate quantity take-off of all the necessary block shapes and sizes for delivery.

Image courtesy of Tidhar Construction.

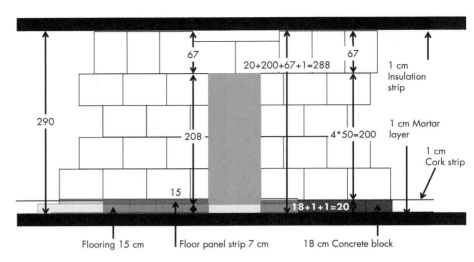

FIGURE 7–2 An isometric view of the layout plan for placing pallets of masonry blocks for partition walls on the story of a reinforced concrete residential building, showing the type of block in each pallet and their placement between the planned locations of shoring poles that support the slab formwork. These visual instructions are provided to crane operators and signalers, ensuring delivery of the right materials to the tight place for the masonry trade crews.

Image courtesy of Tidhar Construction.

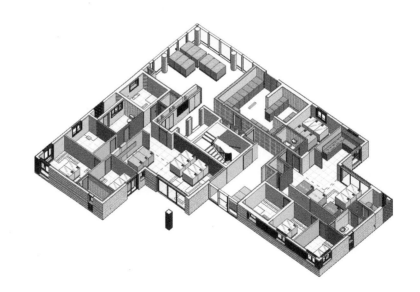

7.2.2 Made-to-Stock and Made-to-Order Component Suppliers

Both MTO and MTS components are produced according to standard designs. Manufacturers provide catalogs of their products, and it is very common for these to be provided as "BIM Object Models" (BOM). There are numerous online portals from which designers and detailers can select products—some of the more well-known portals are listed in Table 5-4, in Section 5.4 of the book, where we describe designers' use of BIM object libraries. In practice, the facility with which these objects can be located and inserted in BIM models is of most use to contractors, because it is often only at the stage of production detailing that the final decisions are made as to which specific products will be used in construction, and from which specific suppliers they will be procured.

Detailing the model with the precise components that will be used in construction has numerous advantages. Specific components may give rise to spatial conflicts and may require specific installation clearances. They may have unique requirements for electrical, plumbing, or other service connections. They can be counted automatically and precisely for order and delivery, and in some cases, they can be tracked as they move through the supply chain to the site, and that information can be displayed using the model.

7.2.3 Engineered-to-Order Component Fabricators

Engineered-to-order (ETO) components include a wide range of products, from basic prefabricated components or precast products to complete Prefinished Prefabricated Volumetric Construction (PPVC) components, as shown in Figure 7–3. PPVC modules are the highest level ETO components. These are complete building modules that are lifted into place in a building, connected to utilities, and are essentially ready for occupation. The Singapore Building

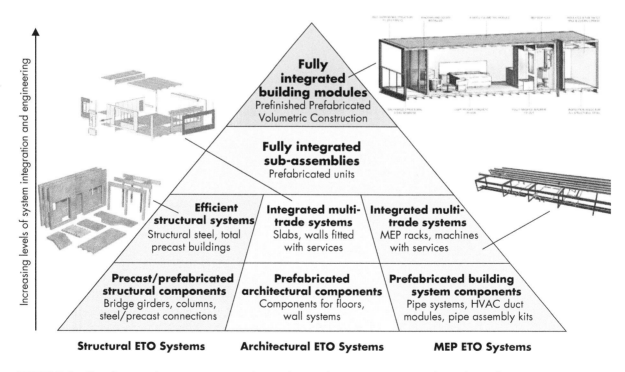

FIGURE 7–3 Classification of components, according to degree of system integration and completion, for use in government programs to promote "Design for Manufacturing and Assembly" (DfMA), based on the classification system used by the Singapore government Building Construction Authority (BCA) for public construction projects incentive schemes.

Construction Authority (BCA) defines PPVC as "a construction method whereby free-standing volumetric modules (complete with finishes for walls, floors and ceilings) are: (a) constructed and assembled; or (b) manufactured and assembled, in an accredited fabrication facility, in accordance with any accredited fabrication method, and then installed in a building under building works." At lower levels, the degree of finishing of the building modules and the degree of system integration reduce, but the common thread is that all of them require project-specific engineering work before they can be fabricated.

ETO producers typically operate production facilities that manufacture components that need to be designed and engineered prior to production. In most cases, they are subcontracted to a building's general contractor or, in the case of a project being executed by a construction management service company, they are subcontracted to the owner. The subcontract typically encompasses detailed design, engineering, fabrication, and erection or installation of their products. Although some companies maintain large in-house engineering departments, their core business is fabrication. Others outsource part or all of their engineering work to independent consultants (dedicated design service providers; see Section 7.2.4). They may also subcontract erection or installation of their product on-site to independent companies.

In addition, there are building construction trades that do not function exclusively as ETO producers but offer significant ETO component content as part of their systems. Examples are plumbing, heating, ventilation and air-conditioning (HVAC), elevators and escalators, and finish carpentry.

7.2.4   Design Service Providers and Specialist Coordinators

Design service providers offer engineering services to producers of engineered-to-order components. They perform work on a fee basis and generally do not participate in actual fabrication and on-site installation of the components they design. Service firms include: structural steel detailers, precast concrete design and detailing engineers, and specialized façade and curtain wall consultants, among others. As one moves up the scale of ETO component classification (Figure 7–3), the need for integration of multiple systems demands closer coordination among architects, building systems designers, and engineering consultants.

Designers of tilt-up concrete construction panels are a good example of design service providers for ETO products in the third class. Their expertise in engineering, designing, and preparing shop drawings enables general contractors or specialized production crews to make large reinforced concrete wall panels in horizontal beds on-site and then lift (or tilt) them into place. This on-site fabrication method can be implemented by relatively small contracting companies, by virtue of the availability of these design service providers.

Specialist coordinators provide a comprehensive ETO product provision service by bringing together designers, material suppliers, and fabricators under a "virtual" subcontracting company. The rationale behind their work is that they offer flexibility in the kinds of technical solutions they provide, because they do not have their own fixed production lines. This type of service is common in the provision of curtain walls and other architectural façades. The 100 11th Avenue, New York, case study (see the *BIM Handbook* companion website); the Dongdaemun Design Plaza, Seoul, case study (Section 10.4); and the Fondation Louis Vuitton, Paris, case study (Section 10.3) are good examples of this kind of arrangement. The designers of the façade system assembled an ad hoc virtual subcontractor composed of a material supplier, a fabricator, an installer, and a construction management firm.

7.2.5 Full-Service Design-Build Prefabricated and Modular Construction

One of the ways to fully exploit the economies of prefabrication and modular construction is to implement the high degree of integration needed within a single full-service, vertically integrated company. In this context, BIM can be used as a hub of information that can flow smoothly through the whole process. Designers can consider the firms' proprietary fabrication and construction capabilities from the earliest steps of schematic design. Throughout the design and detailing process, company standards can be applied through the use of BIM component libraries that are pre-configured to use the proprietary construction methods.

This business model goes against the common wisdom of general contractors reducing their internal staff to a minimum, outsourcing as much of the work as possible, which has traditionally been the response of companies to the uncertainties and instability of demand for construction work in their local regions. Yet where production is moved off-site, and information can be managed with BIM and production IT systems, there appears to be renewed value in the full-service model. **Katerra**, a full-service company based in California, adopted this model and achieved remarkable market value in a relatively short time. Katerra provides mass-customization with intensive use of computer software. It prefabricates floor systems and exterior and interior wall panels in the company's own plants.

7.3 THE BENEFITS OF A BIM PROCESS FOR SUBCONTRACTOR FABRICATORS

Figure 7–4 shows a typical traditional information and product flow for ETO components in building construction. The process has three major parts: project acquisition (preliminary design and tendering), detailed design (engineering and coordination), and fabrication (including delivery and installation). The process includes cycles that allow the design proposal to be formulated and revised, repeatedly if necessary. This typically occurs at the detailed design stage, where the fabricator is required to obtain feedback and approval from the building's designers, subject not only to their own requirements but also to the coordination of the fabricator's design with other building systems also in development. There are many problems with the

FIGURE 7–4 Typical traditional information and product flow for a fabricator of ETO components.

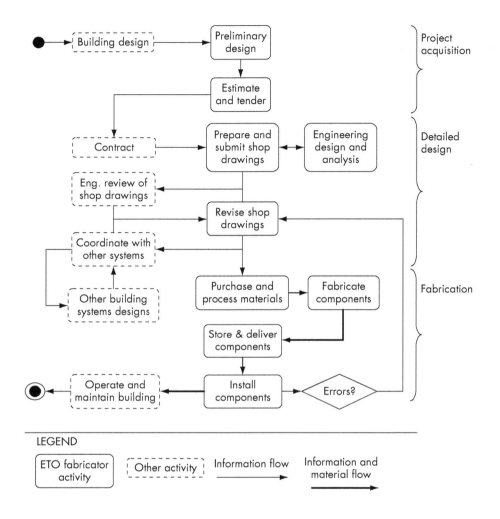

existing process. It is labor intensive, with much of the effort spent producing and updating documents. Sets of drawings and other documents have high rates of inaccuracies and inconsistencies, which are often not discovered until erection of the products on-site. The same information is entered into computer programs multiple times, each time for a distinct and separate use. The workflow has so many intermediate points for review that rework is common and cycle times are long.

Leveraging BIM can improve the process in several ways. First, BIM can improve the efficiency of most existing steps in the traditional 2D CAD process by increasing productivity and eliminating the need to manually maintain consistency across multiple drawing files. With deeper implementation, however, BIM changes the process itself by enabling degrees of prefabrication that remain prohibitive in coordination costs with existing information systems. When implemented in the context of lean construction techniques, such as with pull flow[3] control of detailing, production, and installation, BIM can substantially reduce lead times and make the construction process more flexible and less wasteful. In this section, the short-term benefits are first explained in an approximated chronological sequence with reference to the process map shown in Figure 7–4. Section 7.4 discusses the more fundamental process change.

7.3.1 Marketing and Tendering

Preliminary design and estimating are essential activities for obtaining work for most subcontractor fabricators. To win a project with a profitable price requires precision in measuring quantities, attention to detail, and the ability to develop a competitive technical solution—all of which demand significant time investments by the company's most knowledgeable engineers. Generally, not all tenders are successful, and companies are required to estimate more projects than are eventually performed, making the cost of tendering a sizable part of the company's overhead.

BIM technology aids engineers in all three of these areas: developing multiple alternatives, detailing solutions to a reasonable degree, and measuring quantities.

For marketing purposes, the persuasive power of a building model for a potential client is not limited to its ability to provide a 3D or photorealistic image of a proposed building design. Its power lies in its ability to adapt and change designs parametrically and better exploit the embedded engineering knowledge, allowing for more rapid design development for satisfying clients' needs to the greatest extent possible. The following excerpt describes the story of a precast concrete estimator's experience using a BIM tool to develop and sell a design for a parking garage:

"To give you some background on this project, we started it as a design-build project for one of the salesmen. Bill modeled the entire garage (240′ wide × 585′ long × 5 supported levels), without connections or reinforcing, in 8 hours. It is composed of 1,250 pieces. We sent PDF images to the owner, architect, and engineer.

The next morning, we had a conference call with the client and received a number of modifications. Bill modified the model by 1:30 pm. I printed out the plan, elevations, and generated a web viewer model. I sent these to the client at 1:50 pm via email. We then had another conference call at 2:00 pm. Two days later, we had the project. The owner was ecstatic about seeing a model

(continued)

---

[3] Pull flow is a method for regulating the flow of work in a production system whereby production at any station is signaled to begin only when an "order" for a part is received from the next station downstream. This is in contrast to traditional methods where production is "pushed" by schedule directives from a central authority. In this context, pull flow implies that detailing and fabrication of components for any particular building section would begin only a short preset time before installation became possible for that section.

of his garage. Oddly enough, it's supposed to be 30 miles from our competitor's plant. In fact, their construction arm is who we will be contracted to.

We figured it would have taken two weeks in 2D to get to where we were in 3D. When we had the turnover meeting (a meeting we have to turn over scope from estimating to engineering, drafting, and production) we projected the model on a screen to go over the scope of work. It went just as we envisioned. It was exciting to see it actually happen that way."

The project referenced in this excerpt—the Penn National Parking Structure—is documented in further detail in the first edition of this book (Eastman et al., 2008), and available from the *BIM Handbook* companion website. The example underscores how shortened response times—obtained using BIM—enabled the company to better address the client's decision-making process. Alternative structural layout configurations were considered. For each, the producer automatically extracted a quantity takeoff that listed the precast pieces required. These quantities enabled the provision of cost estimates for each, allowing the owner and general contractor to reach an informed decision concerning which configuration to adopt.

7.3.2 Reduced Production Cycle Times

The use of BIM significantly reduces the time required to generate shop drawings and material takeoffs for procurement. This can be leveraged in three ways:

- To offer a superior level of service to building owners, for whom late changes are often essential, by accommodating changes later in the process than is possible in standard 2D CAD practice. Making changes to building designs that impact fabricated pieces close to the time of fabrication is very difficult in standard practice. Each change must propagate through all of the assembly and shop drawings that may be affected and must also coordinate with drawings that reflect adjacent or connected components to the piece that changed. Where the change affects multiple building systems provided by different fabricators or subcontractors, coordination becomes far more complex and time-consuming. With BIM platforms, the changes are entered into the model and updated erection and shop drawings are produced almost automatically. The benefit is enormous in terms of time and effort required to properly implement the change.
- To enable a "pull production system" where the preparation of shop drawings is driven by the production sequence. Short lead times reduce the system's "inventory" of design information, making it less vulnerable to changes in the first place. Shop drawings are produced once a majority of changes have already been made. This minimizes the likelihood that additional changes will be needed. In this "lean" system, shop drawings are produced at the last responsible moment.

- To make prefabricated solutions viable in projects with restricted lead times between the contract date and the date demanded for the commencement of on-site construction, which would ordinarily prohibit their use. Often, general contractors find themselves committing to construction start dates with lead times that are shorter than the time required to convert conventional building system designs to prefabricated ones, due to the long lead times needed for production design using 2D CAD. For example, a building designed with a cast-in-place concrete structure requires, on average, two to three months for conversion to precast concrete before the first required pieces can be produced. In contrast, BIM systems shorten the duration of design to a point where more components with longer lead times can be prefabricated earlier.

These benefits derive from the high degree of automation that BIM systems are capable of achieving, when attempting to generate and communicate detailed fabrication and erection information. Parametric relationships between building model objects (that implement basic design knowledge) and their data attributes (that enable systems to compute and report meaningful information for production processes) are the two features of BIM systems that make these improvements possible. This technology is reviewed in detail in Chapter 2.

A reduction in cycle time can be achieved by exploiting automation for the production of shop drawings. The extent of this benefit has been explored in numerous research projects. In the structural steel fabrication industry, fabricators reported almost a 50% savings in time for the engineering detailing stage (Crowley, 2003b). The General Motors Production Plant case study, reported in the first edition of this book, documented a project with a 50% reduction of overall design-construction time compared to traditional design-bid-build projects (although some of this reduction can be attributed to the lean management and other technologies that were used in addition to 3D models of the structural steel). An early but detailed evaluation of lead-time reduction in the case of architectural precast concrete façade panels was performed within the framework of a research project initiated by a consortium of precast concrete companies (Sacks, 2004). The first Gantt chart in Figure 7–5 shows a baseline process for engineering the design of an office building's façade panels. The benchmark represents the shortest theoretical duration of the project using 2D CAD, if work had been performed continuously and without interruption. The benchmark was obtained by reducing the durations measured for each activity in the actual project to the net number of hours that the project team worked on them. The second Gantt chart shows an estimated timeline for the same project, if performed using an available 3D parametric modeling system. In this case, the reduction in lead time decreased from the baseline minimum of 80 working days to 34 working days.

7.3.3 Reduced Design Coordination Errors

In the introduction to this chapter, we mentioned the need for fabricators to communicate construction intent to designers. One of the reasons for this is

FIGURE 7–5 (A) A benchmark of production lead time for engineering design and detailing of architectural precast façade panels using 2D CAD. (B) An evaluation of a comparable lead time using 3D parametric modeling (Sacks, 2004).

Reproduced from the *Journal of Computing in Civil Engineering* 18(4), by permission of the American Society of Civil Engineers.

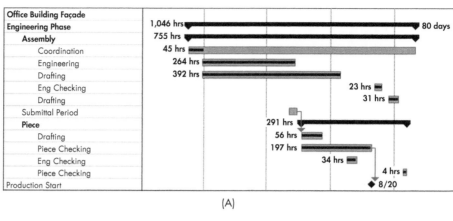

(A)

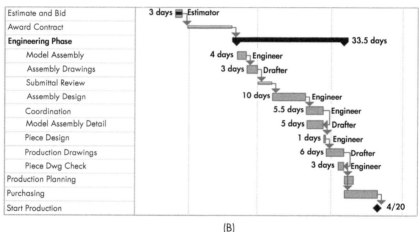

(B)

that the information obtained through the submittal and approval process is essential to the design team as a whole. It allows the team to identify potential conflicts inherent in the design. A physical clash between two components, where they are destined to occupy the same physical space, is the most obvious problem, and is termed a hard clash. Soft clashes occur when components are placed too close to one another, albeit not in physical contact, such as rebars that are too close to allow for the proper placing of concrete, or pipes that require adequate space for insulation. Soft clashes are sometimes referred to as clearance clashes. Logical clashes are a third type and include constructability problems, where certain components obstruct the construction or erection of other components, and access problems, where access needed for operation, service, or dismounting of equipment is obstructed.

When design coordination is incomplete, hard clashes[4] are discovered on-site during installation of the second component. Regardless of who carries the legal and financial liability for the resulting rework and delays, the

---

[4] See Section 6.7 for a detailed definition of clash types.

fabricators inevitably suffer. Construction is leaner when work is predictable and uninterrupted.

BIM offers numerous technical benefits that improve design coordination at all stages. Of particular interest to fabricators is the ability to create integrated models of potentially conflicting systems at production-detail levels. BIM tools for model integration, such as **Autodesk Navisworks Manage** and **Tekla BIMsight**, import models from various platforms into a single environment for identifying clashes. The clashes are identified automatically and reported to the users (this application is discussed in Chapter 6, in Section 6.7). Current technology limitations prevent the resolution of clashes directly, because one cannot make corrections in the integrated environment and then port them back to the originating platform. It is possible, however, to generate a record of the problem in a BIM Collaboration Format (BCF) file, which can then be opened in the original BIM platform itself. This allows engineers to see the problem in the same view in the BIM platform, where they can implement any changes needed to correct the issue. Repeating the cycle of importing the models to the review software enables close to real-time coordination, especially if the detailers for the trades are co-located.

To avoid design coordination conflicts, the best practice is for detailed design to be performed in parallel and within collaborative work environments involving all of the fabricating trades. This avoids the almost inevitable need for rework in the detailed design, even when conflicts in the completed designs have already been identified and resolved. Most BIM Execution Plans include specific provisions for system coordination in advance of detailing, and for collaborative processes to resolve clashes if they do occur. In BIM "Big Rooms," where designers, contractors, and trade subcontractor partners are co-located, detailers for plumbing, HVAC, sprinkler systems, electrical conduits, and other systems detail their systems in close proximity with one another and in direct response to the progress of fabrication and installation of the systems on-site. Experience in many projects around the world has repeatedly shown that under these conditions, very few coordination errors reached the job site itself.

Another significant waste occurs when inconsistencies appear within the fabricator's own drawing sets. Traditional sets, whether drawn by hand or using CAD, contain multiple representations of each individual artifact. Designers and drafters are required to maintain consistency between the various drawings as the design development progresses and further changes are made. Despite quality control systems of various kinds, entirely error-free drawing sets are rare. A detailed study of drawing errors in the precast concrete industry, covering some 37,500 pieces from various projects and producers, showed that the costs of design coordination errors amount to approximately 0.46% of total project costs (Sacks, 2004).

Two views of drawings of a precast concrete beam are shown in Figure 7–6. They serve as a good example of how discrepancies can occur. Figure 7–6(A) shows a concrete beam in an elevation view of the outside of the building; and Figure 7–6(B) shows the same beam in a piece fabrication shop drawing. The external face of the beam had brick facing, which is fabricated by placing the bricks face down in the mold. The shop drawing should have shown the back of the beam up, with the bare concrete (internal to the building) face-up in plan view. Due to a drafting oversight, the inversion was not made and the

FIGURE 7-6 Drawing inconsistency for a precast concrete spandrel beam: (A) elevation, (B) piece fabrication shop drawing drawn in mirror image in error, and (C) the beams in place with mismatched end connection details (Sacks et al., 2003).

Reproduced from the Journal of the Precast/ Prestressed Concrete Institute 48(3), with permission of the Precast/Prestressed Concrete Institute.

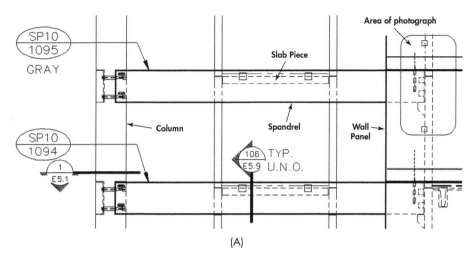

(A)

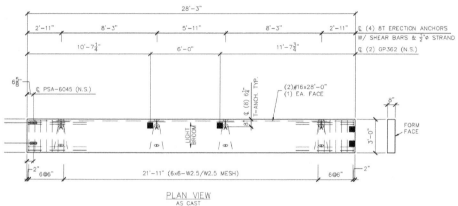

PLAN VIEW
AS CAST

(B)

(C)

beam was shown with the external face up, which resulted in all eight beams in this project being fabricated as "mirror images" of the actual beams needed. They could not be erected as planned—see Figure 7–6(C)—which resulted in expensive rework, reduced quality, and construction delays.

7.3.4 Lower Engineering and Detailing Costs
BIM reduces direct engineering costs in three ways:

- Through the increased use of automated design and analysis software
- Almost fully automated production of drawings and material takeoffs
- Reduced rework due to enhanced quality control and design coordination

One major difference between BIM and CAD is that building information objects can be programmed to display seemingly "intelligent" behaviors. This means that the preprocessing of data for analysis software of various kinds, from thermal and ventilation analyses to dynamic structural analyses, can be performed directly from BIM data or within the BIM platform itself. For example, most BIM platforms used for structural systems enable the definition of loads, load cases, support conditions, material properties, and all other data needed for structural analyses, such as finite element analysis.

It also means that BIM systems can allow designers to adopt a top-down design development approach, where the software propagates the geometric implications of high-level design decisions to its constituent parts. For example, the fine details of shaping pieces to fit to one another at connections can be carried out by automated routines based on premade custom components (*families*). The work of detailing the designs for production can, to a large extent, be automated. Apart from its other benefits, automated detailing directly reduces the number of hours that must be consumed to detail ETO components and to produce shop drawings.

Most BIM systems produce reports, including drawings and material takeoffs, in a highly automated fashion. Some also maintain consistency between the model and the drawing set without explicit action on the part of the operator. This introduces savings in the number of drafting hours needed, which is particularly important to fabricators who previously spent the lion's share of their engineering hours on the tedious task of preparing shop drawings.

Various estimates of the extent of this direct productivity gain for engineering and drafting with the use of BIM have been published (Autodesk, 2004; Sacks, 2004). One set of controlled experiments was undertaken for the case of preparing construction drawings and detailing rebar for cast-in-place reinforced concrete structures using a BIM platform with parametric modeling, customizable automated detailing routines, and automated drawing preparation (Sacks and Barak, 2007). The buildings had previously been detailed using 2D CAD, and the hours worked were recorded. As can be seen in Table 7–1, the reduction in engineering and drafting hours for the three case study projects

Table 7–1   Experimental Data for Three Reinforced Concrete Building Projects

Hours Worked	Project A	Project B	Project C
Modeling	131	191	140
Reinforcement detailing	444	440	333
Drawing production	89	181	126
Total 3D	664	875	599
Comparative 2D hours	1,704	⟍ 1,950	760
Reduction	61%	55%	21%

fell in the range of 21 to 61%. (Figure 7–7 shows axonometric views of the three cast-in-place reinforced concrete structures modeled in the study.)

7.3.5   Increased Use of Automated Manufacturing Technologies

Computer numerically controlled (CNC) machinery for various ETO component fabrication tasks has been available for many years. Examples include laser cutting and drilling machines for structural steel fabrication; bending and cutting machines for fabricating reinforcing steel for concrete; saws, drills, and laser projectors for timber truss manufacture; water jet and laser cutting of sheet metal for ductwork; pipe cutting and threading for plumbing; as well as others. However, the need for human labor to code the computer instructions that guide these machines proved to be a significant economic barrier to their use.

Two-dimensional CAD technology provided a platform for overcoming data input barriers by allowing third-party software providers to develop graphic interfaces, where users could draw the products rather than coding them alphanumerically. In almost every case, the developers found it necessary to add meaningful information to the graphics that represented the pieces to be fabricated by creating computable data objects that represented building parts. They could then automatically generate parts and material takeoffs.

The parts, however, continued to be modeled separately for each fabrication stage. When changes were made to building systems, operators had to manually revise or reproduce the part model objects to maintain consistency. Apart from the additional time required, manual revision suffers the drawback that inconsistencies may be introduced. In some cases, such as for the structural steel fabrication industry, software companies addressed this problem by developing top-down modeling systems for updating within assemblies and parts, so that a change would propagate almost entirely automatically to the affected pieces. These developments were constrained to certain sectors, such as the structural steel industry, where market size, the scale of economic benefit from use of the systems, and technological advances made investment in software development economically viable. These applications evolved into fully object-oriented 3D parametric modeling systems.

BIM platforms model every part of a building using meaningful and computable objects, and so provide information from which the data formats

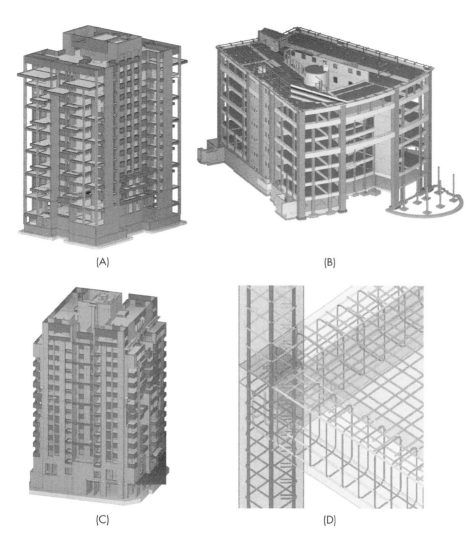

(A)

(B)

(C)

(D)

FIGURE 7–7 Axonometric views of projects A, B, and C. These models (A–C), prepared as part of an experiment to evaluate 3D modeling productivity, contain complete rebar details. The close-up image (D) shows detailed rebars in a balcony slab and supporting beams.

required for controlling automated machinery can be extracted with relative ease. Unlike their 2D CAD–based predecessors, however, they also provide straightforward ways to store and show the logistical information needed for managing the fabrication processes, including links to construction and production schedules, product tracking systems, and so forth.

7.3.6 Increased Preassembly, Prefabrication, and Modular Construction

By removing or drastically reducing the overhead effort required to produce shop drawings, BIM platforms make it economically feasible for companies to prefabricate a greater variety of pieces for any building project. Automatic maintenance of geometric integrity means that making a change to a standard piece and producing a specialized shop drawing or set of CNC instructions demand relatively little effort. Construction of structurally diverse and unique buildings, such as the Walt Disney Concert Hall in Los Angeles (Post, 2002), Dublin's Aviva Stadium (see the *BIM Handbook* companion website), the Fondation Louis Vuitton building in Paris, and the Hyundai Motor Studio in Goyang (the latter two are case studies 10.3 and 10.2 respectively), has become possible; and increasingly more of the standard parts of buildings can be prefabricated economically.

The trend toward prefabrication is encouraged by the relative reduction in risk associated with parts not fitting properly when installed. Each trade's perception of that risk, or of the reliability of the design as a whole, is strongly influenced by the knowledge that all other systems are similarly and fully defined in 3D and reviewed together. This is true not only for prefabricated modular parts, but also for simpler, linear building systems. Because the cost of detailing and coordinating the layout of many routed systems (such as pipes and electrical trays) using 2D drawings was prohibitive, they were often simply left for the contractors to route on-site. Each subsequent contractor would have a more difficult job routing their system as ceiling space became occupied. Parametric 3D modeling of all building systems enables teams to allocate and reserve spaces for each participating system, and to coordinate to resolve any space conflicts that do arise.

With few exceptions, 2D CAD did not give rise to new fabrication methods, and it did little to aid the logistics of prefabrication off-site. BIM, on the other hand, is already enabling not only greater degrees of prefabrication than could be considered without it but also prefabrication of building parts that were previously assembled on-site. Because BIM supports close coordination between building systems and trades, integrated prefabrication of building modules that incorporate parts of multiple systems is now feasible. For example, Crown House Technologies, a UK MEP contractor, developed a sophisticated system for hospital projects in which large sections of pipes and plumbing fixtures are preassembled on stud frames and then rolled into place. Construction of the Staffordshire Hospital in the United Kingdom provided an excellent example (Court et al., 2006; Pasquire et al., 2006). Many other projects around the world have applied this approach with great success; the St. Joseph Hospital project in Denver, Colorado (case study 10.5) is another good example. Figure 6–14, taken from the Hyundai Motor Studio project (case study 10.2), shows how components of HVAC, plumbing, sprinkler, electrical, and communication systems can be assembled together in a module for simple installation in the ceiling on-site.

Likewise, modular construction rests heavily on the ability of design and construction teams to achieve highly detailed integrated design, information, production, and control processes. Coordinating the physical and logistical aspects of integration to this degree is only possible given the richness and reliability of the information provided by BIM. The information needs for modular construction are discussed in Section 7.5.2.

BIM is also used to facilitate the design, detailing, fabrication, and erection of proprietary prefabricated building systems. Companies that have developed proprietary and/or patented building systems find that they can use dedicated parametric BIM design tools to rapidly configure, detail, and manufacture their structural systems. For example, Prescient Co. Inc. offers a structural system (see Figure 7–8) that is designed and configured using a dedicated add-on application for Revit that supports design, manufacturing, and erection.

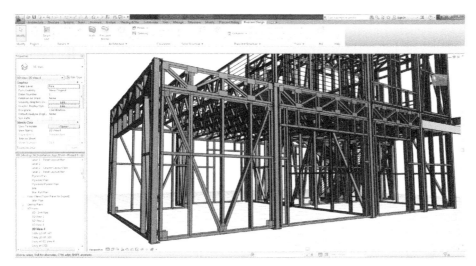

FIGURE 7–8 (Top) Prescient Co. Inc.'s proprietary BIM design add-on for Revit. (Bottom) A manufactured building frame.

Images courtesy of Prescient Co. Inc.

The DIRTT case study (see the *BIM Handbook* companion website) shows the same practice, but in the context of interior fit-out or remodeling works.

DIRTT is a Canadian company that designs, manufactures, and installs interior partitions, mostly but not only for office spaces. DIRTT is an acronym for "Doing It Right This Time," which reflects the idea that a "design for manufacture and assembly" (DfMA) approach, fully integrated with an end-to-end BIM software solution, can outperform traditional methods of interior design and construction. The components of their plug-and-play construction solutions are produced off-site in factories across North America. Prefabricated wall modules are installed once they arrive on-site, and plug-and-play electrical fittings are added, as are modular case-goods accessories where applicable. To avoid disposal to landfills when spaces are renovated, DIRTT's product is designed for complete reuse in new wall configurations. To make this work, all components installed are recorded in a database that makes them available for reconfiguration into new solutions once they are dismantled.

To achieve a supply chain in which the products are sustainable, custom designed for each customer, and flexible enough for that envisioned reuse, DIRTT needed a comprehensive design, manufacturing, delivery, and tracking software platform, but none existed. To accomplish these goals, the software needed to provide unlimited configurability, and the product needed to match the software capability. Those goals could only be accomplished by creating a new software platform in unison with the product design. DIRTT's *ICE* software was the result. For details on the capabilities of DIRTT's *ICE* system, please see the *BIM Handbook* companion website.

7.3.7 Quality Control, Supply Chain Management, and Lifecycle Maintenance

Numerous avenues for applying sophisticated tracking and monitoring technologies in construction have been proposed and explored in various research projects. They include the use of radio-frequency ID (RFID) tags for logistics; comparing as-built structures to design models with laser scanning (LIDAR); monitoring quality using image processing; and reading equipment "black box" monitored information to assess material consumption. Many more are described in the "Capital Projects Technology Roadmap" devised by FIATECH (FIATECH, 2010).

RFID tracking for ETO components has moved from research to practice, with significant success reported in numerous projects. The Meadowlands Stadium project built by Skanska in New Jersey is an excellent example (Sawyer, 2008). Some 3,200 precast concrete components were tracked through fabrication, shipment, erection, and quality control using RFID tags read by field staff using rugged tablet PCs (Figure 7–9, top). The tag IDs corresponded with the virtual objects in the building model, which allowed clear visualization and reporting of the status of all precast pieces. Figure 7–9,

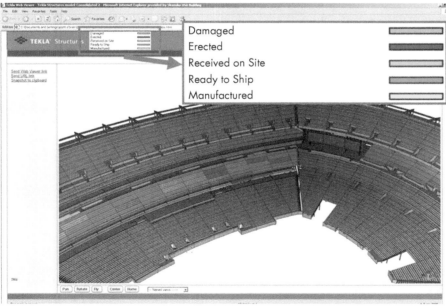

FIGURE 7–9   (Top) Field personnel use rugged tablet PCs to query information about precast pieces and their production, delivery, erection, and approval status from a color-coded model of the stadium. (Bottom) The PCs are equipped with readers to capture information from RFID tags attached to the precast concrete pieces.

bottom, shows a screen shot of the Tekla model in a web viewer, with color-coding of the pieces as recorded using software and hardware provided by Vela Systems. The major benefit is that day-to-day operational decisions that have far-reaching cost implications can be made on the basis of clear, accurate, and up-to-date information.

The Maryland General Hospital project, reported in a case study available in the *BIM Handbook* companion website, illustrates how an information system using barcode tags, used for tracking major mechanical and electrical equipment during construction, became an invaluable asset for lifecycle maintenance. For manufacturers of ETO products for construction, three main areas of application will be:

- Monitoring of the production, storage, delivery to the site, installation location, and quality control of ETO components using GPS and RFID systems
- Supporting the installation or erection of components and quality control using LIDAR and other surveying technologies
- Providing lifecycle information about components and their performance using RFID tags and sensors

A common thread that runs through all of these tracking systems is the need for a building model to carry the information against which monitored data can be compared. The quantity of data that is typically collected by automated monitoring technologies is such that sophisticated software is required to interpret them. For this interpretation to be meaningful, both the designed state of the building product and the as-built realization, involving both geometry and other product and process information, must be available in a computer-readable format.

7.4   GENERIC BIM SYSTEM REQUIREMENTS FOR FABRICATORS

In this and the following section, we define the system requirements that ETO component fabricators, design service providers, and consultants should require from any software platform they are considering. This section defines generic requirements common to all types of fabrication and places special emphasis on the need for fabricators to participate actively in compiling comprehensive building models as part of collaborative project teams. The following section expands the list of requirements to include specialized needs of specific types of fabricators.

Note that the most basic required properties of BIM platforms, such as support for solid modeling, are not listed, because they are essential for all users and almost universally available. For example, the solid modeling capabilities that all fabricators require for clash detection and volumetric quantity takeoffs are provided in all BIM software because section views cannot be produced automatically without them.

7.4.1   Parametric and Customizable Parts and Relationships
The ability to automate design and detailing tasks to a high degree—and for building models to remain coherent, semantically correct, and accurate even as

they are manipulated—are cornerstones for reaping the benefits of BIM for fabricators. Creating models would be excessively time-consuming and impractical if operators were required to generate each and every detailed object individually. It would not only be time-consuming but also highly error-prone if operators were required to actively propagate all changes from building assemblies to all of their detailed constituent components.

For these reasons, fabricators must have software systems that support parametric objects for their system and that manage relationships between objects at all levels (parametric objects and relationships are defined in Chapter 2). The structural steel connection shown in Figure 7–10 illustrates this requirement. The software selects and applies an appropriate connection according to its predefined rules. Setup and selection of rule sets for a project may be done by the engineer of record or by the fabricator, depending on the accepted practice, and may or may not include rules to respond to changes in the loads applied. If the profile shape or parameters of either of the connected members are subsequently changed, the geometry and logic of the connection updates automatically.

An important aspect to evaluate is the degree to which customized parts, details, and connections can be added to a system. A powerful system will support nesting of parametric components within one another; modeling of geometric constraints, such as "parallel to" or "at a constant distance from"; and application of generative rules that determine whether a component will be created in any given context.

While BIM design intent applications allow users to assign layers to a wall section in terms of a 2D section, some architectural BIM design applications include parametric layout of nested assemblies of objects, such as stud framing, within a layer of a generic wall. This allows generation of the detailed framing and derivation of a cut lumber schedule, thereby reducing waste and allowing for faster erection of wood or metal stud–framed structures. In large-scale structures, similar framing and structural layout options are necessary operations for fabrication. In these cases, objects are parts that

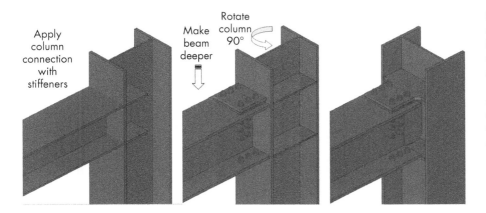

FIGURE 7–10 Structural steel connection in Tekla Structures. The software applies the connection selected by the operator (left to middle) and automatically updates the customized connection when the beam is made deeper and the column is rotated (middle to right).

are composed into a system—structural, electrical, piping, and the like—and the rules determine how the components are organized. Components often have features, such as connections, that are custom designed and fabricated. In the more complex cases, each of the system's parts are then internally composed of their constituent parts, such as steel reinforcing in concrete or complex framing of long-span steel structures.

A distinct set of BIM design applications have been developed for modeling at the more detailed fabrication levels. These tools provide different object families for embedding different types of expertise (see Table 7–2). They are also related to different specific uses, such as materials tracking and ordering, plant management systems, and automated fabrication software. Structural steel fabrication was one of the first domains for which such tools were developed. Initially, these were simple 3D layout systems with predefined parametric object families for connections and editing operations that trimmed members for steel connections (**Tekla Structures**, for example, began as a steel detailing software called **XSteel**). These capabilities were enhanced to support automatic connection design based on loads and member sizing. With associated CNC cutting and drilling machines, these systems have become an integral part of automated steel fabrication. In a similar manner, systems have been developed for precast concrete, reinforced concrete, metal ductwork, piping, and other building systems.

In fabrication modeling, detailers refine their parametric objects for well-understood reasons: to minimize labor, to achieve a particular visual appearance, to reduce the mixing of different types of work crews, or to minimize the types or sizes of materials. Standard design-guide implementations typically address one of multiple acceptable approaches for detailing. In some cases, various objectives can be realized by using standard detailing practices. In other circumstances, these detailing practices need to be overridden. A company's best practices or standard interfacing for a particular piece of fabrication equipment may require further customization. In future decades, design handbooks will be supplemented in this way, as a set of parametric models and rules.

Through the decade since publication of the first edition of the *BIM Handbook* in 2008, there has been a significant move toward consolidation of BIM software, with the major vendors acquiring many of the smaller domain-specific software tools. Many of the software tools for structural steel, reinforced concrete, and MEP detailing and fabrication in particular have been acquired. Some have been removed from the market, while others continue to be provided as part of broader suites of software. Most of those no longer available belonged to a class of fabrication-level CAD systems that were not fully fledged parametric object modeling tools. Rather, they were traditional B-rep modelers with a vendor-provided library of object classes, and many used the AutoCAD platform. Within these traditional CAD platforms, users select, parametrically size, and lay out 3D objects with associated attributes. Object instances and attributes can be exported and used in other applications, such as for bills of material, work orders, and fabrication. These systems work well when there is a fixed set of object classes to be composed using fixed rules. Appropriate

Table 7–2 BIM Software for Subcontractors and Fabricators

BIM Software	Building System Compatibility									Functionality	Vendor
	Structural steel	Precast concrete	CIP concrete	Mechanical/HVAC	Electrical	Plumbing/sprinkler	Curtain Walls	Timber/metal framing	Solar power		
Tekla Structures	✓	✓	✓				✓	✓	✓	Modeling, detailing, coordination	Trimble
Revit	✓	✓	✓	✓	✓	✓	✓	✓	✓	Modeling	Autodesk
AECOsim	✓	✓	✓	✓	✓	✓	✓	✓		Modeling	Bentley
Allplan Engineering	✓	✓	✓							Modeling, detailing	Nemetschek
Allplan Architecture	✓	✓	✓							Modeling	Nemetschek
SDS/2 Design Data	✓									Fabrication detailing	Nemetschek
ProSteel	✓									Modeling, detailing	Bentley
Structureworks		✓								Modeling, detailing, layout, production tracking	Structureworks LLC
ProConcrete			✓							Modeling, detailing	Bentley
aSa Rebar Software			✓							Estimating, detailing, production tracking	Applied Systems Associates, Inc.
DDS-CAD				✓	✓	✓		✓	✓	Modeling, detailing, analysis	Nemetschek
Field Link for MEP				✓	✓	✓				Layout on site	Trimble MEP
Graphisoft MEP Modeler				✓	✓	✓				Modeling	Nemetschek
Fabrication CADmep, ESTmep, CAMduct				✓	✓	✓				Modeling, detailing	Autodesk
DuctDesigner				✓						Modeling, fabrication detailing	Trimble MEP
CADPIPE HVAC and Hanger				✓						Modeling, fabrication detailing	Orange Technologies Inc.
CADPIPE Electrical and Hanger					✓					Modeling, fabrication detailing	Orange Technologies Inc.
CADPIPE Commercial Pipe						✓				Modeling, fabrication detailing	Orange Technologies Inc.
PipeDesigner						✓				Modeling, fabrication detailing	Trimble MEP
SprinkCAD						✓				Modeling, detailing	Tyco Fire Protection Products
Graphisoft ArchiGlazing							✓			Modeling	Nemetschek
SoftTech V6							✓			Modeling, estimating, detailing	Softtech
Framewright Pro								✓		Modeling, detailing	Cadimage
MWF—Metal Wood Framer								✓		Modeling, detailing, coordinating, manufacture	StrucSoft Solutions

applications include piping, ductwork, and cable tray systems. Among the tools of this type that are still available are Trimble MEP's **DuctDesigner** and **PipeDesigner**, Tyco's **SprinkCAD**, and Orange Technologies' **CADPIPE** suite.

The advantage of the more modern BIM-based fabrication tools is that users can define much more complex structures of object families and relations among them than is possible with 3D CAD, without undertaking programming-level software development. With BIM, a curtain wall system attached to columns and floor slabs can be defined from scratch by a knowledgeable nonprogrammer. Such an endeavor would require the development of a major application extension in 3D CAD.

7.4.2 Reporting Components for Fabrication

The ability to automatically generate production reports for each individual ETO component in a building is essential for fabricators of all kinds. Reporting may include preparation of shop drawings; compiling CNC machinery instructions; listing constituent parts and materials for procurement; specifying surface finish treatments and materials; and listing hardware required for installation on-site, and so forth.

In prefabrication of any type of ETO component, it is important to be able to group the components in different ways to manage their production (i.e., procurement of parts, preparation of forms and tools, storage, shipping, and erection). Precast concrete parts and fabricated formwork pieces for cast-in-place concrete are commonly grouped according to their molds, so that single molds can be used for multiple parts with minor modifications between each use. Reinforcing bars must be produced and bundled in groups according to their association with building elements.

To support these needs, BIM applications should be able to group components according to criteria specified by operators on the basis of their geometric information, order of assembly, supplier, and other classifications, and also meta-data (defining origin and ownership of the data, status, and IDs). In the case of geometric shapes, the software should be able to distinguish between parts on the basis of the degree to which the pieces are similar or dissimilar. For example, timber trusses might be given a primary identifier for grouping those trusses with the same overall shape and configuration, while a secondary identifier could be used to distinguish subgroups of one or more trusses with minor differences within the primary group. If a generic truss family were given the type identifier "101," then a subgroup of a few trusses within the generic "101 family" might include a particular member with a larger profile size that is otherwise the same as a "101" and might be named subfamily "101-A."

In some applications, prefabricated ETO components will require that some of the constituent parts be delivered loose to the job site, such as weld plates for embedding in reinforced concrete elements. These too must be grouped and labeled to ensure delivery to the right place at the right time. Where parts must be cast into or bolted onto the building's structure, they may need to be delivered in advance to other subcontractors or even to other fabricators. All of this information must be generated and applied to the objects, preferably automatically, within the BIM platform.

7.4.3 Interface to Management Information Systems

A two-way interface to communicate with procurement, production control, shipping, and accounting information systems is essential to fully leverage the potential benefits listed in Section 7.3. These may be stand-alone applications, parts of a comprehensive enterprise resource planning (ERP) suite, or provided as a "Software as a Service (SaaS)" solution for construction supply chain management, such as **ManufactOn**. The goal is to monitor and control design, ordering, manufacturing, shipping, installation, quality control, and turnover of ETO products. The major advantage of a cloud-based system is that multiple independent companies can be given access to collaborate on a project, thus exposing the status of materials and products to all. This reduces uncertainty and improves the predictability of production planning, thus making construction leaner. Data collection may be manual or automated with bar-code and QR code readers, or with the more powerful radio-frequency identification (RFID) technology. RFID tags have been shown to be feasible for precast concrete components (Ergen et al., 2007), and applied successfully in industry, in projects such as the Meadowlands Stadium and others discussed in Section 7.3.7.

To avoid inconsistencies, the building model should be the sole source for part lists and part production details for the full operation. Fabrication is performed over time, during which changes may continue to be made to the building's design. Up-to-date information regarding changes made to pieces in the model must be available to all of a company's departments at all times if errors are to be avoided. Ideally, this should not be a simple file export/import exchange but an online database link. Minimally, the software should provide an application programming interface, so that companies with access to programming capability can adapt data exchanges to the requirements of their existing enterprise systems.

7.4.4 Interoperability

By definition, subcontractors and fabricators provide only part of a building's systems. The ability to communicate information between their BIM platforms and those of the designers, general contractors, and other fabricators is essential. Indeed, one may conceive of a comprehensive building model as consisting of the full set of system models maintained in the distinct BIM platforms of the numerous design and construction trades, even if there is no one unified database. No single fabrication platform is able to address all aspects of building construction fabrication today, and we do not expect this situation to change.

The technical aspects of interoperability are discussed thoroughly in Chapter 3, including both its benefits and limitations. Suffice it to say that for the purposes of BIM platform selection by subcontractors and fabricators, the capability to import and export models using an appropriate industry exchange standard should be considered mandatory. Which standard is most important depends on the industry sector: for structural steel the CIS/2 format is essential; for most other sectors the IFC format will likely be most useful.

7.4.5 Information Visualization

A 3D building model viewer is a very effective platform for entering and visualizing management information, particularly for erectors and general contractor staff outside the fabricator's organization. Customizable functions for generating model displays that are colored according to a variety of production status data are highly beneficial.

Two good examples are the use of 4D CAD techniques for production planning of a construction operation and the use of a model interface to pull the delivery of prefabricated parts to the job site in a just-in-time configuration. In the first, a building model that included the structural members and the resources (cranes) and activities was used for step-by-step planning and simulation of the erection sequence for steel and precast concrete elements for an underground subway station roof in London (Koerckel and Ballard, 2005). Careful planning was essential so that the project team could meet a strict 48-hour time limit for erection, during which train traffic was suspended. For a detailed description of 4D CAD techniques and benefits, please refer to Section 6.9 in Chapter 6.

The second example is illustrated by Figure 7–9 (top), which shows field personnel consulting a building model at the Meadowlands Stadium project described in Section 7.3.7. Instead of consulting a spread of drawings and paper reports, which are often out of date, to select pieces for manufacture and delivery, project managers can plan work with high reliability. The effort of coordinating between multiple sets of drawings and lists and the resulting human errors are eliminated. Indeed, information visualization of this kind, where a site supervisor can simply point and click on a color-coded model to compile delivery lists, as shown in Figure 7–9 (bottom), enables the pull flow control paradigm advocated by lean construction thinking.

Fabricators of a wide range of ETO components can also exploit BIM models to prepare step-by-step animated 3D instructions, delivered on hand-held devices, to guide workers in making and installing their products. The **Structureworks XceleRAYtor** application automatically compiles a sequence of detailed, color-coded, and dimensioned graphic instruction screens to guide workers in setting up the embeds and rebars needed to prepare a mold for casting a concrete piece, as illustrated in Figure 7–11. It can be used with an overhead laser to project the parts needed in each step directly onto the bed in the correct position. It is but a small additional stretch of the imagination to consider that a camera placed above the bed could be used to check, using machine vision, that each embed and rebar is correctly placed before authorizing the pour. The same tool is also used for compiling and delivering erection sequences to workers on-site, including automated preparation of loading lists. Apart from the quality and productivity gains in the plant, this process entirely obviates the need for shop drawings, eliminating many hours of non-value-adding time from the process.

7.4.6 Automation of Fabrication Tasks

The selection of a BIM software platform should reflect the opportunities and plans for automation of the fabrication tasks. These vary with each

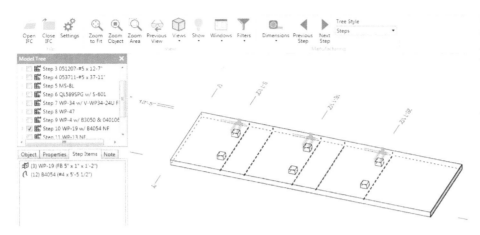

FIGURE 7–11 Step 10 in a sequence of assembly steps for assembling the various embeds and rebars needed in a mold before pouring a precast concrete piece in a fabrication plant. The 3D view shows only the pieces required in this step, and the items needed are listed in the tree at left.

Image courtesy of Structureworks LLC.

building system. Some companies will already have CNC machines of different kinds, such as rebar bending and cutting machines, laser cutters for steel profiles or plates, or sophisticated conveyor and casting systems for precast concrete. For some fabricators, these technologies may be drivers for adopting BIM into their existing production methods. For others, they will be new options, and BIM will enable their introduction; this is the case for 3D printing and various forms of robotic construction, for which 3D modeling is a necessity.

In either case, it is important to consider the information requirements and the interfaces that are supported by the BIM software. Two-dimensional laser-cutters and rebar bending machines require drivers that generate numerical control instructions; 3D printing requires fully closed BREP solid geometry before printing instructions can be generated. Robotic construction equipment, such as Fastbrick Robotics' automated bricklaying machines, require not only 3D geometry, but also information about the materials and other building systems with which their products are integrated. Information from the BIM model must be processed to provide the format needed for machine operation.

7.5 SPECIFIC BIM REQUIREMENTS FOR FABRICATION

There are numerous ways to reduce the quantity of human work required for building construction, such as prefabrication, modular construction, robotics, and 3D printing. The common denominator for all of these is the need for detailed, precise, and complete product and process information. Providing this information is the key contribution that BIM makes to enabling automation in construction. Yet the types of information needed vary with each application. The geometry, fabrication processes, and other factors differ and place unique requirements on BIM tools.

7.5.1 Traditional ETO Component Fabricators

This section describes specific BIM requirements for fabricators of the more common kinds of ETO products, and Table 7–2 provides a short list of software packages (available at the time of publication) for each class of fabricator. The software packages are listed, along with explanations of their functionality for each domain. The list is by no means exhaustive or complete, but it provides an overview of the kinds of systems available.

Structural Steel: With steel construction, the overall structure is divided into distinct parts that can be easily fabricated, transported to the site, erected, and joined, using minimal material quantities and labor, all under the necessary load constraints defined by the structural engineers. Simply modeling the structure in 3D with all detailing of nuts, bolts, welds, plates, and so forth is not sufficient. The following are additional requirements that should be met by steel detailing software:

- **Automated and customizable detailing of steel connections:** This feature must incorporate the ability to define rulesets that govern the ways in which connection types are selected and parametrically adapted to suit specific situations in structures.
- **Built-in structural analysis capabilities, including finite element analysis:** Alternatively, as a minimum, the software should be able to depict and export a structural model, including the definition of loads in a format that is readable by an external structural analysis package. In this case, it should also be capable of importing loads and reactions back to the 3D model.
- **Output of cutting, welding, and drilling instructions directly to computer numerically controlled (CNC) machinery:** This capability is being extended to include assembly. Assembly requires even more extensive geometry and process information.

Precast Concrete: Information modeling of precast concrete is more complex than modeling structural steel, because precast concrete pieces have internal parts (rebar, prestress strands, steel embeds; see Figure 7–12), a much greater freedom in shapes, and a rich variety of surface finishes. These were among the reasons why BIM software tailored to the needs of precast concrete became available commercially much later than for structural steel.

The first two needs specified for structural steel—automated and customizable detailing of connections and built-in structural analysis capabilities—apply equally to precast concrete. In addition, the following requirements are specific to precast concrete:

- The ability to model pieces in a building model with geometric shapes different from the geometry reported in shop drawings. All precast pieces are subject to shortening and creep, which means their final shape is different than that which is produced. Precast pieces that are eccentrically prestressed become cambered when prestress cables are

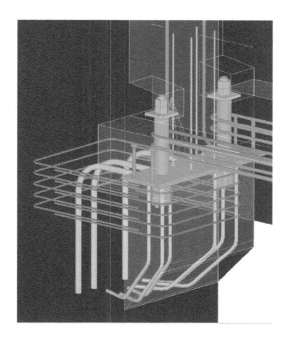

FIGURE 7–12 Reinforcing bars and other embeds in a *Tekla Structures* parametric column-corbel-beam connection for precast concrete construction. The connection layout can be adjusted to fit the section sizes and the layout of the columns and beams. Parametric modeling operations can include shape subtraction and addition operations that create reveals, notches, bullnoses, and cutouts defined for connections to other parts.

released after curing. The most complex change occurs when long precast pieces are deliberately twisted or warped. This is commonly done with long double tee pieces in parking garages and other structures to provide slopes for drainage, by setting the supports of one end at an angle to those of the other end. The pieces must be represented with warped geometry in the computer model, but they must be produced in straight prestressing beds. Therefore, they must be rendered straight in shop drawings. This requires a relatively complex geometric transformation between the assembly and the shop drawing representations of any intentionally deformed piece.

- Surface finishes and treatments cannot simply be applied to faces of parts but often have their own distinctive geometry, which may require subtraction of volume from the concrete itself. Stone cladding, brick patterns, thermal insulation layers, and so forth are all common examples. Special concrete mixes are used to provide custom colors and surface effects but are usually too expensive to fill the whole piece. As a result, the pieces may be composed of more than one concrete type, and the software must support the documentation of volumes required for each type.

- Specialized structural analyses of individual pieces—to check their resistance to forces applied during stripping, lifting, storage, transportation, and erection, which are different from those applied during their service life in a building—are required. This places special emphasis on the need for integration with external analysis software packages and an open application programming interface.

- A precast piece's constituent parts must be grouped according to the timing of their insertion: cast into the unit at time of fabrication, cast into or welded onto the building foundation or structure, or supplied loose (bundled with the piece) to the site for erection.
- Output of rebar shapes in formats compatible with fabrication control software and automated bending and cutting machines.

Reinforcement and Formwork for Cast-in-place Concrete: Like precast concrete, cast-in-place reinforced concrete has internal components that must be modeled in detail. All of the requirements for structural analysis, generating and reporting rebar shapes for production and placing, and for measuring concrete volumes are equally valid for cast-in-place concrete.

CIP concrete, however, is quite different from both structural steel and precast concrete, because cast-in-place structures are monolithic. They do not have clearly defined physical boundaries between components, such as with columns, beams, and slabs. Indeed, whether the concrete volume at the components' intersection is considered part of one or part of the other component's joint framing is determined based on the reporting needs. *Autodesk Revit's* joint geometry feature begins to address this need, and for standard cases parameters that give one element type priority over another can be set to automate this behavior (such as setting beams to always be shortened where they intersect with columns). Likewise, the same rebars may fulfill a specific function within one member and a different function within a joint, such as with top steel in a continuous beam that serves for shear and crack resistance within the span but also as moment reinforcement over the support.

Another difference is that cast-in-place concrete can be cast with complex curved geometries, with curvature in one or two axis directions and variable thicknesses. Although nonuniform multicurved surfaces are rare, domes are not uncommon. Any company that encounters curved concrete surfaces in its construction projects should ensure that the descriptive geometry engine of any modeling software can model such surfaces and the solid volumes they enclose. A third difference is that, unlike steel and precast components, CIP concrete structures are partitioned differently for analysis and design than for fabrication. The locations of pour stops are often determined in the field and do not always conform to product divisions, as envisioned by the designers. Nevertheless, if the members are to be used for construction management as well as for design, they must be modeled both ways (Barak et al., 2009).

Lastly, CIP concrete requires layout and detailing of formwork, whether modular or custom designed. Some modular formwork manufacturing companies provide layout and detailing software, which allows users to graphically apply standard formwork sections to CIP elements in 3D. The software then produces the detailed bills of material required and the drawings to aid laborers in erecting the modular forms. PERI, for example, a major formwork and scaffolding manufacturer and supplier, provides a parametric library of its products for *Tekla Structures*. Figure 7–13 shows a BIM model of formwork designed for construction of a concrete pylon for a railway bridge in Germany.

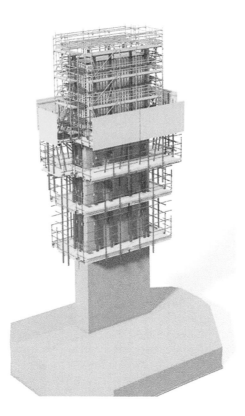

FIGURE 7–13 Rendering of the formwork configuration for casting of a tall concrete pylon for a railway bridge.

Image Courtesy of PERI GmbH, Weißenhorn, Germany.

Curtain Walls and Fenestration: Curtain walls include any wall closing system that does not have a structural function in that it does not carry gravity loads to the foundations of a building. Among custom-designed and fabricated curtain walls—essentially involving ETO components—aluminum and glass curtain walls are typical. They can be classified as *stick systems*, *unit systems*, or *composite systems*. Fenestration ETO products include all window units that are custom-designed for fabrication and installation in a specific building, with profiles of steel, aluminum, timber, plastic (PVC), or other materials.

Stick systems are built in-situ from metal profiles (usually aluminum), which are attached to the building frame. They are similar to structural steel frames in that they are composed of longitudinal extruded sections (vertical mullions and horizontal transoms) with joints between them. Like precast façade panels, their connections to the structural frame must be detailed explicitly for every context. They place a unique requirement on modeling software, because they are highly susceptible to changes in temperature, which cause expansion and contraction; as such, their joints must be detailed to allow for free movement without compromising their insulating or aesthetic functions. Joints with appropriate degrees of freedom and sleeves to accommodate and hide longitudinal movement are common. Stick systems require only assembly modeling, with minimal piece fabrication detailing (needed only to support cutting profiles to the right length in the shop). The ability to plan erection sequences in order to accommodate tolerances is critical.

Unit systems are composed of separate prefabricated pieces installed directly onto the building's frame. A key feature for modeling is the need for high accuracy in construction, which means that dimensional tolerances for the building's structural frame should be modeled explicitly.

Composite systems include unit and mullion systems, column cover and spandrel systems, and panel (strong back) systems. These require not only detailed assembly and piece fabrication details but must also be closely coordinated with a building's other systems.

Curtain walls are an important part of any building model, because they are central to all analyses of building performance other than overall structural analysis (i.e., thermal, acoustic, and lighting). Any computer simulation that can be performed on a model will need the relevant physical properties of the curtain wall system and its components—not only its geometry. Models should also support local wind and dead load structural analyses for the system components.

Most curtain wall modeling routines that are commonly available in architectural BIM platforms allow for preliminary design only and have no functionality for detailing and fabrication. The 100 11th Avenue, New York, apartment building (the case study is available on the *BIM Handbook* companion website) has a complex curtain wall whose design and fabrication are a good example of BIM platform use for design and analysis. On the other hand, proprietary software applications are available for detailing and estimating the curtain wall and fenestration systems of numerous fabricators. These applications are intended for modeling individual windows or curtain wall sections, without compiling them into whole building models. Due to the nature of the steel and aluminum profiles used in most curtain walls, some companies have found mechanical parametric modeling platforms, such as **Solidworks** and **Autodesk Inventor**, to be useful.

Mechanical, Electrical, and Plumbing: Three distinct types of ETO component systems are included in this category: ducts and machinery for HVAC systems; piping runs for liquid and gas supply and disposal; and routing trays and control boxes for electrical and communication systems. These three systems are similar both in nature and in the space they occupy within a building, but they also depend on specific requirements for detailing and fabrication software.

Ducts for HVAC systems must be cut from sheet metal sections, fabricated in units that can be conveniently transported and maneuvered into position, and then assembled and installed in place at a building site. Duct units are three-dimensional objects and often have complex geometries. Chillers, pumps, diffusers, and other machinery have strict space and clearance requirements and interface with both electrical and plumbing systems—their locations and orientations demand careful coordination.

Piping for supply and disposal of various liquids and gases is composed of extruded profiles that also incorporate valves, bends, and other equipment.

While not all piping is engineered to order, sections that require cutting, threading, or other treatments must be done in a workshop prior to delivery to be considered ETO components. In addition, spools of piping components that are preassembled as complete units prior to delivery and/or installation are also considered pre-engineered, even if most of their constituent parts are off-the-shelf components.

Although electrical and communication cables are largely flexible, the conduits and trays that carry them may not be, which means their layout must be coordinated with other systems.

The first and most generic requirement for these systems to be supported by BIM is that their location, orientation, and routing in space must be carefully coordinated. Routing requires easy-to-follow or color-coded visualization and functions for identifying clashes between systems. Figure 7–14, which was prepared by a general contractor (the Mortenson Company) for coordination purposes, is an excellent example of how a building's MEP systems can be modeled, checked, and prepared for fabrication, production, and installation. Although physical clash detection is available in most piping and duct software, in many cases soft clash detection is also needed. Soft clash detection refers to certain requirements, where minimum clear space must be maintained between different systems, such as the minimum distance between a hot water pipe and electrical cables. Similarly, a piece of equipment may need to be dismounted for inspection or repair, so that the path for access to it and for its removal must be kept free of interference. The software must allow users to set up rules that define verifiable spatial constraints between different pairs of systems when clash checks are performed.

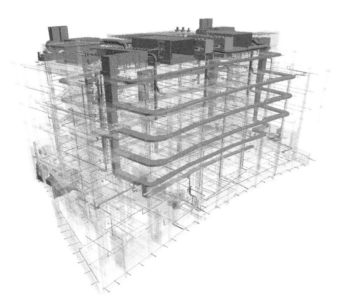

FIGURE 7–14 A model view showing a building's MEP systems with transparent building structure components, prepared by a general contractor (Mortenson) for construction coordination.

Image courtesy of Mortenson.

A second generic requirement is the grouping of objects for production and installation logistics. Numbering or labeling components must be performed on three levels: a unique part ID for each piece; a group ID for installation spools; and a production group ID that the system assigns based on the collection of identical or largely similar parts for fabrication or procurement. Grouping of parts for site delivery, with collections of separate components belonging to duct runs and pipe spools, is particularly important. If any part is missing or cannot fit into place due to dimensional changes or fabrication errors, productivity degrades and the workflow is disrupted. To avoid this, BIM systems must provide material takeoff lists and seamless integration with logistics software for labeling schemes to allow complete and correct collections of parts to be pulled to the work-face at the right time.

Unique BIM requirements for each of the systems are as follows:

- Most duct sections are fabricated from flat sheet metal. Software should generate cutting patterns—unfolded from 3D geometric shapes—and translate the data into a format appropriate for plasma cutting tables or other machinery. The software should also offer optimization of the nesting pattern to minimize off-cut waste.
- Piping spools are commonly represented in symbolic isometric drawings. Software should enable display in multiple formats, including full 3D representation, line representation, and symbolic form, as well as 2D plans, sections, and isometric views.
- Duct sections, piping spools, and modular MEP racks are good candidates for prefabrication. Software should provide tools to generate assemblies, fabrication and installation instructions, and bills of materials automatically. *Stabiplan's **STABICAD***, for example, provides a Revit add-on tool and object libraries (see www.mepcontent.eu/MEP for modeling of MEP assemblies at LOD 400), compilation of part lists, and preparation of prefabrication instructions (see Figure 7–15). With the prefab sheets and cutting lists generated from the model, there is no need to measure, cut, or fabricate pipes on-site, and there are no offcuts to transport away as waste.

Software applications capable of generating detailed models and fabrication information for MEP systems were made available earlier than for other building systems. This was mainly because ducts, pipes, and the like are generally composed of distinct parts, which have standard geometries that are independent of local conditions at the interfaces between parts. Solid modeling and Boolean operations were not needed, and self-contained parametric parts could be added by programming purpose-built routines. It was therefore possible to provide fabrication-level modeling on the basis of generic CAD software, which lacked more sophisticated parametric and constraint modeling capabilities.

As we discussed toward the end of Section 7.4.1, the drawback of CAD-based applications, as opposed to BIM-based applications, is that

(A) (B)

(C) (D)

FIGURE 7–15 MEP assemblies designed and prefabricated for installation in a housing project: (A) Design model, (B) Fabrication, (C) Shipping to site, (D) Installed.

Images courtesy of Stabiplan.

CAD platforms do not maintain logical integrity when changes are entered. Neighboring duct sections should adjust when changes are made to individual sections or to a duct run as a whole. When a duct or pipe that penetrates a slab or wall moves, the hole in the slab or wall should either also be moved or healed if it is no longer needed. Also, some MEP applications lack the import and export interfaces needed for industrywide interoperability, such as support for IFC models.

Given their popularity, subcontractors and fabricators are likely to continue using CAD-based tools for some time. Among the tools of this type that are still available are **Trimble MEP's DuctDesigner** and **PipeDesigner**, **Tyco's SprinkCAD**, and **Orange Technologies' CADPIPE** suite (see Table 7–2). The resulting "mixed use" of BIM models with MEP systems detailed in CAD tools is apparent in the Sutter Medical Center case study (see the *BIM Handbook* companion website). For this reason, it is important to ensure that any CAD-based platform is capable of supporting file formats that can be uploaded into design integration software (see Section 2.5.2).

7.5.2 Modular Construction

The most comprehensive ETO products for construction are modular prefabricated units that are assembled to together to form whole buildings or major parts of buildings (see Figure 7–3). The NTU Student Residence Hall Project in Singapore, detailed in Case Study 10.7, is an excellent example of the use of PPVC modules. The steel frames for the modules were fabricated in Taiwan, they were shipped to Singapore, and the finishing work and building systems were applied in a factory in Singapore.

Many people consider modular construction to be particularly suited to sectors such as branded hotels, student accommodation, high-rise residential buildings, and hospital units, due to the uniformity of their geometry, and indeed there are many examples of such construction. Tide Construction and Vision Modular Systems' 29-storey Apex House tower in north London; "True Glasgow West End", a 592-room complex built with modules fabricated by China International Marine Containers (CIMC); and the modular room units installed in Saint Joseph Hospital in Denver, Colorado, by Mortenson, described in Case Study 10.5, are all examples. However, BIM and parametric design and detailing tools mean that the engineering cost for modular buildings with much more varied geometry can be reduced. The variety of form of modular buildings is therefore likely to grow as the scale of modular production for construction grows and BIM becomes thoroughly integrated in the DfMA process.

In a report published by the UK's Construction Leadership Council (CLC) reviewing the construction labor model, subtitled "Modernise or Die," Mark Farmer called for increased use of modular construction (Farmer, 2016). The report makes the case for modernization of the construction industry and confirms the essential role of BIM in providing the information needed:

"PreManufacture – Many different terms are used in the realm of construction innovation including 'off-site manufacture' 'modern methods of construction' or 'pre-fabrication'. This review uniformly adopts the term pre-manufacture as a generic term to embrace all processes which reduce the level of on-site labour intensity and delivery risk. This implicitly includes a 'design for manufacture & assembly' approach at all levels ranging from component level standardisation and lean processes through to completely pre-finished volumetric solutions. It also includes any element of on-site or adjacent to site temporary or 'flying' factory or consolidation facilities which de-risk in-situ construction, improving productivity and predictability. 'Industry 4.0' is a term often used to reference the fourth industrial revolution underpinned by cyber-physical 'smart' production techniques. It is however clear that in many respects, construction has not even made the transition to 'industry 3.0' status which is predicated on large scale use of electronics and IT to automate production. It is important therefore to see this as the immediate goal and to use terminology and definitions based on industrial strategy benchmarks that reflect this current reality."

"…. Building Information Modelling (BIM) …[is] a critical change agent for the industry, completely intertwined with the move to manufacturing led approaches discussed above."

At the time of writing, there were no BIM tools available that provided specific capabilities for modular construction. Because of the significant industrial engineering knowledge content, some fabricators of modular units find mechanical engineering CAD packages, such as **Solidworks** or **Autodesk Inventor,** to be useful. These may be appropriate for the manufacturing stage, but they do not have the capabilities for building design that are essential for the schematic and design development stages. Handover of information from a BIM platform to a manufacturing one is not trivial. There appears therefore to be a "vacuum" of opportunity for a modular construction-specific tool within a BIM platform.

7.5.3 3D Printing and Robotic Construction

3D printing, or additive manufacturing (AM), is a rapid prototyping technology that produces a product by adding and binding multiple layers of materials on top of each other. With the increasing availability of BIM data, 3D printing has made significant progress in construction. It became popular in architectural education with the development of affordable 3D printers in the early 2000s, but it was not until 2008 that a practical approach was proposed for buildings. Currently, three types of 3D printing technologies are deployed in the AEC industry. They are contour crafting, binder jetting, and fused deposition modeling (FDM).

Contour crafting is the most commonly used and the most advanced method for 3D building printing. A printing nozzle deposits successive layers of concrete paste or similar quick-setting cementitious material to generate a building or to produce building elements. The method was first proposed in 2008 by Behrokh Khoshnevis, a professor of Industrial and Systems Engineering at the University of Southern California (USC). Winsun, a precast concrete producer in China, has played an important role in commercializing and popularizing contour crafting technology. In 2014, the company built 10 houses within 24 hours to demonstrate its capabilities. Winsun does not print buildings on-site; instead, they print components at a plant and assemble them on-site in a method similar to precast concrete construction. A Russian company, Apis Cor, has developed an on-site 3D building printing system that has an extending boom that rests on and rotates around a fixed turntable. Apis Cor printed its first building, a 38 m^2 home, in December 2016. Its system can print an area of up to 132 m^2 (4 to 8.5 m in diameter).

Binder jetting nozzles spray a binder (glue) onto a thin layer of 3D printing materials layer by layer to 3D-print a product. Binder jetting is also known as the powder bed method because it spreads a 3D print material in a powder form on a production bed before it sprays a binder on the 3D printing material. Later, excessive 3D printing material is removed. D-shape was the most well-known AEC 3D printing company to use binder jetting. The surfaces of products printed by D-shape resembled the texture of coral reefs because D-shape used sand as the main 3D printing material.

Fused deposition modeling melts and binds a 3D printing material to form a shape. Since concrete cannot be melted and bound, other types of materials such as steel or plastics are used for FDM. A well-known example is a

3D-printed steel bridge being built by MX3D, a robotic 3D printing company in the Netherlands. Branch Technology and ETH Zurich used similar FDM approaches to print reinforced structures. Branch Technology's Cellular Fabrication (C-Fab) technology 3D-prints a wire-framed structure using carbon fiber-reinforced plastic and fills in the gaps with spray foam insulation. SHoP, a New York architecture firm, used C-Fab to 3D-print the largest 3D printed pavilion in the world in Miami, Florida, in 2017. On the other hand, ETH's Mesh Mould technology 3D-prints a steel wire frame, which plays a dual role as reinforcement and concrete mold at the same time, and fills the gaps with zero-slump concrete.

Regardless of the method used, four steps are required to 3D-print a building:

1. The first step is to filter and select the objects to be printed from a BIM model and to export 3D geometry information to a computer-aided manufacturing (CAM) program that controls the 3D printer. Each type of 3D printer has its own CAM application.
2. Next, options for 3D printing such as print quality and print paths are set up in the CAM software.
3. Large-scale on-site 3D printing machines require a calibration process to determine the base point and the orientation.
4. Finally, the 3D-printer is run to build a building or building objects.

Despite the rapid growth of research and interest in 3D printing technologies, there are still many limitations and challenges to be overcome before they become competitive with existing construction methods. The problems concern scalability and mobility of machines, weak resistance to lateral loads (wind and earthquakes), mixed-material printing, quality of surface finishes, difficulties creating cantilevered members, and so on. Nevertheless, the idea of being able to model a building in a BIM platform and then have a machine simply fabricate the building precisely, quickly, and with no further human input, is sufficiently attractive and appealing that people are likely to continue exploring the possibilities.

Robotic construction, on the other hand, may have more potential in the short term. R&D efforts toward robotic construction in the late 1980s (see Warszawski, 1990, for example) did not come to fruition in industry due to the expense of industrial robots, the lack of mature navigation tools and vision tools, and the high setup costs (including the need for extensive programming of each task due to the lack of building information models). Those conditions have changed—specifically, BIM is now common. Robotic construction tools that use model information, such as Fastbrick Robotics' Hadrian X, are reaching the tipping-point of commercial application. The FastBrick approach is similar to 3D printing using contour crafting in that it lays down successive layers of material to form walls, but it solves a range of problems by using solid bricks rather than a viscous cementitious material that needs to flow through pipes and set.

7.6 ADOPTING BIM IN A FABRICATION OPERATION

A robust management strategy for the adoption of BIM must concern aspects beyond software, hardware, and the training of engineering staff, because of its range of impact on workflows and people.

BIM systems are a sophisticated technology that impacts every aspect of a fabrication subcontractor's operations, from marketing and estimating through engineering, procurement of raw materials, fabrication, shipping to installation on-site, and maintenance. BIM does not simply automate existing operations that were previously performed manually or used less sophisticated software; it enables different workflow patterns and production processes.

BIM systems directly improve engineering and drafting productivity. Unless a company experiences sustained growth in sales volume through the adoption period, the number of people needed for these activities will be reduced. Downsizing may be threatening to employees whose energy and enthusiasm is critical for changing work procedures. A thorough plan should account for this impact by considering and making provisions for all staff, both those selected for training and those for whom other tasks may be found. It should aim to secure involvement and commitment at an early stage.

7.6.1 Setting Appropriate Goals

The following guideline questions may help in setting goals for an effective adoption plan and for identifying the actors inside and outside the company who should be party to the plan. They apply equally to fabrication companies with in-house detailing capabilities and to companies that specialize in providing engineering detailing services.

- How can clients (building owners, architects, engineering consultants, and general contractors) benefit from fabricators' enhanced proficiency using BIM platforms? What new services can be offered that presently are not? What services can be made more productive, and how can lead times be shortened?
- To what degree can building model data be imported from upstream sources, such as from architects' or other designers' BIM models?
- How early in the process will models be compiled, and what are the appropriate levels of detail for models? Some fabricators are called upon to propose general design solutions at the tendering stage, where a low level of detail model can be an excellent tool for communicating a company's unique approach. Others are restricted to tendering on the

designers' solution only, so that modeling begins with detailing only once a contract has been won.

- If a model has been prepared for tendering, how much of the information compiled is useful for the engineering and detailing phase that follows if the project is won?

- How and by whom will the company's standard engineering details be embedded in custom library components in the software? Will libraries be compiled at the time of adoption or incrementally as needed for the first projects modeled?

- Can BIM offer alternative modes of communicating information within the company? This requires open discussion with different departments to ascertain real needs. Asking a production department head, "How do you want your shop drawings to look?" may miss the point in a BIM adoption, where alternative forms of presenting the information may be possible.

- How will information be communicated to designers and consultants in the submittal process? BIM-capable architects and engineering consultants are likely to prefer to receive the model rather than drawings. How will review comments be communicated back to the company?

- To what degree will building models be used to generate or display management information? What is needed (software, hardware, programming) to integrate BIM systems with existing management information systems, or will new management systems be adopted in parallel? Most BIM platform vendors provide not only fully functional authoring versions but also model integration and model viewing versions (see Section 2.6), which are likely to be adequate for production or logistics departments and personnel.

- What is the appropriate pace of change? This will depend on freeing up the time of those individuals committed to the company's BIM adoption activities.

- How and to what degree will the existing CAD software be phased out? How much buffer capacity should be maintained during the adoption process? Are there any clients or suppliers who will not move to BIM and may therefore require that a limited CAD capacity be maintained?

- What are the needs and capabilities of any suppliers to whom engineering work is outsourced? Will they be expected to adapt? Will the company provide them some support in making the transition to BIM, or will they be replaced with BIM-savvy engineering service providers?

7.6.2   Adoption Activities

Once software and hardware configurations have been selected, the first step will be to prepare a thorough adoption plan, starting with definitions of the goals to be achieved and selection of the right staff to lead the adoption, both as managers and as first learners. Ideally, the adoption plan will be developed together with or by the selected leaders in close consultation with key people from the production and logistics departments companywide. The plan should detail timing and personnel commitments for all of the following activities:

- **Training engineering staff to use the software.** A word of caution: 3D object modeling is sufficiently dissimilar in concept from CAD drawing that some experienced CAD operators find the need to "unlearn" CAD behavior a serious barrier to effective use of BIM software. As with most sophisticated software, proficiency is built with practice over time; staff should not be trained until the organization can ensure that they can devote time to continued use of the software in the period immediately following the training.

- **Preparation of custom component libraries, standard connections, design rules, and so forth.** For most systems and companies, this is a major task, but on the other hand it is a key determinant of the level of productivity that can be achieved. Different strategies can be considered. Custom components can be defined and stored incrementally as needed on the first projects performed; a large proportion of the libraries can be built ahead of time; or a mixed approach is possible. Larger companies may elect to dedicate a specially trained staff member to compile and maintain part libraries, because parametric modeling libraries are considerably more complex and sophisticated than those used with 2D CAD.

- **Customization of the software to provide drawing and report templates suitable for the company's needs.** Immediately after training, the "first learners" can be tasked with "ghosting" a project. This involves attempting to model a project that is being produced in parallel using the standard CAD software. Ghosting provides an opportunity to explore the breadth of a real project, while not bearing responsibility to produce results according to production schedules. It also reveals the limitations of training and the degree of customization that will have been achieved.

- **Seminars and/or workshops for those impacted but who are not direct users**—other departments within the company, raw material and processed product suppliers, providers of outsourced services, and clients—to inform them of the capabilities, enlist their support, and solicit ideas for improved information flows that may become possible. In one such seminar at a precast concrete company, the manager of the rebar cage assembly shop was asked to comment on various options for shop drawing dimensioning formats. Instead, he responded by asking if he could have a computer for 3D viewing of rebar cages color-coded by bar diameters, which he felt would enable his team to understand the cages they were to tie in a fraction of the time they currently needed to interpret 2D drawing sets.

7.6.3 Planning the Pace of Change

The introduction of new BIM workstations should be phased. The personnel undergoing training are likely to remain unproductive during their training and less productive than with CAD platforms during the early period, as they progress along a learning curve. The first people trained are also likely to be unproductive for a longer period than most others, because they will have to customize the software to suit company-specific products and production practices. In other words, there is likely to be a need for *additional* personnel at the early stages of adoption, followed by a fairly sharp drop. This can be seen in the total number of personnel needed, as shown in the last row of each adoption plan in Table 7–3.

Table 7–3 shows a feasible plan for a phased replacement of a company's existing 18 CAD workstations with 13 BIM workstations. It lists the numbers of CAD and BIM workstations planned for operation in each of the first four periods following the introduction of BIM software. It is based on estimates for two unknowns: the degree of expected productivity gains and anticipated rate of growth in business volume, if any. The rate of growth in volume can be expressed conveniently in terms of an equivalent number of CAD workstations needed to cope with the volume (the table shows two options, ignoring and considering growth in work volume). The rate of productivity gain used to prepare this table is 40% and is based on the number of hours required to

Table 7–3 An Example of Staged Adoption of BIM Workstations for a Fabricator's Engineering Department

Adoption periods	Start	P1	P2	P3	P4
Plan ignoring growth in work volume					
Equivalent CAD workstations required	18	18	18	18	18
CAD workstations operating	18	18	13	3	
CAD workstations saved			5	15	18
BIM workstations added		3	6	2	
BIM workstations operating		3	9	11	11
Total workstations	18	21	22	14	11
Plan considering growth in work volume					
Equivalent CAD workstations required	18	18	19	20	21
CAD workstations operating	18	18	14	5	
CAD workstations saved			5	15	21
BIM workstations added		3	6	3	1
BIM workstations operating		3	9	12	13
Total workstations	18	21	23	17	13

produce the same output using BIM as would be produced using CAD. In terms of drawing production, that translates to 60% of the hours currently spent using CAD. This is a conservative estimate based on available measures from research, as detailed in Section 7.3.4.

Table 7–3 also demonstrates how downtime for training and reduced productivity at the start of the learning curve can be accounted for. A simplifying assumption in this regard is that the BIM workstations introduced in each period will only become fully productive in the period that follows. Thus, there is no reduction in CAD workstations in the first adoption period, despite the addition of three BIM workstations. In the second period, the reduction in CAD workstations is five and is equal to the number of BIM workstations that become productive (three, the number added in the preceding period) divided by the productivity ratio (3 ÷ 60% = 5).

The increase in personnel needed during the first adoption period may be ameliorated by outsourcing or by overtime, but it is likely to be the main cost item in a BIM adoption cash flow plan and usually significantly costlier than the software investment, hardware, or direct training costs. Companies may decide to stagger the adoption gradually to reduce its impact; indeed, planning period durations may be reduced over time (integrating new operators is likely to be smoother once more colleagues have made the conversion and as the BIM software becomes more deeply integrated in day-to-day procedures). In any event, from a management perspective, it is important to ensure that the resources needed for the period of change will be recognized and made available.

7.6.4 Human Resource Considerations

In the longer term, the adoption of BIM in a fabricator's organization is likely to have far-reaching effects in terms of business processes and personnel. Achieving the full benefits of BIM requires that estimators, who are commonly among the most experienced engineers in a fabrication organization, be the first to compile a model for any new project, because it involves making decisions about conceptual design and production methods. This is not a task that can be delegated to a draftsperson. When projects move to the detailed design and production stages, it will again be the engineers who are capable of applying the correct analyses to models and, at least, the engineering technicians who will determine the details. For trades such as electrical, HVAC and piping, communications, and so forth, detailing should be done in close collaboration with a general contractor and other trades to ensure constructability and correct sequencing of work, which again requires extensive knowledge and understanding of the domain.

As observed in Chapter 5 on the topic of BIM for the design professions, here too the skill set required of BIM operators is likely to result in a decline of the traditional role of drafting. Companies should be sensitive to this in their adoption plan, not only for the sake of the people involved but because BIM adoption may be stifled if the wrong people are expected to pursue it.

Chapter 7 Discussion Questions

1. How does BIM enable new construction methods and new architectural designs? Use examples from modern buildings built with BIM to support your answers.

2. Select a specific building type and construction method, and compile a list of 10–12 kinds of subcontractor that might work on such a project. Classify the subcontractors (trades, suppliers, and fabricators) on two scales: according to the quantity of work performed on-site and according to the type of components they use. Is there any correlation between the two classifications?

3. List three examples of engineered-to-order (ETO) components of buildings. Why do fabricators of ETO components traditionally prepare shop drawings? How can BIM reduce the cycle time for marketing, detailed design, fabrication, and erection of ETO components in construction? Use the three examples of ETO components you provided to illustrate your answers.

4. What are the ways in which BIM can facilitate the work of subcontractors and fabricators? Which of the wastes defined by lean construction can be reduced? (The wastes are rework, unnecessary processing steps, unnecessary movement of people, equipment and materials, inventories, waiting, and overproduction).

5. What are the features of BIM systems that enable "push of a button" changes to details of the kind shown in Section 7.6?

6. Imagine that you are assigned responsibility for the adoption of BIM in a company that fabricates and installs HVAC ducts in commercial and public buildings. The company employs six detailers who use 2D CAD. Discuss your key considerations for adoption and outline a coherent adoption plan, citing major goals and milestones.

7. What type of contractual relationship best serves the needs of a subcontractor doing prefab work, with emphasis on the ability to benefit from the use of BIM?

8. What kinds of technologies (field and office) are available to align the information needs of subcontractors, suppliers, and general contractors with respect to material flows, fabrication and delivery of components, and installation of assemblies?

9. How does BIM influence the economic viability of pre-assembly, prefabrication, and modular construction? How will it contribute to 3D printing and robotic construction in the future?

Facilitators of BIM Adoption and Implementation

8.0 EXECUTIVE SUMMARY

Although "information" is paramount in BIM, the nontechnical aspects of "process," "people," and "policy" must be considered too. This chapter focuses on facilitators of BIM, including mandates, requirements, roadmaps, maturity models, measures, guides, education and training, legal, security and best practice issues.

Many countries have mandated BIM on public projects to design, build, and manage their projects "better, faster, cheaper, safer, and greener" and many more are following suit. Experience teaches that a long-term strategic plan is required to bring a national construction industry to a level where the broad societal benefits of BIM can be achieved. For this reason, most countries release BIM roadmaps in concert with their BIM mandates. BIM guides have also been developed and updated as the industry reached each milestone on the roadmap. At the time of writing, more than 100 BIM guides were publicly available. Sometimes as part of a BIM guide and sometimes as an independent tool, numerous BIM maturity models were developed and released as a means to monitor and manage the status of BIM implementation at various levels.

People are always at the center of any technology innovation. Many BIM training and certification programs have been developed around the world to educate and foster the skills needed. Collaboration between project participants is so essential in BIM that a majority of BIM roadmaps were developed using "level of collaboration" as the main framework. Projects that involve a high level of collaboration cannot be free of legal and security risks, and many BIM guides recommend action on legal and security issues. Overall, accumulated knowledge and experience become best practices and are eventually coded in BIM guides. This creates a cyclic process of project execution, evaluation, and evolution.

8.1 INTRODUCTION

The four core elements of business process reengineering are technology, people, process, and policy. While Chapters 2 and 3 focus on technological aspects of BIM and Chapters 4 to 7 discuss process changes in addition to technological innovation in each discipline, this chapter focuses on the social, strategic, organizational, and other issues that facilitate BIM adoption and implementation. The following main topics are discussed in each section:

- **BIM mandates**: This section discusses the significance of government BIM mandates and reviews the status of mandates around the world. It introduces the different motivations and requirements, challenges and considerations in preparing government BIM mandates.
- **BIM roadmaps, BIM maturity models, and BIM measures**: These are closely related concepts. This section introduces the different types and provides examples of each.
- **BIM guides**: This section introduces publicly available BIM guides by region and by organization. It provides a detailed review of BIM LOx, BIM information requirements, and BIM execution planning.
- **BIM education and training**: People are the core element of BIM. This section describes BIM training and certification programs in industry and university education programs around the world.
- **Legal, security, and best practice issues**: BIM is grounded on tight collaboration among project participants. However, legal and security issues are unavoidable in any highly collaborative project. This section discusses the responsibilities and rights of BIM project participants regarding BIM data. It describes different approaches to BIM service fee structures, discusses the importance of social aspects of BIM, and explains the cyclic relationship between BIM guides, BIM projects, and best practices through BIM project execution, evaluation, and evolution.

8.2 BIM MANDATES

Construction owners, both public and private, are increasingly mandating the use of BIM for their projects. Mandates are often announced by public or private owners in memorandums or public notices that are publicized to the design and construction industry. They are implemented as contractual requirements for service providers. This section focuses on BIM mandates issued by government and other public owners. It first discusses the importance of government BIM mandates and then reports the status, motivations, and requirements of the BIM mandates around the world. It concludes by discussing the challenges and considerations for government BIM mandates.

8.2.1 Significance of Government BIM Mandates

Both public and private sector organizations mandate BIM on their projects, but private sector mandates have less impact on the industry than public sector mandates. Why do the government BIM mandates attract more attention on the part of the industry?

First, a government BIM mandate has a great impact on the industry's awareness of BIM. For example, a series of BIM surveys conducted by the National Building Specification for the UK showed that 43% of respondents were unaware of BIM in 2011, when the BIM mandate was first announced. In 2012, the number dropped to 21%, and in 2013 to 6%. The 2012 SmartMarket Report "The Business Value of BIM in South Korea" showed that two years after the BIM mandate began in South Korea, only 3% of Korean respondents were unaware of BIM.

Second, a large proportion of construction projects, particularly infrastructure projects, are public projects and many companies rely heavily on these public projects.

Third, unlike the BIM mandates of private companies, government BIM mandates are closely related to government policies, regulations, and administration systems, such as the e-Submission system of Singapore. When governments announce BIM mandates, they also generally release a strategic roadmap to change or improve their regulations, standards, and systems to support the changes required by their BIM mandate. BIM guides are also continuously updated according to new BIM requirements.

Fourth, private companies keep the detailed plans and guidelines for their BIM mandate internal, making it difficult for the public to know details about them.

These are only a few reasons and there might be more. The subsequent sections review government BIM mandates in detail.

8.2.2 The Status of Government BIM Mandates around the World

Public organizations in Europe, the U.S., and Asia started mandating BIM in the years leading up to 2010. The first BIM mandates on public projects were announced in 2007 by Norway, Denmark, and Finland. In the U.S., the General Services Administration (GSA) announced that it would mandate BIM on all its projects starting from 2008. In Asia, South Korea mandated BIM on public projects from 2010. Since then, over 15 countries around the world have mandated or announced a plan to mandate BIM. Table 8–1 summarizes them.

Table 8-1 BIM Mandates around the World (by Target Year)

Country	State/Organization	Target Year	Requirements
Norway	Statsbygg	2007–2010	"One-Five-Fifteen-All": One project in 2007, five projects in 2008, fifteen projects in 2009, and all public projects from 2010 were required to use IFC.
Denmark	bips/MOLIO	2007–2013	From January 2007, all public projects over EUR 3M were required to use IFC as a requirement for BIM. In 2013, the Danish government expanded the scope of the BIM mandate to public building projects over EUR 0.7M or projects over EUR 2.7M with loans or grants from government authorities to use ICT/BIM.
Finland	Senate Properties	2007	All public projects are required to use IFC/BIM. Since 2012 after the Common BIM Requirements (COBIM) was released, Senate Properties and major construction companies has mandated BIM on their projects using COBIM as a guide. Finland began a program called KIRAdigi, which includes a plan to make BIM a part of the building permit process.
US	GSA	2008	GSA has mandated BIM on all its major projects (approximately over USD 35M) that involve appropriations from the U.S. government based on the GSA Guide Series.
	Wisconsin	2010	The State of Wisconsin announced that all public projects with a budget of USD 5M or more and all new construction with a budget of USD 2.5M or more must use BIM from 2010.
South Korea	Ministry of Land, Infrastructure, and Transport (MoLIT)/Public Procurement Service (PPS)	2010–2016	At least two projects in 2010, at least three projects in 2011, all "total service" projects over KRW 50B in 2012, and all "total service" projects from 2016 were required to use BIM. A "total service" project is a project whose entire procurement and construction process is planned and managed by PPS.
Singapore	Building and Construction Authority (BCA)	2013–2015	By 2013, all new building projects larger than 20,000 m^2 were required to use "Architecture BIM e-submission." By 2014, all new building projects larger than 20,000 m^2 were required to use "Engineering BIM e-submission." By 2015, all new building projects larger than 5,000 m^2 were required to use "Architecture and Engineering BIM e-submission."
UK	UK BIM Task Group/The Cabinet Office	2016	In 2011, the UK government announced that it would mandate BIM on all public projects at the UK BIM Level 2 by 2016.
China	Hong Kong Housing Authority	2014	In 2014, the Hong Kong Housing Authority mandated BIM on all its projects.
	Hong Kong government	2017–2018	In January 2017, the Hong Kong Policy Address specified that the Hong Kong governmental departments should actively request consultants and contractors to use BIM. From January 2018, the Hong Kong government mandated BIM on government projects exceeding HKD 30M.
	Hunan Province	2018–2020	The Hunan Province planned to mandate BIM on all public design and construction projects exceeding RMB 60M or 20,000 m^2 by late 2018 and on 90% of all new buildings in Hunan Province by 2020.

Table 8–1   (continued)

Country	State/Organization	Target Year	Requirements
China	Fujian city	2017	The city of Fujian selectively mandated BIM on some projects exceeding RMB 100M by 2017.
	National government	2020	Based on the government's Twelfth Five-Year Plan, A-class housing and 90% of new construction projects were required to use BIM by late 2020.
Dubai	Dubai Municipality	2014	In 2014, Dubai Municipality mandated the use of BIM tools for buildings that are 40 stories or taller, for facilities and buildings that cover over 300,000 ft^2, for hospitals, universities, and other special buildings, and those delivered by an international party.
Italy		2016	On January 27, 2016, the Italian government announced that public projects over EUR 5,225,000 must meet the Level 2 BIM of the UK BIM roadmap from October 18, 2016.
France	The Centre Scientifique et Technique du Batiment (CSTB)	2017	In 2014, France announced that it would develop 500,000 houses using BIM by 2017.
Spain	Ministry of Development	2018–2019	In 2015, the Ministry of Development of Spain announced that it was planning to mandate BIM in the public sector from March 2018, public construction projects from December 2018, and infrastructure projects from July 2019.
	Catalonia Municipal Government	2020	In February 2015, the Catalonia Municipal Government formed a group named "Construim el Futur" ("We Build the Future") to set up a plan to mandate BIM by 2020.
Germany	Federal Ministry of Transport and Digital Infrastructure	2020	The Germany government planned to mandate BIM on all infrastructure projects by 2020 and potentially also on building construction projects.
Israel	Ministry of Defense	2016	All projects must be delivered with BIM by 2019.

8.2.3 Motivations

Government BIM mandates are motivated by various factors:

- The construction industry is central in all economies, but has relatively low productivity compared to the other industries (Egan, 1998; Teicholz, 2004).
- The opportunity to improve the quality and management of building and infrastructure projects through the lifecycle of a project.
- Governments sought to improve management of public facilities and assets by repurposing BIM data produced during the design and construction phases. This motivation naturally led to the mandatory submission of IFC or COBie "as-built" models as part of the BIM requirements.
- The desire for "informed decision making" based on BIM data. This was one of the strongest motivations for the UK BIM Task Group.

- The increasing demand for sustainable and environmentally friendly design and construction. The Kyoto Protocol in 1997 and the Paris Agreement in 2015 are significant in this regard. BIM is recognized to be an effective tool for achieving sustainability goals (Bernstein et al., 2010; Krygiel and Nies, 2008).
- The desire to maintain or expand global leadership in the construction sector.

There may be more, but these motivations reflect a strategic approach to enable project participants to plan, design, construct, operate, and manage their buildings and other facilities "better, faster, cheaper, safer, and greener."

8.2.4   BIM Requirements

The early BIM mandates simply required submission of design data in IFC or other BIM formats. As more knowledge and experience about BIM were gained, the requirements became more complex and explicit. One such example is the Korea Power Exchange headquarters project, which began in 2009. Although the roadmap for the BIM mandate in South Korea officially began in 2010, seven public projects in South Korea had already been asked to use BIM before 2010.

The Dongdaemun Design Plaza case study, introduced in Section 10.4, and the Korea Power Exchange headquarters project were two of them. The BIM requirements for the Korea Power Exchange headquarters project were very specific and each of them was evaluated and scored during the design evaluation process. In addition to submitting design BIM models in IFC, three more categories of requirements were stipulated: (1) automated checking of spatial requirements; (2) automated checking of the basic design quality; and (3) BIM-based energy performance evaluation. Each category had subrequirements. For example, the basic design-quality check included hard- and soft-clash-free design, and satisfaction of regulations related to egress and fire safety, the disability laws, and staircase designs. Each team used over ten applications including Rhino, Revit, SketchUp, Robot, Midas, Ecotect, IES Virtual Environment, and Solibri Model Checker. IFC was recommended for data exchange. However, a meeting with project participants after the tendering process revealed that the industry and the software applications were not yet sufficiently mature to fulfill all the requirements. This motivated the birth of the BIM mandate roadmap of South Korea for incremental adoption of BIM described in Table 8–1.

In 2013, when the Danish government expanded the scope of its BIM mandate, it required seven items: (1) coordinated use of information and communication technology, (2) management of digital building objects, (3) use of digital communication and a project website, (4) use of digital building models, (5) digital quantity-takeoff and bidding, (6) digital delivery of building documentation, and (7) digital inspection.

On May 31, 2011, the UK Cabinet Office announced that the government would mandate Level 2 BIM on its projects from April 2016. Subsequently it released a series of BIM guides starting with PAS 1192-2 (BSI 2013), released in 2013. PAS 1192-2 specifies "information management for the capital/delivery phase of construction projects using BIM," which requests submission of three documents: a Master Information Delivery Plan (MIDP); a BIM Execution Plan (BEP); and Employer's Information Requirements (EIR). PAS 1192-3 specifies "information management for the operational phase of assets using BIM," and recommends explicit specification of asset information requirements and submission of asset information according to COBie-UK-2012. PAS 1192-4 specifies details on collaborative production of COBie-UK. PAS 1192-5 specifies security-related requirements. There are more specifications for the BIM mandate, and the number is expected to grow. Some will become contractual requirements, and some will remain simply as guidelines.

The national-level BIM guides specify minimum requirements. Each project can expand the list of requirements and may add new or detailed requirements depending on the needs of a project. For example, some projects add the specific methods of using BIM, the minimum number of BIM specialists on a team (managers and coordinators), or the use of specific platforms or a BIM server.

8.2.5 Challenges and Considerations

As described earlier, government BIM mandates greatly increase awareness of BIM in the industry. However, that does not mean that the government-driven BIM mandates immediately produce benefits for industry. To create a positive impact of a BIM mandate on projects, the following points should be considered.

- Building owners, as well as industry professionals, need to be educated about BIM. Where owners are ignorant and/or indifferent, the expected returns are minimal. In the worst cases, the entire project can be mismanaged with detrimental results.
- Watch out for "BIM wash"—a superficial way of conducting and delivering BIM services. Many early BIM-mandated projects were conducted by consultancies to satisfy the minimum requirements, such as submitting models in the IFC format. To avoid BIM wash, a well-planned and incremental strategy to get the industry involved is needed.
- A clear definition of BIM handover data is required. For example, many owners simply request submission of IFC or COBie files without thinking about what information is truly needed for facility management.
- Be patient. It takes time for people to learn how to use BIM efficiently and effectively. As Jan Karlshoj, vice chair of buildingSMART Nordic, explained in an interview in 2016 (Karlshoj, 2016), "[Denmark] took seven to eight years since BIM was mandated to see the benefits from the new way of working. . . . It took a couple of years after the mandate to get all contractors on board and another three to four years before it became part of the handover. All things considered, the clients have only been implementing this for a few years; therefore, we still have a lot to learn."

8.3 BIM ROADMAPS, MATURITY MODELS, AND MEASURES

BIM maturity model, BIM measure, BIM roadmap, BIM mandate, and BIM guide are inseparable concepts (Figure 8–1). A BIM maturity model is a benchmark tool for assessing the level of BIM implementation on a project, in an organization, or across a region. A BIM measure is an individual key performance indicator (KPI) that may be used in a BIM maturity model. BIM implementation requires time and incremental steps. A BIM roadmap is a plan to reach target competency levels as measured using a BIM maturity model. A BIM mandate defines target goals at each stage of a BIM roadmap. A BIM guide is a set of detailed instructions to help users fulfil the mandate.

8.3.1 BIM Roadmaps

Since the early 2000s, when BIM began to be perceived as the future direction of the AEC industry, many companies developed roadmaps to adopt BIM in their organization. For example, Skanska Finland had a roadmap to begin the first BIM project in 2005 and to gain clear business benefits by 2013 through the expansion of scope of BIM adoption to residential projects by 2008, to commercial projects by 2009, and to global projects by 2009 (see Sacks et al., 2017, Chapter 5).

The earliest BIM roadmap developed by a public organization was that of the US Army Corps of Engineers (USACE). The initial USACE roadmap, released in 2006, had seven milestones based on the number of projects and the compliance level (in terms of percentage) with the National BIM Standards (NBIMS). It had ambitious goals to incrementally implement BIM in all USACE district projects, based on NBIMS by 2010, to achieve the full

FIGURE 8–1 The relationships between BIM roadmaps, BIM maturity models, BIM mandates, BIM guides, and BIM measures.

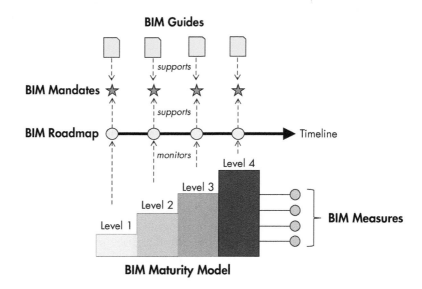

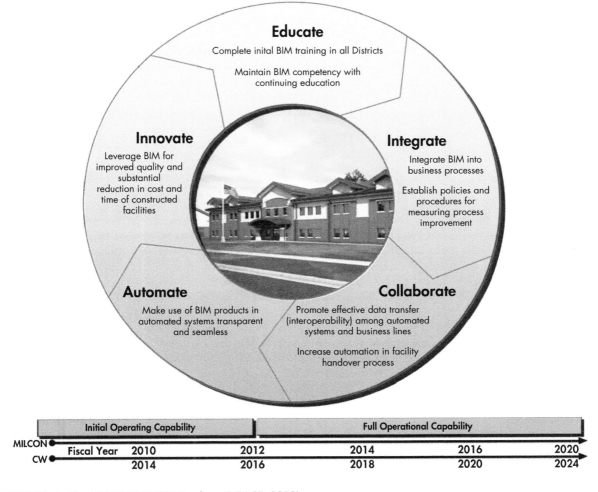

FIGURE 8–2 The USACE 2012 BIM Roadmap (USACE, 2012).

operational capability defined by NBIMS by 2012, and automation of lifecycle tasks by 2020. A revised roadmap released in 2012 pushed back the target date for achieving the full operational capability to 2020, and it redefined the BIM maturity levels as a cyclic process of five steps—Educate, Integrate, Collaborate, Automate, and Innovate—rather than a linear incremental process (Figure 8–2).

Since the USACE roadmap, many BIM roadmaps have been developed and released to the public. Each one reflected a different philosophy and strategy. However, they can be roughly grouped into five groups.

The first group is defined by the *level of collaboration*. For example, the BIM roadmap, published by the Australian Institute of Architects and the

Cooperative Research Center (CRC) for Construction Innovation in 2009, categorized the BIM maturity status into three levels: *Isolated, Collaborative,* and *Integrated.* The USACE roadmap is similar to the Australian model. Similarly, the Canadian BIM roadmap released in 2014 specifies five levels: *Independent, Coordinated, Collaborative, Integrated,* and *Unified/Optimized* (Figure 8–3). McCallum categorized the different levels of BIM collaboration in layman's terms, calling them *Lonely BIM, Shy BIM, Friendly BIM,* and *Social BIM* (McCallum, 2011). The UK BIM roadmap is based on the "Bew-Richards BIM maturity model" and can also be categorized in this group. buildingSMART Australasia compared the UK maturity model and its own model and mapped Levels 0 and 1 of the UK model to its Isolation phase, Level 2 to the Collaboration phase, and Level 3 to the Integration phase (Figure 8–4). Unsurprisingly, the UK BIM Level 1 is often referred to as the Lonely BIM phase.

The second group categorizes BIM roadmaps based on the *scope of BIM projects.* Examples include the BIM roadmaps of Singapore BCA, South Korea MOLIT and PPS, Scandinavian countries, and other countries with a BIM mandate. For example, Singapore BCA uses the gross floor area. Denmark, South Korea, China, and the State of Wisconsin use the total project value. China uses the percentage of projects. France use the number of units. Dubai uses the number of stories and the gross floor areas. The open BIM roadmap for super-tall buildings of South Korea uses the project phase. Spain uses the type of project. See Table 8–1 in Section 8.2.2 for more details and examples.

The third group defines BIM roadmaps based on *the core value* to achieve at each phase. The BIM Roadmap published by PPS of South Korea and buildingSMART Korea in 2009 divided the BIM roadmap into the establishment phase (3 years), the implementation phase (3 years), and the advancement and settlement phase (4 years). Each phase had a specific goal: *design quality improvement, budget reduction,* and *business innovation,* respectively. Each of these goals was supported by specific execution strategies and sub-goals in five categories: (1) policy promotion, (2) standards development and adoption, (3) technology acquisition and diffusion, (4) project implementation, and (5) education and dissemination.

The fourth group defines BIM roadmaps based on *BIM uses.* For example, the BIM 2030 Roadmap discussed in Chapter 9 (Section 9.6) defines five levels of BIM use, beginning from the least technically challenging ones: Level 0 Marketing BIM, Level 1 Early Coordination BIM, Level 2 Two-Track BIM, Level 3 Full BIM, Level 4 Lean BIM, and Level 5 Artificial Intelligence BIM. Company BIM roadmaps often use this approach.

The last group includes BIM roadmaps with a unique approach. For example, the BIM roadmap of the UK High Speed Two (HS2) rail project takes a descriptive approach in contrast with the prescriptive approach of typical roadmaps. HS2 uses a cartoon to describe what to achieve at different points (Figure 8–5). The National BIM Blueprint of Australia uses a process map to illustrate the relationships between eight categories: (1) procurement, (2) BIM guidelines, (3) education, (4) product data and libraries, (5) process and data exchange, (6) regulatory framework, (7) national BIM initiative, and (8) industry.

Roadmap v 1.0 | 26.11.2014 | Copyright © buildingSMART Canada 2014

Roadmap to Lifecycle Building Information Modeling in the Canadian AECOO Community

	level 0	level 1	level 2	level 3	level n.
Technology	Isolated	Networked	Interoperable	Integrated	**Unified**
Organization	Independent	Coordinated	Collaborative		
Process	Ad Hoc	**Defined**	Managed	Optimized	
	2014		◆ 2017		2020+

Engage:
Foster engagement from government, industry and academia by promoting BIM in Canada. (1.0.0)

- Create a movement to BIM (1.1.0)
- Engage public owners & push for strong leadership at federal, provincial and municipal levels (2.1.0)
- Inform the community through outreach programs and promotion (1.3.0)
- Form constituent organizations (1.4.0)
- Support constituent organizations through coaching and strong leadership (1.5.0)

Desired state:
- Broad industry support and full engagement of government sectors, private sectors and academia
- Constant reporting of success stories, lessons learned and best practices

Develop:
Develop guidelines, protocols, technical codes and standards to facilitate the use of BIM in the Canadian AECOO community. (2.0.0)

- Develop and communicate a national BIM strategy (2.1.0)
- Develop national BIM Standard (2.2.0)
- Develop BIM Guidelines (practice manuals, toolkits, etc.) (2.3.0)
- Review BIM Standards and Guidelines (2.4.0)
- Develop specifications for Canadian BIM certifications (2.5.0)
- Develop best practices and BIM body of knowledge (2.6.0)

Desired state:
- Complete and coherent toolkits
- Unified software platform
- Rigorous certification standards, data exchange definitions, and protocols

Educate:
Develop training and educational programs to develop the core BIM capabilities in the Canadian AECOO community. (3.0.0)

Provide impetus for a national BIM mandate

- Build a community of practice of parties offering BIM education and training in Canada (3.1.0)
- Develop reference curriculum for BIM education in Canada (3.2.0)
- Develop BIM training packages for AECOO community stakeholders
- Provide accreditation for institutions (3.3.0)
- Provide certification for individuals (3.4.0)

Comprehensive national BIM mandate

Desired state:
- Defined and accepted educational standards
- Integrated educational programs
- Robust and recognized certification and accreditation process

Deploy:
Create and implement collaborative project delivery environments that foster the use of BIM in the Canadian AECOO community. (4.0.0)

- Develop standardized contractual language with the legal community for BIM deployment (4.1.0)
- Develop and adopt standardized contracts that facilitate BIM implementation (4.2.0)
- Use of delivery modes that foster collaborative project delivery environments (4.3.0)
- Develop standardized requirements facilitating the passage to open data and information deliverables (4.4.0)

Desired state:
- Widespread and consistent client demand
- Ongoing deployment of program and frameworks
- Prevalence of collaborative project delivery modes

Evaluate:
Measure, evaluate and assess the impact and maturity of BIM within the Canadian AECOO community. (5.0.0)

- Develop metrics and Key Performance Indicators for consistent performance and capability assessment (5.1.0)
- Develop a maturity model/ capability assessment tool (5.2.0)
- Provide a platform to allow maturity modeling and capability assessment of the AECOO community (5.3.0)
- Establish a national performance assessment and benchmarking framework (5.4.0)
- Communicate and compare performance and maturity levels (5.5.0)

Desired state:
- Consistent metrics & measurement processes
- Continuous evaluation of community maturity
- Support for measurement and benchmarking effort

Sustain:
Adopt and maintain the transition to BIM and collaborative project delivery practices within the Canadian AECOO community. (6.0.0)

- Document and promote success stories through Canadian case studies (6.1.0)
- Establish partnerships between academia and industry to encourage knowledge creation and innovation (6.2.0)
- Maintain buyin and engagement from agencies, professional associations and stakeholders (6.3.0)
- Maintain and communicate best practices and BIM body of knowledge (6.4.0)
- Align & maintain Canadian BIM standards and guidelines with international initiatives (6.5.0)

Desired state:
- Constant progression of BIM use in the Canadian AECOO community
- Maintained standards, guidelines and protocols

FIGURE 8–3 The Canada BIM Roadmap (bSC, 2014).

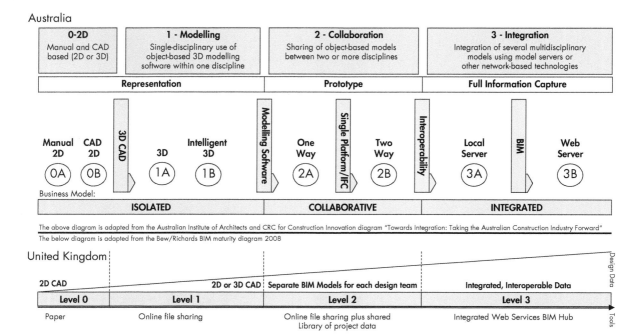

FIGURE 8–4 A comparison between the Australian and UK BIM maturity models (buildingSMART Australasia, 2012).

FIGURE 8–5 The UK High Speed 2 (HS2) BIM Roadmap (HS2, 2013).

These roadmaps are used as a basis for BIM mandates and are usually supported by a BIM guide, which is updated at each stage. For example, the UK BIM roadmap and the mandate are supported by the detailed descriptions of the BIM Level 2 requirements in the PAS 1192 series and in BS standard documents. Similarly, the MOLIT/PPS guide of South Korea was updated at each stage of the MOLIT/PPS BIM Roadmap.

BIM roadmaps tend to describe the goals, action plans, and BIM requirements for the short-term (typically 4–5 years) relatively specifically, but those beyond the short-term remain vague. For example, the UK BIM roadmap provides clear guidelines for BIM Level 2, but those for BIM Level 3 are less so. Chapter 9 discusses the future directions of BIM in more detail.

8.3.2 BIM Maturity Models

As the famous saying goes, "What cannot be measured, cannot be managed." A BIM maturity model is a framework to quantify and manage the level of BIM proficiency in an organization or across a project team. BIM maturity models generally have two axes: the areas of interest (evaluation criteria) and the maturity levels with score values. By combining these two, the BIM maturity level in each area of interest and the total maturity score can be calculated. Some BIM maturity models are defined at a high (macro) level with a small number of areas of interest, but many are defined at a very detailed level with multiple depths of areas of interests and several maturity levels. Different BIM maturity models are available for assessing individuals, project teams, organizations, or whole industry sectors and/or regions. Table 8–2 summarizes the BIM maturity models by main evaluation target.

The first two models introduced in Table 8–2 have the simplest form. The "level of expertise" model asks a very simple question: What is your level of BIM expertise, beginner, moderate, or expert? This question was first used by SmartMarket Report: The Value of BIM series from 2007. Since then, this question has been used by many BIM surveys. The Individual Competency Index (ICI) is not very different. It categorizes the level of BIM expertise into five levels: none, basic, intermediate, advanced, and expert. A more complex form of the BIM maturity model for individual evaluation might be the BIM certification criteria for BIM professionals discussed in Section 8.5.

The second set of models aims to evaluate the level of BIM maturity at a project level. For example, **the BIM Excellence Project Assessment (BIMe) is** composed of two models: one for complete projects and the other for current projects (ChangeAgents AEC Pty Ltd., 2017). Complete projects are evaluated using the past performance indicators as benchmarks, and the current projects are evaluated using process metrics. The model uses the cost certainty index (the difference between estimated costs and actual costs) as the key indicator. Examples of model uses include clash detection, structural analysis, and cost estimation.

Another example, **the BIM Success Level Assessment Model (SLAM)** does not measure the capability maturity level; it evaluates the degree of success. The BIM SLAM is composed of six steps. It begins by laying out the *BIM goals* of a project by core project members similar to the development process of a BIM

Table 8–2   BIM Maturity Models by Evaluation Target

Evaluation Target	Model	Year	Organization
Individual	Level of Expertise	2007	McGraw Hill Construction
	Individual Competency Index (ICI)	2013	ChangeAgents AEC, Pty. Ltd.
	Various BIM certification models	n.d.	Various organizations
Project team	BIM Excellence (BIMe)	2011	ChangeAgents AEC, Pty. Ltd.
	BIM Success Level Assessment Model (SLAM)	2014	Yonsei University
Project team, Organization, or Industry sector	NBIMS Capability Maturity Model (CMM)	2007	NIBS
	IU BIM Proficiency Matrix (BPM)	2009	Indiana University
	VDC Scorecard/bimSCORE	2009/2013	Stanford CIFE/ Strategic Building Innovation, Inc.
	BIM Maturity Matrix (BIm^3)	2010	ChangeAgents AEC, Pty. Ltd.
	BIM QuickScan	2012	TNO
	The Organizational BIM Assessment Profile (BIM Maturity Measure, BIMmm)	2012	Penn State CIC
	BIMCAT	2013	University of Florida
Macro-level Evaluation (Region/Industry)	Diffusion of Innovations (DoI)	1962	University of New Mexico
	Hype Cycle model	1995	Gartner Inc.
	slim BIM model	2012	Yonsei University
	BIM engagement index	2013	McGraw Hill Construction
	Macro-BIM adoption model	2014	ChangeAgents AEC

execution plan. Different weight values can be assigned to each goal. The second step defines *BIM uses* to achieve the project goals. The third step defines the *BIM key performance indicators (KPIs)* related to the BIM goals and uses. The BIM SLAM provides a set of commonly used KPIs for different BIM goals and uses them as candidates for the BIM KPIs of the project. The final set of KPIs is selected considering the *measurability, collectability,* and *comparability* of each KPI. The fourth step is to define unit measurements—atomic information items required to collect KPI data. The fifth step is to create *work templates* that allow project members to collect unit measurement data during a daily work process without additional work. The final step is to *evaluate* the collected data against the historical data of past projects or the goals of the current project and to *share* the status of the project on a construction dashboard to promote collaboration (Won and Lee, 2016).

The third set of models are most versatile and complex. They can be deployed to assess the BIM maturity level of a project team, of an organization, or of an industry. **The BIM Capability Maturity Model (BIM CMM)** is one of the earliest. It was developed by the National Institute of Building Sciences in 2007 based on the Capability Maturity Model (CMM) concept used in software development. It is accompanied by Interactive CMM (I-CMM), an Excel-based BIM CMM tool. The BIM CMM evaluates the level of BIM maturity in 11 areas of interest: (1) data richness, (2) lifecycle views, (3) change management, (4) roles or disciplines, (5) business process, (6) timeliness/response, (7) delivery method, (8) graphical information, (9) spatial capability, (10) information accuracy, and (11) interoperability/IFC support. Different weight values can be assigned to the areas of interest. BIM experts evaluate each area on ten levels using the BIM CMM Chart as a guideline. The level of a project is categorized into Platinum (90 and over), Gold (80 and over), Silver (70 and over), Certified (50 and over), and Minimum BIM (30 and over) (McCuen et al., 2012).

The IU BIM Proficiency Matrix (BPM) developed by Indiana University in 2009 is similar to the BIM CMM in that it also uses a matrix of the areas of interest and the maturity level as a basic framework (Indiana University Architect's Office, 2009). The BPM has eight areas of interest and four levels of BIM maturity. The eight areas of interest are (1) physical accuracy of model, (2) IPD methodology, (3) calculation mentality, (4) location awareness, (5) content creation, (6) construction data, (7) as-built modeling, and (8) FM data richness. Since each area has four levels, the maximum total BIM score is thirty-two.

The BIM Maturity Matrix (BIm^3) developed in 2009 in Australia is another model that uses a matrix structure similar to the BIM CMM (Succar, 2010). To overcome perceived drawbacks of the CMM (overlapping and unclear areas of interest and lack of areas related to collaboration and cultural issues), it categorized five evaluation areas: technology, process, policy, collaboration, and organization. These areas were based on the people, process, technology, and policy (PPTP) framework, which is the basic framework used in business process reengineering. Each area of the BIM Maturity Matrix was categorized into five levels—namely, initial (ad-hoc), defined, managed, integrated, and optimized levels—similar to those of the original CMM in software engineering.

The Center for Integrated Facility Engineering (CIFE) at Stanford University developed **the VDC Scorecard**, which later became the basis for **bimSCORE**, a commercial version of the VDC Scorecard (Kam et al., 2016). The name was inspired by the Balanced Scorecard, which was developed in business management to extend project or organization evaluation to incorporate nonfinancial information. The VDC Scorecard assesses the BIM performance of a project or an organization in four areas: planning, adoption, technology, and performance. The scoring of each area uses a percentile system against the industry norm using the following five levels as a guideline: (1) conventional practice (0%–25%), (2) typical practice (25%–50%), (3) advanced practice (50%–75%), (4) best practice (75%–90%), and (5) innovative practice (90%–100%). The evaluation areas break down into three depths. The four areas of interest are subcategorized into ten dimensions, and the ten dimensions into fifty-six measures. Different weights can be assigned to each area and dimension. This four-tier system makes the coverage of the VDC Scorecard/bimSCORE more complete than that of any other models, but at the same time completing the evaluation takes a long time. Nevertheless, it has been applied to analyze the status of numerous BIM projects in the United States, Singapore, China, Hong Kong, and South Korea.

The BIM QuickScan, developed by TNO in the Netherlands in 2012, evaluates BIM projects in four chapters: (1) organization and management, (2) mentality and culture, (3) information structure and flow, and (4) tools and applications. The four chapters are subcategorized into ten areas: strategy, organization, resources, partners, mentality, culture, education, information flow, open standards, and tools. These areas are evaluated using a maximum of 50 KPIs in the form of a multiple-choice questionnaire. In additional to the BIM QuickScan, several BIM maturity models were developed by BIM consulting firms in the Netherlands such as **BIM Measure Indicator, BIM Success Predictor,** and **BIM Success Forecasters** (Sebastian and van Berlo, 2010).

The Organizational BIM Assessment Profile or **the BIM Maturity Measure/Measurement (BIMmm)** is a maturity model developed by Pennsylvania State University (Penn State) as part of the BIM Planning Guide for Facility Owners (CIC, 2013). It is a matrix of six areas of interest and six maturity levels. The six areas of interest are (1) strategy, (2) BIM uses, (3) process, (4) information, (5) infrastructure, and (6) personnel. The BIM Maturity Measure/Measurement (BIMmm) is the new name given by Arup, a global design and engineering firm, after adding interactive features to Penn State's Excel-based "Organizational BIM Assessment Profile" tool. The model is the same. Although its name declares that it was initially developed for BIM assessment at an organizational level, Arup adopted the model and deployed it to assess the BIM maturity level of hundreds of its BIM projects.

The last group of models are the ones deployed to understand the level of BIM maturity (BIM adoption/implementation, to be more specific) at an industry or a regional level. They are often referred to as *macro-level BIM maturity models*. **The diffusion of innovation (DOI) model** and **the hype cycle model** are generic technology adoption models, not BIM-specific, dating from the 1960s and 1995, respectively. The DOI model uses the main user type as the basis for determining the status of technology adoption. The users are categorized into five groups: innovators, early adopters, early majority, late majority, and laggards. The hype cycle model classifies the technology adoption into five stages: technology trigger, peak of inflated expectations, trough of disillusionment, slope of enlightenment, and plateau of productivity. A global survey in 2015 showed that a majority of respondents from BIM-leading regions such as North America, Europe, Oceania, and Asia perceived that they reached the slope of enlightenment and were heading toward the plateau of productivity (Jung and Lee, 2015b).

The BIM Engagement Index was developed by the McGraw Hill Construction Research and Analytics to quantify the level of BIM engagement in different regions (Bernstein et al., 2014). Similar to the **slim BIM model** developed in 2012 (Jung and Lee, 2015a), it evaluates the level of BIM engagement using three indices: depth of BIM implementation, level of BIM proficiency, and years of using BIM. Each area is categorized in three to four levels with different scoring systems. The total sum represents the BIM engagement level of a region. It has been used by the SmartMarket Report series since 2013.

There are many more BIM maturity models than can be presented here. They include BIM maturity models used at companies, specific disciplines, or specific regions. However, the ones listed previously should be enough as a starting point for readers seeking a BIM maturity model suitable for their organization, or one that can be tailored for a specific purpose.

8.3.3 BIM Measures

When a company sets out to adopt BIM, senior managers commonly ask how much it will cost, how soon will BIM provide returns on investment, and how can progress be monitored. BIM measures are the key performance indicators that can be used to provide answers. BIM measures are ideally monitored over the long term, but they can also be used as one-time measures to quantify benefits in case study projects. Naturally, they include standard construction project measures, such as schedule, cost, and quality performance.

Figure 8–6 lists 13 measures used in 18 studies related to BIM benefits. They include the impact on *schedule* and *cost*, the *return on investment (ROI)*, the number of *requests for information (RFI)*, *change orders (CO)*, *amount of rework,* and *defects. Productivity* is another traditional index. Although they appeared less frequently in the studies, *energy consumption, risks, safety-related accidents, claims,* and *waste* are also critical KPIs. In addition to these, *carbon footprint, inspection pass rate, issue resolution time*, the numerous KPIs defined in the various BIM maturity models, and many other indices used in construction projects are also useful measures of BIM impact.

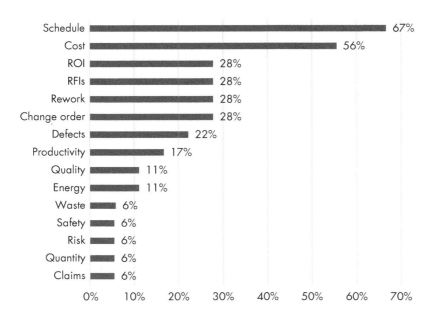

FIGURE 8–6 Commonly used BIM measures, updated from Won (2014).

8.4 BIM GUIDES

A BIM guide is *a collection of best practices for implementing BIM in a project*. Guides evolve continuously as people learn how to use BIM effectively and efficiently. The number and the scope of BIM guides are rapidly increasing. As of 2015, Cheng and Lu (2015) identified 123 BIM guides published in 14 countries. BIM guides can strongly influence project participants' behavior when they are given legal authority through inclusion in construction contract clauses.

This section introduces BIM guides by region and organization. It then reviews the guides according to three special topics: level of detail/level of development (LOx), information requirements, and BIM execution planning.

In practice, several terms—such as manual, handbook, protocol, guidelines, requirements, project specifications, and standard—are used with the BIM prefix, and most of them are interchangeable with the term BIM guide. In this book we use the term *BIM guide* to denote a document developed to help BIM users implement BIM effectively and efficiently. The term *BIM standard* denotes a guide, information requirements, or a protocol that is approved by an international standard organization such as ISO. BIM standards are reviewed in Section 3.3.2.

8.4.1 BIM Guides by Region and Organization

BIM guides are commonly categorized into international, national, project, and facility levels by application scope and into public organization, private organization, and university by publisher type. BIM guides on international, national, project, and facility levels have an inheritance relationship. In other words, BIM guides for individual projects or facilities can be developed by elaborating guidelines specified in a national-level BIM guide or by adding new contents. The level of detail increases as the scope of application narrows down. That is, project or facility level BIM guides are more detailed than national guides. Perhaps the closest thing to an international-level BIM guide is the ISO international framework for BIM guidance (ISO/TS 12911, 2012). Given the overwhelming number of guides available, we provide a brief historical review of some of the key national guides.

The earliest BIM guides were published in the United States and Europe. In the United States, the "Contractor's Guide to BIM" was published in 2006 by the Associated General Contractors of America (AGC, 2006). Since the depth of knowledge and experience related to BIM projects was shallow at that time, the Contractor's Guide to BIM was more of an introduction to BIM and BIM processes than a prescriptive technical guide to best practice. In 2007, the General Services Administration (GSA) started publishing the BIM Guide Series (01-08) (GSA, 2007). In the same year, the National Institute of Building Sciences published the first parts of the National BIM Standard (NBIMS-US) (NIBS, 2007), and the National Institute of Standards and Technology published the General Buildings Information Handover Guide (NIST, 2007). While these guides focused on modeling and implementation issues, the American Institute of Architects (AIA) published contract guidelines, such as AIA E201

Digital Data Protocol Exhibit (AIA, 2007b) and AIA C106 Digital Data Licensing Agreement (AIA, 2007a).

In Europe, Denmark published a series of BIM guides such as 3D Working Method in 2006, and English versions in 2007 (bips, 2007). The early Danish BIM guide series focused on 3D object-based CAD, rather than BIM, and lacked technical and procedural details similar to the Contractor's Guide to BIM in the United States. In 2007, Senate Properties of Finland published BIM Requirements for Architectural Design, which later became a basis for the Common BIM Requirements (COBIM) series (01-13) (buildingSMART Finland, 2012). In 2017, the EU BIM Task Group published the EU BIM Guide for the European public sector.

Singapore published a BIM-related guide in 2008, but the scope was limited to an e-Submission process (BCA, 2008). BIM guides that covered the wide range of BIM-related issues were published in Hong Kong in 2009 (HKHA, 2009), in Australia in 2009 (CRC, 2009), in South Korea in 2010 (MLTM, 2010), and in Singapore in 2012 (BCA, 2012). Japan, Taiwan, and China have also published national BIM guides.

Since then, the number and the scope of BIM guides has increased exponentially and they influence one another. Older BIM guides have been updated several times. Among the many BIM guides, the COBIM series, the GSA BIM Guide series, and the NBIMS-US are the most comprehensive and consequently influenced many others. A detailed historical review of BIM guides can be found in Cheng and Lu (2015).

The BIM Guides project team of buildingSMART International analyzed 81 BIM guides to develop a common framework for BIM guides. The team identified that most BIM guides have two parts: a document overview, a general introduction that describes intended use, scope and audience; and document contents, which provides the technical details in five subsections, as listed below (bSI, 2014a; Keenliside, 2015):

Part A: Document Overview

General overview, including descriptions of intended use and audiences

Part B: Document Content

- **Project definition and planning** section includes definitions of project phases, BIM roles, model element definitions, BIM maturity levels, BIM functions and use cases, and other issues related to project definition and planning.
- **Technical specifications** section includes BIM object classification systems, modeling requirements, file formats, LODs, information exchange requirements (IDM/MVD), and other technical requirements.
- **Implementation processes** section discusses the scope and definition of deliverables and handovers, BIM management and planning, process maps and workflows such as collaboration procedures, quality check/quality control protocols, and other issues related to implementation.

- **Supporting tools** section specifies issues related to selection of software and hardware including BIM servers, security issues, data exchange protocols, and tool-related issues.
- **Legal aspects** section includes fee structure, contractual issues, procurement strategies, intellectual property provisions, liability, risks, insurance, and other legal issues.

Hwang and Lee (2016) analyzed 40 national-level BIM guides and reported that the issues related to BIM maturity, hardware selection, process maps, fee structures, procurement strategies (including IPD), and liability, risks, and insurances were relatively less discussed. Sacks et al. (2016) analyzed 15 national-level BIM guides and reached a similar conclusion. Hardware selection might not be a critical issue in the near future as the computing power of devices increases exponentially. As we gain more experience and knowledge about the other issues, the empty slots will be filled in.

8.4.2   BIM Guides by Topic

A good BIM guide should cover all issues critical to BIM implementation. Many of the issues are discussed in general BIM guides, but some are discussed as special topics in specific BIM guides. This section reviews BIM guide issues related to BIM LOx, information requirements, and BIM execution planning.

BIM LOx. A model is an abstraction of the real world and is supposed to include only the essential information required for a project, not everything. Otherwise, the effort and time to generate a new model, or to update a model to reflect new requirements and changes, would be unreasonable. Modeling effort and time increase as the amount of information, the number of objects in a model, and the number of revision cycles increase.

Furthermore, given the relative ease with which detailed information could be added, the pitfall of overspecification too early in design is real. For example, a model used in an early phase of a project for mass studies does not require a high level of detail, whereas a model used during the construction phase for steel fabrication does require a high level of detail.

Thus determining the appropriate level of detail of models to meet their purposes is critical for efficient project implementation. This issue was recognized from the first days of BIM adoption in the early 2000s. The main questions were "What are the appropriate levels of detail for generating models for different purposes?" and "How can the contractual requirements for the level of detail of BIM models be specified?" These were initially referred to as the *level of detail (LOD)* issues, borrowing the term used in computer graphics to represent the varying degree of complexity of a 3D model by the distance of objects in a model: The closer an object is, the higher the level of detail is. However, the term *level of detail* was soon replaced by the *level of development (LOD)* to emphasize that the level of detail might not increase even if a project progressed to a later design phase. That is, a higher *level of development* number does not necessarily mean a higher *level of detail*. A good example is that the BIM models required by the FM phase generally require lower levels of detail than the BIM models used during the construction phase.

After several years of discussions, "3D Working Method"—the first official document related to LOD—was published in 2006 by bips, a Danish building knowledge center, and translated into English in 2007 (bips, 2007). This document uses the term "Information Level" instead of LOD, and categorizes Information Levels into six, yet the general concept is the same as that of LOD.

A significant publication that strongly influenced the industry and the succeeding LOD guides was published in 2008, *AIA Document E202: The Building Information Modeling Protocol Exhibit* (AIA, 2008). At the same time, the *Model Progression Specification* (MPS) was also published by Webcor Builders, Vico Software, and the AGC (Vico Software et al., 2008). The two documents are similar in that both use LOD 100 to LOD 500 and provide a template for specifying LODs for model elements. One major difference is that the MPS uses LOD as an acronym for Level of Detail, whereas the AIA Document E202 uses LOD as an acronym for Level of Development.

AIA Document E202 was influential because it was designed as a general guide to be used in tandem with design contracts, and it has been used as a basis for specifying LOD of BIM models by many BIM projects throughout the world. AIA Document E202 includes definitions of each LOD and a Model Element Table that can be used to specify different LODs for each model element in a BIM model. Figure 8–7 shows an example of the LOD Model Element Table. Document E202 was updated in 2013 (*AIA G202-2013 Project BIM Protocol Form*) to add one more level, LOD 350, and more detailed descriptions and examples of each LOD.

Since 3D Working Method and AIA Document E202 were published, numerous LOD guides have been based on them, with or without variations. LOD guides such as those of New York City, Penn State, USACE, Taiwan, Hong Kong, and Singapore BCA use LOD 100 to LOD 500 as defined by AIA Document E202. The New Zealand guide (2014) also uses LOD 100 to LOD 500, but elaborates them into four subcategories: Level of detail (LOd), Level of accuracy (LOa), Level of information (LOi) and Level of coordination (LOc). The UK took a slightly different approach, defining seven Levels of Definition following the UK classification of a project lifecycle. It distinguishes level of geometric data from level of nongeometric data, calling them Level of Model Detail (LOD) and Level of Model Information (LOI), respectively.

Model Elements Utilizing CSI UniFormat™			LOD
A Substructure	A10 Foundations	A1010 Standard Foundations	
		A1020 Special Foundations	
		A1030 Slab on Grade	
	A20 Basement Construction	A2010 Basement Excavation	
		A2020 Basement Walls	

FIGURE 8–7 An example of the LOD Model Element Table (AIA, 2008).

South Korea also developed BIM Information Level (BIL 10-60) based on the AIA LOD with minor differences in the number of information levels and the information required by each level (bSK, 2016). The term *LOx* is used as a generalized term for these numerous LOD-related terms.

Despite the popularity of the LOD guides as a simple and practical tool for specifying the work scope of BIM information producers in a contract, they cannot provide explicit definitions of information requirements and always leave room for disagreement among project participants. For example, let us assume that models related to excavation work (such as A2020 Basement Walls in Figure 8–7) were specified to be modeled at LOD 300 in a contract, but some parts of a basement wall were needed at LOD 400. This type of situation, which requires further negotiation during a project among project participants, is common in practice. Thus, it is important to understand that the LOD guides are *general modeling guides*, not intended for explicit or rigorous definitions of information requirements, as are MVDs. The next section describes guides related to more specific and explicit information requirements, including MVDs.

BIM Information Requirements. To acquire all the information needed from one phase to another or from one application to another, an explicit information specification is required. A set of explicit information items required for a specific process is called *Information Requirements (IR)* or a *Model View Definition (MVD)* in ISO 29481 Information Delivery Manual (IDM) (ISO TC 59/SC 13, 2010), or the *Employer's Information Requirements (EIR)* in PAS 1192-2 (BSI, 2013). Well-known examples of such information requirements are Construction Operations Building Information Exchange (COBie) initially developed by the U.S. Army Corps of Engineers (Nisbet and East, 2013), and COBie-UK, a version of COBie adapted for the UK industry (BSI, 2014b). COBie specifies information required for asset management. By having such an explicit specification for information requirements, it is possible to check automatically whether all required information is submitted. For this reason, many projects require submittal of handover data in COBie format.

Once more MVDs like COBie become available, contractual requirements for deliverables will be changed to use them in place of LOD specifications. Nevertheless, the quality of information (i.e., whether the submitted data is correct or not) still cannot be checked using MVDs. To check the quality of handover information, rule-based or semantic/ontological approaches can be taken. For example, consider this rule: "If a room exists, its floor-to-ceiling clearance must be at least 3.3m, it must be enclosed by walls, and it must have at least one door." A system can check whether a room satisfies these conditions. More complex rule checking is also possible based on inference rules that use ontological definitions of *room, floor, ceiling, wall, door,* and associated classes. More technical details about IDM/MVD are provided in Section 3.3.5.

BIM Execution Planning. As the number of BIM projects rapidly increased toward the end of the first decade of the new millennium, owners increasingly demanded preparation of a BIM execution plan as part of bidding packages.

At that time, there were no standard BIM execution plan guides. Many contractors, such as DPR, Mortenson, and the Beck Group, prepared their own guides for BIM execution planning, but a more structured and generalized approach was needed. The Pennsylvania State University (Penn State) developed and published the first version of its BIM Project Execution Planning (BEP) Guide in 2010 (CIC, 2010), and that document became the most widely used reference for developing BIM execution plans, and indeed other BEP guides. The Penn State BEP guide calls for four steps:

1. Identify BIM goals and uses.
2. Design BIM project execution process.
3. Develop information exchanges.
4. Define supporting infrastructure for BIM implementation.

Through these four steps, the following 14 sets of information are expected to be gathered:

- BIM project execution plan overview
- Project information
- Key project contacts
- Project goals and BIM uses
- Organizational roles and staffing
- BIM process design
- BIM information exchanges
- BIM and facility data requirements
- Collaboration procedures
- Quality control
- Technological infrastructure needs
- Model structure
- Project deliverables
- Delivery strategy and contract

BEP guides for specific uses other than construction itself have also appeared. In 2012, Penn State published a BEP Guide for Facility Owners, and in 2014 the University of Florida proposed a BIM execution planning method for green building projects (Wu and Issa, 2014).

8.5   BIM EDUCATION AND TRAINING

What might be the most challenging issue in adopting BIM? Organizations often respond to this question by saying "people issues." A study by Won et al. (2013b) on the critical success factors for BIM projects backs up this claim.

Out of ten critical success factors, nine were related to people and procedural issues rather than technical issues. This section focuses on people issues. It discusses transition of senior staff, BIM roles and responsibilities, and how the industry and universities around the world are teaching and training people.

8.5.1 Transition of Senior Staff

The greatest challenge in implementing new design and construction technologies is the intellectual transition required of senior team leaders. These senior staff, often partners, have decades of experience with clients, design development procedures, design and construction planning and scheduling, and project management, and that experience represents part of the core intellectual competence of any successful firm. The challenge is to engage them in the transition in a way that enables them to realize both their own expertise and also the new capabilities that BIM offers. Among the several potentially effective ways to address this challenge are:

- Team partners with young, BIM-savvy staff, who can integrate the partner's knowledge with the new technology.
- Provide one-on-one training one day a week or on a similar schedule.
- Host a small exercise for teams that includes training for partners in a relaxed off-site location.
- Visit firms that have made a transition to BIM, and attend workshops and online webinars.

Similar transition issues exist with other senior staff, such as project managers, and similar methods may be used to facilitate their transition. For example, BIM technology has new associated overhead costs beyond that of software investment. As firms already know, system management, often management responsibility of the Chief Information Officer (CIO), has become a crucial support function for most firms. IT dependency expands as it supports greater productivity in the same way that electricity has become a necessity for most kinds of work. BIM inevitably adds to that dependency.

No method is guaranteed. The transition of an organization is largely cultural. Through their actions, support, and expression of values, senior associates communicate their attitudes toward new technology to the junior members within the organization. Issues related to new BIM roles and responsibilities and transition of junior staff are discussed in the following sections.

8.5.2 BIM Roles and Responsibilities

BIM also created new roles and responsibilities. Barison and Santos (2010) identified various new roles created by BIM such as BIM manager, BIM modeler, BIM consultant, and BIM software developer. In their subsequent study (Barison and Santos, 2011), they analyzed 22 BIM job advertisements to understand the skills (competencies) required for a BIM manager. Uhm et al. (2017) extended the study and analyzed 242 BIM job advertisements around the world to analyze different types of BIM jobs and required skills. Uhm et al.

identified 35 different terms used for BIM jobs and grouped them into eight types based on their roles and relationships by using social network analysis. For example, in job advertisements, the roles of CAD manager, Revit manager, and VDC manager were defined as the same as those of BIM manager. Thus, CAD, Revit, VDC, and BIM managers are identified and categorized as the same role. Table 8–3, adapted from Uhm et al. (2017), summarizes job

Table 8–3 Job Competencies Required for Major BIM Roles (Adapted from Uhm et al., 2017).

Required Job Competencies		BIM Project Manager	BIM Manager	BIM Coordinator	BIM Technician
a) Job competencies required more by high-level BIM roles					
Experience	Average minimum years of experience	7.3 years	5.8 years	4.5 years	2.4 years
	Related work experience	73%	52%	52%	40%
Leadership skills	Leadership	20%	17%	4%	4%
	Management of personnel resources	27%	15%	—	—
	Having control over unit or department	20%	17%	4%	—
Language skills	English language	33%	6%	7%	8%
	Foreign language	27%	2%	7%	—
License, Higher Education	License, certificate, or registration	33%	6%	4%	4%
	Graduate degree	33%	6%	4%	4%
b) Job competencies required more by low-level BIM roles					
Computer skills	Computers/Electronics	7%	23%	26%	—
	Interacting with computers	67%	77%	81%	84%
	Drafting, laying out and specifying technical devices, parts, and equipment	20%	48%	63%	76%
Domain-Specific Knowledge	Mechanical	—	8%	15%	16%
	Evaluating information to determine compliance with standards	20%	29%	37%	44%
General	Cooperation	13%	38%	43%	60%
	Thinking creatively	20%	21%	22%	52%
	Providing high quality products	7%	10%	19%	20%

The percentage number indicates the number of job postings that include a certain competency element divided by the total number of job postings for the specific job type.

competencies needed for BIM project manager, BIM coordinator, BIM manager, and BIM technician. The required competencies are categorized by the U.S.'s Occupational Information Network (O*NET) competency classification.

In general, longer work experience, higher leadership skills, better language skills, and higher education were required in order of BIM project manager, BIM manager, BIM coordinator, and BIM technician. The average years of experience required for BIM project manager were 7.3 years, for BIM manager 5.8 years, for BIM coordinator 4.5 years, and for BIM technician 2.4 years. On the other hand, computer skills and domain-specific knowledge were required more by low-level BIM roles.

These are high-level requirements for BIM roles. Detailed requirements for each BIM job may differ by project or by organization. Here is an example of skills required by a BIM coordinator.

What Skills are Needed for a BIM/VDC Coordinator in a Construction Contracting Company? What Education is Needed?

Oralia Cruz is a VDC coordinator at Lease Crutcher Lewis, an over-130-year-old construction company based in Seattle, Washington, and Portland, Oregon. In 2017, she worked, prepared, and applied a BIM model on a USD 12M kitchen retrofit project for a Tech Giant company in downtown Seattle. In previous kitchen refits, at least 1% had been spent on rework. On this project, the cost of rework was zero. Oralia's USD 25,000 modeling cost helped Lewis avoid USD 120,000 of budgeted contingency money.

Oralia defines her job responsibilities as a VDC coordinator as these:

- MEP and design coordination
- 3D modeling via the latest technologies in BIM software
- 4D sequencing
- Design team integration/support

She adds to this list the general duties of a BIM detailer:

- Responsible for creating and maintaining federated models for project engineer's review, field inspection, punchlist background, field instruction, and more
- Reviewing and documenting design document and coordination conflicts
- Providing general BIM tech support for project engineers
- Providing field construction quality control support, resolving field disputes through model verification
- Providing field subcontractors with the most current coordinated information
- Providing modeling for change order verification, for rough order of magnitude (ROM) estimates, to fill in model aspects where scope has changed, to support design teams, and the like

- Interpreting the construction documents and building a base model
- Dividing the model in the way that work will be installed
- Working with the field to understand how they work and what information they need
- Providing a great level of detail and adding objects that may impact scope of work
- Providing accurate material quantities
- Developing work package drawings
- Communicating conflicts in model both real and potential
- Producing information and drawings, beyond work package development, that are helpful to the project team
- Communicating model information to trades not involved in modeling
- Developing the as-built model through the duration of the project

Her educational path to this career included a two-year Associate of Applied Science Degree in Architectural Engineering Drafting from North Seattle Community College, with related certificates in "Computer Aided Drafting for Design and Construction" and "Building Information Modeling for Design and Construction," and an eight-month Certificate in Construction Management from the University of Washington.

It's important to identify the responsibilities and skill sets required for different BIM roles, because they are the basis for designing education and training programs for BIM. The next sections describe BIM education and training efforts around the world.

8.5.3 Industry Training and Certificate Programs

The Contractor's Guide to BIM (AGC, 2006), one of the earliest guides, says, *"Whether the design is issued in the form of 2D printed documents or a 3D electronic media or in a combination of both, the responsibilities of the members of the project team remain unchanged. The important issue is to ensure that project team members thoroughly understand the nature and exactitude of the information that is being conveyed."*

This recommendation is still valid. Even if BIM becomes standard practice, people's fundamental roles remain the same. Designers still design, contractors build, and so on. The pedagogical question is how to change the education and training of practitioners, because although their responsibilities remain the same, the tools they should use are fundamentally different. Existing practitioners are not the only target of such education and training programs. People who can take on the new BIM roles listed in the previous section are another issue. Some jobs, such as CAD drafters, are disappearing, and those people need training to gain new skills.

In summary, training and certificate programs have three goals: (1) to teach existing practitioners how to conduct their job with new tools; (2) to equip people on disappearing jobs with new skills; and (3) to foster new BIM specialists. The following are a few examples of such training and certificate programs.

The AGC offers the AGC Certificate of Management—Building Information Modeling (CM-BIM). After completing the four AGC BIM Education Program course units listed below, candidates can take an exam to qualify for the AGC CM-BIM certificate.

- Unit 1: BIM 101: An Introduction to Building Information Modeling
- Unit 2: BIM Technology
- Unit 3: BIM Contract Negotiation and Risk Allocation
- Unit 4: BIM Process, Adoption, and Integration

buildingSMART Korea (bSK) has offered certificate programs for BIM technician and BIM (CM) coordinator since 2013, and planned to offer certificate programs for BIM modeler and BIM manager. The bSK certificate is cross-certified by buildingSMART International, buildingSMART Singapore, and Singapore BCA. The minimum eligibility criteria for the certificates is to fulfill either one of the academic degree requirements, the BIM-relevant experience requirement, or the certificate requirement listed in Table 8–4. For example, the BIM coordinator certificate applicant requires either a Bachelor's degree, five years of BIM-relevant experience, or two years of experience after acquiring the BIM technician certificate. The BIM manager certificate requires the longest experience (ten years) followed by the BIM (CM) coordinator certificate (five years), the BIM technician certificate (three years), and the BIM modeler certificate (no experience).

The certification process is composed of a written test and a practical skill test. Table 8–5 lists test subjects. The written test includes various topics, such

Table 8–4   Minimum Eligibility Criteria for the bSK BIM Certificates

Eligibility Criteria (either one of)	BIM Modeler	BIM Technician	BIM (CM) Coordinator	BIM Manager
Academic Degree	No requirement	Associate's degree	Bachelor's degree	Associate's degree and 8 years of practice, Or Bachelor's degree and 6 years of practice
BIM-Relevant Experience		3 years	5 years	10 years
Certificate		BIM modeler certificate	2 years after acquiring a BIM technician certificate	3 years after acquiring a BIM coordinator certificate

Table 8–5   Test Subjects for the bSK BIM Certificates

Test Subject		BIM Technician	BIM Coordinator	BIM CM Coordinator
Written Test	Basic concept and theory	O	O	O
	Interoperability and IFC	O	O	O
	PPS's FM BIM Guide	O	O	O
	MOLIT's Architectural BIM Guide		O	O
	Architectural BIM	O	O	
	Parametric Design and BIM	O	O	
	Freeform Design and BIM	O	O	
	Green BIM		O	
	BIM CM Process and Tasks			O
	BIM Execution Planning			O
	BIM Collaboration and 4D			O
Practical Skill Test	Architectural BIM	O	O	
	Green BIM	O	O	
	BIM Quality Assurance	O	O	O
	Communication BIM	O	O	
	Integrated BIM	O	O	
	Interim Estimate BIM	O	O	

as the PPS's FM BIM Guide and the MOLIT's BIM Guide, as well as basic BIM concepts and methods. The practical skill test assesses the knowledge and skills of various ways of using BIM such as for quality assurance, architectural design, interim estimating, and Green BIM. Test subjects for the BIM coordinator and the BIM CM coordinator are separate. The tests for the BIM CM coordinator include more subjects on construction and project management than those for the general BIM coordinator. bSK plans to add "Government Policy and BIM" and "BIM Project Procurement Methods" to the subject lists for BIM managers.

The BCA Academy of Singapore offers the Certificate of Successful Completion (CSC) for BIM planning; architectural, MEP, and structural BIM modeling; MEP coordination; and BIM management. While the certificate programs of the other countries focus on roles, the BCA's certificate programs focus on tasks. That is, a person may take several courses to acquire certificates in different areas. The BIM planning course is designed mainly for building developers and facility managers, the BIM modeling courses for BIM modelers, the MEP coordination course for BIM coordinators, and the BIM management course for BIM managers. Table 8–6 lists test subjects for the Singapore BCA BIM certificate tests.

Table 8–6   Test Subjects for the Singapore BCA BIM Certification

Test Subject	BIM Planning	BIM Modeling	BIM for MEP Coordination	BIM Management
BIM Fundamentals	O	O		O
BIM Technology				O
BIM Design Process	O			O
Design Coordination and Documentation	O		O	O
Design Analysis				O
Construction Planning and Coordination (4D BIM and 5D BIM)	O			O
BIM Company Deployment Plan				O
BIM Project Execution Plan				O
BIM to Field			O	
BIM Tool User Interface		O		
Modeling a Project		O	O	
Project Documentation		O		
e-Submission Project Template		O		
Worksets and Worksharing		O		
Design Object Library creation		O		
BIM for FM	O			
BIM Adoption (Singapore BIM Roadmap and Guide)	O			
BIM Strategy and Planning	O			
BIM Case Study from Developer/Owner's Perspective	O			

The Hong Kong Construction Industry Council (CIC) provides the Certified BIM Expert program. The Certified BIM Expert program is structured on three levels:

- Level I: Basic
- Level II: Architecture, Structure, MEP, Revit Families
- Level III: Architecture, Structure, MEP, Construction Management, Cost Management, BIM Management

At the time of writing, the Hong Kong CIC provided only Level I: Basic BIM training and certification, but it planned to expand the program to cover a broader scope including civil projects and construction and cost management. For example, the Construction Management program would include these nine subjects:

- Information-focused BIM
- Application-focused BIM

- Integration-focused BIM
- Level of detail and level of development
- Contractual implication of BIM model
- BIM in prefabrication and manufacturing
- Material delivery
- Quantity takeoff and preparation for bills of quantities
- Roles and responsibilities

In the UK, two public organizations—the British Standards Institute (BSI) and the Building Research Establishment (BRE)—provide BIM certificate programs. The BSI provides three types of BIM certificates, called: BSI Kitemark for BIM Design and Construction; BSI Kitemark for BIM Asset Management; and BSI Kitemark for BIM Objects. While the other certification programs focus on the knowledge level of individuals, the BSI's Kitemark certification program focuses on the compliance of a company's standardized process and procedures for BIM implementation with the BIM Level 2 specified in British standard BIM guides such as PAS 1192-2:2013, BS 1192:2007, BS 1192-4:2014, PAS 1192-3:2014, and BS 8541. See Table 8–7 for details.

BRE provides both individual and company level BIM certificates. The company level BIM certification is similar to that of the BSI Kitemark. The BRE's BIM Level 2 Business Systems Certification assess a company's BIM capability in the following areas:

- Company BIM skills and training records
- Software tools

Table 8–7   Assessment BIM Guides for BSI Kitemark BIM Certificates

Certificate Type	Assessment BIM Guides
BSI Kitemark for BIM Design and Construction	PAS 1192-2:2013 Specification for information management for the capital/delivery phase of construction projects using building information modeling (BIM)
	BS 1192:2007 Collaborative production of architectural, engineering and construction information. Code of practice.
	BS 1192-4:2014 Collaborative production of information. Fulfilling employer's information exchange requirements using COBie. Code of practice.
BSI Kitemark for BIM Asset Management	PAS 1192-3:2014 Specification for information management for the operational phase of assets using building information modeling (BIM).
BSI Kitemark for BIM Objects	BS 8541: Library objects for architecture, engineering and construction: Part 1: Identification and classification Part 3: Shape and measurement
	Part 4: Attributes for specification and assessment

- IT strategy and infrastructure
- Compliance with PAS 1192:2 2013 methods and processes
- CAD/BIM documentation confirming the above
- Compliance with PAS91-2013, Section 4.2, Table 8
- Project case studies

As the minimum requirements for certificate application, BRE requires the following three parties:

- A task team, which can set up and execute a BIM execution plan, a staff training schedule, a Task Information Delivery Plan, Common Data Environment procedures, and other BIM-related procedures and plans
- A lead supplier, which can set up and perform task team assessment procedures and Master Information Delivery Plan
- An employer, which can provide Employers Information Requirements, supply chain assessments, and staff for project information

The BRE offers two types of BIM certificates for individuals:

- BIM Informed Professional: This certificate is designed for policy makers, advisors, educators, and construction professionals who are implementing the BIM process. It requires detailed knowledge of BIM and the BIM process.
- BIM Certificated Practitioner: This certificate is designed for project-based construction professionals and project or task information managers. It requires practical-level knowledge about BIM and the BIM process.

These are only a few examples of BIM training and certificate programs among the many certificate programs offered by private and public organizations around the world, including those in Southeast Asian countries and Brazil. New certificate programs will be more rigorous than these because they will build upon the existing ones.

In addition to the training and certification programs offered by public organizations, some labor unions provide BIM training programs for existing practitioners, especially in the United States and in Scandinavian countries. It is not rare to meet former laborers who have become senior BIM detailers or 4D-based schedule managers through these schemes.

Thus far, we have discussed BIM training and certificate programs provided by public organizations. Many large design, engineering, and construction firms have also developed and run internal BIM training programs. Many of them hold periodic workshops and provide internal resources for knowledge sharing among employees (websites, blogs, and so on) Examples include the Turner University and the HOK BIM Solutions website. Medium- and small-sized firms rely heavily on the BIM training programs offered by private BIM service providers and platform vendors. Most of these focus on training for operation of BIM tools. Nevertheless, it is expected that courses related to planning, coordinating, and managing projects, project information, and processes will be increasingly available.

8.5.4 University Education Programs

This section introduces several approaches that universities are taking to incorporate BIM in their curricula. Before discussing the different approaches, we consider several challenges to setting up BIM degree programs, or to changing degree programs to reflect the changes wrought by BIM.

- The first challenge is to narrow the educational-philosophical gap among faculty members regarding the impact of BIM on traditional architectural and civil education. Some will not see the necessity of change in education due to BIM, just as some faculty members in 1980s and 1990s did not perceive the impact of CAD on the industry and on education. Some even forbade students from using CAD at school.
- The second challenge is the balance between various fields of study. A department is normally composed of several research areas. Although BIM is an enabling technology for many fields of study, each field is rapidly changing and has new demands. Thus, it is challenging to put much weight on any one field of study (such as BIM) and change the entire course structure to accommodate it.
- Even if a department's structure allows a relatively easy transformation from an existing program to a new program, transformation requires time, especially where the department runs an accredited education program. An exit strategy for existing students will be required.
- Existing faculty members need to learn BIM before they can incorporate it into their courses and teach students. This may generate resistance and take some time to resolve.

The latter three issues may be easier to solve than one might think, because many classes already use BIM tools or are based on BIM concepts. For example, structural engineering classes are taught using 3D analysis tools. Scheduling classes teach project scheduling and 4D simulation tools based on lean concepts. Lighting classes use BIM-based lighting simulation. Moreover, many students are already using BIM design tools inside and outside design studios.

The efforts to incorporate BIM into an existing undergraduate curriculum can be classified into three models. The first model assumes that BIM is already being taught or will be taught as part of existing classes as discussed earlier. This approach makes no or minimum changes in an existing curriculum on the undergraduate level. Instead, universities in this category provide an integrated design-engineering studio to undergraduate senior students as a capstone class and advanced BIM classes to graduate students. Many universities follow this model. Some examples include the Department of Construction Management at the University of Washington, Seattle; the Department of Architecture and Architectural Engineering at Yonsei University, South Korea; and the Department of Civil Engineering at the Hong Kong University of Science and Technology.

The second model takes an intermediate approach and adds a couple of new introductory BIM classes to their existing undergraduate program. The BIM classes focus mostly on BIM tools and basic BIM concepts. The graduate-level education is similar to that of the first model. Examples are the Technion–Israel Institute of Technology and the Escola Politécnica da USP in Brazil.

The third model takes a more aggressive approach and turns an existing program into a BIM-specialized one or adds an entirely new BIM-specific degree program. Many undergraduate degree programs have adopted this approach to cope with the industry demand. In the case of South Korea, the government funded several universities to develop such BIM-specialized programs.

Many universities that have faculty members competent in BIM or pursue BIM-related research offer graduate-level BIM degree programs. These courses include not only the classes directly relevant to BIM theories, methods, standards, and tools, but also the classes related to BIM-enabling technologies such as data mining and management, parametric modeling, interoperability, requirements engineering, computational flow dynamics, algorithmic design, and construction automation.

In addition, some universities run a BIM training and/or certificate program as part of their continuing education program or a Master of Science program. Examples include the BIM for Construction Management (CM) program at Georgia Institute of Technology (Georgia Tech), Stanford University, the University of Washington (UW), Tallinn University of Technology, and Tallinn University of Applied Sciences in Estonia (Table 8–8).

These are but a few examples. Various education models such as distance learning, Massive Open Online Courses, and flipped learning on BIM will increase in the future.

8.5.5 Considerations for Training and Deployment

BIM is a new IT environment, requiring training, system configuration, library and document template setup, and adaptation of design review and approval procedures, often combined with new business practices. These need to be developed incrementally, side by side with existing methods, so that learning problems do not jeopardize the completion of current projects.

We encourage preparation of a detailed deployment plan for any firm considering the change to BIM; adoption should not be ad hoc. The more grounded the plan is in relation to a company's strategic goals, the more successful adoption is likely to be. The following sections address a range of issues to consider.

Training usually starts with one or a small number of IT specialists who can then plan system configurations and introduce a training program for the rest of the firm. System configuration includes hardware selection (BIM tools demand powerful workstation hardware), server setup, plotting and printing configurations, network access, integration with reporting and project accounting, setup of libraries (described in Section 5.4.2), and other company-specific system issues.

Table 8–8   BIM Courses Offered by the BIM Certificate Programs at Universities

Topic	Georgia Tech	Stanford	UW
Introduction	Introduction to BIM	VDC overview	• Introduction to BIM • BIM technology fundamentals
BIM for Design		3D object-oriented modeling of facility designs	
BIM for Engineering		Model-based analysis of 3D models	
BIM for Construction Management	• BIM and Construction Management • BIM and Field-Related Technologies	• 4D modeling, animation, and analysis • Organization modeling and analysis	• Planning for success • Scheduling with BIM • Quantities and component tracking • BIM in the field
BIM for Fabrication		• Production planning, control, and optimization for design and construction processes • Supply chain configurations in support of VDC	
BIM for Facility Management	BIM for Facility Management		Facilities and asset management
BIM for Collaboration		• Process modeling and analysis • Interactive collaborative design • Integrated project modeling of the functional intent, design, and performance of the project product, organization, and process	• Coordination and clash prevention • BIM for project reviews • Capstone workshop
BIM Standards and the Future	BIM Standards and the Future	Students can qualify for VDC certification by completing specified courses and experience	

Early projects should focus on the basic skills needed for modeling buildings and producing drawings, including incremental definition of object libraries and getting the basics down before undertaking more advanced integration efforts. After the basics of project management have been realized, the door is open to a variety of extensions to take advantage of the multiple integration and interoperability benefits that BIM offers.

An important note of caution during the early phase of BIM adoption is to avoid providing too much model detail too soon. Because methods of project definition and detailing are partially automated in BIM, it is possible, if details are defined too quickly, for a design concept to be misinterpreted. Detailed models are easy to realize while still in the conceptual design phase but may lead to errors and client misunderstanding by inadvertently making overreaching decisions that become hard to reverse. BIM users should appreciate this issue and manage the level of detailing explicitly. Careful preparation of the project-level LOD guide provided to consultants and collaborators has also been found to be worthwhile. Early involvement of all key project partners is recommended, but the point at which each begins modeling will depend on their roles. For example, detailed MEP 3D layout should not be done until later in the process to avoid multiple revisions. On the other hand, curtain wall consultants and fabricators may be brought in earlier to help plan and coordinate structural connections and detailing.

On larger projects, architects represent only one partner in an overall design team. Collaboration requires engineering, mechanical, and other specialty consultants. Procedures for coordination via model reviews and backed up by data exchange methods must be worked out, and this is best achieved by preparing a BIM Execution Plan (BEP; see Sections 1.9.1, 4.5.1, and 8.4.2). Given the benefits of and the need for close collaboration among designers, a Big Room (Obeya) arrangement is preferred even for firms new to BIM (see Section 4.5.4 and the case studies in Chapter 10).

8.6   LEGAL, SECURITY, AND BEST PRACTICE ISSUES

BIM requires and encourages close collaboration among project members. In an ideal world, harmony would prevail among project team members in a collaborative and integrated environment, and there would be no security breaches nor legal disputes. Unfortunately, reality is different. This section therefore discusses legal, security, and associated best practice issues for BIM.

8.6.1   Legal and Intellectual Property Issues

Legal and intellectual property issues are not new in design, engineering, and construction projects. However, in BIM projects, the ownership and rights to information are a key aspect due to the digital and collaborative nature of the material. Questions frequently asked in BIM projects include:

- Who owns the information?
- Who owns the copyright of a BIM model?
- Who has the right to use a model?
- Who has the right to change a model?
- Who is responsible for the problems caused by errors in digital information?

The first four questions sound similar in that they are all related to the rights to BIM data, but they are different in legal terms. One can own a digital model, but that does not mean that one can freely change the model (design) due to copyright issues. Yet it would be disastrous if team members were denied the right to use or change a model in a BIM project. Who then has the right to use or change a model?

BIM guides from the United States, Finland, South Korea, and Singapore unanimously say that the client is the owner of digital models and information as well as the other deliverables. For example, Section 6.12, "Responsibilities and Rights," in the PPS BIM Guide of South Korea (PPS, 2016), claims that PPS has the right to use BIM data and the contractors are responsible for errors in IFC models and drawings generated from BIM models.

Section 2.4.2 in the GSA BIM Guide Series 01 insists that the Public Building Service (PBS) has the ownership and rights of digital data and other deliverables.

"For all GSA projects, PBS has ownership of and rights to all data and other deliverables developed and provided by the A/E [architect and/or engineer] in accordance with the applicable provisions of the A/E contract. These rules extend to Building Information Models and associated data developed for GSA projects."

Section 4.3 "Rights to the use of building information models" in the COBIM Series 11 "Management of a BIM project" of Finland (buildingSMART Finland, 2012) states that the client has the ownership and right to use digital data. It continues to explain that any designer who does not want to transfer the copyright to the client should submit a proposal about how to work together with team members as part of the tender document.

"The client has the right to use the models.... If the designer considers that the relinquishment of the libraries and objects used in the models either to other parties during the project or to the client at the end of the project links with copyright-related, designer competition privilege-based or other similar legal problems, the designer should mention these in his/her tender. As an appendix to the tender, there should be a proposal about how the problems concerned may be resolved so that the designer can relinquish the models required by BIM-based cooperation to other parties during the project as well as, with regard to building use, maintenance and repairs, the usable models to the client at the end of the project.... With respect to possible property sales, the transfer of operational rights to the transferee must be separately entered."

The Singapore BIM guide (BCA, 2013) distinguishes the model owner from the model author and model users. In general, the client is the model owner. A modeler or a designer is the model author. Model users are project participants who are allowed to use or check the models, but do not have the right to change the models. Section 3.3, "BIM Objective and Responsible Matrix," in the Singapore BIM guide, provides a table to specify the model authors and the model users for different models used in a project.

"The model author is a party responsible for the creation and maintenance of a specific model to the level of detail prescribed in the BIM Project Objectives and Responsibility Matrix. In creating and maintaining the model, the model author does not convey any ownership right of the model.... The Employer [owner] may specify for ownership of the model in the Principal Agreement.... Model users are parties authorized to use the model on the project.... Where inconsistency is found in the model, the model user shall promptly notify the

model author for clarification. The model users shall make no claim against the author in connection with the use of the model. The model users shall also indemnify and defend the model author against all claims from or related to subsequent use or modification by the model users."

Lawsuits attributed to the responsibilities and rights issues related to BIM are rarer than was anticipated. Nevertheless, lawyers advise that the responsibilities and rights of project participants should be clearly stated in contracts to avoid any unnecessary dispute or conflict between project participants during or after a project.

8.6.2 Cyber Security for BIM

Unfortunately, some of the significant benefits of BIM can be exploited by people with malicious intent. BIM concentrates all the information about a building in one easily accessible model and provides a platform for automation of building operation. This potentially exposes three vulnerabilities:

- Cyber-attacks on the BIM models during design and construction, whether for purposes of ransom or sabotage
- Unauthorized access to building models during design and construction for military, criminal, or commercial espionage
- Cyber-attacks on a building during the operational phase through BIM-supported building automation systems and facility maintenance systems .

The first and second vulnerabilities are no different in principle from the vulnerability of CAD-based design and construction, because the threat is to the online databases. The defense strategies are therefore not unique to the use of BIM. Project collaboration websites such as *structshare.com* provide a construction collaboration service with multilayered cyber-security that was designed for military and government applications.

However, once compromised, BIM models are far easier to understand and use than sets of 2D drawings. This is particularly relevant where the threat arises from less sophisticated organizations. Prisons, courthouses, police stations, military buildings, banks, bridges, and many other public and private buildings and other infrastructure are all more vulnerable when their BIM models are readily accessible to those who pose a threat.

In response to the second threat, the UK BIM Task group has developed PAS 1192-5:2015: "Specification for security-minded building information modelling, digital built environments and smart asset management." This document outlines the concerns and various procedures that can be incorporated in an organization's BIM Guides and/or in a project BIM Execution Plan.

Perhaps the most effective approach to the first and second vulnerabilities is to apply the Big Room concept in which all designers and other model users are physically co-located. Apart from the benefits outlined in Chapters 5 and 6, this has the major advantage that the computer systems used can be entirely isolated from the outside world, thus minimizing the threat of cyber-attack or theft of digital information.

The vulnerability of a building to cyber threats during its operation phase is different. In theory, an attacker can gain control of the operation of a building through online building control systems based on BIM models. Isolating systems is one option, but where MEP systems are linked to supplier's control centers or mobile apps are used to interface into the building operation systems, isolation is impractical, and appropriate cyber protection measures must be applied.

8.6.3 Best Practices and Other Social Issues

In social science terms, a BIM model is a "boundary object," which facilitates discussions and collaboration between project participants (Forgues et al., 2009; Neff et al., 2010). Depending on how project participants interact with each other using the "boundary object," the outcomes will vary greatly. Park and Lee (2017) presented an example of the way in which design coordination strategies can affect the social dynamics between team members in terms of information control and eventually the productivity of a project. Although BIM was deployed in the project described, only drawings were accepted as the legal submittal. By changing the sequence of MEP coordination, a BIM coordinator could gain more access to and more control over information. As a result, the average coordination time per drawing was reduced from 59.2 hours to 26.4. The frequency of design changes per drawing dropped from 2.13 to 0.42. The first building, constructed before the BIM coordinator had access to the data, was delayed by 9.3 months, while the second building on the same site was completed without any delay. Interest in BIM case study research on best practices and social interactions like the one above is increasing, as opposed to earlier case studies that focused on the benefits. The annual workshop series "When Social Science Meets Lean and BIM," which began in 2013 in Europe, reflects this interest.

Best practices, guides, execution plans, and projects have a positive feedback relationship through execution, evaluation, and evolution of BIM use in projects (Figure 8–8). BIM execution plans are developed on the basis of BIM guides. Projects are run according to their BIM execution plans. Through case studies, best practices are derived and documented. Best practices in turn inform the authors of BIM guides. As we gain more knowledge about BIM use, the benefits are likely to grow.

Acknowledgments

We thank Arto Kiviniemi at the University of Liverpool; Jan Karlshoj at the Technical University of Denmark; Carrie Dossick at the University of Washington; Jennifer Whyte at Imperial College London; Jack Cheng at the Hong Kong University of Science and Technology; Zhiliang Ma at Tsinghua University, China; Ergo Pikas at the Tallinn University of Technology, Estonia; Timo Hartmann at TU Berlin, Germany; Eduardo Toledo Santos at the University of Sao Paulo, Brazil; Xiangyu Wang at Curtin University, Australia; and Jeong Han

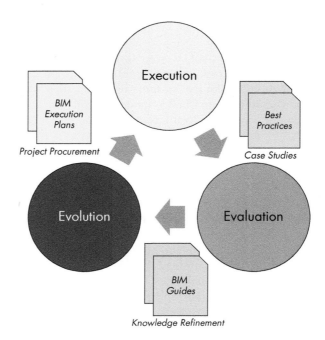

FIGURE 8–8 The positive feedback relationship of BIM execution plans, best practices, and guides through BIM project execution, evaluation, and evolution.

Woo at the Milwaukee School of Engineering, U.S., for sharing their knowledge and experience about BIM mandates, guides, education, and training programs of their schools and regions.

Chapter 8 Discussion Questions

1. Are government BIM mandates for public projects beneficial? What impacts do they have? What are the advantages and disadvantages of a government BIM mandate?

2. Imagine an industry or region that has not yet adopted BIM or lags behind BIM adoption. Compile a BIM roadmap for the industry or the region. Explain why you set up your BIM roadmap in the way that you did.

3. If you had to monitor and manage a BIM project using only one index, which index would you use and why do you think the index is important? What are the things that you expect to monitor using the index?

4. Specify a project or an organization and choose or develop a BIM maturity model that is most appropriate for your project or organization. Explain why your BIM maturity model works best for your project or organization.

5. Review three existing BIM guides. If you were asked to develop a BIM guide, what would you add to existing BIM guides and why do you think that the contents are important?

6. What do you think should be taught to undergraduate and graduate students of architecture or of civil engineering in BIM courses, and why?

7. If you were asked to develop a certificate program for different types of BIM professionals, how would you structure the certification program for them? What would be your minimum criteria and how would you validate that the professionals fulfill the requirements?

8. In what ways can the use of BIM compromise the security of the built environment? What can be done to make projects secure?

The Future: Building with BIM

9.0 EXECUTIVE SUMMARY

BIM is not a thing or a type of software but a business information process that ultimately involves broad changes in the construction industry. BIM represents a new way of compiling both product and process information. If the invention of technical drawing of plans, projections, cross-sections, and details was the first revolution in construction information, BIM is the second revolution. The shift from paper drawing to computer drawing was not a paradigm change: BIM is.

A wide variety of owners demand BIM use, and nationwide governmental mandates for BIM use for all public construction have been adopted throughout the world. The mandates are supported with standard BIM contract terms and detailed BIM guides and standards, all of which have a broad transformative effect on national construction industries. New skills and roles are developing. Almost universally positive return on investment values have been reported by both design firms and construction contractors, with those actively measuring return on investment reporting that it exceeded their initial estimates. A survey conducted by McGraw-Hill Construction in early 2007 found that 28% of the U.S. AEC industry was using BIM; that number grew to 49% by 2009 and to 71% by 2012. In 2007, only 14% of users surveyed considered themselves to be expert or advanced. By 2009, 42% did, and by 2012, 54% did. Other BIM surveys also show that the percentage of BIM users in other regions are also growing rapidly.

Information from BIM models is no longer constrained to design offices or construction site offices; it is readily available in the field on mobile devices. The lack of appropriately trained professional staff, rather than the technology itself, is still the current bottleneck for most companies. The greatest demand is for people who have experience both in modeling and in construction. Although pioneering universities and colleges are replacing their drafting classes with courses that educate architects and engineers in BIM, BIM-savvy graduates generally lack experience in construction practice.

The technology trends include the development of automated checking for code conformance and constructability using building information models. Some vendors have expanded the scope of their BIM tools, while others offer more discipline-specific functionality, such as construction management functions. It is becoming more common for building product manufacturers to provide 3D catalogs; and BIM is helping to make globalization of fabrication for increasingly complex building subassemblies economically viable.

Yet the "BIM revolution" is still very much a work in progress. The principles were outlined in 1975; BIM began to spread into broad commercial practice around the turn of the century, and it is now well established as best practice for design and construction. As it develops and its use becomes more widespread, the extent of its impact on the way in which buildings are built will become more apparent. With the benefit of the hindsight of the last 40-something years, we attempt in this chapter to extrapolate what progress can be expected within the next decade. The coming years are likely to see much broader adoption of basic BIM tools. BIM will contribute to a higher degree of prefabrication, greater flexibility and variety in building methods and types, fewer documents, far fewer errors, less waste, and higher productivity. Building projects will continue to perform better, thanks to better analyses and exploration of more alternatives, fewer claims, and fewer budget and schedule overruns. The pressure to leverage BIM models to provide datasets for operation and maintenance is growing. These are all improvements on existing construction processes.

Numerous societal, technical, and economic drivers will determine the development of BIM in the midterm future (up to 2025). The latter part of this chapter identifies the drivers and obstacles in the timeframe leading up to 2025. We reflect on the likely impacts of the drivers on BIM technology, on the design professions, on the nature of construction contracts and the synergy between BIM and lean construction, on education and employment, and on statutory and regulatory processes.

Among the major BIM developments expected by 2025: thoroughly digital design and construction; growth of a new culture of innovation in construction; diverse and extensive off-site prefabrication; strong progress in automated code-compliance checking; increased application of artificial intelligence; globalization of fabrication in addition to design; and continued strong support for sustainable construction. Beyond 2025, BIM will be characterized first by its strong support for lean workflow improvements, and later by its service as a platform for a variety of artificial intelligence applications.

The big picture is that BIM facilitates early integration of project design and construction teams, making closer collaboration possible and facilitating off-site fabrication. This will help make the overall construction delivery process faster, less costly, more reliable, and less prone to errors and risk. This is an exciting time to be an architect, an engineer, or any other AEC industry professional.

9.1   INTRODUCTION

BIM is changing the way buildings look, the way they function, and the ways in which they are built. Throughout this book, we have intentionally and consistently used the term BIM to describe a sequence of activities (*building information **modeling***), rather than an object (as in *building information **model***). This reflects our belief that BIM is not a thing or a type of software but a human activity that ultimately involves broad process changes in construction. In this chapter, we aim to provide two perspectives on the future of building using BIM: *where BIM is taking the AEC industry,* and *where the AEC industry is taking BIM.*

We begin with a short introduction describing the conception and maturation of BIM until the present (year 2017). We then provide our perspectives on what the future holds. The forecast is divided into two timeframes: a fairly confident forecast of the midterm future that looks ahead to 2025, and a more speculative forecast looking beyond 2025. The midterm forecast reflects current market trends—many of which are discussed in earlier chapters of this book—and then reviews current research. The forecast beyond 2025 relies on analyses of likely drivers and a fair amount of intuition. In the longer-term, beyond 2030, potential advances in hardware and software technologies, as well as business practices, make it foolish to predict anything reliably, and so we refrain from speculation.

After 2025, construction industry analysts will reflect, with the benefit of hindsight, on the process changes that will have occurred by then. They will likely find it difficult to distinguish definitively between such influences as BIM, lean construction, and performance-driven design. In the absence of each other, these techniques could, theoretically, flourish on their own. Researchers have cataloged some 55 positive interactions between BIM and lean construction (Sacks et al., 2010). We address some of these synergies in Sections 9.3 and 9.4. Their impacts, however, are complementary in important ways, and they are being adopted simultaneously. Practical examples of their synergies are apparent in the case studies of the Mapletree Business Park II and the St. Joseph Hospital projects (in the following chapter), and of the Sutter Medical Center and the Crusell Bridge projects (in the *BIM Handbook* companion website).

BIM technology continues to develop rapidly. Just as the concepts of how BIM tools should work drove their technological development, a renewed vision of the future of building with BIM—emphasizing workflows and construction practices—is now needed. Readers who are considering the adoption of BIM tools for their practices and educators teaching future architects, civil engineers, contractors, building owners, and professionals should all understand not only the current capabilities but also the future trends and their potential impacts on the building industry.

9.2 BIM BEFORE 2000: PREDICTING TRENDS

The concept of computer modeling for buildings was first proposed when the earliest software products for building design were being developed (Bijl and Shawcross, 1975; Eastman, 1975; Yaski, 1981). Progress toward BIM was restricted first by the cost of computing power and later by the successful widespread adoption of CAD. But idealists in academia and the construction software industry persisted, and the research needed to make BIM practical continued to move forward. The foundations for object-oriented building product modeling were laid throughout the 1990s (Gielingh, 1988; Kalay, 1989; Eastman, 1992). Parametric 3D modeling was developed both in research and by software companies for specific market sectors, such as structural steel. Current BIM tools are the fulfillment of a vision that has been predicted, by many, for at least three decades.

In 1975, Chuck Eastman published an article in the *AIA Journal* describing a "Building Description System." In the article, he described how the system would support generation and use of building information: "Designing would consist of interactively defining elements.... It should be possible, then, to derive sections, plans, isometrics, or perspectives from the same description of elements.... Any change of arrangement would have to be made only once for all future drawings to be updated. All drawings derived from the same arrangement of elements would automatically be consistent ... any type of quantitative analysis could be coupled directly to the description. All data preparation for analyses could be automated. Reports for cost estimating or material quantities could be easily generated.... Thus BDS will act as design coordinator and analyzer, providing a single integrated database for visual and quantitative analyses, for testing spatial conflicts and for drafting.... Later, one can conceive of a BDS supporting automated building code checking in city hall or the architect's office. Contractors of large projects may find this representation advantageous for scheduling and materials ordering" (Eastman, 1975). The article was particularly visionary in its title: it did not limit its vision to "the use of computers for drawing" (what we would call CAD), but proposed "The Use of Computers Instead of Drawings."

In another example of prescient writing, in 1989 Paul Teicholz made some 92 predictions about technology trends and their impact on the AEC industry (Teicholz, 1989). Almost all of the generic statements concerning the development of personal computers, local area networks, the nature and function of databases, graphics, and computer communications, which were already work in progress at the time, have been fulfilled. The few predictions about operating systems were all incorrect. Table 9–1 lists 32 predictions

Table 9–1   Predictions Made in 1989 and an Evaluation of Their Fulfilment by 2017

Prediction (from Teicholz, 1989)	Assessment of Fulfilment Status
Conceptual Design	
The generation of conceptual design from user requirements will remain a major challenge.	Yes
For plant design, where the rules are perhaps better defined than for other areas (say architecture practice), the use of expert systems may allow quick generation of prototype designs.	No. Expert systems for design automation are not yet common.
Space layout (block diagramming) will be facilitated by expert systems that can reason about 3D space.	Available as optimization tools, but not in expert systems per se.
In order to reduce construction cost, the design will reflect the tools and (automated) methods used in the field.	Implemented
All design areas will use the computer for simulation of conceptual (preliminary) designs, i.e., simulating how the design will "work" and the impact it will have on its environment.	Common practice
The environmental impact of a structure will be studied and perhaps presented using simulation models. This will facilitate interaction with the owner and outside agencies (permits, environmental impact, loans, etc.).	Common practice
The data generated during the conceptual design phase will be used to initiate downstream functions.	Common practice
Detail Design	
The process of detail design will be done by fewer engineers using CAD/CAB systems that will automate many of the lower-level design functions.	Common practice
Engineering analysis will be completely integrated with the design applications so that analysis and design can be done interactively.	Available
Expert systems that are integrated into the design application will check for standards (rules, guidelines, etc.) in such areas as building codes, company practice, constructability, operability, and maintainability.	Available and under development
The end products of detail design will be a 3D graphic database, the object data about the structure (material codes, sizes, weights, etc.) and the knowledge base (specifications) for the project.	Implemented—this is BIM
From this information it should be able to develop a reasonable schedule and cost estimate using expert systems that are tailored to particular types of structures (e.g., high-rise office building, ammonia plants).	The functionality is available, but not using expert systems per se.
Bidding Process	
The database created during the detail design process will be used to prepare the cost estimate.	Available
The material quantities can be extracted and combined with the construction productivity knowledge of the contractor.	Available
This knowledge can be captured in a company database and used with an expert system that will apply this data to a specific project.	Available
Estimators will review an estimate rather than starting from scratch. This should speed the generation of a bid and allow more time for thought about alternative work methods.	Available
Procurement	
The project database will be used to extract the bill of materials (quantities, descriptions, sizes, etc.).	Common practice

Table 9-1 (*continued*)

Prediction (from Teicholz, 1989)	Assessment of Fulfilment Status
The date material is needed will be defined by relating work packages to schedule activities (also defined in the database). Thus, as changes are made to the design, the corresponding changes can be made to the bill of material and required delivery dates.	Available
The process of issuing requisitions and purchase orders will become electronic. Contractors, owners, and vendors will use an "electronic marketplace" to issue and respond to requisitions, issue purchase orders, arrange transportation, and perhaps even financing.	Available, not in widespread use
Standard material codes will be used in the design database to allow easy specification of material and tracking (via bar codes) after the material arrives at the site.	Available
Contractors will expedite material using electronic messages generated by the material system (in addition to the manually generated messages).	Available
Vendors will increasingly use their computers to link with the material requirements of the project to allow "just in time" delivery, thereby reducing lay down areas and cash investment in inventory.	Available
Project Control	
The project design database and knowledge base become the starting point for the cost, schedule, material control, change order, and other control systems. These systems all have a common starting point, and all require a work breakdown structure (WBS) that is tied to the design (though they may not use the same WBS). Thus, changes to the 3D model and associated data will have their corresponding impact on these control systems.	Available
Graphic output will be used to relate the feedback from a control system (e.g., to show the activities on the critical path, to show which work packages have the required material on hand, to show the work performed by a given foreman which is over budget, etc.).	Available
Graphic output will tend to replace printouts as the preferred mode of communication.	In progress
Expert systems will be used to develop and critique project schedule (networks).	No
Field practice (work methods)	
The use of a 3D model for walkthrough analysis will become standard practice for complex and/or fast moving projects.	Common practice
The same database will be used to control the movement of machines and robots that are used for material movement, pipe bending, fabrication, painting, etc. These tools will have digital controls that are fed from project specific data.	Available for some types (pipe bending, rebar fabrication), under development for others
Workers will be trained to control and repair these automated tools. There will be less need for unskilled workers and more for workers with robotics and computer skills.	Not yet
Facility Management	
The "as-built" database will become the starting point for the management and repair of the facility.	Available, not in widespread use
Modifications to the facility over its useful lifetime will be recorded in this database so that the management systems will remain useful.	Available, not in widespread use
Administrative systems used for normal maintenance, repair, and charge-out (billings and rentals) will all be linked to this facility database.	Available, not in widespread use

unique to the AEC industry. As, can be seen, the majority have indeed been fulfilled. The penultimate statement about detailed design is the most significant regarding BIM: *"The end products of detail design will be a 3D graphic database, the object data about the structure (material codes, sizes, weights, etc.) and the knowledge base (specifications) for the project."* It clearly outlines the three aspects of building information that BIM encompasses: form, function, and behavior.

BIM technology crossed the boundary between research concept and viable commercial solution roughly around 2000, as evidenced by the white papers on BIM published by major software companies (including Autodesk, Bentley, and Graphisoft) in the early 2000s. It is well on the way to becoming as indispensable to building design and construction as the proverbial T-square or hammer and nail. The transition to BIM, however, is not a natural progression from computer-aided drafting (CAD). It involves a paradigm shift from drawing to modeling. Modeling provides different abstractions and model development processes, leading to new ways of designing and building. These are still being sorted out. BIM also facilitates—and is facilitated by—a concurrent shift from traditional competitive project delivery models to more collaborative practices in design, construction, and facility management.

It is evident then that the concept of BIM itself was clearly formulated and understood for roughly 15 years before the various computing hardware and software required for its implementation became available (around 1990), and some 25 years before it became common commercial practice (circa 2000). When the technology matured, BIM was a self-fulfilling prediction, in that the existing ideas were implemented. The point, however, is that where modes of use can be imagined that are clearly more efficient than current practice, and the current technology developments are underway, we can make fairly intelligent guesses about future practice by extrapolation.

9.3   DEVELOPMENT AND IMPACT OF BIM: 2000 TO 2017

Since BIM was recognized in the early 2000s by the AEC industry as a means to revolutionize the labor-intensive and inefficient practice (Laiserin, 2008), BIM has had significant impacts on stakeholders of the AEC industry on all levels, from owners to subcontractors, from designers to component suppliers. This section reviews the development and impact of BIM up to 2017 on various stakeholders in AEC including owners, contractors, suppliers, educators, and authorities, and also on the project documentation practice and software applications.

Given the relative inertia of the construction industry and its highly fragmented structure (Chapter 1), BIM adoption is by no means complete across the industry. Paper drawings—or at least 2D drawing formats that can be communicated electronically—remain common forms of construction documentation. Indeed, full adoption of BIM in any firm requires two to three years to become effective. Thus, while significant industry-wide productivity gains have yet to be measured, cost and schedule reductions have been recorded for large numbers of projects. Local effects are sometimes dramatic; building forms once considered impractical—due to either technical or budget constraints—are considered viable.

9.3.1   Impact on Owners: Better Options, Better Reliability

Owners have experienced improvements in the quality and nature of services available and an overall increased reliability of the project budget, program compliance, and delivery schedule. Advanced owners are leading their project teams to adapt and expand their BIM-related services. Chapter 4 and several of the case studies describe owners who were introduced to or who demanded new processes and deliverables, and Chapter 8 discussed the ways in which they have communicated their needs. Designers and builders routinely deliver building information models and provide services related to analyzing, viewing, and managing the model's development.

In the early project phases, owners expect 3D visualizations and conceptual building information models with programmatic analysis (see Chapter 5 for a discussion of these tools). With the increasing availability of 3D viewers, owners have many options to view project models and use them for marketing, sales, and evaluation of designs in the site context. Building models are far more flexible, immediate, and informative than computer renderings of buildings produced by using CAD technologies. They also enable owners and designers to generate and compare more design options early in the project, when decisions have the most impact on the project and lifecycle costs.

These technical developments have had different impacts for different owners, depending on their business incentives. Owners who build to sell find that they can demand and achieve much shorter design durations for conceptual design and construction documentation. On the other hand, owners who have an economic interest in the lifecycle costs and energy efficiency of their buildings can exploit the conceptual design stage for an in-depth study of the behavior of each alternative building design. Savvy owners—with the perception that conceptual-level models can be developed and evaluated rapidly—can demand higher design quality. In an effort to optimize building design, they can demand thorough exploration of more alternatives, in terms of construction cost, sustainability, energy consumption, lighting, acoustics, maintenance and operations, and other criteria. Figure 9–1 illustrates an example of early stage design optimization for a hospital operating room.

We note, however, that like any powerful technology, BIM too is open to abuse. First-time (and often one-time) construction clients may not be familiar with BIM and its potential uses and, as a result, may not adequately engage the design team in assessing the project's subtler goals regarding function, cost, and time-to-delivery. If designers are not disciplined, they can develop fairly detailed designs rapidly and create building models that appear convincing and appealing. If the vital stage of conceptual design is short-circuited, premature production level modeling can lead to a lot of rework later in the process. In the

FIGURE 9-1 Example of a component-based simulation of an operating room, allowing the owners and designers to compare different equipment. The equipment components include parameters and behaviors, ensuring that proper clearances and distances are maintained.

Image courtesy of View22 and GE Healthcare.

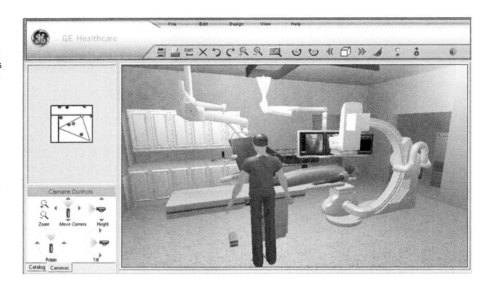

worst cases, inadequately designed buildings that do not meet the clients' needs may be built. Building clients unfamiliar with the capabilities that BIM technology offers are advised to educate themselves and select knowledgeable design consultants in order to obtain professional design services that exploit the technological capabilities of BIM to achieve the desired objectives of the project.

As the use of 4D and BIM coordination by contractors becomes more commonplace, owners increasingly appreciate the power of these tools to improve budget and schedule reliability as well as overall project quality. More owners demand the use of BIM in the construction phase. Owners with adequate experience can take advantage of IPD contracts that allow full, early participation of designers and contractors, with gain-share/pain-share arrangements that contribute to superior team alignment, improved design, cost-saving opportunities at every stage of the lifecycle, and reduced design and construction time. Without BIM tools and processes, this would not be possible.

Postconstruction, owners are increasingly aware of the value of the model for facility management, as discussed in Chapter 4. The trend set by efficient delivery of as-built information directly from the commissioning process in the field into BIM datasets, as exemplified in the Stanford University Medical Center, Howard Hughes Medical Center, and the Medina Airport case studies in Chapter 10, and the Maryland General Hospital case study in the *BIM Handbook* companion website, encourages owners to adopt BIM-based facility management systems. These are all examples of increased use and maturation of BIM-based facility management products.

9.3.2 Impact on the Design Professions

Designers have achieved productivity gains at the construction stage and deliver higher-quality design services. The three main drivers for broad adoption are: (1) client demand for enhanced quality of service; (2) productivity gain in preparing documentation; and (3) contractor demand to support virtual construction.

Architecture and engineering firms already face a workplace with changing roles and activities. Junior architects are expected to demonstrate proficiency with BIM as a condition of employment, in the same way that CAD proficiency was required since the 1990s. Some downsizing has already occurred among staff members dedicated to document-producing activities. New roles have emerged with titles such as the building modeler or model manager, requiring design and technical know-how. The introduction of Big Rooms for collaborative design and construction management (some, but not all, in the context of IPD contracts), represents a major change to many designers' working environments. Working together with designers from all disciplines in a single project-specific office space, with frequent coordination meetings centered on an integrated building model representation, represents a significantly different way of working compared with the way designers function in their own office.

Little's Law (Hopp and Spearman, 1996, Little and Graves, 2008), which relates cycle times and levels of work-in-progress to throughput, explains that for any given workload, reducing cycle times means that the level of work in progress is reduced. The implication is that firms should be able to reduce the number of projects they have in active design at any given time in their practices. Thus, some of the waste inherent in moving employees' attention from one project to another at frequent intervals may be reduced. As detailing and documentation production phases become increasingly automated in various areas of engineering, cycle times for processing are becoming significantly reduced. These trends were already witnessed in the Crusell Bridge and the 100 11th Avenue New York case studies (see the *BIM Handbook* companion website).

9.3.3 Impact on Construction Companies

Construction companies seek to develop BIM capabilities for competitive advantage both in the field and in the office. They use BIM for 4D CAD and for collaboration, clash detection, client reviews, production management, and procurement. In many ways, they are in a better position than most other participants in the construction supply chain to leverage the short-term economic benefits of ubiquitous and accurate information.

Chapters 6 and 7 explained how BIM contributes to reducing construction budgets and schedules, as a result of better-quality designs (i.e., fewer errors) and by enabling greater degrees of prefabrication. A positive effect of the ability to develop design details fairly early in the process is that rework, which commonly results from unresolved details and inconsistent documentation, is mostly eliminated. These effects have already been reported broadly across the industry, and are evident in most of the case studies in Chapter 10.

The richness and ready availability of information in a building model enables novel applications for planning work on-site, including aspects other than cost and schedule. Construction safety is a key concern, and BIM is used to plan work to identify hazards such as exposed floor penetrations, unprotected edges, dangerous materials, and exposure to equipment, as the example shown in Figure 9–2 illustrates. The concept of *virtual construction* is no longer familiar only to the research community. Roles such as *VDC coordinator* and *BIM detailer* are now common in construction contracting companies.

9.3.4   Impact on Building Material and Component Suppliers

Building product manufacturers now provide 3D catalogs. Products as diverse as JVI mechanical rebar splices, Andersen windows, and many others can be downloaded as 3D objects with relevant data and inserted parametrically into models from several online sites. Content libraries such as BIMObject.com, SmartBIM, MEPCOntent and other similar tools provide large repositories of building product content for BIM. Content is increasingly accessible through search engines. Product libraries are primarily developed for the most common BIM tools, such as RVT file type families, but all are supported in varying degrees.

9.3.5   Impact on Construction Education: Integrated Education

Since 2006, leading schools of architecture and civil engineering have been teaching BIM to undergraduates from their first year, and that trend has spread in parallel with the adoption of BIM in the design professions (Sacks

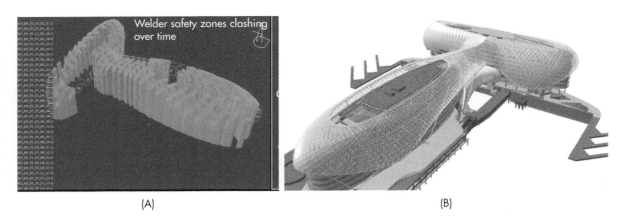

(A)   (B)

FIGURE 9–2   The Yas Island Formula One building. (A) The physical spaces that model the weld crew's workspaces to find unsafe interferences. (B) The overall frame of the structure.

Architect: Asymptote Architecture. Images courtesy Gehry Technologies.

and Barak, 2010). It appears that students are able to grasp the concepts and become productive using BIM tools more quickly than they were with CAD tools. Chapter 8 described a variety of university level courses that require students to use BIM and outlined formal curricula development efforts. Some examples include buildingSMART International's effort (Pikas et al., 2013 and Uhm et al., 2017).

9.3.6 Impact on Statutory Authorities: Model Access and Review

Despite predictions of adoption of statutory processes in which BIM models would be used for building permitting processes by statutory authorities, very few authorities have adopted the technology to the point where they can accept BIM model submissions. Singapore's Building Construction Authority (BCA) allows voluntary BIM model submissions of architectural models (since October 2016) and of structural and MEP models (since October 2017) using native formats (ArchiCAD, Revit, Tekla Structures, or Bentley AECOsim), and these are evaluated manually by BCA employees. The New York City Department of Buildings encourages construction companies to submit 3D site safety plans, offering early identification of risks, faster approvals, and better service. Given the progress made in BIM technology, the potential for greater impact in this area remains, but clearly more time is needed for statutory authorities to develop their business processes. More details on BIM mandates and requirements are provided in Chapter 8.

9.3.7 Impact on Project Documentation: On-Demand Drawings

Drawings are unlikely to disappear until digital display technologies are flexible and hardy enough for everyday use on-site, but the use of isometric and other 3D views with sequential assembly views and bills of material are already being used to facilitate crew operations. The case studies of the Mapletree Business Park II project, the Victoria Station Upgrade project, and the St. Joseph Hospital project in Chapter 10 all show examples of this use. The use of tablet computers in the field to view models with views defined on demand is also an everyday practice on leading projects.

One function of drawings in today's construction industry is for documentation of business transactions in the form of appendices to construction contracts. Already, however, there are indications that building information models can better serve this purpose, partly because of their improved accessibility to nonprofessionals. A technical and legal hurdle that remains to be resolved is the notion of *signing* a digital model, or even its individual components. Another is the issue of whether access to models in the future, as applications develop and old versions are no longer supported, will remain reliable. Both of these issues have been resolved in other business fields, and the economic drivers are strong enough to ensure that they will be resolved for building models too. Solutions may take advantage of advanced encryption technologies, third-party archiving of original model files, neutral view-only formats, blockchain and other techniques. In practice, a growing number of project participants already choose to build according to models, rather than drawings. Legal practice will have to keep pace with commercial practice.

9.3.8   Impact on BIM Tools: More Integration, More Specialization, More Information

The ready availability of BIM platforms has encouraged a new wave of plug-in applications for a wide variety of design and construction applications. They include tools for architectural conceptual design, layout and fabrication tools for new materials and building surfaces, green building design and evaluation, interior design, and a host of other areas.

Almost all major BIM vendors have **integrated analysis software interfaces** within their design modeling software, whether through acquisition of the analysis software companies or through close alliances with them. This is largely the result of competition between the vendors in their efforts to provide comprehensive suites of software, driven in part because the issue of interoperability remains insufficiently resolved. The trend began with embedded structural analysis software, continued with energy analysis, and is likely to be pursued further with acoustic analyses, estimating, building code compliance, and planning compliance.

The demand for object-level BIM servers (as opposed to file servers) has not grown as quickly as predicted. Given the large and growing size of BIM project files and the difficulties inherent in managing model exchanges, the **demand for BIM servers** with the potential for managing projects at the *object* level, rather than at the file level, was expected. Systems such as Aconex, PlanGrid, FinalCAD, and BIM 360 Field are all numerous and widely used, but object server solutions like BIM 360 Glue remain rare. The issues are discussed in detail in Chapter 3, which also lists and details some of the BIM servers that are already available. The technology for object-level exchanges already exists within those BIM systems that enable multiple users to access the model simultaneously, including locking mechanisms for individual objects and management of the update process. Given that transactions are primarily incremental updates of objects and their parameters (as opposed to complete model exchanges), the actual amount of data that needs to be transferred is fairly small, certainly much smaller than equivalent sets of files. However, we expect that the use of object level cloud servers will continue to evolve slowly.

Model viewer software such as DWF viewers, Tekla's and Bentley's web viewers, 3D PDF, and others reviewed in Chapter 2 have become important tools, due to their simplicity. A wide variety of applications—including quantity takeoffs, basic clash checking, and even procurement planning—can be used as information consumers only; they do not need to update information to BIM models. This has greatly increased the number of users of BIM models throughout the AEC industry.

9.4   CURRENT TRENDS

Market and technology trends are good predictors of the near-term future in any field, and BIM is no exception. The trends observed reveal the potential direction and influence BIM will have in the construction industry. All of these process and technology trends were formative in our attempt to look ahead at the future of building with BIM, in the following sections. BIM, however, is not developing in a vacuum. It is a computer-enabled paradigm change, and so its future will also be influenced by developments in Internet culture and by other similar and less predictable drivers.

9.4.1 Process Trends

Around the world, public and private owners increasingly mandate BIM use. The intrinsic value that the quality of information BIM provides to building clients is perhaps the most important economic driver for BIM systems and their adoption. Improved information quality, building products, visualization tools, cost estimates, and analyses lead to better decision making during design and less waste during construction, reducing both first costs for construction and lifecycle costs. Together with the value of building models for maintenance and operations, these are powerful motivators for clients to demand the use of BIM on their projects.

While the UK Government BIM Mandate has received much publicity, many other governments and major public and private construction clients have issued mandates for the use of BIM on their projects. Section 8.2 described these and outlined their powerful effect. These mandates make discussion of BIM ROI essentially superfluous, as they reflect a broadly held conviction that BIM provides overall benefits to society. This appears to be an "irresistible force" that will ensure eventual replacement of CAD with BIM in the AEC industry. Many of the case studies in Chapter 10 already reflect the key leadership role played by construction owners, all of whom are motivated by the economic benefits they perceive to be inherent in building with BIM.

Demand for people with new skills. The productivity gain for the documentation of design implies downsizing of drafting staff in building design practices of all kinds. On the other hand, many architects, engineers, and construction professionals are now needed for building information modeling roles. Architectural designers are sought who can effectively develop well-defined models that can support different assessments, for energy or cost/value. Engineers who can extract the analysis models needed to carry out structural or energy analyses and propose improvements to the building model design are in demand. Construction engineers who can leverage the information in a model to takeoff quantities, estimate costs, plan construction using simulations, and manage and control production on-site are sorely needed.

New management roles have developed. In design firms, model managers fulfill two basic roles. At the company level, they provide system and software support services. At the project level, they work with project teams to update the building model; guarantee origin, orientation, naming, and format consistency; and coordinate the exchange of model components with internal design groups and external designers and engineers. New roles and responsibilities are discussed in Section 8.4.2.

BIM Process and Technology Trends

Process Trends

- Owners are mandating BIM and changing contract terms to enable its use.
- New skills and roles are developing.
- Successful implementations in construction have led to corporate wide uptake by general contractors.
- The benefits of integrated practice are receiving wide review and being tested intensively in practice.
- Standards are now available in many countries and development efforts are underway in many others.
- Green building is increasingly demanded by clients.
- BIM and 4D CAD tools have become common tools in large construction site offices.

Technology Trends

- Automated checking for code conformance and constructability using building information models is being intensively researched, with developments in application of AI techniques.
- Major BIM platform vendors are adding functionality and integrating design assessment capabilities, providing even richer platforms for use.
- Building product manufacturers are beginning to provide parametric 3D catalogs.
- BIM tools with construction management functions are increasingly available.
- BIM is encouraging prefabrication for increasingly complex building subassemblies, which can be procured globally.

BIM use among architects, engineers, and contractors has become mainstream. In 2007, only 28% of the AEC industry in the United States was using BIM, but that number grew to 49% by 2009 and 71% by 2012. In 2007, only 14% of BIM users considered themselves to be expert or advanced, but here too, growth was rapid: 42% by 2009, and 54% by 2012 (Figure 9–3) (Young et al., 2007, Young et al., 2009, Bernstein et al., 2012). These figures regarding BIM adoption are difficult to interpret in detail because the survey questions were changed slightly from year to year, and because terms such as "expert user" are open to interpretation by the respondents. Nevertheless, the general trend of BIM use is quite clear. This trend is not limited to the United States, but many surveys show that the rapid increase of BIM use is global.

Successful implementations in construction have led contractors to reengineer their processes to take corporate-wide advantage of the benefits they have identified. In the first two editions of the *BIM Handbook*, most case studies reported design applications of BIM. In this edition, the Mapletree Business

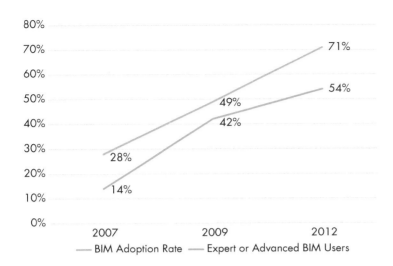

80%

70% ⌐ 71%

60%

50% ⌐ 54%
         49%
40%   42%

30%
    28%
20%

10% ⌐ 14%

0%
    2007   2009   2012
—— BIM Adoption Rate —— Expert or Advanced BIM Users

FIGURE 9–3 The trend of BIM use in the U.S. from 2007 to 2012.

Data Source: SmartMarket Report series

Park II, the St. Joseph Hospital, the NTU Student dormitories, and the Hyundai Automobile Complex in Chapter 10 all focus on construction contractor use of BIM. Among the case studies in the *BIM Handbook* companion website, the Sutter Medical Center project showed how BIM is essential in enabling the close collaboration needed in integrated project delivery (IPD) projects, including lean pull flow control for detailing of MEP systems, resulting in a high degree of off-site preassembly.

Owners are increasingly aware of the value of BIM for facility operation and maintenance. Three of the case studies in Chapter 10 (Medina Airport, Stanford Medical Center, and Howard Hughes Medical Center) highlight the way in which owners are benefiting directly from FM systems that apply BIM model data to operations and maintenance. The COBie exchange standard (Construction Operations Building information exchange) (BSI 2014a) for handover of equipment lists, product data sheets, warranties, and other as-built information has been adopted broadly.

The value of collaboration in construction projects is more widely recognized. Leading AEC firms and owners increasingly recognize that future building processes will require integrated practice of the whole construction team and will be facilitated by BIM. All members of the building team, not only the engineering consultants but contractors and fabricators, are recognized to have valuable input for design. This is leading to new forms of partnerships, with more design-build projects, more construction firms incorporating their own design offices, and more innovative and intensive teaming. Although IPD contracting *per se* has not developed at the rate expected, partnering, alliancing, and IPD are more widely known and understood than in the past. Alliancing is now the preferred method for procuring major infrastructure projects in Australia, for example (Morwood et al., 2008). One aspect of growing collaboration is that projects prepare explicit definition of workflows for supporting project development and completion. Workflow planning, in the form of BIM Execution Plans (BEP), is a feature of many large projects; the hand-offs, with content specifications and levels of detail, are the new "milestones."

Big Rooms. The increasing use of dedicated project-specific spaces for co-location of designers and builders is one practical expression of deepening collaboration across firms. With increasing amounts of information available electronically and as building information models incorporate more process annotations, information visualization is becoming central to the overall work process. Multi-display environments enable project teams to interact with the building information model and the entire information space. Team members can simultaneously view the model, the schedule, specifications, tasks, and relationships between these views.

Standardization efforts have borne fruit. In 2006, the American Institute of Steel Construction amended its code of standard practice to require that a 3D model, where it exists, be the representation of record for design information. In the United States, the National Institute for Building Sciences (NIBS) continues to facilitate industry definition of a set of National BIM Standards, which aims to precisely specify data exchanges within specific construction workflows. Numerous industry interest groups have prepared "Model View Definitions" as part of this effort[1] and all major BIM tool vendors now support, to a lesser or greater degree, some form of IFC standard exchange. In the UK, the British Standards Institution has hosted the development of a series of *British Standard* and *Publicly Available Specification (PAS) documents* to support broad adoption of BIM in the AEC industry, mostly in response to the UK government's BIM Mandate, which called for thorough adoption of BIM for public construction by April 2016. These are all detailed in Chapter 8, Section 8.3.1.

BIM is helping to make the fabrication of increasingly complex building subassemblies economically and globally viable. Large curtain wall system modules (see the 100 11th Avenue, New York City, case study in the *BIM Handbook* companion website) and prefinished prefabricated construction (PPVC) units (see the NTU North Hills case study in Chapter 10), are but a few of the many examples of modular construction that BIM is making economically viable (for more, see Section 7.5.2). The need for transport time allowances means that lead times for design are short, and the modules must be fabricated right the first time. BIM produces reliable and error-free information and shortens lead times. It allows a larger portion of a project to be prefabricated off-site, which reduces costs, increases quality, and simplifies the construction process.

Green building is demanded by a public conscious of the threats of climate change. BIM helps building designers achieve environmentally sustainable construction by providing tools for the analysis of energy needs and for accessing

---

[1] Some MVDs are coordinated on the "IFC Solutions Factory" website (see www.blis-project.org/IAI-MVD/).

and specifying building products and materials with low environmental impact. BIM tools can also assist in the evaluation of projects for LEED compliance. In response to demand, vendors have embedded energy analysis tools within BIM platforms, although doubts regarding the accuracy of energy consumption analyses remain. The U.S. Federal Department of Energy is funding new research to improve the tools for building energy simulation.

9.4.2 Technology Trends

Automated model verification tools for checking program and code compliance are the subject of continuing research and development. Innovative companies, such as Solibri, EPM, and SmartReview, have developed model-checking software using IFC files and are intent on extending their capabilities. Coordination between complex building systems using superimposed 3D models is becoming common, and checks go beyond identification of physical clashes.

"Code-compliance checking software can potentially re-engineer the building permit process. Instead of waiting weeks for a building office to make a decision on whether the plans comply and the permit can be issued, the architect could present a certified plan review report along with the BIM. If the building department officials accept the certified plan review report, the permit could be issued 'over the counter,' eliminating days, weeks, or months of delay."

Mark Clayton, SmartReview

Peripheral hardware is linking the virtual BIM world to the physical construction world. The continued development of laser scanning, photogrammetry, drones, radio-frequency identification (RFID) technology, augmented, mixed and virtual reality systems, and portable computers is enabling data transfer in both directions between BIM and construction site.

The effort to develop a range of wearable communication tools led by French construction company Bouygues is an excellent example of innovation in this area. Figure 9–4 illustrates the concept, which includes a heads-up display with built-in camera, a vest with warning signals and sensors, construction boots with sensors in the soles, and a sleeve that provides a display and buttons.

Rapid improvements in the areas of virtual, augmented, and mixed reality are particularly significant peripheral tools for BIM. Section 6.12.1 discussed the growing role of augmented reality in bringing BIM information into the field during construction and directly to operations and maintenance workers in functioning buildings. The spread of mobile computing has made both virtual and augmented reality tools more readily accessible, and designers and builders continue to come up with new ways to exploit them to deliver project information.

3D printing and robotic construction. Section 7.6.3 outlined a range of initiatives in this area. What is striking is that most of these are now commercial start-up efforts, no longer the preserve of long-term funded research initiatives. Although most of the 3D printing efforts must still overcome a range of obstacles related primarily to material technology and delivery, robotic construction

FIGURE 9–4 A collection of online equipment designed to improve the safety of operatives in the field and the ergonomics of their working environment. The system was developed by the Ideas Laboratory, a shared innovation laboratory based in Grenoble, France.

Image courtesy of Bouygues Construction, a partner in the Ideas Laboratory (project developed with Suez, Air Liquide & CEA).

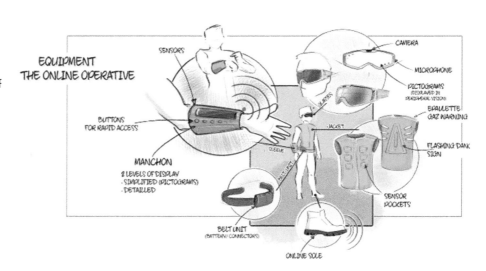

machines like FastBrick Robotics' Hadrian appear to be poised to enter mainstream construction. They universally depend on BIM for their operation.

9.4.3 Integrative Process and Technology Trends

Lean Construction and BIM are developing in tandem. Lean construction (Koskela, 1992; Ballard, 2000) and BIM are progressing hand in hand, with many of the predicted synergies between them becoming reality. BIM and Lean are complementary in several important ways.

When applied to building design, lean thinking implies reduced waste through the elimination of unnecessary process stages that provide no direct value to the client, such as producing drawings; concurrent design to eliminate errors and rework, as far as possible; and shortened cycle durations. BIM enables all of these goals. The need to efficiently produce highly customized products for discerning consumers is a key driver of lean production (Womack and Jones, 2003). An essential component is the reduction of cycle times for individual products because it helps designers and producers better respond to clients' (often changing) needs. BIM technology can play a crucial role in reducing the duration of both design and construction, but its main impact is felt when the design phase duration is effectively reduced. Rapid development of conceptual designs, strong communication with clients through visualization and cost estimates, concurrent design development and coordination with engineering consultants, error reduction and automation in producing documentation, and facilitated prefabrication all contribute to this effect. Thus, BIM is becoming an indispensable tool for construction, not only because of its direct benefits, but because it enables lean design and construction.

Clearly defined management and work procedures are another aspect of lean construction, as they allow structured experimentation for systematic improvement. Leading construction companies like Lease Crutcher Lewis, DPR, and Mortenson in the United States, Fira Oy and Skanska in Finland, Tidhar Construction in Israel, and many others have created their own specifications for BIM and Lean practices, thus defining their "Company Way" of doing things,[2] described in books such as *Integrating Project Delivery* (Fischer et al., 2017) and *Building Lean, Building BIM: Changing Construction the Tidhar Way* (Sacks et al., 2017).

Lean production management software tools for construction are maturing. Entirely new production management information systems for construction have been introduced and are developing rapidly. Most of these are cloud "software as a service" (SAAS) solutions that support the four planning levels of the Last Planner System.[3] Some, such as vPlanner and touchplan.io, do not use the BIM model, while others, such as VisiLean, work directly with the model. The latter system and others like it are based on the "KanBIM" research prototype (Sacks et al., 2010), which demonstrated how BIM models could be leveraged to provide crew leaders at the work face not only with product information, but with process information. Process information enables them to "see" the status of shared equipment, what other teams are doing, where materials are along the supply chain, what spaces are available for work, and so forth, all of which enables them to make intelligent choices about their own work progress. Figure 9–5 shows a typical interface.

9.4.4 Trends in BIM Research

BIM has become a leading topic of interest for researchers in the fields of Architecture, Engineering and Construction Management. The European

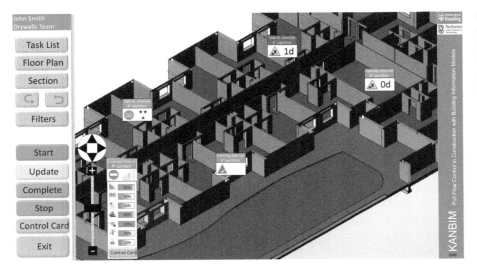

FIGURE 9–5 An example of a KanBIM user interface, displayed on a large-format touch screen for use on the construction site (Sacks et al., 2010).

---

[2] The "company way" term is inspired by the "Toyota Way" (Liker, 2003).

[3] A lean construction work planning and control system (see Ballard, 2000).

Union's 7th Framework and its Horizon 20-20 schemes, the National Science Foundation in the United States, and many other national research foundations all fund BIM research. A recent review paper (Zhao, 2017) identified no fewer than 614 research papers on various BIM topics, published between 2005 and 2016 in journals listed in the Web of Science core collection database. A similar paper that reviewed a broader set of 1,874 publications found that the key research areas included automated and parametric design, interoperability (including IFC), implementation and adoption, green building, quality inspection, and 4D/5D modeling (Li et al., 2017).

Some of the most promising developments in BIM research are in two closely related topics, **semantic enrichment** and **semantic web services**. Research in these areas has the potential to provide novel solutions for BIM that exploit developments in artificial intelligence, for overcoming the interoperability problems that still retard BIM development, for enabling generic object-level BIM servers, and for applying new tools to automate aspects of design and analysis.

Maintaining integrity across different design models (e.g., architectural versus structural versus construction) is imperative, as changes are made to the different models by their respective disciplines. Unfortunately, interoperability tools like the IFC standard, still do not support coordination beyond visual inspection and the identification of physical clashes in geometry. Managing changes across different systems—involving loads (structural or thermal) or other performance relations—is increasingly recognized as an important and limiting condition. Smart automated transactions, implemented on BIM servers, will be needed to augment and increasingly replace the manual updates of special-purpose model views that are required for synchronization. These may be automatic or resolved by an analyst. Research will need to determine the nature of the relationships between building objects that are implemented in different discipline-specific systems.

Semantic enrichment of building models refers to the automatic or semiautomatic addition of meaningful information to a digital model of a building or other structure by software that can deduce new information by processing rules (Belsky et al., 2016) or by applying machine-learning (Bloch et al., 2018) (see also Section 3.6.2.). Domain expert knowledge is used to recognize or infer the semantics of a given building information model, and the new information is added to the model. As Figure 9–6 shows, a semantic enrichment engine can identify and add aggregation relationships (i.e., objects belong to groups), functional relationships (such as "object 1 is connected to object 2"), and parameters to what would otherwise be "dumb" geometry. The key idea is that by using semantic enrichment, any domain-specific BIM tool might be able to import generic IFC files directly, recognize the intent of the model objects, and manipulate the information as if the model were prepared specifically for that tool. Artificial intelligence approaches, such as rule-inferencing or machine-learning using artificial neural networks, have been tested in research, and have shown promising results in domains that include precast concrete, reinforced concrete highway bridges, and high-rise residential apartment buildings.

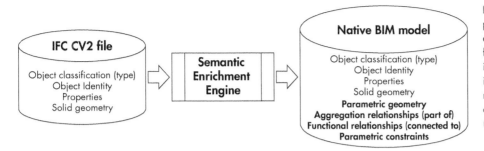

FIGURE 9–6 The SEEBIM prototype semantic enrichment engine uses forward-chaining rule inferencing to add semantic information to building models defined in IFC coordination view 2.0 (Sacks et al., 2017).

Semantic Web Services In the past ten years, an increasing number of industry developments and research initiatives have focused on the usage of linked data and semantic web technologies for the management of building data. The semantic web was introduced as a concept in 2001 by Tim Berners-Lee and aimed at transforming the World Wide Web of documents into a World Wide Web of data (Berners-Lee et al., 2001). Research on this topic for the construction industry similarly aims to express BIM models as online graphs of building data, using the Web Ontology Language (OWL) and Resource Description Framework (RDF). An overview of recent initiatives in the building industry can be found in Pauwels et al. (2017).

The main advantages of expressing building data using these technologies is to make use of a broad range of tools for (1) seamless linking to data outside the building industry (geography, materials, products, infrastructure, regulations), (2) querying data, and (3) reasoning with data. Each of these three—linking, querying, and reasoning—can be done using out-of-the-box query engines and query languages that are also widely used outside the construction industry. This enables swift and agile usage of data: quick linking to other data, querying the data for subsets, and performing small checks using reasoning engines.

The main strands of research and development revolve around an ifcOWL ontology, which is a semantic web version of the IFC schema. Using that ontology, one can express any BIM model in a semantic web graph and readily deploy the available technologies. Since most companies continue to work with BIM models as files, exploitation in the industry thus far is primarily for downstream processes: exporting the data into an RDF format and querying and reasoning downstream.

9.4.5 Obstacles to Change

As a counterpoint to the positive trends discussed in the previous section, BIM faces numerous obstacles to progress. These include technical barriers, legal and liability issues, regulation, inappropriate business models, resistance to changes in employment patterns, and the need to educate large numbers of professionals.

Construction is a collaborative endeavor, and BIM enables closer collaboration than CAD; however, this will require that workflows and commercial relationships support an increase in the sharing of both liabilities and rewards. BIM tools and IFC file formats do not yet adequately address support for the management and tracking of changes to models, nor are contract terms sufficiently developed to handle these collective responsibilities.

The distinct economic interests of designers and contractors are another possible barrier. In construction business models, only a small portion of the economic benefits of BIM now accrues to designers. The major payoffs go to contractors and owners. Some BIM guides call for redistribution of milestone payments for designers (see Section 8.6.1), shifting payments to earlier design stages in recognition of the fact that more information is generated earlier in the process (as reflected in the MacLeamy curve, shown in Figure 5-1). Yet these are the exception rather than the rule, and none of the guides call for increased design fees. Similarly, the necessary business and contractual arrangements for performance-based design, likely associated with formal commissioning, have not yet been worked out.

In the economic context, cheap construction labor has been, and remains, a retarding factor for innovation and technology adoption in construction. Yet cheap labor cannot build the more sophisticated buildings that are increasingly in demand, with the result that the industry is not homogeneous; some projects both drive and benefit from technological innovations such as BIM, while others cannot exploit it effectively.

BIM developers cater primarily to the design professions because of their large numbers. However, the challenge for BIM is the increasingly specialized software needed for specialized functions, ranging from project feasibility evaluation (such as DESTINI Profiler) to concept design, but especially to different contracting and fabrication systems. The development of BIM software is capital-intensive and software vendors will have to assume the commercial risk of developing sophisticated tools for construction contractors.

The major technical barrier is the need for mature interoperability tools. Moore's Law in practice suggests that hardware will not be a barrier, and this appears to be the case. The development of standards has been slower than expected, largely because there is a lack of a business model that will allow its funding to be addressed in a capitalist economy. Meanwhile, the lack of effective interoperability continues to be a serious impediment to collaborative design.

9.5 VISION 2025

Recent years have witnessed the transition of BIM to accepted mainstream practice and the realization of many of the ideas of BIM visionaries. The next few years will see increasing numbers of successful implementations, changes in the building industry, and new trial uses and extensions of what can be achieved with BIM beyond its use today. With the knowledge of the arc of development to date, considering current trends and the drivers and obstacles to change, we now turn to extrapolate into the future. We assess developments in the areas of construction processes and technology, the ways in which building information is delivered, design services, building product specifications, code-checking, construction management practices, employment, professional roles, and the integration of building information into business systems.

9.5.1 Thoroughly Digital Design and Construction

Design and construction will become thoroughly digital, with BIM providing the information backbone for construction projects. The Internet of Things (IoT) will provide new streams of input data, from tower cranes, concrete pumps, building monitoring systems, cameras, and sensors carried by workers and by drones, to construction materials in the supply chain, and many more. All of these streams will need to be interpreted and the results integrated with the building model. The information will be used in many different ways that are unavailable today. For example, with location monitoring, a drill may identify the materials through which it expects to pass (from the BIM model) and recommend to its operator both the mode of action and the appropriate drill bits. A worker may be alerted to a fall hazard near an unprotected opening. Comprehensive information will provide situational awareness for construction crews, allowing them to make better decisions that prioritize mature work packages in safe conditions over work that is not ready for them.

Information collected on-site during construction and during a building's life will also feed back into design. It will become possible to calibrate performance simulations with actual performance data, and for the first time, sufficient data sets for machine learning will become available. BIM and the Internet level the playing field in terms of access to building information at both the project and industry-wide levels. Information flow becomes near instantaneous, and collaboration among all concerned within a project can become synchronous, which is a paradigm change from traditional asynchronous workflows. Traditional workflows with sequential generation, submittal, and reviews of drawings—which can be iterative and wasteful due to rework—are no longer appropriate. The professional and legal constructs that have evolved in relation to these workflows are equally unsuitable for collaborative design and construction processes, with shortened cycle times and closely integrated information flows.

While academic research has a role to play in defining new concepts and measures of information flow that promote integrity and value, it is likely that trial-and-error efforts by industry pioneers—driven by practical imperatives—will be the primary source of new BIM workflows. New contractual forms, job descriptions, commercial alignments, and procurement arrangements will need to be synthesized, tested, and refined. These will need to be adapted and sometimes redefined to fit with local codes, union practices, and other controlling contextual issues. Such efforts will support and stimulate the development of new tools in both academia and industry.

Digital construction will extend beyond the boundaries of project sites, linking BIM models with Precinct Information Modeling (PIM), City Information Modeling (CIM) or "Smart City" systems. The interfaces between BIM models and GIS systems will be mediated through mapped data exchange standards. Mappings between the IFC and the CityGML schema are well developed (Isikdag, 2014). BIM model data provides city information systems with data on the internal spatial layout and assets of buildings, while GIS systems provide designers and builders of individual projects with detailed information about their site and its utility infrastructure.

Architectural, engineering, and construction education will continue to evolve, sometimes leading but mostly lagging behind developments in industry. The shift to a fully digital process will require graduates who are not only competent in a digital work environment, but who are also able to adapt and learn new work processes throughout their careers.

9.5.2 A New Culture of Innovation in Construction

Traditionally, construction has had very low levels of investment in R&D and little innovation. The fragmented, modular structure of the industry has stifled integral innovations (i.e., innovations that cross organizational boundaries in their implementation; Sheffer, 2011). Yet the availability of BIM models opens the door to a wide range of technological innovations that require detailed product and process information. As Figure 9–7 shows, the number of construction technology start-up companies founded each year already increased dramatically from 2010 to 2015.

Since the early 1990s and throughout the period during which BIM evolved, the academic research community generated many conceptual applications for building models that could not be implemented in practice because object-oriented building model data was unavailable. BIM tools were neither sufficiently mature nor were they in widespread use. Examples include automated control of construction equipment, such as cranes, robotic pavers, and concrete surface finishers; automated data collection for performance monitoring; construction safety planning; electronic procurement and logistics; and many others. While there are still hurdles to overcome, technical progress in computing power, remote sensing technologies, computer-controlled production machinery, distributed computing, information exchange technologies, and other technologies have opened new possibilities that software vendors are exploiting. The increasing power of mobile computing, location, identification, and remote sensing technologies (GPS, RFID, laser scanning, and so forth) all allow for greater use of building information models in the field, which enable faster and more accurate construction.

The ready availability of digital building information and the means to store and manipulate large amounts of data is not the only enabler of innovation in construction. A digital design and construction industry fosters innovation because people have a positive attitude to technology and the willingness and ability to put new tools to work. BIM has brought about the growth of a construction culture that welcomes innovation. We expect therefore that there will indeed be exponential growth in the number of construction tech start-ups, incubators, innovation labs, and so on. They will bring real-time monitoring and control, laser-scanning and photogrammetry reviews using drones and/or fixed cameras, and changes to the way that

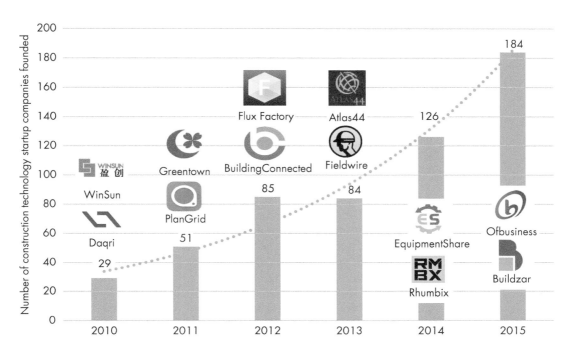

FIGURE 9–7 Number of construction technology start-up companies founded, 2010–2015.

Data source: Tracxn Technologies Private Limited.

construction crews are managed. Production control will become possible with far greater detail than is possible today.

9.5.3 Off-site Construction

As discussed in Chapter 7, BIM facilitates prefabrication and preassembly, making their engineering coordination essentially error-free, and thus more economical than previously possible. With the pressures for better, quicker, and less expensive buildings, modular design and manufacture of larger and more complex custom-building parts will become widespread. There will be more multitrade racks, bathroom units, hotel rooms, stair units, and other modular products. BIM enables mass customization, so that the benefits of factory production with good quality control and automated machining can be obtained without compromising on design variation. Building sectors where BIM and associated construction technologies are applied will become more like manufacturing, with much of the work done by off-site vendors who create modules that are shipped to the job-site and assembled into finished buildings.

In the same way that semiconductor fabrication plants undertake for-hire chip fabrication, prefabrication plants for construction may support custom numerical control (CNC) fabrication with little or no manual input for precast concrete, steel welded systems, and a few types of exterior carbon fiber reinforced plastics. Fabrication plants will rely on model data provided by the designers to generate CNC instructions, needing only minimal checking by the component producer. This will reduce the costs associated with custom fabrication, bringing them closer to that of standard construction and spreading their capital investments over many projects. 3D printing, as described in Section 7.6.3, will have a major role to play in this regard.

Two caveats are needed here. First, BIM-enabled integration of highly developed design and commercial information—facilitating prefabrication and preassembly—will lead to a construction industry aligned more with other manufacturing industries, with a minimum of activity performed on-site; yet this does not imply mass production, but lean production of highly customized products. Each building will continue to have unique design features, but BIM will enable their prefabrication in ways that ensure compatibility when all parts are delivered. Second, this will not apply equally to all of the construction industry. As we discuss in the paragraphs on the period beyond 2025 in Section 9.6, there is likely to be a growing divergence between two branches of the construction industry: one that is highly dependent on BIM and other technologies, and another that continues to apply on-site construction methods with cheap labor and low productivity.

9.5.4 Construction Regulation: Automated Code-Checking

Checking building design models for compliance with code requirements and planning restrictions is the focus of intensive research. All over the world, owners, designers, and builders press statutory authorities to accelerate the granting of construction permits, with the expectation that BIM models can be analyzed efficiently and quickly for this purpose. Similarly, sophisticated construction clients will drive the development of automated design review software for different building types.

This functionality could be provided in one of two ways:

- Application service providers sell/lease code-checking software plug-ins embedded in BIM software tools. The plug-in extracts local requirement data from online databases maintained by the service provider, as a service to local jurisdictions. Designers check their designs continuously as they evolve.
- External software directly checks a neutral model file, such as an IFC file, for code compliance. The designer exports the model and the check is run on the IFC model on a web server.

Both developments are possible, although the former has an advantage for users; providing feedback directly to the model will make fixing problems easier than receiving an external report that needs interpretation before edits can be made. Because design is an iterative process—and designers will want to obtain feedback, make changes, and check again—it may be preferred.

A number of tools for model checking are already available on the market (some are reviewed in Section 2.5.3), but key obstacles to broad use remain:

- Model checking for any particular aspect requires that the model objects be tailored precisely to the intended meaning of the objects defined in the particular code, standard, regulation, or specification under consideration. For example, consider an attic space with a sloped internal ceiling. If a jurisdiction determines that spaces with headroom greater than 2.20m are primary space, while areas with less than 2.20m headroom are ancillary space, then the space objects in the model must be divided at the 2.20m headroom contour to facilitate checking for compliance to area restrictions. Existing model checking tools require extensive preprocessing by users each time a check is performed, which is onerous and error-prone.
- The diversity and range of building code checkers needed leads to the recognition that hard-coding rules is not the best way to define and implement them. As with other software applications, hard-coding generates tools that are too expensive to write and debug and are inflexible for making changes. Instead, high-level and special-purpose rule definition languages are needed, facilitating the general development of rule-checking in buildings (Eastman et al., 2009).

The good news is that researchers in industry and academia are making progress to solve these issues. Artificial intelligence techniques, particularly those that apply machine learning, are being applied to enable semantic enrichment of models, thus automating code-specific preprocessing. New ways to express rules and conditions without embedding them in computer code are also under development, which will allow nonprogrammers to write and edit checking rules. Given the increasingly positive climate and culture for innovation in construction technology, this is an area that is likely to see rapid growth.

9.5.5 Artificial Intelligence in Construction

Another technical area that may introduce further developments that influence BIM systems is euphemistically referred to as *artificial intelligence*. Progress in natural language interfaces, semantic web technologies (including generic inferencing tools), and deep learning will all be applied within BIM platforms for a range of purposes, such as code checking, quality reviews, intelligent tools for comparing versions, design guides, and design wizards.

In particular, AI tools that apply machine learning are likely to become increasingly relevant as the population of BIM models available for learning routines grows. Consider for example the case of model checking—without an extensive case base of models with their checking results, there is no resource for training model checking systems. As jurisdictions begin to accept

BIM models for permitting applications—as is already the case in Singapore, for example (see Section 9.3.6)—the necessary databases will grow.

Another significant application for AI in general and machine learning in particular is to support acquisition of as-built information. The trend toward the use of laser scanning and/or photogrammetry for acquiring geometry in the field for use in design or construction management is still hampered by the high cost of interpreting the point clouds and generating meaningful building objects that can be used in a building information model. This is a time-consuming endeavor that limits the technology's use, but recent developments suggest that solutions may be at hand. In the EU Infravation *SeeBridge* project, researchers trained software to identify shapes in point clouds and thus reconstruct the 3D geometry of reinforced concrete highway bridges. The solid geometry thus obtained was classified using forward-chaining rule-based inferencing, and the technique was also applied to aggregate the objects, to infer structural connections, to build grids of axes, and to propose sensible extensions for bridge elements that were partially occluded in the scans. The result was a BIM model that could be used for bridge maintenance.

This period should also see increasingly smoother transitions from design models to construction models. Software *wizards*—using parametric templates of work packages with embedded construction methods—will be applied to rapidly compile a construction model from a design model. Ideas like the *recipes* in the *Vico Office* suite are an early indication of what can be expected. For example, a parametric template for a post-tensioned flat slab will lay out the formwork design and determine labor and equipment inputs, material quantities, and delivery schedules based on a generic slab object in a design model. A resulting construction model can be analyzed for cost, equipment, and logistic constraints and for schedule requirements; and the alternatives can be similarly compared. Thus, construction planning will be greatly enhanced. The parametric templates will also serve as a repository for corporate knowledge, in as far as they will embed an individual company's way of working into these software applications.

ALICE (ArtificiaL Intelligence Construction Engineering), a tool developed by a start-up company based on academic research, is an early sign of things to come. The software begins with a BIM model, applies recipes that encapsulate construction methods to generate candidate activities, generates large numbers of candidate construction plans with different crew sizes and method options, and then identifies the optimum plan.

As BIM becomes ubiquitous, designers will prefer to specify building products that offer information to be inserted directly into a model in electronic form, including hyperlinked references to the suppliers' catalogs, price lists, and so forth. Rudimentary electronic building product catalogs available today will evolve into sophisticated and intelligent product specs, including information that enables structural, thermal, lighting, LEED compliance, and other analyses, in addition to the data now used for specifying and procuring products. The ability of some products to support their direct use in simulation tools, especially lighting and energy analyses, will become important extensions to their current challenge of geometric integration. The basic challenges for realizing high levels of semantic search will have been addressed, and new capabilities that allow for searches based on color, textures, and shape will become available.

9.5.6 Globalization

Globalization resulted from the elimination of barriers to international trade (Friedman, 2007). In construction, architecture and engineering design firms have worked across the world for many years, but the physical fabrication of buildings has remained almost entirely local. Now, however, both the Internet and BIM tools are facilitating increasing degrees of globalization in construction, not only in the design and parts supply but in the fabrication of engineered-to-order components of increasing complexity. Highly accurate and reliable design information creates the possibility of moving the production of building parts to more cost-effective locations, because pieces can be shipped great distances with a high degree of confidence that they will fit correctly when installed.

The fabrication of the steel and glass panels of the curtain wall system for the 100 11th Avenue, New York City, case study project (in the *BIM Handbook* companion website) was an early example, and the continuing trend is evident in the NTU North Hills project case study in Chapter 10, where PPVC modules produced in Taiwan were finished and installed in Singapore. The accuracy and reliability of production data prepared using BIM enables building products and assemblies that would traditionally be procured locally to be made anywhere in the world. Competition in the construction fabrication area is spreading globally.

9.5.7 Support for Sustainable Construction

Sustainability introduces new dimensions to the costs and values of buildings and construction. The true costs of building and facility use, when looked at from the point of view of worldwide sustainability issues, have not yet been brought to the marketplace. The pressure to make all residences zero net energy usage, and to make larger facilities energy producers rather than consumers, is growing. These affect the pricing of materials, of transport costs, and the ways in which buildings are operated. Architects and engineers will be tasked with providing much more energy-efficient buildings that use recyclable materials, which means that more accurate and extensive analyses will be needed. BIM systems will need to support these capabilities.

Research is needed to address the various types of model geometry needed for different types of analyses. While most people are familiar with the need for stick and node models for structural analysis, few are aware of the need for tessellation structures of single bounded surfaces to represent separately managed energy zones within a building. Automatic methods for tessellation are needed for preprocessing models for energy analysis and for panelization of irregularly-shaped building facades. Another type of geometric abstraction will be necessary for enclosing spatial volumes for computational fluid dynamics. Such models use heuristics to determine which geometric features are required for capturing essential air flows. Further development of automated geometry abstractions is needed if these analyses are to move into everyday use. New semantic enrichment techniques may be applied to expedite the pre-processing of model data that is needed.

Green or sustainable construction practices are likely to get a boost from BIM, because building information models can be analyzed for compliance with energy consumption standards, for their use of green construction materials, and for other factors included in certification schemes like LEED. The ability to automatically assess building models will make the enforcement of new regulations more practical. Such capabilities are already available through gbXML. Some building codes already require that energy analyses be performed on all buildings to comply with standards for energy consumption. The use of performance-based standards, as opposed to prescriptive standards, is likely to increase. All of these trends will put great pressure on developing better metrics for addressing the accuracy of energy and sustainability models. The first energy calculation tools integrated within BIM tools are already available, which means that BIM will facilitate the push for sustainable buildings.

Research on the integration of multiple types of analysis, as well as the development of new types of energy systems and the need to analyze them, will lead to a new generation of energy simulation tools. For example, to show the interaction of heat flows with natural convection, the output from a simulation of energy radiation to internal materials within a space will be used as input for a computational fluid dynamics (CFD) model. On the equipment side, the need to integrate smart electrical grid capabilities, where the utility companies manage the level of power provided to buildings with local renewable energy systems such as photovoltaics, will require a new generation of tools to model their behavior. The new tools will be modular so that mixes of different types of energy-producing and energy-consuming systems can be modeled. Multi-criteria optimization methods are available, such as genetic algorithms of various kinds, but utility functions that can express the integrated performance of buildings with respect to different functions will be needed. Developing these relationships would allow parametric models to automatically vary to search for performance objectives dealing with weight, solar gain, energy use, and other objectives. This would enable new levels of comprehensive performance-based design, for example at the mechanical equipment level and the building envelope level, that are not possible today.

9.6 BEYOND 2025

Looking beyond the medium term, we can only paint the picture of BIM and its role in a changing construction industry in broad brushstrokes.

Perhaps the key change is that thanks to BIM's function as a digital information platform, the construction industry itself is becoming an increasingly digital industry. Adoption of BIM is not uniform across the industry, however, and this is not only due to conservative attitudes or lack of education—there are economic forces at play that obstruct BIM adoption in some sectors. Cheap labor is one; industry fragmentation to cope with risk is another. It is becoming increasingly likely that two quite different sectors will emerge, each performing different projects: on the one hand, large, sophisticated information-driven construction companies, fully exploiting BIM and increased automation; and on the other hand, labor-driven construction companies, based primarily on cheap labor. The case study projects in the next chapter represent the first sector. These projects are built by designers and builders with high levels of technical expertise, they use the latest BIM platforms and tools, and they make optimal use of them. As a result, they use less labor and have higher productivity than non-BIM projects. Given the local nature of many construction projects and the small size of the majority of them, it is quite possible that the divide between these sectors will persist for some time. In the remainder of this section, we refer to the construction sector that is applying BIM and other information technologies.

The chart in Figure 9–8, prepared by the Building Informatics Group at Yonsei University in Seoul, South Korea, succinctly describes BIM along a trajectory that culminates in the 2030s with a period called AI BIM. The end of the current decade (2010s) is called Full BIM (or Level 3 BIM, as it is loosely defined in the BS PAS 1192 series and other BS standard documents). "Lean BIM" is an appropriate collective term for the practices expected in the next decade (2020s), as the synergies of Lean and BIM adoption influence the ways in which BIM supports better flows of information, materials, equipment, spaces, and teams in design and in construction based on lean manufacturing and construction concepts. The following decade is called the AI BIM period, because the most significant changes to the ways in which BIM is applied are likely to be the result of the growing use of AI in society in general and its application in construction in particular.

Another intriguing possibility is that information technology will change the role of general contracting companies entirely by enabling clients, designers, suppliers, and trade crews to coordinate their transactions through new platform services. Online platforms such as Amazon, Uber, and many others have radically changed the way their respective industries operate. The services provided by a general contractor are not only transactional, they include assumption of risk, coordination, quality control, financing, and more. Yet if distributed solutions could be found for these functions to be provided independently, with emphasis on identifying a mechanism for fair distribution of risk, then platform aggregators could contract and schedule design and construction work with much greater flexibility than general contracting companies can do today. BIM would play a critical role in such a digital construction platform, providing the definitive product and process model around which all participants in a project would work.

No less than it has done since its advent, BIM continues to make this an exciting time to be a designer, a builder, or any other AEC industry professional.

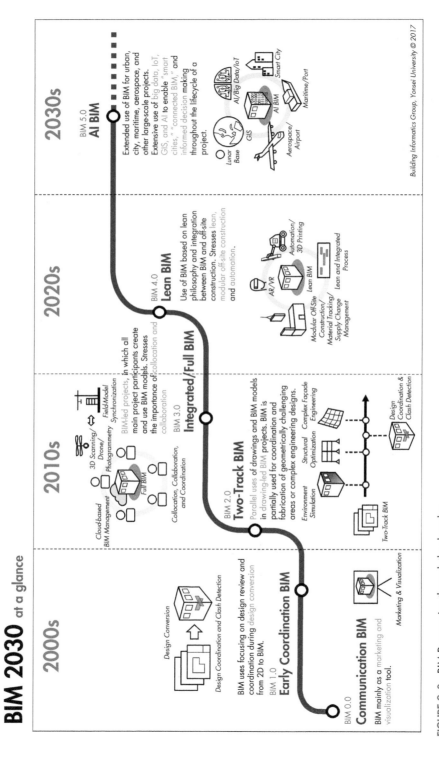

BIM 2030 at a glance

| 2000s | 2010s | 2020s | 2030s |

BIM 0.0

Communication BIM

BIM mainly as a marketing and visualization tool.

Marketing & Visualization

BIM 1.0

Early Coordination BIM

BIM uses focusing on design review and coordination during design conversion from 2D to BIM.

Design Conversion

Design Coordination and Clash Detection

BIM 2.0

Two-Track BIM

Parallel uses of drawings and BIM models in drawing-led BIM projects. BIM is partially used for coordination and fabrication of geometrically challenging areas or complex engineering designs.

Environment Simulation

Structural Optimization

Complex Facade Engineering

Two-Track BIM

Design Coordination & Clash Detection

BIM 3.0

Integrated/Full BIM

BIM-led projects, in which all main project participants create and use BIM models. Stresses the importance of collocation and collaboration

Cloud-based BIM Management

3D Scanning/ Drone/ Photogrammetry

Field-Model Synchronization

Full BIM

Collocation, Collaboration, and Coordination

BIM 4.0

Lean BIM

Use of BIM based on lean philosophy and integration between BIM and off-site construction. Stresses lean, modular offsite construction and automation.

AR/VR

Lean BIM

Automation/ 3D Printing

Modular Off-Site Construction/ Material Tracking/ Supply Change Management

Lean and Integrated Process

BIM 5.0

AI BIM

Extended use of BIM for urban, city, maritime, aerospace, and other large-scale projects. Extensive use of big data, IoT, GIS, and AI to enable "smart cities," "connected BIM," and informed decision making throughout the lifecycle of a project.

Lunar Base

GIS

AI/Big Data/IoT

Smart City

AI BIM

Aerospace/ Airport

Maritime/Port

Building Informatics Group, Yonsei University © 2017

FIGURE 9–8 BIM Progression through the decades.

Graphic courtesy of Building Informatics Group, Yonsei University.

Features of Lean BIM, the 2020s	Features of AI BIM, the 2030s
• Integration with Lean Construction management and tools, such as the Last Planner System and other pull planning methods • Increased use of manufacture-to-order (MTO) or engineer-to-order (ETO) components produced off-site • Construction automation • 3D printing • Material tracking and supply chain management • Modular off site construction • Use of IDM/MVD for automated data exchange • Virtual and Augmented Reality applications	• Data-driven decision-making processes for design, construction, and FM/AM • Automated data processing and exchange • Automated production for on-site and off-site construction • Semantic and intelligent information interfacing technologies • BIM data science (big data) • IoT-based manufacturing • IoT-based project and facility management • AI-based design, engineering, and model quality checking • IDM/MVD for automated data exchange and information requirements checking, IDMs/MVDs at each LOD • Integration of Smart Cities, GIS, and BIM

Acknowledgment

The authors are grateful to Dr. Pieter Pauwels for the paragraphs on semantic web services.

Chapter 9 Discussion Questions

1. To what extent are the trends of BIM development that are reported in Section 9.4 evident in the region in which you work or study? Conduct a short survey among practitioners and discuss any possible differences you find between the local trends and best practice. What are the reasons for the differences?

2. What are the most important issues in BIM technology that require research for their development?

3. Based on a survey of industry, market, and demographic changes, discuss the future of BIM in the context of potential changes in the architecture, engineering, and construction industry.

4. Identify a few of the primary barriers to BIM implementation in your environment and discuss how they can be overcome.

5. Artificial intelligence is being applied increasingly to many technologies. List three possible ways in which AI could be applied in the context of BIM, and for each case, describe how you envisage it working and what benefits it would bring.

6. What changes are field BIM technologies likely to bring to the construction site?

CHAPTER 10

BIM Case Studies

10.0 INTRODUCTION

In this chapter, we present eleven case studies of projects in which BIM played a significant role. They represent the experiences of owners, architects, engineers, contractors, fabricators, and even construction crews and a facility maintenance team—all pioneers in the application of BIM. All the case studies are new to this edition. The case studies in the first and the second editions are available at the *BIM Handbook* companion website. The case studies listed in Table 10–0–1 represent a broad range of public and private building and infrastructure projects from different regions including Asia, Europe, North America, and the Middle East. The case studies also cover various types of projects in terms of function, including medical, residential, office, museum, exhibition hall, multicultural complex, airport, and railway station projects.

Taken as a whole, the case studies cover the use of BIM across all phases of the facility delivery process (as shown in Table 10–0–2) by a wide range of project participants. Three case studies focus on the use of BIM during the operation, maintenance, and facility management phase. Each case study

Table 10–0–1 Brief Descriptions of the Case Study Projects

Project	Client Type	Main Use	Region	Status*
10.1 National Children's Hospital, Dublin	Public	Hospital complex	Europe	Under construction
10.2 Hyundai Motorstudio, Goyang	Private	Exhibition hall	Asia	Completed
10.3 Fondation Louis Vuitton	Private	Museum	Europe	Completed
10.4 Dongdaemun Design Plaza	Public	Multicultural complex	Asia	Completed
10.5 Saint Joseph Hospital	Private	Healthcare facility	North America	Completed
10.6 Victoria Station, London Underground	Public	Underground railway station	Europe	Due for completion in 2018
10.7 North Hills Residential Hall NTU	Public	Student housing facility	Asia	Completed
10.8 Mapletree Business City II	Private	Business office park	Asia	Completed
10.9 Prince Mohammad Bin Abdulaziz International Airport	Public-Private Partnership	Airport	Middle East	Completed
10.10 Howard Hughes Medical Institute	Private	Healthcare facility	North America	FM system implemented
10.11 Stanford Neuroscience Health Center	Private	Hospital	North America	FM use case tested

*Status of the projects at the time of writing

demonstrates a diverse set of benefits to various organizations, resulting from the implementation of BIM tools and processes. Table 10–0–3 indexes the case studies according to a list of commonly identified BIM benefits. The wide variety of software and technologies used in each phase is compiled in Table 10–0–4. These tables are guides for readers both to compare the case studies and to quickly find those that match a reader's specific interests.

No single project has yet realized all or even a majority of BIM's potential benefits, and it is doubtful that all of the benefits that the technology enables have been discovered or even identified. Each case study presents the salient aspects of the BIM process and focuses on the ways each team used the available tools to maximum benefit. We also highlight the many lessons that these teams learned as they encountered challenges in implementing the new technologies and processes.

Most of the projects were complete at the time of publication, but some of the projects were still in progress, preventing a full review or complete assessment of the benefits. Naturally, research was limited by the available information. Architecture, engineering, construction, fabrication, and real estate development are competitive fields, and organizations are often reluctant

Table 10–0–2   Case Studies by Phase of Lifecycle

Case Study	Feasibility	Schematic Design	Design Development'	Construction Documentation	Construction	Operation and Maintenance
Case studies from the 1st and 2nd editions of the BIM Handbook (available on the BIM Handbook companion website)						
Hillwood Commercial Project, Dallas, Texas (1e, 2e)	O	O				
Sutter Medical Center, Castro Valley, California (2e)	O	O	O	O	O	
U.S. Coast Guard (1e, 2e)		O	O			
National Aquatics Center, Beijing, China (1e)		O	O	O		
Aviva Stadium, Dublin, Ireland (2e)		O	O	O	O	
100 11th Avenue, New York City (1e, 2e)		O	O	O	O	
Music Center, Helsinki, Finland (2e)		O	O	O	O	
One Island East Project, Hong Kong (1e, 2e)			O	O	O	
General Motors Plant, Flint, MI (1e)			O	O	O	
Penn National Parking Structure, Grantville, Pennsylvania (1e)				O	O	
Federal Office Building, San Francisco (1e)			O	O		
Federal Courthouse, Jackson, Mississippi (1e)			O	O		
Camino Group Medical Building, Mountain View, California(1e)				O	O	
Marriott Hotel Renovation, Portland, Oregon (2e)				O	O	
Maryland General Hospital, Baltimore, Maryland (2e)					O	O
Crusell Bridge, Helsinki, Finland (2e)			O	O	O	
Case Studies in Chapter 10						
10.1 National Children's Hospital, Dublin, Ireland	O	O	O	O		
10.2 Hyundai Motorstudio, Goyang, South Korea	O	O	O	O	O	
10.3 Fondation Louis Vuitton, Paris, France		O	O	O	O	
10.4 Dongdaemun Design Plaza, Seoul, South Korea		O	O	O	O	
10.5 Saint Joseph Hospital, Denver		O	O	O	O	
10.6 Victoria Station, London Underground		O	O	O	O	O
10.7 Nanyang Technological University Student Residence Halls, Singapore		O	O	O	O	
10.8 Mapletree Business City II, Singapore		O	O	O	O	O
10.9 Prince Mohammad Bin Abdulaziz International Airport, Medina, UAE						O
10.10 Howard Hughes Medical Institute, Chevy Chase, Maryland						O
10.11 Stanford Neuroscience Health Center, Palo Alto, California						O

1e: *The BIM Handbook* 1st Edition

2e: *The BIM Handbook* 2nd Edition

Table 10-0-3 BIM Benefits Described in the Case Studies

Benefits	National Children's Hospital	Hyundai Motorstudio	Fondation Louis Vuitton	Dongdaemun Design Plaza	Saint Joseph Hospital	Victoria Station, London Underground	Nanyang Technological University Student Residence Halls	Mapletree Business City II	Prince Mohammad Bin Abdulaziz International Airport	Howard Hughes Medical Institute	Stanford Neuroscience Health Center
Cost reduction		O		O	O	O			O		O
Time saving		O		O	O	O	O	O	O		O
Enhanced design quality	O	O	O	O	O		O	O			
Better end-user requirements capture	O	O		O	O	O	O				
Request for Information (RFI) reduction								O			
Rework reduction	O	O		O			O	O	O		
Waste reduction	O								O		
Safety improvement		O			O				O		
Communication/decision-making improvement		O		O				O			O
Reduced energy consumption	O						O	O	O		
Improved asset and facility management	O						O	O	O	O	
Improved resource management	O								O		O
Accurate impact analysis										O	O
Facilitated modular or offsite prefabrication		O	O	O	O		O				
Others		O		O						O	O

to disclose their enterprise expertise. Nevertheless, most organizations and individuals were extremely helpful and made significant efforts to share their stories and provide images, information, and important insights. We have tried to identify the key issues of each project, not just success stories, but also the problems that had to be solved and the lessons learned from dealing with them.

Acknowledgments

The authors wish to acknowledge and thank Kyungha Lee, Jehyun Cho, Namcheol Jung, Yongshin An, Wonjun Kim, Taesuk Song, Kahyun Jeon, and Daeyoung Gil at the Building Informatics Group of Yonsei University for their review of the case studies and software applications.

Table 10-0-4 BIM Uses, Software, and Technologies Used for the Case Studies

Phase	BIM Uses	Software	Technologies
10.1 National Children's Hospital			
Feasibility	Site Analysis	Revit, AutoCAD	Laser Scanning
	Phase Planning	Revit, AutoCAD	CAD
Design	Existing Conditions	Revit	Modeling
	Design Authoring	Revit, Dynamo, NBS Create	Virtual Reality (VR), Augmented Reality (AR)
	3D Coordination	Navisworks	Clash Detection
	Cost Estimation	CostX	Analysis
	Structural Analysis	Dynamo, Tekla Structural Designer 2015, SCIAEngineer 16	Structural Modeling and Analysis
Preconstruction	3D Coordination	Navisworks	Virtual Reality (VR), Augmented Reality (AR), Laser Scanning
	Cost Estimation	CostX	Relational Database
	Other Engineering Analysis	Dynamo, Tekla Structure, Designer 2015, SCIAEngineer16	Virtual Reality (VR), Augmented Reality (AR), Laser Scanning
10.2 Hyundai Motorstudio			
Construction Documentation	Design Review	Navisworks	IFC
	Design Review	Fuzor	Virtual Reality
Construction	Design Authoring	CATIA, Tekla Structures, Digital project, Revit Architecture, Revit MEP, AutoCAD MEP	IFC
	Existing Conditions	Trimble Realworks	Laser Scanning
	3D Coordination	Autodesk Recap	Laser Scanning
	Digital Fabrication	Digital Project	Prefabrication
	Phase Planning	Navisworks	IFC
10.3 Fondation Louis Vuitton			
Design and Construction	Collaboration	GT Global Exchange (GTX, Trimble Connect)	Cloud-based Project Management
	Design Authoring, Engineering, Detailing, and Design Review	Digital Project Tekla Structures, BoCAD, Solidworks, Autodesk products, Rhinoceros, Grasshopper, ANSYS, NASTRAN, Sofistik3D, 3DVia Composer, Solibri	
	Existing Conditions		Laser Scanning
	Digital Fabrication	Digital Project	Prefabrication

Table 10-0-4 (*continued*)

Phase	BIM Uses	Software	Technologies
10.4 Dongdaemun Design Plaza			
Schematic and Design Development	Design Authoring	Rhinoceros	
Construction Documentation	Design Authoring, 3D Coordination, and Construction Documentation	Rhinoceros, Digital Project, Revit, AutoCAD	
	Structural Analysis	MIDAS, Tekla Structures	
	Other Engineering Analysis		Wind Simulation
Construction	3D Coordination	Rhinoceros, Digital Project, Revit, Tekla Structures	
	Structural Analysis	MIDAS, Tekla Structures	
	Digital Fabrication	Rhinoceros, Digital Project, AutoCAD	Multipoint Stretch Forming
	Design Authoring	Rhinoceros, AutoCAD	IFC
10.5 Saint Joseph Hospital			
Construction Documentation	3D Coordination	Revit, BlueBeam	IFC
	Phase Planning	Primavera P6, Synchro	Others
	Structural Analysis		Others
Construction	Digital Fabrication	Revit, BlueBeam	Prefabrication
	3D Control and Planning	Navisworks	Virtual Reality (VR)
	3D Coordination	Revit, BlueBeam	COBie
10.6 Victoria Station, London Underground			
Schematic Design	Feasibility	Bentley Triforma, Bentley AECOsim	Modeling
	Layout	Legion Modeling	Crowd Simulation
	Collaboration Archiving	Bentley ProjectWise	File Sharing, Cloud
Design Development	Design Authoring, 3D Coordination	Triforma, AECOsim	Modeling
	Collaboration Archiving	ProjectWise	File Sharing, Cloud
	Structural Analysis	STAAD, Hevacomp	Finite Element Method
Construction Documentation	Design Reviews	Triforma, AECOsim	Modeling
	Drawing	Microstation	CAD
Construction	Existing Conditions	Triforma, AECOsim	
	Collaboration	ProjectWise	
	Phase Planning	AECOsim	4D Simulation

(*Continued*)

Table 10–0–4 *(continued)*

Phase	BIM Uses	Software	Technologies
10.7 North Hills Residential Hall, NTU			
Design	Design	Revit	Modeling
	Structural Analysis	ETABS	FEM
	Other Engineering Analysis	PHOENICS	CFD
Construction	Data Sharing	Google Drive	Cloud File Sharing
	Construction Planning and Sequencing	Autodesk Navisworks	4D Simulation
	Clash Detection and 3D Coordination	Autodesk Navisworks	Clash Detection
	Digital Fabrication	AutoCAD	CAD
10.8 Mapletree Business City II			
Design	Design	Revit	Modeling
	Design review	Unity	Virtual Reality (VR)
	Collaboration	Autodesk A360	Model Sharing
	Existing Conditions		Laser Scanning
Construction	Construction Planning and Sequencing	Navisworks, Revit	Clash Detection 4D Simulation
	Layout	Autodesk Point Layout Add-in	Total Station Survey
	As-built	Autodesk A360	Augmented Reality (AR)
10.9 Medina Airport, UAE			
O&M	Maintenance Scheduling	EcoDomus-FM	
	Space Management/Tracking	Navisworks	Laser Scanning
	Asset Management	IFS, EcoDomus-FM	
	Record Model	Aconex, Revit, Navisworks EcoDomus PM	
10.10 Howard Hughes Medical Institute			
O&M	Facility Management	EcoDomus	
	Existing Conditions	Revit	
	Database	EcoDomus	
	Building System Analysis	Revit	
	Impact Analysis	EcoDomus, Database	
10.11 Stanford Neuroscience Health Center			
O&M	Tested for Facility Management	EcoDomus	
	Tested for Asset Management	Revit, Maximo	

10.1   NATIONAL CHILDREN'S HOSPITAL, DUBLIN

10.1.1   Introduction

The new National Children's Hospital (NCH) in Dublin, Ireland, is the largest, most complex, and most significant investment project ever undertaken in healthcare in Ireland. The NCH site is centrally located within Dublin City at the St James's Campus. NCH will bring together into one entity three existing hospitals: Our Lady's Children's Hospital Crumlin, Temple Street Children's University Hospital, and the National Hospital in Tallaght. The ultimate aim is to share the presence of this new hospital facility with St. James's Adult Hospital and, in time, also the Coombe women's and infants' university hospital by integrating them into a single health campus. These hospitals will merge to form the Children's Hospital Group before transition to the new facilities.

The first contracts for construction were awarded in July 2016, but only for one section. At the time of writing, construction had begun, but the case study deals only with the design phase.

The client requested the use of BIM, as they believed it offered a qualitative advantage to project development and delivery by facilitating more efficient design option studies and development and coordination of design information. The client expected that during construction BIM would derive significant improvements in cost, value, and carbon performance through the use of open sharable asset information.

BIM was requested to a Level 2 standard (as defined in PAS 1192-2:2013), which involved all parties using their own 3D CAD models, but not necessarily working on a single, shared model. As BDP (Building Design Partnership, the co-lead design firm) had worked on a number of hospitals in the UK at a Level 2 standard, this standard was seen as a realistic level of expectation to which all the members of the multidisciplinary design team could aspire. The client required that all stakeholders must be involved with the design, which normally would result in difficulties for the design team with regard to the presentation of technical information to nonspecialists.

All hospital projects present a complex array of issues, but pediatric facilities pose a number of unique challenges because of the age range of the children and young people and the close participation of their extended families. The inclusion of multiple stakeholders, including the staff of the existing hospitals, clinical leads, and local residents, carried the potential challenge of the design team having to rely on laypeople, with no knowledge of design, to augment their understanding of the required functionality of the space. A BIM model offered the opportunity to visualize space easily, therefore improving an awareness of underutilized spaces, as well as being used by the whole team to further collaboration techniques, as it offered an easier way of interpreting the project requirements. Collaboration was key in the NCH design process, and BIM was an essential tool that helped nonspecialized end users to contribute more effectively during the construction process. The early application of BIM was crucial in demonstrating the visual impact on the surrounding area. BIM was implemented from early project conception and was used as a key tool in obtaining planning permission. With the requirement to meet the UK BIM

Level 2 standard, BIM offered the opportunity for the design team to generate room data from the model, apply complex algorithms in generating roof panels, use advanced augmented reality practices, and apply innovative methods of analysis.

10.1.2 Motivation for the Project

An integral goal of the project was to pursue synergies, including an energy center, facilities management (FM) services, materials management, environmental waste management service, central sterile service department, logistics, helipad, medical gas services, water supply services, and main public drainage services. The children's hospital will provide in-patient care and all surgery (including day surgery), while the satellite centers at Tallaght Hospital and Connolly Hospital will provide urgent care and outpatient care. The proposed Children's Research and Innovation Centre, which is an integral part of the new children's hospital, will be co-located with the existing academic facilities on the campus at St James's Hospital. This maximizes clinical linkages and creates a center of excellence for both pediatric and adult healthcare research.

Much of the current infrastructure in existing children's hospitals is not compatible with contemporary healthcare needs, and the current duplication and triplication of some services across the three pediatric services in Dublin was unsustainable. Co-location of the new children's hospital with St. James's Hospital provides access to the greatest breadth and depth of adult subspecialties to optimally support the new children's hospital.

10.1.3 The Building

The building will be three stories tall above street level along the South Circular Road and four stories along its southern elevation, and it will be four stories tall along its northern and eastern elevations with the same parapet height as the southern side. The public entrance is located about midway along the northern side, with two further entrances into the hospital on the eastern side for self-presenting patients and ambulances accessing the Emergency Department. The building will provide a number of landscaped and recreational areas, including courtyard gardens at ground level and a significant garden covering most of the building footprint at Level 04, which will have the benefit of fresh air and distant views to the city. The ward block rises to seven stories above ground level, comprising three levels of wards, with an additional plant area enclosed on the roof space. The oval shape of the ward block reduces its impact on near and middle distance views and assists in reducing the impacts on microclimate effects. The new hospital will accommodate 380 children as in-patients, each in their own individual room with en-suite bathroom and facilities for a parent to comfortably stay with their child. In addition, there will be 87 day care beds.

The new hospital will have state-of-the-art operating theaters, including specialized theaters for heart surgery, neurosurgery, and orthopedics. The theater areas will have dedicated rooms for emergency and general surgical procedures, as well as interventional theaters. The design also encompasses a

FIGURE 10–1–1   NCH and its surroundings.

Image courtesy of BDP.

52-bed family accommodation building adjacent to the new children's hospital. A helipad and a two-level underground car park are also to be constructed. Figure 10–1–1 illustrates the layout of the building within its proposed new environment, while Figure 10–1–2 details the main entrance to the NCH.

10.1.4 The NCH Project

The National Pediatric Hospital Development Board (NPHDB) is responsible for overseeing the building of the hospital. The board's members have combined experience and expertise in architecture, planning, engineering, and procurement to bring this very large and complex project to completion.

BDP, a major international practice of architects, designers, engineers, and urbanists, and O'Connell Mahon Architects are the co-lead designers on the project. They were contracted by the NPHDB as lead consultants and architects to design the building to a Level 2 BIM standard in collaboration with ARUP (M&E Engineering), Linesight (Cost Consultant), and O'Connor Sutton Cronin (OCSC), among others. The initial cost estimate for the hospital was in the region of €650 million, excluding fit out costs. The finished complex is expected to be completed by 2019, and to become fully operational by 2020. Ground works began on the first phase in July 2016.

BDP used their BIM knowledge from the very beginning to offer a qualitative advantage to the project development process, maximizing collaboration between design team members, identifying conflicts in design drawings, and maximizing accuracy in the scheduling and measuring of building elements.

FIGURE 10–1–2 NCH entrance.

Image courtesy of BDP.

Initially, Murphy Surveys conducted a series of laser scans of surrounding buildings, streetscape, site features, topography, visible and underground services, and so on. BDP requested 2D CAD files of the elevations and 3D DWG files of all the levels, which they then imported into Revit to create an overall topography in BIM. Figure 10–1–3 gives a virtual view of the existing site, while Figure 10–1–4 details the position of the NCH in relation to its surroundings.

10.1.5 The BIM Execution Plan (BEP)

A full Level 2 BIM collaborative environment was a contractual requirement for the project by the client on the advice of BDP, who have been using the BIM process successfully since 2011. For public sector projects in Ireland there is a requirement to use the Government Construction Contracts Committee (GCCC) form of contract. In order for BIM to work with the GCCC form, the contracts were adapted with both the Construction Industry Council (CIC) BIM protocol (a supplementary legal agreement that is incorporated into professional service appointments and construction contracts by means of a simple amendment) and a BIM Execution Plan (BEP), which was introduced as an additional legal document. Already at the design stage, a conscious effort

Existing Site

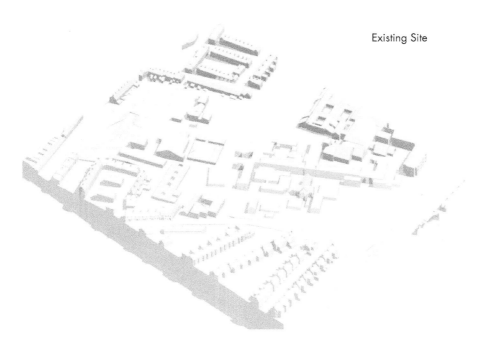

FIGURE 10–1–3 Existing site.

Image courtesy of BDP.

Construction

- Substructure
- Structure
- Internal Partitions
- Primary Plant Routes
- External Envelope

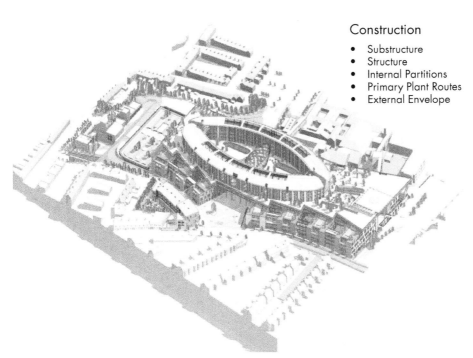

FIGURE 10–1–4 Position of the NCH in relation to its surroundings.

Image courtesy of BDP.

was made to address future problems, such as intellectual property rights, contractual issues, and more. An important feature within the contractual framework was the requirement that the NPHDB retain ownership of the model. The CIC protocol stated that the design team will have no liability to the contractor in connection with any use, amendment, modification, or alteration of the building information models provided by the employer, whether for the permitted purpose or otherwise.

The client requested that the contractor should produce, update, and deliver a federated construction BIM model. This involved amalgamating models to be created by each of the relevant subcontractors, incorporating all construction installations, assemblies, and components along with their associated COBie information throughout the construction process to provide an accurate, data-rich "as built" BIM and Asset Information Model (AIM) prior to substantial completion. Due to the large size of the project, the model was split into a number of different discipline-specific models. These included models for the site, M&E, external envelope, internal layout, and Fixtures Furniture and Equipment (FF+E), as shown in Figure 10–1–5. The client requested that any information generated within the BIM must be suitable to transfer to the NPHDB computer-aided FM software application.

An Employer Information Requirements (EIR) document, which detailed the client's requirements and expectations with regard to BIM, was prepared. The EIR enabled the design team to understand the needs of the client from an early stage. It detailed roles and responsibilities, technical issues, submittals, and the management of models. It also detailed team training, which was provided by the BIM managers within each organization (or by an external consultant) to all team members, to allow them to access, view, and print from the model. The BIM manager was also responsible for establishing software protocols for the successful delivery of the project and the coordination of meetings on-site, undertaking clash detection, and proposing any required solutions. To enhance this process, BDP entered into a three-year Global Enterprise Business Agreement with Autodesk. The agreement provided BDP with unlimited access to all Autodesk software, including Autodesk project support, to assist in the development of procedures, workflows, and overall BIM implementation.

The Project Revit Manual, an internal document, defined the working procedures and best practices for BIM adoption. This document ensures that the modeling practices would align with the BIM Level 2 aspirations as the team grows, and ant team members joining the project through its lifetime have a single point of reference for all methods and conventions in use on the project. This document is updated as the working practice evolves. BDP also provided its own in-house training. Any potential staff working on the project had to undertake a BIM knowledge smart test. The test provides an indicator of a person's BIM knowledge. The results enable training to be tailored to help individuals reach their necessary BIM maturity through either in-house or online training.

The BEP was structured in accordance with the RIBA Plan of Work 2013, PAS 1192-2:2014, PAS 1192-3:2014, BS 1192:2016, BS 8541—Pts 1-4:2012, BS 1192:2007, and AIA Document E202 2008. The BEP outlined the role of

Site

Structure

Internal

Landscape

M&E

Envelope

Container File

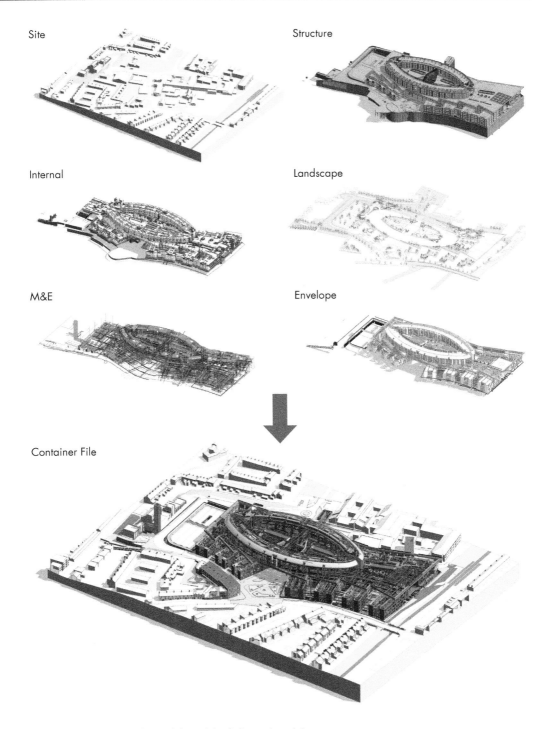

FIGURE 10-1-5   Discipline-specific models and the federated model.

Image courtesy of BDP.

each design team member with regard to modeling requirements, collaboration, and coordination procedures. Data was held in the Common Data Environment (CDE), which was structured in accordance with PAS 1192:2 (i.e., work in progress, shared, published documentation, and archive folder). To facilitate coordinated and efficient working, each design team made its design data available for project-wide formal access through a shared repository. Prior to sharing, data was checked, approved, and validated as "fit for coordination."

10.1.6　Visualization, Simulation, and Design Optimization

The NPHDB requested the facility to download the model in IFC file format at any time. A robust system of document management was implemented, which was held and managed in the CDE. The system allowed all project team members to upload documents and data to a shared area that could be accessed easily while providing an auditable repository of information.

BIM was used in a number of areas for simulation and design optimization. As the project progressed, virtual illustrations and videos were used to demonstrate the visual impact of the hospital on the surrounding areas. An example of this is the Luas, which is a tram/light rail system that serves the Dublin area and stops outside the hospital. A number of 3D images and videos were used to demonstrate how these works will be undertaken, as illustrated in Figure 10–1–6. Videos can be viewed at the NCH website (www.newchildrens hospital.ie/design-vision/video/). Figures 10–1–7 and 10–1–8 illustrate rendered views used to communicate the emerging design to the building users.

BDP has integrated modeling workflows with cloud rendering services and now use Google Cardboard as the primary visualizing tool for presentations.

FIGURE 10–1–6　NCH in relation to LUAS Light Rail.

Image courtesy of BDP.

FIGURE 10–1–7   Patient room user view.

Image courtesy of BDP.

FIGURE 10–1–8   Atrium user view.

Image courtesy of BDP.

By adopting this immersive technology, staff members of the NCH were placed inside a virtual representation of their building, which enabled an understanding of design proposals and further permitted them to engage with the design. Figure 10–1–9 provides a view of what the client would see if wearing the Google Cardboard glasses.

NBS Create, a specification authoring tool for BIM, allows for compilation of a specification by adding system outline clauses. It enabled BDP to synchronize their specification with the Revit model using a plugin, and allowed the full

FIGURE 10-1-9   Google
Cardboard view.

Image courtesy of BDP.

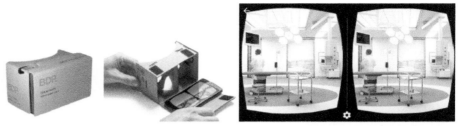

Google Cardboard, a visualisation tool where project stakeholders are placed 'inside' a virtual representation of their building.

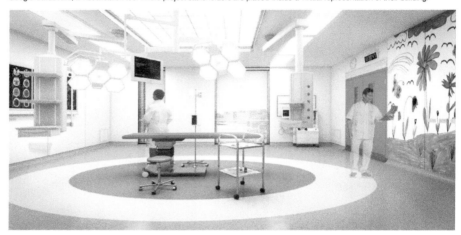

use of BIM objects from the National BIM Library, using UniClass to reference their model, view, and component names.

With 6,500 rooms, the NCH facility maintenance database requires about half a million FF+E objects that need to be embedded with information that must be coded, coordinated, and specified. Codebook, a software designed to produce room data sheets as an output of the BIM process, was used to input or export information on the room properties and FF+E within the Revit models. The database was hosted on Codebook's servers, which can provide backup and restore support. This ensured all data was accessible to the client and several consultants. Table 10-1-1 provides information on some of the fields required to be populated, and Figure 10-1-10 illustrates this in relation to an operating theater that can be viewed within the model.

Dynamo software reduces the requirement for manual repetitive tasks as it enables the establishment of custom workflows in Revit. As it extends BIM using the data and logic environment of a graphical algorithm editor, it was used for rapid design development. For instance, the external consultant for building services used Dynamo software to analyze the roof panels based on their slope angle. Within Dynamo all curtain panels were selected by family type. This panel area was then computed and the now remapped result range was linked to a color range that enabled automatic overriding of panel colors within the view. This process is illustrated in Figure 10-1-11.

Table 10-1-1   Codebook Information Fields

Criteria	Fields to be Completed				
Standard Information	Project	Department	Room	Room Number	
Design Criteria	Room Code	Room Label	Room Name	Room Number	
Design	Template Name	Room Instance Code	Area Required	Room Type	Room Notes
	SOA* Line Number	SOA Quantity of Rooms	SOA Room Area	SOA Total Area	Sub Department Code
Occupancy	Room in Use	Number of Occupants	Number of Staff/ Visitors	Personnel	
Windows	Internal Glazing				
Doorsets	Security				
Observation	Observation Required	Observation Type			
Fire	Fire Enclosure				
Other Notes					

*SOA = Schedule of Areas.

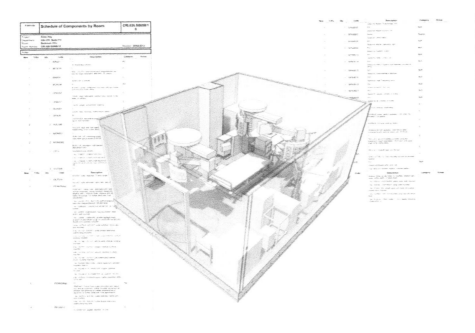

FIGURE 10-1-10   Codebook data for an operating theater.

Image courtesy of BDP.

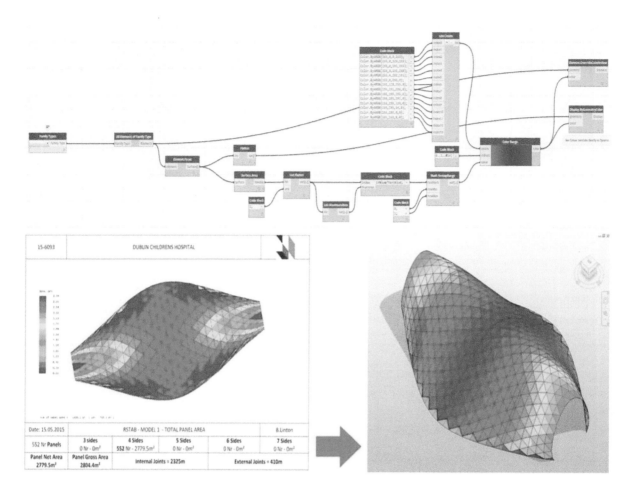

FIGURE 10-1-11   Analysis of roof panels by area in Dynamo.

Image courtesy of BDP.

Navisworks Manage was the main tool used at an early stage for clash detection. Clash resolution meetings were held, where appropriate, for each work stage, and clash detection reports were included within monthly design team reports. The clashes were designated within three levels as follows: Level 1 clashes (services versus structures and architectural); Level 2 clashes (services versus services), and Level 3 clashes (all other clashes). A clash reduction analysis graph, as shown in Figure 10-1-12, was issued to members of the design team to keep them informed. It enabled all parties to follow the progress in resolving clashes per designated clash test with the overall aim that the graph sets a continuous falling slope equating to a reduction of clashes. For example, the purple line in the graph represents the structure versus containment clash test, which began at 1,300 clashes on January 1, 2015, and subsequently fell to

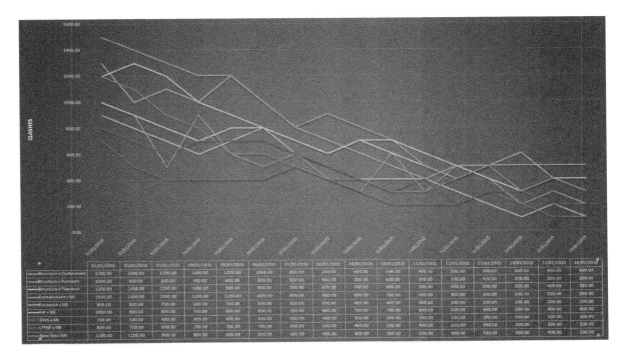

FIGURE 10–1–12　Clash reduction analysis.

Image courtesy of BDP.

400 clashes by January 16, 2015. During construction, the design team could coordinate specialist subcontractor design elements using this clash detection protocol.

The quantity surveyor (Linesights) worked closely with BDP to ensure that information was embedded in the form of coding for each element in the model, allowing effective analysis in CostX and approximate calculation of quantity take-offs. As information such as cost per square meter is related to the model element, the client was afforded better understanding of different design iterations and greater cost certainty, particularly early in the design process. Figure 10–1–13 provides an illustration of a quantity takeoff with regards to the walls within CostX by using some of the available 3D tools. From this dimension groups were created, which were then used to take off building elements within the model, such as skirting boards, architraves, and the like.

The Level of Development (LOD), which was outlined in the BEP, followed the standard fundamental requirements (i.e., a minimum LOD 100; the Model Element may be graphically represented with a symbol or other generic representation) up to LOD 500. (Model Element is a field-verified representation in terms of size, shape, location, quantity, and orientation.)

The possession of structured data and information requirements about the organization in relation to its asset(s)—in the form of an Asset Information

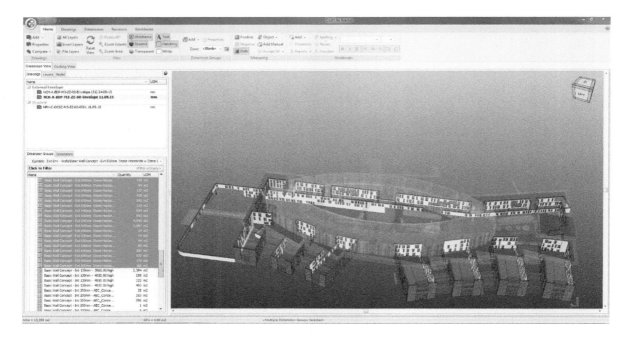

FIGURE 10-1-13   Take-off within CostX.

Image courtesy of BDP.

Requirement (AIR) document and COBie drops, which are aligned to project stages, and represent the information required and the level of development of that project stage—has enabled a greater control of the asset requirements of the client.

Structural frame and finite element analysis and design for the New Children's Hospital was primarily carried out using two structural programs, Tekla Structural Designer 2015 and SCIA Engineer 16. Both programs can import 3-D Revit frame models and can be used for the structural analysis of structural steel and reinforced concrete construction. Both linear and nonlinear analyses were carried out for different short- and long-term load conditions.

10.1.7   Summary of BIM Benefits

A virtual model can help predict and avoid potential risks. It enables clash detection, improving the quality of the design and removing associated risk. Planners can reduce the impact on surrounding areas to the building site by mapping best access routes for the delivery and removal of materials to ensure relatively unrestricted traffic flow. The use of BIM can enhance the involvement of the client in the design process, ensuring better management of space within the hospital (i.e., theater, plant, nurse stations, and so on) and aiding functionality. As the GCCC forms of contract are fixed price, the contractor can use

BIM to predict elements of risk with greater accuracy and be better positioned to absorb this risk.

Early collaboration within the design team ensured clarity of vision, roles, and requirements. The BIM contractual documents, as outlined in the EIR, were essential to this and the client's understanding and expectations. Guidance documents such as the Project Revit Manual ensured that a live system could help with training needs. Another notable lesson learned was the importance of aligning management and training practices from the multidisciplinary design team with cultural differences in order to streamline the digital workflow.

Overall the NCH has provided a significant stepping stone for Ireland's construction industry on its BIM journey. The application of BIM and its associated processes has enabled the intelligent management of information, which has delivered significant benefits. The application of innovative technologies empowered an eclectic range of client stakeholders to gain a closer understanding of the project concept than a traditional approach would have allowed, with expected continued benefits across the complete lifecycle of the project, enhanced by application of the AIM to driving value. Other expected benefits include use of the AIM by the Facilities Management team to view space and perform "what-if" analyses, study maintenance and access, and ensure sufficient provision of space as equipment requirements fluctuate in conjunction with ongoing medical advances.

Acknowledgments

Dr. Alan Hore, Dublin Institute of Technology (DIT); Dr. Barry McAuley, CitA BIM Innovation Capability Programme & DIT; and Professor Roger West, Trinity College Dublin, compiled this case study together with the authors. We are grateful to Sean O'Dwyer, Dominic Hook, and Zucchi Benedict, all from the Building Design Partnership (BDP).

10.2 HYUNDAI MOTORSTUDIO GOYANG, SOUTH KOREA
Five Challenges and Resolutions

10.2.1 Project Overview

Hyundai Engineering & Construction (Hyundai E&C) is a top-five general contractor in South Korea. Hyundai E&C has developed its application of smart construction processes using BIM through managing such projects as the Qatar National Museum (budget $550 million USD, 2011–2017).

From 2013 until its completion in 2016, Hyundai E&C was focused on the Hyundai Motorstudio Goyang project (Figures 10–2–1 and 10–2–2). The final total project budget for construction was $170 million USD. This project has various interesting characteristics. It is a multipurpose building mainly used for exhibition halls for automobile products. It has a steel-framed structure with a mega truss structure and free-form exterior panels. The irregular geometric shape of the building was challenging for the project team in terms of space

FIGURE 10-2-1 BIM model image of Hyundai Motorstudio Goyang.

Image courtesy of Hyundai E&C.

FIGURE 10-2-2 Completed Hyundai Motorstudio Goyang.

Photo by Sejun Jang.

utilization, and exterior and interior design during the design and construction phases. Many change orders were made during the construction phase, and BIM played a key role in resolving the issues caused by the frequent design changes to this project.

The planned construction schedule was 39 months from breaking ground. Due to the various design changes and additional facilities required by the owner, this was extended by five months to 44 months. Associated with these changes, was an increase in budget from $120 million to $170 million USD. Construction started in March 2013 and was completed in November 2016.

The client was Hyundai Motor Group. Delugan Meissl Associated Architects (DMAA), the international architectural firm, provided design services, including concept design, while Hyundai Architects & Engineers Associate (HDA), the domestic architectural firm, undertook the construction documentation. Since HDA was a sister company of Hyundai E&C, it became, practically, a design-build project.

The general contractor, Hyundai E&C, participated in the detailed design phase to assist in the design from the aspect of constructability. Major subcontractors (e.g., steel, concrete, and MEP) participated in the design coordination during the construction documentation phase. The major subcontractors worked with the general contractor to refine the design to suit the site conditions and materials.

The most critical goals for the owner were:

- The final quality of construction
- Achieving a trend setting design

The owner of this project, Hyundai Motor Company, had an ambitious goal: to build the most attractive automobile exhibition facility in the world. Consequently, they wanted to review the development of the building's details and space programs more frequently and in more detail than the traditional design review process with 2D drawings. A BIM-based design coordination process was adopted to meet these needs by improving coordination and change management between client, designer, general contractor, and subcontractors.

Hyundai E&C was preparing to become a BIM-based construction and project management company, capable of managing the entire lifecycle of a project from initial feasibility to operation and management by utilizing BIM. Hyundai E&C was also trying to shift its target markets from common buildings such as apartment complexes, factories, and office buildings to high-technology-oriented buildings, such as complex buildings, hospitals, and data centers. Hyundai Motorstudio Goyang was one of the major projects that Hyundai E&C selected as a pilot project for this transition, and implemented the process innovation with staff from both construction site and headquarters.

The Hyundai Motorstudio Goyang project had five challenges:

1. A complex spatial arrangement
2. Free-form-patterned exterior panels
3. A mega truss structure
4. A perception gap between project participants
5. Schedule reduction

To resolve these five challenges, various BIM-related techniques were deployed:

- The spatial design complexity was managed using a BIM-based coordination process between client, designer, contractor, and subcontractor.

- Parametric modeling was used through BIM for panelizing the façades and for detailing the free-form-patterned exterior panels.
- 3D laser scanning was used for quality control of the mega truss structure.
- Virtual reality (VR) devices and 4D simulation were used to facilitate communication between various project participants.
- Multi-trade prefabrication was applied for reducing schedule and increasing productivity.

Detailed explanations and examples of each of the challenges and solutions are presented below.

10.2.2 Complex Spatial Arrangement: BIM-Based Design Coordination

The Hyundai Motorstudio consists of various facilities (car showrooms, theaters, a 3D experience room, automobile repair facilities, a cafeteria, childcare facilities, sports facilities, and more). For the engineering and construction of these facilities, specialized subcontractors (e.g., motor repair machine, dust inhalation) were involved in the design coordination phase in addition to the more common subcontractors (e.g., steel, concrete, glazing, and MEP). Due to the characteristics of the project, design coordination was expected to be the most challenging part of the process, and it required the coordination of more stakeholders than would be required for a typical project. Methods were needed to increase the efficiency of design coordination.

Repeated coordination meetings with too many participants lead to inefficient decision-making. A two-tiered coordination process (Figure 10–2–3) was used on this project and streamlined the decision-making process, allowing decisions to be made at the right level by the right participants. A Tier 1 meeting is attended by client, designer, general contractor, and the relevant major subcontractors (e.g., steel, concrete, and MEP) and a Tier 2 meeting is attended by general contractor and subcontractors (e.g., glazing, façade, door, and catwalk subcontractors). Detailed descriptions follow.

Tier 1 meetings mainly focused on constructability, major design errors, and the direction of design development, not elimination of clashes and minor design errors. Constructability issues could not be resolved solely by consultation between subcontractors. They required input from GC and designer with subsequent modifications of design. Design errors that required changes of architectural design and/or had significant effect on the cost were classified as major design errors. In addition, Tier 1 meetings lead to agreement between client and designer regarding the direction of development of detailed shop drawing. A BIM model at level of development (LOD) 250~350, developed by an outsourced BIM firm (ArchiMac), was utilized for the coordination meeting. Miscellaneous materials (e.g., pipe branches, electrical hard conduit) were excluded from the scope of the (LOD 250-350) BIM model. This was done to make the BIM model faster and because it was not relevant to the client or designer for the Tier 1 meetings. Minor clash

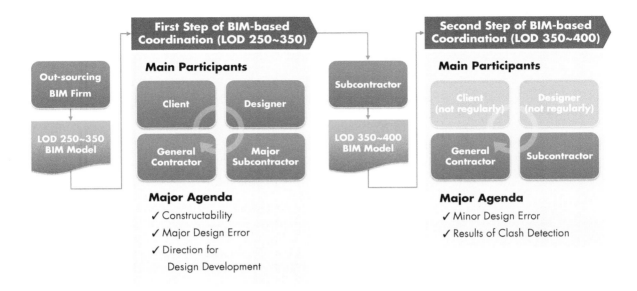

FIGURE 10–2–3   Two-tiered coordination process.

Image courtesy of Hyundai E&C.

detection was the responsibility of the general contractor and so was excluded from the Tier 1 meeting agenda. Comprehensive optimization was conducted for major trades. In one case, as a result of catwalk design optimization, the steel quantity was reduced by 35.7%, which resulted in cost reduction.

Tier 2 meetings focused on minor design errors and construction clashes. The client and designer did not regularly participate in these Tier 2 coordination meetings. They only attended for critical resolution meetings when issues could result in significant changes. Contractually, the responsibility for resolution of detail design errors lies with the various subcontractors. It is inefficient to resolve these through coordination meetings if the issue can be resolved directly between the relevant subcontractors and has no significant impact on costs. BIM models at LOD 350-400, developed by subcontractors for 3D shop drawings, were used for the Tier 2 coordination meeting. Construction objects that could be resolved in the field (e.g., supporting hangers, flexible pipe) were excluded from the scope of BIM modeling. It was not efficient to solve all clashes and errors through BIM. Hyundai E&C has already learned lessons from spending too much time in coordinating everything through BIM. The two-tiered system worked because participants were only called to meetings that were strictly relevant to their function.

10.2.3   Free-Form Patterned Exterior: Panelization

The second challenge was the difficulty of designing the free-form-patterned exterior anodized panels, which had a total area of nearly 13,940 m^2.

Anodizing is an electrochemical process that provides corrosion resistance for the aluminum panels used for the exterior cladding and allows the use of delicate color tones on exterior panels.

The key stage in this task was detailed design of the free-form-patterned panels for manufacturing and construction. The concept design did not include the details of each panel. Therefore, it was necessary to design each panel. The other main issue in the construction phase was the question of how to install the panels while maintaining the open joint gap between the irregularly shaped panels, and how to divide and connect the tiny edge panels of the exterior façade (Figure 10–2–4). Hyundai E&C, the general contractor, conducted panelization through the façade BIM model. The process was carried out with SteelLife, a façade subcontractor.

To resolve these design and construction issues, a panelizing method using BIM was applied in the design phase. Digital Project software was used for parametric modeling. The panelizing method could be divided into three steps.

The first step was to review the initial façade design based on the construction phase documents (Figure 10–2–5). Through this process a zoning plan for the panels was developed. In this step, the number and type of panels corresponding to each zoning were determined. This step was considered the most critical process of the BIM panelizing since the subsequent processes would be affected by the initial façade zoning plan.

The second step was to set up the parametric design and the algorithms for interactions between the panels (Figure 10–2–6). The positional design parameters of the panels were connected so that all these design parameters would be revised if any parameter was revised.

FIGURE 10–2–4 Façade panels.

Photo by Sejun Jang.

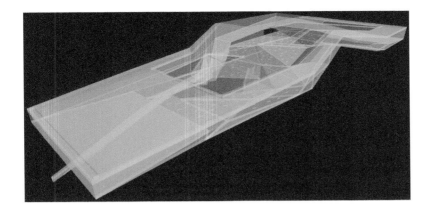

FIGURE 10–2–5   Façade design model before panelization.

Image courtesy of Hyundai E&C.

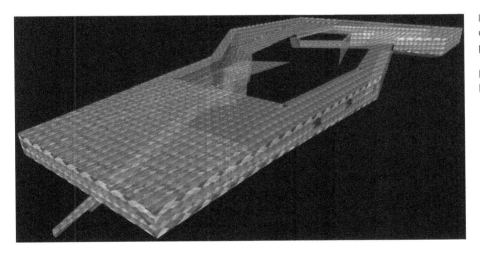

FIGURE 10–2–6   Façade design model after panelization.

Image courtesy of Hyundai E&C.

The third step was to add the detail design for installation (Figure 10–2–7). After detailing the panels based on the façade zoning plan, secondary steel structure and metal connectors such as brackets and plates had to be designed. These designs were needed for installation of the exterior panels.

The BIM-based panelizing method served many purposes. It enabled optimization of the number of panel types by changing the façade shapes (as was done for the Dongdeamun Design Plaza Project in Seoul, South Korea, which is the subject of Section 10.4). It also enabled design of the detailed panels without changing the façade (as was done for the Qatar National Museum Project). The priority for both the client and the architect was to connect the panel patterns smoothly, and this was more important than cost reduction. Accordingly, Hyundai E&C applied different types of design on every edge of the façade, instead of decreasing the number of panel types.

FIGURE 10-2-7   Façade construction model showing the structural subframe.

Image courtesy of Hyundai E&C.

10.2.4   Mega Truss Structure: Laser Scanning

The third challenge was maintaining quality control for the mega truss structure, which weighed 3,644 tons (Figure 10–2–8). The truss structure had two key features that had to be addressed:

FIGURE 10-2-8   A mega truss steel structure of Hyundai Motorstudio Koyang.

Image courtesy of Hyundai E&C.

1. Construction consists of a floating structure some 12.3 m above ground level.
2. The longest length of the truss structure is 32.2 m.

These features require strict management of quality control during the construction phase. The long cantilever span can sag continuously as load is added during construction, creating significant dimensional tolerance problems.

The deflection of the truss was predicted in the design phase. Sag deflection of about 50 mm to 100 mm was expected and precambering was planned so that it would settle into its correct designed position after installation. Monitoring the actual deflection against the designed deflection was crucial because the following trades (i.e., glazing, exterior panel) would have to be redesigned if the deflection exceeded the expected tolerance. The team deployed 3D laser scanning to monitor the deflection of the truss efficiently and accurately during construction (Figure 10–2–9). Trimble TX5 and TX8 3D laser scanners were used. Scans were performed at nearly 40 different scanning stations on the site. The laser scanning required 20 minutes per station, for a total scanning time of two days.

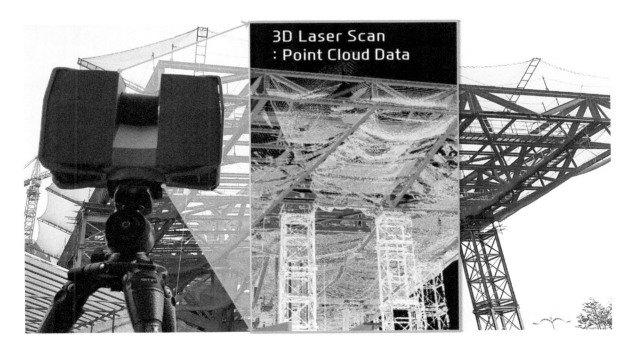

FIGURE 10–2–9   3D laser scanning for quality control of the steel structure.

Image courtesy of Hyundai E&C.

The original scan data was acquired and transferred to point cloud data using Trimble RealWorks, a specialized software for post-processing scan data. The point cloud data was merged with the BIM model. The next step was to analyze the difference between the designed and the actual constructed truss position (Figure 10–2–10). In this way, the deflection of the steel structure could be measured and reviewed easily using 3D laser scanning data. Analysis of the merged data from point cloud and BIM model identified design and construction issues for the curtain wall and exterior panel trades. These issues were relayed to each trade's managers for the managers to resolve in line with their trade's design and construction plans.

The trade manager for the installation of exterior panels trusted the original construction documents and tried to install the exterior panels on this basis. However, analysis of the 3D scanning data would have identified the critical panel installation issues. The design and construction plan could then have been revised to resolve the issues (e.g., redesign the secondary structure to support

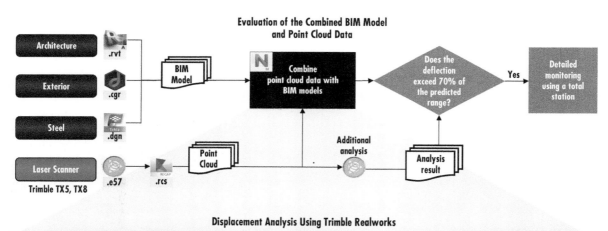

FIGURE 10–2–10   A work process for 3D laser scanning.

Image courtesy of Hyundai E&C.

the panels and their brackets for the various types, sizes, and positions). 3D laser scanning has potential benefit for construction quality management work, and it could reduce the risk of construction time and cost caused by rework (Figures 10–2–11 and 10–2–12).

Despite these advantages, the use of 3D laser scanning was still in the experimental phase because the legal ground rules for measurement quality had not yet been established. 3D laser scanning is a little less accurate than the comparable existing measurement tool, a total station. Total stations and laser scanners have a similar observational equipment error of ±2 mm per 100 m, but a 3D laser scanner has more cumulative error than a total station. The first cumulative error occurs in the process of measuring the reference point on the point cloud because the target (the reference point) moves finely with wind or vibration. This, however, does not account for the difference between laser scanners and total stations because total stations suffer from the same issue. The second cumulative error is generated when combining the point clouds acquired from different stations into a single point cloud through the registration process. The third issue has to do with the scanning resolution. For example, if the scanning resolution is set to achieve the point spacing of 5 mm, the minimum distance between two measured points will be 5 mm. If the target measurement point is located somewhere between two actual measured points, the measured location of the target point will be a couple of millimeters

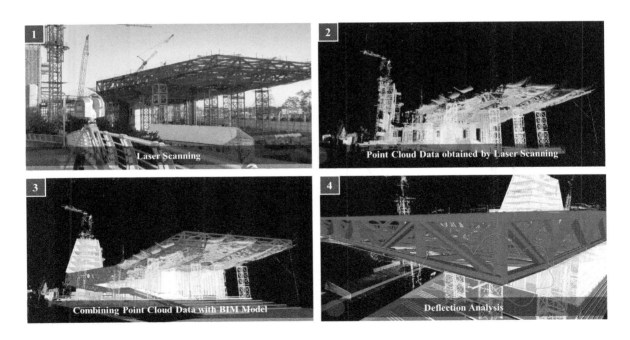

FIGURE 10–2–11   A scanning process for design analysis.

Image courtesy of Hyundai E&C.

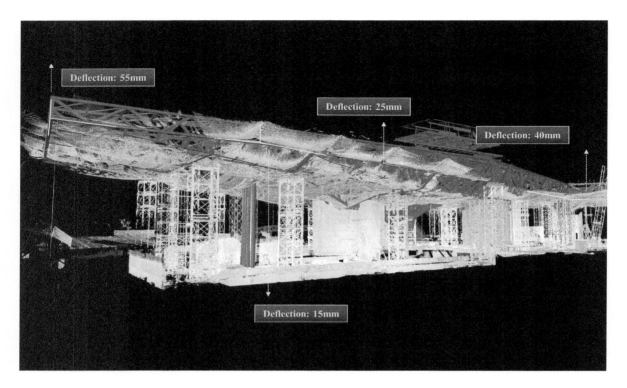

FIGURE 10–2–12 A design analysis result based on 3D laser scanning.

Image courtesy of Hyundai E&C.

off from the actual location of the target point. Due to these cumulative error issues, a total station was used as the main measuring instrument rather than a laser scanner. In addition, there is still no standard yet for quality checks using laser scanning in South Korea.

Despite the disadvantages, laser scanning was used in this project because it could measure the deflection of the truss structure at any point that the contractor would like to examine with one scan. Wherever the deflection exceeded 70% of the predicted deflection, more precise measurement was carried out using a total station.

10.2.5 Perception Gap between Participants: VR and 4D Simulation

BIM is used to visualize various issues during coordination meetings. However, even if everyone in the meeting looks at the same BIM model, the reality they perceive is different. We refer to this problem as a "perception gap."

The first aspect of the perception gap arises from the perceived textures or colors of the finish materials in a model. Since experienced contractors and subcontractors use similar materials over and over, they can imagine what the final finishes will look like even if the BIM model is not photo-realistically rendered. This is, however, a challenging task for inexperienced clients and others. One of the clients in this project commented, "It seems to require considerable practice to understand and imagine the actual building by looking at a BIM model."

The second aspect arises from construction details. Well-trained contractors and subcontractors can imagine construction details even if a BIM model is created at a low LOD and does not include them. However, contractors or clients who have relatively little experience with a certain type of work may not be able to find potential problems with the same BIM model.

There was a risk of delaying decision making during design coordination due to the perception gap among various participants. Fuzor rendering software was used to prevent coordination delays. The increased realism of the rendered BIM model for the client's specific areas of concern allowed detailed texture mappings and walk-through simulations with an avatar.

The change to the position of air vents on the exterior panels was a major change where the application of VR techniques provided the means to resolve problems. The initial design of the exterior panels for air vents planned to use approximately 30 perforated panels on the side wall of the structure. The client and designer were concerned with this design due to its potential to spoil the beauty of the building. For intuitive design review, virtual reality (VR) was deployed. The rendered BIM model was ported an Oculus Rift VR headset and this provided more realistic visual services for the client, apparently affording the client a better understanding of the current design. The use of VR devices was a win-win strategy because the client could choose options for design with clearer understanding and the contractor could encourage the clients to make decisions earlier than usual. Through the VR-based review, the client and designer decided to relocate most of the perforated panels from the side to the front of the structure. The number of perforated panels for air vents on the side wall was reduced from 30 to 10, and 20 panels were relocated to the front of the building to minimize the impact on the aesthetics of the building (Figure 10–2–13).

The problem caused by the perception gap was not limited to the finish and detail issues, but also occurred while examining the construction sequences. The construction sequence of a specific trade was obvious to the subcontractor who was in charge. However, it was difficult for the other subcontractors to imagine the construction sequence simply by looking at a BIM model of the trade's work. The 4D simulation was applied to narrow the perception gap in this construction sequence problem.

Most of the building area was covered by the mega truss structure. As mentioned earlier, managing the deflection of the truss was a major risk for this project, but there was another construction risk. During the construction of the truss, construction work and material and manpower movements at the lower level were prohibited due to safety issues. For this reason, the construction sequence and material movement plans in the project had to be adjusted to the

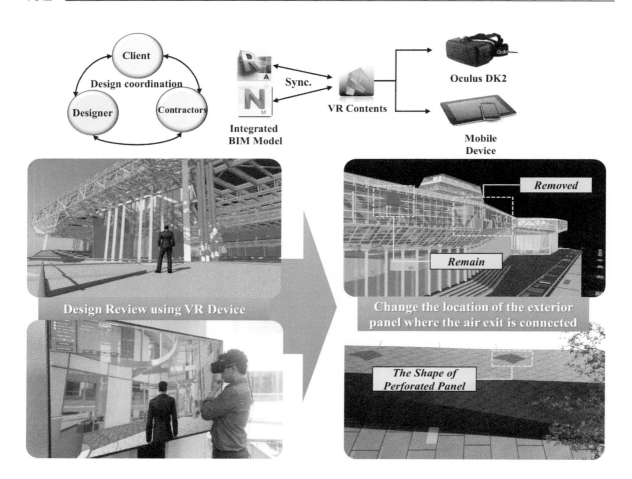

FIGURE 10–2–13   Utilization process of VR and an example.

Image courtesy of Hyundai E&C.

schedule of the truss structure. A coordination meeting was held to determine the construction sequence. At the beginning of the coordination meeting, an attempt was made to coordinate the construction schedule by color-coding the BIM model. However, those engineers who had no experience with steel construction found it difficult to understand the precise construction sequence and construction equipment plans. The color-coded BIM model was upgraded to a 4D simulation. The visualized construction sequence allowed participants to clearly understand and optimize the construction schedule and movement plans through the coordination meetings. The construction sequence of the truss structure reflected the working positions and material movement paths of other subcontractors (Figure 10–2–14).

FIGURE 10–2–14 Use of 4D simulation.

Image courtesy of Hyundai E&C.

In the early 2000s, when BIM was introduced to South Korea, 4D simulation was expected to be used to effectively describe each step of the building process. Contrary to the expectation, the effectiveness of 4D has been questioned due to the time it takes to create a 4D simulation. This case study demonstrates that 4D simulation is most effective when it is used for the high-risk construction areas that need communication between various participants, rather than for the areas that are built mainly by a single subcontractor.

10.2.6 Needs for Schedule Reduction: Multi-trade Prefabrication

During the project, the client's requirement to incorporate new design trends was accommodated but at a cost of increasing the construction period by more than five months. Despite this situation, the client wished to shorten the construction period to allow early opening of the facility to the public.

To catch up with the delayed project schedule caused by frequent design changes and meet the new deadline, the contractor decided to deploy multi-trade prefabrication. Single-trade prefabrication is common today. However, the biggest limitation of single-trade prefabrication is that it impacts only a single trade and does not reduce the schedule for the whole project. Multi-trade prefabrication was applied to the four floors of the office tower.

Corridor ceilings, in particular, were the most complex spaces for MEP (Mechanical, Electrical, and Plumbing) elements. Therefore, the team planned to manufacture the corridor's MEP systems as prefabricated racks at a factory, and to subsequently install them on-site.

The design of the MEP prefabricated modules was started two months before the installation date (Figure 10–2–15). Manufacture of the modules started one month before the installation date and took one week per floor (four modules). Installation of the MEP modules for all four floors took a single day (see Figure 6–14 in Chapter 6, Section 6.10).

MEP multi-trade prefabrication was used to reduce the construction schedule and also to improve productivity. The application of multi-trade prefabrication was effective for the first purpose, schedule shortening. However, it failed to achieve the second purpose of improving productivity. Overall, the

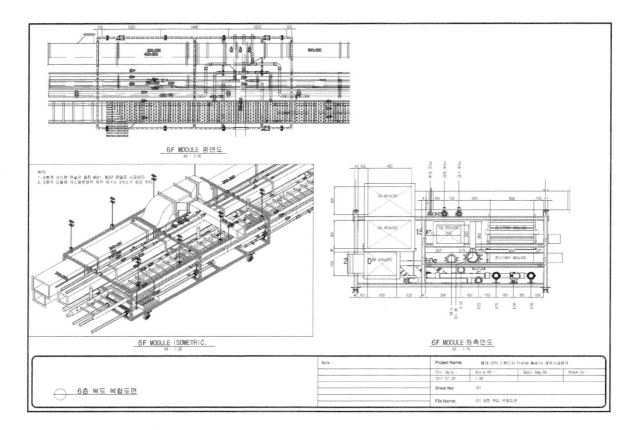

FIGURE 10–2–15 Shop drawing for multi-trade prefabrication (for manufacturing).

Image courtesy of Hyundai E&C.

multi-trade prefabrication increased labor input by 13.5%, but the productivity increased floor by floor as the workers' learning curve improved (Table 10–2–1).

The original plan had allocated one month for the sequential installation of the MEP trades on one floor. Therefore, the MEP prefabrication module could shorten the on-site schedule by one month. Productivity was measured using the labor input (person-days) as a metric. This was compared with the South Korean government labor input standard as a baseline. The multi-trade prefabrication input includes hours required at the factory for manufacturing and hours on-site for installation.

Table 10–2–2 lists BIM applications used during the project.

Table 10–2–1   Comparison of Person-Days Input Between the South Korean Government Standard and Multi-trade Prefabrication

Basis	Person-Days	Ratio to the South Korean Government Standard
South Korean Government Labor Input Standard	114.3	100
Overall Multi-trade Prefabrication	129.7	113.5
Fifth Floor		137.0
Sixth Floor		121.6
Seventh Floor		98.6
Eighth Floor		95.6

Table 10–2–2   BIM Uses and Tools

BIM Use	BIM Tools
BIM Modeling	CATIA
	Tekla Structures
	Digital Project
	Revit Architect
	Revit MEP
	AutoCAD MEP
Integrated File Management	Navisworks
Laser Scanning Data Management	Realworks
	Autodesk Recap
4D Simulation	Navisworks
Virtual Reality	Fuzor

10.2.7 Lessons Learned and Conclusion

The Hyundai Motorstudio Goyang project employed a wide variety of techniques in construction, visualization, panelization, measurement, and coordination as well as management skill in implementing an overall BIM strategy. These approaches do not always result in effective project management, change control, project development, and construction. The success of a project using BIM as the overarching management tool depends on the engagement of all participants, from client to suppliers; their being able to access, understand, and implement the input data that they require from the BIM; and their ability to supply the data needed by other users. BIM is still a relatively new working technique, and all participants are endeavoring to tailor their work practices to its new requirements. The techniques employed on the project met with varying degrees of success, and it is expected that this range of successes will vary from project to project. The major lessons learned include the following:

- Too many cooks spoil the broth. It is inefficient for all project participants to attend all BIM coordination meetings. To make coordination meetings efficient, the meetings can be categorized by coordination agenda and project phase, and only directly related participants to the meetings should be invited.

- The panelization method was used to make the design and construction details of the irregular façades. It was possible to quickly generate details of numerous exterior panels using parametric modeling techniques although the efficiency did not correlate with the cost for façade work. The cost depended on the client's design preferences and design changes.

- Laser scanning can acquire the shape and geometry of the surrounding area faster than a total station. However, the cumulative error of a laser scanner was larger than that of a total station. Moreover, there is yet no legal inspection standard for laser scanning. Thus, it is desirable to use a laser scanner and a total station together: a laser scanner as a measurement tool to quickly find potentially risky points, and a total station to check them further in detail. For example, the overall deflection of the truss structure was monitored regularly using a laser scanner and then checked using a total station only when precise measurement was required.

- Project participants interpreted the BIM model differently depending on their role and experience. This perception gap resulted in a delay in coordination meetings and decision making. Photo-realistic rendering, virtual reality, and 4D simulation were helpful in reducing the perception gap and facilitating decision-making processes.

- Multi-trade prefabrication can shorten a schedule by reducing on-site work. However, in order to obtain a positive effect on productivity, the target building should be large enough to generate the learning effect.

Acknowledgments

This case study was prepared with the close collaboration of Sejun Jang, Dong-min Lee, and Jinwoo Kim at Hyundai E&C. We are indebted to them and to all of the exceptional people at Hyundai E&C who contributed to this project and to this case study.

10.3   FONDATION LOUIS VUITTON, PARIS

10.3.1   Introduction

Designed by Frank Gehry and opened in October 2014, the Fondation Louis Vuitton (FLV; previously known as the Foundation for Creation) is a new exhibition space that hosts a permanent art collection, performances, lectures, and various rotating exhibitions. This project won the 2012 BIM Excellence Award, a prestigious recognition given by the American Institute of Architects, and it is considered a milestone that will take us to a new era in the use of building information technology.

The building is located in the Jardin d'Acclimatation, a children's park with ducks, ponies, and other small animals within the Bois du Boulogne, a public park on the western edge of Paris. The building puts forward an ambitious architectural and construction paradigm that demonstrates new construction methods and an equally new spatial character, especially with respect to its novel use of materials and fabrication technology. The fluid and sinuous sketch that Frank Gehry produced as a reference indicates his intention to create an organic architectural body that presents a visual dialogue with its natural surroundings and at the same time relates to the city of Paris. This relation is shown in Figures 10–3–1 and 10–3–2.

FIGURE 10–3–1   Fondation Louis Vuitton (FLV) by Frank Gehry.

Image courtesy of Fondation Louis Vuitton; © Iwan Baan / Fondation Louis Vuitton.

To highlight and respect the presence of nature, the architect used free-form transparent glass, a material that provides a unique visual separation between inside and outside. The use of glass of course is not new. Recent glass-based landmarks by Gehry include the Nationale Nederlanden building in Prague, the Conde Nast Cafeteria in New York, and the Novartis HQ building in Basel. More than a century earlier, Joseph Paxton designed and assembled the Crystal Palace in Hyde Park, London. What is new with Gehry's project is the use of glass in what appears to be a free-form manner (see Figure 10–3–3). With the multilayered complexity of building skin, intermediate structure, and shading "sails," the project posed unique challenges in multi-fabricator version control, detailed variable design generation tasks, model synchronization, tolerances, structural analysis of variable beams and connections, variable surfaces, fabrication, and construction.

Another objective of Frank Gehry was that the FLV should be open and adaptable to support different styles of environment. A recent "blanket" of the FLV was applied by Daniel Buren to demonstrate this potential (see Figure 10–3–4).

In what follows, we describe Gehry's project in some detail, focusing on its multilayered enclosed shell assembly and the extensive use of parametric 3D modeling that made its fabrication possible.

10.3.2 Project Design Workflow and Software Technology

Gehry's office has been a pioneer of the use of computer technology in architecture. In the late 1980s, a partner at Gehry Partners LLP, Jim Glymph, researched and then introduced CATIA, 3D software by Dassault Systèmes used in the aerospace industry. Since then, the office has been able to extend the boundaries and demonstrate the ability to build architectural geometries that were imaginable but impossible to construct up to that time. Adopting CATIA

FIGURE 10–3–3 Free-form use of glass in the sails of the Fondation Louis Vuitton.

Image courtesy of Nassim Saoud.

(A)

(B)

FIGURE 10–3–4 (A and B) Daniel Buren, a French artist known for his in-situ works, has covered the 3,584 pieces of glass making up the building's 14 sails in brightly colored filters.

Photos courtesy of Michael Arons.

led to Gehry's office establishing a relationship with Dassault Systèmes in France, applying it to many memorable multicurved surface buildings: the Guggenheim Museum in Bilbao, Spain; the Walt Disney Concert Hall in Los Angeles; the Stata Center at MIT; and many others. From this cooperation, a version of CATIA with some accommodation to building product modeling, called Digital Project, was developed to facilitate both the software environment and interfaces in the AEC domain. They also developed the conventions of object assemblies, facilitating the way that Gehry and partners managed surface assemblies. This collaboration has been beneficial for both parties; the way the software has been used by Gehry has influenced the way Dassault Systèmes thinks about the software they produce. Since then, the architectural practice has had an influence on the tools used in the automobile and aerospace industries (Friedman et al., 2002). Gehry Technologies was acquired in 2014 by Trimble Inc.

From the beginning, the process adopted for the FLV was structured to be a highly collaborative effort that involved more than ten different companies and their software: Digital Project, SketchUp, various Autodesk software, BoCAD, SolidWorks, ANSYS, NASTRAN, Sofistik3D, 3DVia Composer, Solibri, Tekla Structures, Rhino 3D, and Grasshopper 3D. Special efforts were made to develop mappings between these programs and Digital Project. To facilitate digital collaboration with so many partners on the project, Gehry Technologies adopted a web-based 3D platform for file management and project collaboration, calling it GT Global Exchange (GTX). The goal was to reach consensus more quickly, reduce change orders in the fabrication phase, and better manage project costs. GTX was the forerunner for a commercial project collaboration platform, called GTeam, and GTeam was in turn rebranded as Trimble Connect.

The workflow process for the FLV was strongly based on the concept of a master model serving as the BIM collaboration platform for both design and fabrication. This master model, hosted in GTX, was cloud-based and always accessible by the various teams at any time. The idea was to create a secure web server where people could access and share all the information carried by the master model. Users could work on the master model directly online from their computer without any 3D authoring application needing to be installed on the local machine.

The master model was composed of two main models that were merged:

- A design detail model, prepared by the architect, was used as a starting point. This was the authoritative design document.
- A detailed working model suitable for construction, prepared and maintained by the contractor with the information acquired from the design model.

The master model was a high-fidelity composite of the two, used for construction, and from which all the information regarding the lifecycle and the facility operation of the FLV could be gathered.

At times during the fabrication phase of the project, there were as many as fourteen teams involved. Some of them used their own software, and the GTX effort harmonized these different platform models and data with Digital Project. Gehry Technologies' role in practice was to coach the other teams on how to interface their workflow with the main DP platform. This involved creating new scripts or customized tools to achieve a more refined level of interoperability.

Another key purpose of the BIM process was to eliminate the common problems and mistakes that emerge from 3D curved surface teamwork. This intent was supported in part by simulation of the real building, but more importantly, through creation of a model that is at the same time more flexible, and is available to anyone in the process at any time. Moreover, this model could collect the information and the knowledge coming from the various competencies in the design process. In this sense, the 3D model could clarify numerous design and engineering issues before they became problems.

10.3.3 Design of the Structure and Sails

The building can be divided assembly-wise into two main components:

- The iceberg
- The sails

The iceberg structure serves as the structural core and houses the major mechanical systems (see Figure 10–3–5). It is covered by a skin made of Ductal concrete panels, and it supports the transparent sails. The unique geometry of the FLV results in a complex set of structural forces to which it must respond. These include the wind load of the sails, the combined gravity loads of the glass sails, and the iceberg skin of super high-strength concrete. The skin over the structure is carried by a set of parametrically defined ribs. They receive the loads and give shape to the exposed surfaces covering the iceberg. An example of the parametric ribs is shown in Figure 10–3–6; the control parameters are provided to define the shapes of the individual ribs.

The icebergs provide structural support to the sails. The sails constitute the exterior visual layer of the building. They give its typical aspect to the whole building construct and are the element inspired by Gehry's sketches. Gehry decided to use glass for the external layer of the building because of the material's qualities. He felt it was important to accentuate lightness and transparency within a site that is rich in natural presence like the Jardin d'Acclimatation. According to Gehry, "Our wish was to conceive a building that would evolve with the passing of the hours and with the changing light so as to create an impression of the ephemeral, and of continual change" (Fondation, 2014). Nevertheless, such a choice was quite new even in Gehry's unconventional architectural vocabulary of shapes and methodology. FLV was the first time that Gehry used glass in such a dramatic and sculpturally expressive way.

The area of the sails is approximately 13,000 square meters (more than 140,000 square feet). The sails façade is visually detached from the main structural body of the icebergs, but is anchored to the body with custom joints.

FIGURE 10–3–5 Iceberg structure and steel framework.

Image courtesy of Gehry Technologies.

FIGURE 10–3–6 Structural ribs support the building's skin. The geometry of the ribs is generated by a set of parameters that define their curvature.

Image courtesy of Gehry Technologies.

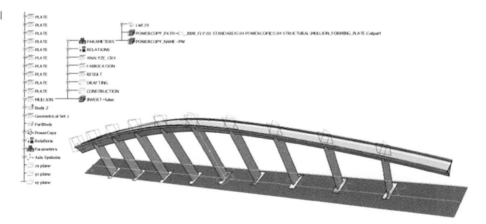

The structural core receives the glass grid sail loads through the extruded aluminum grid for the glass panels, as shown in the model view in Figure 10–3–7.

10.3.4 Model Analyses

The sail structure was studied by the Centre Scientifique et Technique du Bâtiment (CSTB), the French national organization providing research and innovation, consultancy, testing, training, and certification services in the construction

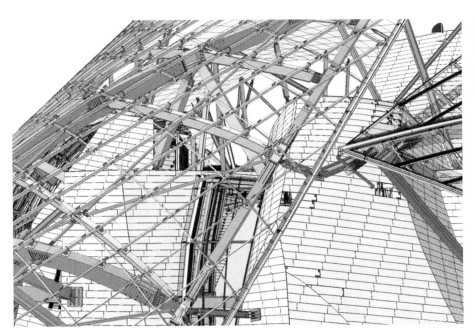

FIGURE 10–3–7   View of the façade and its assembly components. The computed view shows the grid that carries the glass panels, with the Ductal concrete panels covering the iceberg structures, and the heavier structural steel elements picking up the glass panel loads.

Image courtesy of Gehry Technologies.

industry. The CSTB appointed RFR and TESS, two engineering companies that specialize in complex structures and sophisticated envelopes, to partner for this effort. Several analyses were made to collect data for fabrication and behavior of the sail's structure. Many measurements were made first on the construction site to evaluate the impact of the environment on the nature of winds encountered in the Paris region. Values collected *in situ* were reproduced in a wind tunnel respecting space, scale, and time dimensions, such as the length of vortices and velocity variations as a function of time. Sensors installed on a mock-up of the project made from sintered powder were used to characterize their effects and quantify pressures present in the structures (Barré and Leempoels, 2009). Several analyses were also done for load transfer, risk of condensation, joint tightness, and fire performance.

The BIM master model was also used to simulate possible scenarios concerning fire safety and crowd flow to better locate emergency exits. The 3D master model was also used to implement a full 4D simulation of the entire building. Predictive information was estimated regarding maintenance and renovation of particular building parts over the course of time.

10.3.5   Generative Detailing Using 3D Intelligent Components

Digital Project has an intelligent parametric object modeling tool called "Power Copy." It is used for advanced replication; its function is to duplicate or instantiate a component, but it also allows one to adapt the component parametrically to its context. For example, when power copying a joint where the angle can be only within a certain radius, Digital Project will check to make sure that this

FIGURE 10-3-8 3D intelligent components. The picture shows different parametric objects that with their embedded intelligence can adjust themselves to the different geometries with which they have to interface.

Image courtesy of Gehry Technologies.

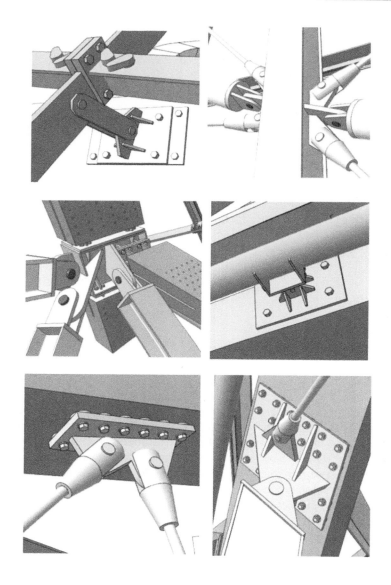

condition is respected, and if it is not, the joint will adapt to reestablish the preset condition. This is a very beneficial tool for design and detailing in 3D, and it was used extensively for the FLV project, in which hundreds of details and components were designed. Some examples are shown in Figure 10-3-8.

What is especially useful is that an architect can design a detail component for a building in a prototype fashion, without knowing all the geometric constraints that the particular component will undertake. The intelligence embedded in the script adjusts the component to the various contexts in which it will be placed. This generative detailing allows the designer to specify, by defining a script, a set of constraints or rules within the component itself. These rules can be very extensive and can include conditional states and optimization of the detail in its particular surrounding. In addition, these intelligent details can be used by other people that do not have that particular expertise. Its purpose is to encapsulate some of the knowledge a particular detail required and make it usable by somebody who does not have all the knowledge going into the detail. It is a way to share and redistribute knowledge among the team members.

10.3.6 Concrete Iceberg Panelization and Optimization for Fabrication

The icebergs are the structural core of the project. They are a series of solid volumes that support the sails, the floating glass canopies that cover most of the building. The icebergs are designed as concrete shells or steel frameworks, and are covered with over 16,000 wall panels. Special technology, implemented and patented by Lafarge in 2008, provides the Ultra High-Performance Concrete (UHPC) adopted in the project (Lafarge, 2014). Bonna Sabla, a French company specializing in precast concrete, started industrial production of the panels in spring 2011.

The BIM model and its parametric characteristics allowed architects and engineers to optimize the 16,000 panels (all of which had unique shape) according to panel size, bounding area, and bounding volume to reduce mold variation. The result of this process was that the number of unique molds was reduced to 1,900, far fewer than the original 16,000 unique panel shapes. This rationalized the fabrication process, as molds could be reused. See Figure 10–3–9.

Each mold shape was made in foam. The ruled surfaces were hot wire cut, as shown in Figure 10–3–10; the nonruled surfaces were routed (Gehry Technologies, 2012). All of these operations were computer numeric controlled (CNC). The casting assembly was realized with a layer of flexible silicon and

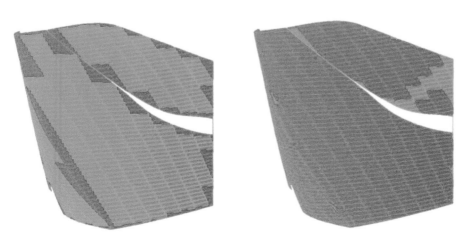

FIGURE 10–3–9 Optimization process of the Ductal panels. The colors indicate association of panels with a family of panels.

Image courtesy of Gehry Technologies.

FIGURE 10–3–10 CNC hot-wire panel cutting machine. It is set up to cut horizontally above the table carrying the mold base. The mold base is cut from the lower surface, then the upper surface is cut. Finally, the shape of the panel profile is trimmed from the stock piece, providing the panel shape, then the positive panel is removed with a negative mold.

Image courtesy of Gehry Technologies.

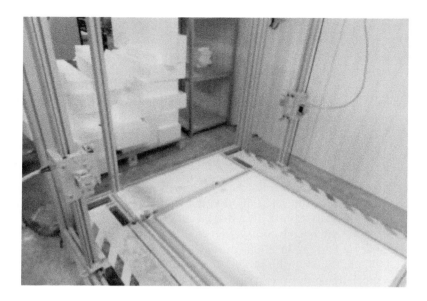

block-outs for the embedded hardware. Once the concrete was poured, the package was placed in a vacuum bag for the 20 hours required for curing. After curing, each individual shape was scanned with a laser scanner to ensure conformance of the surface to the design shape. Finally, each of the panels was numbered and a radio frequency identification (RFID) tag was applied to help track all the elements to ensure installation in their proper location on the iceberg structure. The panels are connected to the structural concrete core with two hundred aluminum ribs that were designed to exactly match the outside curvature of the iceberg. Stiffening elements are located underneath every joint of the Ductal tiles. These aluminum panels are connected to the concrete structure by specially designed spacers. The aluminum cladding ribs were fabricated by Iemants N.V. Iemants refined a highly automated process that allowed the fabrication of these pieces with careful control over small tolerances (Pouma/Iemants, 2012).

10.3.7   Fabrication of the Glass Sails

The FLV building has fourteen sails, formed with 3,584 panels, each of which was custom-made with a CNC type of fabrication and run through an optimization process; this process helped the team find the best fit for each panel making up the fourteen sails (see Figure 10–3–3). Final tolerance verification was done on a global level for the whole sails canopy structure. For the sail elements, three different levels of optimization studies were undertaken to iterate the information and data through the design process:

- A surface level optimization, where the 3D intelligent component adjusts itself on the sail surface with a power copy operation

- A local surface deformation, where the different panels optimize themselves according to their families
- A global project optimization, where entire elements are checked for consistency and tolerances

The process used to size, make, and place the glass panels had six steps:

1. The process starts from a **parametric definition** of a developable panel, defined for curvature from the architectural model, with triangulated control points taken at corner points of the panels. Since all surfaces were on complex curved surfaces, the panels were all placed relatively within the tolerance spaces set up by the architect's model. This spatial model is the reference for defining the control points of the master model.

2. In the second step, **adaptive instantiation**, the parametric developable panel was placed in all of the locations on grids. The panel geometry adjusted to fit the constraints of each panel location. The result was a set of 16,000 unique panels. Figure 10–3–11 shows a typical section.

3. **Convergent optimization** applied goal-seeking algorithms to reduce the variability of the panels within the bounds of acceptable deviation from the original surface. At this point a first level of optimization was used to drive any nonlinear design conditions or deformations towards a more controlled linear shape. This reduced the number of unique panels by merging panel designs based on similarity and tolerances. Figure 10–3–12 shows color-coded visualization of the optimization process.

4. In the **frequency analysis** step, the number of individual panels that belong to each of the resulting groups was counted, identifying the most common panel shapes.

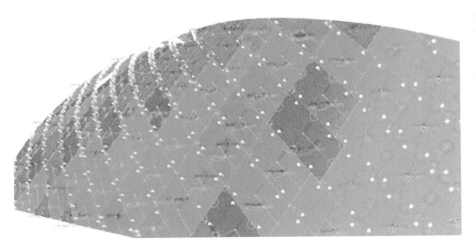

FIGURE 10–3–11 Adaptive instantiation of the panels. A 3D intelligent component (Power Copy), which carried information regarding the geometry, material, and installation constraints, was placed in each grid location on the surface, thus adapting each of the components to its own location. The panel connections are indicated with the white spots.

Image courtesy of Gehry Technologies.

5. **Family decomposition.** In this step, the final set of panel families is chosen, and each panel is assigned to belong to the family with the closest geometry conformance.

6. Given that the panel geometries were changed from their original instantiation in the grid, an additional **tolerance verification** step was performed to ensure that any deviations would fall within acceptable bounds.

The glass panels for the sails were fabricated using a large CNC cylindrical glass bending machine. The panels were heated to 800 degrees F and then run through a set of cylindrical rolls that can adjust their position to accommodate the curvature to be impressed into the panel.

10.3.8   Integrated Use of the BIM Model

The BIM model was used during all the phases of the project, from design through construction. At all times the Digital Project 3D master model was considered the sole source of validation for changes and procedures. Because of its high-fidelity details, embracing knowledge from all the various competencies involved in the project, the model allowed visualization of all the possible problems and supported development of solutions in time to avoid problems. This helped save time and money and reduced mistakes that could have resulted due to poor integration of information in the drawings and incomplete individual comprehension of the project.

All of the contractors were required to develop 3D studies of their work. This obligation helped save time in the fabrication of the components since the majority were fabricated by using a CNC machining process. All the fabricated parts were laser scanned and compared with the 3D model to verify their geometry and tolerances. Corrections were made where needed before installation, and each panel in the model was updated to match the as-built state after placement. This practice was rendered necessary due to the complex geometry: by laser checking the elements before their installation, the team was able to optimize the assembly operation.

During construction, fabricators took the 3D master model and derived information that was important for their part of the job. Some of them built their own 3D model of the building using the BIM tools they were accustomed to working with, while others subcontracted back to Gehry Technologies to provide consultancy, including modeling of detailed 3D fabrication information that could be reintegrated into the 3D BIM master model.

Scripting was a big component of the process. Over 150 Visual Basic scripts were implemented within Digital Project. One of the challenges in this situation was to manage the modifications that were made to the model over time, and to make all the other team members aware of them. 3D projects often have many interdependent files, and any modification can propagate and require changes in different parts of the model. People working on the project need to be aware of the modifications that affect them. It is essential for a team to be able to track all the changes, when they were made, and by whom. This is what led to the adoption of a versioning system that tracked the modifications made throughout the process and facilitated communication among the various stakeholders involved in every phase of the project. The tool used for this purpose is a French Open Information System called Batiwork (Batiwork, n.d.). A system that works with CATIA, this versioning system facilitated the 3D validation process of the modifications made by different teams.

All the information regarding the project was integrated into the BIM model (occupancy information, wall types, finish, and so on). This effort to collect all this information was of a particular value for all the team that will have to work with the building during its lifecycle. Owner and building operators, maintenance staff, museum curators, and all other players will have a resource full of valid information and data to be used for managing and optimizing their activities.

At the time the project was developed, the use of tablet computers was not yet common. Most of the communication on-site was done with more traditional methods, including paper drawings. If the construction were to have started now, the communication flow on site would probably rely more heavily on the use of 3D visualization tools, such as tablets and smart phone cameras.

10.3.9 Lessons Learned

In France, as in most of Europe, during the design development phase designers hand off the documentation to the contractors, who then develop the details for fabrication for which they will be responsible. This project adopted a different approach, in which designers and contractors have much closer relationships. At the design development phase, all consultants, builders, and engineers were housed in one building on-site. Over 300 people shared the same location during construction, and this factor was key to making the process successful. The Paris headquarters used GTX to constantly communicate with consultants and fabricators who were not on-site. Moreover, the team from Gehry Technologies was always conscious that the different teams involved in the process used different tools. Each tool had potential and limitations, and GT wanted to leave freedom to each team to create geometries in the environment that was most efficient for them. Their effort was to focus in the creation of a common environment in which to drop all the different created content without worrying about the system in which they were created. To this purpose, GTX, the cloud-server-shared master model, was extremely beneficial. To track all of the changes and the various design iterations, a BIM-connected SQL database was implemented, with a versioning system that allowed the various teams to benefit from a query service.

The construction process also benefitted from the flexibility of workflows that the use of GTX allowed. This flexibility allowed the integration of many different workflows and techniques that were being used by different fabricators and subcontractors, leaving each free to work in the system to which they were more accustomed. For example, for fabrication of the aluminum cladding, the Digital Project model was imported into Rhino and then Grasshopper. This digital environment allowed the fabricators to develop specific scripts in VB.Net and Python that led the aluminum cladding fabricator, Iemants, to implement an automated system for producing the panels.

Tolerances and assembly are inherent challenges when free-form 3D surfaces are involved. The use of 2D drawings easily results in serious problems during prefabrication and assembly. Throughout the project, control point elements were placed and tracked that could be placed in the 3D construction as the building was erected, minimizing dimensional variations as assembly progressed. Tolerance management was part of the design and erection processes.

10.3.10 Conclusion

With the Fondation Louis Vuitton building, we see the evolution of the use of building information modeling. This project shifts the focus toward a cloud-based coordination server that helped distribute project information and data among the members of a worldwide project team through the use of a shared 3D BIM model. This effort helped eliminate many of the problems that commonly derived from poor communication and technological organization. It accelerated the design process and reduced the mistakes that come from the lack of information and knowledge. Enhanced parametric modeling integrated the project with advanced automated CNC fabrication processes and tight quality control that benefited the entire chain of production.

The FLV is made up of multiple layers of structure, glass shading surfaces, and thin-formed high strength concrete panels, with a structural steel frame tying them together. This organization allowed clear articulation of the structural system connections and allowed Gehry Partners to use the Power Copy parametric modeling technology together with scripted functions and other solvers to efficiently engineer the connections, concrete panels, and glass sails. Extensive use of parametric modeling also enabled optimization and perfection of the fabrication and erection of the building's unique components. Without BIM, this building might never have been attempted.

Acknowledgments

This case study was prepared by Mauro Buffa and Chuck Eastman. The authors are grateful to Andrew Witt, Director of Research at Gehry Technologies, and to Dennis Shelden, CTO at Gehry Technologies, for their support.

10.4 DONGDAEMUN DESIGN PLAZA, SEOUL, SOUTH KOREA
BIM to Fabrication

10.4.1 Introduction

The Dongdaemun Design Park (DDP) is a branch of the National Museum of Modern and Contemporary Art, located at the center of Seoul, South Korea. The general project information is in Table 10–4–1. Since its opening in 2014, the gigantic spaceship-looking exterior, with its embedded LED lights, has attracted over 20,000 visitors per day, and the number is still growing (Figure 10–4–1). The cladding that gives the spaceship-like appearance is composed of over 460,000 parts, including 46,000 aluminum panels and 10 substructure parts per panel to support each panel, and excluding the LED lights and fasteners. The number of parts in the exterior cladding of DDP is larger than the number of parts in a Boeing 737 airplane, which is composed of 367,000 parts. The aerodynamic shape of DDP could not have been formed without the ability to fabricate a total of more than 45,000 façade panels, including 20,000 double-curved panels, within a limited timeframe and budget. A solution to "mass customizing" façade panels was urgently needed.

Nevertheless, the enormous number of panels and technical challenges were not the only problems faced by the DDP project. DDP, which cost about 2.4% of Seoul's annual budget, was the most significant outcome of the "Design Seoul" campaign pushed by the former mayor of Seoul. Naturally, it was at the epicenter of a political debate.

Moreover, the project was located at a historical site. Seoul, which has been the capital of South Korea since 1392, used to be protected by a fortress wall and four main gates—the North, South, East, and West Big Gates. Around each gate, large markets were formed. After 600 years, Dongdaemun, which means the "East Big Gate" in Korean, became the hub of the Asian fashion market. During the period of Japanese rule, a sports complex called the Dongdaemun Stadium was built near Dongdaemun, on top of the fortress wall and the military facilities of the Joseon Dynasty. The DDP was built at the site where the

Dongdaemun Stadium used to stand. The stadium floodlights were intentionally left at the current DDP site as a design element to show the historical background of DDP. During the demolition and excavation work for DDP, the project team discovered the exact locations of the ruins of the fortress wall and military facilities of the Joseon Dynasty. Zaha Hadid Architects (ZHA) had to redesign a large portion of DDP to incorporate the historical ruins as a new design element. These were just a few of many technical and nontechnical challenges the project faced.

10.4.2 Challenges during the Design Phase

DDP was the first large public project in Korea to deploy BIM during the design and construction phases. In November 2006, when the international design competition was announced, the number of small BIM projects started to increase in Korea. In 2008, when ZHA and its local architectural firm, Samoo Architects and Engineers (Samoo), were busy developing construction

Table 10–4–1   Project Summary

Project	Dongdaemun Design Plaza (DDP)
Location	Seoul, Republic of Korea
Owner/client type	Public
Contract	Design-Bid-Build (DBB)
Use and occupancy	Exhibition Halls, Conference Hall, Design Museum and Exhibition Pathway, Design Labs and Academy Hall, Media Center, Seminar Rooms, and Designers Lounge
Structure	Steel-framed structure, Reinforced Concrete (RC), etc.
Gross floor area(m^2)	86,574 m^2
Site area	65,000 m^2
Number of floors	4 floors/3 basement floors
Maximum height	29 m
Project duration	International Design Competition: April 2007–August 2007
	Demolition of the Dongdaemun Stadium: December 2007–February, 2009
	Dongdaemum Historical Culture and Park opened on October 27, 2009.
	Dongdaemum Design Plaza opened on March 21, 2014 (Original planned completion date: December 26, 2011)
Design and construction cost	Initial budget approx. US$ 200 million
	Final cost approx. US$ 370 million

documents, more than 30 large BIM projects were in progress in the private and public sectors.

ZHA and Samoo won the international design competition for DDP in August 2007, but the design development and construction documentation did not start until several months later because the contractual negotiation over the design fee and other details between ZHA and the city of Seoul took longer than anticipated (Figure 10–4–2).

Based on their experience, both ZHA and Samoo knew that the DDP project would require the use of BIM, although its use was not mandated. ZHA chose Rhino as a main design tool. Samoo had experience in developing construction details using CATIA for the Incheon International Airport Transportation Center, which had the shape of a flying bird. Samoo chose CATIA as the main design tool for the exterior surface of the building. Han-All Technology, a CATIA expert firm with a background in mechanical engineering, was hired to model the exterior surface and substructures. The main structural frames were designed using Revit and AutoCAD.

In addition, Group5F, Evolute, and Ebener participated in the project as façade consultants for the panelization and rationalization (optimization) of the exterior surface. Rationalization is a process for increasing the number of

FIGURE 10–4–2   DDP project timeline.

repetitive patterns while decreasing the number of double-curved panels, as these are very expensive to fabricate. Each cycle of panelization and rationalization had a great impact on the project schedule because every detail had to be rebuilt from scratch, based on the geometry of the new exterior surface proposed by the façade consultant team and ZHA. For example, the exterior surface was initially divided into approximately 14,000 panels, but the final number of exterior panels ended up being over 45,000. Since the number of panels and the relationships radically changed with each panelization and rationalization cycle, the parametric relations defined between geometric elements in a given model became useless. Interoperability issues also became a critical bottleneck, even between these small numbers of software applications.

The interoperability issue was partially relieved by developing scripts that would automatically rebuild panels and substructures in a CATIA model from a new Rhino surface model and control points. However, the construction documentation phase was too short to mature the scripts, as well as the data exchange process. The interoperability process was matured by Gehry Technologies, which was hired later during the construction phase. The interoperability process is described in detail later in the "BIM to Fabrication" section of this case study.

Even after several cycles of panelization and rationalization of facades, the percentage of double-curved panels was still approximately 50% of the 45,133 panels (Figure 10–4–3). Contrary to general perception, none of the free-form buildings with metal facades, including the Walt Disney Concert Hall, the Bilbao Guggenheim Museum, and the Experience Music Project (EMP), had been built using truly double-curved metal panels. The Walt Disney Concert Hall and the Bilbao Guggenheim Museum used a series of single-curved panels to form a freely curved shape, which was achieved through many iterations of the Gaussian curvature analysis and design rationalization processes. EMP had a more complex shape than the Walt Disney Concert Hall and the Bilbao Guggenheim Museum. The surface of EMP was recursively subdivided until each piece reached a size that could be cold-bent on site. These approaches are much less expensive than using double-curved panels, but gaps between panels are

Panel Type	Quantity (piece)	Area (m²)	Ratio (%)	Flat	Single Curved	Double Curved
Flat	13,841	9,492	29			
Single curved	9,554	7,455	22			
Double curved	21,738	16,281	49			
Total	**45,133**	**33,228**	**100**	**29%**	**22%**	**49%**

FIGURE 10–4–3   Distribution of panel types.

Image courtesy of Gehry Technologies.

unavoidable (Figure 10–4–4). Since ZHA allowed only a 2 mm tolerance in the 25 mm spacing between panels, no options other than fabricating the panels in double-curved shapes were available. Yonsei University (Yonsei) was hired as a technical advisor to survey and review the state-of-the-art metal processing techniques, including dieless forming and explosive forming. Yonsei was unable to find a metal processing technique that was sufficiently fast and affordable to meet the project deadline and the budget based on existing methods. Therefore, they suggested that the project team develop a new metal processing machine based on the existing multipoint forming technique, as had been deployed in the fabrication of the twisted built-up columns of the Beijing Olympic stadium known as the Bird's Nest.

To make the situation even more complicated, historical remains were found on-site during the excavation, toward the end of the construction documentation phase, as mentioned in the introduction. The project had to be stopped and redesigned to cope with the newly found remains. Since the start and end dates of the construction were contractually fixed, the time available

FIGURE 10-4-4 Intended gaps between panels at EMP, Seattle.

Photo by Ghang Lee.

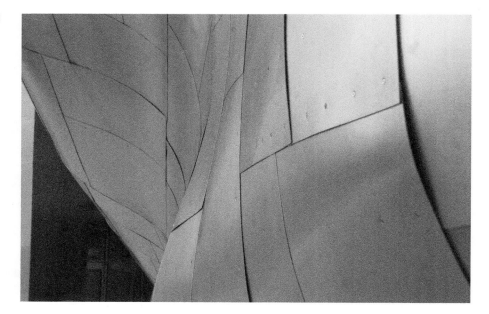

to resolve the façade panel fabrication method and details was too short, and the fabrication issues passed over into the construction phase.

10.4.3   Challenges during the Construction Phase

Combinations of the multiple problems described in the previous section made the project a fast track project, even though the project had been contracted as a typical design-bid-build project. Demolition and excavation began in December 2007, but the official construction process did not begin until March 2009 (Figure 10-4-2). The project was divided into two parts: the history and culture park and the design plaza. The park area was scheduled to open first, in October 2009, six months after the construction began, and the design plaza two years later in December 2011, before the term of the presiding mayor ended (Figure 10-4-2). The design plaza was the main building, while the history and culture park was composed of low-rise buildings with free-form shapes. The history park included a café and exhibition halls for the remains and relics of the old fortress wall and military facilities, as well as a trail along the remains of the old fortress (Figure 10-4-5).

The project was very tight in terms of both schedule and budget. Figures 10-6 and 10-7 compare the schedule and cost of DDP with those of similar projects. The floor area of 18,552 m^2 was built in one year in the case of DDP, which was four times faster than that of exhibition facilities constructed

FIGURE 10–4–5   Dongdeamun History and Culture Park (DHCP).

Photo by Ghang Lee.

between 2012 and 2014 in South Korea, and at least 1.3 times faster than that of buildings designed by ZHA (Figure 10–4–6).

In terms of construction costs, DDP is approximately 132% to 177% more expensive than the final construction cost of other exhibition facilities built in South Korea between 2012 and 2014, around the same time when DDP was completed, (Figure 10–4–7). Considering the complexity of DDP, this was a very tight budget.

The Samsung Construction and Trade (C&T) consortium won the project. However, being apprehensive about the project, and especially the cost and the details associated with the façade panels, Samsung C&T and the city of Seoul underwent a long contractual negotiation process. The final resolution was that the city of Seoul would hire the design team (ZHA + Samoo) again as

FIGURE 10–4–6 Comparison of the constructed floor areas per year (m²) between DDP and the other buildings designed by ZHA, and also between DDP and the other exhibition facilities in S. Korea constructed between 2012 and 2014 based on actual schedules.

Updated from Lee and Kim, 2012.

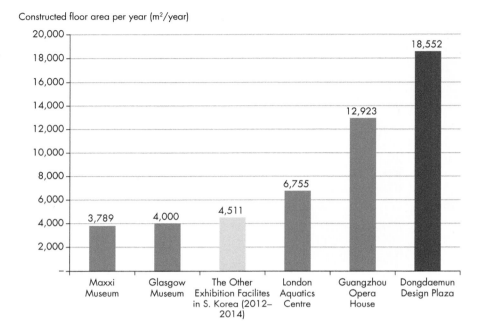

Constructed floor area per year (m²/year)

FIGURE 10–4–7 Comparison of the final construction costs per m² between DDP and the other exhibition facilities in South Korea constructed between 2012 and 2014.

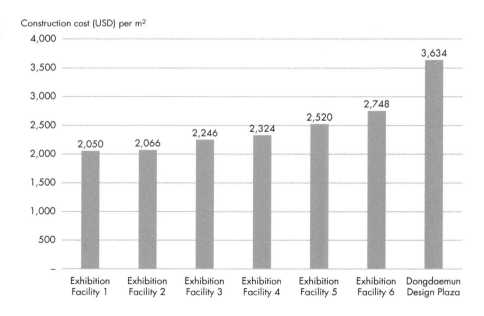

Construction cost (USD) per m²

Table 10-4-2   The Construction Project Team

Roles	Participants
Owner/Client	City of Seoul
Design Architect, Construction Administration	Zaha Hadid Architects (ZHA)
Architect of Record, Construction Documentation, Construction Administration	Samoo Architects & Engineering (Samoo)
Façade Consultant	Group 5F, Evolute, Ebener
Main Contractor	Samsung Construction and Trade (Samsung C&T) Consortium
BIM Consultant	Gehry Technologies (GT) Korea
Construction Management	Consortium of Kunwon Engineering, Global Team Space Engineering & Consulting (GTS E&C) and Heerim CM
Cladding	Consortium of Iljin Aluminum, SteelLife, and Steel E&C (ISS)

a construction administrator (CA), in addition to a construction management (CM) team and a new BIM team as a BIM consultant (Table 10–4–2).

In May 2009, approximately two months after Samsung C&T was hired, Gehry Technologies (GT) Asia was hired as a BIM consultant and founded GT Korea as a contractual entity. The first assignment of GT was to develop BIM models for the low-rise buildings of the park areas within three months. This was an extremely short period to set up a BIM process and develop BIM models from designs with unfixed details, especially when the project team members were very pressured by the short schedule and skeptical about the usefulness of BIM. Against all the odds, the BIM models were built and vertically divided at every 30 cm to produce cross-sections of the buildings. The cross-sections were used to fabricate the ribs of the concrete forms. At that time, concrete forms for the buildings in the park area were still being made manually by carpenters based on cross-sectional drawings, instead of sending the cross-section data from BIM models directly to a computerized numeric control (CNC) machine, even though CNC was not a new technology in the Korean construction industry. Nevertheless, this process made the project team members start to appreciate the necessity of BIM in this geometrically complex project.

After completion of the history and culture park, the BIM process started to take shape. The BIM contract specified the role of the BIM consultant as a communication channel to organize and integrate BIM services into the construction process, in addition to the roles as a BIM modeler, trainer, and technical supporter. The BIM consultant specified the data exchange flow, as well as a process to incorporate design changes into the BIM models. The data were exchanged using a Digital Project (DP) model as the master BIM model between Rhino, Tekla Structures, AutoCAD, Midas, and Revit. At the beginning of the project, no resolution process existed for settling conflicts arising from the differences in the designs of the different trades. By defining the DP model as the master BIM model, and by also setting up a process to resolve conflicts between the designs of the different trades through weekly and irregular BIM meetings, the BIM process was settled down. The project members became used to the BIM process, although the conflicts caused by the innate geometrical differences between a Rhino model (the architectural design model) and a DP model (the master model in the data exchange process) were inevitable. In those cases, the Rhino model, as a geometric representation of the architect's design intents, took priority; however, giving a Rhino model the highest priority as a design model caused quite a few problems, due to the geometric inaccuracy of Rhino because of its nature as a surface modeler. The conflicts could be resolved through meetings and negotiations, but many project members felt that the effort and time for the negotiation process could have been reduced by contractually defining the DP model (a model produced by a solid modeler) as the model with the highest priority. Although the BIM process was organized and settled down, the fabrication of the façade panels still remained a major technical challenge.

10.4.4   BIM to Fabrication

The exterior panels of DDP were 4-mm-thick aluminum panels. The sizes of the panels differed by curvature, but the typical size was 1.6 m × 1.2 m. The greater the curvature, the smaller the panel. The façade design was modified and elaborated multiple times during the construction phase, but the data exchange was quite seamless because of the maturation of the scripts and the data-conversion process from a Rhino model into a DP model with details of panels and substructures. Figure 10–4–8 describes the data exchange process in detail. First, an updated Rhino model was exported to DP as an IGES model. Second, a wireframe model was generated using DP templates and scripts. Third, the locations of space-frame units were corrected to align themselves to the centroid of each panel using an Excel spreadsheet and DP templates. Fourth, panels and rod bars were created. Fifth, panel data were extracted from subdivision of the panels. Sixth, each panel was automatically numbered with a unique panel identification number using a DP template. Seventh, panels were automatically classified into certain panel types for fabrication and cost estimation based on shape information. Eighth, perforated panel models were generated. Ninth, the final model with substructures and pattern details was generated. Tenth, drawings and fabrication data were automatically generated from the final model.

A consortium of Iljin Aluminum, SteelLife, and Steel E&C (ISS) was hired as the cladding subcontractor. SteelLife led the development of a new machine to fabricate double-curved aluminum panels. The new machine used a hybrid approach of multipoint forming and stretch forming. Thus, the method was referred to as the multipoint stretch forming (MPSF) method. The machine

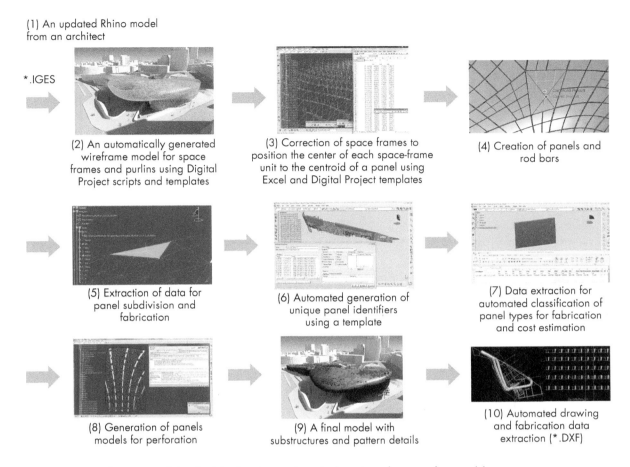

(1) An updated Rhino model from an architect

*.IGES

(2) An automatically generated wireframe model for space frames and purlins using Digital Project scripts and templates

(3) Correction of space frames to position the center of each space-frame unit to the centroid of a panel using Excel and Digital Project templates

(4) Creation of panels and rod bars

(5) Extraction of data for panel subdivision and fabrication

(6) Automated generation of unique panel identifiers using a template

(7) Data extraction for automated classification of panel types for fabrication and cost estimation

(8) Generation of panels models for perforation

(9) A final model with substructures and pattern details

(10) Automated drawing and fabrication data extraction (*.DXF)

FIGURE 10–4–8 Generation of details of the façade panels and substructures from a surface model.

Image courtesy of SteelLife.

consisted of 1,200 posts, each of which was controlled by a DC motor, an encoder, and a reduction gear. The height of each post was generated from panel shape information contained in a BIM model. In addition, a method was developed for the automatic detection of the panel shape that was the closest to the panel shape in the BIM model from the surface of a process sheet metal using a laser scanner. The correctly shaped panel would then be cut out from processed sheet metal by using a laser cutter attached to a robot arm. The neck of the robot arm was automatically rotated to keep the direction of the laser perpendicular to the double-curved surface, so that cuts did not have a sharp edge. Ribs were welded around the cut panels (Figure 10–4–9).

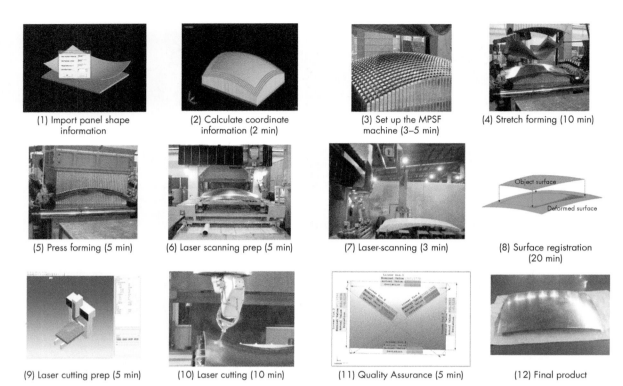

(1) Import panel shape information

(2) Calculate coordinate information (2 min)

(3) Set up the MPSF machine (3–5 min)

(4) Stretch forming (10 min)

(5) Press forming (5 min)

(6) Laser scanning prep (5 min)

(7) Laser-scanning (3 min)

(8) Surface registration (20 min)

(9) Laser cutting prep (5 min)

(10) Laser cutting (10 min)

(11) Quality Assurance (5 min)

(12) Final product

FIGURE 10–4–9   Multipoint stretch forming process.

Image courtesy of SteelLife.

The new machine was developed during the construction phase through four cycles of mock-up tests (Figure 10–4–10). After two years of trial and error, the project team was able to achieve the required quality for the panels: 2 mm tolerance in 25 mm spacing between panels (Figures 10–4–10 and 10–4–11). The fabrication cost per panel dropped from the initial US$ 7,000 to an average of US$ 250-400 per m², including the flat panels. The production time was reduced from several hours to an average of 15 to 70 minutes per m², including the changeover time. Initially, the total time required to produce 40,000 pieces was estimated to be 20,000 days (approximately 58 years). Nevertheless, using the BIM to fabrication method, it took approximately one year to produce more than 45,000 panel pieces.

Another challenge of the DDP project was to make irregularly shaped interior concrete structures. Several traditional methods were tested, but the expected quality could not be achieved and the finishes could not be covered up because the structures were designed to be exposed concrete structures. The MPSF was used to create steel concrete forms with a finish quality of 0.5 mm variances compared to the model (Figure 10–4–12). After the project, the as-built BIM models were submitted and kept for maintenance purposes.

FIGURE 10–4–10   Mock-up tests.

Photo by Ghang Lee.

FIGURE 10–4–11   Installed façade panels.

Photo by Ghang Lee.

(A)   (B)

FIGURE 10–4–12   Use of MPSF in concrete work: (A) Assembled concrete forms fabricated using MPSF. (B) Exposed concrete structures.

Photo by Ghang Lee.

Since the conclusion of the DDP project, the MPSF developed though the DDP project has been deployed in other irregularly shaped buildings, such as the Yeosu Expo Theme Pavilion. The application of this technology did not end with the architectural domain, but was expanded to the ship and airplane industries (Figure 10–4–13).

10.4.5   Lessons Learned

Many lessons were learned through the DDP project. The following summarizes the lessons and considerations for using BIM for an irregularly shaped building project from the organization, operations, design and construction timeline, master BIM model requirements, data exchange and handover, and contracting perspectives.

Organization

- The project participants must be truly collaborative partners and not be in an adversarial or a mere contractual relationship with one another.
- One firm in the project team must be designated to manage the master BIM model and coordinate with the stakeholders.
- One person or team with BIM experience must be solely dedicated to BIM management and operations.

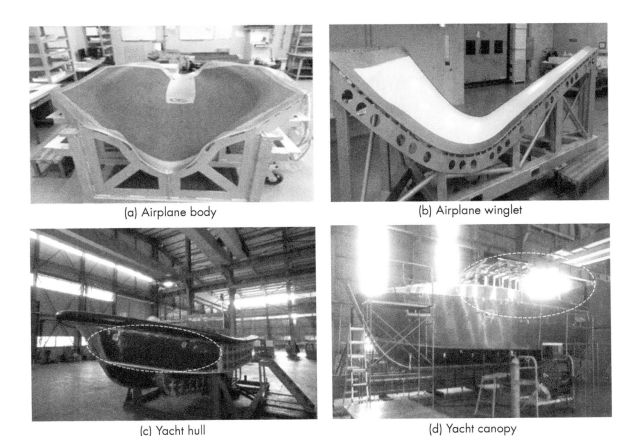

(a) Airplane body

(b) Airplane winglet

(c) Yacht hull

(d) Yacht canopy

FIGURE 10–4–13 Application of MPSF in ship and airplane manufacturing.

Image courtesy of SteelLife.

- Subcontractors without BIM capacity must be excluded. If their participation is absolutely necessary, contractual obligations and training are essential.
- 4D or 5D require additional dedicated staff to manage these areas.

Operations
- Approval processes must be established to accommodate design changes to the master and related BIM models.
- The BIM team must be shielded from unnecessary, repetitious, or time-consuming information requests through a gatekeeper process for prioritizing requests.

Design and Construction Timeline

- Compared to traditional buildings, the complex forms of irregularly shaped buildings are more susceptible to clashes and complications brought about by design changes. Feasibility analyses generally take longer to perform. Therefore, an adequate design timeline must be allocated, otherwise poor quality and completion delays may result.

- For the same reasons, the construction timeline may take substantially longer. Installing curved formwork for an irregularly shaped building requires considerably more effort. Since the challenges associated with the form may differ for each building, there is no set formula for anticipating the additional time required for construction; however, according to project samples, the annual construction area for an irregular building typically runs at 4,000–7,000 m², and the maximum area does not exceed 10,000 m² except for DDP and the Guangzhou Opera House.

Master BIM Model Requirements

- It is almost unavoidable to have multiple BIM models for different trades. Nevertheless, there must be only one master BIM model that can be a reference to other BIM models. Even apparently insignificant differences between models may cause confusion in translation to construction.

- The system for creating the master BIM model must be able to generate construction drawings directly.

- The system for the master BIM model must be able to generate specifications for accurate CNC fabrication of the building elements.

- BIM model files for irregularly shaped buildings tend to be large. Systems that can handle large files are an absolute necessity.

- Considering all these, a solid modeler is more suitable as a master BIM model tool than a surface modeler, especially during the construction documentation and construction phases, although a surface modeler might be an efficient and powerful design tool during early design phases.

Data Exchange and Handover

- A single project may have multiple software systems dedicated to various fields. Before the start of the project, the participants must define and agree on the data exchange formats (file formats, exchange methods, etc.).

- Before the project, a survey must be conducted of the software systems that the project participants use to optimize results and interoperability.

- If an owner is to require information handover for facility and asset management after project completion, the owner must have an explicit list of information requirements (submittals) and a clear idea of what to do with the information during the maintenance and operation phase before the construction phase, so that the contractor and the BIM team can collect the required information during construction. It will be too late to discuss what should be submitted to the owner during construction.

Contracting

- Design changes are inevitable if all aspects of the project are not studied in detail. Design and construction methodologies such as "fast track," which may increase the number of design changes, should be avoided for irregularly shaped buildings.
- The contract must include provisions that limit the number of design changes. Design changes in irregularly shaped buildings have greater implications than in traditional buildings.
- Costs that reflect maximum input from engineering and construction consultants early in the design phase must be included to prevent further issues during construction.
- If BIM cannot be applied to all areas of the project, priority must be given to processes where its use can be maximized. In the case of the DDP, architecture, structure, and MEP were the areas of highest priority, followed by lighting, with electrical work, earthwork, and landscaping taking the lowest priority.
- The contract must specify which model will be the master BIM model and who will manage it, and what the process is for making design changes.
- Provisions that will promote trust, cooperation, and data exchange between the project participants must be included in the contract.

10.4.6 Conclusion and Future Outlook

The number of irregularly shaped buildings is increasing so rapidly that buildings with diagonal or mildly curved shapes are no longer perceived as irregularly shaped buildings. And this trend will persist.

DDP is a controversial project beyond its political symbolism. In most successful BIM projects, either cost reduction or schedule is identified as the main benefit from BIM. However, in case of DDP, both schedule and budget were almost doubled compared to the initial plan. For this reason, some people viewed this as a failed case, although some claimed that the initial budget and schedule were not realistic considering the complexity of the project compared to similar buildings (Figures 10–4–6 and 10–4–7). Despite all these controversies, the reason that DDP is worthy as a BIM case study is the technological advancement it made. There was one important role of BIM that all the DDP project team members agreed upon even if each team member perceived the effectiveness of BIM differently. They unanimously said that the DDP project could not have been finished without BIM, regardless of how much money or time was poured into the project.

At one time, architectural, engineering, and construction (AEC) technologies such as a method to design and build an invincible fortress or a method to produce geometrically accurate drawings were regarded as the state-of-the-art technology or sometimes a nation's top secrets. However, the AEC industry these days is a beneficiary of advanced technologies developed in other industries, and it is losing its impact as a technology leader. The DDP project, in the area of BIM to fabrication technology, shows the possibility of the AEC industry becoming a technology leader with advances and increasing demand for 3D printing, 3D scanning, and other BIM and construction-automation-related technologies.

Acknowledgments

The authors wish to acknowledge and thank the DDP project team, including the City of Seoul, ZHA, Samoo, Samsung C&T, GT Korea, Kunwon Engineering, GTS, Heerim CM, Iljin Aluminum, SteelLife, and Steel E&C for their support and help.

10.5   SAINT JOSEPH HOSPITAL, DENVER
BIM Enables Speed and Quality through Prefabrication Solution

Opened to its first patient on December 13, 2014, the new Saint Joseph hospital is a model for the future of healthcare, with increased outpatient focus and the efficiency to help lower escalating operating costs. The new 77,233 gross m² (831,327 gross sf) hospital includes 365 patient rooms, 42 emergency room beds, five fast-track emergency room beds, 21 operating rooms, including two hybrids, two robotic surgery suites, two parking garages, food service/support areas, labs, laundry, a helipad, and a chapel. See Figure 10–5–1.

The $623 million project (total project costs) included construction of the new hospital for $389 million along with associated demolition of the existing hospital, which brought Mortenson's total construction contract to $405 million. Building a large hospital in a dense urban location presented numerous challenges on its own, yet the daunting challenge on the new Saint Joseph Hospital—to build this very large and complex project in 30 months—created extra pressures for the design and construction team. The project, a replacement hospital for an existing facility adjacent to the new site, had to go "beyond fast-track" to "psycho track," according to Rob Davidson, principal for H+L Architecture, one of three architectural firms that led the design team.

The project's schedule was driven by regulatory deadlines that required the new hospital to be open and operational by January 1, 2015. The first private hospital established in Denver, the original Saint Joseph Hospital was

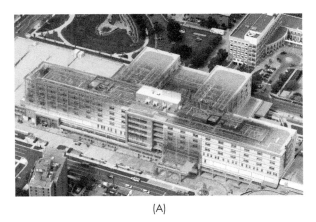
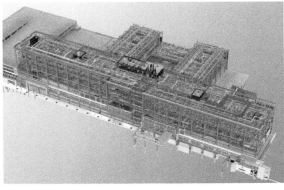

(A)   (B)

FIGURE 10–5–1   (A and B) General view of the hospital project BIM model.

Image courtesy of Mortenson.

founded by four of the Sisters of Charity of Leavenworth who arrived from Kansas with the challenge to provide care to the needy. It had undergone various modernizations and expansions over the years, but the hospital was aging and could no longer meet current code regulations, let alone new ones. "When I got here in January of 2010, the clock was ticking," says Bain Ferris, the CEO (until retirement in 2015) of Saint Joseph Hospital, owned by SCL Health Systems (SCL hereafter).

10.5.1 Organizational Structure and the Collaboration Agreement

A project of this scale and importance required a truly collaborative and integrated project team. Mortenson Construction and the architectural design team, comprised of H+L Architecture, Davis Partnership, and ZGF, along with MEP engineer Cator Ruma & Associates and civil/structural engineer Martin/Martin, came together to set the parameters and expectations of how the teams were going to work together. While the design and construction (CM at Risk) contracts were separate, the entire team created and signed a written collaboration agreement to ensure all parties bought in to the project's guiding principles and customer success factors, and adhered to an integrated project delivery approach. The agreement clearly states the intent: "This Agreement is intended to supplement the Separate Agreements by aligning the Parties and their interests toward achieving a successful Project through integrated project delivery." See Figure 10–5–2.

FIGURE 10–5–2   The organizational structure bound by the collaboration agreement.

Image courtesy of Mortenson.

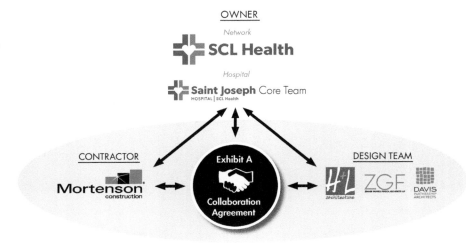

Goals of the Collaboration Agreement

Involve the parties early in the project.
Create alignment of the parties toward common goals.
Create a culture of cooperation among the parties.
Create an open environment for sharing information.
Integrate leadership early in the decision-making process.
Integrate operation, design, and construction knowledge.

Facilitate construction of the project virtually, before construction of the project physically, through the use of Building Information Modeling ("BIM") tools and other available technologies for design and construction planning, with a focus on:

- Ensuring completeness of documentation
- Reducing redundancy and conflicts
- Improving efficiency, coordination, means, and methods
- Increasing opportunities for the use of prefabrication and off-site construction
- Creating strong relationships to continue through project completion, activation, and warranty

The 18-page collaboration agreement further defined the owner's criteria for success, individual project roles, the purpose of the Project Core Team and Owner Architect Contractor (OAC) teams, and the decision-making processes, including advising trade partners. The written collaboration agreement also outlined the specific responsibilities for managing and communicating the schedule, phases, subphases, and fast-track delivery, as well as the design and construction models. This collaboration agreement helped set the foundation for the BIM Execution Plan and supported the concurrent production capabilities of prefabrication, which required design decisions to be made much earlier than they would have been made in a typical linear process.

10.5.2 The BIM Execution Plan

A detailed BIM Execution Plan was developed based on the goals set in the Collaboration Agreement. The project was "IPD-like" in that all parties participated in the development of the BIM Execution Plan. Because each of the individual entities involved in the collaboration agreement contributed to creating it, there was full buy-in to the rules of the agreement. It was referenced often, especially at the beginning of the project, whenever a potential issue arose and solutions were more easily agreed upon because the entire team was able to say, "We have our name on it."

The BIM Execution Plan required the design and construction teams to update their models as changes were released, and RFIs were answered by their respective contracts with the owner. The team used Revit, Bluebeam, and Box along with estimating software MC2 and Primavera P6 and Synchro scheduling software. Weekly structured upload/download times were scheduled for each design entity to post to a private FTP site, so that everyone knew their responsibility for coordinating their respective scope. "The review process was ongoing, each team checking each other's work as it was released. The collaboration was extensive, and we kept each other in check," said Chris Boal, Integrated Construction Manager for Mortenson's Denver office.

The BIM Execution Plan provided a detailed LOD (Level of Development) with MEAs (Model Element Author) for each scope of work. This was further broken out into multiple drawing work packages that were required as deliverables in order for Mortenson to keep track on the schedule (examples are shown in Figures 10–5–3, 10–5–4, and 10–5–5). The LOD used for this project was based on the AGC and AIA's LOD tables, which followed CSI format.

Multiple Platforms were used for the exchange of information.

- FTP site:
    - The design team posted weekly model updates to a private FTP site provided by the Core & Shell Architect
- Box.com (cloud hosted information):
    - Hosted the "field set" of drawings (most current drawings with RFIs posted) for the entire project team. All stakeholders, from the owner, design team, construction team, and trade partners, to on-site and off-site craft workers, utilized this set day to day.
    - 3D MEP/FP (Mechanical, Electrical, Plumbing/Fire Protection) systems coordination with all affected trade partners.
    - Coordination model posting for project team, especially for use in the field on mobile devices.
    - Prefab warehouse information exchange with site team. Posting the status of prefab elements, and when to expect delivery for on-site installation.

Design Package		Title	BIM Deliverable	Comments
No.	Date			
DP #1		Demolition/ROW/Detention/Utilities	2D and 3D	PDF files and 2D CAD (sheet layout)
DP #2		Shoring & Excavation	2D	PDF files and 2D CAD (sheet layout)
DP #3		Parking Structure	3D**	PDF files and 3D (Civil 3D and/or Revit)
DP #4		Surface Parking	2D	PDF files and 2D CAD (sheet layout)
DP #5a		Hospital Foundations	3D**	PDF files and 3D (Civil 3D and/or Revit)
DP #5b		Hospital Superstructure	3D**	PDF files and 3D (Civil 3D and/or Revit)
DP #6		CUP	3D**	PDF files and 3D (Civil 3D and/or Revit)
DP #7		Hospital Core and Shell	3D**	PDF files and 3D (Civil 3D and/or Revit)
DP #8		Hospital Interiors/Finishes	2D	PDF files and 2D CAD (sheet layout)
DP #9		Demolition of Existing Hospital	2D	PDF files and 2D CAD (sheet layout)

**Provide sheet layouts with the 3D file

FIGURE 10–5–3   BIM Deliverables Schedule: Construction.

Image courtesy of Mortenson.

Design Phase		Title	BIM Deliverable	Comments
Phase	Date			
General Development Plan		GDP Approval	2D	PDF files
Zoning		Zoning Approval	2D	PDF files
Wastewater		Wastewater Plan-Final Review	2D	PDF files
Concept Design		Concept Design Approval	2D and 3D	PDF files, 2D CAD (sheet layout) and 3D (SketchUp model)
Schematic Design		Final SD Submittal	2D and 3D	PDF files, 2D CAD (sheet layout) and 3D (SketchUp, Revit and/or Civil 3D)
Design Development Core/Shell		DD Submittal Core/Shell	2D and 3D	PDF files, 2D CAD (sheet layout) and 3D (SketchUp, Revit and/or Civil 3D)
Design Development Interiors		100% DD Documents	2D and 3D	PDF files, 2D CAD (sheet layout) and 3D (SketchUp, Revit and/or Civil 3D)
Construction Documents		CDs for Summary	3D**	PDF files and 3D (Civil 3D and/or Revit) at each summary package

**Provide sheet layouts with the 3D file

FIGURE 10–5–4   BIM Deliverables Schedule: Design.

Image courtesy of Mortenson.

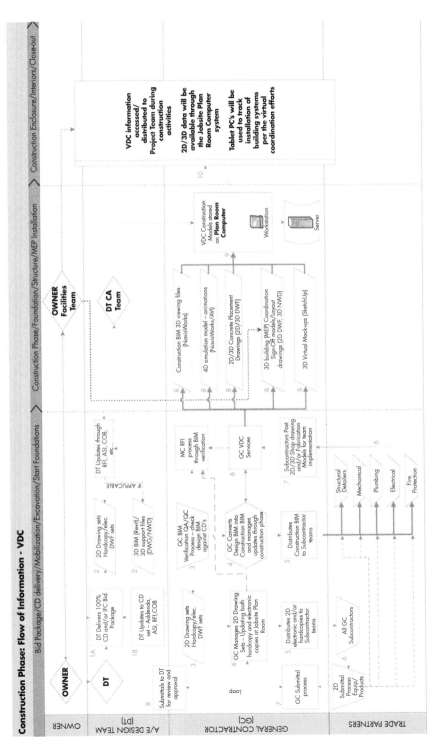

FIGURE 10-5-5 Design Phase and Construction Phase BIM Workflow Diagrams.

Image courtesy of Mortenson.

473

Due to the extensive BIM Execution Planning process, there were no interoperability issues. The BIM Execution Plan allowed the team to agree upon a VDC tool for each scope of work.

The only major obstacles to communication were the issues that are characteristic of trying to get a hospital built in a short amount of time. "We needed information from the design team at a fast pace, and Mortenson was building at the same fast pace, so that constant communication was key," said Boal. "The model was the baseline for every decision. We looked at it and drilled down into it to make quicker decisions. It helped people understand the problem quickly so that we could make a decision quickly. The result was nimbler decision making and subsequent progress in design. The 4D was very useful as a communication tool to the owner, including to the C-level (CEO, chief operating officer, chief nursing officer), to ensure progress was happening as planned and to communicate what decisions needed to be made."

10.5.3   Simulations and Analyses

BIM and VDC processes were used early in the design to verify all design concepts for the owner, including visualizations for city code officials and inspectors, design coordination, and ongoing communication with all project stakeholders throughout the design development process.

Chris Boal, the Integrated Construction Manager, recalled: "The model was used to drive schedule estimates after the baseline schedule was developed in Primavera P6, and we then used Synchro to continue to develop and visualize the 4D schedule. As always, this was incredibly effective to get the entire team to review the schedule from a holistic point of view. Additionally, load calculations were initiated from the model elements to aid in structural analyses. With the team collaborating through models and other VDC tools, in general it reduced the amount of time needed to answer project RFIs, again helping keep the project on track."

10.5.4   BIM Support for Prefabrication

BIM was implemented from the project's start—it was a must to ensure everything was perfectly coordinated to meet the aggressive schedule. The efforts of the VDC Team were also crucial to ensuring that the benefits of the team's BIM expertise transitioned to flawless execution when the team decided to pursue prefabrication on a grand scale, which was likely the most impactful solution to meet the requirement to complete this 77,233 gross m^2 (831,327 gross sf) hospital in just 30 months. Though prefabrication is not a new concept, the continued progression of detailed building information modeling and virtual design and construction expertise have enabled important advances in its implementation. The biggest opportunities for repetitive prefabrication strategies on the Saint Joseph Hospital included exterior panel systems, multitrade racks (MTRs), patient room head walls, bathroom pods, doors and hardware, and other miscellaneous "kitted" and preassembled components. Early design coordination and decisions were critical to ensure the prefabricated components met the design requirements.

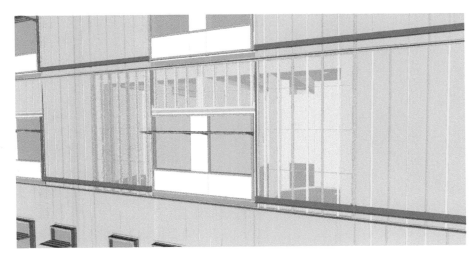

FIGURE 10–5–6 SJHP exterior panel coordination model.

Image courtesy of Mortenson.

Exterior Panels: The BIM was instrumental in the entire prefabrication approach of the New Saint Joseph Hospital facades. (See Figure 10–5–6.) The prefabrication strategy included 346 prefabricated enclosure panels with an average size of 30′ × 15′. Panel mock-up production began at a very early stage to allow for a trial assembly and test of the process. The team received valuable feedback to inform the balance of the fabrication and installation process, ensuring success during final installation. These adjustments included:

- Integrating a lifting apparatus into the panels
- Trucking more panels in at a time
- Connection details to the slab/structure
- As-built survey points, recorded after each concrete slab pour, to ensure proper dimensions and fit of each panel

Multitrade Racks: Before the structure reached its fourth story, work began on the assembly of 166, 25-foot, multitrade racks (MTRs) at a leased warehouse about five miles away from the job site. The units included an engineered Unistrut structure containing mechanical piping, HVAC systems that were insulated and labeled, electrical, cable tray, and pneumatic tube systems, which allowed a plug-and-play installation, connecting the racks along patient tower corridors. An MTR mock-up was produced very early on for everyone to evaluate from a design, assembly, quality, and installation point of view, and it proved to be very valuable in informing the final design and construction on all MTRs. (See Figure 10–5–7.)

The MTR mock-up was also used to practice delivery, hoisting, and installation logistics on the project site in advance of production. From this process, the team learned to incorporate pick points and how to properly, but easily, brace the piping systems to secure them for travel.

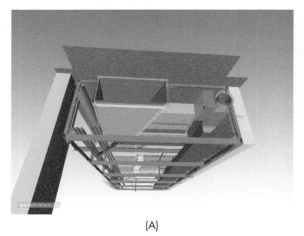

(A)

(B)

FIGURE 10–5–7   (A) BIM model of a multitrade rack. (B) A photograph of the same rack installed in the building.

Image courtesy of Mortenson.

Patient Head Walls: 376 patient head walls were also assembled at the off-site warehouse. Again, virtual and physical mock-ups and BIM and VDC collaboration tools helped ensure these critical patient safety elements came together flawlessly in the field. Testing the head wall approach ahead of time realized significant schedule savings by resolving coordination issues, a specific example being that the medical gas hookups were installed in precisely the right location on the prefabricated head walls. The finished head walls arrived at the site pretested and ready for operation once installed in the patient rooms. Due to the way the team assembled and installed the head walls, the project achieved very high levels of sound reduction on the patient room demising walls; in most cases they tested out to be Sound Transfer Class 55 or greater, which is typically very difficult to achieve in a hospital wall full of pipes, conduits, and back boxes.

Bathroom Pods: Virtual and physical mock-ups also provided solutions for the 440 prefabricated bathroom pods, enabling very efficient production and delivery. For example, after inspection and evaluation of the bathroom pod mock-up, the team realized that the ceiling height on the bathroom pods could be reduced from 275 cm (9′) to 241 cm (7′-11″), enabling more pods to be loaded on a standard semitruck that would be delivering the finished product from Eggrock, the pod manufacturer, resulting in an $111,000 cost savings on the pod transportation alone. This decision did not compromise the design because the owner preferred a lower ceiling height in the bathroom. Another design change that occurred was the removal of the exterior window in the shower due to moisture buildup and maintenance concerns. A more typical, traditional team might have tried to communicate the difficulties of building bathroom systems, along with the maintenance and safety challenges they present "on paper" drawings, but the physical mock-up proved its value. Providing the owner with the opportunity to see the real-life example allowed critical design changes to be made early in the process, before the structure of the building had even started construction.

Thus, prefabrication is yet another example of the benefit of the upfront buy-in of the team to the Collaboration Agreement. The process enabled earlier design decisions and subsequent production on items that would have typically come much later in a linear process.

10.5.5   Ensuring Metrics Help Inform Future Efforts

Expectations of the value and impact from prefabrication have continued to grow as it has become more widely adopted and a wider range of options for standardized products have become available. The team realized the impact that prefabrication would have and wanted to rely on more than anecdotal evidence for the evaluation of that impact. With that goal in mind, Mortenson established a process and provided resources for a professor and student from the University of Colorado to conduct a study of the impact of the prefabricated elements. Overall, the study concluded that for every dollar spent on prefab, approximately $1.13 was returned as a quantifiable benefit to the project. (See Figure 10–5–8.)

Benefit-to-Cost Ratio

= [total direct site-built cost + total indirect schedule cost savings

+ total incident cost avoided] / [total prefab cost]

= 1.13

BENEFIT-TO-COST RATIO

Based on value-based cost-benefit analyses performed on the most significant performance drivers for prefabrication (schedule, cost, and safety), the benefit-to-cost ratio of the project was 1.13. Approximately 13% of every dollar spent on prefabrication was expected to be returned as a quantifiable benefit to the project.

FIGURE 10–5–8   Benefit-to-cost ratios for the four types of prefabricated modules.

Image courtesy of Mortenson.

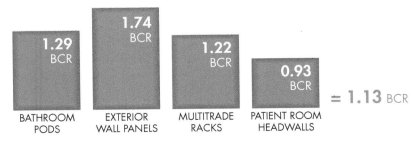

BATHROOM PODS	EXTERIOR WALL PANELS	MULTITRADE RACKS	PATIENT ROOM HEADWALLS
1.29 BCR	1.74 BCR	1.22 BCR	0.93 BCR

≐ 1.13 BCR

Table 10–5–1 Results for Prefabrication of the Different Elements

Prefab Element	Schedule Reduction	Indirect Cost Savings	Direct Cost	Required Labor for Off-site Fabrication	Diverted Labor Off-site	Off-site Prefabrication Safety Incidents*	Job Site Production Loss Prevention
Exterior Wall Panels	41 days	$2.4 M	3.7% saving	5,000 hours	33,000 hours	2 incidents	$0.5 M
Bathroom Pods	52 days	$3.1 M	4.6% increase	27,700 hours	78,000 hours	4 incidents	$1.4 M
Multitrade Racks	20 days	$1.2 M	21.7% increase	NA	24,000 hours	1 incidents	$0.4 M
Patient Room Headwalls	0 days	$0	7.6% increase	1,300 hours	16,000 hours	1 incidents	$0.3 M
Total	72 days	$4.3 M	6.0% increase	29,500 hours	150,500 hours	7 incidents	$2.6 M

*Estimates based on the rate of OSHA-defined safety incidents per labor-hour worked on the project on site and the number of hours diverted off-site.

In addition to the significant quantifiable results shown in Table 10–5–1, the use of prefabrication substantially decreased on-site congestion. Although difficult to put a number on this, it was immediately evident that hallways were less crowded, and there were fewer lifts on the exterior and interior of the building and significantly less material, noise, and dust. The use of prefabrication made the project safer and more predictable. For these reasons, the craft workers were excited to work in both the warehouse and on-site.

The BIM also supported procurement as it was utilized to check quantities for many scopes of work, including structural steel, concrete, mechanical equipment, doors, headwalls, prefab wall panels, and prefab bathroom pods.

10.5.6 Risk and Safety Benefits of BIM and Prefabrication

BIM and prefabrication led to many favorable scenarios that helped reduce risk. For the enclosures, the prefabrication allowed the building enclosure to advance very quickly, enabling interior work to begin in a protected environment, which could not have happened with traditional methods of construction. For the MTRs, the assembly was conducted in a controlled environment at standing level and resulted in a safer and higher quality product with reduced overhead work. For the owner and for the Authorities Having Jurisdiction (AHJs), there was a great benefit to being able to see and inspect the work at "bench height" in the warehouse before the MTRs were hoisted and installed at above-ceiling height. It allowed for quicker inspections as well as better visibility and thus understanding of access to the systems.

For the craft workers, prefabrication of the MTRs became a project perk, as they preferred to work in the controlled environment of the warehouse (most of the assembly occurred through the winter months). The project benefited greatly from the additional safety of being able to do a lot of work at bench height versus working on ladders and lifts. The safety benefits quantified in the prefabrication study showed a total of seven safety incidents were estimated to have been avoided.

10.5.7 BIM in the Field

Models were used extensively in the field to help with on-site coordination. (See Figure 10–5–9.) The craft workers for the MEP/FP subcontractors were required to redline their shop drawings to reflect any deviations to the approved shop drawings. This information was then relayed back to the model detailers to make the revisions and post them for the rest of the team. If any modifications required additional 3D coordination to confirm the system would fit, the team would coordinate immediately and post the information back to the model.

10.5.8 BIM for Facility Management

The owner's FM staff was involved, and as the project progressed, the team held multiple "user group" meetings and used the models to get feedback from the teams that would be working in each department. The owner desired detailed information regarding their MEP/FP systems, including zone shutoff valves for the hydronic systems, AHU (Air Handling Unit) zones, and medical gas shutoff locations.

At the time of the project, SCL investigated whether they had the staff to utilize the model parameter data, and if it would fit into their legacy work order system, so they did not specify asset information handover for facility maintenance at the end of the project. When the contracts were being bought out, the owner requested typical as-built documents, models (Design and Construction), O&Ms, and warranty information. During the project, Mortenson was able to discuss different FM deliverable options within the market with the hope of educating SCL on what was available for them to utilize with their new facility. Mortenson demonstrated the benefits of mobile information in the hands of the FM staff, and how it would increase productivity. It included training on model use, data collection from the model, geolocation of model elements, and how the FM staff could respond to emergencies quickly.

(A)   (B)

FIGURE 10–5–9 (A and B) Using the BIM model in the field.

Photos courtesy of Mortenson and Colorado State University.

10.5.9 Lessons Learned: Best Practices

BIM was used constantly and consistently to explain expected outcomes: from design renderings and enclosure virtual mock-ups to 4D sequence models and 3D phase plans; and from 3D MEP/FP coordination clash detection to operating room (OR) and Lab in-wall system coordination, including headwall coordination. The model was used to explain outcomes throughout the project.

Among the key takeaway lessons from the project:

- Enable/allow the team to contribute to and create their own agreements so that there is full and complete buy-in. This is key to everything going forward.
- Use the right tools and empower users. Innovation breeds innovation, so empower each individual to make his or her own processes better within the team guidelines. This "respect for people's" approach is a baseline Lean principle. To go from 42 to 29.5 months' project duration, the graphics and better visualization were essential.
- Communicate, communicate, communicate: a message that still resonates today. If we can't communicate what our software tools are providing, then those tools lose their usefulness. Communicate to the field, to the executives, to the customers, and to the neighbors.
- Be willing to look beyond tradition. The client and the design team must adjust their conventional approach to the design progression. Decisions often made late in the design process must be considered and locked in place significantly earlier. An example in this case study is that the proposed solution required the designer to make decisions on tile much earlier in the project than they were accustomed to doing. It may be more uncomfortable for some, as they'd typically expect to not have to deal with something like that until much later, but the Collaboration Agreement served as a guidepost to remind the team that they needed these types of decisions earlier, not later. This reflects the earlier accumulation of design information with BIM as illustrated in the MacLeamy curve (see Figure 5-1 in Section 5.2).
- Some of the lessons learned in this project relate directly to prefabrication.
- The decision to pursue prefabrication must be made extremely early and be agreed upon by all major parties. Realistic cost, schedule, safety, and quality expectations should be addressed early. The general contractor and subcontractors must be involved in the earliest possible design phases to steer decisions, take on design responsibility where appropriate, provide constructability input and dictate the content and timing of design packages. The many benefits of prefabrication are significantly reduced the longer the design evolves without prefabrication in mind.
- Repetitive construction should be a strong reason to consider prefabrication as it greatly improves efficiency in a warehouse setting. However,

repetition does not necessarily dictate that prefabrication is the right choice. At a minimum, a detailed cost and schedule analysis should be performed to understand the true impact of each prefabrication assembly.

- Construction scheduling must be looked at through a new lens. Rapid installation of prefabricated assemblies will require multiple successor activities to be accelerated and performed much earlier than usual to avoid vacant areas.
- Before any prefabrication moves into mass production, an intense on-site, full mock-up must be reviewed and 100% functionally tested. Painstaking inspections must be performed as early as possible. Should any quality-related issue arise, the impact is compounded many times due to the rapid production of these assemblies. Any repetitive deficiencies result in costly repairs and have a significant impact on schedule and jobsite morale. Additionally, the cost burden and coordination to correct any mistakes becomes a challenge from a contracting and cost issue standpoint.

Bain Ferris, the client's CEO, had this to say about the project and the role of BIM: "One of the things I asked was, 'Can you get this project done in this time frame?' Their (Mortenson's) answer was, 'We can, if you can make decisions. So, I'd ask if there was a decision that needed to be made, that we get it a week ahead and if the question was formed correctly, we'd make the decision and we have. And that's a real partnership. Mortenson was disciplined about their 4D model and their process and how to manage the process."

Acknowledgments
This case study was prepared with the close collaboration of Nancy Kristof and Chris Boal at Mortenson. We are indebted to them and to all of the exceptional people at Mortenson who contributed to this project and to this case study, and to Matt Morris and his colleagues at Colorado State University.

Online Sources
Project prefab video links:

- www.youtube.com/watch?v=cbKIOHrYSWM
- www.youtube.com/watch?v=EER_Qkr1qTU
- www.youtube.com/watch?v=yiT8oGR4YSc
- http://mortenson.strxur.com/owner-and-gc-talk-transparency-and-tools/
- www.bluebeam.com/us/solutions/case-studies/mortenson-video.asp
- www.usengineering.com/portfolio-item/exempla-saint-joseph-hospital-heritage-project-denver-co/

10.6   VICTORIA STATION, LONDON UNDERGROUND

This case study demonstrates the use of Building Information Modeling (BIM) along with digital engineering on London Underground's Victoria Station Upgrade Project (VSU). It highlights the positive impact that BIM and technology has had on a project that used it from the earliest opportunity. Adopting BIM on a project with significant engineering challenges resulted in the use of an extreme jet grouting ground treatment solution that was managed and constructed virtually before being physically constructed using the data-rich information model.

10.6.1   History

Victoria mainline station is the second busiest railway terminus in London and dates from the 1860s (Figure 10–6–1). Victoria Station is a major commuter hub and serves south London and the south of England as well as passengers traveling by train to and from Gatwick Airport. There are two connected

FIGURE 10–6–1   A historical image of Victoria Mainline Station.

Image courtesy of Taylor Woodrow BAM Nuttall (TWBM).

London Underground stations at Victoria, which were built more than a century apart, with what is now the District & Circle line station opening in 1868, and then the Victoria line station opening in 1969.

The District line part of the underground station opened on December 24, 1868, when the Metropolitan District Railway (MDR, now known as the District Line) opened the first section of its line between South Kensington and Westminster stations. The MDR connected to the Metropolitan Railway (later the Metropolitan line) at South Kensington. The line was originally operated by steam locomotives, creating the necessity to leave periodical gaps in the tunnel roof open to the air for ventilation, before being electrified in 1902–3. The new Victoria underground station opened on March 7, 1969, when the third phase of the line began operating south of Warren Street. Victoria served as the temporary terminus of the line while the final phase was under construction to Brixton.

10.6.2 The Project

At Victoria Underground Station, the passenger demand is anticipated to continue to grow from 82m passengers per annum in 2006 to 100m in 2020. This will result in more frequent and longer station and ticket hall closures at peak times in order to provide crowd control. In 2013, with new trains and improved signaling, the timetable was revised, which increased the number of trains per hour from 28 to 33. The resulting increase in capacity only served to add to the likelihood of passenger congestion. By 2020 it was predicted that the station would need to be closed for more than half of the daily peak hour in order to ensure the safety of passengers and smooth running of the services.

Congestion at Victoria Station (Figure 10–6–2) is not a new phenomenon, and a minor interchange scheme was implemented in 1989 to deal with the

(A)

(B)

FIGURE 10–6–2 (A and B) Congestion at Victoria Station.

Image courtesy of Taylor Woodrow BAM Nuttall (TWBM).

problem. That scheme introduced an additional interchange staircase between the District & Circle platforms and Victoria lines and provided an extension of the lower concourse. Previous options for easing the congestion at Victoria Station included adding a new running tunnel with greater platform capacity and providing an additional escalator to the existing platforms, but this could only be achieved by extending the platforms by 30 m. Both of these options were rejected due to the potential for cost and disruption issues.

A third option looked at a phased incremental approach, devised in conjunction with Land Securities as part of their major retail and commercial development on the northern side of Victoria Street. The scope of the phased approach included the following:

- Build a new ticket hall to the north with step free access to the Victoria Line.
- Connect the interchange concourse at subsurface level with step-free access to the District & Circle lines and better eastbound interchange.
- Add escalator capacity from the existing Victoria Station ticket hall to the interchange concourse, and enlarge the existing Victoria Station ticket hall with better westbound interchange.

These points formed the basis of the proposed upgrade.

The scheme settled on a new ticket hall and a new entrance to be built on Bressenden Place on the north side of Victoria Street with escalator and step free links down to the far north end of the Victoria line to link the platform tunnels, the South ticket hall, and the District & Circle ticket hall with new passenger tunnels (Figures 10–6–3 and 10–6–4). Step-free access will be provided by eight new lifts. The new Bressenden Place entrance will extract around 40% of customers from the existing ticket hall to be nearer the offices and shops of

FIGURE 10–6–3 The new entrance in Bressenden Place.

Image courtesy of Taylor Woodrow BAM Nuttall (TWBM).

FIGURE 10–6–4 The new ticket hall.

Image courtesy of Taylor Woodrow BAM Nuttall (TWBM).

Victoria Street, saving around seven minutes on-street journey time compared to their current journey from the existing south ticket hall. The project is due for completion in 2018, and the construction cost is £510 million. When the station upgrade is completed, the project will have delivered:

- nine new escalators
- eight new lifts
- 280 m of new tunnels
- 20 new ticket gates
- one new ticket hall
- one enlarged ticket hall
- three new entrances

To construct the new station in one of the busiest areas of London, the construction team will have created 280 m of new tunnels and used:

- 930 piles (the deepest being 50 m and the largest diameter pile 2,100 mm)
- 23,000 m³ of reinforced concrete
- 50,000 m³ of spoil removal
- 2,700 interlocking jet grout columns

The new tunnels vary in diameter from 4.5 m to 9.0 m, and the new ticket hall boxes are up to 15 m deep. When finally completed in 2018, the project will have taken 6 ½ years to construct.

The junction of Wilton Road and Victoria Street is a major road and pedestrian traffic thoroughfare in this area of London. It was important that the level of disruption caused by the construction be kept to a minimum and in

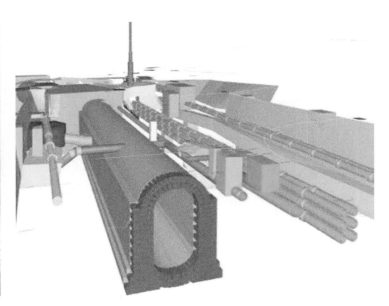

FIGURE 10–6–5 The exposed existing Victorian sewer and other buried utilities. These utilities were laser scanned and then modeled and put into the 3D model.

Image courtesy of Taylor Woodrow BAM Nuttall (TWBM).

order to achieve this, the project team decided on a top-down construction process. The construction site is very congested with a number of major existing infrastructure elements to consider including pipelines, sewers, power, and communication cables that needed to be avoided or diverted (Figure 10–6–5).

Construction of the new ticket hall box and tunnels took place beneath the foundations of a number of existing buildings. Three of these buildings—the Victoria Place Theatre, Apollo Theatre, and National Rail Station north façade—are listed by National Heritage as having national special architectural or historic interest. There are significant constraints on any structural change or construction activity that would impact a listed building. The St. Stephens Tower miniature, or "Little Ben," on the traffic island at the junction of Victoria Street and Vauxhall Bridge Road, is also listed and required special consideration, planning, and approval regarding the works.

The secant piles that form the new walls of the Bressenden ticket hall are located within 3 m of an existing Victorian brick culvert that carries the River Tyburn. The new passenger tunnel that links the new ticket hall to the Victoria line passes under the culvert and over the southbound Victoria line running tunnel. Tolerance was a huge consideration in the design because the new escalator tunnel fits in between the two Victoria line platform tunnels with a meagre 300 mm to spare. Managing tight tolerances and clearances between the existing and new structures was essential to safe and successful delivery of the project.

Due to the complexity of the existing site and of the resulting project required to deliver the solutions, it was decided at a very early stage to use BIM. The project team created an information model incorporating detailed 3D laser scan surveys of the existing assets and utilized 3D digital engineering tools to manipulate and visualize data about the asset and the construction site. Collaborative working was seen as essential to facilitate high-quality designs and reduce risk. This was achieved through the use of a common data environment by the contractor, subcontractors, and client.

10.6.3 Engineering Challenges

The existing tunnels at Victoria Station are shallow: the crown of the District & Circle lines are 2.5 m below the surface and the crown of Victoria line tunnels are approximately 14 m below ground level. The existing ground conditions in which the new tunnels were to be constructed are formed of made ground sitting on London clay, which overlies water-bearing terrace gravels. In order to prevent any disturbance to the existing tunnels and surrounding buildings during the excavation on the new tunnels, the ground had to be stabilized. The ground treatment process chosen to stabilize the clay and the gravels was jet grouting (Figure 10–6–6).

The process of jet grouting involves inserting a hollow drill bit into the ground and injecting cement grout at pressure so that it mixes with surrounding

(A) (B)

FIGURE 10–6–6 (A and B) Jet grouting at Victoria.

Image courtesy of Taylor Woodrow BAM Nuttall (TWBM).

material, the objective being to create a stable concrete mass through which to safely construct the new tunnels. An additional benefit is that the concrete mass would also create an impermeable barrier to keep the new works dry.

Jet grout concrete columns are 1.6 m in diameter, each column overlapping with its neighbors by a minimum of 150 mm, with close control of the dimensions and location. The resultant is a mass of interlocking weak concrete columns. To ensure the required coverage was achieved, jet grout columns of diameters of 1.4 m and 1.8 m were also used. In all, a total of 2,700 jet grout columns were constructed.

Two major general contractors, Taylor Woodrow and BAM Nuttall, formed a joint venture (TWBN), and they delivered the project under an NEC Option C[1] design and construct contract with shared gain/pain. Mott MacDonald, a multidisciplinary engineering, management, and development services consultancy, developed London Underground's (LU) concept design, helped steer the project through the statutory Transport & Works Act processes, and is now working as the designer for TWBN.

LU completed the site acquisition in March 2011, and site preparation began in summer 2011. The sprayed concrete lining (SCL) tunneling started in summer 2012 adjacent to the North ticket hall and advanced southward. Work on the South ticket hall began in October 2012. The new North ticket hall opened on January 25, 2018. At the time of writing, the project as a whole was due to be completed by the summer of 2018.

10.6.4 The Role of BIM

To manage the daunting challenges and risks of the Victoria Station Upgrade (VSU), the project team used Building Information Modeling (BIM) on a scale that was unprecedented in the UK when work commenced in 2006. Up until that point BIM had only been used for smaller and simpler construction projects. BIM focuses on the creation and use of an information model of the physical asset and is a process that incorporates 3D design, simulation and analysis, quantity surveying, and a host of other tools. A key aspect of BIM is enabling more collaborative ways of working through the requirement for a Common Data Environment, which provides a platform for creation, management, and exchange of information across the project team. London Underground (LU) initiated this approach because without a spatially accurate, fully coordinated 3D model, it would have been very difficult to visualize and coordinate the project. (See Figure 10–6–7.)

When design got underway in 2006, BIM was very much in its infancy in the UK with the BS1192 Standard not yet published. VSU pushed the use of BIM far beyond anything previously attempted in the UK and set standards

---

[1] Option C is a target cost contract from the NEC family of construction contracts, with an activity schedule where the outturn financial risks are shared between the client and the contractor in an agreed proportion. www.neccontract.com/Products/Contracts/Engineering-Construction-Contract/NEC3-Engineering-and-Construction-Contract-ECC-/NEC3-Engineering-and-Construction-Contract-Option-1

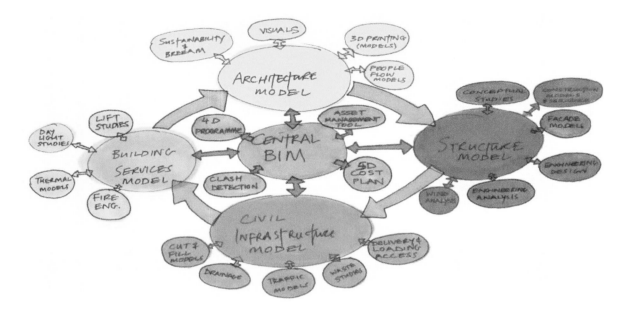

FIGURE 10-6-7   The BIM concept.

Image courtesy of Taylor Woodrow BAM Nuttall (TWBM).

internationally. Use of BIM on the project predated the Government Construction Strategy. Indeed, VSU was a reference point during development of the strategy and remains an exemplar in terms of information model maturity. Lessons learned and benefits realized have influenced the BIM strategies for other major infrastructure projects like Crossrail and the Transport for London Bank Station Capacity Upgrade.

The VSU information model incorporated 18 discrete design disciplines and provided a clear understanding for all parties as to how the entire project would fit together. Although predating BS1192:2007, the BIM working process was built around:

- collaboration between the client and the project supply chain
- a single, unified system for data creation, management, and sharing
- a coordinated information model

To maximize interoperability between disciplines, the project used Bentley Systems ProjectWise as the preferred collaboration software wherever possible. The ProjectWise system was supplied by Mott MacDonald, who were responsible for managing the CAD data and the BIM process between the multidisciplinary design teams and the client. WAN access was also available for remote design team members who required access to the data.

Mott MacDonald, and later Taylor Woodrow Bam Nuttall, used Bentley Triforma and Bentley AECOsim to create the 3D models from the VSU information model. London Underground use London Survey Grid (LSG) as their preferred coordinate system, which takes into consideration the curvature of the earth. When dealing with a large linear asset such as a railway, using this type of system is critical when dimensioning because the error between the flat Ordnance Survey coordinates and the curved LSG coordinates will become greater as the distances increase. The Bentley suite of programs was selected because of the in-built coordinate systems within the software, which enabled the team to work easily with the more accurate LSG system.

3D and animated PDFs extracted from the information and 3D models were used for communications across the design team, which removed the need for engineers to be trained in CAD platforms. This reduced the number of face-to-face meetings and the number of hard copies required and therefore saved time and money. The PDFs were also an essential tool in making information accessible to nontechnical stakeholders.

Location of the planned work in a heavily built-up and congested part of London introduced restrictions in size of the construction site. The ability to prefabricate became essential to the construction strategy of the project. The use of BIM processes on the project allowed the design team to develop a high level of confidence in the quality of the data produced that underpinned the VSU information model. Consistent ways of working and improved collaboration provided the assurance needed that design was fully space-proofed to enable the offsite fabrication.

Finite Element Analysis programs, such as STAAD and Hevacomp, used data directly from the model, and there were bidirectional design processes in place to assist the design workflow. This enabled the engineers to use the model data, perform their engineering design tasks, and then input the revised design directly back into the model. This resulted in reductions in time taken for the design tasks and made information available more quickly to the project team members.

BIM and Jet Grouting. The scale of jet grouting on VSU was unprecedented in the UK; it was the first use of jet grouting in conjunction with sprayed concrete lined (SCL) tunneling. The VSU information model was data rich from the collated survey and geological data, and several 3D models were created to inform, design, plan, and validate the jet grouting process. Each SCL tunnel was first created virtually, and this helped the team to identify gaps within the grout columns ahead of commencement of works (Figure 10–6–8 and 10–6–9). The 3D models also showed untreated zones within the jet grouting, obstructions in the tunnel face, and any anomalies in geology. This helped the team to decide on critical remedial measures before the start of tunneling.

BIM was used to virtually plan the coordination, position, and orientation of the 2,700 jet grout columns. A unique identification code was assigned to each of the columns in the model (Figure 10–6–10). The unique identification code aided the construction sequencing and enabled the works team to identify and ensure that the orientation and position of every jet grout was correct.

3D "as-built" risk reduction model

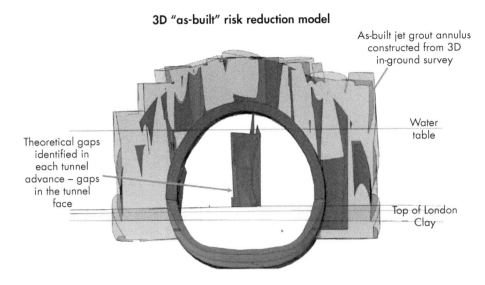

As-built jet grout annulus constructed from 3D in-ground survey

Water table

Theoretical gaps identified in each tunnel advance – gaps in the tunnel face

Top of London Clay

FIGURE 10–6–8   A gap highlighted in the 3D model between the jet grouts.

Image courtesy of Taylor Woodrow BAM Nuttall (TWBM).

Actual gaps in the tunnel face

FIGURE 10–6–9   The same area of the jet grouting during excavation.

Image courtesy of Taylor Woodrow BAM Nuttall (TWBM).

Using BIM allowed the design team to manage risks. For example, the 3D model allowed 2D extraction of the columns to run engineering overlap checks and acted as a visual representation of potential problems (Figure 10–6–11). The information model was used to perform a reverse "clash detection" process, ensuring that there were no voids within the consolidated ground that may have compromised constructing the tunnels (i.e., water ingress into the works).

The ground treatment contractor, Keller, identified that the grouting rigs on-site could use the location/angle/depth data directly from the 3D model. (See Figure 10–6–12.) The normal failure rate for jet grouting is 5–10%; on VSU only two columns had to be redrilled, representing failure rate of 0.00074%.

FIGURE 10–6–10   Unique ID codes for all the jet grouts.

Image courtesy of Taylor Woodrow BAM Nuttall (TWBM).

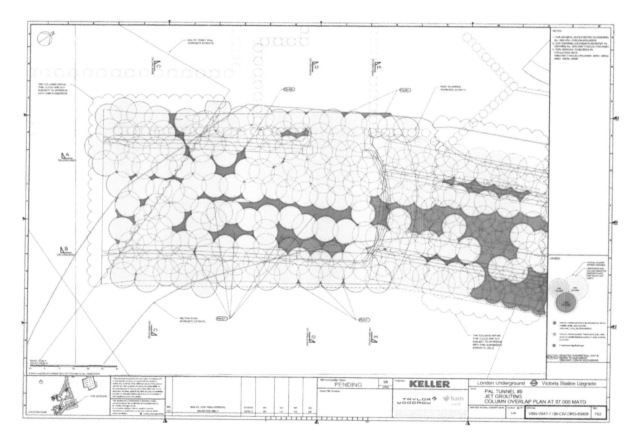

FIGURE 10–6–11   A 2D section cut highlighting areas over jet grout overlap and potential areas for concern.

Image courtesy of Taylor Woodrow BAM Nuttall (TWBM).

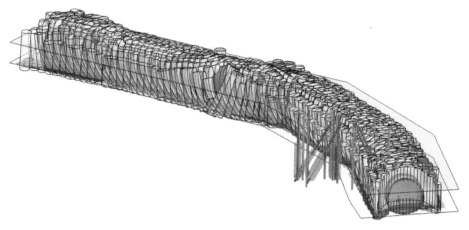

FIGURE 10–6–12 The full extent of the jet grouting around the proposed tunnel.

Image courtesy of Taylor Woodrow BAM Nuttall (TWBM).

By employing BIM to support the jet grouting process, the project avoided potential costs of up to £4 million.

The levels of improved accuracy, efficiency, and mitigation of risk have led Keller to now apply the same technology and approach on other projects. Through embracing BIM, Keller have demonstrated that it is practical for subcontractors to rapidly develop the level of BIM maturity needed to achieve government efficiency targets set for all centrally funded capital programs and projects.

Further Uses of BIM. Another area where BIM played a key role was the construction of the District & Circle line underpass. The project required a tunnel to be constructed under the existing District & Circle brick arch tunnel. The issue with the construction was the lack of space to construct a conventional tunnel below the existing brick arch tunnel, and the preferred design solution selected was to construct a concrete box underpass.

Taylor Woodrow Bam Nuttall Joint Venture (TWBN) was responsible for the delivery of the District & Circle underpass. The slab was cast during a six-day window between Christmas and New Year's Eve 2014. This required an extended possession of the railway in order to minimize the impact to the traveling public. This slab formed the roof of the underpass for the Paid Access Link tunnels (PALs).

The railway had to be reopened by New Year's Eve, which is one of the London Underground network's busiest periods during the entire year. TWBN produced a 4D sequencing model to ensure that the works could be completed in the allotted time frame and make the construction teams familiar with the tasks required to complete the works. The works were completed, and the railway was reinstated, tested, and handed back to London Underground on December 30, 10hrs 45min earlier than the critical cutoff time of 01:00 on New Year's Eve.

Pedestrian modeling of the existing, temporary, and new station layouts was used prior to construction to ensure that there were no areas of congestion

FIGURE 10–6–13 Legion model of the extended south ticket hall.

Image courtesy of Taylor Woodrow BAM Nuttall (TWBM).

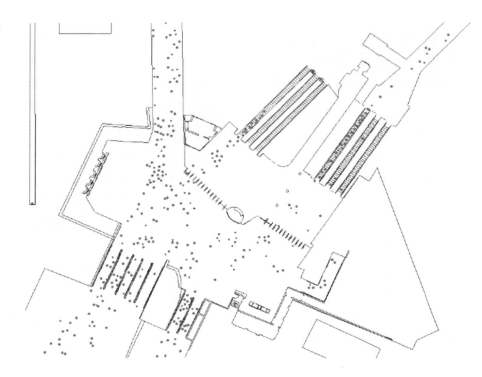

within the station during the construction phase of the works. Due to the nature of the project, some areas of the existing station had to be closed while works were carried out, while ensuring that the passenger flows were kept moving at a desired rate. To do this London Underground used Legion modeling software (www.legion.com) with data from the VSU information model to predict passenger movements within the station. Within the Legion model, varying numbers of passengers can be added, and the virtual passengers can be assigned different behaviors to make the computer simulation as realistic as possible. The model is used to highlight areas of congestion during different scenarios: fire evacuation, escalator/lift replacement, and so on. (See Figure 10–6–13.)

The model was also used to show contractors the sequencing of works within the Bressenden entrance plant room (Figure 10–6–14). The plant room is very congested, and the equipment had to be installed in a particular sequence to ensure the plant room was completed with no clashes on-site and within the program timeframe.

There were a number of difficult interfaces for the project team to engineer within the project, particularly where sprayed concrete lining tunneling interfaced with the more traditional methods of mining such as squareworks. One of these interfaces was around Shaft No.2 near the Bressenden Place entrance, shown in Figure 10–6–15. Modeling these interfaces in 3D enabled the project team to confidently make design decisions based on the 3D data within the information model, as the model allowed the interface to be viewed from every

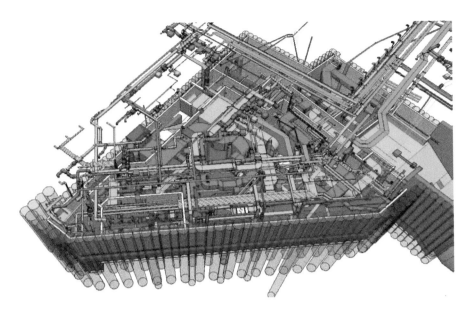

FIGURE 10–6–14
Bressenden Place entrance plant room.

Image courtesy of Taylor Woodrow BAM Nuttall (TWBM).

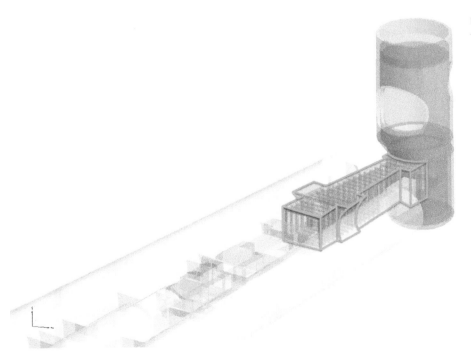

FIGURE 10–6–15 The vertical Shaft No.2 interfacing with the squareworks tunnel (highlighted in blue).

Image courtesy of Taylor Woodrow BAM Nuttall (TWBM).

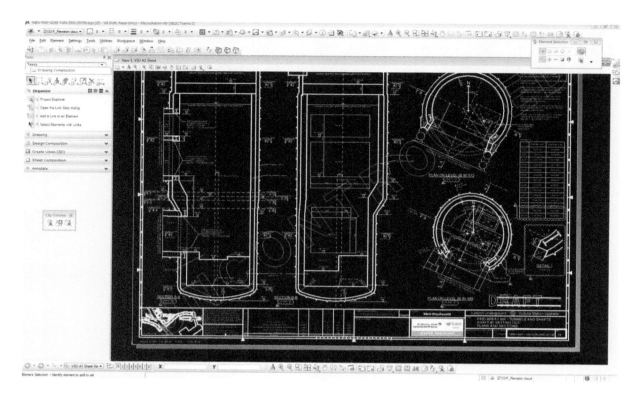

FIGURE 10–6–16   CAD drawing of Shaft No.2 created from the model.

Image courtesy of Taylor Woodrow BAM Nuttall (TWBM).

conceivable angle, and therefore there were no surprises when they started to construct the tunnels. TWBN also produced a 4D model of this area to clarify the sequence of works and ensure that the correct tunnel rings were delivered to the work site as and when required; this was key as the vertical Shaft No.2 had to fit within the two Victoria Line running tunnels.

The VSU information model was also used to support engagement with stakeholders and the public. The design team had a 3D print produced, which gave access and understanding to a large number of stakeholders who would otherwise have struggled with traditional engineering drawings and information formats (Figures 10–6–16 and 10–6–17). The team also procured a holographic print of the completed station with the surrounding buildings (Figure 10–6–18), once again to give stakeholders a 3D view of the project. Using the 3D print and the hologram improved the projects team's ability to communicate the design and construction intentions to a wide audience. This contributed to timely feedback and modification if required, avoiding any potential cost and delay associated with changes further down the project program.

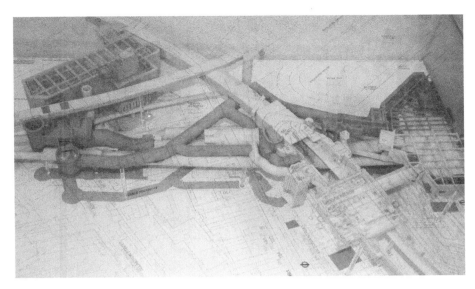

FIGURE 10–6–17 3D print of Victoria Station Upgrade.

Image courtesy of Taylor Woodrow BAM Nuttall (TWBM).

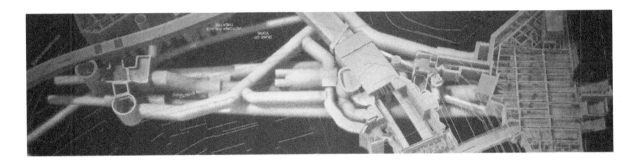

FIGURE 10–6–18   Holographic print of Victoria Station Upgrade.

Image courtesy of Taylor Woodrow BAM Nuttall (TWBM).

10.6.5 BIM Benefits to the Project

As the project moved towards completion in 2018, the richness of the information contained within the VSU model was improving from being based on data from the "as designed" state to the "as-built" state. During the construction phase, the model enabled Taylor Woodrow Bam Nuttall (TWBN) to understand and resolve issues on-site earlier and more easily than would have otherwise have been possible.

The model has enabled TWBN to check the as-built works against specifications and validate any anomalies. The data within the single integrated model matured as the project progressed and supported the continuous review and testing of the design for constructability throughout the design and construction process. In 2018, the as-built information model will be handed over to London Underground at the completion of the works to be used to maintain and operate the asset.

The use of BIM model coordinates feeding directly into the jet grouting rigs improved the accuracy level up to a new level. This alone saved the project approximately £4 M and several days in program by not having to redrill some 270 additional jet grouts.

Using 4D technology was extremely beneficial to aid the project teams in understanding how particularly complex areas of the project are to be constructed. This enabled the team to build and rebuild these areas in a virtual environment to find the optimum safe method and effective sequence of works to deliver the project.

Faster, more accurate design was enabled through applying BIM to VSU. Availability of a single and accurate information model helped deliver time and cost savings by allowing checks for structural, architectural, and building services clashes within the model prior to any construction activities taking place. An example of time saving was on the design of the ticket halls where, if the architect revised the location of an opening within a slab, the engineer would normally have needed to recalculate the load paths and, if necessary, any additional reinforcement required. The use of Finite Element Analysis software with its bidirectional link to the VSU information model meant that the load paths and reinforcement areas were automatically calculated.

Finally, Keller (the ground treatment contractor) understood the benefits of BIM by seeing improvements in accuracy, efficiency, and mitigation of risk on VSU. They subsequently committed their organization to embracing BIM and became BIM Level 2 compliant within two years. This demonstrates to all contractors and subcontractors that BIM is worth a look.

10.6.6 Postscript

"There are known knowns; that is to say there are things we know we know.

We also know there are known unknowns; that is to say we know there are some things we do not know.

But there are also unknown unknowns—the ones we don't know we don't know."

BIM allows us to model what we know we know.

BIM allows us to prepare for what we know we don't know.

BIM allows us to react to what we don't know we don't know.

Acknowledgments

The Victoria Station Upgrade case study was prepared by Meir Katz, a Technion graduate student; and Steve Wright and Paul Carr of Transport for London. The authors are very grateful for their cooperation and contribution. The postscript paraphrases a quotation by Donald Rumsfeld, 2002.

10.7 NANYANG TECHNOLOGICAL UNIVERSITY STUDENT RESIDENCE HALLS, SINGAPORE
Building Information Modeling (BIM) for High-Rise Prefinished Prefabricated Volumetric Construction (PPVC) in Singapore

10.7.1 Introduction

The new Student Residence Halls at the Nanyang Technological University (NTU), Singapore, were built through the integration of Building Information Modeling (BIM) and Prefinished Prefabricated Volumetric Construction (PPVC) technologies. This case study describes the philosophy, principles, techniques, and practical applications of utilizing BIM for PPVC in this project.

Singapore's productivity in the construction sector has improved to achieve the target productivity improvement of 2% to 3% per annum, and the Building and Construction Authority (BCA) of Singapore is continually looking for ways to achieve higher productivity gains. To that end, BCA promotes prefabrication and assists and encourages the private sector by giving grants through diverse incentive schemes. As a result, the Singapore construction industry is experiencing an evolution of building construction methods using new productive technologies such as Design for Manufacture and Assembly (DfMA). DfMA is an approach to design that focuses on ease of manufacture (off-site) and efficiency of assembly (on-site), which coincides with BCA's plan to raise construction productivity, reduce its reliance on foreign labor, and provide a safer work environment at construction sites.

A DfMA solution begins by understanding the end product, the site constraints, and key drivers. The PPVC technique represents a very attractive DfMA solution and is considered to be a new productive game-changing construction technology. For PPVC, modules complete with internal finishes, fixtures, and fittings are manufactured in factories, and then transported to construction sites for installation in a Lego-like manner. BCA has also set in place policies and strategies for adoption of BIM, as an advanced information technology and a key tool for Virtual Design and Construction (VDC) to be used throughout the construction process.

10.7.2 Project Overview

The Nanyang Technological University (NTU), represented by the NTU Office of Development & Facilities Management (ODFM), decided to use Prefinished Prefabricated Volumetric Construction (PPVC) for its new development of a 1,673-unit student hostel and apartment accommodation located along the Nanyang Crescent-North Hill, Singapore. Construction commenced in June 2014 with a planned duration of 26 months; construction took approximately 19 months, costing a total of about S$196 million.

FIGURE 10–7–1   A typical steel PPVC module.

Image courtesy of Moderna Homes Pte Ltd.

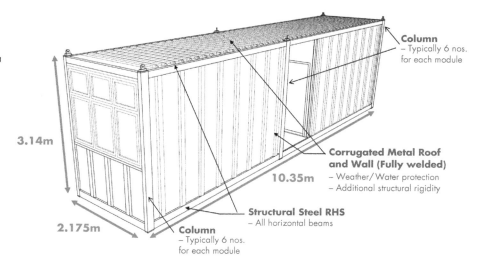

The project site layout consists of six blocks of student hostel units, a multipurpose hall, and one carpark. Each block has 13 stories with communal facilities. The total gross floor area (GFA) of the entire development is approximately 54,000 m², 29,400 m² of which are PPVC modules (approximately 60% PPVC). There are 1,213 steel modules, 11 structural modules, and 40 architectural (single- and double-occupancy) modules, with typical dimensions of 2.175 m width, 10.35 m length, and 3.14 m height. Typical story height is 3.15 m and internal ceiling height is 2.75 m. The total estimated tonnage is 4,442 tons. Modules were prefabricated off-site with a certain level of furnishing and then transported to site for installation. Figure 10–7–1 shows the components of a typical Steel PPVC Module.

Three high-capacity tower cranes were deployed for this project. The tower cranes had a 24-ton tip load lifting capacity at 24 m radius; each architectural PPVC module typically weighed 8 to 21 tons, while smaller modules weighed approximately 6 to 8 tons. The 1st to the 4th–5th stories were built using conventional reinforced concrete (RC) construction comprising the podium levels, dining hall, shops, meeting rooms, and cultural dance rooms. PPVC modules were installed above the 4th–5th story, but the core walls were built using reinforced concrete. Figure 10–7–2 shows the integration of conventional construction for podium and PPVC for tower as the typology for a typical building in the project. The figure illustrates the following details:

- Conventional construction of podium floors to handle sloping terrain at site
- Transfer slab between conventional construction and steel PPVC modules
- Centralized conventional construction services and circulation cores for lateral stability of PPVC modules

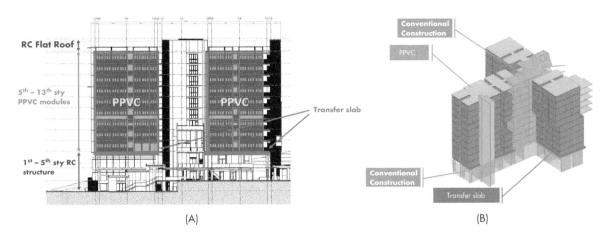

FIGURE 10–7–2 Integration of PPVC with conventional construction (hybrid approach of PPVC and cast in-situ works). (A) Elevation view. (B) 3D view.

(A) Image courtesy of Moderna Homes Pte Ltd). (B) Image courtesy of P & T Consultants Pte Ltd.

Initially, at the start of the Design Phase, the project was planned to be built using the conventional cast-in-situ construction methods, but a few months into the Design Phase, with NTU's support and after further evaluation and planning, the project adopted PPVC technology. The motivation to change from conventional to PPVC was NTU-ODFM's understanding of BCA's push for adoption of game-changing construction technologies to raise productivity and the university's willingness to assist the government in its national productivity agenda. As the leading technological university, NTU decided to adopt the challenge and be the first of the early adopters of PPVC in the design and construction of the Residential Halls at North Hill. Design planning was done with clear demarcation of PPVC and conventional construction to facilitate separation of contract packages.

According to BCA Regulations in 2013–2014, all new developments with a gross floor area in excess of 20,000 m² were required to use BIM for architectural submission, while use of BIM in mechanical and electrical (M&E) and civil and structure (C&S) was voluntary. On this basis, BIM was used from the beginning of the project, primarily to comply with the regulations.

While the benefits of using BIM and PPVC independently are striking, more benefits were reaped by using BIM for PPVC. Taking into consideration key factors such as site constraints, the delivery of the PPVC modules, the client's design brief, the project budget, and the timeline, the team decided right from the start to deploy BIM from design to fabrication to assembly of the PPVC modules. Designing and constructing the PPVC modules with BIM enabled a comprehensive design coordination process and made construction

FIGURE 10–7–3 BIM representation of NTU PPVC project. (A) North perspective view. (B) Bird's-eye view.

Images courtesy of P & T Consultants Pte Ltd.

(A)

(B)

management more effective. Figure 10–7–3 shows two rendered BIM representations of the NTU PPVC project.

BIM facilitated integration of the different roles/disciplines to enhance coordination and communication. As a consequence, there were fewer errors, greater consistency, and more clarity. The applications of BIM during the four principle stages of PPVC, as observed in the project, are summarized in Figure 10–7–4.

Design
- 3D Visualisation, Site layout Planning, quantity takeoff, Schedule and Cost Planning
- Conflict, Interference and collision detection
- Standardization of BIM Families (BIM library)
- MEP coordination and Fabrication Process

Manufacturing and Assembly
- Generation of detailed shop drawings based on completed BIM model
- Error-free fabrication and assembly of modules

Logistics and Transportation
- Schedule Coordination of the modules
- Tracking of the modules' status
- JIT delivery

Installation
- On-site coordination for modules installation's planning and construction management
- Lay out the modules locations with positioning system and surveying equipment through referencing to BIM model
- Managing and tracking the construction process and progress, Inventory Checking, Quality controlling
- Providing a complete construction schedule for material ordering, fabrication, delivery and on-site installation of each building system

FIGURE 10–7–4 Applications and benefits of BIM in PPVC stages.

10.7.3 Project Organization/Management

Table 10–7–1 lists the project team members and their roles.

10.7.4 PPVC Workflow

Design Stage. Off-site modular construction requires more coordination during design and construction than traditional methods do. Early planning was paramount; one of the reasons for this was because the dimensions of the modules dictated the necessary structural supports. Details such as the exterior finishes, material specifications, and elevations also had to be decided before the modules could be fabricated. Therefore, adoption of PPVC forced the project stakeholders to make decisions as early as possible to reap maximum benefits. The design stage included the following studies:

1. **PPVC feasibility study**, which included layout planning, cost study, project timeline, technical considerations, and site constraints. The key

Table 10–7–1   Project Team

Role	Company Name
Developer/Owner	Nanyang Technological University (NTU), Office of Development and Facilities Management (ODFM)
Architect	P & T Consultant Pte Ltd. with Guida Moseley Brown Architects
Main Contractor	Singapore Piling and Civil Engineering Pte Ltd., BBR
PPVC Specialist	Moderna Homes Pte Ltd.
PPVC Design Engineer	Ronnie & Koh Consultants Pte Ltd.
C&S, M&E Engineer	BECA Carter Hollings & Ferner (S.E. Asia) Pte Ltd.
Quantity Surveyor	Franklin+Andrews Pte Ltd.
Factory (steel chassis production)	• Hsinchu, Taiwan (Chu Rong Steel Industry Co Ltd.), 367 boxes • Zhangjiagang, China (Maristar Container Manufacturing Co Ltd.), 230 boxes • Senai, JB, Malaysia (Kong Hwee Iron Works & Construction (M) SdnBhd), 475 boxes • Loyang Way, Singapore (Technics Steel Pte Ltd.), 132 boxes
Factory (fit-out processes)	• Jln Terusan yard, Singapore • Jurong Port Road yard, Singapore

considerations were: (1) assessment of suitability for PPVC to meet project requirements; (2) consider inherent site constraints; (3) cost analysis with government grants; and (4) considerations on project timeline with probably more deliberate tender evaluation process.

2. **PPVC design planning**, which included demarcating PPVC and non-PPVC construction components, phasing of building developments, project time planning, and packaging of building contracts. The key considerations were: (1) early involvement of approved PPVC specialist; (2) integrating PPVC and non-PPVC; (3) construction sequencing in PPVC on-site installation; and (4) contract packaging and planning to consider architectural and M&E components required at early stages of works due to off-site assembly system.

3. **PPVC concept design**, which included study of modular layout, modular design, and standardized dimensions, building height limitations, and integration with overall design. The key considerations were: (1) optimize/minimize the variations of modular sizes and configurations; (2) layout to consider technical height limit of PPVC; (3) layout with non-PPVC cores for lateral stability, which lead to minimizing additional bracing required for PPVC; and (4) typical module design to incorporate bracing for rigidity of individual boxes for hoisting.

4. **PPVC design development**, which included study of services coordination, structural integration, architectural façade, and cost estimates. The key considerations to note were: (1) early consultation with authorities for atypical design and construction details; (2) effective PPVC design coordination with BIM modeling; (3) design of PPVC modules to maximize off-site automated assembly and minimize onsite subassembly works; and (4) incorporate variations, staggering, subassemblies for unique façade outlook.

Manufacturing and Off-site Fabrication and Assembly Stage. After design finalization, the fabrication drawings and details were sent to the overseas factory (e.g., in Taiwan) for production of the PPVC modules, which included consideration of mechanical and electrical systems. The skeleton boxes were made of galvanized metal (hot-dip galvanized steel structure). Figure 10–7–5 (A to D) shows the process of welding the boxing and bracing plates to form a complete module. Figure 10–7–5 (E) shows the insides of a semi-complete module skeleton. The modules were furnished later at the fit-out yard in Singapore, which was located near the construction site. Once at the fit-out yard, the skeletons were fitted with windows and M&E services. They were clad with a fireboard that is required for fire safety according to Singapore's regulation and code, as shown in Figure 10–7–5 (F), following which the aluminum cladding was applied. The last step in the fit-out yard included tiling and painting of the modules.

Transportation and On-site Delivery Stage. The modules were transported by trailer to the site as needed—in other words, just in time (JIT) delivery. Modules whose width exceeded the limit set in the regulations by the Land Transport Authority (LTA) of Singapore were transported at night. There was a maximum buffer time of 1 night where 3 to 6 modules could be stored in a storage area near to the tower crane on site. However, these modules were immediately installed in the following morning. Figure 10–7–6 (A and B) illustrates transportation from the fit-out yard to the site. The module was temporarily sealed with waterproof material to protect it from weather conditions during transport.

Installation Stage. Once the modules arrived on site, they were connected either vertically or adjacent to one another using nuts and bolts. A small percentage of the finishing works were performed on site to seal the joints between the PPVC modules. Figure 10–7–6 (C and D) illustrates the process of lifting the module for installation while Figure 10–7–6 (D) also shows the completed building after the modules have been installed. There were three high-capacity tower cranes on-site that were used for PPVC installation.

FIGURE 10–7–5 Factory production. (A to D) Welding of boxing plates and bracing plates on to assembled module. (E) Semi-completed module. (F) Installation of fireboard at the fit-out yard.

Photos courtesy of Moderna Homes Pte Ltd.

(A)

(B)

(C)

(D)

(E)

(F)

(A)

(B)

(C)

FIGURE 10–7–6 (A and B) Transportation of a module from fit-out yard to site. (C and D) Lifting and installation of PPVC modules at site, installed modules at site.

Photos courtesy of Singapore Piling & Civil Engineering Pte Ltd., BBR

(D)

Each crane was strategically positioned in such a way that two modules could be hoisted simultaneously (anti-collision of cranes). They were relocated between the blocks under construction.

The number of modules received via shipping ranged from 10 to 24 modules in a day. The fit-out yard produced three to six modules in a day. On-site, a crew of seven workers needed only 40 minutes to install a module and were very comfortable with lifting and installing 6–8 modules in a day. The process of installation starts from installing the first layer of PPVC modules, followed by steps of tightening of bolts, collar plates, waterproofing at joints, and inspection by client and main contractor. After that, the following layers of PPVC modules can be installed.

10.7.5 BIM Implementation

Modularity and repetitive elements of the PPVC modules allowed for parallel design and technical coordination to be performed through BIM, which enabled greater productivity and construction efficiency. The repetitive nature of the elements did not hinder the consultants from designing varied yet functional layouts with the PPVC modules. Figure 10-7-7 illustrates the framework for using BIM for collaboration between different disciplines in this project.

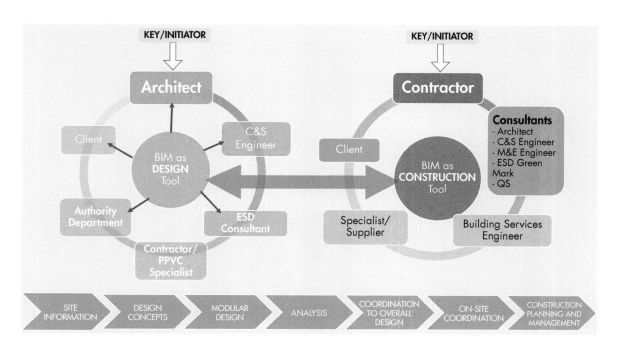

FIGURE 10-7-7 BIM as a tool for collaboration between different disciplines.

Images courtesy of P & T Consultants Pte Ltd.

10.7.6 Parametric PPVC Library

Typical PPVC module designs with different types are shown in Figure 10–7–8.

PPVC modules were about 60% of the overall project scope. The consultants of the project developed a library of parametric BIM families for PPVC

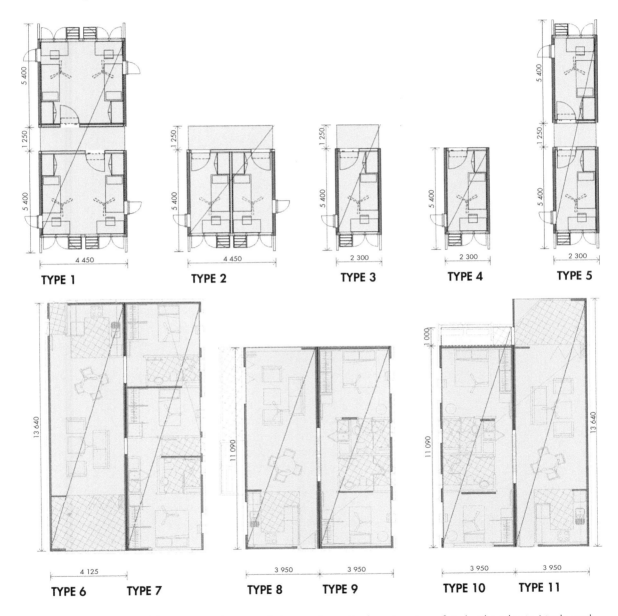

FIGURE 10–7–8 PPVC modules customized to meet design requirements of varying sizes of student hostel units (single- and double-occupancy rooms) and faculty apartments. Types 1 and 2 are each composed of two modules in actual construction.

Images courtesy of P & T Consultants Pte Ltd.

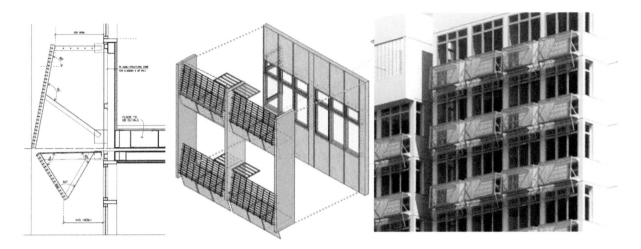

FIGURE 10-7-9   Detailed and comprehensive design development of users' design features with BIM modeling, clothes rack, and façade features.

Images/Photos courtesy of P & T Consultants Pte Ltd.

modules, which facilitated the design of the PPVC modules. It also eased the quantification of building parts/materials, and hence the cost analysis, due to modularization and repetition. PPVC BIM libraries enabled the consultants to study, understand, and visualize the assembly of the components and the interfaces between the modules, the external façades, and the cast-in situ works in a 3D environment.

The façade subassembly was customized to project design requirements and created a unique and non-monotonous façade design. Off-site assembly of façade components in an automated PPVC factory with QA/QC ensured good workmanship and reduced the need for scaffolding works at height. The unique identity of the façade design as a subassembly can be seen in Figure 10-7-9. Vertical sun-shading and aluminum screens were used, which formed part of the subassembly elements as lightweight attachments.

BIM Applications in the Design Stage. In this project, coincidently all the collaborators used Autodesk Revit. For planning and design, BIM was used to select the most suitable site area and plan the layout for project development. Figure 10-7-10 shows use of the BIM model for site layout planning. It illustrates 3D visualization of undulating topography/terrain against podium and tower block configuration. BIM was used for earthwork cut and fill analysis, as shown in Figure 10-7-11.

BIM was used to analyze the integrity of the building by assessing its safety and durability. Since PPVC has very low tolerance (2–3 mm) requirements to comply with design standards, BIM reduced conflicts that were not

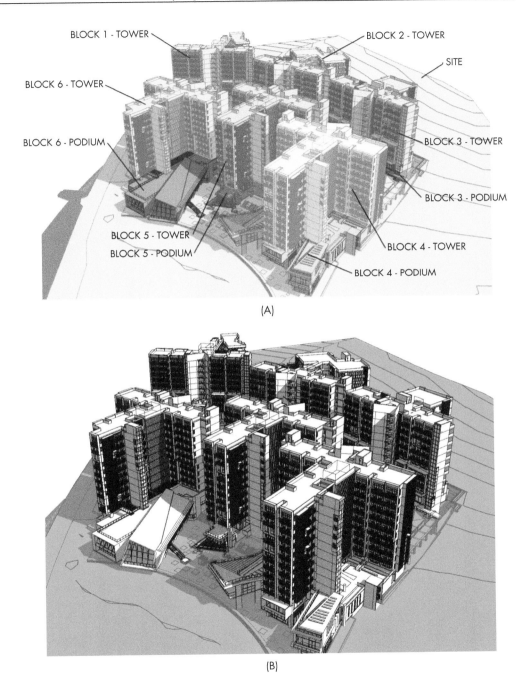

(A)

(B)

FIGURE 10-7-10 (A and B) 3D BIM model of project site layout planning.

Images courtesy of P & T Consultants Pte Ltd.

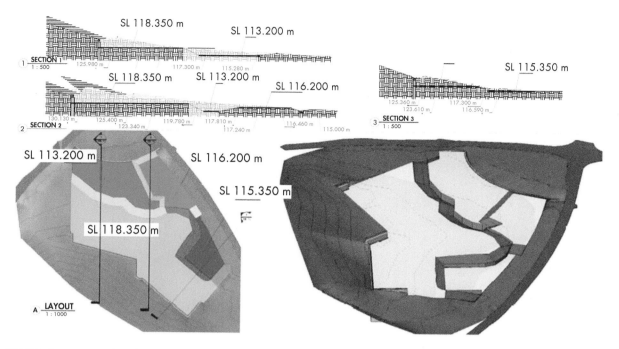

FIGURE 10–7–11   Earthwork cut and fill of soil volume in BIM.

Images courtesy of P & T Consultants Pte Ltd.

obvious to the eye, which minimized downstream risks. Figure 10–7–12 and Figure 10–7–13 illustrate the high consistency and accuracy achieved by using BIM for structural and MEP studies respectively, which minimized errors and discrepancies.

BIM was used for environmental analysis and for calculation of the optimal concrete usage index (CUI). BIM was used to study the 3D space as a green sustainable living environment by ensuring adequate wind flow velocity across each unit, achieving the prerequisite requirement for Green Mark Platinum (Figure 10–7–14 and Figure 10–7–15). BCA Green Mark is a green building rating system to evaluate a building for its environmental impact and performance. BIM was also used to perform a 3D study of the massing and orientation of the building to help in achieving the optimum CFD result for Green Mark Platinum (Figure 10–7–16).

With the help of the visualizations through BIM, the client was given a clear picture of the finished product, and the project stakeholders were able to discuss the practicality of the construction. It facilitated the design coordination of PPVC modules and reduced errors and adjustments on-site. Early and precise coordination was required for integrating elements cutting

RFEM ANALYSIS

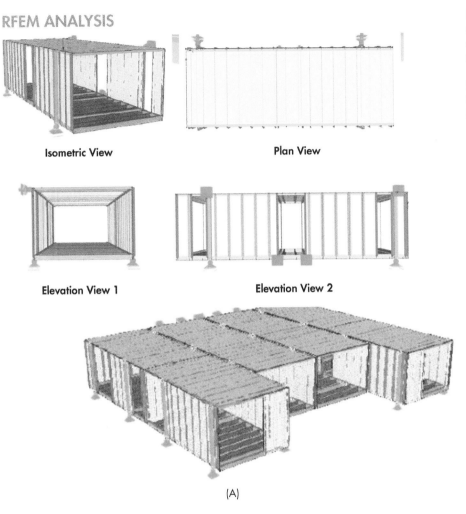

Isometric View

Plan View

Elevation View 1

Elevation View 2

(A)

FIGURE 10–7–12 (A, B, and C) High consistency and accuracy from BIM for structural studies.

Images courtesy of Singapore Piling & Civil Engineering Pte Ltd., BBR.

vertically and horizontally across multiple PPVC modules/floors, such as services shaft/risers/ducts, and so on, to ensure exact integration of the PPVC modules during on-site installation without the need for on-site modifications. Detailed coordination on connection and interfacing details was done between PPVC modules and between PPVC main and subassemblies.

The sequence and method of PPVC construction was particularly coordinated during design in order to:

- Provide adequate access for delivery of PPVC modules
- Ensure clear zoning and demarcation for ease of hoisting activities
- Integrate conventional and PPVC construction

LATERAL LOAD ANALYSIS

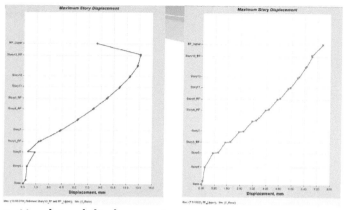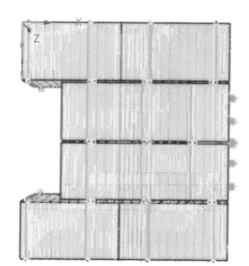

- Max lateral displacement,
  - X-direction : 13.6mm (1/3150) < 1/500, OK
  - Y-direction :   7.5mm (1/5710) < 1/500, OK

(B)

DEFLECTION ANALYSIS

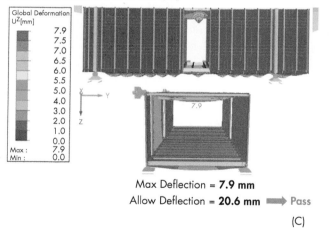

Max Deflection = **7.9 mm**
Allow Deflection = **20.6 mm** ➡ Pass

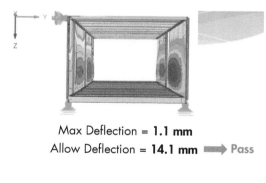

Max Deflection = **1.1 mm**
Allow Deflection = **14.1 mm** ➡ Pass

(C)

FIGURE 10–7–12   (continued)

MEP INTEGRATION STUDY

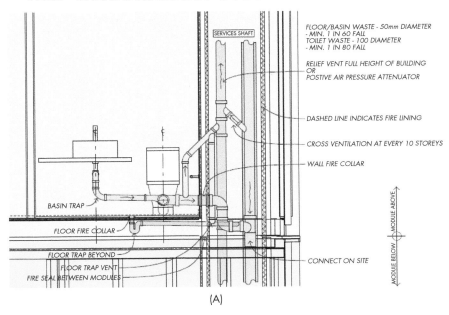

FLOOR/BASIN WASTE - 50mm DIAMETER
- MIN. 1 IN 60 FALL
TOILET WASTE - 100 DIAMETER
- MIN. 1 IN 80 FALL

RELIEF VENT FULL HEIGHT OF BUILDING
OR
POSTIVE AIR PRESSURE ATTENUATOR

DASHED LINE INDICATES FIRE LINING

CROSS VENTILATION AT EVERY 10 STOREYS

WALL FIRE COLLAR

SERVICES SHAFT

BASIN TRAP

FLOOR FIRE COLLAR

FLOOR TRAP BEYOND

FLOOR TRAP VENT
FIRE SEAL BETWEEN MODULES

CONNECT ON SITE

MODULE ABOVE
MODULE BELOW

(A)

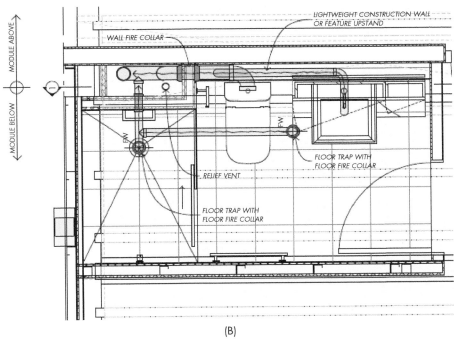

LIGHTWEIGHT CONSTRUCTION WALL
OR FEATURE UPSTAND

WALL FIRE COLLAR

FLOOR TRAP WITH
FLOOR FIRE COLLAR

RELIEF VENT

FLOOR TRAP WITH
FLOOR FIRE COLLAR

MODULE ABOVE
MODULE BELOW

(B)

FIGURE 10–7–13 (A, B, and C) High consistency and accuracy from BIM for MEP studies.

Images courtesy of Singapore Piling & Civil Engineering Pte Ltd., BBR.

FIGURE 10–7–13 *(continued)*

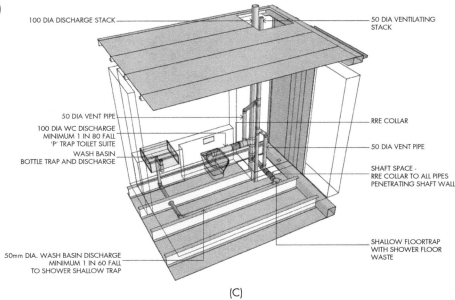

100 DIA DISCHARGE STACK

50 DIA VENTILATING STACK

50 DIA VENT PIPE
100 DIA WC DISCHARGE
MINIMUM 1 IN 80 FALL
'P' TRAP TOILET SUITE
WASH BASIN
BOTTLE TRAP AND DISCHARGE

RRE COLLAR

50 DIA VENT PIPE

SHAFT SPACE -
RRE COLLAR TO ALL PIPES
PENETRATING SHAFT WALL

50mm DIA. WASH BASIN DISCHARGE
MINIMUM 1 IN 60 FALL
TO SHOWER SHALLOW TRAP

SHALLOW FLOORTRAP
WITH SHOWER FLOOR
WASTE

(C)

2D CAD drawings were exported from the BIM model and used for off-site fabrication. They facilitated understanding of the fabrication process and were used to get subcontractors' inputs. This was done at the outset of the design phase, which helped the consultants to better incorporate fabrication considerations and constraints into their design.

BIM Applications during Construction. During the construction phase, the BIM model was used as a reference by the main contractor instead of the traditional 2D drawings. The model was passed by the consultant to the main contractor using a common data sharing account set up by NTU on Google Drive. It was used for construction planning, estimation, sequencing and scheduling, safety simulations, temporary occupation permit (TOP) compliances, project progress monitoring, clash detection between elements and services, and project coordination. Figure 10–7–17 shows how BIM was used by the main contractors to perform conflict resolution to mitigate construction errors and inefficiencies.

BIM was helpful in detecting uncoordinated parts of the buildings that may have compromised users' safety and functionality. It was specifically useful for identifying low headroom, hidden corners, tripping hazards, low safety barrier heights, and more.

BIM enhanced planning and operations of the tower cranes for PPVC modules, and was used to plan their locations and utilization on-site in order to optimize the reach for hoisting and installation of the PPVC modules.

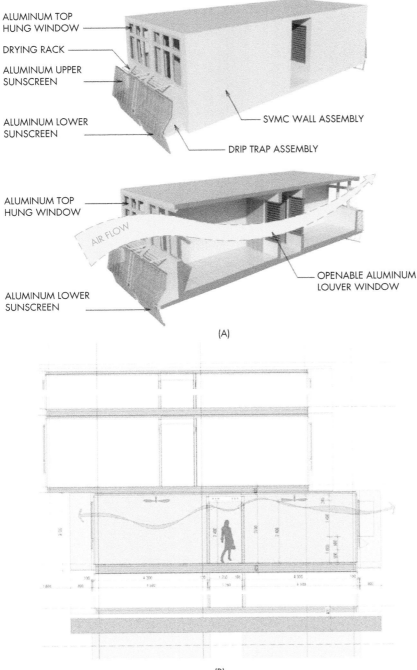

ALUMINUM TOP HUNG WINDOW

DRYING RACK

ALUMINUM UPPER SUNSCREEN

ALUMINUM LOWER SUNSCREEN

SVMC WALL ASSEMBLY

DRIP TRAP ASSEMBLY

ALUMINUM TOP HUNG WINDOW

AIR FLOW

ALUMINUM LOWER SUNSCREEN

OPENABLE ALUMINUM LOUVER WINDOW

(A)

(B)

FIGURE 10–7–14 (A and B) Passive design studies on ventilation performance for green mark platinum.

Images courtesy of P & T Consultants Pte Ltd.

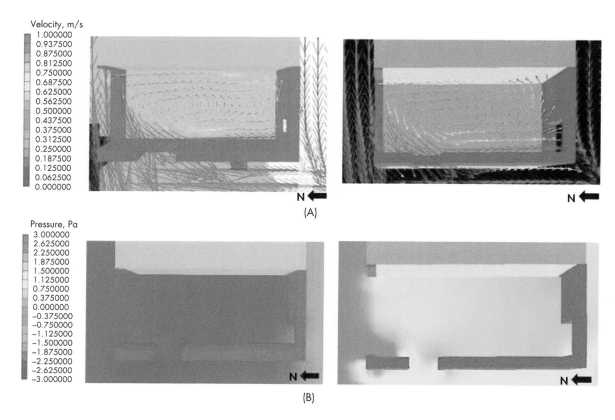

FIGURE 10-7-15   (A and B) Wind velocity and pressure profile.

Images courtesy of BECA Carter Hollings & Ferner (S.E Asia) Pte Ltd.

Subsequently, the main contractor used Autodesk Navisworks to conduct 4D simulations, including simulation for PPVC construction planning and sequencing (as shown in Figure 6-9 in Chapter 6).

10.7.7   Benefits Realization

In comparison with a conventional construction process, the DfMA process allows manufacturing of modules simultaneously with on-site construction work (or even prior to it). This flexibility allowed for a faster construction period. Ideally, the PPVC modules for one block could be installed within a month if everything went as planned, and assuming that there were no concrete slabs to be cast between modules. The greatest time saving was in the duration for on-site work, which was reduced by a third compared to the conventional method. The duration of PPVC work on-site lasted only four months, whereas, in general, the conventional method would have taken 12 months.

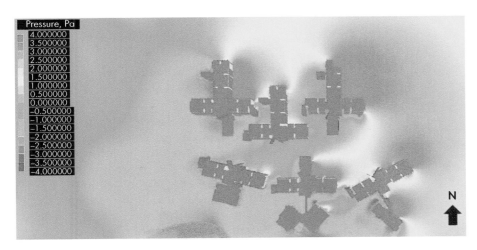

FIGURE 10–7–16 Computational fluid dynamics study (CFD) of the site.

Images courtesy of BECA Carter Hollings & Ferner (S.E Asia) Pte Ltd.

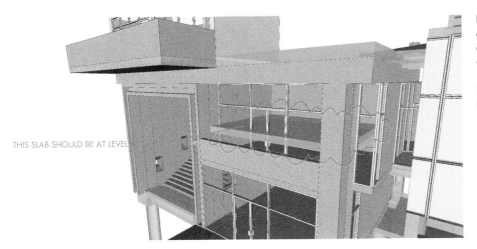

THIS SLAB SHOULD BE AT LEVEL

FIGURE 10–7–17 BIM for clash detection to minimize errors during construction coordination

Images courtesy of P & T Consultants Pte Ltd.

The main benefits observed in the project were as follows:

- Enabling effective planning of the hoisting and operations of the tower crane for PPVC modules through BIM
- Reduction in construction time in comparison to conventional construction
- Concurrent on-site and off-site construction; off-site fabrication and assembly of PPVC modules in a controlled factory environment enabled reduction in site labor requirement
- Shorter cycle time for floor construction, from 14 to 21 days for conventional construction to approx. four days for on-site installation of PPVC modules (with production of three PPVC units per day)

- Consistency in quality in controlled factory environment; higher quality control and assurance by means of automation in the fabrication and assembly process
- Minimize labor-intensive works at construction site; estimated savings of labor hours about 20%

The downside for adoption of PPVC was that it was 10% to 15% costlier than conventional construction methods. As early adopters of PPVC technology and with no local reference information, the advice received from the contractors and a PPVC specialist pointed to time savings in the range of 15% to 20% and that the cost might be comparable to conventional, at best. However, the owner (NTU ODFM) did caution that PPVC was not locally tested with many variable factors that could affect the estimated benefits. Specifically, technical and market-acceptance uncertainties are reckoned as major issues affecting industry's acceptance of the changes to workflow and regulatory requirements, and these could have attributed to the cost increase, given that this was the first project using PPVC. The Singapore Minister of National Development, Mr. Lawrence Wong, claims, "With greater adoption of PPVC and new technologies, the cost differential will come down." The premium is due to prototyping, but with more repetitive adoption and greater economies of scale, the cost will go down, and PPVC is expected to become highly economical even without government grants. These grants are not the only incentive for going ahead with PPVC; a developer has to look at the construction technology holistically.

10.7.8 Conclusion and Lessons Learned

The NTU Student Residence Hall project was an early success story in Singapore's DfMA integrated with BIM journey. It was the first public high-rise PPVC project that was designed and constructed using BIM, in Singapore. This case study has shown the practical application and usefulness of BIM for PPVC, ensuring the successful design and delivery of the PPVC modules. The main target of PPVC adoption was productivity growth with less reliance on foreign labor at site. Sustainability, environmental improvements, construction safety, and user comfort complete the picture for a complete and holistic view of how mind-set change and adoption of game-changing technologies can help to revive the construction industry to be as attractive as other "good-looking" industries.

Through the use of productive technologies, the project has reaped many benefits, such as time savings, consistency in quality, safer and controlled automated processes, and better design coordination. BIM acted as a catalyst in facilitating the integration of different construction technologies in a single building development, as it was effective in designing and integrating prefabricated building parts with speed and accuracy. BIM especially helped to overcome the challenge in the interfacing between the two different forms of construction (hybrid approach of PPVC and cast in-situ works). Monitoring and tracking of the fabrication, assembly, delivery, and installation using BIM sequencing and scheduling helped the contractor to manage inventory on-site and off-site more effectively.

Using BIM for PPVC has reaped the following main benefits:

BIM Use	Benefits
3D Visualization	• Provided better coordination with the manufacturers, contractors, and PPVC specialist • Facilitated design coordination of PPVC modules and reduced errors and adjustments on-site • Facilitated the demarcation of the PPVC modules with the conventional construction and the integration of the various design parts/packages
Standardization of BIM Families	• Facilitated design of the PPVC modules and enhanced the design production • Eased the quantification of building parts/materials, and hence the cost analysis due to modularization and repetition
Onsite Coordination	• Eased the technical coordination and integration in the off-site assembly of parts and onsite installation of the PPVC modules
Construction Planning & Management	• Facilitated the construction planning, sequencing, and management on-site, particularly in integrating and coordinating the works for PPVC and conventional construction • Enhanced logistics and inventory management of PPVC assembly parts throughout the fabrication process from overseas manufacturing plants to local offsite assembly yards and on-site installation • Enhanced the effectiveness of documentation during construction • Allowed for monitoring of progress, particularly the production rate of off-site PPVC module fabrication and work rate of on-site PPVC installation

Source: BCA (2015)

The major learning points from using BIM and PPVC for NTU project are summarized as follows:

- Create an object library of standard "BIM Families" for the PPVC modules including the connection details required for installation.
- Optimize the variable permutations by minimizing the variations of the PPVC modules with standardized interfacing. Greater standardization of components (modular design and standardized dimensions) will help to ensure even greater benefits on future projects.
- Utilize BIM capabilities for coordination of PPVC and conventional construction elements.
- Design to be "construction-ready" particularly for fabrication, assembly, delivery, and installation on-site.
- Early involvement of the specialist subcontractor was crucial to developing the BIM and PPVC strategies.

It is expected that future PPVC projects would be able to reach maximum potential savings and realize the true productivity and economy of BIM for PPVC technology. In addition, as BIM capability increases across the entire construction supply chain, once BIM is completely implemented for the whole process from design to construction and facility management, the industry in Singapore will be even better placed to deliver successful PPVC projects using BIM. BIM integration with robotics to facilitate automated fabrication is an interesting area that needs further R&D to implement for future PPVC projects. BIM can be used as a design tool for integrating the various modes of construction technologies such as PPVC, prefabricated bomb shelters, and prefabricated bathroom units (PBUs).

Acknowledgments
This case study was written by Meghdad Attarzadeh, Tushar Nath, Angela Lee, and Professor Robert Tiong.

10.8 MAPLETREE BUSINESS CITY II, SINGAPORE

10.8.1 Introduction
Mapletree Business City II (MBC II) is the second phase of Mapletree Business City precinct, the new heartbeat of the Alexandra Business Corridor. Located at the fringe of the city on a site of 43,727 m^2, this business park features 124,884 m^2 of gross floor area integrated in a confluence of work and play. The project owner is Mapletree Business City Pte Ltd., and the project was procured with a REDAS Design and Build Conditions of Contract (3rd Edition) contract. Total project cost was S$338.8 million.

Table 10–8–1 outlines the different phases of the project, and Figures 10–8–1 and 10–8–2 show rendered views.

As can be seen in Figure 10–8–3, the project is a business park development, consisting of four office building blocks, a two-story car park podium, a single-story amenity block, and a landscape e-deck on top of the car park podium. The four blocks comprise:

- Block 80: 30 stories
- Block 70: 8 stories
- Block 60: 6 stories
- Block 50: 5 stories

The construction contract for Mapletree Business City II was based on the REDAS Design & Build Contract with an option module for Employer's Architectural Design. The main contract was awarded in January 2014. After the award, the architectural BIM model from DCA was made available to Shimizu Corporation, to be used for construction planning purposes.

The building form is a single curved mass linking four blocks of large floor areas together; this requires extensive coordination of M&E, structural, and architectural disciplines to achieve this seamless form. The building

Table 10–8–1 Project Details and Outline of Phases.

Project Name	Mapletree Business City II		
Project Owner	Mapletree Business City Pte Ltd.		
Contract Type			
Project Cost	S$338.8 million		
Project Timeline	**Phase**	**Commencement Date**	**Completion Date**
	Phase 1: Blocks 50 & 60, drop-off, Alexandra Terrace entrance bridge, part of first-story carpark	February 21, 2014	October 20, 2015 (20 Months from Contract Commencement)
	Phase 2: Blocks 70 & 80, second-story landscape e-deck, remaining first-story and mezzanine carpark.	February 21, 2014	April 20, 2016 (26 Months from Contract Commencement)
	Phase 3: F&B at second-story e-deck	February 1, 2016	July 31, 2016 (6 Months from Contract Commencement)

FIGURE 10–8–1 Mapletree Business City II.

Image courtesy of DCA Architects Pte Ltd.

FIGURE 10–8–2   Mapletree Business City II.

Image courtesy of DCA Architects Pte Ltd.

floor-to-floor height is 4.55 m and the clear ceiling height is 3.2 m. The lush landscape concept, with over 1,000 trees at the e-deck level (Figure 10–8–4), requires complex coordination of services running at the carpark levels with the limitation of required clear headroom height due to the sunken planters.

Project Collaboration Team. The core collaboration BIM team comprised a design team and a construction team. The design team was led by DCA Architects Pte Ltd. and included SHMA Co Ltd. (landscape architect), Mott MacDonald Singapore Pte Ltd. (mechanical and electrical), and P&T Consultants Pte Ltd. (civil and structural). The construction team included Shimizu Corporation (the main contractor) and the prime subcontractors, namely Bintai Kindenko Pte Ltd. and APP Engineering Pte Ltd.

Mapletree Business City II was procured using the REDAS Design & Build form of contract. The main contract was awarded in January 2014. Civil and structural (C&S) and mechanical, electrical, and plumbing (MEP) consultants were appointed by the client at the outset, before the tender was awarded for this design & build project. The C&S and MEP consultants did not adopt BIM at the preliminary stage but provided information for the architect to incorporate in their model for submission to the regulatory authorities. Separate C&S/MEP consultants were engaged by the main contractor after award of the contract.

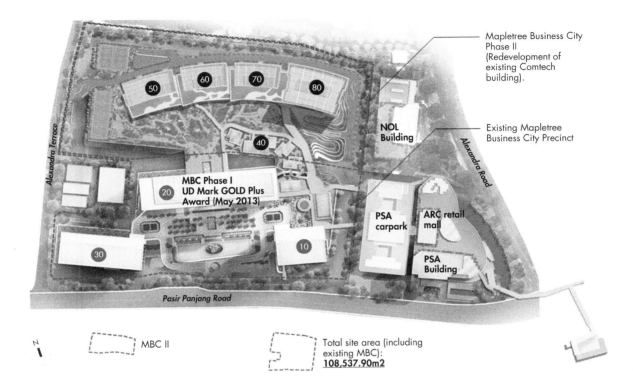

FIGURE 10–8–3 Site plan.

Image courtesy of DCA Architects Pte Ltd.

Since 2009, when DCA architects first used BIM in the Reflections at Keppel Bay project, DCA saw the potential of using BIM to achieve a higher level of coordination between disciplines. The company has defined its goals and objectives for BIM enhancement over the years. With their experience and technical expertise in BIM, they have communicated and demonstrated the effectiveness of BIM to their clients, describing the advantages that BIM can contribute to the quality of a project.

During the pre-tender stage, DCA exported DWG format for the other consultants for their review and feedback. Only an architectural BIM model was available at this stage, and it was divided into a few RVT files as can be seen in Figure 10–8–5.

The regulatory authorities of Singapore accept RVT (Revit) and DWF in both 2D and 3D formats. They view the model and check compliance with their requirements but do not evaluate the designs. The authorities can check some of the conditions for permitting, like gross floor area verification and envelope control (setback, buffer zone, and the like), in the native Revit model.

FIGURE 10–8–4 Lush landscape e-deck of Mapletree Business City II.

Image courtesy of DCA Architects Pte Ltd.

FIGURE 10–8–5 Model management with linked files.

Image courtesy of DCA Architects Pte Ltd.

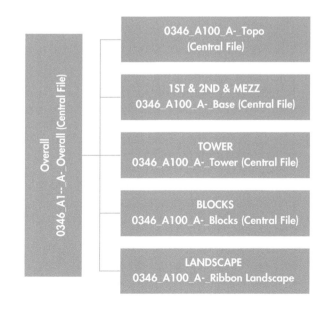

DCA Architects Pte Ltd. started modeling in BIM for Mapletree Business City II project at the preliminary design stage, in 2013. The client was forward thinking and responded positively to this initiative by DCA Architects Pte Ltd. The tender therefore required the main contractor, Shimizu Corporation, to use BIM for the project throughout the construction stage in collaboration with DCA and the employer, effectively harnessing the full advantage of BIM in Mapletree Business City II.

The conditions were explained in the BIM implementation requirements document that was incorporated in the main contract tender. Shimizu in turn required BIM from their subcontractors. As the main contractor, they carried out meetings to coordinate the modeling within their departments and with their subcontractors by appointing an experienced, skillful BIM manager on site.

Project Goals and Team Preparation. The key BIM goals were set by the team and outlined in the BIM execution plan as follows:

Goal Description	Potential BIM Uses
Find and resolve most of the conflicts before construction starts and reduce the number of construction errors and the extent of rework on site.	3D coordination on site
Increase quality of shop drawing and documentation process.	Production of shop drawings
Hand over an accurate BIM as-built model.	Facilities management

The project team for Mapletree Business City II embarked on the BIM collaboration effort in early 2014, responding to BCA's encouragement for the construction industry to tap into the benefits of implementing BIM. Shimizu and DCA both applied for and utilized funds from the Singapore government's BCA's BIM Fund to upgrade their BIM-related IT infrastructure and to cover part of the costs incurred in training.

Training was essential to bring the BIM teams to a level of proficiency to enable their work on the project. The BIM capabilities and resources of each project team member prior to and during the project coordination are described in Table 10–8–2.

The shared commitment of the whole project team—the client, the consultants, the general contractor, and the subcontractors—to implement BIM for Mapletree Business City II meant that all partners had to acquire the BIM capabilities necessary to fully utilize the models for the benefit of the coordination and execution process.

The architect prepared the BIM implementation requirements for the contractor, for and on behalf of the client. The BIM implementation requirements for the contractor were as follows:

- To provide standard infrastructure, such as a BIM coordination room with the required hardware and software

Table 10–8–2 Training and Resources

DCA's Training Program	Personnel Type	No. of Trainees	Timeframe	Training Provider
Specialist Diploma in BIM	BIM Coordinator	1	Nov 2014	BCA Academy
BIM Management	Technical Manager	1	Jan 2013	BCA Academy
Autodesk Revit	Designer/Architect	1	Dec 2011	IMAGINIT
	Architectural Associate	1	Apr 2012	
	Architectural Associate	1	Mar 2013	
	Architectural Associate	1	Sep 2013	
	Modeler/Drafter	1	Dec 2011	
	Modeler/Drafter	1	Mar 2012	
Shimizu's Training Programme	Personnel Type	No. of Trainees	Timeframe	Training Provider
BIM Management	Arch Coordinator	1	May 2014	BCA Academy
Navisworks	Planning Manager	1	Aug 2014	In-house
	Structural Engineer	4		
	Arch Coordinator	4	June 2015	
	Modeler/Drafter	8		
Autodesk Revit	Modeler/Drafter	4	June 2014	OJT

- To develop/update the received design intent BIM model/2D drawings from all major trades and resolve conflicts with all applicable parties prior to construction
- To employ a skilled BIM manager and develop the required BIM execution plan together with owner and architect
- To follow standard collaboration procedures
- To follow standard BIM modeling quality control procedures and level of development specifications
- To prepare and follow a submission/coordination schedule with deliverables itemized
- To refer to the latest Singapore BIM guide and particular conditions
- To transfer/submit the as-built/record BIM models to the owner

10.8.2 Communication and Collaboration Issues

As this was a partial design-build (DB) contract, after award of the contract the main contractor, Shimizu, was responsible for collating the respective BIM models and information from the various consultants to put together the overall model for technical coordination and clash detection. The project team continued to participate in two weekly meetings: technical meetings, where the BIM model was used for coordination purposes, and weekly BIM coordination

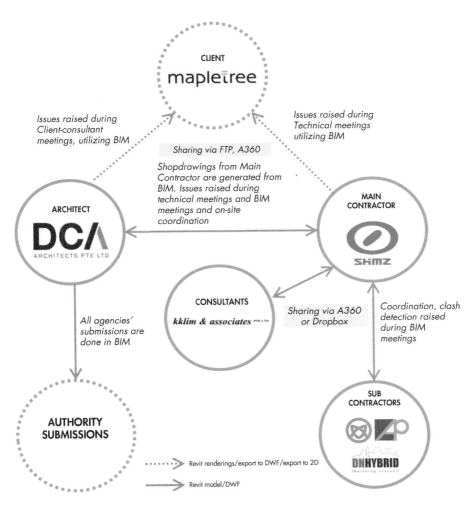

FIGURE 10-8-6 Collaborative work process.

Image courtesy of DCA Architects Pte Ltd.

meetings, where clash detection was run and errors found were presented and resolved.

The collaborative work process diagram between the various parties is shown in Figure 10–8–6.

10.8.3 BIM Coordination Meetings

In the BIM coordination meetings, Autodesk Navisworks Manage was used for the reviews and native Revit models were updated immediately if necessary. Two screens were used to conduct the meetings. The first showed the image or figure to highlight the issue, while the other showed the BIM model. Figure 10–8–7 illustrates the setup for these meetings and a 3D section view of the federated BIM model, and Figure 10–8–8 is an example of record of an issue raised and its solution.

FIGURE 10-8-7   (A and B)
Technical and BIM
coordination meeting with
federated BIM model.

Image courtesy of DCA
Architects Pte Ltd. &
Shimizu Corporation.

(A)

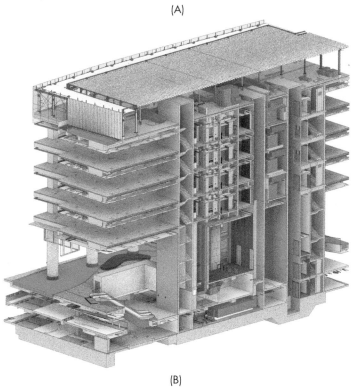

(B)

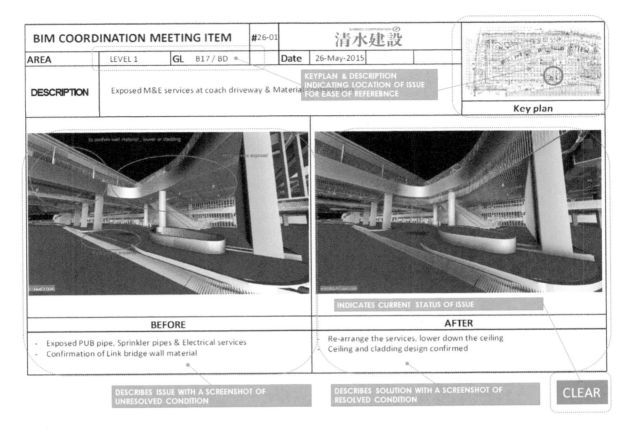

FIGURE 10–8–8 BIM coordination meeting report sample.

Image courtesy of DCA Architects Pte Ltd. & Shimizu Corporation.

Design and construction changes were tabled for discussion in the BIM coordination meetings. The main contractor incorporated the revisions (e.g., structure, M&E, architectural finishes, and so on) in the model and shared the model with the team for coordination, integrating input, and feedback from the architect, C&S, M&E, and client.

The BIM coordination meetings were scheduled weekly to keep pace with construction sequence. Based on the structural casting schedule, the contractor planned the meetings typically four weeks ahead. This would allow all parties to resolve the major coordination issues in the model within one week prior to the issuance of shop drawings. The detail coordination for architectural and M&E trades were subsequently discussed and coordinated in the BIM technical meetings.

10.8.4 BIM Execution Planning

The BIM execution plan considered the roles and responsibilities of each design partner. Shimizu employed a construction BIM manager, as per the contract requirements, to work closely with the architectural BIM manager. In all there were seven people directly responsible for maintaining the model, as outlined in Table 10–8–3. Their roles and responsibilities were defined in the BIM Execution Plan, shown in Table 10–8–4.

10.8.5 Data Exchange

Model data were exchanged via FTP and A360. A360, a cloud-based collaboration system, was introduced and used to share the BIM model in Navisworks format. After each weekly technical meeting, BIM models were uploaded to the A360 to share the information among the project team members. Marked-up images of the model were then shared (Figure 10–8–9). Whenever necessary, native BIM models were uploaded to a shared FTP site for sharing among the team members. The project team did not face any major issues in coordination and communication. Ownership of the intellectual property of the BIM model was addressed by adopting BCA's BIM guidelines, which specifies that the models or model aspects prepared by the respective parties remains their intellectual property.

Using the CSIxRevit plug-in, the project team was able to export the proposed structural model from Revit and send it to the structural engineers to perform structural analysis in SAP 2000. As a result, the structural engineers saved considerable time.

Table 10–8–3 BIM Modeling Personnel

ROLE	ORGANIZATION	LOCATION
Architectural BIM Manager Architectural BIM Modelers	DCA Architects Pte Ltd.	DCA's Office
Contractor BIM Manager Contractor BIM Coordinator (Archi) Contractor BIM Coordinator (C&S) Contractor BIM Coordinator (MEP) Contractor BIM Modelers	Shimizu Corporation	Site Office
Sub-Con BIM Coordinator (Electrical) Sub-Con BIM Coordinator (ACMV) Sub-Con BIM Coordinator (Fire)	Bintai Kindenko Pte Ltd.	Site Office
Sub-Con BIM Coordinator (Plumbing, Sanitary & Gas)	APP Engineering Pte Ltd.	APP's Office

Table 10–8–4   BIM Roles and Responsibilities Defined in the BIM Execution Plan

ROLE	RESPONSIBILITIES IN MODEL MANAGEMENT	BIM RESPONSIBILITIES
BIM Manager (Consultant)	• Check BIM models to follow design intent and contract requirements • Develop BIM strategy with main contractor BIM manager	• Design reviews • Model exchange
BIM Manager (Main Contractor)	• Determine BIM uses on project • Develop and execute the project BIM execution plan • BIM model quality control • Coordinate BIM schedule ahead of actual construction • Manage/resolve clash detections for both minor and major clashes and present during the BIM meetings • Sharing BIM activities	• Oversight • Manage BIM execution • Manage 3D coordination • Manage model exchange • Manage phase planning • Assist cost estimation
BIM Coordinators (Main Contractor)	• Receive/create BIM for constructability study and field use • Determine interference checking responsibilities	• Coordinate with design team and subcontractors • Clash detection • Model exchange
BIM Modelers (Main Contractor)	• Develop/update BIM models according to BIM schedule • Generate construction drawings including structural precast elements' shop drawings from BIM model for site factory	• Design authoring • Record Modeling (as-built)
BIM Coordinators (Subcontractor)	• Develop BIM models and documents from design development stage to construction stage	• Coordinate with main contractor • Model user and review • Model exchange

10.8.6   Productivity Gains

The use of BIM helped reduce the number of RFIs on the project—only 48 RFIs were issued throughout the 18-month construction period. DCA estimated that without BIM, approximately **22 times as many** RFIs would have been issued. Their estimate is based on data from projects of similar type and complexity executed previously using conventional methods. In a previous project designed by DCA Architects that had 180,000 m^2 gross floor area of offices and 9,000 m^2 of retail space and a food and beverage court, 1,555 RFIs were issued. Using the gross floor area as an indicator of project size, the number of RFIs expected for MBC II was 1,028.

The team estimated that for the coordination of a typical floor office area, the team saved about 358 hours using the BIM process, compared to a conventional process, as shown in Table 10–8–5.

FIGURE 10–8–9   Reviewing and marking up models in A360.

Image courtesy of DCA Architects Pte Ltd. & Shimizu Corporation.

Table 10–8–5   Productivity Gain for Coordination of Office Area

WORK SCOPE	CONVENTIONAL PROCESS (HOURS)	BIM PROCESS (HOURS)	TIME DIFFERENCE (HOURS)
Internal coordination (M&E)	32	16	−16
Internal coordination (M&E + STR + ARCH)	16	8	−8
BIM coordination meeting	0	6	+6
RFI preparation	5	1*	−4
RFI approval process	336**	0	−336
TOTAL	**389**	**31**	**−358**

*Part of BIM meeting
**Based on two week review and approval time

10.8.7   Innovative Uses of BIM

Design Options. During the Design Development stage, the architect explored several design options in Revit to achieve a balance between cost and aesthetic requirements for the employer. In particular, they sought an optimum curtain wall module for the curved façade (Figure 10–8–10). Several design options were prepared, which were presented to the client with perspective views and renderings for accurate representation. With BIM, the extent of glass curtain walls and mullions could be easily summarized in a schedule, which was subsequently provided to the quantity surveyor for costing.

Virtual Reality. Virtual reality views were prepared for the design review, using Autodesk A360 panoramic rendering and Google Cardboard. The rendered BIM model could be seen with Google Cardboard by scanning the QR codes (Figure 10–8–11) provided by the A360 cloud software.

A virtual tour of the project was conducted using 3D technology at BCA's Centre for Lean and Virtual Construction before the actual construction was completely finished (see Figure 10–8–12). The objective was to explore the potential of the new technology for it to be shared with the developer in future design review process.

Code Checking. Customized Revit families with parametric code-checking features were prepared and used to check for compliance with some of the regulatory requirements. For example, to comply with the Singapore Building Construction Authority's (BCA) Code on Accessibility, special door families were created with solid volumes to represent maneuvering space for both push and pull sides (see Figure 10–8–13). In this way, the interference check tool in Revit would highlight any clash into the maneuvering space as shown in the lower part of the figure.

3D Printing for Visualization. BIM helped the project team to study interfaces between the various disciplines, the existing topography, sloping structures such as ramps and more complex features of the landscaping feature such as the terracing ribbons, undulating food and beverage (F&B) roof, and walkways. The design intent of the F&B roof was conceptualized using BIM. The complexity of its undulating roof structure could not be captured in 2D alone. Therefore, the architect compiled a separate BIM model for study of the roof, incorporating the details and other requirements during coordination. Once the study model was deemed feasible and locked in, it was merged with the master model and became a reference for the main contractor to develop further.

During the detail coordination stage, further BIM coordination was conducted between the architect and the engineers appointed by Shimizu to incorporate all the structural and MEP requirements and to make sure the aesthetic was not compromised. Physical models of complex areas were printed, using a 3D printer for better visualization, to facilitate communication, and to resolve interfacing issues (see Figure 10–8–14).

FIGURE 10–8–10
(A and B) Two façade
modulation options
considered at the design
development stage.

Image courtesy of DCA
Architects Pte Ltd.

(A)

(B)

FIGURE 10–8–11   A QR
code for viewing a
panoramic rendering with
Google Cardboard.

Image courtesy of DCA
Architects Pte Ltd.

(A)   (B)

FIGURE 10-8-12   (A and B) Immersive virtual reality viewing of the BIM model.

Image courtesy of DCA Architects Pte Ltd.

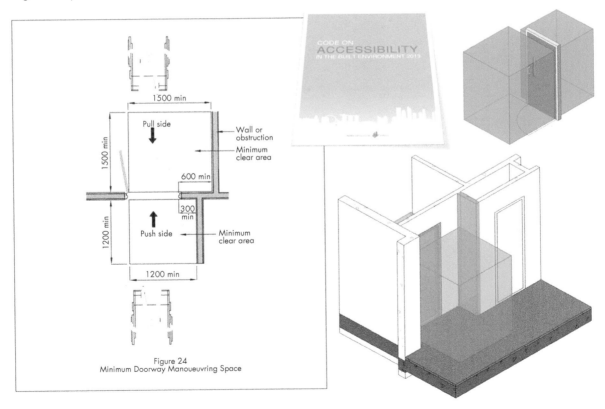

FIGURE 10-8-13   A custom Revit family that includes clearance volumes for doors that open on two sides, to enable automated code-checking for accessibility using clash-checking.

Image courtesy of DCA Architects Pte Ltd.

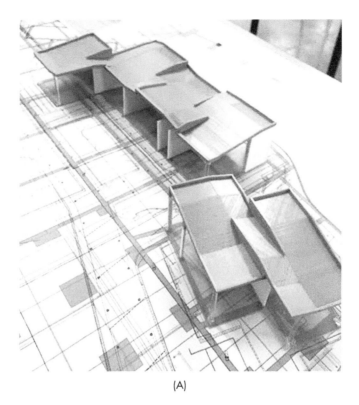

(A)

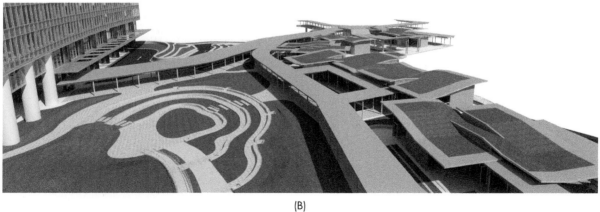

(B)

FIGURE 10–8–14   (A and B) Outputs from a 3D printer versus a rendering of the design intent BIM model.

Image courtesy of DCA Architects Pte Ltd. & Shimizu Corporation.

Virtual Mock-up. During the construction stage a detailed mock-up of the reinforcement column was modeled in Revit for the design of the complex rebar reinforcements. Where a column transitions from a rectangular to a circular arrangement, a prefabricated circular reinforcement cage was needed to increase the productivity of the site work. In order to avoid rework, the complex reinforcement was modeled in Revit to determine the precise specs for the cage, as shown in Figure 10–8–15. This process avoided coordination issues and additional costs, minimized scheduling, and connected BIM with the physical world. This allowed the rebar cage to be fabricated off-site accurately, and installed and positioned seamlessly on site.

Shop Drawings Generation for the Fabrication of Structural Precast Elements. Coordinated information from the BIM model was used as the basis for preparation of fabrication shop drawings for the structural precast elements (see Figure 10–8–16).

Delivery of the As-Built Model for FM. The as-built BIM model was handed over to the client upon project completion. As an optional function for operation and maintenance, the as-built BIM models can be uploaded onto an iPad, enabling facility managers to easily identify or detect the routing of concealed services, as can be seen in Figure 10–8–17.

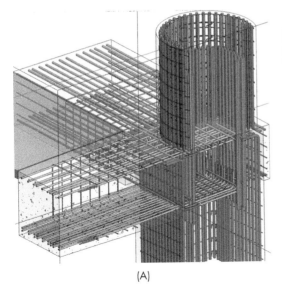

(A)   (B)

FIGURE 10–8–15   (A and B) BIM reinforcement detailing.

Image courtesy of Shimizu Corporation.

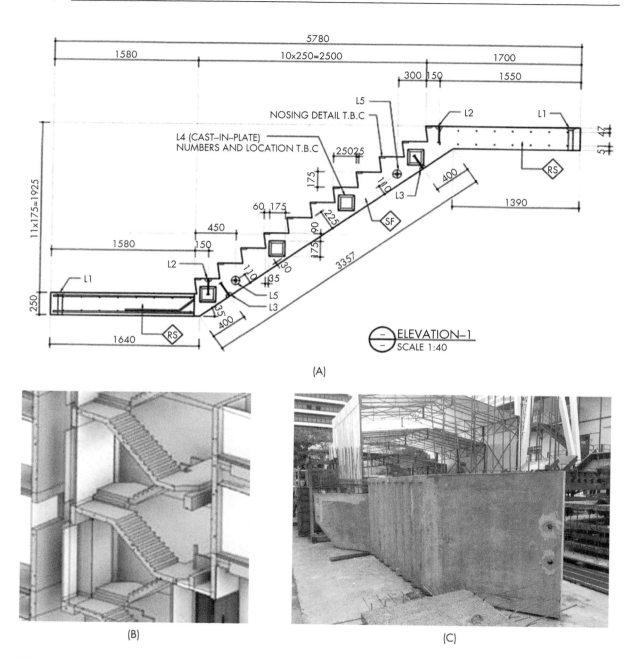

(A)

(B)

(C)

FIGURE 10–8–16   (A, B, and C) A precast concrete stair unit. (A) BIM model. (B) shop drawing. (C) Precast piece.

Image courtesy of Shimizu Corporation.

FIGURE 10–8–17 Detecting routing of concealed services with the as-built BIM model on iPad.

Image courtesy of Shimizu Corporation.

10.8.8   Simulation and Analysis

Sun Path Analysis. During the construction stage, the client requested a revision to the landscape design near the restaurant outlets as follows:

- Additional lawn area to provide a park-like setting instead of hardscape
- A new trellis shading structure for outdoor lawn areas
- To provide shady trees

BIM was used to conduct sun path studies of the landscaping area adjacent to the F&B blocks. The aim was to determine the feasibility and exposure of light to turfed areas under trellised spaces. The sun path study also helped determine relevant plant species in the various shaded areas. The annual direct sunlight received for each area was computed. The landscape consultant was then able to recommend the extent/profile of a new landscape solution that could establish a shady environment, and suitable plant species that require minimum sunlight exposure were proposed. Figure 10–8–18 illustrates the process. Design review sessions with the client and consultant were shortened as the analysis efficiently addressed areas of concern.

4D Simulation. 4D simulation is a useful and powerful method for communicating and visualizing project milestones. 4D modeling was implemented to support the construction planning and the impacts on the installation and design. Using a combination of both Revit and Navisworks, a workflow was established that enabled the project team to effectively plan and schedule different phases of construction, identifying potential problems, and evaluating

REVISED LANDSCAPE SCHEME

Zoysia Grass and Axonopus grass
selected based on daily direct sunlight
exposure from BIM sun path study

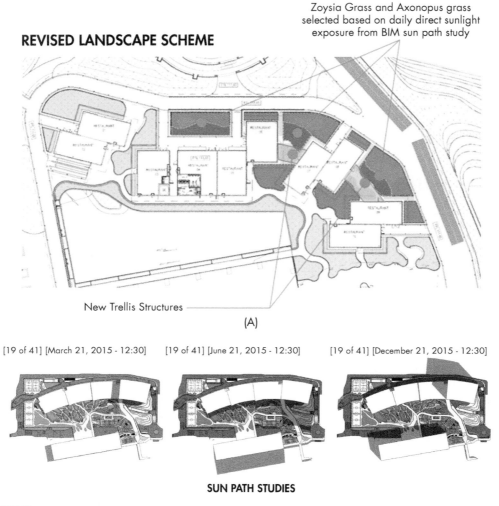

New Trellis Structures

(A)

[19 of 41] [March 21, 2015 - 12:30]   [19 of 41] [June 21, 2015 - 12:30]   [19 of 41] [December 21, 2015 - 12:30]

SUN PATH STUDIES

LANDSCAPE AT F&B AMENITIES BLOCK DEVELOPED FROM SHADING ANALYSIS

(B)

FIGURE 10–8–18   (A and B) Final landscape design after the sun path study in the BIM model.

Image courtesy of DCA Architects Pte Ltd.

Plan (Nov 2014- Jun 2015)

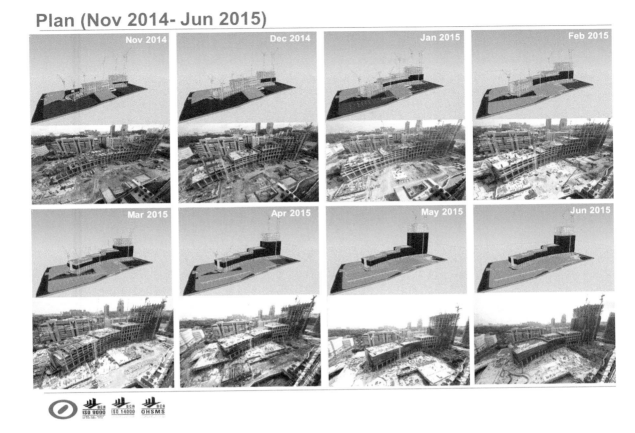

FIGURE 10–8–19 BIM scheduling compared with site progress photos.

Image courtesy of Shimizu Corporation.

alternative solutions. A monthly progress visualization, such as the one shown in Figure 10–8–19, which juxtaposed BIM construction phases and real-time photographic images, allowed the project team to track the schedule against the work done on-site and inform the client.

BIM was not only used to determine the major milestones of the project, but also to plan and implement a construction cycle schedule on the typical floor, as illustrated by the sequence of images in Figure 10–8–20. Thus the construction sequence could be shown and easily explained to other parties, including daily floor cycles organized into morning and afternoon shift works.

4D Simulation to 5D Cost Estimation for Complex Ribbon Landscape. The landscape ribbons are located adjacent to Block 80 and the main drop off and pick up ramp. This complex feature was introduced midway during the

FIGURE 10–8–20 (A and B) 4D construction sequence and floor cycle simulation.

Image courtesy of Shimizu Corporation.

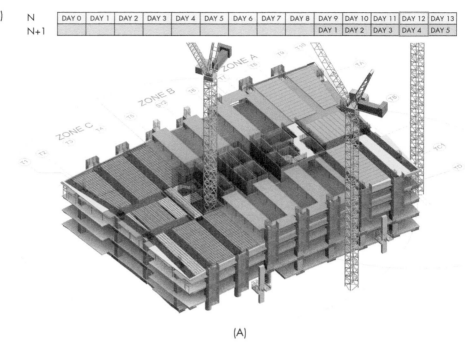

| N | DAY 0 | DAY 1 | DAY 2 | DAY 3 | DAY 4 | DAY 5 | DAY 6 | DAY 7 | DAY 8 | DAY 9 | DAY 10 | DAY 11 | DAY 12 | DAY 13 |
| N+1 | | | | | | | | | | | DAY 1 | DAY 2 | DAY 3 | DAY 4 | DAY 5 |

(A)

construction stage. BIM enabled the team to study options and calculate material quantities in order to achieve the most efficient solution in terms of cost and construction method. The landscaping feature required the study of height with consideration of structure, authority requirements, and aesthetics. The design intent model was developed by the architectural consultants and eventually provided to the main contractor to be further developed and refined. A 4D model was used to plan and understand the logistics and sequence for the construction of this complex structure. These are shown in Figures 10–8–21 and 10–8–22.

The proposed design contained complex areas with three-dimensional, free-formed shapes. As there would be difficulty to take off the material quantity using the conventional methods, the BIM model became a useful tool for visualization and quantity takeoffs in Revit. Elements could be extracted from the Revit model that contain information parameters such as concrete volume, formwork area, and so on.

10.8.9 BIM in the Field

Autodesk Point Layout. The crews on-site used the Autodesk "Point layout" add-in to identify the coordinate points and export information to the surveyors for their input to the robotic total station. The surveyor was able to select the points from the BIM model via the iPad (Figure 10–8–23).

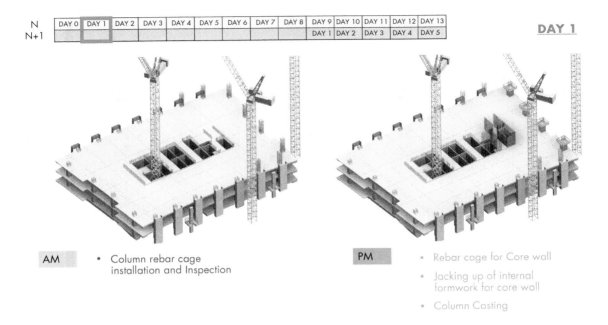

| N | DAY 0 | DAY 1 | DAY 2 | DAY 3 | DAY 4 | DAY 5 | DAY 6 | DAY 7 | DAY 8 | DAY 9 | DAY 10 | DAY 11 | DAY 12 | DAY 13 |
| N+1 | | | | | | | | | | DAY 1 | DAY 2 | DAY 3 | DAY 4 | DAY 5 |

DAY 1

AM
- Column rebar cage installation and Inspection

PM
- Rebar cage for Core wall
- Jacking up of internal formwork for core wall
- Column Casting

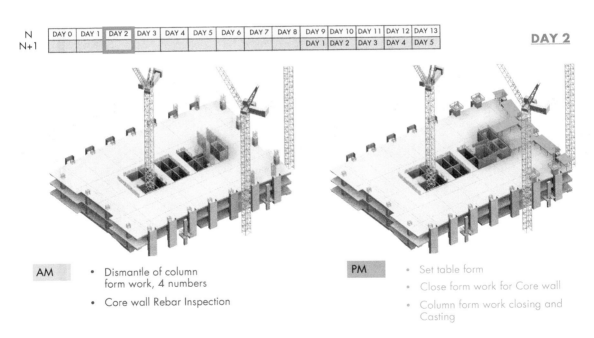

| N | DAY 0 | DAY 1 | DAY 2 | DAY 3 | DAY 4 | DAY 5 | DAY 6 | DAY 7 | DAY 8 | DAY 9 | DAY 10 | DAY 11 | DAY 12 | DAY 13 |
| N+1 | | | | | | | | | | DAY 1 | DAY 2 | DAY 3 | DAY 4 | DAY 5 |

DAY 2

AM
- Dismantle of column form work, 4 numbers
- Core wall Rebar Inspection

PM
- Set table form
- Close form work for Core wall
- Column form work closing and Casting

FIGURE 10–8–20 (continued)

N	DAY 0	DAY 1	DAY 2	DAY 3	DAY 4	DAY 5	DAY 6	DAY 7	DAY 8	DAY 9	DAY 10	DAY 11	DAY 12	DAY 13	
N+1										DAY 1	DAY 2	DAY 3	DAY 4	DAY 5	**DAY 3**

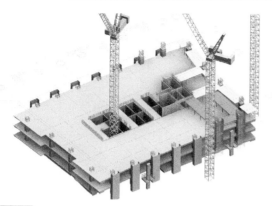

AM
- Dismantle of column form work, 4 numbers
- Set table form
- Core wall form work closing
- Erection of scaffold for PC half slab at lift lobby

PM
- Core wall form work closing
- Set table form
- Install Hollow Core Slab, PC half slab
- Core wall form work closing
- PC Beams installation

N	DAY 0	DAY 1	DAY 2	DAY 3	DAY 4	DAY 5	DAY 6	DAY 7	DAY 8	DAY 9	DAY 10	DAY 11	DAY 12	DAY 13	
N+1										DAY 1	DAY 2	DAY 3	DAY 4	DAY 5	**DAY 4**

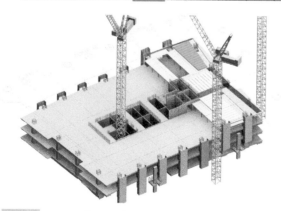

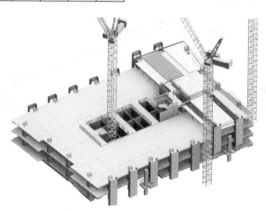

AM
- Installation of Hollow Core slab
- Installation of PC slab & beams
- Rebar for spandrel and RC beam
- Formwork closing for core wall

PM
- Installation of Hollow core Slab
- Installation of Half Slab at Lift Lobby
- Rebar for Post tensioning beams
- Laying of tendons PT beams
- Formwork closing for core wall

FIGURE 10–8–20   (continued)

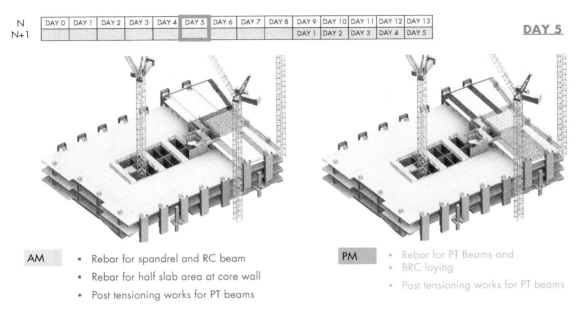

DAY 5

| N | DAY 0 | DAY 1 | DAY 2 | DAY 3 | DAY 4 | DAY 5 | DAY 6 | DAY 7 | DAY 8 | DAY 9 | DAY 10 | DAY 11 | DAY 12 | DAY 13 |
| N+1 | | | | | | | | | | DAY 1 | DAY 2 | DAY 3 | DAY 4 | DAY 5 |

AM
- Rebar for spandrel and RC beam
- Rebar for half slab area at core wall
- Post tensioning works for PT beams

PM
- Rebar for PT Beams and
- BRC laying
- Post tensioning works for PT beams

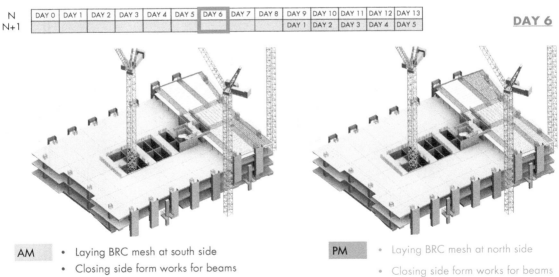

DAY 6

| N | DAY 0 | DAY 1 | DAY 2 | DAY 3 | DAY 4 | DAY 5 | DAY 6 | DAY 7 | DAY 8 | DAY 9 | DAY 10 | DAY 11 | DAY 12 | DAY 13 |
| N+1 | | | | | | | | | | DAY 1 | DAY 2 | DAY 3 | DAY 4 | DAY 5 |

AM
- Laying BRC mesh at south side
- Closing side form works for beams

PM
- Laying BRC mesh at north side
- Closing side form works for beams

FIGURE 10-8-20 (*continued*)

| N | DAY 0 | DAY 1 | DAY 2 | DAY 3 | DAY 4 | DAY 5 | DAY 6 | DAY 7 | DAY 8 | DAY 9 | DAY 10 | DAY 11 | DAY 12 | DAY 13 | **DAY 7** |
| N+1 | | | | | | | | | | DAY 1 | DAY 2 | DAY 3 | DAY 4 | DAY 5 | |

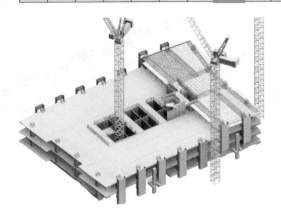
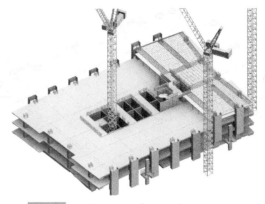

AM
- Laying BRC mesh at north side
- Final adjustment of PT works and Completion
- Beam side formwork

PM
- Beam side formwork
- Cleaning and final check of Formwork alignment, rebar works and PT works
- Rebar, and PT works inspection.

| N | DAY 0 | DAY 1 | DAY 2 | DAY 3 | DAY 4 | DAY 5 | DAY 6 | DAY 7 | DAY 8 | DAY 9 | DAY 10 | DAY 11 | DAY 12 | DAY 13 | **DAY 8** |
| N+1 | | | | | | | | | | DAY 1 | DAY 2 | DAY 3 | DAY 4 | DAY 5 | |

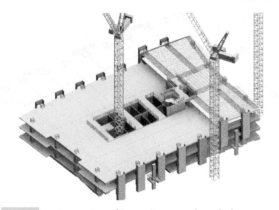
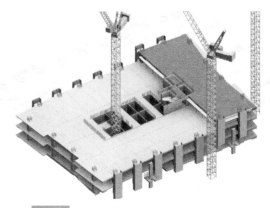

AM
- Inspection of Beam Form work and alignment.
- Setting of level pegs and marking of casting level
- Final cleaning and Inspection

PM
- Casting of wall, Beam and Slab.

(B)

FIGURE 10–8–20 (continued)

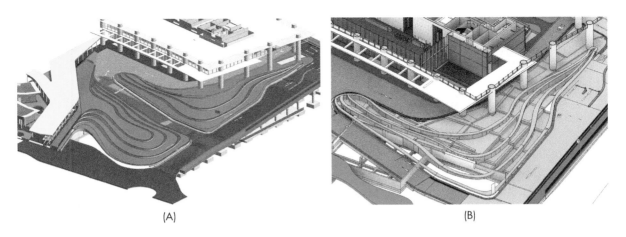

(A)

(B)

FIGURE 10–8–21   (A and B) Complex Ribbon Landscape.

Image courtesy of DCA Architects Pte Ltd. & Shimizu Corporation.

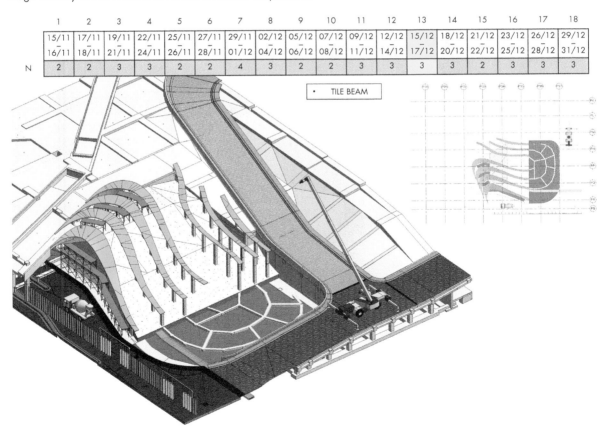

	1	2	3	4	5	6	7	8	9	10	11	12	13	14	15	16	17	18
	15/11 16/11	17/11 18/11	19/11 21/11	22/11 24/11	25/11 26/11	27/11 28/11	29/11 01/12	02/12 04/12	05/12 06/12	07/12 08/12	09/12 11/12	12/12 14/12	15/12 17/12	18/12 20/12	21/12 22/12	23/12 25/12	26/12 28/12	29/12 31/12
N	2	2	3	3	2	2	4	3	2	2	3	3	3	3	2	3	3	3

TILE BEAM

FIGURE 10–8–22   4D simulation of complex ribbon landscape.

Image courtesy of Shimizu Corporation.

FIGURE 10–8–23   Selecting the points from the BIM model via the iPad.

Image courtesy of Shimizu Corporation.

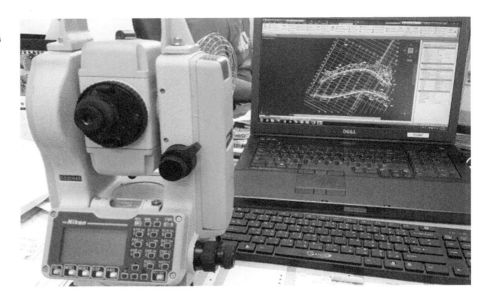

As described above, the ribbon structure was a variation introduced during the construction stage. It was also the final structural construction of the project, and so had to be completed within a very short time frame. With such a complex design forming a key entrance feature of the project, expectations were high. With the close collaboration between the architects, engineers, and contractor, the model was adjusted accurately with all the interfacing details to achieve the desired effect. The 3D model shown in Figure 10–8–24 was

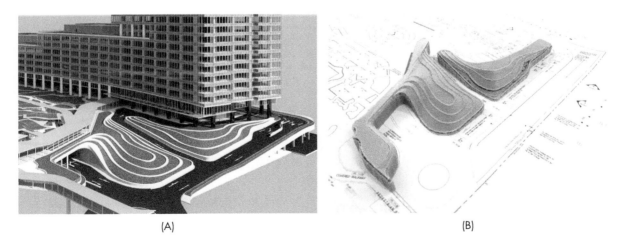

(A)   (B)

FIGURE 10–8–24   Design intent of the ribbon landscape feature. (A) BIM model. (B) 3D print.

Image courtesy of DCA Architects Pte Ltd. & Shimizu Corporation.

(A)   (B)

FIGURE 10–8–25   (A and B) In-progress and completed ribbon landscape.

Image courtesy of DCA Architects Pte Ltd. & Shimizu Corporation.

printed to facilitate the visualization, especially for workers on-site to understand the form. The coordinate points were accurately determined with "point layout" to facilitate marking on-site. The entire foundation, structure, finishes, and planting were completed in only 8 weeks (see Figure 10–8–25).

BIM 360 Glue and iPad on Site. To support the project team to verify the works carried out on-site, the BIM model was delivered to mobile devices, such as iPads, by uploading it in BIM 360 Glue, which enabled the construction team to access the BIM models and review them on-site (shown in Chapter 6, Figure 6–15).

Changes made on-site were tracked and incorporated into the as-built BIM model. Changes were marked on the iPad directly during the site inspections, and photos were taken for record. The construction team then briefed the modelers in the site office for them to update the BIM model to reflect the changes made in the field.

BIM Board. The project team was looking for a method to communicate information from the BIM models to the site team. One of the methods they devised was the BIM board shown in Figure 10–8–26, on which Shimizu displayed printed 3D images from the BIM model for all workers. This proved to be especially useful for discussion with subcontractors, and easy for the workers to understand the works scheduled in the morning and the afternoon shifts. It is particularly useful for workers drawn from a pool of different nationalities and for those who have just started work on-site, as they can quickly see what works are planned for the day with 3D images and detailed tasks.

FIGURE 10–8–26   Photo of
BIM board on-site.

Image courtesy of Shimizu
Corporation.

10.8.10 Conclusion

Risk Reduction. The use of BIM enabled a better understanding of the issues
involved, facilitated communication among the project team and with the
authorities, and thus contributed both to avoiding or reducing risk and to
improved productivity. Risk to the construction budget and schedule can be
minimized with an accurate BIM model, providing clarity to all parties and
accurate measurement of material quantities. Some examples:

- For Phase 1 completion, the BIM model was used to present the project's
  status to the BCA in order to address their concerns for the safety and
  protection of the public from ongoing construction works. The hazard
  zones for tower crane hoisting operations and the layout of protective
  hoardings near public areas were all modeled accurately to address these
  risks (see Figure 10–8–27).
- 3D views were incorporated in the construction drawings and the shop
  drawings and displayed prominently around the construction site. This
  allowed the site workers to better visualize the complex interfacing,
  reducing unwanted mistakes on-site, and thereby reducing the risk to
  the construction schedule.

The high-level milestones of the project timeline remained unchanged. The
detailed level of coordination achieved using **BIM** validated its **effectiveness in
ensuing prompt decision making** throughout the design development stage and
on-site **to meet timely completion** for Temporary Occupation Permit (TOP)
1 within 20 months and Temporary Occupation Permit (TOP) 2 in 26 months.

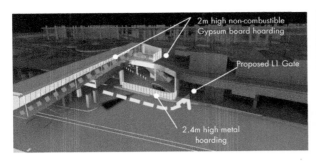

2.4m high metal hoarding.

1.8m high non-combustible Gypsum board hoarding.

FIGURE 10-8-27   Temporary Metal Hoarding in BIM.

Image courtesy of DCA Architects Pte Ltd. & Shimizu Corporation.

Without BIM, there would clearly have been situations where traditional coordination would have resulted in unforeseen circumstances in coordination, such as undetected clashes or poor interfacing, that would have required redesign and rework and would have caused delay. BIM enabled the project team to visualize every corner and to address issues in 3D effectively. With BIM, the opportunities for discrepancies across 2D drawings were greatly reduced, and all areas were visualized and reviewed in the model, both of which reduce the risk of human error, whether in design or in communication.

Challenges and Solutions. MBC II adopted BIM processes throughout the project successfully and the building was completed on schedule. Nevertheless, there were some aspects in which BIM could have been leveraged to improve the process even more:

- Ideally the whole consultant team should be involved at an early stage together with the client. In this project, the architect had to model the information provided by the C&S, M&E, and landscape architect.
- A method of contract procurement that allows for early contractor involvement is preferable. This would give the team a better head start to select optimum construction methods, and would likely have made construction crews more productive and cost effective.
- From the point of view of technology, more supporting tools could be adopted, such as point cloud data to capture existing information for part of the addition or alteration works within the development.
- The client's facility maintenance team should be involved in design and construction so that they understand the building and the BIM model to be handed over for their operational and maintenance purposes.

Acknowledgments

This case study was prepared by Vincent Koo and Min Thu of DCA Architects, Pty. Ltd., Singapore and with the support of many of the Mapletree project team and of Tai Fatt Cheng and others at the Singapore Building Construction Authority. We are extremely grateful to them all for sharing their deep practical experience of working with BIM.

10.9 PRINCE MOHAMMAD BIN ABDULAZIZ INTERNATIONAL AIRPORT, MEDINA, UAE
Building Information Modeling Facilities Management Integration

10.9.1 Project Information

Established through the public-private partnership (PPP) model, Prince Mohammad Bin Abdulaziz International Airport in Medina is the first airport privatization in Saudi Arabia. It is the main entry point for visitors to the Kaaba and those arriving on pilgrimage to the two Holy Cities of the Islamic World (see Figure 10–9–1).

The airport was developed and is now being operated by the consortium company Tibah Airports Development Company Limited, formed by the following Joint Venture (JV): TAV Airports of Turkey and Saudi Oger Limited and Al Rajhi Holding Group, both of Saudi Arabia. The JV entered into a contract

FIGURE 10–9–1 Medina Airport.

Image courtesy of TAV Construction.

in October 2011 with the Civil Aviation Authority of Saudi Arabia (GACA) to build and operate the airport under a 25-year concession, securing a US$1.2 billion financing package from a club of Saudi Arabian banks.

The 25-year concession has been structured as a Build-Transfer-Operate (BTO) project so that GACA retains ownership of the airport infrastructure during the operation phase of the contract. The consortium, through the special purpose vehicle incorporated for the project, Tibah Airports Development Company Limited, will be responsible for the management of the airport, including airside and landside operations. GACA will continue to act as regulator and will be responsible for air traffic control operation. The consortium and its lenders are taking passenger demand risk and will share revenues generated under the concession with GACA.

The expansion will increase capacity to eight million passengers per year through the construction of the new terminal building, apron, and rapid exit taxiways. Capacity is expected to be further increased to 16 million passengers per year by the end of the concession period.

The key principles of the architectural design are integration with existing airport facilities; a simple, coherent layout with well-defined routes for passenger circulation, safety, and security; as well as operational efficiency, flexibility, adaptability, and expansion potential. The design and construction of the new terminal and airside infrastructure were completed during July, 2012–February, 2015 by a large project team located in multiple countries (see Table 10–9–1).

Medina Airport is the first airport to be certified LEED Gold by USGBC in the MENA (Middle East and North Africa) region. In 2015, the airport also won the ENR's Global Best Projects Award as the best project in the airports/ports category.

Project highlights:

- 156,940 m^2/Terminal Building and Concourses
- 8,000,000 passengers per year/Terminal Design Capacity
- 14,320 tons/Structural Steel Works
- 89,161 m^3/Concrete Works
- 10,000,000 m^3/Excavation Works
- 2,800,000 m^3/Filling Works
- 1,500,000 m^2/Runway, Taxiway, Apron Area
- 32 units/Passenger Boarding Bridges
- 93 units/Lifts, Escalators, Travelators
- 2,200 baggage per hour/Baggage Handling System Capacity

10.9.2 Novel/Innovative Use of BIM

The use of BIM within the Middle East has been evolving. Following the lead of several countries around the world, the use of BIM is becoming mandated in the Middle East, such as the January 1, 2014, mandate by the Dubai Emirate Municipality where the use of BIM has become a requirement for buildings

Table 10–9–1   Key Parties and Their Roles in the Project

Client/Grantor	General Authority of Civil Aviation (GACA) of Saudi Arabia
Concessionaire	Tibah Airports Development Company Limited
	Joint Venture composed of TAV Airports Holding (Turkey), Al Rajhi Holding Group CJSC, Saudi Oger Limited (Saudi Arabia)
Independent Engineering	Halcrow Group Limited (UK)
Lenders	Consortium of National Commercial Bank (NCB), Arab National Bank (ANB), Saudi British Bank (SABB)
Lenders Technical Advisors	Intervistas Consulting Inc.
Main Contractor	Madinah Airport Joint Venture composed of TAV Tepe Akfen Investment Construction and Operations (Turkey) with Al Arrab Contracting Company CJSC) (Saudi Arabia)
Main Designer	Scott Brownrigg (formerly GMW Architects UK)
Airside Infrastructure Works & MEP + Structural Concept Design	URS/Scott Wilson (UK)
Structural Steel Design	Çakıt Engineering (Turkey)
Reinforced Concrete Design	OSM Engineering (Turkey)
Mechanical Design	Moskay Engineering (Turkey)
Electrical Design	HB Teknik (Turkey)

that are "above 40 floors," "larger than 300,000 square feet," and "specialized buildings such as hospitals, universities, and all that is similar to that." While BIM can bring benefit to all size projects, the mandate on only large and special projects reflects an understanding of the associated transition cost and difficulty for small projects in a market where BIM capable companies and staff have only recently been developing.

The trend is clear; projects are increasingly requiring BIM execution. Foreseeing the expanding need to implement BIM on projects, TAV Integrated Solutions (TAV-IS) had been established within TAV construction to formalize and commercialize the combined design, construction, and operation know-how of TAV construction and TAV airports based on available tools and technologies created for the built environment industry.

The use of BIM was not specified by the client and being a fast track project within a joint-venture with partners without BIM resources, its implementation was not planned for construction of the Medina Airport. Currently, the main drivers for BIM use are the project requirements as specified in the Employer's Information Requirements (EIR). The resources for BIM execution are budgeted to be compliant with the EIR during tender phase, otherwise the tooling and staffing for BIM is currently seen as an additional cost. Difficulty in staffing BIM positions or training existing staff and finding subcontractors with the BIM capabilities are other limiting factors.

The use of a BIM system as a repository for all design, construction, and operational assets for facilities management had been discussed as a need for TAV-operated airports within TAV airports and construction circles. So the timing, scope, and size of the Medina project was ideal to develop a BIM infrastructure specifically for facilities management as a benchmark within the company. This BIM-FM project was funded by Tibah and implemented by TAV-IS. Through this effort TAV will have formulated and implemented the complete range of information mobility, providing a broad reference and template to future projects and other airports.

The CEO of TAV Airports Holding is an avid supporter of TAV-IS and its initiative to develop the use of BIM and technology throughout company operations. The scope and budget of the BIM-FM integration in Medina was presented to the Tibah board of directors and received approval to proceed. In line with TAV-IS initiatives, the main objective was to combine all design and construction information using BIM to integrate with Facilities Management (FM) workflow and systems that will be actively used during the lifetime of the facility. With this integration, all construction, maintenance, and asset information becomes accessible to staff operating the terminal through a single easily navigable graphical interface. Figure 10–9–2 shows an aerial photo of the terminal with the BIM model showing the general system routings.

The added value of BIM as an FM tool are as follows:

- Visual interface to complete facility information
- Asset database developed within BIM effort and direct population of CMMS
- Access to equipment documentation through BIM model
- Ability to view and track end-to-end system and subsystem connectivity
- Mobile visual tool to access and add or update data to CMMS database from site
- Basis for energy analyses for upgrades and renovation scenarios to assess impact and return on investment

The following summarize the two main milestones:

- Develop a federated BIM model of the terminal, including all discipline systems:
  - BIM LOD 500 modeling: gathering construction specification, documents, and drawings; modeling the terminal and systems
- Organize and integrate BIM with facility management and operation objectives; integrate physical equipment and system information of the terminal:
  - BIM-FM library development, training, and integration: workshop and training with consultants and stakeholders to determine FM library requirements and guidelines
  - BIM-FM data validation and Computerized Maintenance Management System (CMMS) integration: implementation and integration of BIM-FM system and as-built validation

FIGURE 10–9–2 (Top)
Medina Airport aerial
view. (Bottom) Mechanical
systems in BIM model.

Image courtesy of TAV
Construction.

10.9.3 Communication and Collaboration

Modeling of the terminal began during the late phases of the construction. All the drawing and construction information packages were acquired directly from the TAV Construction staff on-site and through Aconex, a cloud-based project document and information management software.

Workshops were organized with several Tibah and TAV Airport Operations staff to determine end user needs and expectations. Critical maintainable assets and systems were identified, along with their relevant attributes useful for site staff. This information was necessary to scope the amount of data to be incorporated within the BIM model.

During pre-engineering, TAV-IS staff and ProCS, the MEP BIM consultant, had to determine all space, element families, system information, system routing-connectivity, and attribute information. The major maintainable systems are MEP related; construction and operational know-how is key to correctly identify and properly model MEP systems.

The bulk modeling from the terminal as-built drawings was done as a joint effort by TAV-IS staff and MEP BIM consultant (ProCS) with the support of a BIM modeling company (Invicta). Continuous QA/QC of the model with feedback from site staff to clarify any issues were essential for producing the right information. The BIM-FM platform Ecodomus-FM (http://ecodomus.com/products/masonry-style/) and the CMMS software IFS (www.ifsworld.com/us/solutions/) were chosen for this project. BIM models were authored using Autodesk Revit and compiled within Autodesk Navisworks and Ecodomus PM (http://ecodomus.com/products/ecodomus-pm/).

A twelve month duration was planned for all the workshops, modeling, integration, and training. The modeling itself was planned to continue for 4–5 months. For an airport terminal this size, under normal circumstances, this is a reasonable amount of time to author a federated BIM model. Tibah updated the room numbering and element tagging scheme, which required the model to the updated. This extended the modeling effort by several months. In the end, the model and integration was completed in 18 months. There are several lessons learned from this for future projects as discussed below.

There were parties participating from seven countries (Turkey, U.S., Russia, KSA, UAE, Egypt, and India) and four continents to realize this BIM-FM integration effort. Regular web meetings were held to touch base on updates, make decisions, or clarify any major concerns with all parties involved.

A web-based project management platform, Basecamp (https://basecamp.com/), was used rather than email to provide coherent communication among all involved parties. All project files, including BIM models, were distributed using TAVcloud, an enterprise hybrid cloud file sharing platform (see Figure 10–9–3). A common communication and file-sharing platform is essential to keep all stakeholders on track with update information, avoiding the splintering that is common with individual emails and attachments.

The main concerns were to author BIM models with accurate information that reflects the as-built conditions and ensure that all asset elements modeled are tagged consistently with the CMMS database and asset registry requirements. Having access to both construction and operations staff on-site was an advantage to clarify issues when drawings or information were not clear.

One challenge to collaboration and communication with such a group spread around the globe was to schedule web meetings around time differences and different holidays. Such meetings were also not always efficient due to connection quality, but this was offset with the use of the web-based project management platform and also by recording screencast videos to share specific issues regarding software use and modeling.

10.9.4 Stakeholder Involvement

Stakeholder involvement throughout the BIM modeling and FM integration workflow is shown in Figure 10–9–4. Each row represents the field of responsibility for each stakeholder. TAV-IS together with Tibah led the authoring and integration effort with the support of a MEP BIM consultant, the BIM-FM platform, and CMMS software vendor.

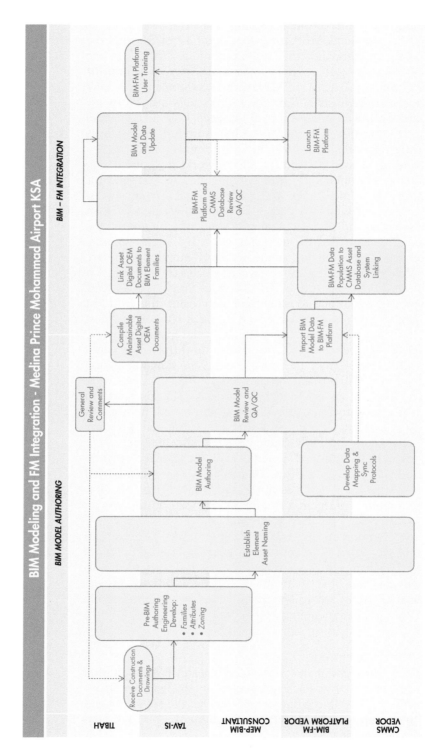

FIGURE 10-9-3 Web-based file and project management tools are essential to provide coherent communication and data exchange across a large group.

Image courtesy of TAV Construction.

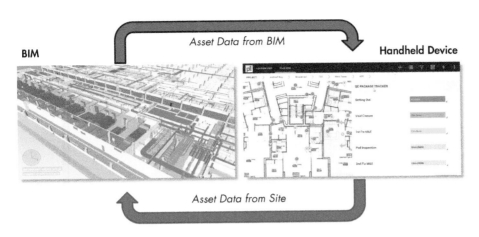

FIGURE 10–9–4 Stakeholder roles within workflow for developing BIM models and FM integration.

Image courtesy of TAV Construction.

All asset element families and respective attributes were developed using the terminal design documents. Models were authored as the asset naming nomenclature was being developed by Tibah and the CMMS software vendor. Modeling was iterative as model information and comments were received. Meanwhile, mapping data protocols between the BIM-FM and CMMS software were developed between the software vendors. Construction and asset documentation were linked to the element families within the BIM-FM platform and the BIM asset data were used to populate the CMMS database.

Once commissioned and operational, the most critical job is maintaining the BIM models, keeping them up to date and synchronized with the CMMS database. This requires a clear lifecycle management plan. The FM/Operations BIM Execution Plan (BEP) defines the authoring requirements, along with the management of the BIM models, for content as well as periodic software version updates to ensure BIM models are accessible in the long term.

The FM/Operations BEP defines model requirements for future projects from minor interior modifications, new expansions, or new buildings within the airport. This guides future stakeholders and projects executed with BIM through the design phase to construction or for postconstruction BIM authoring to be integrated with the existing BIM-FM platform. Figure 10–9–5 shows the schematic relationship between how BEPs are derived for future projects.

Asset data is managed on site by Tibah staff while the models are managed by TAV-IS. Changes in site conditions are registered on-site either manually or through the platform mobile devices interface (see Figure 10–9–6). This data is aggregated and used to update the BIM models periodically. Site conditions are forwarded to TAV-IS for BIM model and platform updates, where the data is synchronized with the CMMS database.

10.9.5 Risk

The return on investment of implementing BIM on a given project is difficult to quantify; however, the project team's experience indicates that costs associated

FIGURE 10–9–5 The BIM execution plan for the overall BIM-FM platform and its relationship to the development of BIM models on future projects. This is essential to ensure that information from future projects can be integrated into the BIM-FM platform.

Image courtesy of TAV Construction.

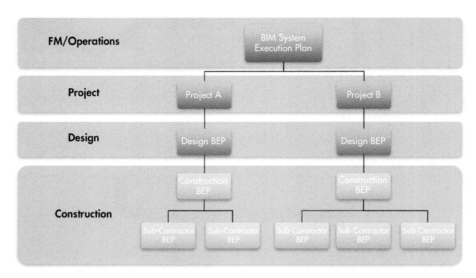

with implementing BIM are offset by efficiency gains and reduced staffing for the functions supported by BIM.

The combined information within the BIM-FM platform will improve the response and service level of the FM operations team to maintain the terminal more efficiently. Responding technicians will have access to the relevant information as shown in Figure 10–9–7 for the task at hand, including element attributes, location, maintenance history, OEM documentation, spare parts, and access/routing information.

In an emergency scenario, where a fire sprinkler is accidently discharged due to damage or false activation, the location of each fire sprinkler and its routing to the shutdown valve is defined as a system within the BIM model. It will be possible to quickly locate the connected shutdown valve and prevent flooding. This is illustrated in Figure 10–9–8.

Using a BIM-FM platform provides a granularity of information several magnitudes greater compared to the CMMS database populated with data manually extracted from printed material or site survey. A total of eleven BIM models were authored for Medina per discipline and floor levels, which, when assembled, provide information on more than 580,000 individual components. The following tables summarize elements tagged specifically for maintainable content within the BIM models. The listed elements define the categories of elements that form the asset tree of the CMMS database (see Table 10–9–2).

Part of delivering a large airport project includes providing technical facilities management through the defect and liability period (DLP), which can be many years. Having the CMMS operational is critical for the airport authority to track contractual key performance indicators (KPI) of the airport operation. Delaying the use of the CMMS system risks improper reporting of KPIs, which could potentially lead to penalties.

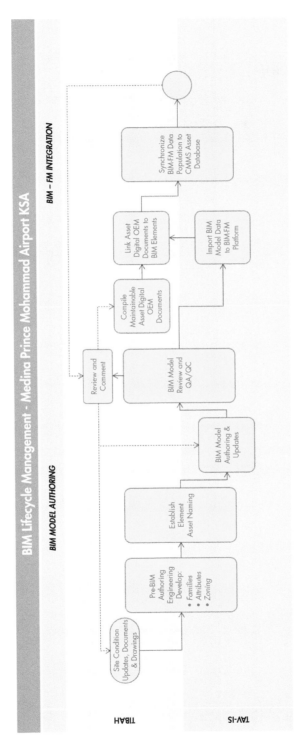

FIGURE 10-9-6 Site conditions are registered and reflected to the BIM models to ensure asset data is up to date and accurate. Models are updated periodically based on the information from the site.

Image courtesy of TAV Construction.

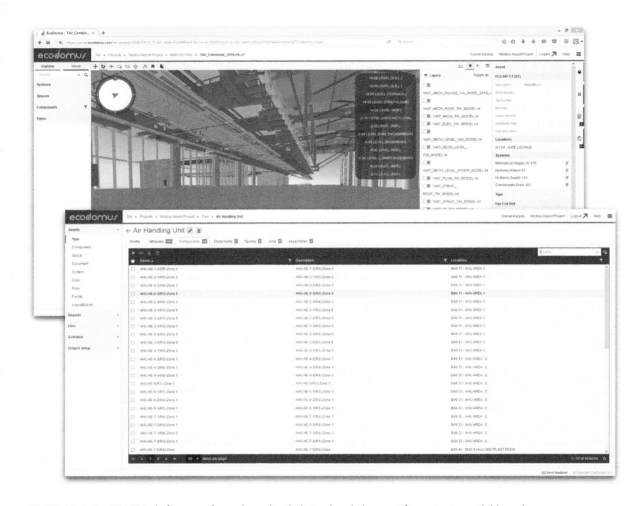

FIGURE 10-9-7 BIM FM platform interface where detailed visual and element information is available to the user.

Image courtesy of TAV Construction.

FIGURE 10-9-8 The relation of each component within a system is defined in the BIM model. This makes it possible to isolate and track connected components per system and/or zone. The figure shows the shutdown valve of the sprinkler system in one of the departure gates in the terminal.

Image courtesy of TAV Construction.

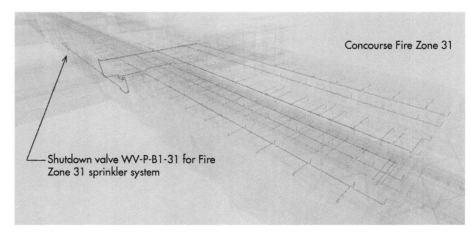

Concourse Fire Zone 31

Shutdown valve WV-P-B1-31 for Fire Zone 31 sprinkler system

Table 10–9–2   Model Elements with Maintainable Content in CMMS Database

BIM Model File Name	Schedule Name	Family Count	Instance Count
1407_STRUC_TAV_MODEL	Structural Column Schedule	86	2,248
	Structural Framing Schedule	5	12,874
	Floor Schedule	18	226
	Wall Schedule	16	340
1407_STRUC_ ROOF_TAV_MODEL	Structural Column Schedule	3	28
1407_ARCH_TAV_MODEL	Door Schedule	26	1,950
	Specialty Equipment Schedule	12	1,242
	Generic Model Schedule	5	1,342
	Casework Schedule	10	120
	Ceiling Schedule	1	776
	Floor Schedule	1	2,861
	Plumbing Fixture Schedule	18	3,237
	Structural Column Schedule	1	675
	Wall Schedule	52	7,781
1407_ARCH_FACADE_TAV_MODEL	Door Schedule	14	195
	Wall Schedule	2	1,110
	Generic Model Schedule	216	2,895
	Panel Schedule	3	13,582
	Mullion Schedule	1	18,635
1407_MECH_LEVEL_000_MODEL	Air Terminal Schedule	8	4,682
	Duct Accessory Schedule	7	1,860
	Mechanical Equipment Schedule	5	1,231
	Pipe Accessory Schedule	9	6,934
1407_MECH_LEVEL_-730_MODEL	Air Terminal Schedule	12	1,448
	Duct Accessory Schedule	10	2,840
	Mechanical Equipment Schedule	31	1,598
	Pipe Accessory Schedule	20	5,873
1407_MECH_LEVEL_OTHER_MODEL	Air Terminal Schedule	9	1,446
	Duct Accessory Schedule	7	1,329
	Mechanical Equipment Schedule	13	711
	Pipe Accessory Schedule	13	3,768
1407_PLUM_TAV_MODEL	Mechanical Equipment Schedule	13	62
	Pipe Accessory Schedule	12	1,425
	Plumbing Fixture Schedule	24	3,068

(Continued)

Table 10–9–2 *(continued)*

BIM Model File Name	Schedule Name	Family Count	Instance Count
1407_FP_TAV_MODEL	Mechanical Equipment Schedule	3	227
	Pipe Accessory Schedule	19	953
	Sprinkler Schedule	3	18,176
1407_ELEC_TAV_MODEL	Communication Device Schedule	2	2,256
	Electrical Equipment Schedule	47	531
	Electrical Fixture Schedule	7	8,036
	Fire Alarm Device Schedule	19	8,629
	Lighting Device Schedule	19	690
	Lighting Fixture Schedule	36	18,361
	Security Device Schedule	2	376
	Total	**840**	**168,627**

Project specifications define delivery of the relevant drawings and documents for operations and their specific formats at the handover phase of the project. In general, several duplicates of hard copies of the documents are required to be delivered in ring binders along with digital copies of these documents on DVDs. The handover packages are usually not convenient for digital processing. Documents may be scanned copies and disparate, which require extensive manual processing. Population of the CMMS database for an airport typically means extracting asset information from tens of thousands of documents. Accessing and organizing relevant data to populate a database for operations manually can be extremely cumbersome.

In many large projects the amount of time FM staff is available on-site before substantial completion is not sufficient to review and extract all the data and populate the CMMS prior to the start of operations. Authoring BIM models with FM in mind expedites populating the CMMS database where all the required information has already been concurrently compiled within the BIM models during the construction phase. The promise of BIM allows data mobility and alleviates the divide between design, construction, and operation of a facility. This significantly reduces the work hours associated with having to extract information from printed documents and drawings to manually populate the CMMS database.

10.9.6 BIM in the Field

The goal of integrating BIM with FM systems is to make all the data accessible to Tibah staff on-site anywhere within the terminal. The BIM-FM platform provides both a web-based interface as well as an application for mobile devices.

Figure 10–9–9 describes the IT infrastructure. All asset information and documentation resides on the BIM-FM platform. The CMMS database is

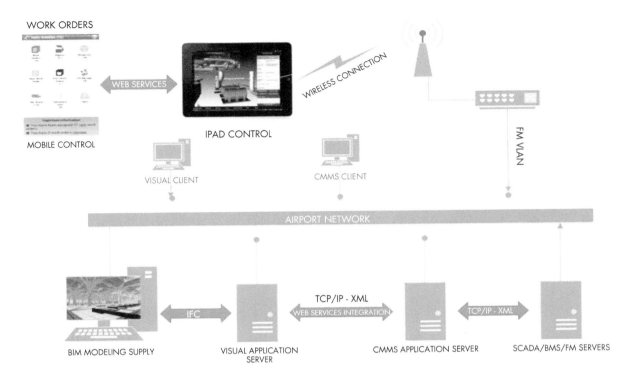

FIGURE 10–9–9 IT infrastructure of the BIM-FM platform and relation to the CMMS application.

Image courtesy of TAV Construction.

populated and synchronized with the BIM-FM platform. Work orders are stored on the CMMS database and server where the data is mapped to the BIM-FM platform. Work orders can be opened or searched through either system and their respective mobile applications. Both systems are accessible throughout the terminal over the airport Wi-Fi network.

The mobile application of the BIM-FM platform provides a means to register the changes on-site by linking photos and documentation to the elements or rooms within the BIM-FM platform. Periodic updates to the BIM models are made based on this data.

10.9.7 Lessons Learned: Problems, Challenges, Solutions

Specification Requirements. As mentioned earlier, the project specifications are the main driver of BIM implementation in the majority of large projects. The details of the BIM requirements for large projects vary greatly. Requirements for the use of BIM for FM purposes are usually very vaguely implied.

The following excerpts are from specifications for a few recent large airport projects:

> "In addition to the CAD submittals, the Contractor shall maintain a Revit model of the construction design, fully coordinated, at LOD 400. This model shall be submitted, via Electronic Document Management System (EDMS), for Engineer's review on a weekly basis, every week's end close of business."
>
> "In addition to the CAD submittals, the Contractor shall submit the As-Built Documentation via a Revit model of the construction design, fully coordinated, at LOD 400."
>
> "The Contractor shall coordinate, document and issue submissions for the construction of this project using a Building Information Modeling (BIM) system in accordance with latest industry best practice and the requirements of Dubai Municipality – Circular No. 196."
>
> "Project Close Out: Prior to Substantial Completion the Contractor shall provide to the Employer a fully compliant BIM Model including the following... All As-Built Information shall include the following... Hand-over to Facility Management team for lifecycle cost and data capture, asset operation and maintenance."

The first three excerpts were the only requirements given in the specifications for BIM on the project, while the last was the only information on the expectations for FM use of BIM.

With the development and adoption of standards such as the widely circulated Publicly Available Standard (PAS) 1192 documents by the British Standards Institute (BSI) and the National BIM Standard-United States (NBIMS-US) by buildingSMART, where both include the COBie (Construction Operations Building Information Exchange) framework, authoring BIM models, compiling documentation for FM after construction will become standardized and clear for all stakeholders.

The expectation of BIM for FM use or a LOD 500 model as part of the project delivery is becoming more common. A clear BIM Execution Plan (BEP) framework based on the Employer's Information Requirements (EIR) within the project specifications is a must to ensure the delivery of BIM models to be useful for FM, especially in the current environment where the definition of LOD (Level of Development) or LOI (Level of Information) outputs can be contentious.

Without a clear BEP, a common misconception is that updating BIM models throughout construction alone will result in a LOD 500 model ready for FM integration. Lack of clarity of the BIM scope on projects has led to variation orders where the client has initially specified a limited scope for BIM. Clients, eventually recognizing the shortcomings of the BIM scope, issue a variation order to ensure they receive an LOD 500 BIM model updated to as-built conditions and populated with the necessary information for FM use. This leads to additional modeling work and onerous edits that could have been avoided with proper specifications.

Early Engagement of FM Stakeholders and Concurrent Data Capture. The impact of having BIM models for FM enhances both the FM services and the asset database while reducing the time and effort to populate the CMMS. It is essential that all FM stakeholders be involved as early as possible by both reviewing and if possible authoring the project specifications.

Review of the BIM models and their content during construction while models are being authored and element information is being captured from various sources would avoid time-consuming rework post construction.

At Medina, asset registry and tagging on-site started after construction was completed and did not benefit from the commissioning and handover processes. The Medina project would have benefitted from early engagement of FM staff in defining tagging and attribute requirements during construction. Subsequent changes in room and tagging nomenclature required several modeling iterations and considerable extra time and expense.

Concurrent data capture with BIM during construction would have made compiling data much easier. The largest part of the effort of modeling was extracting information from construction documents. Had subcontractors been contractually required to deliver information using COBie, it would have greatly reduced the overall effort to create BIM models for FM use.

The use of the document management software Aconex during the project, however, greatly reduced the effort to access the documents and drawings themselves. During construction, all documents are added to Aconex consistently with abundant meta-data. This made it convenient to filter through all the documents to link to element families or individual elements directly. Aconex has developed its own BIM interface, called "Connected BIM," where BIM models in IFC format are imported and viewed within the Aconex interface. This way the links between BIM elements and documents can be established within one platform.

Element Tagging. Developing a common tagging scheme that would uniquely identify all maintainable equipment consistent for assets within the CMMS database and BIM models can be a challenge. There are several ways to uniquely identify equipment that may vary based on the chosen software and the preferences of the operations team.

There may be several unique equipment identifiers used in parallel that are necessary to capture as attribute information, yet not particularly useful to tag elements within the BIM models:

- Barcode tag numbers
- Equipment serial numbers
- As-built shop drawing tags
- Object IDs compiled of several naming levels

Some operators may simply prefer to use equipment tags found on the as-built drawings. This may not be possible in large projects where there may be several subcontractors working on the same systems in different zones of the

Table 10–9–3   An Object ID Scheme

Object ID Naming Levels	Description
Level 1: System Code	<u>AA</u>: Two-digit system code as defined by Tibah i.e., 04 for HVAC System
Level 2: Subsystem Code	<u>BB</u>: Two-digit Subsystem code as defined by Tibah i.e., 01 for Air Condition Units under HVAC system
Level 3: Room Number	<u>CCCC</u>: Terminal room number as defined by Tibah i.e., M281
Level 4: Unique ID	<u>DDD</u>: Numbering restarting at each room. i.e., 1,2,3, etc.

FIGURE 10–9–10
An object ID scheme.
Image courtesy TAV
Construction.

Level 1	Level 2	Level 3	Level 4
System Code	Subsystem Code	Room Number	Unique ID

building who may not follow the same tagging scheme, or worse, use inconsistent tagging, which leads to duplicate tags rendering the as-built drawing tags useless for unique identification.

Tibah and the CMMS software vendor developed an Object ID scheme for Medina for the asset database. The Object ID is compiled as described in Table 10–9–3 and Figure 10–9–10, and assigned to each piece of equipment within the BIM models as an instance parameter. This enables equipment to be filtered by system and location.

Example Object ID for the three air condition units in Room M281:

1. 0401M2811
2. 0401M2812
3. 0401M2813

A tagging scheme that includes human readable system and location (building, level, room, system code, and so on) information is desirable for practical reasons, as was done in Medina. Equipment location within the tag is extracted automatically from room spaces defined in BIM models. There is difficulty with equipment spanning multiple rooms. BIM authoring tools may not be able to register such equipment automatically. These elements need to be manually assigned to a given physical space and tagged accordingly.

Another difficulty arose with the Unique ID number for multiple pieces of equipment within the same room space. Manual equipment tagging was done post BIM modeling where equipment numbering increased incrementally, progressing from room to room. However, in the BIM models the Unique ID was reset to one at each room.

The consequence of this difference in Unique ID numbering from room to room is that a particular element in the BIM model may not map to the actual physical location. This is not prohibitive for asset management, yet this difference was corrected manually based on site surveys.

Room Space Definition. Room space volumes must be defined for all spaces in the model to provide location information as part of the tagging for all elements. To ensure equipment tags are unique, every single volume where there is equipment needs a uniquely defined room space. It is an important challenge to define each room in an airport terminal where there are different room heights, ceiling voids, shafts, and technical rooms spread at different locations or intertwined.

One challenge with room naming is that their designation at the design stage and the naming used during construction may be different, or spaces may be redefined when operations begin. This was the case in Medina, and this required a lot of manual rework in the BIM models. Areas like risers and shafts that were not defined in design documents also had to be defined.

Rooms are defined as volumes in the models based on the 2D plan areas on the drawings and the height of each room or area. These room volumes need to be defined so that they include all elements within the specific room area. This is usually up to the slab soffit, generally above the ceiling. Room volumes need to be unique and cannot overlap so as to ensure the associated tagging is also unique. Several checks are done, both from visual information and from schedules, to ensure that all equipment are captured within a room volume.

The height of a room or space can become tricky in a terminal with high ceiling spaces and islands of irregular elevated slabs served with local suspended ceilings are common. An example case is shown in Figure 10–9–11, where large room spaces are dissected to identify elements in a rational way for FM purposes.

System Definition. It is a main requirement and challenge to have all MEP systems within the BIM models connected to provide the visual information of the individual connected pipe and/or duct networks per equipment.

A particular equipment may be a part of multiple systems. For example, an air handling unit (AHU) is connected to the following three different systems with multiple routings as shown in Figure 10–9–12.

1. Hydronic systems: supply and return water piping
2. Air duct systems: fresh, supply, return, and exhaust air ducts
3. Electrical system

Systems definitions are necessary to track the connections, for example, between a particular AHU to the pump bringing the cold water to the unit. Having an element as part of multiple separate systems may cause difficulties both due to limitations of BIM authoring software and for filtering purposes when you have a piece of equipment connected to more than one system.

Large projects like the Medina Terminal result in large BIM model files. When these models are typically divided by discipline and level or zone, the

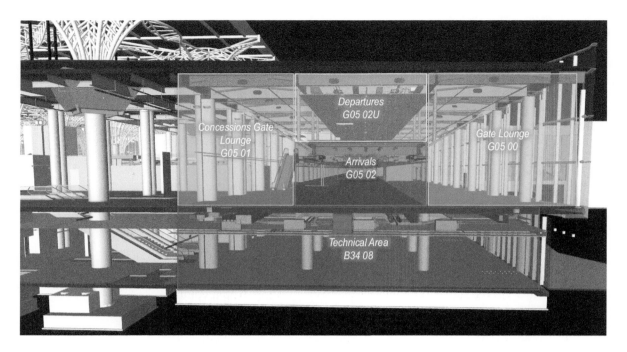

FIGURE 10-9-11   Section view of the terminal concourse showing the room space volume definition used as part of asset naming.

Image courtesy of TAV Construction.

FIGURE 10-9-12   Typical air handling unit (AHU) with its various connected systems.

Image courtesy of TAV Construction.

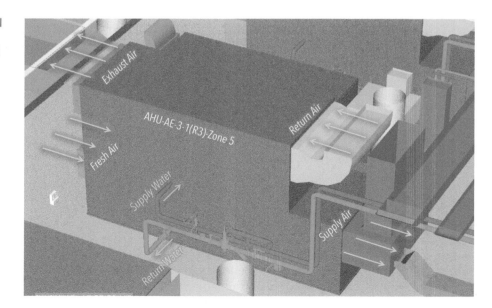

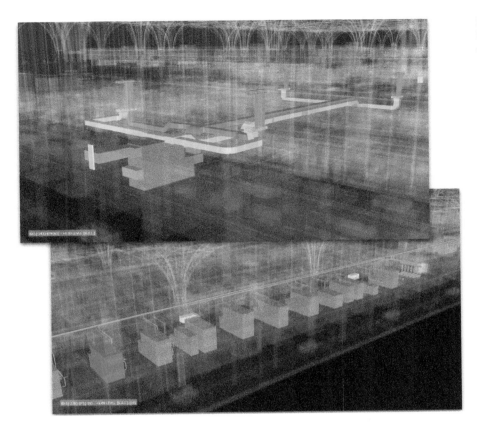

FIGURE 10–9–13 Air handling unit (AHU) shown with both the connected supply/return water supply system and air duct routing to areas the unit is serving.

Image courtesy of TAV Construction.

integrity of the system definitions cannot be maintained. Shared parameters TAV_System and TAV_Subsystem are added to the models, which are used to bind equipment to various systems across multiple BIM model files. These parameters are assigned to each equipment to identify the multiple systems they are a part of. This allows for filtering and visualizing the routing of the system network within the model or BIM-FM platform interface, as shown in Figure 10–9–13.

10.9.8 Conclusion and Future Outlook

As part of an initiative to extend the use of BIM and technologies throughout TAV projects and operated airports, a BIM infrastructure for facilities management was developed at the Medina Airport that provided a benchmark within the company for its other airports and airport clients.

The BIM-FM platform developed combines all design and construction information and integrates with facilities management (FM) workflow and systems that are used during the lifetime of the facility. The data compiled with BIM provided the asset database for the CMMS software with all relevant element attribute information and relevant documentation. With this integration, all construction, maintenance, and asset information is accessible to staff operating the terminal through a single easily navigable graphical interface.

Developing the BIM models and integration with FM systems required a collaborative effort with several different contributors dispersed around the world. The use of a web-based project management platform for coherent communication and cloud base file sharing for keeping all stakeholders on track with update information was essential to the success of this effort.

Implementing BIM for FM use first and foremost requires clear specifications to ensure that data content and organization are sufficient for the intended purpose and integration. A comprehensive FM/operations BIM execution plan is necessary to ensure that BIM models are maintained and that BIM models developed for future projects, from minor interior modifications to new expansions to new buildings within the airport, are consistent with the BIM-FM platform.

Among the challenges for developing a BIM infrastructure for FM, early stakeholder engagement to determine appropriate asset organization, content, and tagging is critical. Room and space definition that are part of asset identification is tricky for the irregular spaces that are typical for airports. Defining system connectivity—especially for elements that are part of multiple systems across multiple BIM models—requires parameter definitions to overcome authoring software limitations.

With BIM, data now has the means to coalesce and become information to be analyzed as never before. Data granularity and its volume achieved around BIM opens the doors for the creation of a searchable dataset for the built environment. Using BIM as a platform to integrate existing FM systems, such as the Computerized Maintenance Management System (CMMS) and Building Management/Automation System (BMS/BAS), means better analytics and performance for operations, energy management, business, and beyond.

Acknowledgments

This case study was prepared with the close collaboration of Ahmet Citipitioglu, Ph.D., P.E., Engineering & Design Director of TAV Construction, and Daniel Kazado, Managing Partner of ProCS Engineering. Further acknowledgments to TAV Integrated Solutions staff for their contributions. Special thanks to Tibah Airports and Dr. Sani Sener, CEO of TAV Airports and TAV Construction, for their vision and support.

10.10 HOWARD HUGHES MEDICAL INSTITUTE, CHEVY CHASE, MARYLAND
Setting Up and Utilizing an FM-Capable BIM

10.10.1 Introduction

The use of BIM technology to improve FM practices and capabilities is a relatively new and rapidly growing/evolving field, one that needs to take into account a number of key issues:

- Facilities managers tend to have a systems-driven viewpoint of their facility, rather than the space- or construction package-driven viewpoint often found in current BIM deliverables to facility owners

- Over time, facilities managers have invested a great deal in well-structured but stand-alone computerized maintenance management system (CMMS) databases, building automation system (BAS) databases, space management databases, and the like, that contain data vital for proper operation of the facility.
- BIM deliverables that focus mainly on transferring maintenance-focused asset data to the facility CMMS potentially miss the opportunity to integrate other valuable data within the BIM with facility data available from the above databases.
- Similarly, the use of a maintenance-focused CMMS to provide the primary means of viewing a BIM, and of interrogating the information within the BIM, potentially misses this same opportunity.

With the advent of BIM as a building systems database (among other things) and the increasing availability of middleware able to extract and integrate information from both the BIM and the above stand-alone databases, the stage is now set for facilities management to leverage this available information in new, imaginative, and effective ways, ways that look beyond a maintenance focus.

This study looks at the work and information flow of the Janelia Research Campus project to generate systems-orientated BIM models that track system linkages and then use these, together with data available in complementary databases, to materially improve a key needed ability and to readily and accurately evaluate and respond to the impacts of a major event or issue.

10.10.2 Background

Howard Hughes Medical Institute (HHMI), the largest private funder of biomedical research in the United States, operates as part of its portfolio Janelia Research Campus, a 689-acre (279 hectare) campus with 1.1 million sf (102,000 m^2) of buildings.

The main research building, built in 2006, covers 600,000 sf (56,000 m^2) and contains about 260 laboratories plus offices, conference facilities, and mechanical spaces. On any given day about 800 people work in the Landscape Building.

The laboratory and peripheral spaces house 51 research groups and 14 scientific shared resource groups. The campus retrofits approximately four new lab spaces per year, the majority with complex MEP and data/communications needs.

The campus is operated, maintained, secured, and expanded by a facilities team of 75 people. At the time of writing, the team had been using BIM as a key platform for about 3 ½ years and over time developed four main objectives for this particular BIM platform:

- Act as the campus repository for as-built and historical engineering and construction information.
- Provide a platform for the management and presentation of needed/critical operational information.

- Provide a rigorous as-built platform for future retrofit projects.
- Provide a platform for engineering analysis of critical system performance and of building performance.

In examining prevalent BIM generation and handover practices, the team saw a focus on generating, and then transferring to the owner's CMMS, mainly space- and asset-related data to facilitate space and maintenance management. While this is certainly necessary for a viable BIM platform, they did not see it as sufficient to meet the stated objectives:

- Such space and asset data constitute only a small portion of the potentially valuable information contained within a BIM.
- A significant amount of typical facility management activities deals with "nonasset" facility elements such as door hardware, paint finishes, carpeting, light fixtures, and the like, the data for which do exist in the BIM.
- While such space and asset data can be associated with a broader context, such as zone or system, a full understanding of critical systems requires that all elements of a system be associated, including ducts, pipes, fittings, and the like. Further, one asset may well function as an element of multiple systems (e.g., a control valve on the hot water feed to an AHU heating coil), and must be able to change system identity, depending on which system is being studied.
- This full understanding is needed to analyze the propagation of the impacts of an event or issue within any given system, and across to other systems. This is discussed further below.

Given the inherent focus of a CMMS system, these problems are not really resolved by using a CMMS as the primary means of viewing and interrogating BIM information.

In summary, there is a need to be able to extract additional data from the BIM and to make use of the valuable data that exists in other campus databases, using a platform different from, but complementary to, platforms such as the facility CMMS.

This assessment led to the concept of an FM-capable BIM, discussed in more detail in Section 10.10.4.

10.10.3 The Challenges

Janelia Facilities' Team Mission is to keep Janelia 100% mission-capable for its science at all times, whatever that science may be. This may mean keeping a 14 ft (4.3 m) high microscope room within ± 0.25 °F (0.14 °C) for four months no matter what the external challenges, or it may mean designing, demolishing, constructing, and commissioning a state-of-the-art optical laboratory suite in three to four months.

This mission and its challenges mean that interactions between the numerous building systems and the scientific community are always complex and dynamic, but also need to be tightly managed well in advance. A rapid and detailed understanding of the impact of any given issue or event across all aspects of our science is therefore *key*. This driving need has led us on a quest for an FM-capable BIM that:

- Understands that managers of highly technical facilities tend to have a systems-driven viewpoint of their facility, which will very likely be different from the space- and construction package-driven viewpoints of the architects, engineers, and contractors usually charged with the generation and handover of BIM deliverables at the end of a project.
- Focuses as much (if not more) on the data content of the BIM deliverable as its geometry.
- Leverages and conforms to the well-structured but often stand-alone computerized maintenance management system (CMMS) databases, building automation system (BAS) databases, space management databases, and the like developed over time by facilities managers (needs to conform to existing naming standards).
- Is primarily intended to help manage operating and maintenance costs, which comprise about 85% of the total cost of ownership of a facility, rather than the approximately 15% incurred during design and construction.
- Provides an efficient platform for architects, engineers, and contractors to execute rapid and accurate retrofit projects.

10.10.4 An FM-Capable BIM

An FM-capable BM must enable the FM team to understand, analyze, and then make well-informed operating decisions about their facility. To be effective, the FM team needs both a broad view and a fine level of detail, together with a large amount of well-integrated data. While some of the needed fine level of detail may be geometry-driven, a significant amount will be data-driven, coming not only from the model but also from the various databases mentioned above.

As an example, an electrical fault could impact a BAS-distributed control panel and degrade control of some of the facility's critical systems; while the electrical feed to the BAS control panel may well be modeled, the controls managed by that panel will very likely be recorded in the BAS control point database; in the Janelia facility database, there are nearly 37,000 control points. Any assessment of the impacts of this electrical issue will require information from both the model and the external database.

We call these external databases "Last Mile" databases as they bridge the gap between the information best housed in the model and the information best housed in the external database, or already available from that database. These considerations, together with the reality that it is neither feasible nor desirable that all FM team members are Revit-capable, led the team to explore the use of visualization/analysis middleware to interrogate, collate, and present the engineering information available from the BIM as well as the detailed engineering, operating, and maintenance information available from the Last Mile databases, and to add database management skills to the FM team.

An FM-capable BIM comprises three key elements: the Revit (or other authoring) model; the Last Mile databases such as the CMMS database, BAS database, and so forth; and visualization/analysis middleware. See Figure 10–10–1.

Janelia's facility team's workflow for setting up a systems-centric model is founded on the primacy of building systems in operating, maintaining, and retrofitting a technical facility and the consequent need to systematically insert systems attributes into a BIM. See Figure 10–10–2.

FIGURE 10–10–1 The key elements of an FM-capable BIM.

Image courtesy of Mark Philip, Director of Facilities.

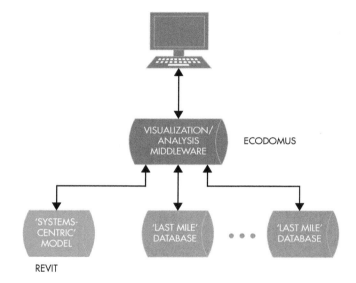

FIGURE 10–10–2 Workflow for setting up a systems-centric model.

Image courtesy of Mark Philip, Director of Facilities.

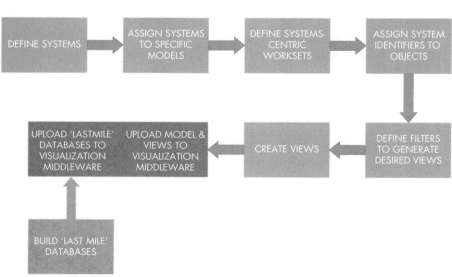

	Building System	BIM Model	LANDSCAPE BUILDING	GUEST HOUSE	STUDIO BUILDING	TOWNHOMES	DIRECTOR'S HOUSE	APARTMENT B	APARTMENT A	COMMERCIAL BUILDINGS
85	531 BUILDING RETURN AIR SYSTEM	Ventilation	X							
86	541 GENERAL EXHAUST AIR SYSTEM	Ventilation	X							
87	542 LAB EXHAUST AIR SYSTEM	Ventilation	X							
88	543 VIVARIUM EXHAUST AIR SYSTEM	Ventilation	X							
89	545 RADIOISOTOPE EXHAUST AIR SYSTEM	Ventilation	X							
90	546 MAIN KITCHEN EXHAUST AIR SYSTEM	Ventilation	X							
91	547 DISHWASHER EXHAUST SYSTEM	Ventilation	X							
92	548 BOB'S KITCHEN EXHAUST AIR SYSTEM	Ventilation	X							
93	549 GARAGE EXHAUST AIR SYSTEM	Ventilation	X							
94	551 KITCHEN EXHAUST RISERS	Ventilation						X	X	
95	552 TOILET EXHAUST RISERS	Ventilation						X	X	
96	553 DRYER EXHAUST RISERS	Ventilation						X	X	
97	554 TRASH SYSTEM EXHAUST	Ventilation						X	X	

FIGURE 10–10–3   System identification, nomenclature, and assignment.

Image courtesy of Mark Philip, Director of Facilities.

The team devotes significant time to identifying systems and their component subsystems in such a way as to be operationally useful and consistent across all campus buildings. This can be deceptively complex because these definitions materially affect the usefulness of any impact analyses later carried out by the FM team. As an example, they found it best to split the main research building's exhaust system into five primary and eight secondary subsystems, each with multiple sub-subsystems. They then assigned each system to a specific model (see Figure 10–10–3).

In the model, they used system-based worksets, both for efficiency and clarity of modeling and to facilitate system-by-system analysis later on. To ensure standardization across models, they define and name system worksets per OmniClass Table 21—for example, 04 30 00 HVAC. In then setting up System Types and System Names, they utilize their internal nomenclature, for example, 543 Vivarium Exhaust Air.

At this point, the workflow moves away from model building to model visualization in ways that will be operationally meaningful and useful. They are careful to define three aspects of a view through the use of filters: which system elements are explicitly made visible, which provide background context, and which are explicitly excluded. Once defined and created, these views are organized in the project browser in an FM area, following Janelia's system definition and naming conventions.

This approach allows the team to efficiently consider either an entire system or focus in on a subsystem, as in Figure 10–10–4, a view of the exhaust subsystem serving one floor of a wing of the main research building.

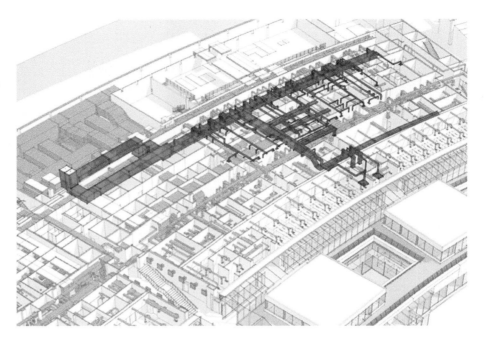

Here subsystem 543.200 Vivarium Exhaust Air Second Floor has been made explicitly visible, while including certain architectural and other HVAC system elements in half-tone for context, and explicitly excluding other MEP elements.

10.10.5 Impact Analysis Using an FM-Capable BIM

One of the key challenges facing any FM team is to determine the impact of an event or an issue on the facility's systems, spaces, functions, and people so that the FM team can develop a sound game plan to respond rapidly and effectively. Often, this work is made difficult and time consuming by a lack of information on hand and a lack of clarity on (or understanding of) the manner in which the facility's systems interact with one another and with the facility's spaces and functions.

One of the basic benefits of any BIM is the availability of information in a structured, accessible manner. A key benefit of an FM-capable BIM, however, is the capability to more rapidly and accurately determine impacts across the facility and the organization it houses, with the potential to materially reduce the costs of the impact on the organization, not only the costs arising from operational losses, but also the costs of developing the response. Janelia's workflow in carrying out impact analyses is summarized in Figure 10–10–5.

Their initial work focused on impacts within electrical systems—in a BIM environment, electrical systems are particularly amenable to impact analysis; proper modeling of these systems inherently creates a hierarchy of

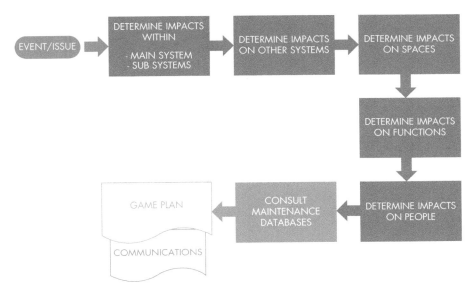

FIGURE 10–10–5   Workflow to respond to an event or issue.

Image courtesy of Mark Philip, Director of Facilities.

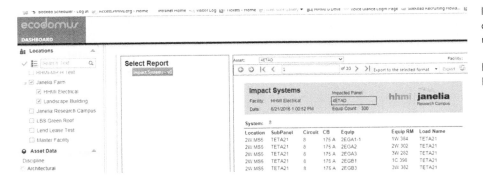

FIGURE 10–10–6   BIM-derived impacted systems report.

Image courtesy of Mark Philip, Director of Facilities.

linearly-propagating impacts within the model, and it is relatively straightforward to extract this information in the form of an automated report.

They have used this capability to help manage two major electrical projects: the replacement of four obsolete main UPS units in a live building, and the parallel installation of a fourth 2 MW emergency generator. They initially ran impact reports directly from the electrical model via middleware to determine the downstream panels and loads that would be affected at each step of the project (see Figure 10–10–6). They supplemented this with database-derived information linking affected loads to affected building systems, and ultimately to affected spaces, functions, and people (see Figures 10–10–7 and 10–10–8).

FIGURE 10–10–7 Database-derived impacted systems report.

Image courtesy of Mark Philip, Director of Facilities.

System: **543 VIVARIUM EXHAUST AIR**

Room	Panel	Circuit	CB	Equip	Circuit Description
	2EMA21	9	75 A/3	EXHAUST FAN (EF) 1	EF-1
	2ETA2V-1	23	75 A/3	EXHAUST FAN (EF) 2	EF-2

FIGURE 10–10–8 Database-derived impacted spaces, functions, and people report.

Image courtesy of Mark Philip, Director of Facilities

Lab Coordinator: Cynthia Sherman

Name: Branson   Kristin   Phone: Number

Room: 2W.316

Panel:	Circuit	CB	Load
2ETA2	29	/2P	WIREMOLD 2W.316
2ETA2	99	/P	WIREMOLD 2W.316

10.10.6 Lessons Learned Thus Far

By the time of writing, a significant amount of the team's BIM work had focused on an as-built model of the main research building on the Janelia campus. They used the experience gained in this exercise to guide modeling of new buildings and retrofit projects, and they were fully aware of the need to manage the impact of the requirements for FM-capable BIM on contractor effort/costs and on model size. In order to meet their defined BIM platform objectives, systems must be modeled as continuous systems; in other words, all relevant objects (including fittings) in a system need to be explicitly identified as belonging to that system. Further, "system continuity" must be validated before one can profitably start to add in system design data and make use of the engineering calculations available in MEP models.

They learned to be explicit up front with contractors about their provision of continuous systems within their models; as part of this, they developed standards around the "system detail" required, including both the validated continuous geometry and the insertion of system design information available, for example, from system process flow diagrams. This, in turn, led them to begin revising standards on the provision of process flow diagrams.

In managing BIM model size and Last Mile databases, they realized the need to decide what data to put into the BIM versus what data to access in parallel with data from the BIM. They were working to define these "insert" versus "access" decisions. Some of the answers appear to be clear: operationally useful information contained in databases routinely supplied by contractors (such as the BAS control point database, access control system database, and fire alarm system database) is likely best accessed via middleware rather than inserted into the BIM. They recognized the need to revise their BIM standards to specify which information they require the contractor to supply in database format versus the information to be submitted in the BIM.

10.10.7 The Path Forward

Janelia Facilities team felt that they had barely scratched the surface of what is possible, over and above standard maintenance and space management activities. They did not yet have good metrics on the benefits of their approach, other than to note that, qualitatively, planning of this work consumed materially fewer work hours than had other electrical shutdowns of similar complexity. This includes the time spent ensuring that lab managers and researchers fully understood (and were able to plan for) the nature and extent of the impacts the projects would have on their scientific work. A key expectation of Janelia campus researchers is that facilities should distract them from their work only when absolutely necessary and only to the least extent possible.

The team acknowledged that their approach may well be superseded as the capabilities of FM-focused platforms evolve and improve, and that they may well migrate the capabilities they were developing to other platforms at some point in the future.

Their planned next areas of focus were:

- Extending impact analysis to other relatively linear building systems such as supply air and exhaust air systems
- Inserting design information into key systems in MEP models and correlating this information with BAS-derived information to facilitate analysis of the actual performance of these systems in the field. In this regard, they had the capability to access real-time operating data in a BIM context through the EcoDomus platform, and planned to steadily extend this capability to provide an integrated environment that facilitates facility management in real time. They see this as preparatory work to being able to utilize the growing network of interconnected smart objects in their world (the Internet of Things), to drive improved operational efficiencies—through, for example, real-time predictive maintenance information.
- Finding ways to intelligently link the MEP models to their associated process flow diagrams, such as the air flow diagram for the example exhaust system discussed earlier (see Figure 10–10–9).

Acknowledgments

Material in this study was originally written by Mark Philip and Mark McKinley of Janelia Research Campus for presentation at the Revit Technology Conference North America in July 2016, and has been adapted for use in this book. The authors thank Igor Starkov of EcoDomus Inc. and Artem Ryzhkov of Synergy Systems for their valued guidance, generation of models, and building of platform capabilities over an extended period.

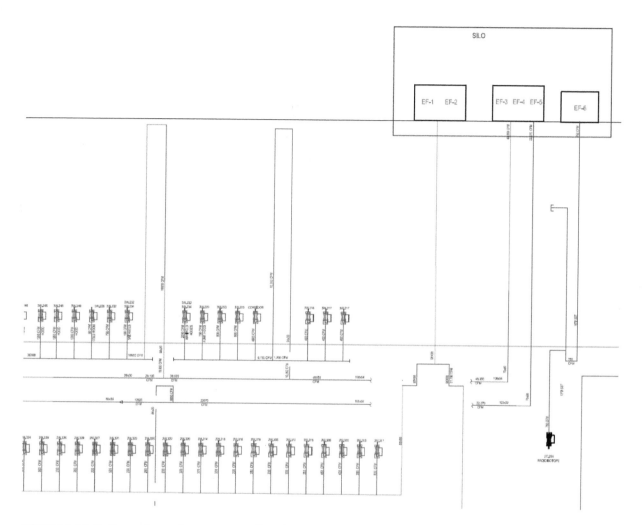

FIGURE 10–10–9   Extract from exhaust air system flow diagram.

Image courtesy of Mark Philip, Director of Facilities.

10.11   STANFORD NEUROSCIENCE HEALTH CENTER, PALO ALTO, CALIFORNIA
BIM Modeling to Support Facility Management

10.11.1   Introduction

In 2013, Stanford Healthcare was in the midst of a major campus expansion with construction of a new hospital, renovation of the existing hospital, and expansion of its clinic portfolio across the Bay Area. As a part of this expansion they envisioned that the construction and building turnover process be done using building information modeling (BIM). During the development of one of their new facilities, the Neuroscience Health Center, they started an ambitious implementation roadmap early in 2014 to evaluate the downstream effects of using BIM as a part of their facilities services. This forward-looking vision resulted in a pilot program in the Neuroscience Health Center building project, which was conducted between 2015 and 2016.

With the Neuroscience Health Center building project (see Figure 10–11–1), Stanford Healthcare Facilities Services along with Stanford planning, design, and construction departments saw an opportunity to utilize building information generated during the design and construction process for facilities management, building operations, and maintenance purposes. There was a vision for the opportunity this would present to other new facilities and mission-critical remodeled areas, so a target state for 2018 through 2021 was established as part of the goal with the following projections:

- Front-end BIM for facilities management specifications are used in the design and construction request for proposals (RFPs).
- Stanford Healthcare is equipped with dedicated BIM staff to monitor models, train staff, and update the BIM models.
- BIM transition plan in place from general contractor—planning, design, and construction (PD&C) responsible for large capital projects to modeling and firm facilities, infrastructure, and safety.
- Utilize in-house BIM modeler for small capital projects—Engineering and Maintenance (E&M) and the Project Management Office (PMO).

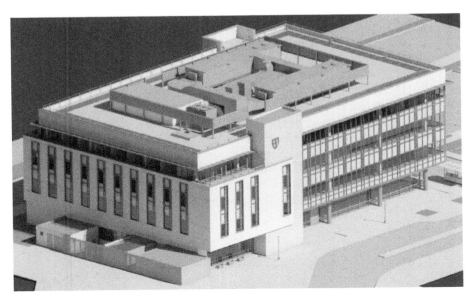

FIGURE 10–11–1 Stanford Neuroscience Health Center building at Hoover Medical Campus.

Image courtesy Stanford Medical Center.

- A BIM model is integrated with the comprehensive enterprise asset management system (EAMS) for asset lifecycle and maintenance management, IBM Maximo.
- The Information Technology Services (ITS) to support BIM software applications.
- Existing buildings are scanned and photographed.

Stanford Healthcare commissioned technology vendors to provide systems necessary to establish the foundation for the lifecycle of BIM.

One of the main drivers behind the initiative was the lack of as-built information and operations and maintenance data available at the end of construction projects resulting in a loss of building information and inefficient handover procedures. The core causes of these issues were inefficient and unreliable transfers of building information from the design and construction process to the Facilities Maintenance and Operations and Maintenance (FMOM), as well as a previous lack of a centralized enterprise asset management system to organize and manage the data. Through the Neuroscience Health Center BIM pilot project study Stanford could determine the value of reducing operational impact through a BIM-enabled process that addresses the three things that matter most that could be improved for Stanford Healthcare:

- Using BIM to improve patient care
- Using BIM to improve patient safety
- Reducing the cost per day for patient care

The following sections elaborate on how this pilot project addressed those areas.

10.11.2 Project Details

The Neuroscience Health Center at Hoover Medical Campus is a new five-story, 92,000 sf (8,547 m^2) building located adjacent to the Hoover Pavilion at 213 Quarry Road. The project broke ground in early 2014 and opened in early 2016. The new facility, which is a comprehensive care destination for all neuroscience patients, includes centralized check-in for all services to increase convenience and efficiency. The building design merges a physically and emotionally supportive care environment with 21 neuroscience subspecialties, providing a streamlined, healing environment for patients suffering from neurological disorders. Building planning included extensive process design work and incorporated feedback from physicians and a neuroscience patient advisory board to address virtually every aspect of the facility, from flooring to lighting.

Project highlights:

- 92,000 sf, five-level building (including basement).
- Approximately $80 million project.

- On-site access to 21 subspecialty areas.
- One of the first PET/MRI machines in North America designated for clinical use.
- The only comprehensive autonomic laboratory, for the diagnosis and treatment of nervous system disorders, on the West Coast (The autonomic nervous system is the part of the nervous system that supplies the internal organs and regulates certain bodily functions: heart rate, digestion, respiratory rate, pupillary response, among others.)
- Patients and caregivers were directly involved in the center's building design to ensure its features accommodated the sensitivities of people with neurological disorders.

10.11.3 The Pilot

The primary goals behind the pilot to utilize building information modeling were:

- to validate three key areas that matter most to Stanford Healthcare leadership:
  - Improve patient care
  - Improve patient safety
  - Reduce the cost per patient day
- to reduce the impact of FM on their patients and use lessons learned to refine the new process.
- to evaluate whether, through captured data and metrics, they could capitalize on the ROI and benefits of a BIM-enabled process determined in the pilot project for the Neuroscience Health Center building, which Stanford Healthcare could then leverage to program future buildings and renovations, as well as to track assets and support building maintenance and management.

Early on there were several areas considered in strategizing around the development of a BIM implementation plan and roadmap. Among these were:

- Review information and data to ensure the understanding of pilot and non-pilot-related activities regarding CAD/BIM/FM/GIS.
- Identify in-progress, pending, and planned new and renovation projects.
- Document the short- and long-term use of the pilot project model and associated data.
- Identify the various levels of facility information and the required technology adoption for each along with necessary software acquisition and training.
- Define stages and timeline for adoption of BIM/FM for new and existing buildings.
- Define the necessary level of detail for upcoming construction project deliverables.

- Provide recommendations for the creation of the BIM Support team.
- Identify staff roles, responsibilities, and qualifications.
- Define necessary technology infrastructure (software, hardware, and server setup).

10.11.4 Making the Case

The Stanford Healthcare team, led by Alex Saleh, began this initiative by assessing the current state of the operations group. That assessment identified a number of issues in a wide range of processes, which were summarized this way: "Operations is unable to efficiently and effectively receive, organize, and retrieve facility, lifecycle asset data and records in the office or field to effectively maintain a lean healthcare system."

Among the issues listed were:

- difficulty in locating proper shut-off valves for utilities.
- worker-specific knowledge: irretrievable loss of information when an employee leaves.
- low work order productivity: inspections, excessive travel, parts mismatch.
- patient experience: reduce troubleshooting of issues in patient rooms and operating environments.
- regulatory compliance reporting: accuracy compromised, excessive effort and time to manage.
- ineffective or poorly organized capital planning.
- field workers spending too much time looking for data and documents and conducting field verification, instead of fixing problems and maintaining the facility.

While there were no specific metrics available then for each of the above conditions, the Stanford Healthcare team was able to quantify the time to execute these items based on workshops conducted with the stakeholders. These are discussed in the pilot execution phase (Section 10.11.7). A high-level plan with goals, targets, and a strategy was presented to the executive teams. The overall goals behind this proof of concept were to:

- increase operational availability through reduced downtime (rooms, equipment, etc.)
- improve access to readily available and improved quality of information
- reduce risk of inadvertent or unnecessary shutdowns
- reduce interruptions to patient care due to building maintenance caused by building surveys, inspections, and troubleshooting
- reduce Patient Care Risk Assessment (PCRA) review time process

These goals would focus on the fundamental problem that underlies the Stanford Facilities Services & Planning division's risk to strategically make timely business decisions; communicate; produce reliable capital plans and maintenance plans; efficiently manage emergency situations, regulatory compliance, and supply chain; and hire and direct its workforce, including prioritization of the work itself.

10.11.5 The Journey

The Stanford Healthcare team led the efforts establish an initial timeline to initiate and implement the BIM pilot that would fit into their overall asset management (AM) implementation roadmap.

Figure 10–11–2 shows the preliminary phase of establishing the framework for putting together the plan and team in place around the BIM pilot, which started in late 2013.

Below is a summary for the pilot framework:

- Utilize the Neuroscience Health Center for the BIM for FM "Proof of Concept."
- Select software vendor for BIM Model development/visualization.
- Select software vendor for enterprise asset management (EAM).
- Develop Guidelines/Business Requirements.
- Obtain proposal from Hoover Project (Neuroscience Health Center).
- Request to proceed.

10.11.6 The Team

The roles for the pilot program were defined as follows:

- **Stanford Healthcare team:** Facility maintenance staff, operations staff were responsible for quantifying the use cases and the execution of the use cases during the pilot period. In addition, they were responsible for

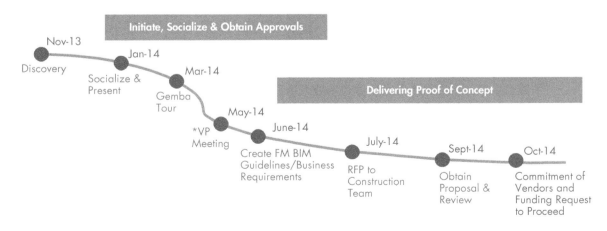

FIGURE 10–11–2 BIM pilot proof of concept framework timeline.

Image courtesy Stanford Medical Center.

the implementation of the Maximo environment. Led by Alex Saleh from the Engineering and Maintenance group, the team also included members from the following groups: Infection Control, Asset Management, PMO, Resource Management, E&M, EH&S, and 500P construction, among others.

- **EcoDomus team:** Responsible for implementation of the EcoDomus software and creation of the pilot use cases within their software, development of the BIM models, and integration of the asset data defined by Stanford as well as the training and support of their technology.

- **Microdesk team:** Selected as the technology and process advisors, responsible for the quality assurance/quality control (QA/QC) review of the BIM models and data, coordination of the pilot program (writing the execution and pilot plan), and analysis of the pilot, as well as development and update of the BIM for FM Guidelines for Stanford Healthcare.

Their involvement throughout the BIM modeling and FM integration workflow is shown in Figure 10–11–3. Figure 10–11–4 illustrates the pilot process workflow.

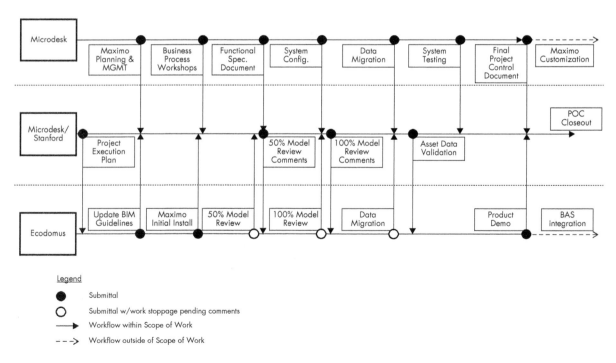

FIGURE 10–11–3   Stakeholder involvement through the pilot evaluation.

Image courtesy of Stanford Medical Center.

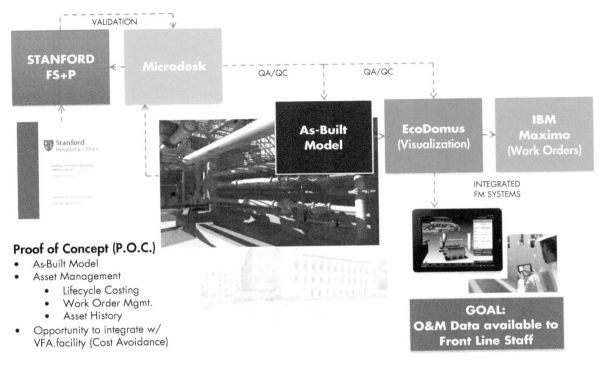

Proof of Concept (P.O.C.)
- As-Built Model
- Asset Management
    - Lifecycle Costing
    - Work Order Mgmt.
    - Asset History
- Opportunity to integrate w/ VFA.facility (Cost Avoidance)

FIGURE 10–11–4 BIM pilot process workflow.

Image courtesy of Stanford Medical Center.

10.11.7 Executing the Pilot

As part of the initiative, Stanford Healthcare commissioned technology vendors to provide systems necessary to develop and execute a strategy to implement a BIM for FM process for the Neuroscience Health Center building. The strategy involved the following activities.

1. Identifying the technology
    The Neuroscience Building pilot was executed using the following technology:
    - BIM software (Autodesk Revit)
    - Middleware (EcoDomus)
        EcoDomus software provides 3D views of facilities in an easy-to-use format for facility managers that links BIM with real-time facility operations data acquired via meters and sensors (building automation systems, BAS) and facility management (FM) software.
        The Middleware package was selected based on its ability to pass data between the two primary platforms, Revit and Maximo.

- EAMS (IBM Maximo)

    IBM Maximo is a comprehensive enterprise asset management system for asset lifecycle and maintenance management, chosen for Stanford's facilities operations.

    A separate project chose this platform for the functions of asset management, work management, scheduling, and its ability to integrate with other Stanford Healthcare Systems. Maximo was subsequently used across the board on existing and new buildings and standards were adopted for its use.

2. Establishing the **project execution plan** for the proof of concept. Microdesk assisted in the development of the Plan.

3. Development of the **as-built BIM model** for the Neuroscience Health Center. This task was performed by EcoDomus.

4. Development of a **DATA dictionary** for key attributes and information required by the Stanford teams. This was determined by the Stanford Healthcare team. Figure 10–11–5 shows a sample of the data dictionary for an air handling unit. Figure 10–11–6 shows the process that was used to merge this data with the as-built BIM model, so that it could be integrated with the Maximo asset management system.

5. Defining relevant areas to evaluate where BIM could have an impact and measure success. Seven **use cases** were identified early on during strategizing to define a baseline case to weigh against a pilot BIM-enabled scenario. The use cases were selected by the Stanford Healthcare team based on the frequency of their use and the ability to define a baseline

FIGURE 10–11–5 Sample data (attributes) for an air handling unit from Stanford's Data Dictionary.

Image courtesy of Stanford Medical Center.

 Stanford HEALTH CARE   MAXIMO DATA DICTIONARY

23-33 25 00   Air Handling Unit

Hierarchical Level: Component
System Association: HVAC
Description: A packaged assembly of air-conditioning equipment, such as coils, filters, humidifiers etc., which provide the treatment of air before it is distributed.

Attribute	Data Type	Unit	Domain / Range of Values
Asset ID	Numeric	N/A	System generated unique id for the entity | barcode
Lawson ID	Numeric	N/A	ID used to reference Lawson Asset
Component Description	ALN	N/A	A narrative description of the entity
Component Type	ALN	N/A	Single Zone, Multi Zone
System (Parent) ID	Numeric	N/A	The system (parent) ID that the component is associated to
Criticality	Numeric	N/A	1, 2, 3, 4, 5
Legacy ID	ALN	N/A	Common name or previous name of the entity
Condition Rating	Numeric	N/A	Condition rating of the component
Inspection Date	ALN	N/A	Date of the last inspection for the condition rating
Year Built	ALN	N/A	Year that the component was constructed
Design Life	Numeric	N/A	Design life

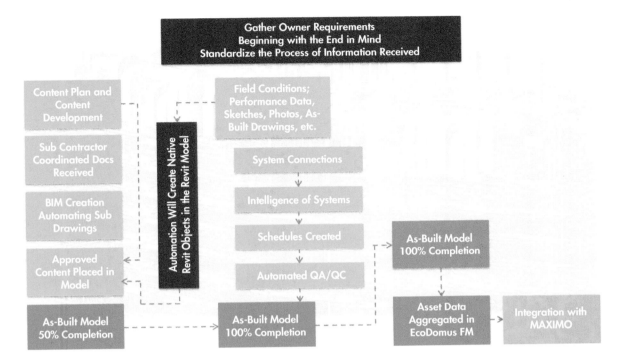

FIGURE 10-11-6 Vision of the FM process development.

Image courtesy of Stanford Medical Center.

quantifiable metric for the time to execute. These were determined by the Stanford Healthcare team with the assistance of EcoDomus. The use cases are defined as follows:

- Use Case 1: Major Plumbing Leak, 2nd-floor Pharmacy, Room #2726A
- Use Case 2: Structural and Fire Safety Analysis
- Use Case 3: Asset Information Entry and Update
- Use Case 4: Integrated Finish Schedule
- Use Case 5: Engineering Staff Training
- Use Case 6: Shutdown Request
- Use Case 7: Infection Control Risk Assessment (ICRA)/Preconstruction Risk Assessment (PCRA) Review

6. Pilot plan implementation: As part of the proof of concept and with the goal to evaluate BIM usefulness and applicability in FMOM processes, a pilot plan was developed for the evaluation of the seven use cases to test relevant aspects in the process. The pilot was conducted systematically with personnel performing work as defined in the use cases and validating the technology and systems used to help accomplish

the various teams' normal work activities. The pilot test was intended to address all business functions within the maintenance management cycle as determined in the use cases.

This implementation plan involved the following:

- Pilot execution plan

    Developed to serve as the framework to be applied for real testing of the use cases.

- Presentation of the pilot plan to the Stanford teams

    Microdesk developed and presented the pilot execution plan to the Stanford team.

- Training Stanford users on the technology
    - Presentation was made on the use cases and how to use the technology.
    - Reference documentation was provided to users for testing.
    - Additional web training was provided as needed.
    - Ecodomus provided assistance around training and support during the implementation.

- *Testing of the technology in the field*

    The pilot testing was performed within a two-week timeframe where the pilot team executed and recorded the results of the seven use cases.

- *User Survey*

    All use cases as listed previously were performed by Stanford facility staff with the purpose of comparing the performance of the current methodology with the new system. One use case was added during the pilot and so details about that use case were not captured in the survey.

    Users were asked to give their impression of the new process and whether it was an improvement compared to the existing (mostly manual) process.

- *Pilot review and analysis*

    Microdesk reviewed and analyzed the results to quantify the benefits and to determine the best approach for wide-scale deployment, as well as to evaluate the use of BIM models for enhancing the maintenance process.

7. Development of the BIM for FM guidelines. As part of the scope Stanford tasked Microdesk with assisting in the development and update of their BIM for FM standards to be incorporated into their BIM guidelines for design and construction.

10.11.8   Use Case Metrics

Next is a breakdown of the seven identified cases defined in conjunction with the Stanford Healthcare teams to assess and quantify tasks and associates' efforts with the goal of comparing the traditional process versus a BIM process and determining a baseline case for current efforts measured in labor hours with Stanford Healthcare data and actual number of annual events per case.

Use Case 1: Major Plumbing Leak, 2nd-floor Pharmacy, Room #2726A

Purpose:

- Identify plumbing systems in the room (as-builts are difficult to interpret and confirm in the field).
  - Determine system relationships is a timely and challenging process.

Current challenges:

- As-builts are difficult to access. Staff is new and sent out to site with limited knowledge of the facility.
- Facilities staff may need to call subcontractors that installed the plumbing system to get additional information.

The time and resources needed to support this use case are shown in Table 10–11–1.

Table 10–11–1   Baseline Processes Associated with a Major Plumbing Leak

No.	Baseline Current Process	Time Spent	Resources/Impact
1	Pharmacy staff calls in a work order stating water leak in room 2726A, which is damaging equipment and pharmaceuticals.	0.5 hrs.	Room is shutdown with negative impact to patient care and to medical equipment.
2	Staff is dispatched to building and investigates source of water leak. They need ladder and equipment to access systems above ceiling. A random selection of tiles are removed to identify leaking system and proper isolation valve.	2.0 hrs.	Information is not easily available. The building engineer is troubleshooting on the fly with minimal building information available. Damage to room and equipment is severe due to leak.
	Total time spent:	2.5 hrs.	
	Impact on operations:		System is shutdown, but may not be the valve that minimizes impact to the facility. Need to investigate material and order replacement parts.

Use Case 2: Structural and Fire Safety Analysis

Purpose:

- Obtain information regarding beams: is it load bearing, how much weight can it support, what walls are firewalls (can a penetration into the wall be made), and so forth.

Current challenges:

- This process involves someone (usually a lead or manager from the vendor team) going out and site verifying what is being asked and then a lengthy process of digging through drawings and reaching out to various PMs, the safety team, and the like.

The time and resources needed to support this use case are shown in Table 10–11–2.

Table 10–11–2   Baseline Processes Associated with Structural and Fire Safety Analysis

No.	Baseline Current Process	Time Spent	Resources/Impact
1	The manager conducts the structural assessment within the facility, red lining the design drawings to identify the beams of interest, searching for the cut sheets and other information in various binders and blueprints.	2.5 hrs.	Drawings (which may be out of date) are heavy to carry, so the manager relies on his memory and goes back and forth between the storage room (location of drawings) and the inspected spaces.
2	The manager completes the assessment report and forwards it to the requestor as an email with a photo attachment.	0.5 hrs.	The email may not be properly catalogued so that future assessments will not benefit from this activity. The photo may be confusing because there are several beams present in the photo.
	Total time spent:	3.0 hrs.	
	Impact on operations:		If information is not found, it may cause significant problems with safety; difficult to maintain and review data.

Use Case 3: Asset Information Entry and Update
Purpose

- Streamline manual data entry into the computerized maintenance management system (CMMS) in use, IBM Maximo.

Current challenges:

- This is done manually, taking time and introducing human errors. It is difficult to keep this information up to date.

The time and resources needed to support this use case are shown in Table 10–11–3.

Table 10–11–3 Baseline Processes Associated with Asset Information Entry and Update

No.	Baseline Current Process	Time Spent	Resources/Impact
1	Construction contractors manually collect information from subcontractors as PDFs and Excel files throughout the project. Typically, there is no standard way of collecting data so that every time the process and data quality are different.	Months	Owners pay per hour of activity, even if it is manual and inefficient. Owners do not see the collected information until the project is over, or sometimes a few months after project completion. Some equipment is difficult to operate since no information is available.
2.	Contractors deliver the collected info to the owner as CDs with PDFs and Excel files and boxes of paper (hundreds of files, dozens of boxes).	Months	Owner pays for all the paper printed and fedexed.
3	Facility managers manually type in all the equipment info into CMMs and then upload documents to various folders.	Years	Data entry is manual and costly, accuracy is poor, and much of the needed data is missing.
	Total time spent:	Years	
	Impact on operations:		If information is not collected properly and not entered on time, it cannot be used properly.

Use Case 4: Integrated Finish Schedule

Purpose:

- Preserve design intent. Add finish attributes to wall and floor finishes

Current challenges:

- Design intent is frequently lost as finishes are replaced.
- Paint quantities are difficult to track without known surface areas to validate vendor estimates and work completed invoices.

The time and resources needed to support this use case are shown in Table 10–11–4.

Table 10–11–4   Baseline Processes Associate with Preserving Design Intent: Material Finishes

No.	Baseline Current Process	Time Spent	Resources/Impact
1	Finishes and color selections are currently turned over as part of the O&M manuals. The material submittals do not specify which surfaces receive which finish material.	N/A Once the information is lost, it cannot be recovered easily.	Design intent and surface finishes are not maintained as designed. Some facilities, such as the Neuroscience building, have incorporated finishes as part of the patient experience and rely on them to assist patient in wayfinding. Maintaining the designed color combinations and finish material is critical for the patient experience.
2	Finish submittals and room finish schedules do not calculate the areas of each applied material. Vendors provide estimates for quantities and work performed for payment which Stanford Health Care has no easy means to verify.	N/A Not possible – high level guess only	Vendor contracts that include cyclical maintenance of paint, carpet, etc. rely on vendor estimates for quantities of work areas and materials. Stanford Health Care has no simple method to validate these quantities and costs.

Use Case 5: Engineering Staff Training

Purpose:

* To bring onboard new building engineering staff and familiarize them with building systems.

Current challenges:

* As-builts are difficult to locate, and verifying systems physically takes time and resources.

The time and resources needed to support this use case are shown in Table 10–11–5.

Table 10–11–5   Baseline Processes Associated with Engineering Staff Training

No.	Baseline Current Process	Time Spent	Resources/Impact
1	New technical staff hired. Supervisor orients staff to the building and explains building components and systems. Series of walks and drawing reviews.	1 month	Supervisor New technical staff
2	New staff shadows existing employees to navigate the building and understand its systems.	1 week	Existing employee New technical staff

Use Case 6: Shutdown Request

Purpose:

- Reduce time required to determine and validate (through field verification, measurement, tracing, and so on) system impacts necessary to perform a safe utility shutdown.

Current challenges:

- As-builts are difficult to interpret and confirm in the field.
- Determining system relationships is a timely and challenging process.
- Facilities staff may need to call subcontractors that installed the plumbing system to get additional information.

The time and resources needed to support this use case are shown in Table 10–11–6.

Table 10–11–6 Baseline Processes Associated with a Shutdown Request

No.	Baseline Current Process	Time Spent	Resources/Impact
1	Contractor submits a utility shutdown request for an electrical panel. Contractor then requests as-built drawings from Facilities and reviews them one received.	1 day	As-built drawings are difficult to interpret and review cannot begin until files are located and received by contractor.
2	Contractor traces the system in the field to verify the conditions.	2 days	System tracing is completed on-site without drawings on hand. Contractor may need to go back and reference the drawings several times. As-built drawings may not be available or accurate; project is delayed. Unforeseen conditions impact project budget cost and time.
3	Facilities receives shutdown request and confirms system and impacts.	2 days	Engineering staff not available to perform system verification
4	Utility shutdown request review by work control within Facilities.	1 day	Management relies on accuracy of field tracing to present impacted systems to departments and leadership.
5	Utility shutdown request approved and building occupants are notified of any impacts. Migration measures (backup power, generator, etc.) are in place during shutdowns.	1 day	Project manager

Use Case 7: Infection Control Risk Assessment (ICRA)/Preconstruction Risk Assessment (PCRA) Review

Purpose:

- Reduce time required to properly review, assess, and approve an infection control risk assessment and a preconstruction risk assessment (through field verification, meetings, follow-ups with project manager, and so on).

Current challenges:

- Risk assessments are based solely on the input of the project manager.
- ICRA and PCRA reviewer are limited with time and resources.
- Reviews require multiple site visits and meetings with the project manager to understand the scope and the impacts.

The time and resources needed to support this use case are shown in Table 10–11–7.

Table 10–11–7   Baseline Processes Associated with Performing an ICRA/PCRA Review

No.	Baseline Current Process	Time Spent	Resources/Impact
1	Project manager (PM) submits an ICRA/PCRA request for a construction activity.	5 days	As-built drawings are difficult to interpret and locate. PM must take photos, create maps and new drawings to show scope and impact.
2	ICRA/PCRA reviewer requires maps, drawings, and photos to understand the impact and scope of the work.	3 days	PM must explain scope, show on photos and maps to demonstrate the work. This results in delays.
3	Meeting is required in field to review the impacts.	2 weeks	PM, ICRA/PCRA reviewer, E&M technical staff and occupants must all meet to understand the scope of the work and the layout of the room and spaces immediately adjacent and above.
4	ICRA/PCRA approved	1 day	Management rely on accuracy of the team to present impacted systems and department to leadership.

10.11.9 Results of Use Cases

The following demonstrates a summary of the use case testing that targeted the Stanford Healthcare facilities and operations group's activities, which had the biggest impact in three major areas:

- Addressing shutdowns (reactive and planned)
- Regulatory compliance (ICRA / PCRA)
- Institutional (tribal) knowledge

Facility Managers using Building Information Models to:

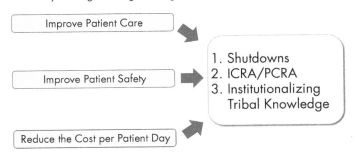

FIGURE 10–11–7   Stanford Healthcare facilities and operations meaningful areas of impact.

Image courtesy of Stanford Medical Center.

Each of these areas compared the traditional processes versus a BIM-enabled process with a baseline case for current efforts measured in labor hours with Stanford Healthcare data for actual number of annual events. Figure 10–11–7 illustrates how the impacts of each use case were analyzed.

1. Addressing SHUTDOWNS: Reactive and Planned

   During the pilot, users had a chance to test and evaluate use cases that had a big impact in patient safety and patient care. Among these were addressing shutdowns both in a reactive and planned scenario using the BIM model process:

   Reactive Scenario (Use Case 1)

   In the pilot, users tested accessing the BIM model on an iPAD to look at the room and system above the ceiling to find a valve for the water supply and pull information about it and its relationship to the system. Recently there had been an event where the wrong valve was shut off to stop a major leak at the Neuroscience Health Center Building since the valves had been mislabeled. Figure 10–11–8 illustrates how each valve was visually related to the piping system it was a part of.

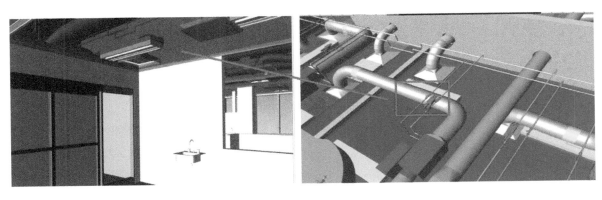

FIGURE 10–11–8   Addressing a plumbing leak on the second floor of the pharmacy, Room #2726A.

Image courtesy of Stanford Medical Center.

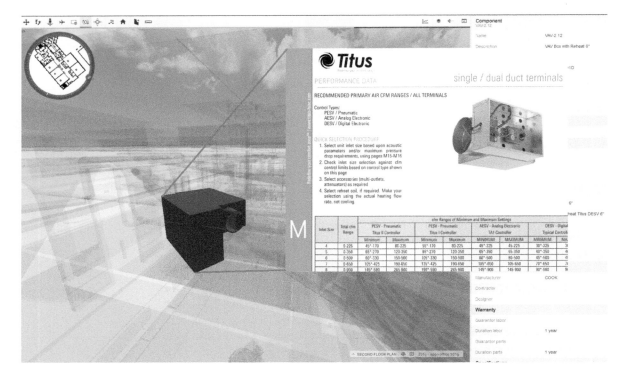

FIGURE 10–11–9   Planned electrical shutdown.

Image courtesy of Stanford Medical Center.

Planned Scenario (Use Case 6)

Users tested accessing the BIM model on an iPad. An example is selecting a VAV component to better understand what rooms are going to lose power and validate system impacts necessary to perform a safe utility shutdown. Figure 10–11–9 illustrates the impacts of shutting down a given electrical supply.

BIM process key distinctions:

- REACTIVE SCENARIO from use case 1 (Baseline average of 2.5 hrs)
  - Time savings = 1.75 hours per instance (70% less time)
  - Scale impact: Number of annual events: 24
- PLANNED SCENARIO from use case 6 (Baseline average of 56 hrs)
  - Time savings: 35 hours per instance (62% less time)

2. Regulatory compliance: ICRA/PCRA (Use Case 7)

Users tested viewing the model on an iPad to access the second floor and visualize Corridor 6 and obtain the information about adjacent spaces that would be affected by the upcoming work, such as the procedure room highlighted in Figure 10–11–10.

FIGURE 10–11–10   Scheduled construction and carpet replacement for corridor 6.

Image courtesy of Stanford Medical Center.

BIM process key distinctions

- Time savings: 78 hours per instance (50% less time)
- Scale impact: Number of annual events: 200

Note: In addition, the BIM process would allow for the review to be done at home or in the office and allows Stanford Healthcare to achieve regulatory compliance going from planned maintenance. It's worth noting that there had been 200 events alone within the current fiscal year at the time.

3. Institutionalize tribal knowledge (Use Cases 2, 3, 4, and 5)

Four additional use cases were tested that currently involved time-consuming tasks around information searching and retrieval, such as looking for as-built drawings and finding resources and documentation, among others.

During the pilot testing phase, users tried pulling and retrieving information required as part of the tasks, addressing the areas shown here with iPads to test field access.

- In one instance users tested by visualizing the structural elements above the MRI room and pulling the information about a beam to determine if it could be penetrated (Use Case 2), as shown in Figure 10–11–11.

- In another instance, users tested by visualizing the second-floor system of firewalls and pulling the information of specific walls to determine their fire rating value (Use Case 2), as shown in Figure 10–11–12.

  Users also tested:

- Visualizing the type of wall in a room and pulling the information about paint type and color scheme (Use Case 4), as shown in Figure 10–11–13.

- Pulling information about any element or equipment in the building by visualizing and isolating rooms and systems to test ease of use in retrieving information and navigating the building (Use Cases 3 and 5), as shown in Figure 10–11–14.

FIGURE 10–11–11   Structural study: hanging heavy items or drilling penetrations.

Image courtesy of Stanford Medical Center.

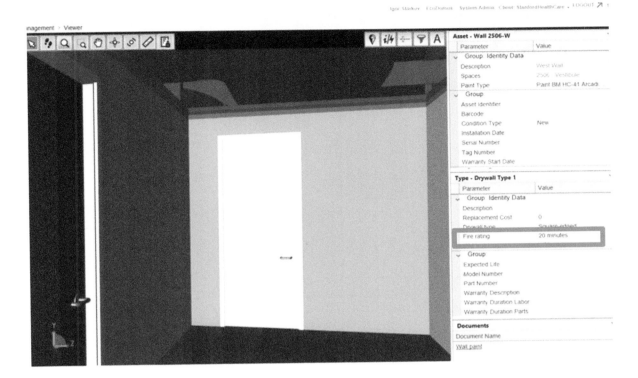

FIGURE 10–11–12   Fire safety analysis: determine fire wall rating value.

Image courtesy of Stanford Medical Center.

BIM process key distinctions:

- Time savings: 308 hours per instance (85% less time)
- Scale impact: Number of annual events: 36

10.11.10   Summary of Benefits

The following summarizes the benefits encountered and envisioned impacting the activities as they pertain to the use cases evaluated.

For addressing shutdown: reactive and planned:

- The direct impact is on time savings per instance or event requiring between 60% and 70% less time.
- Stanford Healthcare can use the infrastructure set up for regionalization of the facilities: growing in its off-site clinics portfolio. With the group the business model changes to support the hospital as well as the off-site clinics.

FIGURE 10–11–13
Preserving design intent:
integrated room finishes.

Image courtesy of Stanford
Medical Center.

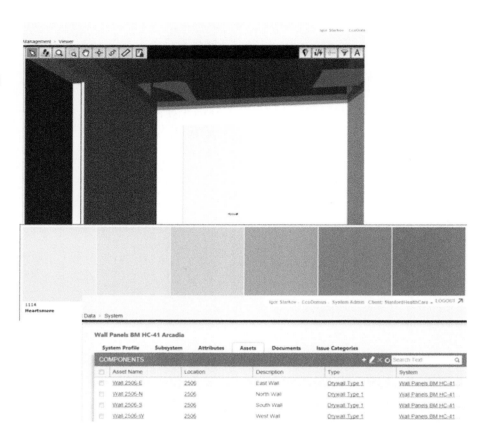

- Systems engineers and management are at the control center in Havens court and can assist field staff in identifying systems and locating optimal shut-off valves that will minimize the impact to the operation of the building.
- There will be a significant reduction in the amount of resources needed to perform a utility shutdown. Contractor time will be reduced, and they will perform a safer and more accurate system verification.

For regulatory compliance: ICRA/PCRA

- Here too, the impact is directly related to time savings per event, in this case a 50% reduction.
- In addition, the BIM process allows for the review to be done at home or in the office and allows Stanford Healthcare to achieve regulatory compliance going from planned maintenance.
- Also, reduce the amount of resources needed to perform a review and reduce time to approve an ICRA/PCRA and perform safer and more accurate system verification and scope verification.

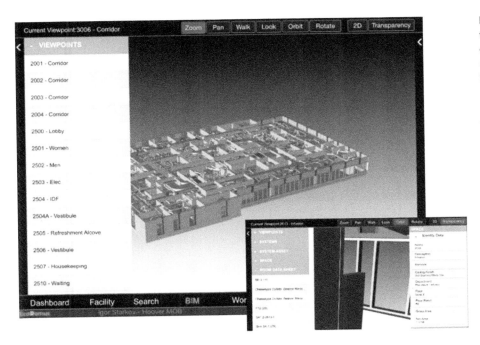

FIGURE 10–11–14 Staff training: understanding complex engineering systems by having access to information.

Image courtesy of Stanford Medical Center.

For institutionalizing tribal knowledge:

- In comparing the results of a single event for the mentioned tasks within the use cases tested, the impact is again on time reduction, which in the case of institutionalizing tribal knowledge is very significant.
- Having the data regarding the different equipment used in the building (i.e., manufacturer, model number, serial number, installation date) would mean that the operations team would not have to manually enter the information into the CMMS system, Maximo.
- Understanding complex engineering systems quickly, new staff can develop operational plans faster.
- Original design finishes can be associated to the building and maintained as designed.
- The structural teams could quickly determine if a wall could be drilled into, or if a team could hang heavy decorations from a beam.

10.11.11 BIM Costs and Impact on Annual Budget

The following methodology was used to determine factored BIM costs:

- User survey data was used to create a factored cost savings.
- The number of annual events was obtained from existing systems.
- Total cost avoidance was calculated based on a 100,000 sf facility.

Table 10–11–8 Cost to Maintain the BIM Model and Maintain It over 5 Years

Facility Size, sf	Total Model Building Cost ($)	Total Soft Cost for 5 yrs ($)	Avg. Cost per sf for 5 yrs ($/sf)
100,000	140,000	83,750	2.24
1,000,000	1,400,000	341,000	1.74
10,000,000	14,000,000	598,000	1.46

- Soft costs were developed to maintain the BIM model based on
  - Consulting time
  - Software costs
  - Staff hires
  - Calculated projected costs over five years

The results of these calculations were as follows:

The initial cost to set up the BIM model with the required information was $1.40/sf ($15.07/m^2), charged to the project. The $1.40/sf was developed from the cost to convert the BIM model from a construction model to a facilities model as well as the cost for a BIM consultant and SHC staff. This cost data for various size facilities is shown in Table 10–11–8.

Based on the above cost analysis for the seven-use case analyses alone, BIM was found to have a direct **4.5%** reduction in cost savings to the following Stanford Healthcare groups:

- Engineering and maintenance
- Environmental, health, and safety
- Facility management

This savings was calculated for a 100,000 sf facility and was equivalent to a reduction of 4% in the cost per patient-day. The savings should increase for a larger facility.

10.11.12 Lessons Learned

Problems/Challenges. During the As-built Model Development Phase:

- Lack of Asset Data in the Models
  Reviewing some of the model areas revealed that some of the building elements were lacking necessary information, and the building model element attributes were missing values. For example, valve type number was blank, which would impact the way the systems are read and

recognized. Additional basic values typically referenced from equipment cut sheets were missing, such as the manufacturer name.

For the most part, this was due to the fact that the construction specs were messy and all over the place, with over 1,000 pages of submittals containing information rejected and approved for the same model elements. This raised the need to add a section in the BIM execution plan (BEP) for FM guidelines and put it up front to avoid the effort required to assemble proper documentation after the fact. The submittals that were in the shared file server site were not digestible; they were all in one big PDF file that was very difficult to understand. In addition, there were many missing values for some of the data that were needed at handover. At one point EcoDomus had to download O&M manuals from manufacturers' websites.

- Model Asset Data Consistency
  In some cases, model elements did not have compliant attributes or attribute information from the Stanford Data Dictionary. Throughout the development of the as-built models, Microdesk compared the project attributes in the FM/O&M model and cross-checked this information with the Data Dictionary provided by Stanford. The Revit families (model elements) did not conform to the standards as laid out in the BIM Guidelines, as shown in Figure 10–11–15.

- Model Data Source
  At a certain stage the data resided in the Middleware application, not in the BIM model.

The above was determined through BIM model audits scheduled at 50%, 75%, and 100% level of completion. The as-built model was checked for its compliance to standards. This involved finding and tracking elements, filtering and isolating elements, and checking consistency across the model elements.

The team looked at various categories of technical and nontechnical factors:

- FMS data integrity
  - Stanford master attributes
- Modeling definition: standards and consistency
  - Naming conventions (element nomenclature for proper mapping into Maximo)
  - Element attribute definition (e.g., manufacturer, model number)
  - MEP systems definition organization; ability to isolate and be viewed separately
- Naming conventions for equipment
  - Types should be succinct, useful, and descriptive. The names provided should allow for easy identification and be easily understood to facilitate the operation, repair, and maintenance of building equipment.

MAXIMO DATA DICTIONARY

23-33 11 00   **Boiler**

Hierarchical Level:	Component
System Association:	HVAC - Heating
Description:	The exterior component of a cooling system that includes a compressor and condensing coil.

Attribute	Data Type	Unit	Domain / Range of Values
Asset ID	Numeric	N/A	System generated unique id for the entity	barcode
Lawson ID	Numeric	N/A	ID used to reference Lawson Asset
Component Description	ALN	N/A	A narrative description of the entity
System (Parent) ID	Numeric	N/A	The system (parent) ID that the component is associated to
Criticality	Numeric	N/A	1, 2, 3, 4, 5
Legacy ID	ALN	N/A	Common name or previous name of the entity
Condition Rating	Numeric	N/A	Condition rating of the component
Inspection Date	ALN	N/A	Date of the last inspection for the condition rating
Year Built	ALN	N/A	Year that the component was constructed
Design Life	Numeric	N/A	Design life
Remaining Useful Life	Numeric	N/A	Remaining useful life estimate
Original Construction Cost	Numeric	$US	Cost of initial construction or purchase cost
Replacement Cost	Numeric	$US	Current replacement value of the component
Manufacturer	ALN	N/A	To be developed on-the-fly
Serial Number	ALN	N/A	Unique identifier for the Component
Model_Number	ALN	N/A	Manufacturer's door model number (catalog id)
Cooling Type	ALN	N/A	Air cooled, Water cooled

Category

Instance Description	Instance Description
Instance Name	Instance Name
InstanceDescription	OmniClassNumber
InstanceName	Sub-Discipline
OmniClassNumber	Type Description
Power	Type Name
Schedule_UniqueId	
Sub-Discipline	
Subcategory	
Tag Number	
Type Description	
Type Name	

(A)   (B)

FIGURE 10–11–15   (A) Revit family model elements that are required to conform to Stanford BIM guidelines. (B) An example of the information carried in the Maximo Data Dictionary for a Boiler.

Figure 10–11–16 shows a 3D view of a mechanical system that allows review of its components and connections.

Resolutions and Takeaways

1. Enhancements to the Stanford Healthcare BIM for FM guidelines must address a number of items, including:
   - The data dictionary is to be referenced in the BIM for FM guidelines and must be part of the contractual document. This will ensure consistent names for all the data and the required level of detail.
   - Updates to the BIM Execution Plan (BEP) are to include more explicit requirements around data requirements and ownership following the BIM for FM standards. Examples of these requirements are:
     - To improve the accuracy of the as-built BIM model by requiring that the as-built condition be scanned so that the scan can be compared

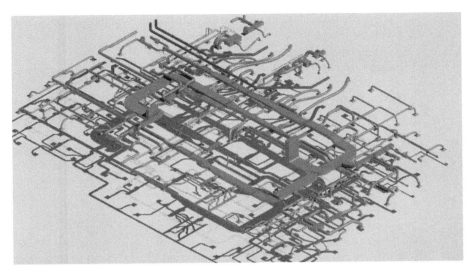

FIGURE 10–11–16
Mechanical system isolation for verification.

Image courtesy of Stanford Medical Center.

to the model. This will catch common errors such as the exact spacing of framing, the location of vents, pipes, valves, and so on. This will allow for validation of the model and ensure that all details are accounted for.

- To develop an as-built delivery schedule that staggers the construction schedule with the potential following sequence:
  - Contractor coordinates subcontractors' as-built and submittal data with the goal to perform modeling throughout construction, as opposed to waiting for the completion of construction.
  - Opportunity to modify delivery schedule to include RFI's, CCD's (Construction Change Directive), and the like.
  - Allows for staff planning and milestone meetings.
- To streamline the close out documentation process
  - Include a documentation submittal requirement as part of Maximo that could be uploaded at close out.
  - Stanford Healthcare will require that all close out documents are in the same consistent PDF format.

2. Addressing data location

One of the key questions concerning as-builts and FM/O&M BIM models is where the data will be stored and how and by whom it will be maintained. Regarding the data location issue, a best practice in the industry is to store the data in the BIM model and not in an external system.

There are several methodologies to approach the maintenance issue. Two common ones are:

- Maintain the as-built model

  In this method, the facility department maintains its data in a view of the construction as-builts, or the facility department submits redline marks to the architect, who maintains the model through ongoing changes, such as merging or splitting rooms.

- Use a separate lifecycle model

  In this method, the facility managers create a separate lifecycle model from the construction as-builts. The facility managers remove detail that is useful for construction but not necessary for day-to-day management and maintain their own changes (for example, merging rooms).

3. Developing a scaling strategy

   The process would involve the development of a stage hierarchy for the new buildings and the ones to be renovated. The following describes the various scenarios under which the solution could be scaled. This approach is broken down into three stages of activity that offer an increasing level of detail of the models and provide a time scaled approach.

   • Stage 1

     Develop an LOD 350 model for the facilities. That would allow for the integration of the BIM model within the asset management solution. This would have an impact on cases such as addressing regulatory compliance (Use Case 7: ICRA/PCRA Review) and institutionalizing tribal knowledge (Use Case 5: Engineering Staff Training).

     In addition, this stage would be used to solve the challenge of the asset data loading presented in Use Case 3: Asset Information Entry and Update. This early stage of development can benefit from incorporating the data needed for this use case because it represents the largest cost savings to the organization

   • Stage 2

     Identify critical systems and prepare a model for them. Expansion of the existing models to include the critical systems would allow for the inclusion of the cases that involved planned and reactive shutdowns (Use Case 1: Major Plumbing Leak and Use Case 6: Shutdown Request) and institutionalizing tribal knowledge (Use Case 2: Structural and Fire Safety Analysis and Use Case 4: Integrated Finish Schedule).

   • Stage 3

     This stage is the final development of a model that reflects the as-built conditions (LOD 500).

4. Technology Support Strategy

   Ensure that training manuals and reference materials are always easily accessible and available to users to avoid reverting to old ways.

10.11.13 Conclusion and Future Outlook

The Neuroscience BIM pilot project proved successful in testing the three major areas that matter most to the facilities and maintenance group at Stanford Healthcare:

1. Patient care
2. Patient safety
3. Cost per patient day

As result, a facility information management subcommittee was created, under the asset management steering group, whose goals were to:

- Determine document library organization and content requirements
- Define record drawing requirements and formats
- Decide level, data transference, and BIM storage/use

Over the next several years, the combination of BIM and facilities management will expand the capabilities of both the facilities and the planning staff. The ability to use as-built models as a tool to explore and validate the operational status of a facility will give planning staff unprecedented access to operational data. The overall trend across the industry is to combine tools such as Revit with operational systems. Additional tools that will be used in this transformation are web-based model viewers and data analytics tools to explore and validate data that is used in operational systems. Overall this blending of technologies will result in a reduction in operational costs and a greatly improved access to information by facility staff. Facilities teams can look forward to providing informed, efficient, and reliable building information for repair and maintenance work. Using integrated information in updated digital files will help monitor, track, and improve operational performance while reducing risk and increasing performance across the asset's lifecycle.

Acknowledgments

This case study was prepared with the close collaboration of Alex Saleh, BRE, CHC, PE Project Support Manager, Stanford University Medical Center, and George Broadbent, Director of Asset Management, Microdesk, Inc. Special thanks to the Stanford Healthcare ITS group and Jennifer Wong for her continued support as an IT resource, and to Stanford Healthcare Planning, Design, and Construction for partnering with facilities and providing the contractor BIM models.

Glossary

4D

A 4D model is a time-dependent view of a BIM model in which objects are associated with activities in a construction plan. 4D models can be viewed as animations, and clash-checks can be run at any point in time to identify space-time conflicts between permanent and/or temporary facilities (e.g., cranes, scaffolding).

5D

A 5D model is a cost-dependent view of a BIM model in which budget line items are associated with specific measurable features of model objects. The purpose is to link budget items with model objects, so that future costs can be forecast and actual costs can be monitored in relation to the BIM model.

As-Built BIM Model

The BIM model(s) prepared during the construction process that reflects all of the changes made to the design model during the construction process. Normally this is an LOD (level of detail) 400 or 500 model that reflects how the facility was actually built.

Asset Information Model (AIM) or Facility Maintenance (FM) BIM Model

The BIM model used by the owner to record the spaces and assets incorporated into the building or other facility. This model is used for location, ownership, and access to product information such as warranties and depreciation values, to support maintenance and personnel move processes. Typically, the Design Intent Model is used as a baseline and then is updated to incorporate all the changes during construction. This is intended to be a lightweight model with enough equipment and systems (connectivity) data to enable FM operations (including space management, equipment maintenance, and asset management).

B-rep (Boundary representation)

3D geometry of a solid shape as defined by its bounding surfaces. Used by most 3D CAD tools for display, clash detection, and measurement to points on surfaces.

BIM application or BIM system

A generic term to denote BIM software, including BIM tools, platforms, or servers used within a BIM environment to support Building Information Modeling. Thus traditional applications such as drafting, rendering, specification writing, and engineering analysis tools are all potentially BIM applications, if workflows and/or data exchange integrates them in Building Information Modeling. The term can be further qualified to denote specific application areas. For example, "BIM Architectural Design Application" is often used to refer to applications used primarily for architectural design, such as Autodesk Revit, Tekla Structures, Bentley AECoSIM, Digital Project, and ArchiCAD.

BIM Collaboration Format (BCF)
BCF is an XML file format intended for exchange and collaborative resolution of clashes and other issues. When BCF files are opened in the BIM platform, the list of clash issues is available. The user's view of the model can be set to focus on and display each issue, together with additional information about the issue.

BIM Execution Plan (BEP) or BIM Project Execution Plan (PxP)
A contractual agreement among the project team that defines how a BIM project will be executed, how the BIM models will be updated over the life of the project, and what information is to be delivered in the various exchanges. It covers the responsibilities of each team member, the technologies used by the team, the level of detail to be used, the naming standards for each kind of object, the data exchange process, and when each type of data will be entered into the model. It also defines how this data will be passed to or integrated with FM systems (if this is part of the team's responsibilities). This plan can be defined by the owner or delegated to a team member by the owner.

BIM environment
A set of BIM platforms and libraries that are interfaced to support multiple information and process pipelines that encompass the various BIM tools, platforms, servers, libraries, and work flows within the project workflows of an organization. A BIM environment is supported by a set of policies and practices that facilitates management of BIM project data.

BIM guide
A BIM guide is a collection of best practices for implementing BIM in a project. It can be also defined as a document that is developed to help BIM users effectively and efficiently make decisions regarding BIM implementation in their projects, so that they can achieve the target goal at each stage of a BIM roadmap or of a BIM execution plan. Synonyms include BIM manual, BIM handbook, BIM protocol, BIM guidelines, BIM requirements, and BIM project specifications. We distinguish BIM guide from BIM standard. (See BIM standard for definition.)

BIM mandate
A requirement and a target goal at each stage of a BIM roadmap.

BIM maturity model
A benchmark tool for assessing the level of BIM implementation of a project, an organization, or a region.

BIM measure or BIM metric
A key performance indicator (KPI) that can be used in a BIM maturity model.

BIM platform

A BIM design application that generates information for multiple uses and incorporates multiple tools directly or through interfaces with varying levels of integration. Most BIM design applications serve not only a tool function, such as 3D parametric object modeling, but also other functions, such as drawing production and application interface, making them also platforms.

BIM process

A process that generates and manages information using BIM applications for design, analysis, fabrication detailing, cost estimation, scheduling, or other use.

BIM roadmap

A national or organizational adoption plan that aims to achieve target levels of capability, defined in a BIM maturity model within a scheduled time frame.

BIM server, model server, Common Data Environment (CDE), or BIM repository

A BIM server is a database management system whose schema is object-based. It is different from existing project data management (PDM) systems and web-based project management systems in that PDM systems are file-based systems, and carry CAD and analysis package project files. BIM servers are object-based, allowing query, transfer, updating, and management of individual project objects from a potentially heterogeneous set of applications.

BIM standard

A BIM guide, information requirements, or BIM-related protocol approved by an international standard organization such as ISO.

BIM tool

A task-specific software application that manipulates a building model for some defined purpose and produces a specific outcome. Examples of tools include those used for drawing production, specification writing, cost estimation, clash and error detection, energy analysis, rendering, and visualization.

Boolean operations

The class of operations allowing editing of shapes by merging two shapes together, subtracting one shape from another, or defining the intersection of two or more shapes. This approach is named after George Boole, who invented the union, intersection, and difference operations on mathematical sets.

Building Data Model or Building Product Data Model

An object schema suitable for representing a building and its supporting data, such as information about building parts, users, energy loads, or processes. A building data model may be used to represent schemas for file exchange, for XML-based web exchange, or to define a database schema for a repository. The main examples of building data models are IFC and CIS/2.

Building Information Modeling (BIM)

A verb or an adjective phrase to describe tools, processes, and technologies that are facilitated by digital, machine-readable documentation about a building, its performance, its planning, its construction, and later its operation. Therefore, BIM describes an activity, not an object. To describe the result of the modeling activity, we use the terms "building information model" in full, "building model," or most simply, "BIM model."

Building Model or Building Object Model

This consists of a digital database of a particular building that contains information about its objects. This may include its geometry (generally defined by parametric rules), performance, planning, construction, and later its operation. A Revit model and a Digital Project model of a building are examples of building models. "Building model" can be considered the next generation replacement for "construction drawings" or "architectural drawings." Downstream in the process, the term "fabrication model" is already in common use as a replacement for "shop drawings."

BIM model checking or model quality checking

For BIM information to be useful for downstream applications—such as functional simulations, code-compliance checking, automated permitting, and so on—it must conform to the semantic content and syntax requirements defined for the receiving applications. Therefore, the move to automated rule checking is critical if the quality assumptions of BIM are to be realized. A wide range of review is available, from checking for the presence and proper naming of objects at each stage of a project (as defined in the BEP), to checking the model for conformance to building codes and other complex requirements.

BIM model integration tools

Model integration tools provide users the ability not only to merge multiple models to form a federated model and to check for clashes, as some of the more sophisticated model viewers do, but they also provide construction management functions that can operate on the integrated models such as clash detection and construction planning.

Building objects

Building objects are the things or parts that make up a building. Objects can be aggregated into higher level objects, such as "assemblies"; assemblies are also objects. More generally, an object is any unit of a building that has properties associated with it. Thus the spaces in a building are also objects. Building objects are a subset of the objects making up a building model. In parts of the text, *element* or *component* is used as a synonym for object.

buildingSMART International (bSI), formerly the International Alliance for Interoperability (AIA)

An international standardization organization that aims to improve data exchange and workflow in the construction industry. It has developed Industry

Foundation Classes (IFC) as a neutral and open specification for BIM as well as other standards for data dictionaries, data modeling methodologies and technologies, and tools. British Standards Institution (BSI) is a different organization.

CIS/2 (CIMsteel Integration Standard/version 2)
A data exchange schema specifically addressed to represent steel in buildings and structures. This standard is endorsed and supported by the American Institute of Steel Construction. It relies on ISO-STEP standard technology.

Clash checking
Checking that the objects in one or more BIM models do not occupy the same space (hard clash) or come too near each other (soft clash) to allow room for maintenance, safety requirements, insulation, and the like.

Construction BIM Model
The BIM model(s) developed by the general contractor (GC) and subcontractors that define the constructed facility in sufficient detail to permit construction operations (procurement, scheduling, accurate locations, and so on), normally LODs 300 to 400.

Construction Operations Building information exchange (COBie)
As defined in the National BIM Standard, United States Version 3, the format for the exchange of information about building assets such as equipment, products, materials, and spaces (see https://www.nationalbimstandard.org/files/NBIMS-US_V3_4.2_COBie.pdf).

Construction Manager at Risk (CM@R)
A form of project procurement where an owner retains a designer to furnish design services and also retains a construction manager to provide construction management services for a project throughout the preconstruction and construction phases. These services may include preparation and coordination of bid packages, scheduling, cost control, value engineering, and construction administration. The construction manager is usually a licensed general contractor and guarantees the cost of the project (guaranteed maximum price, or GMP). The owner is responsible for the design before a GMP can be set.

CSG (Constructive Solid Geometry)
A method of solid modeling that builds up complex shapes by combining simple shapes using the Boolean operations. It stores shapes by the tree of operations used to construct the shape. This is a core capability of parametric modeling.

Design-Bid-Build (DBB)
A form of project procurement where the client (owner) hires an architect, who then develops a design together with other design consultants. This is recorded on drawings that become the basis for bids from one or more contracts. The lowest responsible bid is selected by the owner, and the contractor

who then proceeds to build the project with subcontractors, fabricators, and material suppliers, who are also usually selected on the basis of lowest responsible bid.

Design-Build (DB)
A form of project procurement where the owner contracts directly with the design-build team (normally a contractor with a design capability or working with an architect) to develop a well-defined building program and a schematic design that meets the owner's needs. The DB contractor then estimates the total cost and time needed to design and construct the building. After all modifications requested by the owner are implemented, the plan is approved and the final budget for the project is established.

Design BIM Model or Design Intent Model
The BIM model(s) developed by the architect or design/engineering consultants to express the building form, layout of spaces, and functional characteristics to allow evaluation of building visualization and performance (energy, design intent, approximate cost, and so on).

Exchange format
A format for laying out data that can be used to exchange information. Example exchange formats are IGES and DXF.

Exchange schema
A method to define the structure of data for exchange abstractly, for possible mapping to different formats, such as a text file, XML, or database. IFC, CIS/2, and ISO15926 are example exchange schemas.

Feature
As applied to design, a part of a shape with a specific purpose. In a CAD system, features are important because they have functional purposes; a connection is a feature on a steel beam, and a window opening is a feature in a wall. Features may or may not be accessible, carry properties, or be editable. Feature-based design supports these capabilities.

IFC (Industry Foundation Classes)
An international public standard schema for representing building information. It uses ISO-STEP technology and libraries.

Integrated Project Delivery (IPD)
This form of project procurement consists of a collaborative alliance of people, systems, business structures, and practices in a process that harnesses the talents and insights of all participants to optimize project results, increase value to the owner, reduce waste, and maximize efficiency through all phases of design, fabrication, and construction.

Integrated Form of Agreement for Lean Project Delivery (IFOA)
A standard form of contractual agreement for IPD projects published as the AIA ConsensusDocs 300.

Interoperability
The ability of BIM applications from multiple vendors to exchange BIM data and operate on that data. Interoperability is a significant requirement for team collaboration and data movement between different BIM applications.

ISO-STEP
International Standards Organization, Standard for the Technical Exchange of Product Model Data; officially ISO 10303 developed and managed by ISO Technical Committee 184 Sub Committee 4. ISO-STEP provides the foundation technologies, tools, and methods for developing interoperability tools and standards in manufacturing, aerospace, shipbuilding, and process and industrial plants. It is the technology basis for IFC, CIS/2, and many other exchange schemas and formats.

Level of Detail, Level of Definition, or Level of Development (LOD)
The required level of 3D modeling (what objects are included in the model and the degree of detail with which each object is modeled) has to be carefully determined depending on BIM goals and model uses during different project phases. Many organizations and project-level BIM execution plans specify LOD as requirements for the subsystem projects at different phases. Typically, lower LODs are used for design (100 to 300) and higher LODs for construction (300 to 400) and turnover (500).

Model View Definitions (MVDs)
An MVD defines a subset of the IFC schema that is needed to satisfy one or many exchange requirements of the AEC industry. The method used by buildingSMART is defined in the Information Delivery Manual, IDM (also ISO 29481).

Model synchronization
The issue of maintaining version consistency across all information in a BIM environment. This includes the methods to address this issue and deals with the issues of change management across multiple tools and platforms.

Non-uniform rational B-spline (NURBS)
Non-uniform rational basis spline is a mathematical model commonly used in computer graphics for generating and representing curves and surfaces. It offers great flexibility and precision for handling both analytic (surfaces defined by common mathematical formulae) and modeled shapes.

Object class or object family
In parametric modeling, object classes are the information structures for defining object instances. Architectural BIM design tools have object classes for Walls, Doors, Slabs, Windows, Roofs, and so forth, while structural BIM tools will have object classes for connections, rebar, pre-stress tendons, and so forth. The object class defines how instances of a class are structured, how they are edited, and how they behave when their context changes.

Object-based parametric modeling

The technology on which most BIM design applications are based. Includes the ability to define individual objects whose shape and other properties can be controlled parametrically. It also applies to assemblies of objects, possibly up to the building scale, allowing the assemblies to be controlled by parameters. Typically used for some form of optimization of the design.

Parametric object

A single object that is created or edited through its parameters and parametric constraints.

Scalability

The issue of how well a system behaves as the data it uses grows in size. Some applications operate well only with small datasets. File-based systems tend to have file size limitations while systems that use a database tend to be much less dependent on file size. Large and complex models may need to be subdivided to allow reasonable response times for updating.

Schema

As applied to databases, the abstract representation or model of data for some use.

Semantic enrichment

Semantic enrichment for BIM models is the application of artificial intelligence techniques to models to supplement information, interpreting their contents in much the way a human expert might. Semantic enrichment identifies implicit information and adds it explicitly to a model. The information added includes object classification, aggregation, identification and numbering, grids and axes, and zoning.

Solid modeling

The general type of geometric modeling where the elements being modeled and operated on are closed and bounded, enclosing a volume. Solid modeling can represent solid shapes. In a sense it could be considered misnamed, because it can also represent the shapes of voids, such as a room. Solid modeling has multiple types of modeling within it, including B-rep, constructive solid geometry, and feature-based modeling.

Transaction

In databases, an operation on a database that updates the data as a single step operation, similar to a "save" on a file system. Transactions may be user controlled or system generated, and have as an important function maintaining the consistency of the data being stored.

Virtual design and construction (VDC)

VDC is the practice of using building information modeling specifically as a first-run study of a construction process. With VDC, designers and builders test both the product and the construction process virtually and thoroughly before executing work in the field to construct the building. They examine integrated multidisciplinary performance models of design-construction projects, including the facilities, work processes, supply chains, and project teams in order to identify and remove constraints, thus improving project performance and the resulting facilities.

Workflow

The sequences of task-related communication among people (normally the project team) to accomplish sequences of tasks and the needed data flows to support those sequences.

References

Adachi, Y. (2002). "Overview of IFC model server framework." European Conference for Process and Product Modeling (ECPPM): eWork and eBusiness in Architecture, Engineering and Construction, Portorož, Slovenia, September 9–11, 367–372.

AGC (2010). *The Contractors' Guide to Building Information Modeling*, 2nd edition. Associated General Contractors of America. Arlington, VA. www.agc.org/news/2010/04/28/contractors-guide-bim-2nd-edition.

AGC (2006). *The Contractors' Guide to BIM*. Associated General Contractors (AGC) of America, Arlington, VA.

AIA (1994). *The Architect's Handbook of Professional Practice*, Washington, D.C., AIA Document B162, American Institute of Architects.

AIA (2007a). "AIA Document C106-2007: Digital Data Licensing Agreement." American Institute of Architects, Washington D.C.

AIA (2007b). "AIA Document E201-2007: Digital Data Protocol Exhibit." American Institute of Architects, Washington D.C.

AIA (2008). "AIA Document E202-2008: Building Information Modeling Protocol Exhibit." American Institute of Architects.

AIA (2013). "AIA Document E203-2013: Building Information Modeling and Digital Data Exhibit." American Institute of Architects.

AIA (2017). *AIA Contract Documents: Integrated Project Delivery (IPD) Family*, www.aiacontracts.org/contract-doc-pages/27166-integrated-project-delivery-ipd-family.

AISC (2017). *AISC Design Guide*, 30 vols. AISC Chicago, IL. www.aisc.org/publications/design-guides/.

Akinci, B., Boukamp, F., Gordon, C., Huber, D., Lyons, C., and Park, K. (2006). "A Formalism for Utilization of Sensor Systems and Integrated Project Models for Active Construction Quality Control." *Automation in Construction*, 15(2): 124–138.

Akintoye, A., and Fitzgerald, E. (2000). "A Survey of Current Cost Estimating Practices in the UK." *Construction Management & Economics*, 18(2): 161–172.

Alberti, L. B. (1988). On the art of building in ten books. MIT Press, Cambridge, MA.

ANSI/X3/SPARC (1975). "Interim Report: Study Group on Database Management Systems 75-02-08." *FDT: Bulletin of ACM SIGMOD*, 7(2), 1–140.

Ashcraft, H. W. J. (2006). "Building Information Modeling: A Great Idea in Conflict with Traditional Concepts of Insurance, Liability, and Professional Responsibility." Schinnerer's 45th Annual Meeting of Invited Attorneys.

Autodesk (2004). "Return on Investment with Autodesk Revit," June 25, 2007. Autodesk website. Autodesk, Inc. http://images.autodesk.com/adsk/files/4301694_Revit_ROI_Calculator.zip.

BACnet. (n.d.). "BACnet Official Website." www.bacnet.org/ (accessed Sept. 14, 2017).

Ballard, G. (2000). "The Last Planner™ System of Production Control." Ph.D. Dissertation, University of Birmingham, Birmingham, UK.

Barak, R., Jeong, Y. S., Sacks, R., and Eastman, C. M. (2009). "Unique Requirements of Building Information Modeling for Cast-in-Place Reinforced Concrete." *Journal of Computing in Civil Engineering*, 23(2): 64–74.

Barison, M. B., and Santos, E. T. (2010) "An Overview of BIM Specialists." *International Conference on Computing in Civil and Building Engineering (ICCCBE)*, Nottingham, UK, June 30–July 2, 141–147.

Barison, M. B., and Santos, E. T. (2011) "The Competencies of BIM Specialists: A Comparative Analysis of the Literature Review and Job Ad Descriptions." *International Workshop on Computing in Civil Engineering 2011*, Miami, Florida, 594–602.

Barré, Christian, and Karine Leempoels (2009), *"Louis Vuitton Foundation for Creation on a Cloud", cstb webzine*, February 2009. Accessed September 25, 2017, www.cstb.fr/archives/english-webzine/anglais/february-2009/louis-vuitton-foundation-for-creation-on-a-cloud.html.

Batiwork (n.d.) The Batiwork Official Website. Accessed September 26, 2017, www.batiwork.fr/.

BCA (2008). "BIM e-Submission Guideline for Architectural Discipline." Building and Construction Authority, Singapore.

BCA (2012). "Singapore BIM Guide Version 1.0." Building and Construction Authority (BCA), Singapore.

BCA (2013). "Singapore BIM Guide Version 2.0." Building and Construction Authority (BCA), Singapore.

Beard, J., Loulakis, M., and Wundram, E. (2005). *Design-Build: Planning Through Development*, McGraw-Hill Professional.

Bedrick (2008). "Organizing the Development of a Building Information Model," *AECbytes Feature*, Sept. 18, 2008. www.aecbytes.com/feature/2008/MPSforBIM.html.

Belsky, M., Sacks, R., and Brilakis, I. (2016). "Semantic Enrichment for Building Information Modeling." *Computer-Aided Civil and Infrastructure Engineering*, 31(4), 261–274.

Berners-Lee, T., Hendler, J., and Lassila, O. (2001). "The Semantic Web." *Scientific American*, 284(5): 35–43.

Bernstein, H. M., Jones, S. A., Russo, M. A., and Laquidara-Carr, D. (2012). *2012 Business Value of BIM in North America*. McGraw Hill Construction, Bedford, MA.

Bernstein, H. M., Jones, S. A., Russo, M. A., and Laquidara-Carr, D. (2014). *The Business Value of BIM in Australia and New Zealand: How Building Information Modeling Is Transforming the Design and Construction Industry*. McGraw Hill Construction, Bedford, MA.

Bernstein, H. M., Jones, S. A., Russo, M. A., Laquidara, D., Messina, F., Partyka, D., Lorenz, A., Buckley, B., Fitch, E., and Gilmore, D. (2010). *Green BIM: How Building Information Modeling is Contributing to Green Design and Construction*. McGraw Hill Construction, Bedford, MA.

Bijl, A., and Shawcross, G. (1975). "Housing Site Layout System," *Computer-Aided Design*, 7(1): 2–10.

BIMserver.org. (2012). "Open Source Building Information Modelserver." www.bimserver.org (accessed May 19, 2012).

bips (2007). "3D Working Method 2006." bips, Ballerup, Denmark.

Bloch, T., and Sacks, R. (2018). "Comparing Machine Learning and Rule-based Inferencing for Semantic Enrichment of BIM Models," *Automation in Construction*, 91: 256–272.

Booch, G. (1993). *Object-Oriented Analysis and Design with Applications* (2nd Edition), Addison-Wesley, New York, NY.

Borrmann, A., and Rank, E. (2009). "Specification and Implementation of Directional Operators in a 3D Spatial Query Language for Building Information Models." *Advanced Engineering Informatics*, 23(1): 32–44.

Boryslawski, M. (2006). "Building Owners Driving BIM: The Letterman Digital Arts Center Story." AECBytes. Sept. 30 2006. 27 June 07. www.aecbytes.com/buildingthefuture/2006/LDAC_story.html.

Braid, I. C. (1973). *Designing with Volumes*. Cambridge UK, Cantab Press, Cambridge University.

bSC (2014). "Roadmap to Lifecycle Building Information Modeling in the Canadian AECOO Community Ver. 1.0." buildingSMART Canada, Toronto, Canada.

BSI (2013). PAS 1192-2:2013 Specification for information management for the capital/delivery phase of construction projects using building information modelling, British Standards Institution, https://shop.bsigroup.com/en/ProductDetail/?pid=000000000030281435.

BSI (2014a). BS 1192-4:2014 Collaborative production of information Part 4: Fulfilling Employers information exchange requirements using COBie. Code of practice, British Standards Institution, http://shop.bsigroup.com/ProductDetail?pid=000000000030294672.

BSI (2014b). PAS 1192-4:2014 Collaborative production of information Part 4: Fulfilling employer's information exchange requirements using COBie. Code of practice, The British Standards Institution, London, UK.

BSI (2015). PAS 1192-5:2015 Specification for security-minded building information modelling, digital built environments and smart asset management, British Standards Institution, https://shop.bsigroup.com/ProductDetail/?pid=000000000030314119.

bSI (2014a). "buildingSMART International BIM Guides Project." www.bimguides.org (accessed Feb. 8, 2016.).

bSI (2017). "IFC Overview Summary." www.buildingsmart-tech.org/specifications/ifc-overview (accessed May 20, 2017).

bSK (2016). "Module 15. BIM Information Level (BIL)." *Korea BIM Standards Version 1.0*, buildingSMART Korea, Seoul, Korea.

buildingSMART Australasia. (2012). "National Building Information Modelling Initiative, Volume 1: Strategy." buildingSMART Australasia, Randwick NSW, Australia.

buildingSMART Finland. (2012). "Common BIM Requirements (COBIM) 2012 v1.0." buildingSMART Finland, Helsinki, Finland.

buildingSMART International (2017). http://buildingsmart.org/.

BuildLACCD (2016). *LACCD Building Information Modeling Standards*, Los Angeles Community College District, LA, 36 pp. http://az776130.vo.msecnd.net/media/docs/default-source/contractors-and-bidders-library/standards-guidelines/bim/bim-design-build-standards-v4-1.pdf?sfvrsn=4.

Cassidy, R. (2017). "BIM for O+M: Less about the Model, More about the Data," *Building Design and Construction* 2/2017, https://www.bdcnetwork.com/bim-om-less-about-model-more-about-data.

Cavieres, A., Gentry, R., and Al-Haddad, T. (2009). "Rich Knowledge Parametric Tools for Concrete Masonry Design: Automation of Preliminary Structural Analysis, Detailing and Specification." *Proceedings of the 2009 26th International Symposium on Automation and Robotics in Construction (ISARC)*, Austin, TX, June 24–27, 2009, pp. 544–552.

Chan, P. S., Chan, H. Y., and Yuen, P. H. (2016). "BIM-Enabled Streamlined Fault Localization with System Topology, RFID Technology and Real-Time Data Acquisition Interfaces." *International Conference on Automation Sciences and Engineering (CASE)*, August 21–24, 2016.

ChangeAgents AEC Pty Ltd. (2017). "About BIM Excellence." http://bimexcellence.com/about/ (accessed August 13, 2017).

Cheng, J. C. P., and Lu, Q. (2015). "A Review of the Efforts and Roles of the Public Sector for BIM Adoption Worldwide." *Journal of Information Technology in Construction*, 20, 442–478.

CIC (2010). *BIM Project Execution Planning Guide, Version 1.0*. Pennsylvania State University, University Park, PA.

CIC (2013). *BIM Planning Guide for Facility Owners, Version 2*. Pennsylvania State University, State College, PA.

CII (2002). Preliminary Research on Prefabrication, Pre-Assembly, Modularization and Off-Site Fabrication in Construction. University of Texas at Austin, July 2002.

CityGML (n.d.). "CityGML Official Website." www.citygml.org/ (accessed Sept. 14, 2017).

Cook, S. (2013). "A Field Study Investigation of the Time-Value Component of Stick-Built vs. Prefabricated Hospital Bathrooms." *Capstone Project Report in Construction Management*, Wentworth Institute of Technology, Boston.

Court, P., Pasquire, C., Gibb, A., and Bower, D. (2006). "Design of a Lean and Agile Construction System for a Large and Complex Mechanical and Electrical Project." *Understanding and Managing the Construction Process: Theory and Practice, Proceedings of the 14th Conference of the International Group for Lean Construction*, R. Sacks and S. Bertelsen, eds., Catholic University of Chile, School of Engineering, Santiago, Chile, 243–254.

CRC (2009). "National Guidelines for Digital Modelling." Cooperative Research Centre for Construction Innovation, Brisbane, Australia.

Crowley, A. (2003a). "CIMSteel Integration Standards Release 2 (CIS/2)." www.cis2 .org/ (accessed Jan. 4, 2005).

Crowley, A. (2003b). "CIS/2 Interactive at NASCC," *New Steel Construction*, 11:10.

CURT (2004). Collaboration, Integrated Information, and the Project Lifecycle in Building Design, Construction and Operation, WP-1202 Architectural/Engineering Productivity Committee of the Construction Users Roundtable (CURT), http://mail.curt .org/14_0_curt_publications.html.

Dakan, M. (2006). "BIM Pilot Program Shows Success." *Cadalyst*. July 19, 2006. www .cadalyst.com/aec/gsa039s-bim-pilot-program-shows-success-3338.

Daum, S., Borrmann, A., Kolbe, T. H. (2017). "A Spatio-Semantic Query Language for the Integrated Analysis of City Models and Building Information Models." In Abdul-Rahman, A. (ed.), *Advances in 3D Geoinformation. Lecture Notes in Geoinformation and Cartography*. Springer, Cham.

Day, M. (2002). "Intelligent Architectural Modeling." *AEC Magazine*, September 2002. June 27, 2007. www.caddigest.com/subjects/aec/select/Intelligent_modeling_day .htm.

Do, D., Ballard, G., and Tillmann, P. (2015). *Part 1 of 5: The Application of Target Value Design in the Design and Construction of the UHS Temecula Valley Hospital*. Project Production Systems Laboratory, University of California, Berkeley.

Duggan, T., and Patel, D. (2013). *Design-Build Project Delivery Market Share and Market Size Report*, Reed Construction Data/RS Means Market Intelligence, Norwell, MA. www.dbia.org/resource-center/Documents/rsmeansreport_2013rev.pdf.

East, E. W. (2007). Construction Operations Building Information Exchange (Cobie): Requirements Definition and Pilot Implementation Standard. Engineering Research and Development Center, Champaign IL Construction Engineering Research Lab, ERDC/CERL TR-07-30, 195.

East, E. W. (2012). "Construction Operations Building Information Exchange (COBie)." www.wbdg.org/resources/cobie.php (accessed May 7, 2012).

Eastman, C. M. (1975). "The Use of Computers Instead of Drawings in Building Design." *Journal of the American Institute of Architects*, March: 46–50.

Eastman, C. M. (1992). "Modeling of Buildings: Evolution and Concepts." *Automation in Construction*, 1: 99–109.

Eastman, C. M. (1999). *Building Product Models: Computer Environments Supporting Design and Construction*. Boca Raton, FL, CRC Press.

Eastman, C. M., and Sacks, R. (2008). "Relative Productivity in the AEC Industries in the United States for On-Site and Off-Site Activities." *Journal of Construction Engineering and Management*, 134: 517–526.

Eastman, C. M., His, I., and Potts, C. (1998). *Coordination in Multi-Organization Creative Design Projects*. Design Computing Research Report. Atlanta, College of Architecture, Georgia Institute of Technology.

Eastman, C. M., Teicholz, P., Sacks, R., and Liston, K. (2008). *BIM Handbook: A Guide to Building Information Modeling for Owners, Managers, Architects, Engineers, Contractors and Fabricators*. John Wiley and Sons, Hoboken, NJ.

Eastman, C. M., Parker, D. S., and Jeng, T. S. (1997). "Managing the Integrity of Design Data Generated by Multiple Applications: The Principle of Patching." *Research in Engineering Design*, 9: 125–145.

Eckblad, S., Ashcraft, H., Audsley, P., Blieman, D., Bedrick, J., Brewis, C., Hartung, R. J., Onuma, K., Rubel, Z., and Stephens, N. D. (2007). *Integrated Project Delivery: A Working Definition*. http://ipd-ca.net/images/Integrated%20Project%20Delivery %20Definition.pdf.

Egan, J. (1998). "Rethinking Construction." Dept. of Trade and Industry, London.

Ergen, E., Akinci, B., and Sacks, R. (2007). "Tracking and Locating Components in a Precast Storage Yard Utilizing Radio Frequency Identification Technology and GPS." *Automation in Construction*, 16: 354–367.

Farmer, M. (2016). *The Farmer Review of the UK Construction Labour Model: Modernise or Die*. Construction Leadership Council (CLC), London, UK, 80.

FIATECH (2010). *Capital Projects Technology Roadmap*. http://fiatech.org/capital-projects-technology-roadmap.html.

FIATECH (n.d.). "FIATECH Official Website." www.fiatech.org/ (accessed Sept. 14, 2017).

Fischer, M., Khanzode, A., Reed, D., and Ashcraft, H. W. (2017). *Integrating Project Delivery*. John Wiley & Sons, Hoboken, NJ.

Fondation (2014). "Press Kit: Opening, October 27th, 2014." Fondation pour la Création Louis Vuitton (2014). Accessed September 26, 2017 https://r.lvmh-static .com/uploads/2015/01/oct-2014flv-press-kit.pdf.

Forgues, D., Koskela, L., and Lejeune, A. (2009). "Information Technology as Boundary Object for Transformational Learning." *ITcon*, 14 (Special Issue on Technology Strategies for Collaborative Working), 48–58.

Francis, R. L., McGinnis, L. F., & White, J. A. (1992). *Facility Layout and Location: An Analytical Approach*. Pearson College Division.

Friedman, M., Gehry, F., and Sorkin, M. (2002). *Gehry Talks: Architecture + Process*, Universe Architecture, New York.

Friedman, T. L. (2007). *The World Is Flat 3.0: A Brief History of the Twenty-first Century*. Picador, New York, NY.

Gallaher, M. P., O'Connor, A. C., John, J., Dettbarn, L., and Gilday, L. T. (2004). *Cost Analysis of Inadequate Interoperability in the U.S. Capital Facilities Industry.* Gaithersburg, MD, National Institute of Standards and Technology, U.S. Department of Commerce Technology Administration.

Gehry Technologies. (2012). "Building Information Evolved: Fondation Louis Vuitton." AIA TAP BIM Awards 2012 Submission, Accessed September 25, 2017, https://network.aia.org/technologyinarchitecturalpractice/viewdocument/foundation-louis-vuitton?CommunityKey=79d8bdfe-0ff1-430c-b5c9-7aef1aa8fd0a&tab=librarydocuments.

Gerber, D. J., and Lin, S.-H. E. (2014). "Designing in Complexity: Simulation, Integration, and Multidisciplinary Design Optimization for Architecture." *Simulation*, 90(8), 936–959.

Gero, J. (2012). *Design Optimization.* Elsevier Science, Amsterdam, The Netherlands.

Gielingh, W. (1988). "General AEC Reference Model (GARM)," *Conceptual Modeling of Buildings*, CIB W74–W78 Seminar, Lund, Sweden, CIB Publication 126.

Glymph, J., Shelden, D., Ceccato, C., Mussel, J., and Schober, H. (2004). "A Parametric Strategy for Free-form Glass Structures Using Quadrilateral Planar Facets." *Automation in Construction* 13(2): 187–202.

Gray, J., and Reuter, A. (1992). *Transaction Processing: Concepts and Techniques*, Morgan Kaufmann, Burlington, MA.

Grose, M. (2016). "BIM Adoption in the MEP World." *Engineering New Record*, 2/2016. https://www.enr.com/articles/40243-bim-adoption-in-the-mep-world.

GSA (2007). "GSA BIM Guide Series." www.gsa.gov/portal/category/101070 (accessed 2017, July 22).

Gurevich, U., and Sacks, R. (2013). "Examination of the Effects of a KanBIM Production Control System on Subcontractors' Task Selections in Interior Works." *Automation in Construction*, 37: 81–87.

Hendrickson, C. (2003). *Project Management for Construction: Fundamental Concepts for Owners, Engineers, Architects and Builders* Version 2.1. June 27, 2007, www.ce.cmu.edu/pmbook.

HKHA. (2009). "Building Information Modelling (BIM) Standards Manual for Development and Construction Division of Hong Kong Housing Authority." Hong Kong Housing Authority, Hong Kong.

Hopp, W. J., and Spearman, M. L. (1996). *Factory Physics*. IRWIN, Chicago.

Howell, G. A. (1999). "What Is Lean Construction—1999?" *Seventh Annual Conference of the International Group for Lean Construction*, IGLC-7, Berkeley, CA.

HS2 (2013). "HS2 Supply Chain BIM Upskilling Study." High Speed Two (HS2) Limited London, UK.

Hwang, K., and Lee, G. (2016) "A Comparative Analysis of the Building Information Modeling Guides of Korea and Other Countries." *ICCCBE 2016*, Osaka, Japan, July 6–8, 879–886.

Indiana University Architect's Office. (2009). "IU BIM Proficiency Matrix." Indiana University Architect's Office, Bloomington, IN.

Isikdag, U. (2014). Innovations in 3D Geo-Information Sciences. *Lecture Notes in Geoinformation and Cartography*, Springer International Publishing, Zurich, Switzerland.

ISO (2013). ISO/IEC 27001:2013 Information Technology, Security Techniques, Information Security Management Systems: Requirements, International Organization for Standardization. International Organization for Standardization, pp. 23, www.iso.org/standard/54534.html.

ISO TC 59/SC 13. (2010). "ISO 29481-1:2010 Building Information Models: Information Delivery Manual, Part 1: Methodology and Format." ISO, Geneva, Switzerland.

ISO/TS 12911. (2012). "PD ISO/TS 12911:2012 Framework for Building Information Modelling (BIM) Guidance." ISO, Geneva, Switzerland.

Jackson, S. (2002). "Project Cost Overruns and Risk Management." *Proceedings of the 18th Annual ARCOM Conference*, Glasgow.

Johnston, G. B. (2006). "Drafting Culture: A social history of architectural graphic standards." Ph.D. Thesis, Emory University, Atlanta.

Jones, S. A., and Bernstein, H. M. (2012). *SmartMarket Report on Building Information Modeling (BIM): The Business Value of BIM*. McGraw-Hill Construction, Washington DC, 72.

Jones, S. A., and Laquidara-Carr, D. (2015). "Measuring the Impact of BIM on Complex Buildings." Dodge Data & Analytics, Bedford, MA.

Jørgensen, K. A., Skauge, J., Christiansson, P., Svidt, K., Sørensen, K. B., and Mitchell, J. (2008). "Use of IFC Model Servers: Modelling Collaboration Possibilities in Practice." Aalborg University & Aarhus School of Architecture, Aalborg, Denmark.

Jotne EPM Technology. (2013). "EDMServer Official Website." www.jotne.com/index.php?id=562520 (accessed February 10, 2013).

Jung, W., and Lee, G. (2015a). "Slim BIM Charts for Rapidly Visualizing and Quantifying Levels of BIM Adoption and Implementation." *Journal of Computing in Civil Engineering*, 04015072.

Jung, W., and Lee, G. (2015b). "The Status of BIM Adoption on Six Continents." *International Conference on Civil and Building Engineering (ICCBE)*, Montreal, Canada, May 11–12, 433–437.

Kalay, Y. (1989). *Modeling Objects and Environments*. New York, John Wiley & Sons.

Kam, C., Song, M. H., and Senaratna, D. (2016). "VDC Scorecard: Formulation, Application, and Validation." *Journal of Construction Engineering and Management*, 0(0), 04016100.

Karlshoj, J. (2016). "A BIM Mandate Lesson from Denmark." BIM+, www.bimplus.co.uk/people/bim-ma4ndate-lesso4n-den7mark/ (accessed July 27, 2017).

Keenliside, S. (2015). "Comparative Analysis of Existing Building Information Modelling (BIM) Guides." *International Construction Specialty Conference of the Canadian Society for Civil Engineering (ICSC)*, Vancouver, British Columbia, Canada, June 8–10, 2015, 293: 1–9.

Kenley, R., and Seppänen, O. (2010). *Location-Based Management for Construction: Planning, Scheduling and Control*. Spon Press, Abington, Oxon, UK.

Khemlani, L. (2004). "The IFC Building Model: A Look Under the Hood." March 30, 2004, *AECbytes*. June 15, 2007, www.aecbytes.com/feature/2004/IFC.html.

Koerckel, A., and Ballard, G. (2005). "Return on Investment in Construction Innovation: A Lean Construction Case Study." *Proceedings of the 14th Conference of the International Group for Lean Construction*, Sydney, Australia.

Koskela, L. (1992). *Application of the New Production Philosophy to Construction*, Technical Report #72, Center for Integrated Facility Engineering, Department of Civil Engineering, Stanford University.

Kreider, R., Messner, J., and Dubler, C. (2010). "Determining the Frequency and Impact of Applying BIM for Different Purposes on Building Projects." *6th International Conference on Innovation in Architecture, Engineering and Construction (AEC)*, Penn State University, University Park, PA, USA.

Krichels, Jennifer (2011). "Gehry's Louis Vuitton Fondation Façade" Fabrikator (Blog), October 2011. Accessed June 13, 2014 http://blog.archpaper.com/wordpress/archives/24715.

Krygiel, E., and Nies, B. (2008). *Green BIM: Successful Sustainable Design with Building Information Modeling*. Wiley, Indianapolis, IN.

Kunz, J. (2012), "Metrics for Management and VDC and Methods to Predict and Manage Them." CIFE, Stanford University.

Kunz, J., and Fischer, M. (2009), "Virtual Design and Construction: Themes, Case Studies and Implementation Suggestions." CIFE Working Paper #097, Version 10, October 2009, Stanford University.

Lafarge (2014), "Louis Vuitton Foundation: Innovation from Head to Toe." May 2011, Accessed June 13, 2014, www.ductal-lafarge.com/wps/portal/ductal/1_1_B_1-News?WCM_GLOBAL_CONTEXT=/wps/wcm/connectlib_ductal/Site_ductal/AllPR/PressRelease_1329390075063/PR_EN.

Laiserin, J. (2008). "Foreword." *BIM Handbook: A Guide to Building Information Modeling for Owners, Managers, Architects, Engineers, Contractors and Fabricators*. John Wiley and Sons, Hoboken, NJ.

Laurenzo, R. (2005). "Leaning on Lean Solutions," *Aerospace America*, June 2005: 32–36.

Lee, G. (2011). "What Information Can or Cannot Be Exchanged?" *Journal of Computing in Civil Engineering*, 25(1): 1–9.

Lee, G., and Kim, S. (2012). "Case Study of Mass Customization of Double-Curved Metal Façade Panels Using a New Hybrid Sheet Metal Processing Technique." *Journal of Construction Engineering and Management*, 138(11): 1322–1330.

Lee, G., Eastman, C. M., and Zimring, C. (2003). "Avoiding Design Errors: A Case Study of Redesigning an Architectural Studio." *Design Studies*, 24: 411–435.

Lee, G., Jeong, J., Won, J., Cho, C., You, S., Ham, S., and Kang, H. (2014). "Query Performance of the IFC Model Server Using an Object-Relational Database (ORDB) Approach and a Tradition-Relational Database (RDB) Approach." *Journal of Computing in Civil Engineering*, 28(2): 210–222.

Lee, G., Park, J., Won, J., Park, H. K., Uhm, M., and Lee, Y. (2016) "Can Experience Overcome the Cognitive Challenges in Drawing-Based Design Review? Design Review Experiments." *ConVR 2016*, Hong Kong, Dec 12–13.

Lee, G., Sacks, R., and Eastman, C. M. (2006). "Specifying Parametric Building Object Behavior (BOB) for a Building Information Modeling System." *Automation in Construction* 15(6): 758–776.

Lee, G., Won, J., Ham, S., and Shin, Y. (2011). "Metrics for Quantifying the Similarities and Differences between IFC files." *Journal of Computing in Civil Engineering*, 25(2): 172–181.

Lee, J.-K., Lee, J., Jeong, Y.-S., Sheward, H., Sanguinetti, P., Abdelmohsen, S., and Eastman, C. M. (2010). "Development of Space Object Semantics for Automated Building Design Review Systems," Design computation working paper, Digital Building Lab, July 2010.

Lee, Y.-C., Eastman, C. M., Solihin, W., and See, R. (2016) "Modularized Rule-Based Validation of a BIM Model Pertaining to Model Views." *Automation in Construction.* 63: 1–11.

Li, X., Wu, P., Shen G. P, Wang, X., and Teng, Y. (2017). "Mapping the Knowledge Domains of Building Information Modelling (BIM): A Bibliometric Approach." *Automation in Construction*, under review.

Liker, J. E. (2003). *The Toyota Way*. McGraw-Hill, New York.

Little, J. C., and Graves, S. (2008). "Little's Law." *Building Intuition, International Series in Operations Research & Management Science*, D. Chhajed and T. Lowe, eds., Springer US, 81–100.

Liu, X., Wang, X., Wright, G., Cheng, J. C. P., Li, X., and Liu, R. (2017). "A State-of-the-Art Review on the Integration of Building Information Modeling (BIM) and Geographic Information System (GIS)." *ISPRS International Journal of Geo-Information*, 6(2).

Love, P. E. D., Zhou, J., Matthews, J., and Luo, H. (2016). "Systems Information Modelling: Enabling Digital Asset Management." *Advances in Engineering Software*, 102: 155–165.

Mauck, R., Lichtig, W., Christian, D., and Darrington, J. "Integrated Project Delivery: Different Outcomes, Different Rules. *48th Annual Meeting of Invited Attorneys*. May 20–22, 2009, St. Petersburg, FL.

MBIE. (2014). "New Zealand BIM Handbook, Appendix C: Levels of Development Definitions." Ministry of Business, Innovation, and Employment, New Zealand.

McCallum, B. (2011). "The Four Approaches to BIM." http://bim4scottc.blogspot.kr/2012/10/the-four-approaches-to-bim.html (accessed Oct. 22, 2015).

McCuen, T. L., Suermann, P. C., and Krogulecki, M. J. (2012). "Evaluating Award-Winning BIM Projects Using the National Building Information Model Standard Capability Maturity Model." *Journal of Management in Engineering*, 28(2): 224–230.

McGraw Hill Construction (2011). "Prefabrication and Modularization: Increasing Productivity in the Construction Industry." *SmartMarket Report*, McGraw Hill Construction.

MLTM. (2010). "Architectural BIM Implementation Guide v1.0." Ministry of Land, Transport, and Maritime Affairs, Daejeon, South Korea.

Morwood, R., Scott, D., and Pitcher, I. (2008). "Alliancing: A Participant's Guide. Real Life Experiences for Constructors, Designers, Facilitators and Clients." Maunsell AECOM, Brisbane, Queensland.

Munroe, C. (2007). "Construction Cost Estimating." American Society of Professional Estimators, June 27, 2007, www.aspenational.com/construction%20cost%20estimating.pdf.

Neff, G., Fiore-Silfvast, B., and Dossick, C. S. (2010). "A Case Study of the Failure of Digital Communication of Cross Knowledge Boundaries in Virtual Construction." *Information, Communication & Society*, 13(4): 556–573.

NIBS (2007). *National Building Information Modeling Standard*, National Institute of Building Sciences, Washington, D.C.

NIBS (2008). *United States National Building Information Modeling Standard, Version 1, Part 1: Overview, Principles, and Methodologies.* http://nbimsdoc.opengeospatial.org/ Oct. 30, 2009.

NIBS (2012). "National BIM Standard - United States Version 2: Chapter 5.2 Minimum BIM," National Institute of Building Sciences (NIBS) buildingSMART Alliance.

Nisbet, N., and East, E. W. (2013). "Construction Operations Building Information Exchange (COBie), Version 2.4." www.nibs.org/?page=bsa_cobiev24 (accessed Jan 31, 2017).

NIST (2007). "General Buildings Information Handover Guide: Principles, Methodology and Case Studies." National Institute of Science and Technology, Washington DC.

NYC (2013). "Building Information Modeling (BIM) Site Safety Submission Guidelines and Standards for Applicants." New York City Department of Buildings. www1.nyc.gov/assets/buildings/pdf/bim_manual.pdf.

Oberlender, G., and Trost, S. (2001). "Predicting Accuracy of Early Cost Estimates Based On Estimate Quality." *Journal of Construction Engineering and Management* 127(3): 173–182.

OmniClass (2017). *OmniClass: A Strategy for Classifying the Built Environment*, OmniClass, www.omniclass.org/.

P2SL (2017). *Target Value Design*, Project Production Systems Laboratory, UC Berkeley, CA. http://p2sl.berkeley.edu/research/initiatives/target-value-design/.

Park, J. H., and Lee, G. (2017). "Design Coordination Strategies in a 2D and BIM Mixed-Project Environment: Social Dynamics and Productivity." *Building Research & Information*, 45(6): 631–648.

Pärn, E. A., Edwards, D. J., and Sing, M. C. P. (2017). "The Building Information Modelling Trajectory in Facilities Management: A Review." *Automation in Construction*, 75: 45–55.

Pasquire, C., and Gibb, A. (2002). "Considerations for Assessing the Benefits of Standardization and Pre-assembly in Construction." *Journal of Financial Management of Property and Construction*, 7(3): 151–161.

Pasquire, C., Soar, R., and Gibb, A. (2006). "Beyond Pre-Fabrication: The Potential of Next Generation Technologies to Make a Step Change in Construction Manufacturing." *Understanding and Managing the Construction Process: Theory and Practice, Proceedings of the 14th Conference of the International Group for Lean Construction*. R. Sacks and S. Bertelsen, eds., Catholic University of Chile, School of Engineering, Santiago, Chile, 243–254.

Pauwels, P., Zhang, S., Lee. Y.-C. (2017). "Semantic Web Technologies in AEC Industry: A Literature Overview." *Automation in Construction* 73 (January) 2017, 145–165. https://doi.org/10.1016/j.autcon.2016.10.003.

PCI (2014). *PCI Design Handbook: Precast and Prestressed Concrete*, 7th edition, Precast/Prestressed Concrete Institute, Skokie, IL.

Pikas, E., Sacks, R., and Hazzan, O. (2013). "Building Information Modeling Education for Construction Engineering and Management. II: Procedures and Implementation Case Study." *Journal of Construction Engineering and Management*, 39(11), 05013002 1–13.

Post, N. M. (2002). "Movie of Job That Defies Description Is Worth More Than a Million Words." *Engineering News Record*, April 8, 2002.

Pouma/Iemants (2012). "Tekla, Icebergs: Louis Vuitton Fondation." Tekla Global BIM Awards, 2012, Accessed September 25, 2017 www.tekla.com/global-bim-awards-2012/concrete-icebergs.html.

PPS (2016). "A Basic Guide to Implementing BIM in Facility Projects v1.31." Public Procurement Service, Daejeon, South Korea.

Proctor, C. (2012). "Construction Firms: It's Prefab-ulous for Some of the Work to be Done Off-site." *Denver Business Journal*, November 9–15, 2012.

Ramsey, G., and Sleeper, H. (2000). *Architectural Graphic Standards*. New York, John Wiley & Sons.

Requicha, A. (1980). Representations of Rigid Solids: Theory, Methods and Systems. *ACM Computer Surv.* 12(4): 437–466.

Robbins, E. (1994). *Why Architects Draw*. Cambridge, MA, MIT Press.

Roe, A. (2002). "Building Digitally Provides Schedule, Cost Efficiencies: 4D CAD Is Expensive but Becomes More Widely Available." *Engineering News Record*, February 25, 2002.

Roe, A. (2006). "The Fourth Dimension Is Time" *Steel*, Australia, 15.

Romm, J. R. (1994). *Lean and Clean Management: How to Boost Profits and Productivity by Reducing Pollution*, Kodansha International.

Roodman, D. M., and Lenssen, N. (1995). "A Building Revolution: How Ecology and Health Concerns Are Transforming Construction," Worldwatch Institute.

Sacks, R. (2004). "Evaluation of the Economic Impact of Computer-Integration in Precast Concrete Construction." *Journal of Computing in Civil Engineering* 18(4): 301–312.

Sacks, R., and Barak, R. (2007). "Impact of Three-Dimensional Parametric Modeling of Buildings on Productivity in Structural Engineering Practice." *Automation in Construction* (2007), doi:10.1016/j.autcon.2007.08.003.

Sacks, R., and Barak, R. (2010). "Teaching Building Information Modeling as an Integral Part of Freshman Year Civil Engineering Education," *Journal of Professional Issues in Engineering Education and Practice*, 136(1): 30–38.

Sacks, R., Barak, R., Belaciano, B., Gurevich, U., and Pikas, E. (2013). "KanBIM Lean Construction Workflow Management System: Prototype Implementation and Field Testing." *Lean Construction Journal*, 9: 19–34.

Sacks, R., Eastman, C. M., and Lee, G. (2003). "Process Improvements in Precast Concrete Construction Using Top-Down Parametric 3-D Computer-Modeling." *Journal of the Precast/Prestressed Concrete Institute* 48(3): 46–55.

Sacks, R., Eastman, C. M., and Lee, G., (2004), "Parametric 3D Modeling in Building Construction with Examples from Precast Concrete," *Automation in Construction*, 13(3): 291–312.

Sacks, R., Gurevich, U., and Shrestha, P. (2016). "A Review of Building Information Modeling Protocols, Guides and Standards for Large Construction Clients." *ITcon*, 21: 479–503.

Sacks, R., Korb, S., and Barak, R. (2017). *Building Lean, Building BIM: Improving Construction the Tidhar Way*. Routledge, Oxford, UK.

Sacks, R., Koskela, L., Dave, B., and Owen, R. L. (2010). "The Interaction of Lean and Building Information Modeling in Construction." *Journal of Construction Engineering and Management*, 136(9): 968–980.

Sacks, R., Ma, L., Yosef, R., Borrmann, A., Daum, S., and Kattel, U. (2017). "Semantic Enrichment for Building Information Modeling: Procedure for Compiling Inference Rules and Operators for Complex Geometry." *Journal of Computing in Civil Engineering*, 31(6), 4017062.

Sanvido, V., and Konchar, M. (1999). *Selecting Project Delivery Systems, Comparing Design-Build, Design-Bid-Build, and Construction Management at Risk*, Project Delivery Institute, State College, PA.

Sawyer, T. (2008). "$1-Billion Jigsaw Puzzle Has Builder Modeling Supply Chains," *Engineering News Record*, April 2008.

Sawyer, T., and Grogan, T. (2002). "Finding the Bottom Line Gets a Gradual Lift from Technology." *Engineering News Record*, August 12, 2002.

Scheer, D. R. (2014). *The Death of Drawing: Architecture in the Age of Simulation*. Taylor & Francis.

Schenk, D. A., and Wilson, P. R. (1994). *Information Modeling the EXPRESS Way*, Oxford U. Press, N.Y.

Schley, M., Haines, B., Roper, K., and Williams, B. (2016). *BIM for Facility Management Version 2.1*, The BIM-FM Consortium, Raleigh, N.C.

Sebastian, R., and van Berlo, L. (2010). "Tool for Benchmarking BIM Performance of Design, Engineering and Construction Firms in Netherlands." *Architectural Engineering and Design Management*, 6(4): 254–263.

Shafiq, M. T., Matthews, J., and Lockley, S. R. (2013). "A Study of BIM Collaboration Requirements and Available Features in Existing Model Collaboration Systems." *ITcon*, 18: 148–161.

Shah, J. J., and Mantyla, M. (1995). *Parametric and Feature-Based CAD/CAM: Concepts, Techniques, and Applications.* New York: John Wiley & Sons.

Sheffer, D. (2011). "Innovation in Modular Industries: Implementing Energy-Efficient Innovations in US Buildings." Dissertation, Department of Civil and Environmental Engineering, Stanford University.

Smoot, B. (2007). Building Acquisition and Ownership Costs. CIB Workshop, CIB.

Solihin, W., and Eastman, C. M. (2015), "Classification of Rules for Automated BIM Rule Checking Development." *Automation in Construction,* 53: 69–82.

Succar, B. (2010). "Building Information Modeling Maturity Matrix." *Handbook of Research on Building Information Modeling and Construction Informatics: Concepts and Technologies,* J. Underwood and U. Isikdag, eds., IGI Global Snippet, Hershey, PA, 65–102.

Teicholz, P, et al. (IFMA), (2013). *BIM for Facility Managers.* Wiley. (ISBN: 978-1-118-38281-3).

Teicholz, P. (2001). "Discussion: U.S. Construction Labor Productivity Trends, 1970–1998." *Journal of Construction Engineering and Management,* 127: 427–429.

Teicholz, P. (2004). "Labor Productivity Declines in the Construction Industry: Causes and Remedies." AECbytes, www.aecbytes.com/viewpoint/2004/issue_4 .html (accessed May 3, 2013).

Teicholz, P. "Technology Trends and Their Impact in the A/E/C Industry." Working Paper No. 2, Center for Integrated Facility Engineering, Stanford University, January 1989.

Thomas, H. R., Korte, C., Sanvido, V. E., and Parfitt, M. K. (1999). "Conceptual Model for Measuring Productivity of Design and Engineering." *Journal of Architectural Engineering* 5(1): 1–7.

Thomson, D. B., and Miner, R. G. (2007). "Building Information Modeling-BIM: Contractual Risks are Changing with Technology." June 27, 2007, https://aepronet.org/ documents/building-information-modeling-bim-contractual-risks-are-changing- with-technology/.

Touran, A. (2003). "Calculation of Contingency in Construction Projects." *IEEE Transactions on Engineering Management* 50(2): 135–140.

Uhm, M., Lee, G., and Jeon, B. (2017). "An Analysis of BIM Jobs and Competencies Based on the Use of Terms in the Industry." *Automation in Construction,* 81: 67–98.

U.S. Census Bureau (2016a). "Construction: Summary Series: General Summary: Value of Construction Work for Type of Construction by Subsectors and Industries for U.S., Regions, and States: 2012," EC1223SG09. www.census.gov/data/tables/ 2012/econ/census/construction.html.

U.S. Census Bureau (2016b). "Construction: Summary Series: General Summary: Employment Size Class by Subsectors and Industries for U.S. and States: 2012." EC1223SG02. www.census.gov/data/tables/2012/econ/census/construction.html.

USACE (2012). "ERDC SR-12-2: The U.S. Army Corps of Engineers Roadmap for Life-Cycle Building Information Modeling (BIM)." U.S. Army Corpos of Engineers, Washinton, DC.

Vico Software, Webcor Builders, and AGC. (2008). "Model Progression Specification." Salem, MA.

Warne, T., and Beard, J. (2005). *Project Delivery Systems: Owner's Manual*. American Council of Engineering Companies, Washington, D.C.

Warszawski, A. (1990). *Industrialization and Robotics in Building: A Managerial Approach*. Harper Collins College Div., New York.

Whitworth, Brian; Whitworth, Alex P. (2010). "The Social Environment Model: Small Heroes and the Evolution of Human Society." *First Monday*, [S.l.], ISSN 13960466. Available at: http://firstmonday.org/ojs/index.php/fm/article/view/3173/2647. Date accessed: August 3, 2017. doi: http://dx.doi.org/10.5210/fm.v15i11.3173.

Whyte, J., and Nikolic, D. (2018). *Virtual Reality and the Built Environment*. Second Edition, Routledge, Abington, Oxon, UK.

Womack, J. P., and Jones, D. T. (2003). *Lean Thinking: Banish Waste and Create Wealth in Your Corporation*. New York, Simon & Schuster.

Won, J. (2014). "A Goal-Use-KPI Approach for Measuring the Success Levels of BIM-Assisted Projects," Yonsei University, Seoul, Korea.

Won, J., and Lee, G. (2016). "How to Tell if a BIM Project Is Successful: A Goal-Driven Approach." *Automation in Construction*, 69: 34–43.

Won, J., Lee, G., and Cho, C.-Y. (2013a). "No-Schema Algorithm for Extracting a Partial Model from an IFC Instance Model." *Journal of Computing in Civil Engineering*, 27(6): 585–592.

Won, J., Lee, G., Dossick, C. S., and Messner, J. (2013b). "Where to Focus for Successful Adoption of Building Information Modeling within Organization." *Journal of Construction Engineering and Management*, 139(11), 04013014.

Wu, W., and Issa, R. (2014). "BIM Execution Planning in Green Building Projects: LEED as a Use Case." *Journal of Management in Engineering*, 31(1), A4014007.

Yaski, Y. (1981). "A Consistent Database for an Integrated CAAD System". PhD Thesis, Carnegie Mellon University, Pittsburgh, PA.

Yeh, I. C. (2006). "Architectural Layout Optimization Using Annealed Neural Network." *Automation in Construction* 15(4): 531–539.

Young, N. W., Jr., Jones, S. A., and Bernstein, H. M. (2007). *Interoperability in the Construction Industry*. McGraw Hill Construction, Bedford, MA.

You, S.-J., Yang, D., and Eastman, C. M. (2004). "Relational DB Implementation of STEP-Based Product Model." *CIB World Building Congress 2004*, Toronto, Ontario, Canada, May 2–7, 2004.

Young, N. W., Jr., Jones, S. A., and Bernstein, H. M. (2007). *Interoperability in the Construction Industry*. McGraw Hill Construction, Bedford, MA.

Young, N. W., Jr., Jones, S. A., Bernstein, H. M., and Gudgel, J. E. (2009). *The Business Value of BIM, 2009*. McGraw Hill Construction, Bedford, MA.

Zhao, X. (2017). "A Scientometric Review of Global BIM Research: Analysis and Visualization." *Automation in Construction*, 80: 37–47.

Index

Note: Page references with *f* and *t* refer to figures and tables.